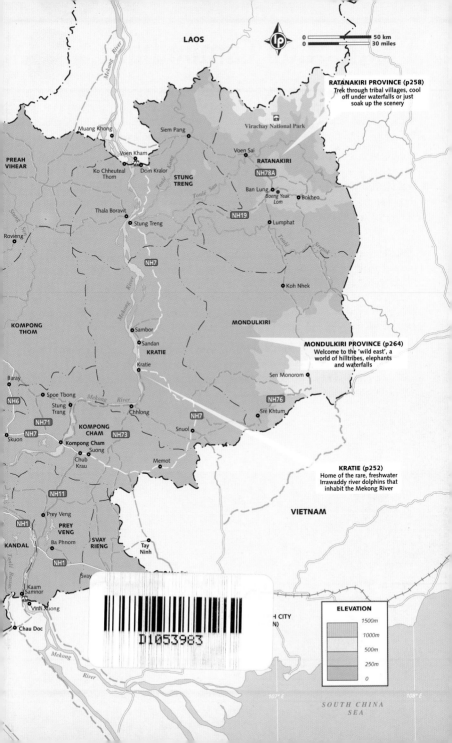

Destination Cambodia

The years of fear and loathing are over. Right now, Cambodia is just about as hot as it gets on the global travel map. Peace has come to this beautiful yet blighted land after three decades of war, and the Cambodian people are embracing the world. Tourism is taking off, but a journey to this little kingdom is still one of Asia's genuine adventures.

Contemporary Cambodia is the successor state to the mighty Khmer empire, which during the Angkor period (9th to 15th centuries) ruled much of what is now Laos, Thailand and Vietnam. The remains of this empire can be seen at the fabled temples of Angkor, monuments unrivalled in scale and grandeur in Southeast Asia. The traveller's first glimpse of Angkor Wat, the ultimate of Khmer genius, is simply staggering and is matched only by a few select spots on earth such as Macchu Picchu or the Taj Mahal.

But behind the brochures, just as Angkor is more than its wat, so too is Cambodia much more than its temples. The south coast is ringed by tropical islands with barely a beach hut in sight. The mighty Mekong River cuts through the country and is home to some of the region's last remaining freshwater dolphins near Kratie. And the northeast is a world unto itself, its wild and mountainous landscapes a home for Cambodia's ethnic minorities and shy wildlife.

Finally there are the people. Cambodians have weathered years of bloodshed, poverty and political instability. Somehow they have come through the experience with their smiles intact; no visitor comes away from Cambodia without a measure of admiration and affection for the inhabitants of this beautiful land.

ANDERS BLOMQV

Highlights

Feel like an explorer of old at Ta Prohm (p162), abandoned to the elements and overrun by nature

Get away from it all on Koh Tonsay (p203)

OTHER HIGHLIGHTS

- Chill out on the beach at Sihanoukville (p184).
- Make a pilgrimage to the mountain sanctuary of Prasat Preah Vihear (p235).
- Leave the lowlands behind with a trip to the rolling hills of Mondulkiri Province (p264).
- Hitch a ride on an elephant (p259) in the rewarding northeast.

Admire the world's finest collection of Khmer sculpture in the stunning National Museum (p81)

Explore the abandoned colonial ruins of Bokor hill station (p199) with its commanding views of the coast below

ANDREW BURKE

RICHARD I'ANSON

Cruise the waterworld of the floating villages (p132) on Tonlé Sap lake

Marvel at the surreal splendour of the Bayon (p156), 216 faces staring eerily out into the forest

MICK ELA

lonely planet

Cambodia

Nick Ray

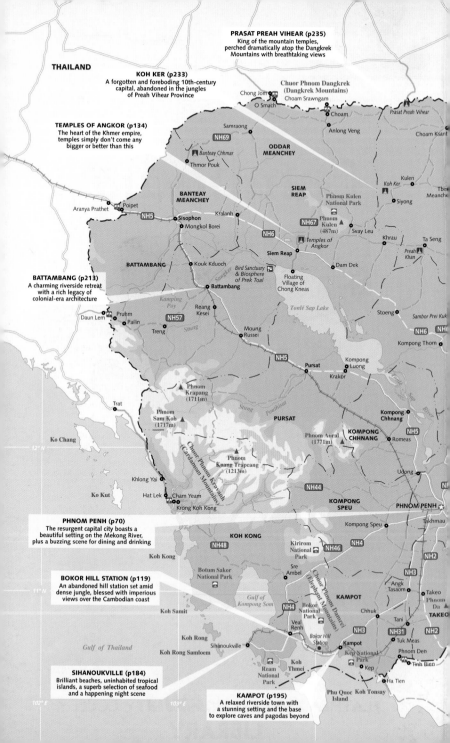

PRASAT PREAH VIHEAR (p235)
King of the mountain temples,
perched dramatically atop the Dangkrek
Mountains with breathtaking views

KOH KER (p233)
A forgotten and foreboding 10th-century
capital, abandoned in the jungles
of Preah Vihear Province

THAILAND

TEMPLES OF ANGKOR (p134)
The heart of the Khmer empire,
temples simply don't come any
bigger or better than this

BATTAMBANG (p213)
A charming riverside retreat
with a rich legacy of
colonial-era architecture

PHNOM PENH (p70)
The resurgent capital city boasts a
beautiful setting on the Mekong River,
plus a buzzing scene for dining and drinking

BOKOR HILL STATION (p119)
An abandoned hill station set amid
dense jungle, blessed with imperious
views over the Cambodian coast

SIHANOUKVILLE (p184)
Brilliant beaches, uninhabited tropical
islands, a superb selection of seafood
and a happening night scene

KAMPOT (p195)
A relaxed riverside town with
a stunning setting and the base
to explore caves and pagodas beyond

Chuor Phnom Dangkrek
(Dangkrek Mountains)

Prasat Preah Vihear

Chong Jom
O Smach
Choam Srawngam
Choam
Choam Ksant

Samraong

Banteay Chhmar
Thmor Pouk

Anlong Veng

ODDAR MEANCHEY

SIEM REAP

Koh Ker
Kulen

Phnom Kulen
National Park

Siyong

Tbe
Meanche

BANTEAY MEANCHEY

Aranya Prathet
Poipet
NH5

Sisophon
Mongkol Borei

Kralanh

NH6

NH69

NH67
Phnom
Kulen
(487m)
Svay Leu

Khrau
Ta Seng

BATTAMBANG

Kouk Kduoch

Siem Reap

Temples of
Angkor

Dam Dek

Preah
Khan

Daun Lem
Pruhm
Pailin

Battambang

Bird Sanctuary
& Biosphere
of Prek Toal

Floating
Village of
Chong Kneas

Stoeng

Sambor Prei Kuk

Reang
Kesei

Kamping
Poy

Tonlé Sap Lake

NH6

NH6

NH57

Treng

Sreng

Moung
Russei

Kompong Thom

Kompong
Luong

Phnom
Krapang
(1711m)

NH5

Pursat

Krakor

Trat

Phnom
Sam Koh
(1717m)

PURSAT

Kompong
Chhnang

Ko Chang

12° N

Chuor Phnom Kravanh (Cardamom Mountains)

Stung Pursat

Phnom Aoral
(1771m)

**KOMPONG
CHHNANG**

Romeas

NH5

Phnom
Kong Trapeang
(1213m)

Udong

Nf

Khlong Yai

Ko Kut

Hat Lek
Cham Yeam

Krong Koh Kong

NH44

**KOMPONG
SPEU**

PHNOM PENH

Takhmau

KOH KONG

NH48

Koh Kong

Kompong Speu

Kirirom
National
Park

NH46
NH4

NH2

Botum Sakor
National Park

Sre
Ambel

NH3

Angk
Tasaom

Takeo

Phnom
Da

Koh Samit

Gulf of
Kompong Som

Chuor Phnom Damrei (Elephant Mountains)

KAMPOT

Chhuk

Tani

TAKEO

11° N

NH4

Veal
Renh

Bokor
National
Park

NH3
NH31

Tuk Meas

NH2

Koh Rong

Sihanoukville

Bokor Hill
Station

Kampot

Phnom Den

Koh Rong Samloem

Koh
Thmei

Kep National
Park

Kep

Tinh Bien

Gulf of Thailand

Ream
National
Park

Ha Tien

Phu Quoc
Island

Koh Tonsay
Island

102° E

103° E

Bow in awe to the mother of all temples, Angkor Wat (p150), the world's largest religious building

Copy the locals and hitch a ride around
Phnom Penh on a *moto* (p107)

Take a dip in the beautiful natural swimming pool
of Boeng Yeak Lom (p261) in Ratanakiri Province

Tantalise your tastebuds with Khmer delicacies at Psar Tuol Tom Pong (p104) in Phnom Penh

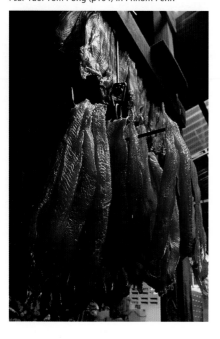

RICHARD I'AN

Tread carefully upon the 5000 silver tiles of the Silver Pagoda (p80), home to a dazzling array of Buddha images

Step back in time to Cambodia's colonial past on the streets of Phnom Penh (p70)

TOM COCK

Contents

Regional Map Contents

Temples of
Angkor p134
Siem Reap
p113

Eastern Cambodia
p242

Northwestern
Cambodia p207

Phnom Penh
p70

South Coast
p178

The Authors

NICK RAY

A Londoner of sorts, Nick is from Watford, the sort of town that makes you want to travel. He lives in Phnom Penh, with his wife Kulikar and young son Julian. He has worked on several guidebooks on Cambodia including Lonely Planet's *Southeast Asia on a Shoestring* and *Cycling Vietnam, Laos & Cambodia*. He also writes for newspapers and magazines, including the *Sunday Times* and *Wanderlust* in the UK. When not writing, Nick is often found foraging around the remote parts of Cambodia as a location scout and manager for the world of TV and film. Motorbikes are a part-time passion and he prefers to take the roads less travelled and is still turning up new trails in Cambodia.

My Favourite Trip

Ouch, that's a tough one...the northeast is always a cracker and the long loop through the wilds of Mondulkiri (p264) and Ratanakiri (p258) with two on the bike is hard to forget. Leaving Stung Treng (p256) for Laos, the boat got marooned in the middle of the Mekong after running aground on a sandbar and out came the bike for some surreal photos. Getting my kicks on Route 66 was a real high, following the old Angkor road from Beng Mealea (p176) to Preah Khan (p166), the ancient bridges providing clues to our progress as we cut through the jungle. Spean Ta Ong (p233) was the ultimate reward, a full 77m-long and guarded by fearsome *naga*, lost in a maze of ox-cart tracks. Then there are the backroads to mainstream destinations, like travelling down NH31 to Kep (p201) and Kampot (p195), and the chance for a ride on the bamboo train (p217). Just turn left or turn right off the trail and there are favourite trips waiting around every corner.

CONTRIBUTING AUTHOR

Dr Trish Batchelor is a general practitioner and travel medicine specialist who works at the CIWEC Clinic in Kathmandu, Nepal, as well as being a Medical Advisor to the Travel Doctor New Zealand clinics. Trish teaches travel medicine through the University of Otago, and is interested in underwater and high-altitude medicine, and in the impact of tourism on host countries. She has travelled extensively through Southeast and East Asia and particularly loves high-altitude trekking in the Himalayas. Dr Batchelor wrote the Health chapter.

LONELY PLANET AUTHORS

Why is our travel information the best in the world? It's simple: our authors are independent, dedicated travellers. They don't just research via the Internet or phone, and they don't take freebies. They visit every place in this book personally, and they take pride in getting all the details right. For more on our authors, visit www.lonelyplanet.com.

Getting Started

Cambodia is kicking! The magnificent temples of Angkor are unrivalled in the region and beyond the rich legacy of the Khmer empire lie the buzzing capital of Phnom Penh, hundreds of kilometres of unspoilt tropical beaches, the mighty Mekong River, a vibrant culture and some of the friendliest people in the region. However, it's not the most sophisticated destination in the world, making it all the more charming for many, so pack some patience and humour. It's full of surprises, a place for an adventure as much as a holiday...welcome to Cambodia!

WHEN TO GO

Cambodia can be visited at any time of year. The ideal time to visit is December and January, when humidity levels are relatively low, there is little rainfall and a cooling breeze whips across the land.

From early February temperatures start to rise until the killer month, April, when temperatures often exceed 40°C. Some time in May or June, the southwestern monsoon brings rain and high humidity, cooking up a sweat for all but the hardiest of visitors. The wet season, which lasts until October, isn't such a bad time to visit, as the rain tends to come in short, sharp downpours. Angkor is surrounded by lush foliage and the moats are full of water at this time of year. If you are planning to visit isolated areas, however, the wet season makes for tough travel.

See Climate Charts (p271) for more information.

Some visitors like to coordinate their trip with one of the annual festivals, such as Bon Om Tuk, the water festival in Phnom Penh, or Khmer New Year (see p276).

COSTS & MONEY

The cost of travelling in Cambodia runs the full gamut from almost free to outrageously expensive depending on taste and comfort. Penny pinchers can survive on as little as US$10 per day, while budget travellers with an eye on enjoyment can live it up on US$20. Midrange travellers can turn on the style with just US$75 to US$100 a day, staying in smart places, dining well and travelling in comfort. At the top end, flash US$200 or more in cash and you can live in luxury.

Accommodation starts from as little as US$2 to US$5 in popular destinations. Spending US$10 to US$20 will add amenities, including aircon, satellite TV, fridge and hot water. Stepping up to US$50, you enter the world of three-star standards or charming mini-resorts. Forking out

---

DON'T LEAVE HOME WITHOUT...

Bring as little as possible. Cambodia has everything you find back home, only a whole lot cheaper. All the soaps and smellies are plentiful, and clothing, shoes and backpacks are available at a fraction of the price in the West. Tampons are available in all major towns and cities, but not in more remote areas.

A Swiss army knife or equivalent comes in handy, but you don't need 27 separate functions, just one blade and an opener. A torch (flashlight) and compass are also useful.

Other handy hints include: ear plugs to block the ever-present noise; a universal plug adaptor; a rain cover for your backpack; and insect repellent to keep the bugs at bay. Finally, the secret of successful packing: plastic bags – not only do they keep things separate and clean, but also dry. That means a lot at the end of a long, wet day.

US$100 and up brings a five-star fling. Don't be afraid to negotiate for a discount if it is low season or traffic is down.

While Cambodian cuisine may not be as well known as that of its neighbours, Thailand and Vietnam, it can compete with the best of them. Snack on the street or chow down in the market on meals starting at just 1000r, or you can pig out for a couple of bucks. Khmer restaurants are a step up in comfort and a local meal will cost US$1 to US$2. Next are the sophisticated Khmer, Asian and international restaurants. Meals start from about US$3 at the cheaper places, more like US$10 with drinks at the smarter ones, and US$50 and beyond is possible if you go wild with the wine list.

Domestic flights link Phnom Penh to Siem Reap and Ratanakiri. Fast boats link several popular destinations in Cambodia and the journey can be more scenic than by road. There is now a healthy selection of bus companies connecting towns and cities throughout Cambodia and prices are rock-bottom. On the rougher roads, share taxis and pick-ups take the strain. Travelling by train is still cheap, but is painfully slow, at an average speed of 20km/h. For ultimate flexibility, some visitors rent a car or 4WD and travel with a guide.

Visitors to Angkor (surely everybody coming to Cambodia) will have to factor in the cost of entrance fees, which are US$20 for one day, US$40 for three days and US$60 for one week. An additional expense is transport to get to and around the ruins, from US$2 for a bicycle, US$6 for a *moto* (small motorcycle with driver), US$10 for a *remorque* (trailer pulled by a bicycle or motorcycle) and US$20 for a car.

Small budget, big budget, it doesn't really matter; Cambodia is the place to be. Soak it up in style.

HOW MUCH?

Hotel room with air-con US$8-20

Restaurant meal US$2-6

Internet access per minute US$0.50-1.50

Cambodia Daily newspaper 1200r

Krama (scarf) 3000r

LONELY PLANET INDEX

Litre of petrol 3000r

Litre of water 500-2000r

Large Angkor Beer US$1.50-2.50

Noodle soup 2000-4000r

Souvenir T-shirt US$2

TRAVEL LITERATURE

The classic Cambodian read is Norman Lewis' *A Dragon Apparent: Travels in Cambodia, Laos & Vietnam* (1951), an account of his 1950 foray into an Indochina that would soon disappear. In the course of his travels, Lewis circumnavigated Tonlé Sap lake, with a pause at Angkor. The book has been reissued as part of *The Norman Lewis Omnibus* (1995).

Written by writers who know and love their countries, *To Asia with Love: A Connoisseur's Guide to Cambodia, Laos, Thailand and Vietnam* (2004), an anthology edited by Kim Fay, is a delightful introduction to Cambodia and the Mekong region for those looking for some inspiration and adventure.

The Coast of Cambodia (2001) by Robert Philpotts is a nice slice of travel literature and guidebook interwoven. Philpotts travelled from Krong Koh Kong to Kompong Trach and had a few adventures along the way.

Amit Gilboa's *Off the Rails in Phnom Penh – Guns, Girls and Ganja* (1998) is a repellent but very popular book dealing with such murky subjects as prostitution and drugs. It feels like he got too close to his subject at times and it's not really a side of Cambodia about which Khmers are proud.

INTERNET RESOURCES

Andy Brouwer's Cambodia Tales (www.andybrouwer.co.uk) A great gateway to all things Cambodian, this site includes comprehensive links to other sites and regular travel articles from veteran Cambodian adventurers, including Andy Brouwer himself.

Biking Asia with Mr Pumpy (www.mrpumpy.net) The definitive website for cyclists passing through Cambodia, it is written with candour and humour by Mr Pumpy's best friend Felix Hude.

TOP TENS

Ancient Temples

Cambodia is truly the temple capital of Asia. The kingdom is littered with the lavish legacy of the god-kings. Choose from majestic mountain-top temples, forbidding and forgotten jungle fortresses, incredible carved riverbeds and pre-Angkorian brick cities.

- Angkor Wat (p150), the Mother of all temples
- Banteay Chhmar (p222), the forgotten fortress of the northwest
- Banteay Srei (p172), the jewel in the crown of Angkorian art
- Bayon (p156) with its 216 enigmatic faces
- Beng Mealea (p176), Angkor-sized but swallowed by jungle
- Kbal Spean (p174), the River of a Thousand Lingas
- Koh Ker (p233), a usurper capital of huge proportions
- Prasat Preah Vihear (p235), king of the mountain temples
- Sambor Prei Kuk (p240), the first temple city in the region.
- Ta Prohm (p162), left as explorers first saw it, nature has run riot

The Cambodian tragedy in words

In stark contrast to the glories of the Angkor empire is the dark void into which the country plunged in the 1970s. A brutal civil war raged for five years, delivering the Khmer Rouge to power. This regime turned the clocks to Year Zero in what was to become one of the world's most radical and bloody revolutions. Read your way through these tumultuous events to understand how it all happened.

- *Brother Enemy* by Nayan Chanda (1985)
- *Derailed in Uncle Ho's Victory Garden* by Tim Page (1995)
- *First they Killed My Father* by Luong Ung (2001)
- *History of Cambodia* by David Chandler (1994)
- *Prince of Light, Prince of Darkness* by Milton Osbourne (1994)
- *River of Time* by Jon Swain (1997)
- *Sideshow: Kissinger, Nixon and the Destruction of Cambodia* by William Shawcross (1979)
- *The Gate* by Francois Bizot (2003)
- *The Pol Pot Regime* by Ben Kiernan (1996)
- *Voices from S-21* by David Chandler (1999)

Adventures

If you are looking for adventures in Asia, then you have come to the right place. The roads may be rough, but the stories will be smooth and stay with you forever. One thing is for sure, an adventure is never far away in Cambodia.

- Beachcomb on the beautiful island of Koh Kong (p181)
- Camp out in the jungle at the temples of Koh Ker (p233)
- Catch a speedboat from Siem Reap to Battambang (p216)
- Go underground to Kampot's cave pagodas (p198)
- Hitch a ride on an elephant (p259) in the remote northeast
- Make the overland pilgrimage to Prasat Preah Vihear (p235)
- Paddle a dugout through the flooded forest of Kompong Phhluk (p133)
- Pan for gold in the wild east town of Mimong (p267)
- Ride the bamboo train in Battambang (p217)
- Take on the winding road to Bokor hill station (p199) by motorbike

Lonely Planet (www.lonelyplanet.com) Summaries on travelling to Cambodia, the Thorn Tree bulletin board and travel news.

Tales of Asia (www.talesofasia.com) This popular website has up-to-the-minute information on overland travel in Cambodia, including webmaster Gordon Sharpless' personal obsession, the Bangkok–Siem Reap run.

The Angkor Portal (http:\\angkor.com) When it comes to links, this site has them, spreading its cyber-tentacles into all sorts of interesting areas.

Itineraries
CLASSIC ROUTES

THE CAMBODIA ENCOUNTER
Two to three weeks

Whether you start in Siem Reap and travel south, or head north to Angkor, this is the ultimate journey, via temples, beaches and the capital.

Hit the **Phnom Penh** (p70) for sights like the impressive **National Museum** (p81), with its excellent Angkorian sculpture collection, and the stunning **Silver Pagoda** (p80), with 5000 silver tiles. There is super shopping at the **Psar Tuol Tom Pong** (p104), and a **nightlife scene** (p102) that rocks at all hours.

Take a speedboat to the **Phnom Da** (p206) temple, then go south to the colonial-era town of **Kampot** (p195). From here, visit the abandoned **Bokor hill station** (p199), the seaside town of **Kep** (p201) and the **cave pagodas** (p198).

Go west to **Sihanoukville** (p184), Cambodia's beach capital, to try the seafood, dive the nearby waters or just soak up the sun. Backtrack via Phnom Penh to **Kompong Thom** (p238) and get a foretaste of what's to come by visiting the pre-Angkorian brick temples of **Sambor Prei Kuk** (p240).

Finish the trip at the temples of Angkor, a mind-blowing experience with which few sights on earth can compare. See the obvious – **Angkor Wat** (p150), perfection in stone; **Bayon** (p156), weirdness in stone; and **Ta Prohm** (p162), nature triumphing over stone – but venture further afield to **Kbal Spean** (p174) or the jungle-clad **Beng Mealea** (p176).

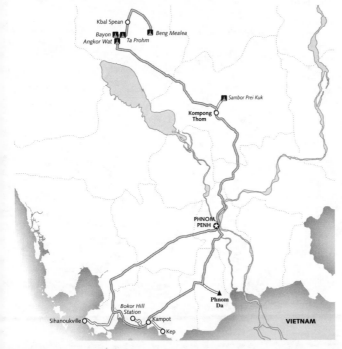

This can be two weeks at a steady pace or three weeks at a slow pace. Public transport serves most of this route. Rent a motorbike for side trips to places like Bokor hill station and Sambor Prei Kuk, and try out a cute little *remorque-moto* at Angkor. More money, less time? Rent a car and set the pace.

THE CAMBODIA EXPERIENCE   One month

Cambodia is only a small country and even though the roads are often bad and travel slow, most of the memorable places can be visited in a month.

Setting out from **Phnom Penh** (p70), take in the beauty of the northeast, following the Run to the Hills itinerary (p20). Make a choice between **Ratanakiri Province** (p258) and **Mondulkiri Province** (p264) to ensure maximum time elsewhere. The gentle hills of Mondulkiri are better for budget travellers as traversing overland is easy, while Ratanakiri is connected to the capital by plane for midrangers seeking adventure. Tough choice... can't decide? Flip a coin, if you can find one in this coinless country.

Head to the south coast, taking the route outlined in The Cambodia Encounter (p17). Take your time and consider a night or two in **Kep** (p201) or one of the nearby islands, and a boat trip from Sihanoukville to explore the maritime wonders of **Ream National Park** (p194). On your way back to the capital, check out **Kirirom National Park** (p111), home to pine trees, black bears and some spectacular views of the Cardamom Mountains.

Then it's time to turn northwest and head to charming **Battambang** (p213), one of Cambodia's best preserved colonial-era towns and a base to discover rural life and ride the bamboo train. Leave in style with a speedboat to **Siem Reap** (p113), passing through stunning scenery along the snaking Sangker River, and turn your attention to the temples of **Angkor** (p134).

Visit all the greatest hits in and around Angkor, but use the extra time to venture further to the rival capital of **Koh Ker** (p233), cloaked in thick jungle, or **Prasat Preah Vihear** (p235) – where it is all about location, location, location – a mountain temple perched precariously atop a cliff-face on the Thai border.

Overlanders can run this route in reverse, setting out from Siem Reap and exiting Cambodia by river into Vietnam or Laos. Entering from Laos, divert east to Ratanakiri before heading south. From Thailand, enter via the south coast and exit via Poipet. Getting about is generally easy, as there are buses on the big roads, taxis on the small roads and buzzing boats on the rivers.

ROADS LESS TRAVELLED

THE LOST TEMPLES OF THE NORTHWEST

The magnificent temples of Angkor are renowned for their splendour, but these represent no more than the capital of what was an unrivalled empire spanning across Southeast Asia. In the steaming jungles of Cambodia, forgotten to the world for centuries, lie several stunning religious monuments that make the perfect excuse to extend your stay by a week or more.

The beauty of this tough trip on rough roads is that it is the alternative, adventurous way to link Cambodia's vibrant capital, Phnom Penh, with sublime Siem Reap, gateway to Angkor. Starting in **Phnom Penh** (p70), head north through **Kompong Thom** (p238) and on to the pre-Angkorian capital of **Sambor Prei Kuk** (p240), Asia's first temple city. Farewell civilisation from here and make the tough journey northwest to the vast jungle temple of **Preah Khan** (p231), one of the largest structures from the Angkorian era.

Continue on to **Koh Ker** (p233), a usurper capital from the 10th century, with a wealth of monuments spread throughout the forest. Travel to Koh Ker via Khvau if you're brave, or go the easy way via **Tbeng Meanchey** (p229), provincial capital of Preah Vihear Province, if you are taking your time.

Last of the temples is the king of the mountain temples, **Prasat Preah Vihear** (p235), the height of Angkorian architectural audacity, its foundation stones stretching to the edge of a precipitous cliff. Breathe in the views as they are simply enormous. From here, it is a long run back to **Siem Reap** (p113) via the former Khmer Rouge stronghold of **Anlong Veng** (p226), where you can visit Pol Pot's cremation site.

This is a tough trip with very little in the way of public transport. Realistically, it is going to take a week and should not be attempted in the wet season. Seasoned motorbike riders can do it on a dirt bike. For less pain, a 4WD is the way to go. It is possible by a combination of pick-up truck and *moto*, but not a whole lot of fun.

RUN TO THE HILLS

Northeast Cambodia is a world unto itself, a landscape of rolling hills and secret waterfalls, and home to a patchwork of ethnic minorities, many of whom still use elephants to get around. It's not only the sights and sounds that are different up here, the temperature is notably cooler, as both Mondulkiri and Ratanakiri Provinces lie at almost 1000m.

Leaving the capital **Phnom Penh** (p70), pass through the bustling Mekong town of **Kompong Cham** (p248) before heading east to **Sen Monorom** (p264), the charming capital of Mondulkiri Province. Spend a few days here to bathe at **Bou Sraa Waterfall** (p266), one of Cambodia's biggest waterfalls, take an **elephant trek** (p265) and explore Pnong villages before heading back to the Mekong at **Kratie** (p252). This attractive little town is the base to encounter one of the rarest mammals on earth, the elusive Irrawaddy river dolphin which lives in ever-dwindling numbers upstream from here.

Push north by express river boat up the Mekong, passing hundreds of tiny islands and sand bars on a very scenic stretch of the river to **Stung Treng** (p256). To the east lies **Ban Lung** (p258), provincial capital of Ratanakiri Province and your base for an adventure to remember. From here plunge into Cambodia's most beautiful natural swimming pool at **Boeng Yeak Loam** (p261), ride an elephant through the rubber plantations to the stunning waterfall of Ka Tieng or visit the medieval **gem mines** (p262) where much of Cambodia's zircon comes from.

On main roads, this trip is easy to manage using share taxis or pick-ups, but until the roads are finished it's a frightening prospect in the wet season. Motorbikers can link Mondulkiri and Ratanakiri Provinces on one of Cambodia's more devilish roads – not for amateurs. Finishing up in Ratanakiri, overlanders can carry on into Laos or fly back to Phnom Penh.

TAILORED TRIP

THE MIGHTY MEKONG

The Mekong River cuts a swathe across Cambodia and is an ideal way to link up the neighbouring countries of Laos and Vietnam. Along the river's banks lie some fascinating towns and it provides a habitat for the rare freshwater Irrawaddy dolphin. Take in the Tonlé Sap tributary and you have the makings of a great adventure on the water.

Crossing into Cambodia from Laos at the Dom Kralor–Voen Kham border crossing, head south to **Stung Treng** (p256) by longtail rocket boat. Make a diversion east to **Ratanakiri Province** (p258) if time allows or continue south by boat to **Kratie** (p252), the best base for dolphin viewing along the Mekong. Head south again through **Kompong Cham** (p248) to the Cambodian capital **Phnom Penh** (p70), and soak up the atmosphere here for a few days and nights.

Next, head northwest, taking a fast boat up the Tonlé Sap river to **Siem Reap** (p113) and the temples of **Angkor** (p134). After a few days to take in these treasures, take a small boat southwest to **Battambang** (p213) along the Stung Sangker, one of the most beautiful boat trips in Cambodia. Return to Phnom Penh by road to pick up a boat taking you to Chau Doc in Vietnam's Mekong Delta. And the adventure doesn't have to stop there, as boats continue all the way to Ho Chi Minh City.

Snapshot

Cambodia is at a crossroads in its road to recovery from the brutal years of Khmer Rouge rule. Compare Cambodia today with the dark abyss into which it plunged under the Khmer Rouge and the picture looks promising, but look to its more successful neighbours and it's easy to be pessimistic. Cambodia must choose its path: pluralism, progress and prosperity or intimidation, impunity and injustice. The jury is still very much out on which way things will go.

Another jury still out is that of the Khmer Rouge trial, sidelined by the politics of the Cold War for two decades, and then delayed by bureaucratic bickering at home and abroad. It is by no means certain that the wheels of justice will turn fast enough to keep up with the rapid ageing of the surviving Khmer Rouge leaders. The Cambodian people deserve justice after so much suffering, but it could be argued that the nation would be better served by a truth and reconciliation commission that cleanses the nation's soul, without seeking revenge. Knowing the truth could prove more cathartic to the average Cambodian than seeing a gang of septuagenarian revolutionaries on trial, 25 years too late.

Corruption remains a way of life in Cambodia. It is the leadership that must set an example but right now that example is take, take, take, and it goes on from the highest government official to lowest paid civil servant. Sometimes it is overt, but it is increasingly covert, with ministers signing off government land to private companies for a steal and contracts being awarded to shadowy business figures with close connections to the leadership. At its worst, it has seen the partial privatization of Cambodia's heritage, with new private roads being bulldozed through to ancient temple sites and hefty tolls levied on foreigners and locals alike for the use of such infrastructure.

But it is not only the locals who know how to play the game. Aid is big business in Cambodia and many smaller nongovernmental organisations (NGOs) have played an impressive role in the getting the country back on its feet. Indeed, there are many who argue that without the parallel state that is the NGO world, there would be many more Cambodians mired in poverty than there are today. However, there are others who contend that many individuals in the bigger, multinational organisations are just riding the gravy train to Geneva, stashing six-figure, tax-free annual salaries, driving the latest 4WDs and renting houses with seven bathrooms. It somehow sticks in the throat when you calculate what this money could be doing if spent directly on the poor rather than subsidising the lifestyle of an international consultant.

Sitting among the dragons of Asia, Cambodia's economy is very much the gecko. Most industries were decimated during the long war years and these days tourism remains the great hope for the future. In Angkor, Cambodia has something with which none of its more developed neighbours can compete, and every Cambodian should thank their inspired ancestors for bequeathing such a legacy. For without the exploding tourism industry, Cambodia's economy would be in much worse shape than it is. The garment industry has been another big money spinner in the past decade, but as Cambodia joins the World Trade Organisation (WTO), there are fears that this industry could vanish overnight when the country is forced to play on a level playing field without favoured access to markets in the US and Europe. The only hope is that Cambodia can

FAST FACTS

Population: About 14 million

Life expectancy: 57.4 years

Infant mortality: 96 per 1000 births

GDP: US$4 billion (2002)

Adult literacy rate: 69.4%

Number of tourists per year: 1 million and rising

Number of monks in Cambodia: 59,470

Annual freshwater fish catch: 290,000-430,000 tonnes per year

Bombs dropped on Cambodia: 539,000 tonnes

Number of psychiatrists in Cambodia: 20

continue to develop good working conditions and sound labour laws to develop a reputation as a country where ethics rank as high as economics when customers choose their clothes, and clothing companies make their orders.

The royal family has been a constant in contemporary Cambodian history and no-one more so than the mercurial monarch King Sihanouk who once again surprised the world with his abdication in 2004. His relatively unknown son King Sihamoni assumed the throne and has brought renewed credibility to the monarchy, untainted as he is by the partisan politics of the past.

But there's a new royal family in town, the Cambodian People's Party (CPP), and they are making plans for the future with dynastic alliances between their pampered offspring. Just look at the roll call of marriages in the past few years and it soon becomes apparent that senior leaders have their eyes firmly on the future and a handover of power to the children of the CPP.

The CPP and the royalist Funcinpec (National United Front for an Independent, Neutral, Peaceful and Cooperative Cambodia) party are once again unlikely bedfellows in government, although real power lies with the CPP as they control the civil service, army and police. It may well be a dance with the devil for Funcinpec, as the party has been steadily shedding support since it won the 1993 election and is now the third force behind the opposition Sam Rainsy Party at the polls. Sam Rainsy continues to berate the country's leaders for their lack of leadership and is making real inroads in urban areas, setting the stage for some spicy showdowns with the CPP in the coming years. Sometimes they get a little too spicy and in early 2005 Sam Rainsy and two of his fellow parliamentarians were stripped of their immunity from prosecution, a disturbing development for democracy in Cambodia.

'Sam Rainsy continues to berate the country's leaders for their lack of leadership...'

Prime Minister Hun Sen has a political guile and cunning unrivalled in Cambodia. Love him or hate him, he has proved himself a survivor, personally as well as politically, for he lost an eye during the battle for Phnom Penh in 1975. With the opposition under his thumb, and a poorly educated electorate, for the time at least, it appears that 'in the country of the blind, the one-eyed man is king'.

The depressing reality of politics in Cambodia is that the political elite have consistently and wholeheartedly betrayed the long-term interests of their people for short-term personal gain. Entering politics is not about national service, but self-service. That Cambodia has made progress in spite of its government and not because of it comes down to the Cambodian people: their tenacity, good humour and instinct for survival. Most Cambodians are hard-working and honest...wouldn't it be good if the same could be said for their politicians?

History

The good, the bad and the ugly is the simple way to sum up Cambodian history. Things were good in the early years, culminating in the vast Angkor empire, unrivalled in the region during four centuries of dominance. Then the bad set in, from the 13th century, as ascendant neighbours steadily chipped away at Cambodian territory. In the 20th century it turned downright ugly, as a brutal civil war lead to the genocidal rule of the Khmer Rouge (1975–79), from which Cambodia is still recovering.

EARLY BEGINNINGS

Cambodia came into being, so the story goes, through the union of a princess and a foreigner. The foreigner was an Indian Brahman named Kaundinya and the princess was the daughter of a dragon king who ruled over a watery land. One day, as Kaundinya sailed by, the princess paddled out in a boat to greet him. Kaundinya shot an arrow from his magic bow into her boat, causing the fearful princess to agree to marriage. In need of a dowry, her father drank up the waters of his land and presented them to Kaundinya to rule over. The new kingdom was named Kambuja.

Like many legends, this one is historically opaque, but it does say something about the cultural forces that brought Cambodia into existence; in particular its relationship with its great subcontinental neighbour, India. Cambodia's religious, royal and written traditions stemmed from India and began to coalesce as a cultural entity in their own right between the 1st and 5th centuries.

Very little is known about prehistoric Cambodia. Much of the southeast was a vast, shallow gulf that was progressively silted up by the mouths of the Mekong, leaving pancake-flat, mineral-rich land ideal for farming. Evidence of cave-dwellers has been found in the northwest of Cambodia. Carbon dating on ceramic pots found in the area shows that they were made around 4200 BC, but it is hard to say whether there is a direct relationship between these cave-dwelling pot makers and contemporary Khmers. Examinations of bones dating back to around 1500 BC, however, suggest that the people living in Cambodia at that time resembled the Cambodians of today. Early Chinese records report that the Cambodians were 'ugly' and 'dark' and went about naked; but a pinch of salt is always required when reading the culturally chauvinistic reports of imperial China concerning its 'barbarian' neighbours.

INDIANISATION & FUNAN

The early Indianisation of Cambodia occurred via trading settlements that sprang up from the 1st century on the coastline of what is now southern Vietnam, but was then inhabited by Cambodians. These settlements were ports of call for boats following the trading route from the Bay of Bengal to the southern provinces of China. The largest of these nascent kingdoms was known as Funan by the Chinese, and may have existed across an area between Ba Phnom in Prey Veng Province, a site only worth visiting for the archaeologically obsessed today, and Oc-Eo

Cambodia's Funan period trading port of Oc-Eo, now located in Vietnam's Mekong Delta, was a major commercial crossroads between east and west and archaeologists here have unearthed Roman coins and Chinese ceramics.

AD 100	600
Indianisation begins: the religions, language and sculpture of India start to take root in Cambodia	The first inscriptions are committed to stone in Cambodia, giving historians a glimpse into the pre-Angkorian period

in Kien Giang Province in southern Vietnam. It would have been a contemporary of Champasak in southern Laos (then known as Kuruksetra) and other lesser fiefdoms in the region.

Funan is a Chinese name, and it may be a transliteration of the ancient Khmer word *bnam* (mountain). Although very little is known about Funan, much has been made of its importance as an early Southeast Asian centre of power.

It is most likely that between the 1st and 8th centuries, Cambodia was a collection of small states, each with its own elites that often strategically intermarried and often went to war with one another. Funan was no doubt one of these states, and as a major sea port would have been pivotal in the transmission of Indian culture into the interior of Cambodia.

What historians do know about Funan they have mostly gleaned from Chinese sources. These report that Funan-period Cambodia (1st to 6th centuries AD) embraced the worship of the Hindu deities Shiva and Vishnu and, at the same time, Buddhism. The *linga* (phallic totem) appears to have been the focus of ritual and an emblem of kingly might, a feature that was to evolve further in the Angkorian cult of the god-king. The people practised primitive irrigation, which enabled the cultivation of rice, and traded raw commodities such as spices with China and India.

> Founded by King Isanavarman I in the early 7th century, Sambor Prei Kuk was originally known as Isanapura and was the first major temple city to be constructed in Southeast Asia.

CHENLA PERIOD

From the 6th century the Funan kingdom's importance as a port of call declined, and Cambodia's population gradually concentrated along the Mekong and Tonlé Sap Rivers, where the majority remains today. The move may have been related to the development of wet-rice agriculture. From the 6th to 8th centuries it was likely that Cambodia was a collection of competing kingdoms, ruled by autocratic kings who legitimised their absolute rule through hierarchical caste concepts borrowed from India.

This era is generally referred to as the Chenla period. Again, like Funan, it is a Chinese term and there is little to support the idea that the Chenla was a unified kingdom that held sway over all of Cambodia. Indeed, the Chinese themselves referred to 'water Chenla' and 'land Chenla'. Water Chenla was located around Angkor Borei and the temple mount of Phnom Da (p206), near the present-day provincial capital of Takeo; and land Chenla in the upper reaches of the Mekong River and east of the Tonlé Sap lake, around Sambor Prei Kuk (p240), an essential stop on a chronological jaunt through Cambodia's history.

The people of Cambodia were well known to the Chinese, and gradually the region was becoming more cohesive. Before long the fractured kingdoms of Cambodia would merge to become the greatest empire in Southeast Asia.

ANGKORIAN PERIOD

A popular place of pilgrimage for Khmers today, the sacred mountain of Phnom Kulen (p175), to the northeast of Angkor, is home to an inscription that tells us in 802 Jayavarman II proclaimed himself a 'universal monarch', or *devaraja* (god-king). It is believed that he may have resided in the Buddhist Shailendras' court in Java as a young man. One of the first things he did when he returned to Cambodia was to reject Javanese

802	889
Jayavarman II proclaims independence from Java, marking the start of the Khmer Empire of Angkor	Yasovarman I moves the capital from Roluos to Angkor, 16km to the northwest

control over the southern lands of Cambodia. Jayavarman II then set out to bring the country under his control through alliances and conquests, the first monarch to rule all of what we call Cambodia today.

Jayavarman II was the first of a long succession of kings who presided over the rise and fall of the Southeast Asian empire that was to leave the stunning legacy of Angkor. The first records of the massive irrigation works that supported the population of Angkor date to the reign of Indravarman I (877–89). His rule also marks the beginning of Angkorian art, with the building of temples in the Roluos area, notably the Bakong (p170). His son Yasovarman I (r 889–910) moved the royal court to Angkor proper, establishing a temple-mountain on the summit of Phnom Bakheng (p163).

By the turn of the 11th century the kingdom of Angkor was losing control of its territories. Suryavarman I (r 1002–49), a usurper, moved into the power vacuum and, like Jayavarman II two centuries before, reunified the kingdom through war and alliances. He annexed the Dravati kingdom of Lopburi in Thailand and widened his control of Cambodia, stretching the empire to perhaps its greatest extent. A pattern was beginning to emerge, and can be seen throughout the Angkorian period: dislocation and turmoil, followed by reunification and further expansion under a powerful king. Architecturally, the most productive periods occurred after times of turmoil, indicating that newly incumbent monarchs felt the need to celebrate and perhaps legitimise their rule with massive building projects.

By 1066 Angkor was again riven by conflict, becoming the focus of rival bids for power. It was not until the accession of Suryavarman II (in 1112) that the kingdom was again unified. Suryavarman II embarked on another phase of expansion, waging wars in Vietnam and the region of central Vietnam known as Champa. He also established links with China. But Suryavarman II is immortalised as the king who, in his devotion to the Hindu deity Vishnu, commissioned the majestic temple of Angkor Wat (p150).

Suryavarman II had brought Champa to heel and reduced it to vassal status. In 1177, however, the Chams struck back with a naval expedition up the Mekong and into Tonlé Sap lake. They took the city of Angkor by surprise and put King Dharanindravarman II to death. The next year a cousin of Suryavarman II gathered forces and defeated the Chams in another naval battle. The new leader was crowned Jayavarman VII in 1181.

A devout follower of Mahayana Buddhism, Jayavarman VII built the city of Angkor Thom (p155) and many other massive monuments. Indeed, many of the monuments visited by tourists around Angkor today were constructed during Jayavarman VII's reign. However, Jayavarman VII is a figure of many contradictions. The bas-reliefs of the Bayon (p156) depict him presiding over battles of terrible ferocity, while statues of the king show him in a meditative, otherworldly aspect. His programme of temple construction and other public works was carried out in great haste, no doubt bringing enormous hardship to the labourers who provided the muscle, and thus accelerating the decline of the empire. He was partly driven by a desire to legitimise his rule, as there may have been other contenders closer to the royal bloodline, and partly by the need to introduce a new religion to a population predominantly Hindu in faith.

For more on the Angkorian period see p134.

For a wild 360 degree tour of the principal temples of Angkor that makes you feel like you are there, take a look at the incredible interactive photographs at www .world-heritage -tour .org/asia/kh/angkor /map.html.

Chinese emissary Chou Ta Kuan lived in Angkor for a year in 1296, and his observations have been republished as *The Customs of Cambodia* (2000), a fascinating insight into life during the height of the empire.

924

Usurper king Jayavarman IV transfers the capital to Koh Ker, but forgets to check the water table first

1112

Suryavarman II commences the construction of Angkor Wat, the mother of all temples

DECLINE & FALL

Some scholars maintain that decline was hovering in the wings at the time Angkor Wat was built, when the Angkorian empire was at the height of its remarkable productivity. There are indications that the irrigation network was overworked and slowly starting to silt up due to the massive deforestation that had taken place in the heavily populated areas to the north and east of Angkor. Massive construction projects such as Angkor Wat and Angkor Thom no doubt put an enormous strain on the royal coffers and on thousands of slaves and common people who subsidised them in hard work and taxes. Following the reign of Jayavarman VII, temple construction effectively ground to a halt, in large part because Jayavarman VII's public works quarried local sandstone into oblivion and the population was exhausted.

Another important aspect of this period was the decline of Cambodian political influence on the peripheries of its empire. At the same time, the Thais were ascendant, having migrated south from Yunnan to escape Kublai Khan and his Mongol hordes. The Thais, first from Sukothai, later Ayuthaya, grew in strength and made repeated incursions into Angkor, finally sacking the city in 1431 and making off with thousands of intellectuals, artisans and dancers from the royal court. During this period, perhaps drawn by the opportunities for sea trade with China and fearful of the increasingly bellicose Thais, the Khmer elite began to migrate to the Phnom Penh area. The capital shifted several times in the 16th century but eventually settled in present day Phnom Penh.

One of the definitive guides to Angkor is *A Guide to the Angkor Monuments* by Maurice Glaize, first published in the 1940s and now out of print. Download it for free at www.theangkor guide.com.

THE DARK AGES

From 1600 until the arrival of the French in 1863, Cambodia was ruled by a series of weak kings who, because of continual challenges by dissident members of the royal family, were forced to seek the protection – granted, of course, at a price – of either Thailand or Vietnam. In the 17th century, assistance from the Nguyen lords of southern Vietnam was given on the proviso that Vietnamese be allowed to settle in what is now the Mekong Delta region of Vietnam, at that time part of Cambodia and today still referred to by the Khmers as Kampuchea Krom (Lower Cambodia).

In the west, the Thais controlled the provinces of Battambang and Siem Reap from 1794; by the late 18th century they had firm control of the Cambodian royal family. Indeed, one king was crowned in Bangkok and placed on the throne at Udong (p108) with the help of the Thai army. That Cambodia survived through the 18th century as a distinct entity is due to the preoccupations of its neighbours: while the Thais were expending their energy and resources in fighting the Burmese, the Vietnamese were wholly absorbed by internal strife.

The commercial metropolis that is now Ho Chi Minh City (Saigon) in Vietnam was, in 1600, a small Cambodian village called Prey Nokor.

FRENCH RULE

Cambodia's long period of bouncing back and forth between Thai and Vietnamese masters ended in 1864, when French gunboats intimidated King Norodom I (r 1860–1904) into signing a treaty of protectorate. French control of Cambodia, which developed as a sideshow to French-colonial interests in Vietnam, initially involved little direct interference in Cambodia's affairs. More importantly, the French presence prevented Cambodia's

1177	1181
The Chams sail up the Tonlé Sap, defeat the Khmers and occupy Angkor for four years	The Chams are vanquished as Jayavarman VII, the greatest king of Angkor and builder of Angkor Thom, takes the throne

expansionist neighbours from annexing any more Khmer territory and helped keep Norodom on the throne despite the ambitions of his rebellious half-brothers.

By the 1870s French officials in Cambodia began pressing for greater control over internal affairs. In 1884, Norodom was forced into signing a treaty that turned his country into a virtual colony. This sparked a two-year rebellion that constituted the only major anti-French movement in Cambodia until after WWII. This uprising ended when the king was persuaded to call upon the rebel fighters to lay down their weapons in exchange for a return to the pretreaty arrangement.

During the next two decades senior Cambodian officials, who saw certain advantages in acquiescing to French power, opened the door to direct French control over the day-to-day administration of the country. At the same time the French maintained Norodom's court in a splendour unseen since the heyday of Angkor, thereby greatly enhancing the symbolic position of the monarchy. The French were able to pressure Thailand into returning the northwest provinces of Battambang, Siem Reap and Sisophon in 1907, in return for concessions of Lao territory to the Thais, returning Angkor to Cambodian control for the first time in more than a century.

> The French did very little to encourage education in Cambodia, and by the end of WWII, after 70 years of colonial rule, there were no universities and only one high school in the whole country.

King Norodom I was succeeded by King Sisowath (r 1904–27), who was succeeded by King Monivong (r 1927–41). Upon King Monivong's death, the French governor general of Japanese-occupied Indochina, Admiral Jean Decoux, placed 19-year-old Prince Norodom Sihanouk on the Cambodian throne. Sihanouk would prove pliable, so the assumption went, but this proved to be a major miscalculation (see the boxed text, opposite).

During WWII, Japanese forces occupied much of Asia, and Cambodia was no exception. However, with many in France collaborating with the occupying Germans, the Japanese were happy to let these French allies control affairs in Cambodia. The price was conceding to Thailand (a Japanese ally of sorts) much of Battambang and Siem Reap Provinces once again, areas that weren't returned until 1947. However, with the fall of Paris in 1944 and French policy in disarray, the Japanese were forced to take direct control of the territory by early 1945. After WWII, the French returned, making Cambodia an autonomous state within the French Union, but retaining de facto control. The French deserved independence it seemed, but not its colonies. The immediate postwar years were marked by strife among the country's various political factions, a situation made more unstable by the Franco-Viet Minh War then raging in Vietnam and Laos, which spilled over into Cambodia. The Vietnamese, as they were also to do 20 years later in the war against Lon Nol and the Americans, trained and fought with bands of Khmer Issarak (Free Khmer) against the French authorities.

INDEPENDENCE & SIHANOUK'S RULE

In late-1952 King Sihanouk dissolved the fledgling parliament, declared martial law and embarked on his 'royal crusade': his travelling campaign to drum up international support for his country's independence.

Independence was proclaimed on 9 November 1953 and recognised by the Geneva Conference of May 1954, which ended French control of Indochina. In 1955, Sihanouk abdicated, afraid of being marginalised

Jayavarman VII dies and the empire of Angkor slowly declines

The expansionist Thais sack Angkor definitively, carting off most of the royal court to Ayuthaya

KING SIHANOUK

Norodom Sihanouk has been a constant presence in the topsy-turvy world of Cambodian politics. A colourful character of many enthusiasms and shifting political positions, his amatory exploits dominated his early reputation. Later he became the prince who stage-managed the close of French colonialism, autocratically led an independent Cambodia, was imprisoned by the Khmer Rouge and, from privileged exile, finally returned triumphant as king, only to abdicate dramatically in 2004. He is many things to many people, a political chameleon, but whatever else he may be, he has proved himself a survivor.

Sihanouk, born in 1922, was not an obvious contender for the throne. He was crowned in 1941, at just 19, with his education incomplete. In 1952 he embarked on a self-styled 'royal crusade' for independence, which culminated in independence from the French in 1953. In 1955 Sihanouk abdicated, and turned his attention to politics, winning every seat in parliament that year.

By the mid-1960s Sihanouk had been calling the shots in Cambodia for a decade. During this period, after innumerable love affairs, he finally settled on Monique Izzi, the daughter of a Franco-Italian father and a Cambodian mother, as his consort.

The conventional wisdom was that 'Sihanouk is Cambodia', his leadership the key to national success. However, as the country was inexorably drawn into the American War in Vietnam and government troops battled with a leftist insurgency in the countryside, Sihanouk increasingly was seen as a liability. With the economy in tatters, his obsessive involvement in the Cambodian film industry (p53) and his public announcements proclaiming Cambodia 'an oasis of peace' suggested a man who had not only abdicated from the throne but also from reality.

On 18 March 1970 the National Assembly voted to remove Sihanouk from office. Sihanouk went into exile in Beijing and joined the communists. Following the Khmer Rouge victory on 17 April 1975, Sihanouk was confined to the Royal Palace as a prisoner of the Khmer Rouge. He remained there until early 1979 when, on the eve of the Vietnamese invasion, he was flown back to Beijing. It was to be more than a decade before Sihanouk finally returned to Cambodia.

Following his return and against all odds, he was back at centre stage again, calling the shots, forming alliances with the Khmer Rouge and breaking them off. After the May 1993 elections, Sihanouk abruptly announced that he was forming a coalition government with himself starring as president, prime minister and military leader. An ambitious move, it failed.

Sihanouk never quite gave up wanting to be everything for Cambodia: international statesman, general, president, film director, man of the people. On 24 September 1993, after 38 years in politics, he took on once again the role of king. In many ways his second stint as king was a frustrating time; reigning rather than ruling, he had to take a back seat to the politicians. He pulled Cambodia through political impasse on several occasions, but eventually enough was enough and he abdicated on 7 October 2004. Many reasons for his abdication were cited (old age, failing health), but most observers agree it was a calculated political decision to ensure the future of the monarchy, as the politicians were stalling on choosing a successor. His son King Sihamoni ascended the throne and Cambodia came through another crisis. However, it will be a hard act to follow, matching the presence of Sihanouk – the last in a long line of Angkor's god-kings.

amid the pomp of royal ceremony. The 'royal crusader' became 'citizen Sihanouk'. He vowed never again to return to the throne. Meanwhile his father became king. It was a masterstroke that offered Sihanouk both royal authority and supreme political power. His newly established party, Sangkum Reastr Niyum (People's Socialist Community Party), won every seat in parliament in the September 1955 elections and Sihanouk was to dominate Cambodian politics for the next 15 years.

1772	1864
The Thais burn Phnom Penh to the ground, another chapter in the story of inflamed tensions that persists today	The French force King Norodom I into signing a treaty of protectorate, which prevents Cambodia being wiped off the map

Although he feared the Vietnamese communists, Sihanouk considered South Vietnam and Thailand, both allies of the USA (which he mistrusted), the greatest threats to Cambodia's security, even survival. In an attempt to fend off these many dangers, he declared Cambodia neutral in international affairs and refused to accept any further US aid, which had accounted for a substantial chunk of the country's military budget. He also nationalised many industries, including the rice trade. In May 1965 Sihanouk, convinced that the USA had been plotting against him and his family, broke diplomatic relations with Washington and tilted towards the North Vietnamese and China. In addition, he agreed to let the communists use Cambodian territory in their battle against South Vietnam and the USA.

These moves and his socialist economic policies alienated right-leaning elements in Cambodian society, including the army brass and the urban elite. At the same time, left-wing Cambodians, many of them educated abroad, deeply resented his internal policies, which did not allow for political dissent. Compounding Sihanouk's problems was the fact that all classes were fed up with the pervasive corruption in government ranks, some of it uncomfortably close to the royal family. Although most peasants revered Sihanouk as a semidivine figure, in 1967 a rural-based rebellion broke out in Samlot, Battambang, leading him to conclude that the greatest threat to his regime came from the left. Bowing to pressure from the army, he implemented a policy of harsh repression against left-wingers.

By 1969 the conflict between the army and leftist rebels had become more serious, as the Vietnamese sought sanctuary deeper in Cambodia. Sihanouk's political position had also greatly deteriorated – due in no small part to his obsession with film-making, which was leading him to neglect affairs of state. In March 1970, while Sihanouk was on a trip to France, General Lon Nol and Prince Sisowath Sirik Matak, Sihanouk's cousin, deposed him as chief of state, apparently with tacit US consent. Sihanouk took up residence in Beijing, where he set up a government-in-exile nominally in control of an indigenous Cambodian revolutionary movement that Sihanouk had nicknamed the Khmer Rouge. This was a definitive moment in contemporary Cambodian history, as the Khmer Rouge exploited its partnership with Sihanouk to draw new recruits into their small organisation. Many former Khmer Rouge fighters argue that they 'went to the hills' (a euphemism for joining the Khmer Rouge) to fight for their king and knew nothing of Mao or Marxism.

THE LON NOL REGIME

Sihanouk was condemned to death *in absentia*, an excessive move on the part of the new government that effectively ruled out any chance for compromise over the next five years. Lon Nol gave communist Vietnamese forces an ultimatum to withdraw their forces within one week, which amounted to a virtual declaration of war, as no communists wanted to return to the homeland to face the Americans.

On 30 April 1970, US and South Vietnamese forces invaded Cambodia in an effort to flush out thousands of Viet Cong and North Vietnamese troops who were using Cambodian bases in their war to overthrow the

During the 1960s Cambodia was an oasis of peace while wars raged in neighbouring Vietnam and Laos. By 1970, that had all changed, as Cambodia was sucked into hell. For the full story, read *Sideshow: Kissinger, Nixon and the Destruction of Cambodia* by William Shawcross (1979).

In Francis Ford Coppola's *Apocalypse Now* a renegade colonel, played by Marlon Brando, goes AWOL in Cambodia. Martin Sheen plays a young soldier sent to bring him back, and the ensuing encounter makes for one of the most powerful indictments of war ever made.

1942	1947
Japanese forces occupy Cambodia, leaving the administration in the hands of Vichy France officials	The provinces of Battambang, Siem Reap and Sisophon, seized by the Thais during the Japanese occupation, are returned

South Vietnamese government. As a result of the invasion, the Vietnamese communists withdrew deeper into Cambodia, thus posing an even greater threat to the Lon Nol government. Cambodia's tiny army never stood a chance and within the space of a few months, Vietnamese forces and their Khmer Rouge allies controlled almost half the country. The ultimate humiliation came in July 1970 when the Vietnamese seized the temples of Angkor.

In 1969 the USA had begun a secret programme of bombing suspected communist base camps in Cambodia. For the next four years, until bombing was halted by the US Congress in August 1973, huge areas of the eastern half of the country were carpet-bombed by US B-52s, killing what is believed to be many thousands of civilians and turning hundreds of thousands more into refugees. Some historians believe the bombing campaign may have killed as many as 250,000 Cambodians. Undoubtedly, the bombing campaign helped the Khmer Rouge in their recruitment drive, as more and more peasants were losing family members to the aerial assaults. While the final, heaviest bombing in the first half of 1973 may have saved Phnom Penh from a premature fall, its ferocity also helped to harden the attitude of many Khmer Rouge cadres and may have contributed to the later brutality of the regime.

Savage fighting engulfed the country, bringing misery to millions of Cambodians; many fled rural areas for the relative safety of Phnom Penh and provincial capitals. Between 1970 and 1975 several hundred thousand people died in the fighting. During these years the Khmer Rouge came to play a dominant role in trying to overthrow the Lon Nol regime, strengthened by the support of the Vietnamese, although the Khmer Rouge leadership would vehemently deny this from 1975 onwards.

The leadership of the Khmer Rouge, including Paris-educated Pol Pot and Ieng Sary, had fled into the countryside in the 1960s to escape the summary justice then being meted out to suspected leftists by Sihanouk's security forces. They consolidated control over the movement and began to move against opponents before they took Phnom Penh. Many of the Vietnamese-trained Cambodian communists who had been based in Hanoi since the 1954 Geneva Accords returned down the Ho Chi Minh Trail to join the Khmer Rouge in 1970. Many were dead by 1975, executed on orders of the anti-Vietnamese Pol Pot faction. Likewise, many moderate Sihanouk supporters who had joined the Khmer Rouge as a show of loyalty to their fallen leader rather than a show of ideology to the radicals were victims of purges before the regime took power. This set a precedent for internal purges and mass executions that were to eventually bring the downfall of the Khmer Rouge.

It didn't take long for the Lon Nol government to become very unpopular as a result of unprecedented greed and corruption in its ranks. As the USA bankrolled the war, government and military personnel found lucrative means to make a fortune, such as inventing 'phantom soldiers' and pocketing their pay, or selling weapons to the enemy. Lon Nol was widely perceived as an ineffectual leader, obsessed by superstition, fortune tellers and mystical crusades. This perception increased with his stroke in March 1971 and for the next four years his grip on reality seemed to weaken as his corrupt brother Lon Non's power grew.

Pol Pot travelled up the Ho Chi Minh Trail to visit Beijing in 1966 at the height of the Cultural Revolution there. He was obviously inspired by what he saw, as the Khmer Rouge went even further than the Red Guards in severing links with the past.

Lon Nol's military press attaché was known for his colourful, even imaginative media briefings that painted a rosy picture of the increasingly desperate situation on the ground. With a name like Major Am Rong, few could take him seriously.

Only a handful of foreigners were allowed to visit Cambodia during the Khmer Rouge period of Democratic Kampuchea. US journalist Elizabeth Becker was one who travelled there in late 1978; her book *When the War Was Over* (1986) tells her story.

Despite massive US military and economic aid, Lon Nol never succeeded in gaining the initiative against the Khmer Rouge, which pursued a strategy of rural attrition. Large parts of the countryside fell to the rebels and many provincial capitals were cut off from Phnom Penh. Lon Nol fled the country in early April 1975, leaving Sirik Matak in charge, who refused evacuation to the end. 'I cannot alas leave in such a cowardly fashion…I have committed only one mistake, that of believing in you, the Americans' were the words Sirik Matak poignantly penned to US ambassador John Gunther Dean. On 17 April 1975 – two weeks before the fall of Saigon (now Ho Chi Minh City) – Phnom Penh surrendered to the Khmer Rouge.

KHMER ROUGE REGIME

Upon taking Phnom Penh, the Khmer Rouge implemented one of the most radical and brutal restructurings of a society ever attempted; its goal was to transform Cambodia into a Maoist, peasant-dominated agrarian cooperative. Within days of the Khmer Rouge coming to power the entire population of the capital city and provincial towns, including the sick, elderly and infirm, was forced to march out to the countryside and undertake slave labour in mobile work teams for 12 to 15 hours a day. Disobedience of any sort often brought immediate execution. The advent of Khmer Rouge rule was proclaimed Year Zero. Currency was abolished and postal services were halted. Except for one fortnightly flight to Beijing (China was providing aid and advisers to the Khmer Rouge), the country was cut off from the outside world.

Francois Bizot was twice caught in the wrong place at the wrong time. First he was kidnapped by the Khmer Rouge, and later (in 1975) he was held by the Khmer Rouge in the French embassy. Read his harrowing story in *The Gate* (2003).

In the eyes of Pol Pot, the Khmer Rouge was not a unified movement, but a series of factions that needed to be cleansed. This process had begun previously with attacks on Vietnamese-trained Khmer Rouge and Sihanouk's supporters, but Pol Pot's initial fury upon seizing power was directed against the enemies of the former regime. All of the senior government and military figures who had been associated with Lon Nol were executed within days of the takeover. Then the centre shifted its attention to the outer regions, which had been separated into geographic zones. The loyalist Southwestern Zone forces under the control of one-legged general Ta Mok were sent into region after region to purify population, and thousands perished.

The Killing Fields (1985) is the definitive film on the Khmer Rouge period in Cambodia. It tells the story of American journalist Sidney Schanberg and his Cambodian assistant Dith Pran during and after the war.

The cleansing reached grotesque heights in the final and bloodiest purge against the powerful and independent Eastern Zone. Generally considered more moderate than other Khmer Rouge factions (although 'moderate' is relative in a Khmer Rouge context), the Eastern Zone was closer to Vietnam. The Pol Pot faction consolidated the rest of the country before moving against the east from 1977 onwards. Hundreds of leaders were executed before open rebellion broke out and set the scene for civil war in the east. Many Eastern Zone leaders fled to Vietnam, forming the nucleus of the government installed by the Vietnamese in January 1979. The people were defenceless and distrusted – 'Cambodian bodies with Vietnamese minds' or 'duck's arses with chicken's heads' – and were deported to the northwest with new, blue *krama* (scarves). Had it not been for the Vietnamese invasion, all would have perished, as the blue *krama* was a secret party sign indicating an eastern enemy of the revolution.

1963	1969
Pol Pot and Ieng Sary flee from Phnom Penh to the jungles to launch a guerrilla war against Sihanouk's government	US President Nixon authorises the secret bombing of Cambodia, which continues until 1973 killing as many as 250,000 Cambodians

---

BLOOD BROTHER NO 1

Pol Pot, Brother No 1 in the Khmer Rouge regime, is a name that sends shivers down the spines of Cambodians and foreigners alike. It is Pol Pot who is most associated with the bloody madness of the regime he led between 1975 and 1979, and his policies heaped misery, suffering and death on millions of Cambodians. Even after being overthrown in 1979 he cast a long shadow over the Cambodian people: for many of them, just knowing he was still alive was traumatic and unjust. He died on 15 April 1998.

Pol Pot was born Saloth Sar in a small village near Kompong Thom in 1925. As a young man he won a scholarship to study in Paris and spent several years there with Ieng Sary, who would later become foreign minister of Democratic Kampuchea. It is here that he is believed to have developed his radical Marxist thought, later to transform into the politics of extreme Maoist agrarianism.

In 1963, Sihanouk's repressive policies sent Saloth Sar and comrades fleeing to the jungles of Ratanakiri. It was from this moment that he began to call himself Pol Pot. Once the Khmer Rouge was allied with Sihanouk, following his overthrow by Lon Nol in 1970 and subsequent exile in Beijing, its support soared and the faces of the leadership became familiar. However, Pol Pot remained a shadowy figure, leaving public duties to Khieu Samphan and Ieng Sary.

When the Khmer Rouge marched into Phnom Penh on 17 April 1975, few people could have anticipated the hell that was to follow. Pol Pot, with the help of others, was the architect of one of the most radical and brutal revolutions in the history of mankind. The year 1975 was proclaimed as Year Zero; Cambodia was on a self-destructive course to sever all ties with the past.

Pol Pot was not to emerge as the public face of the revolution until the end of 1976, after returning from a trip to his mentors in Beijing. He granted almost no interviews to foreign media and was seen only on propaganda movies produced by government TV. Such was his aura and reputation that by the last year of the regime a cult of personality was developing around him and busts were produced.

He was fervently anti-Vietnamese, a sentiment fuelled by the fact that the Vietnamese considered the Cambodian revolution of secondary importance to their own. Fittingly, it was the Vietnamese that turned out to be his greatest enemy, invading Cambodia on 25 December 1978 and overthrowing the Khmer Rouge government. Pol Pot and his supporters were sent fleeing to the jungle near the Thai border, from where they spent the next decade launching attacks on government positions in Cambodia.

Pol Pot spent much of the 1980s living in an armed compound in Thailand, and with the connivance of both China and the West was able to rebuild his shattered forces and once again threaten the stability of Cambodia. Throughout the 1980s and 1990s his enigma increased as the international media speculated as to the real fate of Pol Pot. His demise was reported so often that when he finally passed away, many Cambodians refused to believe it until they had seen his body on TV or in newspapers. Even then, many were sceptical and rumours continue to circulate about exactly how he met his end.

It is still not known exactly how many Cambodians died at the hands of the Khmer Rouge during the three years, eight months and 21 days of their rule. The Vietnamese claimed three million deaths, while foreign experts long considered the number closer to one million. In early 1996, Yale University researchers undertaking ongoing investigations estimated that the figure was around two million.

Hundreds of thousands of people were executed by the Khmer Rouge leadership, while hundreds of thousands more died of famine and disease.

1970	**1973**
Sihanouk is overthrown by Lon Nol and Prince Sirik Matak, and sentenced to death *in absentia;* the civil war begins	Sihanouk visits his Khmer Rouge allies at Phnom Kulen, an unfortunate propaganda victory for Pol Pot

Meals consisted of little more than watery rice porridge twice a day, meant to sustain men, women and children through a back-breaking day in the fields. Disease stalked the work camps, malaria and dysentery striking down whole families; death was a relief for many from the horrors of life. Some zones were better than others, some leaders fairer than others, but life for the majority was one of unending misery and suffering.

As the centre eliminated more and more moderates, Angkar (the organisation) was now the only family people needed and those who did not agree were sought out and destroyed. The Khmer Rouge detached the Cambodian people from all they held dear: their families, their food, their fields and their faith. Even the peasants who had supported the revolution could no longer maintain their support. Nobody cared for the Khmer Rouge by 1978, but nobody had an ounce of strength to do anything about it…except the Vietnamese.

For a fuller understanding of the methodical machine that was the Khmer Rouge's interrogation and torture centre of S-21, read the classic but chilling *Voices from S-21* by David Chandler (1999).

VIETNAMESE INTERVENTION

From 1976 to 1978, the xenophobic government in Phnom Penh instigated a series of border clashes with Vietnam, and claimed the Mekong Delta, once part of the Khmer empire. Khmer Rouge incursions into Vietnamese border provinces left hundreds of Vietnamese civilians dead. On 25 December 1978 Vietnam launched a full-scale invasion of Cambodia, toppling the Pol Pot government two weeks later. As Vietnamese tanks neared Phnom Penh, the Khmer Rouge fled westward with as many civilians as it could seize, taking refuge in the jungles and mountains on both sides of the Thai border. The Vietnamese installed a new government led by several former Khmer Rouge officers, including Hun Sen, who had defected to Vietnam in 1977. The Khmer Rouge's patrons, the Chinese communists, launched a massive reprisal raid across Vietnam's northernmost border in early 1979 in an attempt to buy their allies time. It failed, and after 17 days the Chinese withdrew, their fingers badly burnt by their Vietnamese enemies. The Vietnamese then staged a show trial in which Pol Pot and Ieng Sary were condemned to death for their genocidal acts.

The social and economic dislocation that accompanied the Vietnamese invasion – along with the destruction of rice stocks and unharvested fields by both sides (to prevent their use by the enemy) – resulted in a vastly reduced rice harvest in early 1979. The chaotic situation led to very little rice being planted in the summer of 1979. By the middle of that year the country was suffering from a widespread famine.

As hundreds of thousands of Cambodians fled to Thailand, a massive international famine relief effort, sponsored by the UN, was launched. The international community wanted to inject aid across a land bridge at Poipet, while the new Phnom Penh government wanted all supplies to come through the capital via Kompong Som (Sihanoukville) or the Mekong River. Both sides had their reasons – the new government did not want aid to fall into the hands of its Khmer Rouge enemies, while the international community didn't believe the new government had the infrastructure to distribute the aid – and both were right.

Some agencies distributed aid the slow way through Phnom Penh, and others set up camps in Thailand. The camps became a magnet for half of Cambodia, as many Khmers still feared the return of the Khmer

1975	1979
The Khmer Rouge march into Phnom Penh on 17 April and turn the clocks back to Year Zero	Vietnamese forces liberate Cambodia from Khmer Rouge rule and install a friendly regime in Phnom Penh

Rouge or were seeking a new life overseas. The Thai military bullied and blackmailed the international community into distributing all aid through their channels and used this as a cloak to rebuild the shattered Khmer Rouge forces as an effective resistance against the Vietnamese. Thailand demanded that, as a condition for allowing international food aid for Cambodia to pass through its territory, food had to be supplied to the Khmer Rouge forces encamped in the Thai border region as well. Along with weaponry supplied by China, this international assistance was essential in enabling the Khmer Rouge to rebuild its military strength. The Khmer Rouge regrouped with food and shelter from willing donors and managed to fight on for another 20 years.

In June 1982 Sihanouk agreed, under pressure from China, to head a military and political front opposed to the Phnom Penh government. The Sihanouk-led resistance coalition brought together – on paper, at least – Funcinpec (the French acronym for the National United Front for an Independent, Neutral, Peaceful and Cooperative Cambodia), which comprised a royalist group loyal to Sihanouk; the Khmer People's National Liberation Front, a noncommunist grouping formed by former prime minister Son Sann; and the Khmer Rouge, officially known as the Party of Democratic Kampuchea and by far the most powerful of the three. The undisputed crimes of the Khmer Rouge were conveniently overlooked to ensure a compromise to suit the great powers.

During the mid-1980s the British government dispatched the Special Air Service (SAS) to a Malaysian jungle camp to train guerrilla fighters in land mine–laying techniques. Although officially assisting the smaller factions, it is certain the Khmer Rouge benefited from this experience. It then used these new-found skills to intimidate and terrorise the Cambodian people. As part of its campaign to harass and isolate Hanoi, the USA gave more than US$15 million a year in aid to the noncommunist factions of the Khmer Rouge–dominated coalition and helped the group retain its seat at the UN assembly in New York. Those responsible for the genocide were representing their victims on the international stage.

For much of the 1980s Cambodia remained closed to the Western world, save for the presence of some aid groups. Government policy was effectively under the control of the Vietnamese so Cambodia found itself very much in the Eastern-bloc camp. The economy was in tatters for much of this period, as Cambodia, like Vietnam, suffered from the effects of a US-sponsored embargo.

In 1985 the Vietnamese overran all the major rebel camps inside Cambodia, forcing the Khmer Rouge and its allies to retreat into Thailand. From that time the Khmer Rouge – and, to a limited extent, the other two factions – engaged in guerrilla warfare aimed at demoralising its opponents. Tactics used by the Khmer Rouge included shelling government-controlled garrison towns, planting thousands of mines along roads and in rice-fields, attacking road transport, blowing up bridges, kidnapping village chiefs, and killing local administrators and school teachers. The Khmer Rouge also forced thousands of men, women and children living in the refugee camps it controlled to work as porters, ferrying ammunition and other supplies into Cambodia across heavily mined sections of the border. The Vietnamese for their

For the fuller flavour of Cambodian history, from the humble beginnings in the prehistoric period through the glories of Angkor and right up to the present day, grab a copy of *The History of Cambodia* by David Chandler (1994).

1980	1985
Cambodia is gripped by famine, as the dislocation of the previous few years means that no rice has been harvested	The Khmer Rouge and its allies are forced to retreat to Thailand

part laid the world's longest minefield, known as K-5, stretching from the Gulf of Thailand to the Lao border, in an attempt to seal out the guerrillas. They also sent Cambodians into the forests to cut down trees on remote sections of road to prevent ambushes. Hundreds, surely thousands, died of disease and from injuries sustained from land mines.

By the late 1980s the military wing of Funcinpec, the Armée Nationale Sihanoukiste, had 12,000 troops; Son Sann's faction, plagued by internal divisions, could field some 8000 soldiers; and the Khmer Rouge's National Army of Democratic Kampuchea was believed to have 40,000 troops. The army of the Phnom Penh government, the Kampuchean People's Revolutionary Armed Forces, had 50,000 regular soldiers and another 100,000 men and women serving in local militia forces.

Between four and six million land mines dot the Cambodian countryside. Lifetime rehabilitation of the country's estimated 40,000 victims costs US$120 million.

UNTAC AT THE HELM

In September 1989 Vietnam, suffering from economic woes and eager to end its international isolation, announced that it was withdrawing all of its troops from Cambodia. With most of the Vietnamese gone, the opposition coalition, still dominated by the Khmer Rouge, launched a series of offensives, bringing the number of refugees inside the country to more than 150,000 by the autumn of 1990.

Diplomatic efforts to end the civil war began to bear fruit in September 1990, when a peace plan was accepted by both the Phnom Penh govern-

---

THE NAME GAME

Cambodia has changed its name so many times over the last few decades that there are understandable grounds for confusion. To the Cambodians, their country is Kampuchea. The name is derived from the word Kambuja, meaning 'those born of Kambu', the mythical founder of the country. It dates back as far as the 10th century. The Portuguese 'Camboxa' and the French 'Cambodge', from which the English name 'Cambodia' is derived, are adaptations of 'Kambuja'.

Since gaining independence in 1953, the country has been known in English by various names before coming full circle:

- The Kingdom of Cambodia
- The Khmer Republic (under Lon Nol, who reigned from 1970 to 1975)
- Democratic Kampuchea (under the Khmer Rouge, which controlled the country from 1975 to 1979)
- The People's Republic of Kampuchea (under the Vietnamese-backed Phnom Penh government from 1979 to 1989)
- The State of Cambodia (from mid-1989)
- The Kingdom of Cambodia (from May 1993)

It was the Khmer Rouge that insisted the outside world use the name Kampuchea. Changing the country's official English name back to Cambodia (which was used by the US all along) was intended as a symbolic move to distance the present government in Phnom Penh from the bitter connotations of the name Kampuchea, which Westerners associate with the murderous Khmer Rouge regime.

1985	1989
Hun Sen becomes Prime Minister of Cambodia, a title he still holds today	Vietnam announces the withdrawal of its forces from Cambodia

ment and the three factions of the resistance coalition. According to the plan, the Supreme National Council (SNC), a coalition of all factions, was to be formed under the presidency of Sihanouk. Meanwhile the UN Transitional Authority in Cambodia (Untac) was to supervise the administration of the country for two years with the goal of free elections.

Untac was successful in achieving SNC agreement to most international human-rights covenants; a significant number of nongovernmental organisations (NGOs) were established in Cambodia; and, most importantly, on 25 May 1993, elections were held with an 89.6% turnout. The results were far from decisive, however: Funcinpec, led by Prince Norodom Ranariddh, took 58 seats in the National Assembly; the Cambodian People's Party (CPP), which represented the previous communist government, took 51 seats; and the Buddhist Liberal Democratic Party (BLDP) took 10 seats. The CPP had lost the election, but senior leaders threatened a secession of the eastern provinces of the country. As a result, Cambodia ended up with two prime ministers: Norodom Ranariddh as first prime minister, and Hun Sen as second prime minister.

Untac was quick to pack up and go home, patting itself on the back for a job well done. Even today, it is heralded as one of the UN's success stories. The reality is that it was an ill-conceived and poorly executed peace because so many of the powers involved in brokering the deal had their own agendas to advance.

It was a travesty that the Khmer Rouge was allowed to play a part in the process after the barbarities it had inflicted on its people; it must have seemed like a cruel joke to the many Cambodians who had lost countless family members under its rule. It rapidly became far more than a cruel joke, as the UN's half-botched disarmament programme took weapons away from rural militias who for so long provided the backbone of the government's provincial defence network against the Khmer Rouge. This left communities throughout the country vulnerable to attack, while the Khmer Rouge used the veil of legitimacy conferred upon it by the peace process to re-establish a guerrilla network throughout Cambodia. It is not an exaggeration to say that by 1994, when it was finally outlawed by the government, the Khmer Rouge was probably a greater threat to the stability of Cambodia than at any time since 1979.

Untac's main goals had been to 'restore and maintain peace' and 'promote national reconciliation' and it achieved neither. It did oversee free and fair elections, however these were later annulled by the actions of Cambodia's politicians. But a lot of people rode the gravy train as it steamed through Cambodia, with an army of highly paid consultants and advisers flying in… 1st and business class of course!

If that wasn't bad enough, the UN presence also kick-started Cambodia's AIDS epidemic, with well-paid overseas soldiers boosting the prostitution industry. Cambodia's AIDS problem is now among the worst in Asia.

Cambodia's turbulent past is uncovered in a series of articles, oral histories and photos in an excellent website called 'Beauty and Darkness: Cambodia, the Odyssey of the Khmer People'. Find it at www.mekong .net/Cambodia.

MACHIAVELLIAN TIMES

As early as 1995 there were two major political incidents that boded ill for democratic politics. The first of these was the ouster of Sam Rainsy, a Paris-educated accountant, from Funcinpec. In mid-1994 Rainsy lost his position as finance minister, a job he had excelled at, largely, it was

1991   **1993**

| The Paris Peace Accords are signed; all parties agree to participate in free and fair elections supervised by the UN | Royalist party Funcinpec wins the popular vote, but the CPP threaten secession in the east to muscle their way into government |

surmised, because of his outspoken criticisms concerning corruption. In May 1995 his party membership was rescinded and one month later he was sacked from the National Assembly. He formed the Khmer Nation Party (now called the Sam Rainsy Party) and found himself the country's leading dissident in no time at all.

The other political headline of 1995 was the arrest and exile of Prince Norodom Sirivudh, secretary general of Funcinpec, former foreign minister and half-brother of King Sihanouk. The prince was allegedly plotting to kill Hun Sen, but it all boiled down to an off-the-cuff joke. Hun Sen, who found himself with the perfect excuse to clear another prominent adversary from his path, was the only one laughing.

DEALING WITH THE KHMER ROUGE

When the Vietnamese toppled the Pol Pot government in 1979, the Khmer Rouge disappeared into the jungle. The regime boycotted the 1993 elections and later rejected peace talks aimed at creating a ceasefire.

The defection of some 2000 troops from the Khmer Rouge army in the months after the elections offered some hope that the long-running insurrection would fizzle out. However, government-sponsored amnesty programmes initially turned out to be ill-conceived: the policy of reconscripting Khmer Rouge troops and returning them to fight their former comrades with poor pay and conditions provided little incentive to desert.

In 1994 the Khmer Rouge resorted to a new tactic of targeting tourists, with horrendous results for a number of foreigners in Cambodia. During 1994 three people were taken from a taxi on the road to Sihanoukville and subsequently shot. A few months later another three foreigners were seized from a train bound for Sihanoukville and in the ransom drama that followed they were executed, probably some time in September, as the army closed in.

The government changed its course during the mid-1990s, opting for more carrot and less stick in a bid to end the war. The breakthrough came in August 1996 when Ieng Sary, Brother No 3 in the Khmer Rouge hierarchy and foreign minister during its rule, was denounced by Pol Pot for corruption. He subsequently led a mass defection of fighters and their dependants from the Pailin area, and this effectively sealed the fate of the remaining Khmer Rouge. Pailin, rich in gems and timber, had long been the economic springboard from which the Khmer Rouge could launch counter-offensives against the government. The severing of this income, coupled with the fact that government forces now had only one front on which to concentrate their resources, suggested the days of civil war were numbered.

By 1997 cracks were appearing in the brittle coalition and the fledgling democracy once again found itself under siege. On 31 March 1997 a grenade was thrown into a group of Sam Rainsy supporters demonstrating peacefully outside the National Assembly. Many were killed and Sam Rainsy narrowly escaped injury. He fled into self-imposed exile, blaming Hun Sen and the CPP for the attack. However, it was the Khmer Rouge that again grabbed the headlines. Pol Pot ordered the execution of Son Sen, defence minister during the Khmer Rouge regime, and many of his family members. This provoked a putsch within the Khmer Rouge leadership, and

The Documentation Center of Cambodia is an organisation established to document the crimes of the Khmer Rouge as a record for future generations. Their excellent website is a mine of information about Cambodia's darkest hour. Take your time to visit www.dccam.org.

1994	1995
The Khmer Rouge target foreign tourists in Cambodia, kidnapping and killing groups travelling by taxi and train to the south coast	Prince Norodom Sirivudh is arrested and exiled for allegedly plotting to kill Prime Minister Hun Sen

the one-legged hardline general Ta Mok seized control of the movement and put Pol Pot on 'trial'. Rumours flew about Phnom Penh that Pol Pot would be brought there to face international justice, but attention dramatically shifted back to the capital.

THE COUP

The 'events' of July 1997, as they are euphemistically known in Cambodia, were preceded by a lengthy courting period in which both Funcinpec and the CPP attempted to win the trust of the remaining Khmer Rouge hardliners in northern Cambodia. Ranariddh was close to forging a deal with the jungle fighters and was keen to get it sewn up before Cambodia's accession to the Association of Southeast Asian Nations (Asean), as nothing would provide a better entry fanfare than the ending of Cambodia's long civil war. In his haste, he didn't pay enough attention to detail and was outflanked and subsequently outgunned by Second Prime Minister Hun Sen. On 5 July 1997 fighting again erupted on the streets of Phnom Penh as troops loyal to the CPP clashed with those loyal to Funcinpec. The heaviest exchanges were around the airport and key government buildings, but before long the dust had settled and the CPP once again controlled Cambodia. The strongman had finally flexed his muscles and there was no doubt as to which party commanded the most support within the military.

The international reaction was swift and decisive. Asean suspended Cambodia's imminent membership, the Cambodian seat at the UN was declared vacant and a freeze was put on all new aid money. This was to have a serious impact on the Cambodian economy over the next couple of years.

Following the coup, the remnants of Funcinpec forces on the Thai border around O Smach formed an alliance with the last of the Khmer Rouge under Ta Mok's control. The fighting may have ended, but the deaths certainly did not: several prominent Funcinpec politicians and military leaders were subjected to extrajudicial executions, and even today no-one has been brought to justice for these crimes. Many of Funcinpec's leading politicians fled abroad, while the senior generals led the resistance struggle on the ground.

As 1998 began the CPP announced an all-out offensive against its enemies in the north. By April it was closing in on the Khmer Rouge strongholds of Anlong Veng and Preah Vihear, and amid this heavy fighting Pol Pot evaded justice by dying a sorry death on 15 April in the Khmer Rouge's captivity. He was cremated on a pyre of burning tyres soon after; an official autopsy was never performed, which bred rumours and gossip in Phnom Penh that rumble on today. The fall of Anlong Veng in April was followed by the fall of Preah Vihear in May; and the big three, Ta Mok, Khieu Samphan and Nuon Chea, were forced to flee into the jungle near the Thai border with their remaining troops.

A SECOND ELECTION

In 1998, it was time for the country's second election, and many observers were pessimistic about the chances for democracy after the tumultuous events of 1997. Funcinpec's network was also in tatters as many of its representatives had either left the country, been murdered or switched allegiances in a bid for political survival. To contest the elections the

When Pol Pot passed away on 15 April 1998, his body was hastily cremated without an autopsy, leading many Cambodians to speculate that he was actually bumped off.

1997	1998
Second Prime Minister Hun Sen overthrows First Prime Minister Norodom Ranariddh in a military coup	Pol Pot passes away on 15 April 1998, forever depriving Cambodians of the chance for justice

To stay on top of recent events in Cambodia, including all the highs and lows of the last decade, check out the Phnom Penh Post website at www.phnompenhpost .com or consider investing in its archived CD-ROM.

opposition formed an alliance called the National United Front (NUF), which brought together Funcinpec and the Sam Rainsy Party, but it was politically expedient rather than personally excellent.

The election result reinforced the reality that the CPP was now the dominant force in the Cambodian political system, but it lacked the two-thirds majority required to govern alone. The opposition cried foul and the subsequent stand-off again plunged Cambodia into a crisis of confidence. As the opposition escalated its campaign for democracy, mass demonstrations began in the capital, which soon descended into rioting, fighting and repression.

King Sihanouk eventually negotiated a settlement, which ended with business as usual, a much-weakened Funcinpec agreeing to govern with a now dominant CPP. The formation of a new coalition government allowed the politicians to once more concentrate on bringing an end to the civil war.

On 25 December Hun Sen received the Christmas present he had been waiting for: Khieu Samphan and Nuon Chea were defecting to the government side. The international community began to pile on the pressure for the establishment of some sort of war-crimes tribunal to try the remaining Khmer Rouge leadership.

Several of the current crop of Cambodian leaders were previously members of the Khmer Rouge, including Prime Minister Hun Sen and Head of the Senate Chea Sim, although there is no evidence to implicate them in mass killings.

After lengthy negotiations, agreement was finally reached on the composition of a court to try the surviving leaders of the Khmer Rouge. The CPP was suspicious of a UN-administered trial as the UN had sided with the Khmer Rouge–dominated coalition against the government in Phnom Penh and the ruling party wanted a major say in who was to be tried for what. The UN for its part rightly doubted that the judiciary in Cambodia was sophisticated or impartial enough to fairly oversee such a major trial. A compromise solution – a mixed tribunal of three international and four Cambodian judges requiring a super majority of two plus three for a verdict – was eventually agreed upon.

This elaborate process was blown apart with the dramatic UN decision to pull out of the process in early 2002, but it now looks like a trial will finally go ahead, as a budget has been approved. What a pity that it comes 25 years too late, when many of the protagonists have already passed away, and that it will only try the limited leadership rather than get to the bottom of the who, how and whys that a truth and reconciliation commission might have untangled.

ELECTION TIME AGAIN

For the latest on political gossip in Cambodia, visit www.khmerintelligence .org, one of the best sources on which rumours are true or false.

Early 2002 saw Cambodia's first ever local elections to select village and commune level representatives, an important step in bringing grassroots democracy to the country. Even with national elections since 1993, the CPP continued to monopolise political power at local and regional levels and only with commune elections would this grip be loosened. However, the commune elections were only really a warm up for the country's third national election in summer 2003.

The elections of July 2003 saw a shift in the balance of power, as the CPP consolidated their grip on power and the Sam Rainsy Party overhauled Funcinpec as the second party. It was to be coalition time again, but this time the politicians wouldn't even sit down and talk. Funcinpec and the

1999	2002
Cambodia finally joins Asean after a two-year delay	Cambodia holds its first ever local elections at commune level, a tentative step in bringing grass roots democracy to the country

LIFE'S A RIOT

What should have been a smooth run-up to the 2003 elections got a little hot, as parts of Phnom Penh burned in the so-called anti-Thai riots of January 2003. Historically relations between Thailand and Cambodia have been a little strained, for reasons that shouldn't need spelling out if you have made it this far in the History chapter. Allegedly, a famous Thai soap star claimed Angkor Wat belonged to Thailand, and this spread like wildfire through the Cambodian media. Prime Minister Hun Sen announced that said actress wasn't worth a patch of grass upon which Angkor Wat was built. Within days the Thai embassy was up in flames and countless other Thai-owned businesses were severely damaged, including the Royal Phnom Penh Hotel and Camshin, the mobile phone company owned by Thai Prime Minister Thaksin Shinawatra.

Rumours spread faster than the fires as to how this happened and many observers feel it was politically motivated to oust the popular governor of Phnom Penh Chea Sophara – even though he was out of town at the time, he was the only one to take the fall. He had annoyed the Thais by building a new road to the Cambodian border temple of Prasat Preah Vihear and annoyed Prime Minister Hun Sen by becoming too popular with the people. There had to be a certain amount of high-level collusion in planning the demonstrations, as had this been an anti-CPP rally, it would have been brought to an end in minutes. Most likely, someone powerful engineered the demos, but severely miscalculated the mood of the street, which rapidly got out of control. The Cambodian government agreed a compensation package for the damaged property and slowly but surely relations began to heal.

Sam Rainsy Party formed another of their 'til death do us part' alliances and negotiations began for a tri-party coalition. After nearly a year of false starts, Funcinpec ditched the Sam Rainsy Party once again and put their heads in the trough for another term. The political impact of these machinations remains to be seen, but it looks like Funcinpec are on a one-way ticket out of the political scene and future contests will be between the entrenched CPP and the upwardly mobile Sam Rainsy Party.

2003	2004
The CPP win the country's latest election, but political bickering prevents the formation of the new government for almost a year	King Sihanouk abdicates from the throne and is succeeded by his son King Sihamoni

The Culture

THE NATIONAL PSYCHE

Since the glory days of the Angkor empire of old, the Cambodian people have been on the losing side of many a historical battle, their little country all too often a minnow amid the circling sharks. Popular attitudes have been shaped by this history, the relationship between Cambodia and its powerful neighbours, Thailand and Vietnam, based on fear – sometimes loathing.

The Thais are loathed for their patronising attitudes towards their smaller neighbour, their unwillingness to acknowledge their cultural debt to Cambodia and the popularly held belief that Angkor belongs to Thailand. Most Khmers think of their Thai neighbours as cultural kidnappers who have aided and abetted Cambodia's decline.

Cambodian attitudes towards the Vietnamese are awkward and ambivalent. Sure they generally loathe them too, but it is balanced with a begrudging respect for their hard work ethic and 'liberation' from the Khmer Rouge regime in 1979 (see p34). When 'liberation' became occupation in the 1980s, most Khmers soon remembered why they didn't like the Vietnamese after all. Many Cambodians feel the Vietnamese are colonising their country and stealing their land, but better the devil you know. If most Cambodians had to choose who they mistrusted more, it would probably be the Thais – at least the Vietnamese understand the suffering of the Cambodian people, as they have suffered too.

At first glance, Cambodia appears to be a nation full of shiny, happy people, but look a little deeper and it soon becomes a country of contradictions. Light and dark, rich and poor, love and hate, life and death – all are visible on a journey through the kingdom, but most telling of all is the glorious past set against Cambodia's tragic present.

Angkor is everywhere: it's on the flag, it's the national beer, it's hotels and guesthouses, it's cigarettes, it's anything and everything. It's a symbol of nationhood, of fierce pride, a fingers-up to the world that says no matter how bad things have become, you can't forget the fact that we, the Cambodians, built Angkor Wat and it doesn't come bigger than that. Jayavarman VII, Angkor's greatest king, is nearly as omnipresent as his temples. The man that vanquished the occupying Chams and took the empire to its greatest glories is a national hero.

Contrast this with the abyss into which the nation was sucked during the hellish years of the Khmer Rouge, which left a people profoundly shocked, suffering inside, stoical on the outside. Pol Pot is a dirty word in Cambodia due to the death and suffering he inflicted on the country (see p32). Whenever you hear his name, it will be connected with stories of endless personal tragedy, of dead brothers, mothers and babies, from which most Cambodians have never had the chance to recover. Such suffering takes generations to heal and meanwhile the country is crippled by a short-term mentality that encourages people to live for today, not to think about tomorrow – because not so long ago there was no tomorrow. No-one has tasted justice, the whys and hows remain unanswered and the older generation must live with the shadow of this trauma stalking their every waking hour.

If Jayavarman VII and Angkor are loved and Pol Pot despised, the mercurial Sihanouk, the last of the god-kings who has ultimately shown his human side, is somewhere in between. Many Cambodians love him

'Angkor is everywhere: it's on the flag, it's the national beer, it's hotels and guest-houses, it's cigarettes...'

FACE IT

Getting to grips with face is the key to success in Asia, and Cambodia is no exception. Having 'big face' is synonymous with prestige, and prestige is particularly important in Cambodia. All families, even poor ones, are expected to have big wedding parties and throw their money around like it is water in order to gain face. This is often ruinously expensive, but far less detrimental than 'losing' face.

Getting angry and showing it by shouting or becoming abusive is impolite; it is also unlikely to accomplish much. Getting angry means loss of face and makes all Asians uncomfortable – take a deep breath and keep your cool. If things aren't being done as they should, remember that there is a shortage of skilled people in the country because the majority of educated Cambodians either fled the country or were killed between 1975 and 1979.

---

as the father of the nation, and to them his portrait is ubiquitous, but to others he is the man who failed the nation by his association with the Khmer Rouge. In many ways, his contradictions are those of contemporary Cambodia. Understand him and what he has had to survive and you will understand much of Cambodia.

LIFESTYLE

For many older Cambodians, life is centred on family, faith and food, a timeless existence that has stayed the same for centuries. Family is more than the nuclear family we now know in the West – it's the extended family of third cousins and obscure aunts (as long as there is a bloodline there is a bond). Families stick together, solve problems collectively, listen to the wisdom of the elders and pool resources. The extended family comes together during times of trouble or times of joy, celebrating festivals and successes, mourning deaths or disappointments. Whether the Cambodian house is big or small, one thing is certain: there will be a lot of people living inside.

For the majority of the population still living in the countryside, these constants carry on as they have: several generations sharing the same roof, the same rice and the same religion. But during the dark decades of the 1970s and 1980s, this routine was ripped apart by war and ideology, as the peasants were dragged from all they held dear to fight a bloody civil war and later forced into slavery. Angkar, the Khmer Rouge organisation, took over as the moral and social beacon in the lives of the people and families were forced apart, children turned against parents, brothers against sister. The bond of trust was broken and is only slowly being rebuilt today.

Faith is another rock in the lives of many older Cambodians, and Buddhism has helped them to rebuild their shattered lives after waking from the nightmare that was the Khmer Rouge. Most Cambodian houses contain a small shrine to pray for luck and the wats are thronging with the faithful come Buddhist Day.

Food is more important to Cambodians than to most, as they have tasted what it is like to be without. Famine stalked the country in the late-1970s, and even today, malnutrition and food shortages are common during times of drought. Rice is a Khmer staple served with every meal and many a Cambodian driver cannot go on without his or her daily fix. For country folk, still the majority of the Cambodian population, we must not forget their fields. Farmers are attached to their land, their very survival dependent on it, and the harvest cycle dictates the rhythm of rural life.

Some 85% of the Cambodian population still live in the countryside, a huge number compared with its more-developed Asian neighbours. Expect urban migration to take off in the next decade.

But for the young generation of teenagers brought up in a post-conflict, post-communist period of relative freedom, it's a different story – arguably thanks to their steady diet of MTV and steamy soaps. Like other parts of Asia before it, Cambodia is experiencing its very own '60s swing, as the younger generation stands up for a different lifestyle than the one their parents had to swallow. This is creating plenty of feisty friction in the cities, as rebellious teens dress as they like, date who they want and hit the town until all hours. But few actually live on their own; they still come home to ma and pa at the end of the day and the arguments start again, particularly about marriage and settling down, as the older generation don't like to see the younger generation living the single life.

Cambodia is a country undergoing rapid change, but for now the traditionalists are just about holding their own, although the onslaught of karaoke is proving hard to resist. Cambodia is set for major demographic changes in the next couple of decades. Currently, just 15% of the population lives in urban areas, which contrasts starkly with the country's more-developed neighbours like Malaysia and Thailand. Increasing numbers of young people are likely to migrate to the cities in search of opportunity, changing forever the face of contemporary Cambodian society. However, for now, Cambodian society remains much more traditional than in Thailand and Vietnam, and visitors need to keep this in mind.

'for now the traditionalists are just about holding their own, although the onslaught of karaoke is proving hard to resist'

Greetings

Cambodians traditionally greet each other with the *sompiah,* which involves pressing the hands together in prayer and bowing, similar to the *wai* in Thailand. The higher the hands and the lower the bow the more respect is conveyed – important to remember when meeting officials or the elderly. In recent times this custom has been partially replaced by handshake but, although men tend to shake hands with each other, women usually use the traditional greeting with both men and women. It is considered acceptable (or perhaps excusable) for foreigners to shake hands with Cambodians of both sexes.

Dress

Both men and women often wear cotton or silk sarongs, especially at home. Men who can afford it usually prefer to wear silk sarongs. Most urban Khmer men dress in trousers and these days most urban women dress in Western-style clothing.

On formal occasions such as religious festivals and family celebrations, women often wear a *hol* (a type of shirt) during the day. At night they change into single-colour silk dresses called *phamuong,* which are decorated along the hems. If the celebration is a wedding, the colours of such garments are dictated by the day of the week on which the wedding falls. The women of Cambodia are generally modest in their dress, although this is fast changing in the bigger towns and cities.

Travellers crossing the border from liberal Thai islands such as Ko Pha Ngan or Ko Chang should remember they have crossed back in time as far as traditions are concerned, and that wandering around the temples of Angkor bare-chested (men) or scantily clad (women) will not be appreciated by Khmers. Nude bathing is a definite no-no!

Visiting Khmers

A small token of gratitude in the form of a gift is always appreciated when visiting someone. Before entering a Khmer home, always remove your

---

DO THE RIGHT THING!

Beck and Call
If you would like someone to come over to you, motion with your whole hand held palm down – signalling with your index finger and your palm pointed skyward could be seen as sexually suggestive.

Deadly Chopsticks
Leaving a pair of chopsticks sitting vertically in a rice bowl looks very much like the incense sticks that are burned for the dead. This is a powerful sign and is not appreciated anywhere in Asia.

Hats off to Them
As a form of respect to elderly or other respected people, such as monks, take off your hat and bow your head politely when addressing them. In Asia, the head is the symbolic highest point – never pat or touch an adult on the head.

It's on the Cards
Exchanging business cards is an important part of even the smallest transaction or business contact in Cambodia. Get some printed before you arrive and hand them out like confetti.

The Right Hand
When handing things to other people, use both hands or your right hand only, never your left hand (reserved for bathroom ablutions).

Time for a Toothpick
When using a toothpick, it is considered polite to hold it in one hand and to cover your open mouth with the other.

---

shoes if the homeowners do so first. This applies to some guesthouses and restaurants as well – if there is a pile of shoes at the doorway, take yours off as well.

Visiting Pagodas

The Khmers are easy-going and may choose not to point out improper behaviour to their foreign guests, but it is important to dress and act with the utmost respect when visiting wats or other religious sites. This is all the more important given the vital role Buddhism has played in the lives of many Cambodians in the aftermath of the Khmer Rouge holocaust. Proper etiquette in Cambodian pagodas is mostly a matter of common sense.

Unlike in Thailand, a woman may accept something from a *lok song* (monk), but must be extremely careful not to touch him in the process. A few other tips:

- Don't wear shorts or tank tops.
- Take off your hat when entering the grounds of a wat.
- Take off your shoes before going into the *vihara* (temple sanctuary).
- If you sit down in front of the Buddha, sit with feet to the side rather than in the lotus position.
- Bow slightly in the presence of elderly or senior monks.
- Putting a small sum of money in the donation box will be much appreciated by residents at the temple and visiting Khmers.
- Never point your finger – or, nirvana forbid, the soles of your feet – towards a monk or a Buddha figure.

POPULATION

Cambodia's first census in decades, carried out in 1998, put the country's population at nearly 11.5 million. With a rapid growth rate of 2.4% a year, the population is now hitting 14 million and is predicted to reach 20 million by 2020.

Phnom Penh is the largest city, with a population of about one million. Other major population centres include Battambang, Siem Reap and Sihanoukville. The most populous province is Kompong Cham, where 14% of Cambodians live.

The much-discussed imbalance of men to women due to years of conflict is not as serious as it was in 1980, but it is still significant: there are currently 93.1 males to every 100 females, up from 86.1 to 100 in 1980. There is, however, a marked imbalance in age groups: more than 40% of the population is under the age of 15.

> Among Cambodia's 24 provinces, Kandal has the densest population with more than 300 people per square kilometre, while Mondulkiri has the sparsest population with just two people per square kilometre.

Ethnic Khmers

According to official statistics, around 96% of the people who live in Cambodia are ethnic Khmers, making the country the most homogeneous in Southeast Asia. In reality, perhaps 10% of the population is of Cham, Chinese or Vietnamese origin.

The Khmers have inhabited Cambodia since the beginning of recorded history (around the 2nd century), many centuries before Thais and Vietnamese migrated to the region. Over the centuries, the Khmers have mixed with other groups residing in Cambodia, including Javanese and Malays (8th century), Thais (10th to 15th centuries), Vietnamese (from the early 17th century) and Chinese (since the 18th century).

Ethnic Vietnamese

Vietnamese are one of the largest non-Khmer ethnic groups in Cambodia. According to government figures, Cambodia is host to around 100,000 Vietnamese. Unofficial observers claim that the real figure may be more like half a million. There is a great deal of dislike and distrust between the Cambodians and the Vietnamese, even among those who have been living in Cambodia for generations. For the Khmers, the

---

KHMER KROM

The Khmer Krom people of southern Vietnam are ethnic Khmers separated from Cambodia by historical deals and Vietnamese encroachment on what was once Cambodian territory. Nobody is sure just how many of them there are and estimates vary from one million to seven million, depending on who is doing the counting.

The history of Vietnamese expansion into Khmer territory has long been a staple of Khmer textbooks. King Chey Chetha II of Cambodia, in keeping with the wishes of his Vietnamese queen, first allowed Vietnamese to settle in the Cambodian town of Prey Nokor in 1620. It was obviously the thin edge of the wedge – Prey Nokor is now better known as Ho Chi Minh City (Saigon).

Representatives of the Khmer Krom claim that although they dress as Vietnamese and carry Vietnamese identity cards, they remain culturally Khmer. Vietnamese attempts to quash Khmer Krom language and religion (the Khmers are Theravada Buddhists, while the Vietnamese practise Mahayana Buddhism) have, for the most part, failed. Even assimilation through intermarriage has failed to take place on a large scale.

Many Khmer Krom would like to see Cambodia act as a mediator in the quest for greater autonomy and ethnic representation in Vietnam. The Cambodian government, for its part, needs to concentrate on the vast numbers of illegal Vietnamese inside its borders, as well as reports of Vietnamese encroachments on the eastern borders of Cambodia.

Vietnamese migrants are always outsiders known as *yuon* (a derogatory term that means 'barbarians'), while the Vietnamese consider the Khmers idle for not farming every available bit of land, an absolute necessity in densely populated Vietnam.

Ethnic Chinese

The government claims that there are around 50,000 ethnic Chinese in Cambodia. Informed observers say there are more likely to be as many as half a million or more in urban areas. Many Chinese Cambodians have lived in Cambodia for generations and have adopted the Khmer culture, language and identity. Until 1975, ethnic Chinese controlled the economic life of Cambodia. In recent years the group has re-emerged as a powerful economic force, mainly due to increased investment by overseas Chinese.

Ethnic Cham

Cambodia's Cham Muslims (known locally as the Khmer Islam) officially number around 200,000. Unofficial counts put the figure higher at around 400,000. The Chams live in villages on the banks of the Mekong and the Tonlé Sap Rivers, mostly in Kompong Cham, Kompong Speu and Kompong Chhnang Provinces. They suffered particularly vicious persecution between 1975 and 1979, when a large part of their community was exterminated. Many Cham mosques that were destroyed under the Khmer Rouge have been rebuilt.

Ethno-Linguistic Minorities

Cambodia's diverse Khmer Leu (Upper Khmer) or *chunchiet* (minorities), who live in the country's mountainous regions, probably number between 60,000 and 70,000.

The majority of these groups live in the northeast of Cambodia, in the provinces of Ratanakiri, Mondulkiri, Stung Treng and Kratie. The largest group is the Tompuon (many other spellings are used), who number around 15,000. Other groups include the Pnong, Kreung, Kavet, Brao and Jarai.

The hill tribes of Cambodia have long been isolated from mainstream Khmer society, and there is little in the way of mutual understanding. They practise shifting cultivation, rarely staying in one place for more than four or five years. Finding a new location for a village requires a village elder to mediate with the spirit world. Very few of the minorities wear the sort of colourful traditional costumes you see in Thailand, Laos and Vietnam. While this may not make for interesting photographs, it takes away that depressing human safari-park feel that surrounds visits to tribal villages in other countries.

Little research has been done on Cambodia's hill tribes, and tourism is only just coming to the northeast. There is much to be concerned about regarding the impact of tourism, development and logging on Cambodia's more isolated tribes. Increasing numbers of Khmers are buying up tribal lands in these remote areas, while some foreigners have been buying old totems from sacred burial grounds in Ratanakiri; neither of which has the long-term interests of the minorities at heart.

MEDIA

Cambodia's media scene looks to be in good shape on paper, with freedom of the press enshrined in the constitution, but the everyday reality is a different story. Funcinpec and the Sam Rainsy Party have far less access to the media than the dominant Cambodian People's Party (CPP),

Lowland Khmers are being encouraged to migrate to Cambodia's northeast where there is plenty of available land. But this is home to the country's minority people who have no concept of property rights or land ownership; this may see their culture marginalised in coming years.

with many more pro-government newpapers and radio and TV stations. Many of the local journalists in Cambodia are corrupt and are happy to accept money to plant stories on behalf of businessmen and politicians, undermining the freedom of the press. Journalists working for pro-opposition media have to exercise a certain amount of self-censorship in the interests of self-preservation, as there have been several cases of politically motivated or revenge killings.

Khmer TV is mostly in the hands of the CPP, including state-run TVK and the private channels Apsara and Bayon, but even the 'independent' channels like CTN aren't that independent when you look into who is funding them. Most of the time the programmes seem to involve karaoke, soap operas, game shows or savage gangster movies imported from Hong Kong and China. They're the good parts – the rest is puerile political propaganda showing politicians engaging in good deeds across the country.

Most urban Cambodians look to cable TV news channels like the BBC and CNN for their news, or tune their radios into BBC World Service or Voice of America. Cambodians in the countryside have little choice but to sit back and soak up whatever they are given.

RELIGION
Hinduism

Hinduism flourished alongside Buddhism from the 1st century AD until the 14th century. During the pre-Angkorian period, Hinduism was represented by the worship of Marinara (Shiva and Vishnu embodied in a single deity). During the time of Angkor, Shiva was the deity most in favour with the royal family, although in the 12th century he was superseded by Vishnu. Today some elements of Hinduism are still incorporated into important ceremonies involving birth, marriage and death.

Buddhism

Buddhism was introduced to Cambodia between the 13th and 14th centuries, and most Cambodians today practice Theravada Buddhism. Between 1975 and 1979 the majority of Cambodia's Buddhist monks were murdered by the Khmer Rouge and nearly all of the country's wats (more than 3000) were damaged or destroyed. In the late 1980s, Buddhism once again became the state religion and today young monks are a common sight throughout the country. Many wats have been rebuilt or rehabilitated in the past decade and money-raising drives for this work are seen on roadsides across the country.

The Theravada (Teaching of the Elders) school of Buddhism is an earlier and, according to its followers, less-corrupted form of Buddhism than the Mahayana school. The Theravada school is also called the 'southern' school, as it took the southern route from India through Southeast Asia while the 'northern' school proceeded north into Nepal, Tibet, China and Vietnam. Because the southern school tried to preserve or limit the Buddhist doctrines, the northern school gave Theravada Buddhism the derogatory name Hinayana, meaning 'Lesser Vehicle'. The northern school considered itself Mahayana (Great Vehicle) because it built upon the earlier teachings.

The ultimate goal of Theravada Buddhism is nirvana or 'extinction' of all desire and suffering to reach the final stage of reincarnation. By feeding monks, giving donations to temples and performing regular worship at the local wat, Buddhists hope to improve their lot, acquiring enough merit to reduce the number of rebirths.

Every Buddhist male is expected to become a monk for a short period in his life, optimally between the time he finishes school and starts a

Buddhism in Cambodia draws heavily on its predecessors, incorporating many cultural traditions from Hinduism for ceremonies such as birth, marriage and death, as well as genies and spirits linking back to a pre-Indian animist past.

career or marries. Men or boys under 20 years of age may enter the Sangha as novices. Nowadays men may spend as little as a week or 15 days to accrue merit as monks.

Animism

Both Hinduism and Buddhism were gradually absorbed from beyond the borders of Cambodia, fusing with the animist beliefs already present among the Khmers before Indianisation. Local beliefs didn't simply fade away, but were incorporated into the new religions to form something uniquely Cambodian. The concept of Neak Ta has its foundations in animist beliefs regarding sacred soil and the sacred spirit around us. Neak Ta can be viewed as a Mother Earth concept, an energy force uniting a community with its earth and water. It can be represented in many forms from stone or wood to termite hills – anything that symbolises both a link between the people and the fertility of their land.

The purest form of animism is practised among the Khmer Leu (see p47). Some have converted to Buddhism, but the majority continue to worship spirits of the earth and skies and the spirits of their forefathers.

'The position of women in Cambodia is in a state of transition'

Islam

Cambodia's Muslims are descendants of Chams who migrated from what is now central Vietnam after the final defeat of the kingdom of Champa by the Vietnamese in 1471. Like their Buddhist neighbours, however, the Cham Muslims call the faithful to prayer by banging a drum, rather than with the call of the muezzin, as in most Muslim lands.

The Khmer Rouge made a concerted effort to discriminate against Cambodia's Cham Muslim community. Muslims were forced to eat pork, even when other Khmers were deprived of meat, and many were singled out for execution for simply refusing to do so.

Christianity

Christianity made limited headway into Cambodia compared with neighbouring Vietnam. There were a number of churches in Cambodia before the war, but many of these were systematically destroyed by the Khmer Rouge, including Notre Dame Cathedral in Phnom Penh. Christianity made a comeback of sorts throughout the refugee camps on the Thai border in the 1980s, as a number of food-for-faith type charities set up shop dispensing Jesus with every meal. Many Cambodians changed their public faith for survival, before converting back to Buddhism on their departure from the camps.

WOMEN IN CAMBODIA

The position of women in Cambodia is in a state of transition, as the old generation yields to the new generation, the conservative to the challenging. Traditionally many women were forced to play the Cinderella role at home while the husband got away with anything. While this trend continues among the older generation, there are signs that women of the young generation won't be walked on in the same way.

While something like 20% of women head the household, and in many families women are the sole breadwinners, men have a monopoly on all of the most important positions of power at a governmental level and have a dominant social role at a domestic level.

Cambodian political and religious policies do not directly discriminate against women, but females are rarely afforded the same opportunities as males. In the 1990s, laws were passed on abortion, domestic violence and trafficking, and these have improved the legal position of women, but they have had little effect on the bigger picture.

As young children, females are treated fairly equally, but as they get older their access to education has traditionally become more restricted. This is particularly so in rural areas, where girls are not allowed to live and study in wats.

Friends of Khmer Culture is dedicated to supporting Khmer arts and cultural organisations. Its website is www.khmerculture.net.

Many women set up simple businesses in their towns or villages, but it is not an easy path should they want to progress further. Women currently make up just 10.9% of legislators in Parliament, even though they make up 56% of the voters. Only 13% of administrative and management positions and 33% of professional positions are held by women nationally. It remains a man's world in the sociopolitical jungle that is Cambodia.

Other issues of concern for women in Cambodia are those of domestic violence, prostitution and the spread of sexually transmitted infections (STIs). Domestic violence is quite widespread but, because of fear and shame, it's not known exactly how serious a problem it is. There is a high incidence of child prostitution and illegal trafficking of prostitutes in Cambodia. See the boxed text, p278, for more on the scourge of child prostitution in Cambodia.

Cambodia has the highest rate of HIV infection in the whole of Southeast Asia. Many families in Cambodia have ended up infected due to the actions of an errant husband. However, infection rates are starting to come under control thanks to the impact of powerful public awareness programmes.

ARTS

The famous Hindu epic the *Ramayana* is known as the *Reamker* in Cambodia; Reyum Publishing have issued a beautifully illustrated book telling the story: *The Reamker* (1999).

The Khmer Rouge's assault on the arts was a terrible blow to Cambodian culture. Indeed, for a number of years the common consensus among Khmers was that their culture had been irrevocably lost. The Khmer Rouge not only did away with living bearers of Khmer culture, it also destroyed cultural artefacts, statues, musical instruments, books and anything else that served as a reminder of a past it was trying to efface. The temples of Angkor were spared as a symbol of Khmer glory and empire, but little else survived. Despite this, Cambodia is witnessing a resurgence of traditional arts and a growing interest in experimentation in modern arts and cross-cultural fusion. A trip to the Royal University of Fine Arts (p85) in Phnom Penh is evidence of the extent to which Khmer culture has bounced back.

Dance

For the full story on all the arts organisations working to preserve and enhance Cambodian performance, pick up a copy of the *Cambodia Arts Directory*, published in 2001 by the UK's Visiting Arts.

More than any of the other traditional arts, Cambodia's royal ballet is a tangible link with the glory of Angkor. Its traditions stretched long into the past, when the art of the *apsara* (nymph) resounded to the glory of the divine king. Early in his reign, King Sihanouk released the traditional harem of royal *apsara* that went with the crown. Nevertheless, prior to the Pol Pot regime, classical ballet was still taught at the palace.

Dance fared particularly badly during the Pol Pot years. Very few dancers and teachers survived, including one old woman who was the only one who knew how to make the elaborate costumes that are sewn piece by piece onto the dancers before a performance. In 1981, with a handful of teachers, the University of Fine Arts was reopened and the training of dance students resumed.

Much of Cambodian royal dance resembles that of India and Thailand (it has the same stylised hand movements, the same sequined, lamé costumes and the same opulent stupa-like headwear), as the Thais learnt their techniques from the Khmers after sacking Angkor in the 15th century. Where royal dance was traditionally an all-female affair (with the exception of the role of the monkey), there are now more male dancers featured.

Music

The bas-reliefs on some of the monuments in the Angkor region depict musicians and *apsara* holding instruments similar to the traditional Khmer instruments of today, demonstrating that Cambodia has a long musical tradition all its own.

Customarily, music was an accompaniment to a ritual or performance that had religious significance. Musicologists have identified six types of Cambodian musical ensemble, each used in different settings. The most traditional of these is the *areak ka*, an ensemble that performs at weddings. The instruments of the *areak ka* include a *tro khmae* (three-stringed fiddle), a *khsae muoy* (singled-stringed bowed instrument) and *skor areak* (drums), among others.

Much of Cambodia's traditional music was lost during the Pol Pot era. The Khmer Rouge targeted famous singers and the great Sin Sisamuth, Cambodia's most famous songwriter and performer, was executed in the first days of the regime.

After the war, many Khmers settled in the USA, where a lively Khmer pop industry developed. Influenced by US music and later exported back to Cambodia, it has been enormously popular.

A new generation of overseas Khmers growing up with influences from the West is producing its own sound. *The Khmer Rouge* is a rap album produced by a young Cambodian-American. It draws heavily on the sound of Public Enemy and Dr Dre, but with a unique Cambodian twist and is well worth seeking out.

Phnom Penh too has a burgeoning pop industry, many of whose famous stars perform at the huge restaurants located across the Japanese Bridge. It is easy to join in the fun by visiting one of the innumerable karaoke bars around the country. Preap Sovath is the current male heartthrob and if you flick through the Cambodian channels for more than five minutes, chances are he will be performing. Soun Chantha is one of the more popular young female singers with a big voice, but it's a fickle industry and new stars are waiting in the wings.

One form of music unique to Cambodia is *chapaye,* a sort of Cambodian blues sung to the accompaniment of a two-stringed wooden instrument similar in sound to a bass guitar without the amplifier. There are few old masters such as Pra Chouen left alive, but *chapaye* is still often shown on late-night Cambodian TV before transmission ends.

Literature

Cambodia's literary tradition is limited and very much tied in with Buddhism or myth and legend. Sanskrit, and later Pali, came to Cambodia with Hinduism and Buddhism and much of Cambodia's religious scripture exists only in these ancient languages. Legend has been used to expound the core Cambodian values of family and faith, as well as obedience to authority.

Architecture

Khmer architecture reached its peak during the Angkorian era (9th to 14th centuries AD). Some of the finest examples of architecture from this period are Angkor Wat and the structures of Angkor Thom. See p142 for more information on the architectural styles of the Angkorian era.

Back in the '60s, Cambodia had a lively music scene. Some of these songs are found on the excellent compilation *Bayon Rock*, available in Phnom Penh's markets.

Cambodia's great musical tradition was almost lost during the Khmer Rouge years, but the Cambodian Master Performers Program is dedicated to reviving the country's musical tradition. Visit its website at www.cambodianmasters.org.

Today, most rural Cambodian houses are built on high wood pilings (if the family can afford it) and have thatch roofs, walls made of palm mats and floors of woven bamboo strips resting on bamboo joists. The shady space underneath is used for storage and for people to relax at midday. Wealthier families have houses with wooden walls and tiled roofs, but the basic design remains the same.

The French left their mark in Cambodia in the form of some handsome villas and government buildings built in neoclassical style – Romanesque pillars and all. Some of the best architectural examples are in Phnom Penh, but most of the provincial capitals have at least one or two examples of architecture from the colonial period. Most modern structures are influenced by the wedding-cake school of architecture from Thailand or China, although a number of buildings are going up in neocolonial style.

> Cambodian architect Vann Molyvann helped shape modern Phnom Penh; some of his best-known buildings include the Olympic Stadium, Chatomuk Theatre and the Cambodiana Hotel.

Sculpture

Even in the pre-Angkorian era, the periods generally referred to as Funan and Chenla, the people of Cambodia were producing masterfully sensuous sculpture that was more than a mere copy of the Indian forms it was modelled on. Some scholars maintain that the Cambodian forms are unrivalled in India itself.

The earliest surviving Cambodian sculpture dates from the 6th century AD. Most of it depicts Vishnu with four or eight arms. Generally Vishnu has acquired Indochinese facial characteristics and is more muscular than similar Indian sculpture, in which divinities tend towards rounded flabbiness. A large eight-armed Vishnu from this period is displayed at the National Museum (p81) in Phnom Penh.

Also on display at the National Museum is a statue of Marinara from the end of the 7th century, a divinity who combines aspects of both Vishnu and Shiva, but looks more than a little Egyptian – a reminder that Indian sculpture drew from the Greeks who in turn learnt from the pharaohs.

> For details on the religious, cultural and social context of Angkorian-era sculpture, seek out a copy of *Sculpture of Angkor and Ancient Cambodia: Millennium of Glory* by Helen Jessup (1997).

Innovations of the early Angkorian era include freestanding sculpture that dispenses with the stone aureole that in earlier works supported the multiple arms of Hindu deities. The faces assume an air of tranquillity, and the overall effect is less animated.

The Banteay Srei style of the late 10th century is commonly regarded as a high point in the evolution of Southeast Asian art. The National Museum has a splendid piece from this period: a sandstone statue of Shiva holding Uma, his wife, on his knee. The Baphuon style of the 11th century was inspired to a certain extent by the sculpture of Banteay Srei, producing some of the finest works to have survived today.

The statuary of the Angkor Wat period is felt to be conservative and stilted, lacking the grace of earlier work. The genius of this period manifests itself more clearly in the architecture and fabulous bas-reliefs of Angkor Wat itself.

The final high point in Angkorian sculpture is the Bayon period from the end of the 12th century to the beginning of the 13th century. In the National Museum, look for the superb representation of Jayavarman VII, an image that simultaneously projects great power and sublime tranquillity.

Cambodian sculptors are rediscovering their skills now there is a ready market among tourists. Both Phnom Penh and Siem Reap are excellent places to buy reproduction stone carvings of famous statues and busts from the time of Angkor.

Handicrafts

With a tradition of craftsmanship that produced the temples of Angkor, it is hardly surprising to find that even today Khmers produce exquisitely carved silver, wood and stone. Many of the designs hark back to those of the Angkorian period and are tasteful objects of art. Pottery is also an industry with a long history in Cambodia, and there are many ancient kiln sites scattered throughout the country. Designs range from the extremely simple, to much more intricate; drinking cups carved in the image of elephants, teapots carved in the image of birds and jars carved in the image of gods.

Cinema

The film industry in Cambodia was given a new lease of life in 2000 with the release of *Pos Keng Kong* (The Giant Snake). A remake of a 1950s Cambodian classic, it tells the story of a powerful young girl born from a rural relationship between a woman and a snake king. It is an interesting love story, albeit with dodgy special effects, and achieved massive box-office success around the region. Sadly, its success also points to the downfall of the Cambodian industry, as bootleg versions soon appeared all over Asia.

The success of *Pos Keng Kong* has heralded a revival in the Cambodian film industry and local directors are now turning out up to a dozen films a year. However, most of these new films are vampire or ghost films and of dubious artistic value.

At least one overseas Cambodian director has had success in fairly recent years: Rithy Panh's *People of the Rice Fields* was nominated for the Palme d'Or at the Cannes Film Festival in May 1995. The film touches only fleetingly on the Khmer Rouge, depicting the lives of a family eking out an arduous existence in the rice-fields. His other films include *One Night After the War* (1997), the story of a young Khmer kickboxer falling for a bar girl in Phnom Penh, and *The Land of Wandering Souls* (1999), which tells the story of rural migrant workers employed to lay a fibre-optic cable to connect Phnom Penh and Bangkok.

The definitive film about Cambodia is *The Killing Fields* (1985), which tells the story of American journalist Sydney Schanberg and his Cambodian assistant Dith Pran. Most of the footage was actually shot in Thailand: it was filmed in 1984 when Cambodia was effectively closed to the West, particularly to filmmakers.

Rithy Panh's 1996 film *Bophana* tells the true story of Hout Bophana, a beautiful young woman, and Ly Sitha, a regional Khmer Rouge leader, who fall in love and are executed for their 'crime'.

The first major international feature film to be shot in Cambodia was *Lord Jim* (1964), starring Peter O'Toole.

SIHANOUK & THE SILVER SCREEN

Between 1965 and 1969 Sihanouk wrote, directed and produced nine feature films, a figure that would put the average workaholic Hollywood director to shame. Sihanouk took the business of making films very seriously, and family and officials were called upon to do their bit – the minister of foreign affairs played the male lead in Sihanouk's first feature, *Apsara* (Heavenly Nymph; 1965), and his daughter Princess Bopha Devi the female lead. When, in the same movie, a show of military hardware was required, the air force was brought into action, as was the army's fleet of helicopters.

Sihanouk often took on the leading role himself. Notable performances saw him as a spirit of the forest and as a victorious general. Perhaps it was no surprise, given the king's apparent addiction to the world of celluloid dreams, that Cambodia should challenge Cannes and Berlin with its Phnom Penh International Film Festival. The festival was held twice, in 1968 and 1969. Sihanouk won the grand prize on both occasions. He continued to make movies in later life and it is believed he has made 28 films during his remarkable career. For more on the films of Sihanouk, visit the website www.norodomsihanouk.org.

Environment

THE LAND

The shape of contemporary Cambodia has come about through a classic historical squeeze. As the Vietnamese pushed southward into the Mekong Delta and the Thais pushed westward towards Angkor, Cambodia shrank. Ironically it was only the arrival of the French that prevented Cambodia going the way of the Chams, a people without a state, and in that sense it was a protectorate that protected.

Cambodia today is 181,035 sq km in size, making it a little over half the size of Vietnam or about the same as England and Wales without Scotland. The country is wider (about 580km east–west) than it is tall (about 450km north–south); to the west it borders Thailand, to the north Thailand and Laos, to the east Vietnam and to the south the Gulf of Thailand.

Cambodia's two dominant features are the mighty Mekong River, which is, incredibly, 5km wide in places, and the vast Tonlé Sap lake – see the boxed text on below for more on this natural miracle. Many visitors take express boats up and down the Mekong, linking towns like Kompong Cham and Kratie. The Mekong, which rises in Tibet, flows almost 500km through Cambodia before continuing, via southern Vietnam, to the South China Sea. At Phnom Penh it splits into the Upper River

Cambodia's highest mountain is Phnom Aural in Pursat Province. At just 1813m, it isn't one of the world's great climbs, but for those ticking off peaks across the planet, it can be climbed in two days.

THE HEARTBEAT OF CAMBODIA

The Tonlé Sap lake, the largest freshwater lake in Southeast Asia, is an incredible natural phenomenon that provides fish proteins and irrigation waters for close to half the population of Cambodia.

The lake is linked to the Mekong at Phnom Penh by a 100km-long channel, also known as the Tonlé Sap (*tonlé* meaning 'river'). From mid-May to early October (the wet season) the level of the Mekong rises rapidly, backing up the Tonlé Sap river and causing it to flow northwest into the Tonlé Sap lake. During this period, the lake swells from 2500 sq km to 13,000 sq km or more, its maximum depth increasing from about 2.2m to more than 10m. Around the start of October, as the water level of the Mekong begins to fall, the Tonlé Sap river reverses its flow, draining the waters of the lake back into the Mekong.

This extraordinary process makes the Tonlé Sap lake one of the world's richest sources of freshwater fish, as flooded forest makes for a fertile spawning ground. Experts believe fish migrations from the Tonlé Sap lake help to restock fisheries as far north as China. The fishing industry supports about one million people in Cambodia and an individual's catch on the great lake can average 100kg to 200kg per day in the dry season.

This unique ecosystem has helped to earn the Tonlé Sap lake protected biosphere status, but this may not be enough to protect it from the twin threats of upstream dams and excessive deforestation. The dams hold uncertain consequences for flow patterns of the Mekong and migratory patterns of fish. Illegal logging loosens topsoil in upland Cambodia and this silt is carried down the country's rivers into the lake. The shallowest areas may in time begin to silt up, bringing disastrous consequences not only for Cambodia, but also for neighbouring Vietnam. Hopefully, action will be taken to do all that is possible to protect this unique natural wonder from further harm, but with the Cambodian population growing by 300,000 a year, the task is going to be a far from easy.

For more information about the Tonlé Sap lake and its unique ecosystem, consider visiting the exhibition about the Tonlé Sap (p118), and the Gecko Environment Centre (p132), both in Siem Reap.

(called simply the Mekong or, in Vietnamese, the Tien Giang) and the Lower River (Tonlé Bassac, or the Hau Giang in Vietnamese). The rich sediment deposited during the Mekong's annual wet-season flooding has made for very fertile agricultural land in the centre of Cambodia. This low-lying alluvial plain is where the vast majority of Cambodians live, fishing and farming in time with the rural rhythms of the monsoon.

In the southwest, much of the landmass between the Gulf of Thailand and the Tonlé Sap lake is covered by a mountainous region formed by two distinct ranges: the Chuor Phnom Kravanh (Cardamom Mountains) in southwestern Battambang Province and Pursat Province, and the Chuor Phnom Damrei (Elephant Mountains) in the provinces of Kompong Speu, Koh Kong and Kampot.

South of these mountains is Cambodia's lengthy coastline, a big draw for visitors on the lookout for isolated tropical beaches. There are islands aplenty off the coast of Sihanoukville (p184), Kep (p201) and Koh Kong (p180), all of which offer promising potential in the years to come.

Along Cambodia's northern border with Thailand, the plains collide with a striking sandstone escarpment more than 300km long and 180m to 550m in height that marks the southern limit of the Chuor Phnom Dangkrek (Dangkrek Mountains). Most visitors only see these mountains if making the overland pilgrimage to Prasat Preah Vihear (p235). In the northeastern corner of the country, the plains give way to the Eastern Highlands, a remote region of densely forested mountains and high plateaus that extends eastward into Vietnam's central highlands and northward into Laos. The wild provinces of Ratanakiri (p258) and Mondulkiri (p264) provide a home to many minority peoples and are taking off as traveller hotspots in Cambodia.

> Not only does Tonlé Sap lake expand to five times its size and 70 times its volume each year, but it is also thought to have the world's highest annual freshwater fish catch of 200,000 tonnes.

WILDLIFE

Despite Cambodia's tragic past, its wildlife is in reasonable shape. The years of war and suffering took their toll on some species, but others thrived in the remote jungles of the southwest and northeast. However, peace time has ironically brought more threats, with the logging industry carving up habitat and the illicit trade in wildlife discovering Cambodia and its exotic meats. Years of interruption mean scientists are only just beginning to effectively catalogue the country's plant and animal life, and several new species may await discovery.

Animals

Cambodia has a weird and wonderful selection of animals, but most of them are extremely hard to see for the casual visitor. The easiest way to see a healthy selection of Cambodia's animal life is to visit the Phnom Tamao Wildlife Sanctuary (p110) near Phnom Penh, which provides a home for rescued animals and includes all the major species. For birders, the best bet is to visit Prek Toal Bird Sanctuary (p132) on the Tonlé Sap lake, home to an incredible concentration of some of the world's rarest large water birds.

> For the inside story on birds in Cambodia, look out for *Cambodia Bird News*, a twice-yearly publication available for US$5 in hotels and bookshops in Phnom Penh and Siem Reap.

Cambodia's larger wild animals include bears, elephants, leopards, tigers and wild cow. Some of the biggest characters in Cambodia are the smaller animals, including the binturong (nicknamed the bear cat), the world's largest population of pileated gibbons in the Cardamoms of the southwest, and the lazy lorises, who hang out in trees all day. The lion, although a familiar sight (in statue form) around Angkor, has never been seen here. Among the country's more common birds are cormorants, cranes, egrets and pelicans. There is also a great variety of butterflies across the kingdom. Four types of snake are especially dangerous and worth avoiding if you have a choice: the cobra, the king cobra, the banded krait and the Russell's viper.

ENDANGERED SPECIES

Tragically it is getting mighty close to checkout time for a number of diminishing species in Cambodia, and extinction may be the only fate awaiting some as the country's forest habitat continues to disappear. Very little is known about the exact numbers of most rare animals because their habitats are extremely remote and limited surveys have only been undertaken in recent years.

Given that much of the country has been off limits for such a long time, some suggest Cambodia harbours animals that have become extinct elsewhere in the region. For the moment it remains conjecture, but as the national park system becomes more effective, hopefully whatever is out there will at least be protected. The kouprey (wild ox) and the Wroughton's free-tailed bat, previously thought to exist in only one part of India but recently discovered in Preah Vihear Province, are the only Cambodian mammals on the Globally Threatened – Critical list, the last stop before extinction. The discovery of an isolated herd of Javan rhinoceroses, one of the rarest large mammal species in the world, in southwestern Vietnam in 1998, suggests that there could be more in nearby Mondulkiri or Ratanakiri Provinces, although there is no evidence to substantiate this.

Other mammals under threat in Cambodia include the Asian elephant, Asian golden cat, Asiatic wild dog, black gibbon, clouded leopard, fishing cat, marbled cat, sun bear and wild water buffalo.

There is a large number of rare bird species in Cambodia, drawn to the area by its rich water resources throughout the year. Larger birds include: the Asian openbill stork, greater adjantant stork, giant ibis and spot-billed pelican. As well as the aforementioned Prek Toal Bird Sanctuary, serious twitchers should consider a visit to Ang Trapeng Thmor

---

ON THE TRAIL OF THE TIGER

In 1995 the Worldwide Fund for Nature (WWF) announced a fundraising campaign to save the tigers of Indochina. Six international nongovernmental organisations (NGOs) are currently trying to protect Cambodia's remaining big cats, although experts fear there may be as few as 150 left in the wild. Millions of dollars have been pumped into studies, surveys and assessments, but the time has come for action, as without a drastic initiative there may soon be no tigers left at all.

Tigers are known to inhabit Virachay National Park in Ratanakiri Province, remote parts of Mondulkiri and Preah Vihear Provinces, and the Chuor Phnom Kravanh (Cardamom Mountains), but they are under serious threat from poachers. The magical powers of potency (mainly sexual) ascribed to tiger parts throughout Asia push up the value of a carcass. Fortunately, some hunters are now employed as rangers, making it easier to educate other hunters about the negative impact of the trade.

The fact that tigers are spread across such geographically diverse areas makes them harder to protect from poachers, so environmental NGOs are giving serious thought to promoting the establishment of tiger sanctuaries similar to those found in India. This would concentrate the remaining tigers in a secure environment and, in time, generate a vast income for Cambodia from ecotourism. The lessons that African conservationists learnt in the 1970s when battling to protect rhinos and elephants may need to be learnt today by a new generation of Cambodian conservationists. It would be a terrible tragedy if this majestic creature were to disappear from Cambodia's forests forever. For insights, stories and links about tigers in Cambodia and what is being done to protect them, visit the website of the Cat Action Treasury at www.felidae.org.

Reserve (p132), home to the extremely rare sarus crane, as depicted on the the bas-reliefs at Angkor. Other rare birds include the greater spotted eagle, Siamese fireback and spot-bellied eagle owl.

Cambodia has some of the last remaining freshwater Irrawaddy dolphins, known as *trey pisaut* in Khmer. There may be as few as 75 left, inhabiting stretches of the Mekong between Kratie and the Lao border, and viewing them at Kampi (p254) is a popular activity. The giant catfish, sometimes reaching 5m in length, is also threatened, due to its popularity on menus from Hong Kong to Tokyo.

Plants

Cambodia has more forest cover than most of its Asian neighbours, and a healthy mangrove belt fringing the coastline. The central lowland consists of the ubiquitous rice paddies, fields of dry crops such as corn and tobacco, tracts of reeds and tall grass, and thinly wooded areas.

In the southwest, virgin rainforests grow to heights of 50m or more on the rainy seaward slopes of the mountains. Nearby, higher elevations support pine forests. In the northern mountains there are broadleaf evergreen forests with trees soaring 30m above the thick undergrowth of vines, bamboos, palms and assorted woody and herbaceous ground plants. The Eastern Highlands are covered with grassland and deciduous forests. Forested upland areas support many varieties of orchid. However, in the past two decades, a great deal of deforestation has taken place – see p58 for more details.

The symbol of Cambodia is the sugar palm tree, which is used for roofs and walls in construction and in the production of medicine, wine and vinegar. Because of the way sugar palms grow – over the years, the tree grows taller but the trunk, which lacks normal bark, does not grow thicker – their trunks retain shrapnel marks from every battle that has ever raged around them. Some sugar palms have been shot clean through the trunk.

For a close encounter with tigers at the temples of Angkor, watch Jean-Jacques Annaud's 2004 film *Two Brothers*, the story of two orphan tiger cubs during the colonial period in Cambodia.

NATIONAL PARKS

Before the civil war, Cambodia had six national parks, together covering 22,000 sq km (around 12% of the country). The long civil war effectively destroyed this system and it wasn't reintroduced until 1993, when a royal decree designated 23 areas as national parks, wildlife sanctuaries, protected landscapes and multiple-use areas. Three more protected forests were recently added to the list, bringing the area of protected land in Cambodia to 43,000 sq km, or around 23% of the country. This is fantastic news in principle, but in practice the authorities don't have the resources, or sometimes the will, to actually protect these areas in any way other than drawing a line on a map. The government has enough trouble finding funds to pay the rangers who patrol the most popular parks, let alone recruiting more staff for the remote sanctuaries.

Cambodia's most important national parks include: Bokor (p199), which occupies a 1000m-high plateau on the south coast overlooking Kampot; Ream (p194), which includes a marine reserve and is just a short distance from Sihanoukville; Kirirom (p111), 675m above sea level in the Chuor Phnom Damrei, 112km southwest of Phnom Penh; and Virachay (p263), for a long period the kingdom's largest park, nestled against the Lao and Vietnamese borders in northeastern Cambodia. Bokor is home to wild elephants and has accommodation available at the summit. Ream has a visitor programme, which includes a boat trip and guided walks, while Kirirom has a basic guesthouse and is popular with Khmers at weekends. There is little in the way of facilities at Virachay, but rangers

Many minority peoples fought with the Khmer Rouge, and Virachay National Park provided a safe haven for some of these families for 25 years until 2004 – they had no idea the war was over and were hiding from the Vietnamese.

OUR FAVOURITE NATIONAL PARKS

Park	Size	Features	Activities	Best time to visit	Page
Bokor	1400 sq km	ghost town, views, waterfalls	trekking, biking, wildlife	Dec-May	p199
Kirirom	350 sq km	waterfalls, vistas, pine forests	viewing hiking, wildlife viewing	Nov-Jun	p111
Ream	150 sq km	beaches, islands, mangroves, dolphins, monkeys	boating, swimming, hiking, wildlife viewing	Dec-May	p194
Virachay	3325 sq km	unexplored jungle, waterfalls, hidden wildlife viewing,	trekking, adventure	Dec-Apr	p263

are keen to welcome visitors and have centres in Voen Sai and Siem Pang. Botum Sokor is a coastal park with endless white-sand beaches; it has much potential for ecotourism, as any casual observer can see on the boat journey between Krong Koh Kong and Sihanoukville.

Among the new protected areas, the Mondulkiri Protected Forest, at 4294 sq km, is now the largest protected area in Cambodia and is contiguous with Yok Don National Park in Vietnam. The Cardamom Protected Forest, at 4013 sq km, borders Phnom Samkos and Phnom Aural Wildlife Sanctuaries, creating a huge protected area in the southwest of almost 10,000 sq km.

ENVIRONMENTAL ISSUES
Logging

The biggest threat to the environment in Cambodia is logging. In the mid-1960s Cambodia was reckoned to have around 75% rainforest coverage. Estimates on coverage today vary, but it is likely that only about 30% of the forest remains. During the Vietnamese occupation, troops stripped away a lot of forest to prevent Khmer Rouge ambushes along highways, but the real devastation began in the 1990s when the wholesale shift from a command economy to a market economy led to an asset-stripping bonanza by the cash-strapped government. Most of Cambodia's primary resources beyond the national parks were signed away to logging companies during the first coalition government's rule, with the acquiescence of both prime ministers. Logging companies set about decimating the forests while the politicians sat back and counted the cash.

International demand for timber is huge, and as neighbouring countries like Thailand and Vietnam enforce much tougher logging regulations while at the same time helping to flout Cambodia's lax restrictions, it's little wonder that foreign logging companies flocked to Cambodia. By the height of the country's logging epidemic, at the end of 1997, just under 70,000 sq km of the country's land area had been allocated as concessions, amounting to almost all of Cambodia's forest except national parks and protected areas. However, even in these supposed havens, illegal logging continued.

The military has been the driving force behind much of the logging in Cambodia; it assists in logging legal concessions under the guise of providing security, and then logs illegally elsewhere. The proceeds from these operations contribute towards the army's grey (undeclared) budget, with its nominal budget already taking up a huge chunk of the government's cash during peacetime. More recently the Thai military has turned up in

---

Cambodia was the first Southeast Asian country to establish a national park, when it created a protected area in 1925 to preserve the forests around the temples of Angkor.

For the uncut story on the logging industry in Cambodia, illegal and legal, pay a visit to the website of Global Witness, an environmental watchdog, at www .globalwitness.org.

Cambodia to build roads in the west of the country. Many of these roads are being cut through the heart of Cambodia's forests and no doubt many logs are disappearing across the border into Thailand, before resurfacing as garden furniture in Europe.

In the short term, deforestation is contributing to worsening floods along the Mekong, but the long-term implications of logging will be far more damaging. Without trees to cloak the hills, the rains will inevitably carry away large amounts of topsoil during future monsoons. There can be no doubt that in time this will have a serious effect on the Tonlé Sap lake, as the shallow waters recede from prolonged siltation – a similar situation to that marking the fall of the Angkorian empire? (See p27 for more.) Combined with overfishing and pollution, these problems may lead to the eventual destruction of the lake – an unmitigated disaster for future generations.

In the last couple of years things have been looking up, as there was no further to look down. Under pressure from donors and international institutions, all logging contracts were effectively frozen at the end of 2001, pending further negotiations with the government. Industrial-scale logging ceased and the huge trucks thundering up and down dirt highways crisscrossing the country disappeared. However, small-scale illegal logging continued across the country, including cutting for charcoal production and burning off for settlement, all of which continue to reduce Cambodia's forest cover. The next big threat may come from commercial plantations, or 'deforestation for development' as the companies involved are trying to pitch it, as many plantations are currently being established around the country.

Cambodia needs a sustainable forestry management plan that protects its natural environment while ensuring the country benefits economically. It is not too late for Cambodia's forests, but without sustained action it soon will be.

DID YOU KNOW?

Back in the early 1990s, Cambodia had such extensive forest cover compared with its neighbours that some environmentalists were calling for the whole country to be made a protected area.

Pollution

Cambodia has a pollution problem, but it is not of the same nature as the carbon monoxide crises in neighbouring capitals such as Bangkok and Jakarta: Phnom Penh is the only city in Cambodia that suffers from air pollution. The country does, however, suffer the ill-effects of an extremely primitive sanitation system in urban areas, and in rural areas sanitary facilities are nonexistent, with only a tiny percentage of the population having access to proper facilities. These conditions breed and

---

DOING YOUR BIT!

Cambodia has a low level of environmental awareness and responsibility, and many locals remain oblivious to the implications of littering. Try to raise awareness of these issues by example, and dispose of all your litter as responsibly as possible.

Cambodia's animal populations are under considerable threat from domestic consumption and the illegal international trade in animal products. Though it may be 'exotic' to try wild meat such as bats, deer, shark fins and so on – or to buy products made from endangered plants and animals – it will indicate your support or acceptance of such practices and add to demand.

Forest products such as rattan, orchids and medicinal herbs are under threat and the majority are still collected from the country's dwindling forests. However, some of these products can be cultivated, an industry with potential for local people to earn additional income while protecting natural areas from exploitation and degradation.

When visiting coral reefs and snorkelling or diving, or simply boating, be careful not to touch live coral or anchor boats on it, as this hinders the coral's growth. Don't buy coral souvenirs.

spread disease, with people being forced to defecate on open ground and urinate in rivers. Epidemics of diarrhoea are not uncommon and it is the number-one killer of young children in Cambodia. This type of biological pollution may not be as immediately apparent as smog over a city, but in the shorter term it is far more hazardous to the average Cambodian.

Damming the Mekong

With a meandering length of around 4200km, the Mekong is the longest river in Southeast Asia, and some 50 million people depend on it for their livelihoods. In terms of fish biodiversity, the Mekong is second only to the Amazon; but with regional energy needs ever spiralling, it is very tempting for a poor country like Cambodia to dam the river and make money from hydroelectric power. Even more tempting for Cambodia is the fact that the United Nations Development Programme (UNDP) and the Asia Development Bank (ADB) would pay much of the construction costs.

Overseeing development plans for the river is the Mekong River Commission (MRC), formed by the UNDP and comprising Cambodia, Thailand, Laos and Vietnam. The odd one out is China, which has around 20% of the Mekong but feels it can do what it wants with the river. China has already completed the first dam project on the upper reaches of the Mekong, and many environmentalists fear that more projects will have an adverse effect down river.

China's dam projects are shrouded in secrecy, but there are thought to be 15 projects planned; one is operational now, another is likely to be up and running by the end of 2005 and another by 2009. Meanwhile, the MRC has plans for 11 dams for the Mekong in Laos and Cambodia.

Environmental concerns focus on a number of issues. For a start, even though the MRC dams planned for the Mekong will be small, it is thought they will flood some 1900 sq km and displace around 60,000 people. Secondly, there are worries about how the dams will affect fish migration – some environmentalists claim that the dams might halve the fish population of the Mekong and perhaps even Tonlé Sap lake. Finally, and perhaps of most concern, is the importance of the annual monsoon flooding of the Mekong, which deposits nutrient-rich silt across vast tracts of land used for agriculture. Environmentalists say even a drop of 1m in Mekong water levels would result in around 2000 sq km less flood area around Tonlé Sap lake, a result with potentially disastrous consequences for Cambodia's farmers. The opening of the first Chinese dam coupled with poor rains already saw the lake at one of its lowest levels in years during 2004, with fish stocks down by half. Imagine what happens when a dozen more dams come on line in a decade?

The Mekong is a huge untapped resource. It is probably inevitable that it will be harnessed to make much-needed power for the region. Local environmentalists hope that this can happen in the context of open discussion and with foresight. Many fear, however, that long-term interests will be scrapped in favour of short-term profits.

Dams are planned for a few other rivers around Cambodia, although if you were to believe some of the ministry maps you would think the government was going to dam every bit of water in the country. The most realistic project is the damming of one of the great northeastern rivers that flows into the Mekong at Stung Treng. Tonlé San, Tonlé Sekong and Tonlé Srepok contribute an estimated 10% to 20% of the Mekong's total flow at Kratie. However, the effects on the local indigenous population, Virachay National Park and fish stocks have not been considered in any detail yet – and perhaps never will be.

For the latest on what is happening along the meandering Mekong River, take a look at the official website of the Mekong River Commission at www.mrcmekong.org.

Food & Drink

It's no secret that the dining tables of Thailand and Vietnam are home to some of the finest food in the world, so it should come as no surprise to discover that Cambodian cuisine is also rather special. Unlike the culinary colossuses that are its neighbours, the cuisine of Cambodia is not that well known in international circles, but all that looks set to change. Just as Angkor has put Cambodia on the tourist map of Asia, so too *amoc* (baked fish with coconut, lemon grass and chilli in banana leaf) will put the country on the culinary map of the world.

Cambodia has a great variety of national dishes, some similar to the cuisine of neighbouring Thailand and Laos, others closer to Chinese and Vietnamese cooking, but all come with that unique Cambodian twist, be it the odd herb here or the odd spice there. The overall impression is that Khmer cooking is similar to Thai cooking but with fewer spices.

Freshwater fish forms a huge part of the Cambodian diet thanks to the natural phenomenon that is the Tonlé Sap lake, and they come in every shape and size from the giant Mekong catfish to teeny, tiny whitebait, which are great beer snacks when deep fried. The French left their mark too, baguettes becoming the national bread and Cambodian cooks showing a healthy reverence for tender meats.

Cambodia is a crossroads in Asia, the meeting point of the great civilisations of India and China, and just as it's culture has drawn on both, so too has its cuisine. Whether its spring rolls or curry that takes your fancy, you will find them both in Cambodian cooking. Add to this a world of dips and sauces to complement the cooking and a culinary journey through Cambodia becomes as rich a feast as any in Asia.

Longteine De Monteiro runs several Cambodian restaurants on the East Coast of the US and she has put together her favourite traditional Khmer recipes at www .elephantwalk.com.

STAPLES & SPECIALITIES

Cambodia's lush fields provide the rice and its abundant waterways the fish that is fermented into *prahoc* (fermented fish paste), which together form the backbone of Khmer cuisine. Built around these are the flavours that give the cuisine its kick, the secret roots, the welcome herbs and the aromatic tubers. Together they give the salads, snacks, soups and stews a unique aroma and taste that smacks of Cambodia. Whatever they are preparing, a Khmer cook will demand freshness and a healthy balance of flavours and textures.

Rice is the principal staple, enshrined in the Khmer word for eating or to eat, *nam bai*, literally 'eat rice'. Many a Cambodian, particularly drivers, will run out of steam if they run out of rice. It doesn't matter that the same carbohydrates are available in other foods, it is rice and rice alone that counts. Battambang Province (p212) is the Cambodia's rice bowl and produces the country's finest yield.

For the taste of Cambodia in a bowl, try the local *kyteow*, a rice noodle soup that will keep you going all day. This full and balanced meal will cost you less than just 2000r in markets and up to US$1 in local restaurants. No noodles? Then try the *bobor* (rice porridge), a national institution, for breakfast, lunch and dinner, and best sampled with some fresh fish and a splash of ginger.

A Cambodian meal almost always includes a *samlor* (traditional soup) which will appear at the same time as the other courses. *Samlor machou banle* (hot and sour fish soup with pineapple and a splash of spices) is popular. Other popular soups include *samlor chapek* (ginger-flavoured

Friends (p94) is one of the best-known restaurants in Phnom Penh, turning out a fine array of tapas, shakes and specials to help street children in the capital. Their new cookbook *The Best of Friends* is a visual feast showcasing their best recipes.

pork soup), *samlor machou bawng kawng* (prawn soup similar to the popular Thai *tom yam*) and *samlor ktis* (fish soup with coconut and pineapple).

Much of the fish eaten in Cambodia is freshwater, from Tonlé Sap lake or the Mekong River. *Trey ahng* (grilled fish) is a Cambodian speciality (*ahng* means 'grilled' and can be applied to many dishes). Traditionally, the fish is eaten as pieces wrapped in lettuce or spinach leaves and then dipped into *teuk trey,* a fish sauce that is a close relative of Vietnam's *nuoc mam,* but with the addition of ground peanuts.

Cambodian salad dishes are also popular and delicious, although quite different from the Western idea of a cold salad. *Phlea sait kow* is a beef and vegetable salad, flavoured with coriander, mint and lemon grass. These three herbs find their way into many Cambodian dishes.

Desserts can be sampled cheaply at night markets around the country. One sweet snack to look out for is the ice-cream sandwich. No kidding; it's popular with the kids and involves putting a slab of homemade ice cream in a piece of sponge or bread. It actually doesn't taste too bad.

Cambodia is blessed with many tropical fruits and sampling these is an integral part of a visit to the country. All the common fruits can be found in abundance, including ch*ek* (bananas), *menoa* (pineapples) and *duong* (coconuts). Among the larger fruit, *khnau* (jackfruit) is very common, often weighing more than 20kg. Beneath the green skin are bright yellow segments with a distinctive taste and rubbery texture. The *tourain* (durian) usually needs no introduction, as you can smell it from a mile off. The exterior is green with sharp spines while inside is a milky, soft interior regarded by the Chinese as an aphrodisiac. It stinks, although some maintain it is an acquired taste – best acquired with a nose peg.

The fruits most popular with visitors include the *mongkut* (mangosteen) and *sao mao* (rambutan). The small mangosteen has a purple skin that contains white segments with a divine flavour. Queen Victoria is said to have offered a reward to anyone able to transport an edible mangosteen back to England. Similarly popular is the rambutan, the interior like a lychee, but the exterior covered in soft red and green spines.

Best of all, although common throughout the world, are the *svay* (mangoes). The Cambodian mango season is from April to May. Other varieties of mango are available year round, but it's the Cambodian ones that are a taste sensation.

For the inside story on Cambodian cooking, including the secrets of the royal recipes, seek out a copy of The Cuisine of Cambodia by Nusara Thaitawat (2000), which includes stunning photography throughout.

DRINKS

Cambodia has a lively local drinking culture, and the heat and humidity will ensure that you hunt out anything on offer to quench your thirst.

TRAVEL YOUR TASTEBUDS

No matter what part of the world you come from, if you travel much in Cambodia, you are going to encounter food that is unusual, strange, maybe even immoral, or just plain weird. The fiercely omnivorous Cambodians find nothing strange in eating insects, algae, offal or fish bladders. They will dine on a duck foetus, brew up some brains or snack on some spiders. They will peel live frogs to grill on a barbecue or down the wine infused with cobra to increase their virility.

To the Khmers there is nothing 'strange' about anything that will sustain the body. To them a food is either wholesome or it isn't; it's nutritious or it isn't; it tastes good or it doesn't. And that's all they worry about. They'll try anything once, even a burger.

Avoid eating endangered species, otherwise they will soon be extinct species.

Coffee, tea, beer, wine, soft drinks, fresh fruit juices or some of the more exotic 'fire waters' are all widely available. Tea is the national drink, but these days it is just as likely to be beer in the glass.

Beer

It's never a challenge to find a beer in Cambodia and even the most remote village usually has a stall selling a few cans. Angkor is the national beer, produced in vast quantities in a big brewery down in Sihanoukville (p184). It is a decent brew and costs around US$1.50 to US$2.50 for a 660ml bottle in most restaurants and bars. Draft Angkor is available for less than US$1 in Phnom Penh and Sihanoukville.

Beer Lao from neighbouring Laos is very drinkable and one of the cheapest ales you can get. Tiger beer is produced locally and is a popular draft in the capital. Most Khmer restaurants have a bevy of 'beer girls', each promoting a particular beer brand. They are always friendly and will leave you alone if you prefer not to drink. Brands represented include Angkor, Heineken, Tiger, San Miguel, Stella Artois, Carlsberg, Fosters and Becks. Cans of beer sell for around US$1 in local restaurants.

A word of caution for beer seekers in Cambodia. While the country is awash with good brews, there is a shortage of refrigeration in the countryside. Go native. Learn how to say *'Som teuk koh'*, ('Ice please'). That's right, drink your beer on the rocks!

Wine & Spirits

Local wine in Cambodia generally means rice wine; it is popular with the minority people of the northeast. Some is super strong and has been fermented for months, other wine is fresher and tastes more like a demented cocktail. Either way, if you are invited to join a session in a minority village, it's rude to decline. Other local wines include light sugar palm wine and ginger wine.

In Phnom Penh and Siem Reap, foreign wines and spirits are sold in supermarkets at bargain prices, given how far they have to travel. Wines from Europe and Australia start at about US$4, while the famous names of the spirit world cost between US$3 and US$10! Yes, a bottle of Stoly vodka is just US$3.50!

Most of the locally produced spirits are best avoided, although some expats contend that Sra Special, a local whiskey-like concoction, is not bad. At around US$1 a bottle, it's a cheap route to oblivion. There has also been a surge in the popularity of 'muscle wines' (something like Red Bull meets absinthe) with enticing pictures of strongmen on the labels and names like Hercules, Commando Bear Beverage and Brace of Loma. They contain enough unknown substances to contravene the Geneva Chemical Weapons Convention and should only be drunk with care.

Tea & Coffee

Chinese-style *tai* (tea) is a bit of a national institution, and in most Khmer and Chinese restaurants a pot will automatically appear for no extra charge as soon as you sit down. Coffee *(kaa fey)* is sold in most restaurants. It is either black or *café au lait,* served with dollops of condensed milk which makes it very sweet.

Water & Soft Drinks

Drinking tap water *must* be avoided, especially in the provinces, as it is rarely purified and may lead to stomach complications (p314). Locally

WE DARE YOU!
Crickets
Duck foetus
Durian
Prahoc
Spiders

DID YOU KNOW?
The closest thing Cambodia has to a national dish is *amoc* (baked fish wrapped in banana leaf with coconut, lemon grass and chilli). Sometimes it arrives more like a soup, served in the shell of a young coconut.

DID YOU KNOW?
When Cambodian men propose a toast, they usually stipulate what percentage of the glass must be downed. If they are feeling generous, it might be just *ha-sip pea-roi* (50%), but more often than not it is *moi roi pea-roi* (100%).

produced mineral water is about 500r per bottle at shops and stalls, though some locals and expats alike doubt the purity of the cheapest stuff. Those with a weak constitution might want to opt for one of the better local brands, such as Pure Drop and Minere, or imported water like Evian.

All the well-known soft drinks are available in Cambodia. Bottled drinks are about 800r, while canned drinks cost about 1500r and more again in restaurants or bars.

Throughout Cambodia, *teuk koh* (ice) is produced with treated water at local ice factories, a legacy of the French. Transporting it often involves dragging huge blocks along the ground, but most people don't worry about this, as it usually gets cleaned off.

Fruit Shakes
Teuk kralohk are popular throughout Cambodia. They are a little like fruit smoothies and are a great way to wash down a meal. Stalls are set up around local night markets some time before dark and the drinks cost between 1000r and 2000r. Watch out for how much sugar goes in if you don't like sweet drinks, and pass on the offer of an egg if you don't want it super frothy.

CELEBRATIONS
Cambodians enjoy celebrating, be it a wedding, a festival or a football match. For a festival, the family coffers are broken open and no matter how much they hold, it is deemed insufficient. The money is splurged on those treats that the family may not be able to afford at other times, such as duck, shrimp or crab. Guests are welcomed and will be seated at large round tables, then the food is paraded out course after course. Everyone eats until they can eat no more and drinks beyond their limit. Glasses are raised and toasts are led, everyone downs-in-one. The secret of standing straight come the end of the night is making sure you have enough ice in your beer.

WHERE TO EAT & DRINK
Whatever your taste, some eatery in Cambodia is sure to help out, be it the humble peddler with her yoke, a market stall, a local diner or a slick restaurant.

It is easy to sample inexpensive Khmer cuisine throughout the country, mostly at local markets and cheap restaurants. For more refined Khmer dining, the best restaurants are in Phnom Penh (p94) and Siem Reap (p125), where there is also the choice of excellent Thai, Vietnamese, Chinese, Indian, French and Mediterranean cooking. Chinese, and to a lesser extent Vietnamese, food is available in towns across the country due to the large urban populations of both of these ethnic groups.

There are no Western fast food chains in Phnom Penh as yet, but there are a few local copycats. The most successful has been Lucky Burger, with four branches in the capital.

There are often no set hours for places to eat, but as a general rule of thumb, street stalls are open from very early in the morning till late at night. Most restaurants are open all day, while some of the fancier places are only open for lunch (usually 11am to 2pm) and dinner (usually 5pm to 10pm).

Quick Eats
Because so much of life is lived outside the home, street food is an important part of everyday Cambodian life. Like many Southeast Asian people,

Cambodians are inveterate snackers. They can be found at impromptu stalls at any time of the day or night, delving into a range of snacky things. Drop into the markets for an even greater range of dishes and the chance for a comfortable seat. It's cheap, it's cheerful and it's a cool way to get up close and personal with Khmer cuisine.

VEGETARIANS & VEGANS

Few Cambodians understand the concept of strict vegetarianism and many will say something is vegetarian to please the customer when in fact it is not. If you are not a strict vegetarian and can deal with fish sauces and the like, you should have few problems ordering meals, and those who eat fish can sample Khmer cooking at its best. In the major tourist centres, many of the international restaurants feature vegetarian meals, although these are not budget options. Cheaper vegetarian meals are usually available at guesthouses. In Khmer and Chinese restaurants, stir-fried vegetable dishes are readily available, as are vegetarian fried rice dishes, but it is unlikely these 'vegetarian' dishes have been cooked in separate woks from other fish- and meat-based dishes. Indian restaurants in the popular tourist centres can cook up genuine vegetarian food, as they usually understand the vegetarian principle better than the *prahoc*-loving Khmers.

> **DID YOU KNOW?**
>
> Most Cambodian meals are cooked in a large wok, known locally as *chhnang khteak*.

EATING WITH KIDS

Family is at the heart of life in Cambodia, so it is hardly surprising to find family-oriented restaurants throughout the country. Most local restaurants will welcome children with open arms, particularly foreign kiddies, as staff don't get a chance to see them up close that often. Sometimes the welcome will be too much, with pinches and pats coming left, right and centre, but such is the way in Cambodia.

Ironically, it is often the upmarket Western restaurants where the reception may be terse if the children are playing up, as some stiff expats seem to have forgotten that they started out life that small. That said, there are plenty of excellent, child-friendly cafés and restaurants in Phnom Penh and Siem Reap serving dishes from home. There are rarely children's menus in any places, but with food so affordable, there is little room to quibble.

Most of the snacks children are accustomed to back home are available in Cambodia…and so much more. It is a great country for fruit and the sweetness of mangosteens or the weirdness of dragon fruit or rambutan is a sure way to get them interested. There is also an incredible selection of vegetarian creations for parents who prefer their children to avoid meat.

There is sometimes monosodium glutamate (MSG) in local Cambodian food. If your child has problems digesting it or you prefer to avoid it, it is better to stick to restaurants with an English-language menu that are used to dealing with tourists.

For more information on travelling with children in Cambodia, see p270.

HABITS & CUSTOMS

Enter the Cambodian kitchen and you will learn that fine food comes from simplicity. Essentials consist of a strong flame, clean water, basic cutting utensils, a mortar and pestle, and a well-blackened pot or two.

Cambodians eat three meals a day. Breakfast is either *kyteow* or *bobor*. Baguettes are available at any time of day or night, and go down well with a cup of coffee.

DOS AND DON'TS

■ *Do* wait for your host to sit first

■ *Don't* turn down food placed in your bowl by your host

■ *Do* learn to use chopsticks

■ *Don't* leave chopsticks in a v-shape in the bowl, a symbol of death

■ *Do* tip about 10% in restaurants as wages are low

■ *Don't* tip if there is already a service charge on the bill

■ *Do* drink every time someone offers a toast

■ *Don't* pass out face down on the table if the toasting goes on all night

---

Lunch starts early, around 11am. Traditionally lunch is taken with the family, but in towns and cities many workers now eat at local restaurants or markets.

Dinner is the time for family bonding. Dishes are arranged around the central rice bowl and diners each have a small eating bowl. The procedure is uncomplicated: spoon some rice into your bowl, and lay 'something else' on top of it.

When ordering multiple courses from a restaurant menu don't worry – don't even think – about the proper succession of courses. All dishes are placed in the centre of the table as soon as they are ready. Diners then help themselves to whatever appeals to them, regardless of who ordered what.

Table Etiquette

Sit at the table with your bowl on a small plate, chopsticks or fork and spoon at the ready. Some Cambodians prefer chopsticks, some prefer fork and spoon, but both are usually available. Each place setting will include a small bowl usually located at the top right-hand side for the dipping sauces.

When serving yourself from the central bowls, use the communal serving spoon so as not to dip your chopsticks or spoon into the food. To begin eating, just pick up your bowl with the left hand, bring it close to your mouth, and spoon in the rice and food.

It is polite for the host to offer more food than the guests can eat, and it is polite for the guests not to eat everything in sight!

COOKING COURSES

If you are really taken with Cambodian cuisine, it is possible to learn some tricks of the trade by signing up for a cooking course but there are very few courses on offer compared with neighbouring Thailand and Vietnam. For those who fall in love with the food, there is no better experience than recreating the real recipes back home. It's also a great way to introduce your Cambodia experience to your friends; no-one wants to hear the stories or see the photos, but offer them a mouth-watering meal and they will all come running!

Currently the only courses are operating in Battambang of all places, at the Smokin' Pot (p215), a cracking little kitchen restaurant that offers a US$7 introduction to the secrets of Cambodian cooking. However, it looks set to become a growth industry in Siem Reap in the coming years, so keep your ear to the ground.

EAT YOUR WORDS
Useful Phrases
Where is a ...?
... neuv ai naa?   ...នៅឯណា?
   restaurant
   resturawn, phowjaniyahtnaan   រេស្តូរង់, ភោជនិយដ្ឋាន
   cheap restaurant
   haang baay, resturawn thaok   ហាងបាយ, រេស្តូរង់ថោក
   food stall
   kuhnlaing loak m'howp   កន្លែងលក់ម្ហូប
   market
   psar   ផ្សារ

Do you have a menu in English?
   mien menui jea piasaa awnglay te?   មានម៉ឺនុយជាភាសាខ្មែរទេ?
I'm vegetarian. (I can't eat meat.)
   kh'nyohm tawm sait   ខ្ញុំតមសាច់
Can I get this without the meat?
   sohm kohm dak sait   សូមកុំដាក់សាច់
I'm allergic to (peanuts).
   kohm dak (sandaik dei)   កុំដាក់(សណ្ដែកដី)
What's the speciality here?
   tii nih mien m'howp ei piseh te?   ទីនេះមានម្ហូបអ្វីពិសេសទេ?
Not too spicy please.
   sohm kohm twœ huhl pek   សូមកុំធ្វើហឹរពេក
This is delicious.
   nih ch'ngain nah   អានេះឆ្ងាញ់ណាស់
The bill, please.
   sohm kuht lui   សូមគិតលុយ

Can you please bring me ...?
sohm yohk ... mao   សូមយក...មក
   a fork
   sawm   សម
   a knife
   kambuht   កាំបិត
   a plate
   jaan   ចាន
   a spoon
   slaapria   ស្លាបព្រា

Food Glossary
BREAKFAST

bread	*nohm paang*	នំបុ័ង
butter	*bœ*	ប៊ឺរ
fried eggs	*pohng moan jien*	ពងមាន់ចៀន
rice porridge	*bobor*	បបរ
vegetable noodle soup	*kyteow dak buhn lai*	គុយទាវដាក់បន្លៃ

LUNCH & DINNER

beef	*sait kow*	សាច់គោ
chicken	*sait moan*	សាច់មាន់
crab	*k'daam*	ក្ដាម

curry	*karii*	ការី
eel	*ahntohng*	អន្ទង់
fish	*trey*	ត្រី
fried	*jien, chaa*	ចៀន, ឆា
frog	*kawng kaip*	កង្កែប
grilled	*ahng*	អាំង
lobster	*bawng kawng*	បង្កង
noodles	*mii* (egg), *kyteow* (rice)	មី, គុយទាវ
pork	*sait j'ruuk*	សាច់ជ្រូក
rice	*bai*	បាយ
shrimp	*bawngkia*	បង្គា
snail	*kh'jawng*	ខ្យង
soup	*sup*	ស៊ុប
spring rolls	*naim* (fresh), *chaa yaw* (fried)	ណែម, ឆាយ៉
squid	*meuk*	មឹក
steamed	*jamhoi*	ចំហុយ
vegetables	*buhn lai*	បន្លែ

FRUITS

apple	*phla i powm*	ផ្លែប៉ោម
banana	*chek*	ចេក
coconut	*duong*	ដូង
custard apple	*tiep*	ទៀប
dragon fruit	*phlai srakaa neak*	ផ្លែស្រកានាគ
durian	*tourain*	ធូរេន
grapes	*tompeang baai juu*	ទំពាំងបាយជូ
guava	*trawbaik*	ត្របែក
jackfruit	*khnau*	ខ្នុរ
lemon	*krow-it ch'maa*	ក្រូចឆ្មារ
longan	*mien*	មៀន
lychee	*phlai kuulain*	ផ្លែគូលេន
mandarin	*krow-it khwait*	ក្រូចខ្ចិច
mango	*svay*	ស្វាយ
mangosteen	*mongkut*	មង្ឃុត
orange	*krow-it pow saat*	ក្រូចពោធិសាត់
papaya	*l'howng*	ល្ហុង
pineapple	*menoa*	ម្នាស់
pomelo	*krow-it th'lohng*	ក្រូចថ្លុង
rambutan	*sao mao*	សាវម៉ាវ
starfruit	*speu*	ស្ពឺ
watermelon	*euv luhk*	ឪឡឹក

CONDIMENTS

chilli	*m'teh*	ម្ទេស
fish sauce	*teuk trey*	ទឹកត្រី
garlic	*kh'tuhm saw*	ខ្ទឹមស
ginger	*kh'nyei*	ខ្ញី
ice	*teuk koh*	ទឹកកក

lemongrass	*sluhk kray*	ស្លឹកគ្រៃ
pepper	*m'rait*	ម្រេច
salt	*uhmbuhl*	អំបិល
soy sauce	*teuk sii iw*	ទឹកសុីអីុវ
sugar	*skaw*	ស

DRINKS

banana shake	*teuk kralohk*	ទឹកក្រឡុក
beer	*bii-yœ*	បៀរ
black coffee	*kaa fey kh'mav*	កាហ្វេខ្មៅ
coffee	*kaa fey*	កាហ្វេ
iced coffee	*kaa fey teuk koh*	កាហ្វេទឹកកក
lemon juice	*teuk krow-it ch'maa*	ទឹកក្រូចឆ្មា
mixed fruit shake	*teuk kralohk chek*	ទឹកក្រឡុកចេក
orange juice	*teuk krow-it pow sat*	ទឹកក្រូចពោធិសាត់
tea	*tai*	តែ
tea with milk	*tai teuk dawh kow*	តែទឹកដោះគោ
white coffee	*kaa fey ohlay (ie café au lait)*	កាហ្វេអូឡេ

Phnom Penh
ភ្នំពេញ

At times beautiful and beguiling, at times chaotic and charmless, Phnom Penh is a crossroad of Asia's past and present, a city of extremes of poverty and excess, but one that never fails to captivate the visitor.

Phnom Penh sits at the confluence of the Mekong, Tonlé Bassac and Tonlé Sap rivers. Long considered the loveliest of the French-built cities of Indochina, its charm, while tarnished, has largely managed to survive the violence of its recent history and the current crop of property speculators.

Most of Phnom Penh's tourist attractions are low-key, which means that many travellers spend only a short time here. This is a pity; Phnom Penh is a city that is rediscovering itself and, after the obligatory sightseeing circuit is completed, a fascinating place to take in at leisure. The French left a legacy of now-crumbling colonial architecture, some of which is being tastefully renovated; the wats (Buddhist temple-monasteries) have come back to life with a passion – monks in saffron robes can be seen wandering around carrying alms bowls; and there are great restaurants all over the city, an ideal warm-up for the lively nightshift.

The riverfront area in Phnom Penh is undoubtedly one of the most splendid in Asia, lined with swaying palms and billowing flags, the mightiest river in Asia, the Mekong, converging and diverging as a backdrop. After many years of neglect, Phnom Penh at last seems to be on the move and, if it can learn from the mistakes of its larger neighbours, it could once again become the 'Pearl of Asia'.

HIGHLIGHTS

- Tread lightly upon the 5000 silver floor tiles at the **Silver Pagoda** (p80) in the Royal Palace
- Step back in time at the **National Museum** (p81), home to the world's finest collection of Angkorian sculpture
- Check out the Art Deco masterpiece that is **Psar Thmei** (p104), Phnom Penh's central market
- Discover a darker side at **Tuol Sleng Museum** (p82), a brutal reminder of the pain of Cambodia's past
- Soak up the city by night, with a happy hour cocktail, a fine meal and a crawl through the **city's bars** (p100)

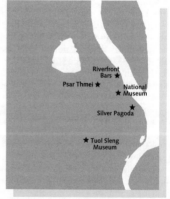

Riverfront Bars ★

Psar Thmei ★

★ National Museum

★ Silver Pagoda

★ Tuol Sleng Museum

- TELEPHONE CODE: 023 ■ POPULATION: 1.2 MILLION ■ AREA: 290 SQ KM

HISTORY

Legend has it that the city of Phnom Penh was founded when an old woman named Penh found four Buddha images that had come to rest on the banks of the Mekong River. She housed them on a nearby hill, and the town that grew up here came to be known as Phnom Penh (Hill of Penh).

The story, however, gives no hint as to why, in the 1430s, Angkor was abandoned and Phnom Penh was chosen as the site of the new Cambodian capital. The move has been much lamented as evidence of cultural decline, but it made a good deal of practical sense. Angkor was poorly situated for trade and subject to attacks from the Siamese (Thai) kingdom of Ayuthaya. Phnom Penh commanded a more central position in the Khmer territories and was perfectly located for riverine trade with Laos and China, via the Mekong Delta. The Tonlé Sap river provided access to the rich fishing grounds of the Tonlé Sap lake.

By the mid-16th century, trade had turned Phnom Penh into a regional power. Indonesian and Chinese traders were drawn to the city in large numbers. A century later, however, Vietnamese incursions into Khmer territory had robbed the city of access to sea lanes, and Chinese merchants driven south by the Manchu (Qing) dynasty began to monopolise trade. The landlocked and increasingly isolated kingdom became a buffer between ascendant Thais and Vietnamese. In 1772 the Thais burnt Phnom Penh to the ground. Although the city was rebuilt, Phnom Penh was buffeted by the rival hegemonic interests of the Thai and Vietnamese courts, until the French took over in 1863. Its population is thought not to have risen much above 25,000 during this period.

The French protectorate in Cambodia gave Phnom Penh the layout we know today. The city was divided into districts or *quartiers*: the French administrators and European traders inhabited the area north of Wat Phnom between Monivong Blvd and the Tonlé Sap; the Chinese merchants occupied the riverfront area south of Wat Phnom to the Royal Palace and west as far as Norodom Blvd; and the Cambodians and Vietnamese lived around and south of the palace. By the time of their departure in 1953, the French had left many important landmarks, including the Royal Palace, National Museum, Psar Thmei (New Market) and many impressive government ministries.

The city grew fast in the post-independence peacetime years of Sihanouk's rule. By the time he was overthrown in 1970, the population of Phnom Penh was approximately 500,000. As the Vietnam War spread into Cambodian territory, the city's population swelled with refugees and reached more than two million in early 1975. The Khmer Rouge took the city on 17 April 1975 and, as part of its radical social programme, immediately forced the entire population into the countryside. Different factions of the Khmer Rouge were responsible for evacuating different zones of the city; civilians to the east of Norodom Blvd were sent east, those south of the palace to the south, and so on. Whole families were split up on those fateful first days of 'liberation' and for many thousands of Cambodians, their experience of the dark days of Khmer Rouge rule depended on which area of the city they had been in that day.

During the time of Democratic Kampuchea, many tens of thousands of former Phnom Penhois – including the vast majority of the capital's educated residents – were killed. The population of Phnom Penh during the Khmer Rouge regime was never more than about 50,000, a figure made up of senior party members, factory workers and trusted military leaders.

Repopulation of the city began when the Vietnamese arrived in 1979, although at first it was strictly controlled by the new government. During much of the 1980s, cows were more common than cars on the streets of the capital, and it was not until the government dispensed with its communist baggage at the end of the decade that Phnom Penh began to develop. The 1990s were boom years for some: along with the arrival of the UN Transitional Authority in Cambodia (Untac) came US$2 billion, much of it in salaries for expats. Well-connected residents were only too happy to assist foreigners part with their money through high rents and hefty price-hikes. Businesses followed hot on the heels of Untac and commercial buildings began to spring up.

The biggest changes to life in Phnom Penh commenced under former mayor Chea Sophara who embarked on a one-man mission to clean up the city. This made him

KNOWING WHEN YOUR NUMBER'S UP

Navigating the streets of Phnom Penh should be pretty straightforward thanks to the grid system put in place by the French. The total and utter lack of an effective house-numbering system, however, makes some guesthouses, restaurants and offices that bit harder to track down. The long years of war, abandonment and reoccupation destroyed the old system and as residents began to repopulate the city, they seem to have picked numbers out of the air. It is not uncommon to drive past a row of houses numbered 13A, 34, 7, 26. Make sense of that and you might get a job as a code cracker. Worse still, several different houses might use the same number on the same street. The long and the short of it is that when you get to a guesthouse or restaurant recommended in this chapter only to discover it appears to have turned into a *prahoc* (fermented fish paste) shop, don't curse us for the bad smell. Just down the road will be another place with the same number – the guesthouse or restaurant you were looking for…unless, of course, it really has gone into the *prahoc* business.

When getting directions, ask for a cross-reference for an address, such as 'close to the intersection of Ph 107 and Ph 182'. The letters 'EO' after a street address stand for *étage zéro* (ground floor).

too popular with Phnom Penh residents for Prime Minister Hun Sen's liking and he was brushed aside in 2003. However, his legacy lives on with roads being repaired, sewage pipes laid, parks inaugurated and riverbanks reclaimed – you can't help feeling Phnom Penh is on the move as a new middle class emerges to replace the thousands eliminated by the Khmer Rouge.

ORIENTATION

A minor hurdle to orientation in Phnom Penh is the frequency with which street names and numbers are changed, depending on the prevailing political winds. The current denominations, which date back to 1993, have settled in, but there is still a chance that some of the numbered streets will change again.

The major boulevards of Phnom Penh run north–south, parallel to the banks of the Tonlé Sap and Tonlé Bassac. Monivong Blvd cuts north–south through the centre of town, passing just west of Psar Thmei. Its northern sector is the main shopping strip and is also home to some of the oldest hotels and travel agents in town. Norodom Blvd runs north–south from Wat Phnom, and is largely lined with administrative buildings; the northern end contains banks, while further south are government ministries. Samdech Sothearos Blvd runs north–south near the riverfront, past the Royal Palace, Silver Pagoda and National Assembly building (Map pp78–9). Sisowath Quay hugs the river and is where many of the city's most popular restaurants and bars are located.

The major east–west boulevards are Russian Blvd in the north of town, Sihanouk Blvd, which passes the Independence Monument and ends just south of Hotel Cambodiana, and Mao Tse Toung Blvd. A ring road of sorts, Mao Tse Toung Blvd, also runs north–south in the west of the city.

Intersecting the main boulevards is a network of hundreds of numbered smaller streets. As a rule of thumb, streets running east–west have even numbers that increase as you go south, while streets that run north–south have odd numbers that increase as you head west.

Most buildings around town have signs with both their building number and *phlauv* (street; abbreviated to Ph) number. Finding a building purely by its address, however, is not always easy, as numbers are rarely sequential. See the boxed text above, and don't forget to pity the postman.

Most buses, taxis and pick-ups arrive in the centre of town around Psar Thmei and it is just a short *moto* (small motorcycle with driver) or taxi ride to most guesthouses and hotels. The train station is just a couple of blocks northwest of here. Boats from Siem Reap, towns on the Mekong, and Vietnam arrive at the tourist boat dock on the Tonlé Sap river at the eastern end of Ph 108. Hundreds of *motos* await, ready to ambush. Phnom Penh International Airport (p288) is 7km west of central Phnom Penh.

Maps

There are few maps that go into greater detail than those in this guidebook. However, for a handy pocket-size map, look out for a free copy of the *Phnom Penh 3-D Map*, which is distributed at the airport and selected bars and restaurants around the city.

Both the *Phnom Penh Visitors' Guide* and the *Phnom Penh Pocket Guide*, freely available in the capital, have maps and listings with good detail on food and drink spots.

The local publications *Phnom Penh Post* and *Bayon Pearnik* include maps with listings, though entries are sponsored by advertisers and are far from comprehensive.

INFORMATION
Bookshops
Prices of new books in Cambodia tend to be higher than elsewhere in the region, but there are now a couple of well-stocked secondhand books offering cut-price reads.

D's Books (Map pp78-9; www.ds-books.com; Ph 240) The newest secondhand bookshop in the capital, a well-stocked outpost of a popular Thai operation.

International Stationery & Book Centre (Map pp78-9; ☎ 218352; 37 Sihanouk Blvd) Mainly devoted to English-language textbooks and dictionaries, but has cheap books on Cambodia.

London Book Centre (Map pp78-9; ☎ 214258; 51 Ph 240) A good place for browsing with plenty of secondhand stock shipped in from the UK, plus cheaper deals if you have something to trade.

Mekong Libris (Map pp78-9; ☎ 722751; 12 Ph 13) Located opposite the main post office, this is the best-stocked French-language bookshop in town.

Monument Books (Map pp78-9; ☎ 217617; 111 Norodom Blvd) Probably the best-stocked bookshop in town, with almost every Cambodia-related book currently in print available. It has a large branch at the international terminal in Phnom Penh Airport.

PHNOM PENH IN...

One Day
If you've only got a day in town, start early with a riverfront stroll to see the mass tai chi and aerobics sessions taking place in front of the **Royal Palace** (p80). Head north to the **Royal University of Fine Arts** (p85) to see a new generation of classical dancers in training. Grab breakfast at one of the riverfront cafés before venturing into the Royal Palace compound to see the dazzling treasures of the **Silver Pagoda** (p80). Next is the **National Museum** (p81) and the world's most wondrous collection of Khmer sculpture. Take lunch at nearby **Friends** (p94) restaurant, giving street children a helping hand into tourism. After lunch, check out the funky architecture of **Psar Thmei** (p104), but save your shopping for the treasure trove that is **Psar Tuol Tom Pong** (p104), more commonly known as the Russian Market. Take a deep breath and continue to **Tuol Sleng Museum** (p82), a savage reminder of Cambodia's tragic past. Sobering indeed and it may be time for a happy-hour drink to reflect on the highs and lows of the day. Take dinner in one of the many good **Khmer restaurants** (p94) in town, before joining the nightshift at some of the **buzzing bars** (p100).

Two Days
With two days, it is easy to get to grips with Cambodia's capital. Start the day as in the one-day itinerary with a visit to the cultural splendours that are the **National Museum** (p81) and **Royal Palace** (p80). In the afternoon, visit the harrowing **Tuol Sleng Museum** (p82) before continuing on to the **Killing Fields of Choeung Ek** (p83), where prisoners from Security Prison 21 were taken for execution. It is a grim afternoon, but essential for understanding just how far Cambodia has come in the intervening years. Wind up with a sunset cruise on the **Mekong River** (p85) with a beautiful view over the Royal Palace.

On the second day, it is time to get serious about shopping. Browse through the Art Deco ziggurat pyramid that is **Psar Thmei** (p104), but save the spending for **Psar Tuol Tom Pong** (p104), a maze of stalls selling everything from textiles and handicrafts to DVDs and cut-price clothing. Keep some cash for the excellent **shops** (p103) that support good causes, all of which stock a solid selection of silk.

In the afternoon, take a look at the **Independence Monument** (p84), modelled on Angkor Wat's central tower, and wander up the riverfront to **Wat Phnom** (p83), where the Khmers prefer to pray for luck. From here it is a short stroll to catch the happy-hour cocktails at the **Elephant Bar** (p100) at Hotel Le Royal, the perfect warm-up for a final fling in Phnom Penh.

www.lonelyplanet.com

PHNOM PENH

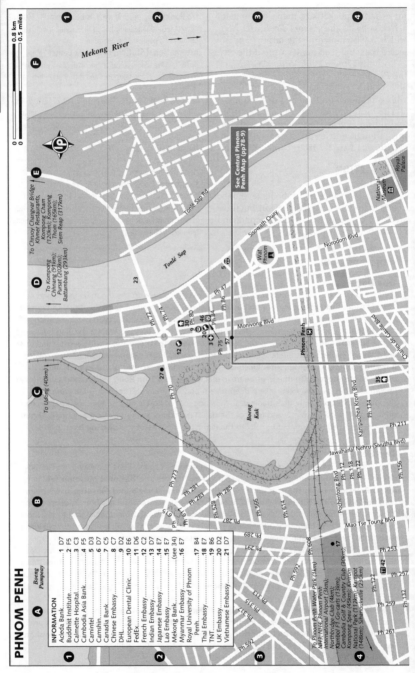

PHNOM PENH

INFORMATION

Acleda Bank...............................	1 D7
Buddhist Institute.......................	2 F5
Calmette Hospital......................	3 C3
Cambodia Asia Bank..................	4 F5
Camintel....................................	5 D3
Camshin....................................	6 D7
Canadia Bank............................	7 C5
Chinese Embassy.......................	8 C7
DHL..	9 D2
European Dental Clinic..............	10 E6
FedEx.......................................	11 D6
French Embassy.........................	12 C2
Indian Embassy.........................	13 D7
Japanese Embassy.....................	14 E7
Lao Embassy..............................	15 E7
Mekong Bank............................	(see 34)
Myanmar Embassy.....................	16 E7
Royal University of Phnom	
Penh......................................	17 B4
Thai Embassy............................	18 E7
TNT...	19 B6
UK Embassy...............................	20 D2
Vietnamese Embassy..................	21 D7

Mekong River

Tonlé Sap Rd

Sisowath Quay

Norodom Blvd

See Central Phnom
Penh Map (pp78–9)

National
Museum

Royal
Palace

Wat
Phnom

Tonlé Sap

Monivong Blvd

Phnom Penh

To Chrouy Changvar Bridge
Khmer Restaurants;
Kompong Cham
(120km); Kompong
Thom (165km);
Siem Reap (317km)

To Kompong
Chhnang (91km);
Pursat (202km);
Battambang (293km)

Charles de Gaulle Blvd

Ph 72

Ph 74

Ph 80

Ph 86

Ph 17

Ph 75

Ph 70

*Boeng
Kak*

Ph 273

Ph 261

Ph 283

Ph 285

Ph 528

Ph 566

Ph 614

Ph 528

Ph 287

Ph 289

Ph 291

Jawaharlal Nehru (Sivutha Blvd)

Pochentong Blvd

Ph 112
Ph 118
Ph 122
Ph 134
Ph 156
Ph 211

Kampuchea Krom Blvd

Mao Tse Toung Blvd

Ph 253

Ph 257

Ph 259

Ph 261

Ph 592

Ph 608

Ph 317

Ph 313
Ph 315

Ph 132

Ph 122

To Phnom Penh Water Park (1km);
NR4; NR3; Pochentong
International Airport (3km);
Northbridge Club (4km);
Kambol F1 Go-carts (13km);
Cambodia Golf & Country Club (80km);
Kompong Speu (45km); Kampot
(148km); Sihanoukville (230km)

To Udong (40km)

0   0.8 km
0   0.5 miles

*Boeng
Pumpeay*

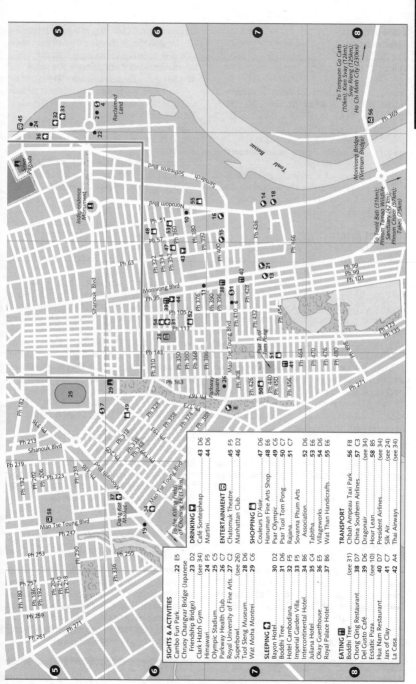

SIGHTS & ACTIVITIES

Cambo Fun Park	**22**	E5
Chruoy Changvar Bridge (Japanese Friendship Bridge)	**23**	D2
Clark Hatch Gym	(see 34)	
Himawari	**24**	F5
Olympic Stadium	**25**	C5
Parkway Health Club	**26**	C7
Royal University of Fine Arts	**27**	C2
Superbowl	(see 26)	
Tuol Sleng Museum	**28**	D6
Wat Moha Montrei	**29**	C6

SLEEPING

Bayon Hotel	**30**	D2
Boddhi Tree	**31**	D6
Hotel Cambodiana	**32**	F5
Imperial Garden Villa	**33**	F5
Intercontinental Hotel	**34**	B6
Juliana Hotel	**35**	C4
Okay Guesthouse	**36**	E5
Royal Palace Hotel	**37**	B6

EATING

Boddhi Tree	(see 31)	
Chong Qing Restaurant	**38**	D7
Del Gusto Cafe	**39**	D6
Ecstatic Pizza	(see 10)	
Hua Nam Restaurant	**40**	D7
Jars of Clay	**41**	C7
La Casa	**42**	A4

DRINKING

Café Sonteipheap	**43**	D6
Martini	**44**	D6

ENTERTAINMENT

Chatomuk Theatre	**45**	F5
Manhattan Club	**46**	D2

SHOPPING

Couleurs D'Asie	**47**	D6
Hanuman Fine Arts Shop	**48**	E6
Psar Olympic	**49**	C6
Psar Tuol Tom Pong	**50**	C7
Rajana	**51**	C7
Sovanna Phum Arts Association	**52**	D6
Tabitha	**53**	E6
Villageworks	**54**	E5
Wat Than Handicrafts	**55**	E6

TRANSPORT

Chbah Ampeau Taxi Park	**56**	F8
China Southern Airlines	**57**	C3
Dragonair	(see 34)	
Hour Lean	**58**	B5
President Airlines	(see 34)	
Silk Air	(see 24)	
Thai Airways	(see 34)	

Emergency

Ambulance (☎ 119)
Fire (☎ 118)
Police (☎ 117)

There are also two 24-hour emergency numbers for the **police** (☎ 366841, 012 999999) in Phnom Penh that will connect you to English-speaking officers. There are emergency numbers with English-speaking operators for Phnom Penh's **ambulance service** (☎ 724891, 426948, 012 808915).

In the event of a medical emergency it may be necessary to be flown to Bangkok. See below for details of medical services in Phnom Penh.

Internet Access

Phnom Penh is now well and truly wired, with prices dropping from US$10 an hour in 1998 to between US$0.50 and US$1 per hour today. There are Internet cafés across the city, although the most convenient those along the riverfront. However, cheaper rates are available in the smaller Internet cafés on the side streets running away from the river and savings can be significant if you are making Internet telephone calls.

Many budget guesthouses also offer some sort of Internet access and in the main backpacker areas, there are several Internet cafés. Those in more expensive hotels should venture out to find an online fix as in-house business centres are overpriced.

Laundry

Most guesthouses around town offer reasonably priced laundry services at around 1000r an item. Cheaper still are the local laundries throughout the city; these are a very worthwhile consideration for those staying in expensive hotels.

Libraries

The National Library (p85) has a small selection of reading material for foreign visitors, but is set in a lovely building. French speakers should call into the **French Cultural Centre** (Map pp78-9; Ph 184). It has a good range of reading material.

Medical Services

Calmette Hospital (Map pp74-5; ☎ 426948; 3 Monivong Blvd; ☿ 24hr) French-administered and the best of the local hospitals.

European Dental Clinic (Map pp74-5; ☎ 211363; 160A Norodom Blvd; ☿ 8am-7pm Mon-Sat) Offers international dental services and has a good reputation.

International SOS Medical Centre (Map pp78-9; ☎ 216911; www.internationalsos.com; 161 Ph 51; ☿ 8am-5.30pm Mon-Fri, 8am-noon Sat) One of the best medical services around town, but with prices to match. Also has a resident foreign dentist.

Naga Clinic (Map pp78-9; ☎ 211300; www.nagaclinic .com; 11 Ph 254; ☿ 24hr) A French-run clinic for reliable consultations.

Pharmacie de la Gare (Map pp78-9; ☎ 526855; 81 Monivong Blvd; ☿ 7am-7pm) A great local pharmacy with English- and French-speaking consultants.

Money

Those looking to change cash into riel need look no farther than jewellery stalls around the markets of Phnom Penh – Psar Thmei (p104) and Psar Tuol Tom Pong (p104) are the most convenient.

A number of upmarket hotels do offer money-changing services, although this is usually reserved for their guests. Many travel agents can also change travellers cheques and offer credit-card advances for a 5% commission or higher. Most banks in Phnom Penh are open from roughly 8.30am to 3.30pm weekdays and 8.30am to 11.30am Saturday.

Cambodia Asia Bank Sisowath Quay (Map pp78-9; ☎ 220381; 349 Sisowath Quay; ☿ 7.30am-9pm); Nagaworld (Map pp74-5; ☎ 210900; Sihanouk Blvd; ☿ 24hr) Cash advances on Visa at 1%, MasterCard at 2%, plus travellers cheques at 2%.

Cambodian Commercial Bank (CCB; Map pp78-9; ☎ 426145; 26 Monivong Blvd) Cash advances on MasterCard, JCB and Visa with a minimum charge of US$5 for transactions under US$250, and 2% thereafter.

Canadia Bank Head Office (Map pp78-9; ☎ 215286; 265 Ph 110); Branch (Map pp74-5; ☎ 214668; 126 Ph 217) Changes travellers cheques of several currencies for a 2% commission, plus free cash advances on MasterCard and Visa.

Foreign Trade Bank (Map pp78-9; ☎ 723466; 3 Ph 114; ☿ 7am-3.45pm Mon-Fri) Lowest commission in town on US dollar travellers cheques at 1%.

Mekong Bank Head Office (Map pp78-9; ☎ 217112; 1 Ph 114); Branch (Map pp74-5; ☎ 424980; cnr Mao Tse Toung & Monireth Blvds; ☿ 3.30-8pm Mon-Sat, 8am-1pm Sun) Cash advances at 2% here. There's also a desk at the airport.

Union Commercial Bank (UCB; Map pp78-9; ☎ 218682; 61 Ph 130) Free cash advances on credit cards, plus travellers cheques at 2% commission.

Those needing to organise an international money transfer can use the Foreign Trade

Bank. However, it may be quicker (and more expensive) to use an international company such as MoneyGram or Western Union. MoneyGram is represented by Canadia Bank, while Western Union can be found at the **Singapore Banking Corporation** (Map pp78-9; ☎ 217771; 68 Ph 214) or **Acleda Bank** (Map pp74-5; ☎ 214634; 28 Mao Tse Toung Blvd).

Post
The **main post office** (Map pp78-9; Ph 13; ☼ 7am-7pm) is in a charming building just east of Wat Phnom. It offers postal services as well as telephone and fax links. There is another branch on Monivong Blvd, near the corner of Sihanouk Blvd. For postal rates see p282.

If you need to get valuables or belongings home in a hurry, there are several international courier companies (p282) represented in Phnom Penh.

Telephone & Fax
The cheapest local and domestic calls in Phnom Penh are available from private booths found throughout the city. Whatever the number you are dialling, private booths will have a selection of telephones to make sure you get the best rate. Local calls start from 300r a minute.

There are public phone boxes operated by Camintel and Telstra in many parts of the city. Nearby will be a local shop that sells phonecards.

Many Internet cafés in Phnom Penh offer telephone services at reasonable prices, including Internet phone calls, which are much cheaper than normal international calls, but involve an irritating delay that turns half the conversation into 'hello?' and 'pardon?'.

For further information on phone and fax services, see p284.

Tourist Information
Due to lack of government funding, you can forget about useful tourist information in Phnom Penh. The tourist office at Phnom Penh International Airport has information on certain hotels around town and can make bookings, but other than this you are effectively on your own.

The **Ministry of Tourism** (Map pp78-9; ☎ 426876; 3 Monivong Blvd) is in a white two-storey building on the western corner of Monivong Blvd and Ph 232, but it offers nothing in the way of handouts for the drop-in visitor.

Travel Agencies
Hanuman Tourism-Voyages (Map pp78-9; ☎ 218356; www.hanumantourism.com; 128 Norodom Blvd) Just south of the Independence Monument, this is a very reliable place to reserve hotels and arrange worldwide flights and cheap regional visas.
PTM Travel & Tours (Map pp78-9; ☎ 364768; 200 Monivong Blvd) Conveniently located near Psar Thmei, this is a good spot for discount flight tickets.
Transpeed Travel (Map pp78-9; ☎ 723999; 19 Ph 106) A popular local agent offering worldwide ticketing and hotel reservations.

DANGERS & ANNOYANCES
Phnom Penh is not as dangerous as many people imagine, but it is still important to take care. Armed robberies do sometimes occur, but statistically you would be very unlucky to be a victim. Guesthouses often make the situation out to be even more dangerous than it is to keep customers in their restaurants.

It pays to take care in crowded bars or nightclubs, particularly the Heart of Darkness. Many pampered children of the elite hang out in popular places, bringing their bodyguards along for good luck. This is fine until a drunk foreigner treads on their toe or they decide they want to hit on a Western girl. Then the problems start and if they have bodyguards with them, it will only end in tears, big tears.

Should you become the victim of a robbery, do not panic and do not, under any circumstances, struggle. Calmly raise your hands and let your attacker take what they want. *Do not* reach for your pockets as the assailant may think you are reaching for a gun! They will probably be as nervous as you, and you will most likely get any documents back later via your guesthouse or embassy, as the robbers often want only cash and valuables. For the time being, even passports and credit cards seem to be returned. Do not carry a bag at night, as it is more likely to make you a target.

It is not sensible to ride a motorbike alone late at night; and if there is one area to avoid after dark, it is Tuol Kork, to the north of Boeng Kak, which is the old brothel quarter and the kind of place where drunk Khmers shoot each other over a karaoke microphone.

If you ride your own motorbike during the day, police will often try to fleece you for the

CENTRAL PHNOM PENH

most trivial of offences, such as turning left in violation of a no left-turn sign. At their most audacious, they try to get you for riding with your headlights on during the day, although worryingly, it doesn't seem to be illegal for Cambodians to travel without their headlights on at night. They will most likely demand US$5 and threaten to take you to the police station for an official US$20 fine if you don't pay. If you are patient and smile, you can usually get away with handing over 1000r or a few cigarettes. The trick is not to stop in the first place by not catching their eye.

The riverfront area of Phnom Penh, particularly places with outdoor seating, attracts many beggars, as does Psar Thmei (p104) and Psar Tuol Tom Pong (p104). Generally, however, there is little in the way of push and shove. For more thoughts, see p272.

SIGHTS

Phnom Penh is a small city and most of the major sights are fairly central. The most important cultural sights can be visited on foot and are located near the riverfront in the most beautiful part of the city.

Royal Palace & Silver Pagoda

ព្រះបរមរាជវាំង/និង វត្តព្រះកែវ

The **Royal Palace** (Map pp78-9; Samdech Sothearos Blvd; admission US$3; ⏱ 7.30-11am & 2.30-5pm) is a striking structure near the riverfront, bearing a remarkable likeness to its counterpart in Bangkok. It stands on the site of the former citadel, Banteay Kev, and looks out on to Samdech Sothearos Blvd between Ph 184 and Ph 240. Visitors are only allowed to visit the palace's Silver Pagoda and its surrounding compound. It is an extra US$2 to take in a camera and US$5 for a video camera. However, photography is not permitted inside the pagoda itself.

CHAN CHAYA PAVILION

Performances of classical Cambodian dance were once staged in the Chan Chaya Pavilion, through which guests enter the grounds of the Royal Palace.

THRONE HALL

The Throne Hall, topped by a 59m-high tower inspired by the Bayon at Angkor, was inaugurated in 1919 by King Sisowath; the present cement building replaces a vast wooden structure that was built on this site in 1869. The Throne Hall was used for coronations and ceremonies such as the presentation of credentials by diplomats. Many of the items once displayed here were destroyed by the Khmer Rouge. In the courtyard is a curious **iron house** given to King Norodom by Napoleon III of France.

SILVER PAGODA

The Silver Pagoda, so named because the floor is covered with over 5000 silver tiles weighing 1kg each, is also known as Wat Preah Keo (Pagoda of the Emerald Buddha). It was constructed of wood in 1892 during the rule of King Norodom, who was apparently inspired by Bangkok's Wat Phra Keo, and was rebuilt in 1962.

The Silver Pagoda was preserved by the Khmer Rouge to demonstrate to the outside world its concern for the conservation of Cambodia's cultural riches. Although some 60% of the pagoda's contents were destroyed under Pol Pot, what remains is spectacular. This is one of the few places in Cambodia where objects embodying some of the brilliance and richness of Khmer civilisation can still be seen.

The staircase leading to the Silver Pagoda is made of Italian marble. Inside, the Emerald Buddha, said to be made of Baccarat crystal, sits on a gilt pedestal high atop the dais. In front of the dais stands a life-size gold Buddha decorated with 9584 diamonds, the largest of which weighs 25 carats. Created in the palace workshops during 1906 and 1907, the gold Buddha weighs in at 90kg. Directly in front of it, in a Formica case, is a miniature silver-and-gold stupa containing a relic of Buddha brought from Sri Lanka. To the left is an 80kg bronze Buddha, and to the right a silver Buddha. On the far right, figurines of solid gold tell the story of the Buddha.

Behind the dais is a standing marble Buddha from Myanmar (Burma) and a bed used by the king on coronation day; designed to be carried by 12 men, its gold work alone weighs 23kg. To either side are silver models of King Norodom's stupa and Wat Preah Keo's library. At the back of the hall is a case containing two gold Buddhas, each decorated with diamonds weighing up to 16 carats; the lower figure weighs 4.5kg, the upper 1.5kg.

Along the walls of the pagoda are examples of extraordinary Khmer artisanship,

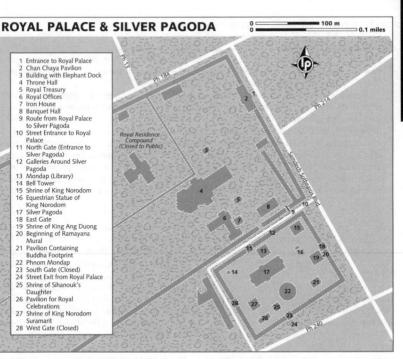

ROYAL PALACE & SILVER PAGODA

1 Entrance to Royal Palace
2 Chan Chaya Pavilion
3 Building with Elephant Dock
4 Throne Hall
5 Royal Treasury
6 Royal Offices
7 Iron House
8 Banquet Hall
9 Route from Royal Palace to Silver Pagoda
10 Street Entrance to Royal Palace
11 North Gate (Entrance to Silver Pagoda)
12 Galleries Around Silver Pagoda
13 Mondap (Library)
14 Bell Tower
15 Shrine of King Norodom
16 Equestrian Statue of King Norodom
17 Silver Pagoda
18 East Gate
19 Shrine of King Ang Duong
20 Beginning of Ramayana Mural
21 Pavilion Containing Buddha Footprint
22 Phnom Mondap
23 South Gate (Closed)
24 Street Exit from Royal Palace
25 Shrine of Sihanouk's Daughter
26 Pavilion for Royal Celebrations
27 Shrine of King Norodom Suramarit
28 West Gate (Closed)

including bejewelled masks used in classical dance and dozens of solid and hollow gold Buddhas. The many precious gifts given to Cambodia's monarchs by foreign heads of state appear rather spiritless when displayed next to such diverse and exuberant Khmer art. The epic of the *Ramayana* (known as the *Reamker* in Cambodia) is depicted on a beautiful and extensive mural enclosing the pagoda compound, created around 1900; the story begins just south of the east gate.

Other structures in the complex (listed clockwise from the north gate) include the *mondap* (library), which housed richly illuminated sacred texts that are written on palm leaves; the shrine of King Norodom (r 1860–1904); an equestrian statue of King Norodom; the shrine of King Ang Duong (r 1845–59); a pavilion housing a huge footprint of Buddha; Phnom Mondap, an artificial hill with a structure containing a bronze footprint of the Buddha from Sri Lanka; a shrine dedicated to one of Prince Sihanouk's daughters; a pavilion for celebrations held by the royal family; the shrine of Prince Sihanouk's father, King Norodom Suramarit (r

1955–60); and a bell tower, whose bell is rung to order the gates to be opened or closed.

National Museum
សារមន្ទីរជាតិ

The **National Museum of Cambodia** (Map pp78-9; admission US$3; 8am-5pm) is home to the world's finest collection of Khmer sculpture. Located just north of the Royal Palace, the museum is housed in a graceful terracotta structure of traditional design (built 1917–20), with a lush courtyard garden providing the perfect backdrop to an outstanding array of delicate objects.

The museum comprises four courtyards, facing a garden. The most significant displays of sculpture are in the courtyards to the left and straight ahead of the entrance. Some highlights include the eight-armed statue of Vishnu from the 6th or 7th century AD, the statue of Shiva (c 866–77) and the sublime statue of Jayavarman VII seated (c 1181–218), his head bowed slightly in a meditative pose. The museum also contains displays of pottery and bronzes dating

---

BATS IN THE BELFRY

The elegant curves of the National Museum make a picturesque sight when framed against the pink and mauve of a sunset. It's also about this time of day that hundreds of bats stream out from the museum's roof, a memorable sight to behold. Most of the bats belong to a recently identified species, the Cambodian freetail.

Some bat experts claim that the National Museum has the largest bat population of any artificial structure in the world. The problem is that bat droppings are corrosive, and until 1994 they were falling through the ceiling, damaging the exhibits. Meanwhile, museum patrons were having to do their sightseeing in a miasma of bat poo.

Fortunately, the Australian International Development Assistance Bureau (Aidab) came to the rescue. In an agreement that saw the 'Treasures of the National Museum of Cambodia' exhibited at the Australian National Gallery, Aidab undertook to help maintain the contents of the museum. It was considered ecologically unsound to remove the bats, so a second artificial ceiling was constructed to stop the droppings falling through. So far it is holding up under the weight.

---

from the pre-Angkorian periods of Funan and Chenla (4th to 9th centuries), the Indravarman period (9th and 10th centuries), the classical Angkorian period (10th to 14th centuries), as well as more recent works. There is a permanent collection of post-Angkorian Buddhas, many of which were rescued from Angkor Wat when the civil war erupted. See p52 for more information.

Unfortunately, photography is prohibited inside the museum. English- and French-speaking guides (from US$2, depending on group size) are available, and there is also a useful exhibition booklet, *The New Guide to the National Museum,* available at the front desk.

The Royal University of Fine Arts (p85) has its headquarters in a structure behind the main National Museum building.

Tuol Sleng Museum
សារមន្ទីរទួលស្លែង

In 1975 Tuol Svay Prey High School was taken over by Pol Pot's security forces and turned into a prison known as Security Prison 21 (S-21). This soon became the largest centre of detention and torture in the country. Between the years 1975 and 1978 more than 17,000 people held at S-21 were taken to the extermination camp at Choeung Ek (opposite).

S-21 has been turned into the **Tuol Sleng Museum** (Map pp74-5; Ph 113; admission US$2; ☺ 8-11.30am & 2-5.30pm), which serves as a testament to the crimes of the Khmer Rouge. It is usually possible to visit any time of day, despite the official opening hours. Entry is on the western side of Ph 113. It costs US$5 to take in a video camera.

Like the Nazis, the Khmer Rouge was meticulous in keeping records of its barbarism. Each prisoner who passed through S-21 was photographed, sometimes before and after torture. The museum displays include room after room of harrowing black and white photographs; virtually all of the men, women and children pictured were later killed. You can tell which year a picture was taken by the style of number-board that appears on the prisoner's chest. Several foreigners from Australia, France and the USA were also held at S-21 before being murdered. Their documents are on display. It is worth paying US$2 to have a guide show you around, as they can tell you the stories behind some of the people in the photographs.

As the Khmer Rouge 'revolution' reached ever greater heights of insanity, it began devouring its own. Generations of torturers and executioners who worked here were in turn killed by those who took their places. During early 1977, when the party purges of Eastern Zone cadres were getting underway, S-21 claimed an average of 100 victims a day.

When the Vietnamese army liberated Phnom Penh in early 1979, there were only seven prisoners alive at S-21, all of whom had used their skills such as painting or photography to stay alive. Fourteen others had been tortured to death as Vietnamese forces were closing in on the city. Photographs of their gruesome deaths are on display in the rooms where their decomposing corpses were found. Their graves are nearby in the courtyard.

Altogether, a visit to Tuol Sleng is a profoundly depressing experience. The sheer ordinariness of the place makes it even more horrific: the suburban setting, the plain school buildings, the grassy playing area where children kick around balls, rusted beds, instruments of torture and wall after wall of disturbing portraits conjure up images of humanity at its worst. It demonstrates the darkest side of the human spirit that lurks within us all. Tuol Sleng is not for the squeamish.

Behind much of the displays at Tuol Sleng is the **Documentation Center of Cambodia** (DC-Cam; www.dccam.org). DC-Cam was established in 1995 through Yale University's Cambodian Genocide Program to research and document the crimes of the Khmer Rouge. It became an independent organisation in 1997 and researchers have spent years translating confessions and paperwork from Tuol Sleng, mapping mass graves and preserving evidence of Khmer Rouge crimes.

French-Cambodian director Rithy Panh's 1996 film *Bophana* tells the true story of Hout Bophana, a beautiful young woman, and Ly Sitha, a regional Khmer Rouge leader, who fall in love but are made to pay for this 'crime' with imprisonment and execution at S-21 prison. It is well worth investing an hour to watch this powerful documentary which is screened here at 10am and 3pm daily.

Killing Fields of Choeung Ek
 វាលពិឃាតជើងឯក

Between 1975 and 1978 about 17,000 men, women, children and infants who had been detained and tortured at S-21 were transported to the extermination camp of **Choeung Ek** (Map pp74-5; admission US$2; ☉ 8-11.30am & 2-5.30pm). They were often bludgeoned to death to avoid wasting precious bullets.

The remains of 8985 people, many of whom were bound and blindfolded, were exhumed in 1980 from mass graves in this one-time longan orchard; 43 of the 129 communal graves here have been left untouched. Fragments of human bone and bits of cloth are scattered around the disinterred pits. More than 8000 skulls, arranged by sex and age, are visible behind the clear glass panels of the Memorial Stupa, which

was erected in 1988. It is a peaceful place today, masking the horrors that unfolded here less than three decades ago.

The Killing Fields of Choeung Ek are 15km from central Phnom Penh and well signposted in English. You'll need to come by *moto* or bicycle, definitely don't walk! To get here, take Monireth Blvd southwest out of the city. The site is 13km from the bridge near Ph 271. Take the left fork when the road splits and pretty soon you will find yourself in rural surroundings. Look out for an archway on the left and it's another kilometre or so down this track. A memorial ceremony is held annually at Choeung Ek on 9 May.

Wat Phnom
វត្តភ្នំ

Set on top of a 27m-high tree-covered knoll, **Wat Phnom** (Map pp78-9; admission US$1) is on the only hill in town. According to legend, the first pagoda on this site was erected in 1373 to house four statues of Buddha deposited here by the waters of the Mekong River and discovered by a woman named Penh. The main entrance to Wat Phnom is via the grand eastern staircase, which is guarded by lions and *naga* (mythical serpent) balustrades.

Today, many people come here to pray for good luck and success in school exams or business affairs. When a petitioner's wish is granted, he or she returns to make the offering promised – such as a garland of jasmine flowers or a bunch of bananas, of which the spirits are said to be especially fond – when the request was made.

The *vihara* (temple sanctuary) was rebuilt in 1434, 1806, 1894 and 1926. West of the *vihara* is a huge stupa containing the ashes of King Ponhea Yat (r 1405–67). In a pavilion on the southern side of the passage between the *vihara* and the stupa is a statue of a smiling and rather plump Madame Penh.

A bit to the north of and below the *vihara* is an eclectic shrine dedicated to the genie Preah Chau, who is especially revered by the Vietnamese. On either side of the entrance to the chamber containing a statue of Preah Chau are guardian spirits bearing iron bats. On the tiled table in front of the two guardian spirits are drawings of Confucius, as well as two Chinese-style figures of the sages Thang Cheng (on the right) and Thang Thay (on the left). To the left of the central altar is an eight-armed statue of Vishnu.

Down the hill from the shrine is a royal stupa sprouting full-sized trees from its roof. For now, the roots are holding the bricks together in their net-like grip, but when the trees die the tower will slowly crumble. If you can't make it out to Angkor (p134), this stupa will give you a pretty good idea of what the jungle can do (and is doing) to Cambodia's monuments.

Wat Phnom can be a bit of a circus. Beggars, street urchins, women selling drinks and children selling birds in cages (you pay to set the bird free – locals claim the birds are trained to return to their cage afterwards) pester everyone who turns up to climb the 27m to the summit. Fortunately it's all high-spirited stuff, and it's difficult to be annoyed by the vendors, who, after all, are only trying to eke out a living. You can also have a short elephant ride around the base of the hill, perfect for those elephant-trekking photos, but without the accompanying sore butt.

It is hardly the most stunning location you are likely to visit in Cambodia, but as a symbol of Phnom Penh, it is a popular spot.

Wat Ounalom
វត្តឧណ្ណាលោម

This **wat** (Map pp78-9; Samdech Sothe aros Blvd; admission free; ☾ 6am-6pm) is the headquarters of the Cambodian Buddhist patriarchate. It was founded in 1443 and comprises 44 structures. It received a battering during the Pol Pot era, but today the wat is coming back to life. The head of the country's Buddhist brotherhood lives here, along with an increasing number of monks.

On the 2nd floor of the main building, to the left of the dais, is a statue of Samdech Huot Tat, fourth patriarch of Cambodian Buddhism, who was killed by Pol Pot. The statue, made in 1971 when the patriarch was 80, was thrown in the Mekong by the Khmer Rouge to show that Buddhism was no longer the driving force in Cambodia. It was retrieved after 1979. To the right of the dais is a statue of a former patriarch of the Thummayuth sect, to which the royal family belongs.

On the 3rd floor of the building is a marble Buddha of Burmese origin that was broken into pieces by the Khmer Rouge and later reassembled. On the front right corner of the dais on this floor are the cement remains of a Buddha stripped of its silver covering by the Khmer Rouge. In front of the dais, to either side, are two glass cases containing flags – each 20m long – used during Buddhist celebrations. The walls are decorated with scenes from the life of Buddha; they were painted when the building was constructed in 1952.

Behind the main building is a stupa containing an eyebrow hair of Buddha. There is an inscription in Pali (an ancient Indian language) over the entrance.

Wat Moha Montrei
វត្តមហាមន្ត្រី

Situated close to the Olympic Stadium, **Wat Moha Montrei** (Map pp74-5; Sihanouk Blvd; admission free; ☾ 6am-6pm) was named in honour of one of King Monivong's ministers, Chakrue Ponn, who initiated the founding of the pagoda (*moha montrei* means 'the great minister'). The cement *vihara*, topped with a 35m-high tower, was completed in 1970. Between 1975 and 1979, it was used by the Khmer Rouge to store rice and corn.

Check out the assorted Cambodian touches incorporated into the wall murals of the *vihara*, which tell the story of Buddha. The angels accompanying Buddha to heaven are dressed as classical Khmer dancers and the assembled officials wear the white military uniforms of the Sihanouk period. Along the wall to the left of the dais is a painted wooden lion from which religious lessons are preached four times a month. The golden wooden throne nearby is used for the same purpose. All the statues of Buddha here were made after 1979.

Independence Monument
វិមានឯករាជ

The **Independence Monument** (Map pp78-9; cnr Norodom & Sihanouk Blvds) is modelled on the central tower of Angkor Wat and was built in 1958 to commemorate the country's independence from France in 1953. It also serves as a memorial to Cambodia's war dead (at least those that the current government chooses to remember) and is sometimes referred to as the Victory Monument. Wreaths are laid here on national holidays. Nearby, beside Samdech Sothearos Blvd, is the optimistically named **Cambodia-Vietnam Friendship Monument**, built to a Vietnamese (and very communist) design in 1979.

Other Sights

The real name of the 700m Japanese Friendship Bridge, which spans the Tonlé Sap river, is the **Chruoy Changvar Bridge** (Map pp74–5). It was blown up during fighting in 1975. Long a symbol of the devastation visited upon Cambodia, it was repaired in 1993 with US$23.2 million of Japanese funding. Those who have seen the film *The Killing Fields* may be interested to note that it was near here on the afternoon of 17 April 1975 – the day Phnom Penh fell – that Khmer Rouge fighters imprisoned and threatened to kill *New York Times* correspondent Sydney Schanberg and four companions.

West of the Chruoy Changvar Bridge is the **Royal University of Fine Arts** (Map pp74–5; Ph 70; 7am-5pm). This is an active school devoted to training students in the arts of music and dance, and is not a tourist attraction. It is possible, however, to drop in early in the morning and watch children rehearsing classical Khmer dance in a pavilion at the rear of the school. Request permission from the teachers to watch the lessons or to take photographs. There is also a circus school here where children learn acrobatics and trapeze, but the thinness of the crash mats makes it painful to observe.

The **French embassy** (p276) on the northern end of Monivong Blvd was for many years used as an orphanage and its apparently larcenous residents were blamed by local people for every theft in the neighbourhood. The embassy has long been back and a high wall surrounds the massive complex. The French have returned to Cambodia in a big way, promoting French language and culture in their former colony. When Phnom Penh fell in 1975, about 800 foreigners and 600 Cambodians took refuge in the embassy. Within 48 hours, the Khmer Rouge informed the French vice-consul that the new government did not recognise diplomatic privileges and that if all the Cambodians in the compound were not handed over, the lives of the foreigners

inside would also be forfeited. Cambodian women married to foreigners could stay; Cambodian men married to foreign women could not. Foreigners wept as servants, colleagues, friends, lovers and husbands were escorted out of the embassy gates. At the end of the month the foreigners were expelled from Cambodia by truck. Many of the Cambodians were never seen again.

There is a cluster of **private language schools** (Map pp78–9) teaching English and French on Ph 184 between Norodom Blvd and the rear of the Royal Palace compound. Between 5pm and 7pm the area is filled with students who see learning English as the key to making it in contemporary Cambodia. This is a good place to meet young locals.

Known collectively as the National Sports Complex, the **Olympic Stadium** (Map pp74–5; near cnr Sihanouk & Monireth Blvds) is a striking example of 1960s Khmer architecture and includes a sports arena and facilities for boxing, gymnastics, volleyball and other sports. It has been closed for renovation for several years, but is due to reopen during the lifetime of this book.

In order to replace the countless Buddhas and ritual objects smashed by the Khmer Rouge, a whole neighbourhood of private workshops making cement Buddhas, *naga* and small stupas has grown up on the grounds of Wat Prayuvong. While the graceless cement figures painted in gaudy colours are hardly works of art, they are an effort by the Cambodian people to restore Buddhism to a place of honour in their reconstituted society. The **Prayuvong Buddha factories** (Map pp78-9; btwn Ph 308 & Ph 310) are about 300m south of the Independence Monument.

The **National Library** (Bibliothèque Nationale; Map pp78-9; Ph 92; 8-11am & 2-5pm Tue-Sun) is in a graceful old building constructed in 1924, near Wat Phnom. During its rule, the Khmer Rouge turned the building into a stable and destroyed most of the books. Many were thrown out into the streets, where they were picked up by people, some of whom donated them back to the library after 1979, while others used them as food wrapping.

ACTIVITIES
Boat Cruises

Boat trips on the Tonlé Sap or Mekong rivers are popular with some visitors. Local tourist boats are available for hire on the

---

SHOOTING RANGES IN THE SIGHTS

Anything goes in Cambodia, or so some Westerners seemed to believe during much of the 1990s. Be it sex, drugs or rock 'n' roll, Cambodia's lack of law enforcement and culture of impunity allowed visitors to do pretty much anything they wanted. The Cambodian military weren't blind to the market opportunities this presented, and with a hefty surplus of weapons from 25 years of civil war, they began to offer their own ammunition reduction scheme involving gung-ho foreigners wanting to do the Rambo thing.

A number of military bases near Phnom Penh were turned into shooting ranges and rapidly became popular places for tourists wanting to try their luck with an AK-47, an M-60 or a B-40 grenade launcher. It wasn't everyone's cup of tea, but it didn't seem that unusual in a poverty-wracked nation – visitors to Vietnam's Cu Chi Tunnels enjoy similar 'opportunities' even today. In a country where public sector incomes are US$20 a month, it shouldn't come as a shock that soldiers are learning to be creative. Travellers on a low budget find it hard to last two days in Cambodia on US$20 – and most don't have a family of five to feed!

The military ranges were an anomaly – loved and loathed in equal measure by visitors to Phnom Penh. By the dawn of the millennium, the government decided enough was enough and that shooting ranges no longer enhanced Cambodia's image as a cultural destination. The ranges were closed and forced underground. However, with the ranges going underground, there was nothing to stop sick Westerners and poverty-stricken soldiers from forming an unholy alliance to shoot live animals. Needless to say, anyone who thinks shooting a cow or chicken is fun is one sick puppy and should not be perverting Cambodia's improving image. Cambodians certainly aren't impressed by this kind of behaviour.

---

riverfront in Phnom Penh and can usually be arranged on the spot for between US$10 and US$20 an hour, depending on negotiations and numbers.

Le Deauville II (Map pp78-9; ☎ 723474) is a sophisticated boat offering a daily cruise with lunch at US$25 per person for 15 people, and a sunset cruise with aperitif at US$12 per person for 10 people.

Mekong Queen (Map pp78-9; ☎ 990382) is a huge converted cargo boat decked out in fairy lights. It offers two-hour afternoon (US$8, 3.30pm) and evening (US$10, 6.30pm) cruises, including a sandwich and tea or coffee. It departs from the tourist boat dock.

Bowling

There is now only one bowling alley in town, the **Superbowl** (Map pp74-5; Mao Tse Toung Blvd; per hr US$9) at Parkway Square. Hourly rates are per lane (any number of bowlers), and shoe hire is US$1 per pair.

Go-carting

There are a couple of go-cart tracks in the Phnom Penh area. The track at Tompuon Go Carts, about 10km across the Monivong Bridge, is pretty small and the carts have seen better days. Much more professional is **Kambol F1 Go-carts** (☎ 210501; per 10min US$7),

about 12km beyond the airport, and 2km off the road to Sihanoukville. It organises races on Sundays, so if you fancy yourself as a new Niki Lauda, turn up then. Prices include helmets and racing suits.

Golf

A round of golf is outrageously expensive by Cambodian standards. Contact **Royal Golf Club** (☎ 366689; NH4; per round Mon-Fri US$35) on the road to Sihanoukville, or **Cambodia Golf & Country Club** (☎ 363666; NH4; per round US$43), if you can't survive without a swing. Shoes and clubs cost US$5 and US$10 respectively at both places.

Gymnasiums

There are plenty of backstreet local gyms in Phnom Penh that charge less than US$1 per hour and have very basic weights. For something more sophisticated, try the **Clark Hatch Gym** (Map pp74-5; Intercontinental Hotel, cnr Mao Tse Toung & Monireth Blvds; per day US$14).

Massage

There are plenty of massage parlours in Phnom Penh, but most are little more than brothels. There are more traditional massage services at most upmarket hotels, but best of all is the **Seeing Hands Massage** (Map pp78-9; per hr

US$4), opposite Wat Phnom, intended to raise funds to empower disabled Cambodians in the capital. The blind masseurs here have been trained for many years and can sort out those niggling aches and pains.

Running
A good opportunity to meet local expatriates is via the Hash House Harriers, usually referred to simply as 'the Hash'. A weekly run/walk takes place every Sunday. Participants meet in front of Phnom Penh train station at 2.45pm. The entry fee of US$5 includes refreshments (mainly a lot of beer) at the end.

Swimming
The Olympic Stadium was closed for renovation in 2000. The stadium itself has since reopened, but the Olympic-size pool still hasn't.

The cheapest swim is at the Royal Palace Hotel (p92; US$3), but the pool is fairly small. Hotel Cambodiana (p93) charges US$6 during the week, US$8 at the weekend. Both the Juliana Hotel (p93; US$8) and the Intercontinental Hotel (p93; US$10) have larger pools.

Himawari (Map pp74-5; ☎ 426806; 313 Sisowath Quay) charges US$10 and this includes access to the gym. The best-value pools are **Parkway Health Club** (Map pp74-5; ☎ 982928; 113 Mao Tse Toung; US$6), which has a pool (indoor, unfortunately), steam bath, sauna and gym, and **Northbridge Club** (☎ 886058; off NH4; US$5), out towards the airport.

WALKING TOUR
What better place to kick off a walking tour of the city (Map p88) than the landmark temple of **Wat Phnom** (1; p83), perched atop the only hill in town. Pray for luck like the locals, or at least pray that you won't fall into one of Phnom Penh's many open drains on this walking tour. Take a look southwest at the fortress that is the under-construction new **US embassy (2)** and wonder to yourself how it is that the security-conscious State Department managed to find the only site in Phnom Penh overshadowed by a hill?

Head west along Ph 92 and pause at the **National Library** (3; p85). Forget about borrowing books, but this is a classic example of French colonial-era architecture. Just along the road is the striking façade of **Hotel**

Le Royal (4; p93), now owned by the Raffles group. Bookmark it for a happy-hour cocktail some time between 4pm and 8pm. Turn left on to Monivong Blvd, the capital's main commercial thoroughfare. Fast approaching on the right is Phnom Penh's **train station (5)**, a grand old building, home to not-so-grand old trains.

Swing southeast towards the dominant dome of **Psar Thmei** (6; p104). This is a market to remember, packed to the gunnels with everything and anything you can imagine and some things you can't, like deep-fried insects and peeled frogs. Browse a while and take in the natural air-conditioning of the immense centre. Don't get liberal with your wallet, however, as sellers here are known to overcharge. That said, it's a great place for cheap local bites.

Continue south on Ph 63 and take a peek at the modern equivalent of the Central Market, aka **Sorya Shopping Centre (7)**. It's pretty sterile after the market, but they have escalator trainers in case you get confused about what to do on a moving staircase!

Snake east on Ph 154 and then south on to Norodom Blvd, before turning left on to Ph 178, a lively strip to browse the many **art shops** (8; p103). Turn right onto Ph 19 before swinging west again, along Ph 240, one of the more fashionable stretches in the capital. Take your pick from one of the many cafés, restaurants or bars along here to recharge the batteries for the second half of the walk.

Head southwards on to Norodom Blvd again and make for the **Independence Monument** (9; p84), which was modelled on the central tower of Angkor Wat and built to commemorate freedom from the French. From here make a loop east and then north towards the city's best known attractions, the striking **Royal Palace and Silver Pagoda complex** (10; p80) and the stunning **National Museum** (11; p81).

Take an hour or more to experience the treasures of the palace and pagoda complex before delving into the world's finest collection of Khmer sculpture from the Angkor period. After an hour or two exploring this magnificent old building, wander east towards the riverfront where the adventure ends. Stroll riverside along Tonlé Sap or duck into a bar or restaurant for a well-earned drink.

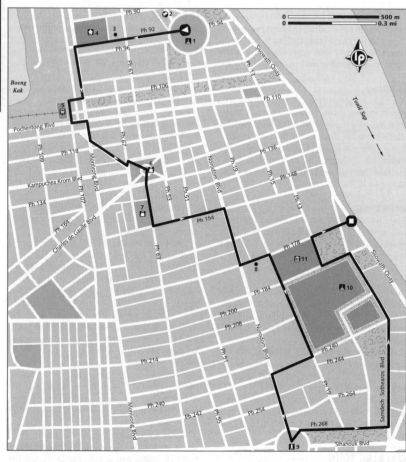

PHNOM PENH FOR CHILDREN

With its chaotic traffic, lack of public parks and open sewers, Phnom Penh is sadly not the most children-friendly city in Asia. Most kiddies will have a lot more fun in Siem Reap (p113), around the temples of Angkor (p134) and down on the beach in Sihanoukville (p184). However, there are a few places that help to pass the time in Phnom Penh.

Just south of Hotel Cambodiana, the **Cambo Fun Park** (Map pp74-5; Hun Sen Park; 5-10pm) is hardly Disneyland, but is the only amusement park in Phnom Penh. By 7pm it is usually packed with school children queuing impatiently to risk their lives on what appear to be some very rickety rides –

the management boasts that the whole thing was built in just 20 days. Stick around to see which rides look the safest or just brave the bumper cars.

Many of the leading hotels have swimming pools (p87) that are open to the public for a fee and the go-cart tracks (p86) might prove popular. **Phnom Penh Water Park** (881008; Russian Blvd; admission US$5; 8am-6pm) with its slides and wave pool is a definite hit with the young-uns and a world away from bustling downtown Phnom Penh.

The most interesting attractions are beyond the city limits and would make good day trips to give the children a break from the chaos of the city. **Phnom Tamao Wildlife Sanctuary** (p110) is a rescue centre for Cambodia's incredible wildlife and the huge enclosures here include tigers, elephants and bears. Further afield is **Kirirom National Park** (p111), with gentle waterfalls and cooler temperatures, plus the kitsch **Kirirom Hillside Resort** (p112), which may not work for adults but is sure popular with children.

TOURS

Anyone arriving in Phnom Penh on an organised trip will have a city tour included. Travelling independently, Phnom Penh is a city best enjoyed at your own pace, without the timetable of a tour. If you really want to have an organised city tour, drop into one of the popular guesthouses around town or contact one of the recommended travel agencies (p77).

FESTIVALS & EVENTS

Chinese New Year (Late January or early February) Is also big in Phnom Penh and dragon dances take place all over the city.

Chaul Chnam (Khmer New Year; mid-April) The capital grinds to a halt for a massive celebration, with a lot of water and talc being thrown about. Big crowds congregate at Wat Phnom, but females should watch out for the overeager attention of young gangs of males.

Chat Preah Nengkal (Early May) The Royal Ploughing Ceremony takes place in front of the National Museum in Phnom Penh and the royal oxen are said to have a nose for whether it will be a good harvest or a bad one.

Bon Om Tuk (Water Festival; late October or November). Boat races are held on the Tonlé Sap river and up to two million people flood the capital for fun and frolics. Very hectic on the riverfront, so book ahead for accommodation.

SLEEPING

The hotel and guesthouse scene in Phnom Penh has come a long way since the bad old days of a handful of decrepit, government-owned places falling apart around their guests. Today there is an excellent range of guesthouses, hotels and luxury palaces to suit all wallets passing through Cambodia's capital.

Affordable guesthouses are springing up all over the city. Some places charge as little as US$2 a room; US$5 will guarantee a small room with a fan. The best hotel deals in Phnom Penh fall in the midrange category and for around US$20 it is possible to get hooked up with air-con, satellite TV and a smart bathroom. Top-end travellers will find that Phnom Penh's best hotels are expensive by regional standards; there is often better value for money at the more comfortable midrange hotels.

Budget

There is no Khao San Rd as in Bangkok, but for many it is good to get away from the ghettoes. There are, however, two popular backpacker strips, one along the eastern shore of Boeng Kak and another around the long-running Capitol Guesthouse along Ph 182 and Ph 111, just west of Monivong Blvd. The area around Boeng Kak has improved considerably, but the rooms in these guesthouses are pretty basic compared with elsewhere in the city. For those who have seen enough of their fellow travellers to last a lifetime, there are several smaller guesthouses spread across the city.

BOENG KAK AREA

Most of the lakeside guesthouses are built on wooden platforms over Boeng Kak, a seriously polluted body of water that no-one should swim in, however many beers they have drunk. The guesthouses used to be rickety shacks with dodgy planking, but are now more solidly built, with great communal areas to while away the day. For some it's like experiencing Ko Pha Ngan in the city, only Boeng Kak isn't quite the Gulf of Thailand.

There are persistent but unfounded rumours that this whole area will be bulldozed in the next few years as part of the zealous beautification drive around the city, so check it out while you can. Sunsets over the lake are not to be missed whether you are staying here or not.

Number 9 Guesthouse (Map pp78-9; ☎ 012 766225; 9 Ph 93; r US$3-8; 🛰) This, the original lakeside pad, now offers an incredible 50 rooms. Rooms over the lake remain simple and a magnet for mosquitoes, but the newer rooms on dry land include some air-con options. The restaurant and chill-out area are draped in verdant plants and the management offers lockers for valuables.

Lakeside Guesthouse (Map pp78-9; ☎ 012 552901; 10 Ph 93; r US$2-7) Another long-running favourite; the rooms with share bathroom are just US$2, while US$5-plus brings a TV. The drinking and dining area (smoking and joking for others) stretches out into the lake and is a mellow place to hang out. There are also lockers here.

Same Same But Different (Map pp78-9; ☎ 012 263332; 11 Ph 93; s/d/tr without bathroom US$2/3/4) The memorable name aside, this pad is same same but the same. The TV has been banished to a separate room, making the restaurant area more sociable.

Floating Island (Map pp78-9; ☎ 990887; 11 Ph 93; r US$3-9; ☒) Upstairs rooms cost US$1 more here – perhaps you are paying for the breeze – rooms with air-con start from US$8. This place definitely has the breeziest terrace in town, a great double-decker drinking den for a serious view of the sunset.

Simon's II Guesthouse (Map pp78-9; ☎ 012 608892; Ph 93; r US$8; ☒) This big wedding cake-style villa is home to the smartest rooms in this part of town, including satellite TV and a bathroom.

Grand View Guesthouse (Map pp78-9; ☎ 430766; Ph 93; r US$3-8; ☒) This combines a touch of Thailand with a veneer of Vietnam; boxy rooms like Bangkok set in a tall, skinny structure like Ho Chi Minh City. Rooms are clean, the stairs endless, but the views of the lake are unrivalled.

Other places worth a look among the many up here include:

Lazy Fish Guesthouse (Map pp78-9; ☎ 012 703368; 16 Ph 93; r US$3-5) A fun little place promising free pool and a free sunset.

Smile Guesthouse (Map pp78-9; ☎ 012 831329; r US$2-5) Tucked down a small alley, English and French is spoken here.

PSAR O RUSSEI AREA

The other budget centre starts near Psar O Russei and heads south along a network of back streets.

Capitol Guesthouse (Map pp78-9; ☎ 724104; capitol@online.com.kh; 14 Ph 182; r US$3-10; ☒) The longest-running budget guesthouse in town offers rooms of every shape and size, some decidedly better than others. It has spilled out from its original home into several nearby annexes, the best being Capitol 3. The cheap-

---

THE AUTHOR'S CHOICE

Spring Guesthouse (Map pp78-9; ☎ 222155; 34 Ph 111; r US$6-9; ☒) This slick looking maroon building is more like a hotel than a guesthouse, and the super new rooms are tempting value. Add US$2 for the privilege of hot water.

---

est deals involve a share bathroom. The restaurant downstairs is a popular budget café, but is more like a bus station these days with all the coaches operated by Capitol Tour coming and going.

Narin Guesthouse (Map pp78-9; ☎ 982554; touch narin@hotmail.com; 50 Ph 125; r US$3-7) Another of the old favourites in town, this is a family-run place with hot showers throughout. Rooms are well looked after and there is a lively terrace for taking some time out. Hotel-like **Narin 2 Guesthouse** (Map pp78-9; ☎ 986131; 20 Ph 111; r US$3-12; ☒ 🖳) is just a few blocks away and has an overwhelming selection of rooms, the price rising with extras like TV and hot water. There are also some top-value rooms for four or more from just US$7.

Tat Guesthouse (Map pp78-9; ☎ 986620; 52 Ph 125; r US$3-5) Right next door to the original Narin Guesthouse, this is a friendly little place to stay with cheap and cheerful rooms. The rooftop restaurant draws a big breeze throughout the day.

Sunday Guesthouse (Map pp78-9; ☎ 211623; 97 Ph 141; r US$4-15; ☒) Rooms here run from basic fan jobs at just US$4 to full blown hotel-style rooms with TV, hot water and fridge. The friendly staff speak good English and can help with travel arrangements.

The King Guesthouse (Map pp78-9; ☎ 220512; 74 Ph 141; r US$3-25) Elvis lives on in Phnom Penh, in name at least! The range of rooms is as wide as the king's girth in the later years of his life, and there is a huge restaurant and a travel centre downstairs. Check out the handouts, with a handy ticklist of what all the rooms include.

Other possibilities in this area include:

Seng Sokhom Guesthouse (Map pp78-9; ☎ 012 898726; sengsokhom@hotmail.com; 22 Ph 111; s/d US$2/3) Popular with long-termers in Phnom Penh for its bargain-basement rooms – not literally in the basement!

Lucky Guesthouse (Map pp78-9; ☎ 218910; 99 Ph 214; r US$6-10; ☒) This guesthouse is expanding into two buildings. Staff here have a good sense of humour, offering 'warm' water rather than hot water.

AROUND THE CITY

Other guesthouses are spread evenly across the city.

Last Home (Map pp78-9; ☎ 724917; 47 Ph 108; r US$2-8; ☒) Another of the old guard of guesthouses that has been around a decade or more; the basic rooms here remain good value. It boasts a good location near Wat

Phnom and the riverfront, plus there's a restaurant and book exchange downstairs.

Boddhi Tree (Map pp74-5; www.boddhitree.com; 50 Ph 113; r US$8-20; 🔀) The location is a touch spooky (opposite Tuol Sleng Museum) but for those who don't get nightmares, this guesthouse has bags of charm. Set in a wooden villa with tastefully decorated rooms, air-con has recently been added to the top-end rooms, plus there is a cracking restaurant in the verdant garden.

Okay Guesthouse (Map pp74-5; 5 Ph 258; r US$2-12; 🔀) Located down a side street near Hotel Cambodiana, this little hideaway has a good location just a stroll away from the riverfront action. Rooms start with share bathroom and top whack brings air-con, TV and hot water. It also has a café downstairs with a teach-yourself board of Khmer phrases and a lively little bar.

Others worth thinking about:

Dara Reang Sey Hotel (Map pp78-9; ☎ 428181; darareangsey@camnet.com.kh; 45 Ph 13; r US$6-16; 🔀) There are hotel-esque rooms here with all the trimmings, plus the restaurant has Khmer prices.

Royal Guesthouse (Map pp78-9; ☎ 218026; 91 Ph 154; r US$5-12; 🔀) Conveniently located between Norodom Blvd and the riverfront, the Royal has a good selection of air-con rooms.

Midrange

For those looking to spend between US$15 and US$50 for a room, there are some excellent deals to be had around town. The average price for a double with air-con, bathroom, satellite TV and laundry service is US$15 to US$20. Some of the fancier midrange places are not that far behind the top-range hotels in comfort, but are pleasingly off the pace in price, at just US$30 to US$50.

As with the budget guesthouses, there is no single midrange hotel area. Probably the best choice, and definitely the best location, is along the riverfront on Sisowath Quay. The area to the southwest of the Independence Monument also has quite a concentration of midrange deals. The stretch of Monivong Blvd between Russian and Sihanouk Blvds is the old hotel district, but this is hardly the most alluring area of town.

RIVERFRONT AREA

California 2 Guesthouse (Map pp78-9; ☎ 982182; www.cafecaliforniaphnompenh.com; 317 Sisowath Quay;

---

r US$15-20; 🔀) Right in the middle of the riverfront action, this little guesthouse remains great value. All rooms include little luxuries like hot water and satellite TV, but it is worth paying more for a room with a view. Breakfast is included at the popular downstairs restaurant and bar.

Hotel Indochine (Map pp78-9; ☎ 724239; indochine htl@camnet.com.kh; 251 Sisowath Quay; r US$10-20; 🔀) The location is great here, but it is worth forking out for the fancier rooms looking over the river, as the cheapies are showing their age. All rooms include TV, fridge and hot water. For more comfort but a smaller view, try their newer place around the corner, **Hotel Indochine 2** (☎ 211525; 28 Ph 130).

Sunshine Hotel (Map pp78-9; ☎ 725684; 253 Sisowath Quay; r US$12-20; 🔀) Next door to the original Hotel Indochine, the Sunshine has lowered its rates, making it serious value for this kind of location. Rooms include TV, fridge and hot water, and the river-view rooms are worth the extra investment.

Bougainvillier Hotel (Map pp78-9; ☎ 220528; www .bougainvillierhotel.com; 277 Sisowath Quay; r US$44-94; 🔀) When it comes to decorative flair, this is one of the best midrange hotels in town. Rooms are finished with a stylish blend of Chinese and Khmer furnishings, including opulent silk drapes, and functional touches like a safety deposit box. The US$67 suites with a large lounge are pretty impressive.

River Star Hotel (Map pp78-9; ☎ 991450; www.river starhotel.com; 185 Sisowath Quay; r US$18-28; 🔀) It may not be the most beautiful hotel in the city from the outside, but once inside things brighten up considerably. Rooms are fully decked out, some offer a river view and there is a lift.

Star Royal Hotel (Map pp78-9; ☎ 219436; www.star royalhotel.com; Sisowath Quay; r US$35-60; ✖ 및) Another hotel where judgements are best reserved until you cross the threshold. Rooms here are almost three-star standard and it is definitely worth requesting a river-view room on the upper floors. Rates include breakfast at the breezy rooftop restaurant.

Foreign Correspondents' Club (Map pp78-9; ☎ 210142; www.fcccambodia.com; 363 Sisowath Quay; r US$45-65; ✖ 및) There are just four elegant rooms at this landmark location. Two have breezy balconies overlooking Tonlé Sap and all include a minibar clearly aimed at the journalists who pass through town – the spirits come in 1L bottles rather than miniatures. Definitely book ahead. Prices include breakfast. The restaurant (p98) of the same name is popular with the expat crowd.

Riverside Hotel (Map pp78-9; ☎ 723318; riverside -hotel@camnet.com.kh; cnr Sisowath Quay & Ph 94; r US$25-35) For three-star standards at two-star prices, this hotel is a real contender. It has a fine location overlooking the Tonlé Sap to the front and Wat Phnom at the back. Rooms include minibar, safety box and breakfast. The only drawback is the hotel is always busy and noisy thanks to the number of weddings that take place in the downstairs restaurant.

Bright Lotus Guesthouse (Map pp78-9; ☎ 990446; 22 Ph 178; r US$14-18; ✖) Occupying a strategic corner location with a top view of the National Museum, Royal Palace, and, if you strain your neck a bit, the riverfront, this guesthouse is one place where it is worth climbing the stairs. All rooms have the same amenities, but US$18 is money well spent for a little balcony.

Other recommendations:

Lyon D'Or (Map pp78-9; ☎ 217710; lyondor@online.com .kh; 12 Ph 110; r US$5-20; ✖) There is a variety of rooms here and a very well-regarded restaurant downstairs (p98).

Tiger Feet (Map pp78-9; ☎ 012 885188; tigerfeetgues thouse@yahoo.com; 9 Ph 118; r US$10; ✖) The elegant rooms here are a bargain right now, but with just three, once word gets out, surely the price will rise. Book ahead.

Tonlé Hotel (Map pp78-9; ☎ 211296; tonle@online. com.kh; 277 Sisowath Quay; r US$35-55; ✖) A smart new hotel with extensive wooden trim. Pay more for the huge rooms at the front.

CENTRAL PHNOM PENH

Golden Gate Hotel (Map pp78-9; ☎ 721161; www.golden gatehotels.com; 6 Ph 278; r US$15-40; ✖ 및) Long popular with the NGO crowd, this hotel is good value for money. Rooms include TV, minibar, bathroom and a free laundry service; the deluxe rooms include breakfast. It's a good idea to book ahead.

Golden Sun Hotel (Map pp78-9; ☎ 721317; golden sun@online.com.kh; 6B Ph 278; r US$13-15; ✖) A few doors down from the Golden Gate, this friendly little hotel has 20 rooms and the rates include free laundry. Some rooms, particularly minisuite 14, are better than others.

Goldiana Hotel (Map pp78-9; ☎ 218490; goldiana .ht@bigpond.com.kh; 10 Ph 282; r US$28-95; ✖ 및 ▣) This huge hotel offers a fair deal considering the facilities include a swimming pool and a fitness centre. Rooms come with all the trimmings, but deluxe rooms are bigger and brighter and include breakfast. The price includes a free transfer from the airport, saving you the US$7 taxi fare.

King Palace Hotel (Map pp78-9; ☎ 217796; 115 Ph 214; r US$15-25; ✖) A new hotel in the centre of town; the rooms here are smart and smartly priced. A lift whisks guests up to the higher floors where there are big views over the bustle of Phnom Penh. Downstairs is a popular restaurant and bar.

Diamond Hotel (Map pp78-9; ☎ 217328; diamond hotel@bigpond.com.kh; 172 Monivong Blvd; s/d US$35/45; ✖ 및) Prices here have remained pegged back due to the busy location. Rooms include wooden floors, comprehensive trimmings and in-room safes, breakfast is included as well.

Other places to consider:

Queen Hotel (Map pp78-9; ☎ 213001; 49 Ph 214; s/d US$25/30; ✖) Large, well-equipped rooms here make it popular with small tour groups.

Princess Hotel (Map pp78-9; ☎ 801809; princess@ camnet.com.kh; 302 Ph 228; r US$30-35) This is a comfortable business hotel, but it's on the noisy Monivong Blvd.

AROUND THE CITY

Bayon Hotel (Map pp74-5; ☎ 430158; bayon@online .com.kh; 2 Ph 75; s/d/ste US$25/35/45, plus 15% tax & service; ✖ 및) This French-run hotel offers tidy rooms that include a video player as well as access to a huge in-house library of films. Downstairs is a very sophisticated French restaurant that has an excellent reputation among the Francophone residents of Phnom Penh.

Royal Palace Hotel (Map pp74-5; ☎ 884823; royal palacehotel@online.com.kh; 93 Monireth Blvd; r/ste

US$35/60;) This hotel's location is un-inspiring, but that is more than adequately reflected in the price. Facilities include a swimming pool and the rooms are extensively furnished. Breakfast is included.

Top End

Walk-in rates at many of Phnom Penh's luxury hotels are high by regional standards. Consider booking through a local travel agent for a better deal, often as much as half the published rates.

Intercontinental Hotel (Map pp74–5; ☎ 424888; www.intercontinental.com; cnr Mao Tse Toung & Monireth Blvds; r US$118;) The city's first five-star hotel, the Intercontinental is Phnom Penh's tallest building, at only 15 storeys. It has a Clark Hatch fitness centre, a swimming pool, a business centre, conference facilities, live music in the lobby bar and the best pillows in Cambodia, but the location is not very central.

Hotel Cambodiana (Map pp74–5; ☎ 426288; www.hotelcambodiana.com; 313 Sisowath Quay; s/d US$102/114;) Weighing in with four stars, this huge hotel is still one of the best options in Phnom Penh, thanks to its fine location on the banks of the Mekong. Rooms on the renovated upper floors are worth the money, as the older rooms are showing their age. Built in 1967, the unfinished structure and its grounds were used as a military base by the Lon Nol government, and by 1975 thousands of refugees from the countryside sheltered under its concrete roof. It has restaurants, bars, a small swimming pool, tennis courts, a health centre, a business centre and shops.

Imperial Garden Villa (Map pp74–5; ☎ 219991; www.imperialgarden-hotel.com; 315 Sisowath Quay; s/d US$120/130;) Right next door to the Cambodiana and dwarfed by its neighbour, this is a three-star hotel with a selection of residential villas as well as standard rooms. Facilities include a pool and tennis courts, but there is no lift.

Amanjaya (Map pp78–9; ☎ 214747; www.amanjaya.com; 1 Ph 154; s/d US$108/120, ste from US$177;) With a stunning location right on the riverfront, this is Phnom Penh's answer to the boutique hotel. The rooms are spacious and smart, and the inspired décor includes hints of Chinese Khmer influence and lavish silk drapes. The corner suites offer commanding views over the river.

THE AUTHOR'S CHOICE

Hotel Le Royal (Map pp78–9; ☎ 981888; www.raffles.com; cnr Monivong Blvd & Ph 92; s/d US$145/155;) This classic colonial-era hotel reopened for business as a Raffles property in 1997 and is Phnom Penh's finest hotel, with a heritage to match its comfort and class. In fact it ranks as one of Asia's grand old palaces, in the illustrious company of the Oriental in Bangkok and the Strand in Yangon. The hotel has a swimming pool, a gym, a spa, a business centre, and bars and restaurants with lavish food and drink. Between 1970 and 1975 most journalists working in Phnom Penh stayed here, and part of the film *The Killing Fields* was set in the hotel (though filmed in Hua Hin, Thailand).

Downstairs is a popular restaurant and bar, K-West, which draws an expat crowd seeking a taste of home.

Sunway Hotel (Map pp78–9; ☎ 430333; www.sunway.com.kh; 1 Ph 92; s/d US$80/95;) In a prime site overlooking Wat Phnom, this hotel has acquired a new neighbour in the shape of the under-construction US embassy. Basically a business hotel, the rooms are slick and clean but not that inspired.

Juliana Hotel (Map pp74–5; ☎ 366070; www.julianacambodia.com; 16 Ph 152; s/tw US$60/70;) The location is easily missed, tucked away down a side street near the Olympic Stadium, but it is worth seeking out for creature comforts at an affordable price. Set in a lush garden with the largest swimming pool in town, facilities include a fitness centre, a sauna, a bar and restaurants.

EATING

Phnom Penh has a cracking selection of restaurants that showcase the best of Khmer cuisine, as well as offering a healthy hitlist of international food that includes Chinese, Vietnamese, Indian, Italian, Mexican, Thai and French. Visitors to Phnom Penh are quite literally spoilt for choice these days. Most local restaurants open around 6.30am and serve food until 9pm or so. International restaurants stay open later, until 11pm or so, but some close between breakfast and lunch or between lunch and dinner.

The best bet for budget dining in Phnom Penh is to head to one of the city's many markets. The dining areas may not be the most sophisticated in the world, but the food is tasty and cheap. The best markets for dining are Psar Thmei (p104), Psar Tuol Tom Pong (p104) and Psar O Russei (p104), which is pretty handy given that these are also the best bets for shopping.

If the markets are just too hot or too claustrophobic for your taste, then look out for the mobile street sellers carrying their wares on their shoulders or wheeling it around in small carts.

Local hole-in-the-wall restaurants are slightly more civilised but still very cheap. Many of the international restaurants around town, and there are plenty of them, are expensive by local standards, but compared with dining in the West, the prices are still absurdly reasonable.

Several of the guesthouses around town have popular restaurants and some tasty food, but with so much good grub available in Phnom Penh it seems a shame to get into the habit of chowing down at the nearest terrace.

Most of the big hotels have in-house restaurants with multinational menus, but prices tend to be high and tax and service is extra, adding up to a multinational-sized bill.

Khmer

Scattered around town are numerous Khmer restaurants that set up outdoor tables and chairs in the evenings. These places rarely have English signs and are as much about drinking beer as about eating, but they're lively places for an inexpensive meal and the food is usually very good. Good hunting grounds include Ph 184 (Map pp78–9) near the French Cultural Centre and Ph 108 (Map pp78–9) just to the east of Norodom Blvd.

Soup chhnang dei (cook-your-own soup) restaurants are very popular with Khmers and are great fun if you go in a group. Other diners will often help with protocol, as it is important to cook things in the right order

---

DINING FOR A CAUSE

There are several restaurants around town that are run by aid organisations to help fund their social programmes in Cambodia. These are worth seeking out, as the proceeds of a hearty meal go towards helping Cambodia's recovery and allow restaurant staff to gain valuable work experience.

Friends (Map pp78-9; ☎ 426748; 215 Ph 13; tapas US$1-2, specials US$3-5) With a prime location near the National Museum, this restaurant, run by NGO Mith Samlanh, has made a real name for itself thanks to a lively little menu of tapas light bites and innovative specials. Try the tangy fish with salsa *verde* or the succulent chicken curry. The shakes are exquisite, or for a shake with a twist, try the raspberry or mango daiquiris. And it's great to know that such good living doesn't come at a cost...in fact it comes with a benefit, giving former street children a helping hand into the hospitality industry. Many trainees at Friends have gone on to work in leading hotels and restaurants in town.

Le Café du Centre (Map pp78-9; Ph 184; mains US$2-4) Also run by Mith Samlanh and helping street kids, this place is in the hidden inner courtyard garden of the French Cultural Centre. The menu is limited but includes some healthy salads, pastas and specials.

Le Rit's (Map pp78-9; ☎ 213160; 14 Ph 310; breakfast from US$3, set menus US$5; ☽ breakfast & lunch Mon-Sat, dinner Wed-Sun) The three-course lunch and dinners here are a relaxing experience in the well-groomed garden. The food comes with a French flourish, while the set dinner is Thai-style. Le Rit's is run by NGO Nyemo and proceeds help disadvantaged women re-enter the workforce.

The Store (Map pp78-9; ☎ 216944; 131 Sisowath Blvd; mains US$1.50-3; ☽ 6am-10pm) Nyemo has also just opened this small café offering light bites and tempting drinks.

Café 151 (Map pp78-9; www.theglobalchild.com; 151 Sisowath Quay) Not far from the Store, this is a small spot offering coffee and shakes with 100% of profits going to help street children.

La Casa (Map pp74-5; Ph 257; mains US$3-5; ☽ Tue-Sun) Set in an old French villa, this place offers a limited menu of French and Khmer dishes, as well as some pastas. It's a long hike out of the city, just off Kampuchea Krom Blvd. Proceeds go to Krousar Thmey (New Family), an NGO helping impoverished and vulnerable children.

THE AUTHOR'S CHOICE

Khmer Borane Restaurant (Map pp78-9; 389 Sisowath Quay; mains US$1.50-3) When it comes to traditional Khmer cooking, this little riverfront restaurant near the Royal Palace has perhaps the best selection of old royal recipes in town. Try the fish in palm sugar, the pomelo salad or the *lok lak* (fried diced beef with a salt, pepper and lemon dip) and you will soon realise Khmer cuisine can rival its neighbours'.

---

so as not to overcook half the ingredients and eat the rest raw. These places also offer *phnom pleung* (hill of fire), which amounts to cook-your-own beef, shrimp, squid (or anything else that takes your fancy) over a personal barbecue.

Dararasmey Restaurant (Map pp78-9; 292 Ph 214; phnom pleung US$3, mains US$2-5) Just off the main Monivong drag, this is the most popular cook-it-yourself restaurant in Phnom Penh, heaving with Khmers every night, and a lively spot to pass an evening as an amateur chef.

Chaay Heng Restaurant (Map pp78-9; cnr Ph 125 & Sihanouk Blvd; mains 6000r) A long-running local restaurant, this place offers a good selection of classic Cambodian cuisine. Be prepared to be ambushed by 'beer girls' as soon as you sit down, with almost as many drink promoters as dishes on the menu.

Goldfish River Restaurant (Map pp78-9; Sisowath Quay; mains US$2-4) Perched on stilts over Tonlé Sap, opposite Ph 106, this is a good Cambodian restaurant for authentic flavours and a cooling breeze. Crab with black pepper is a delight, but there is something for everyone on the extensive menu. Save some space for the tasty banana flambées.

Sa Em Restaurant (Map pp78-9; 379 Sisowath Quay; mains US$1-3) More of a spit-and-sawdust place than some, this atmospheric little diner on the riverfront is great value for the location. Simple dishes like fried rice and noodles are cheap and filling, and large Angkor beers are just US$1.50.

Ponlok Restaurant (Map pp78-9; 212025; 319 Sisowath Quay; mains US$2-5) For a bird's-eye view of the riverfront, the 3rd floor of this large local restaurant is a winner. The English-language menu takes visitors on a guided tour of Khmer classics, but prices are slightly higher than most local restaurants.

Khmer Surin (Map pp78-9; 363050; 9 Ph 57; mains US$3-6) Onwards and upwards, this place has expanded beyond belief in the last few years thanks to its popular menu of Cambodian and Thai food. There are now three levels to choose from, but the middle floor is the most atmospheric with floor cushions, flowering plants and antique furnishings.

Amoc Café (Map pp78-9; 2 Ph 278; mains US$3-6) is under the same ownership as Khmer Surin, with a similar theme, and is named in honour of one of Cambodia's national dishes. It serves delicious *amoc* (fish coconut curry in a banana leaf), as well as a maze of Khmer and Thai favourites.

Sugar Palm (Map pp78-9; 220956; 19 Ph 240) One of the newer venues on fashionable Ph 240, this lovely little restaurant-bar offers authentic Khmer flavours in refined surroundings. Warm up downstairs with a drink before heading up to the balcony for a memorable meal.

Chinese

There are numerous Chinese restaurants around Phnom Penh, many offering an authentic taste of the Middle Kingdom. There are several real-deal Chinese restaurants along Ph 136, opposite the Phnom Penh Public Transport bus station, with names like Peking and Shanghai. These are the perfect place for a meal before or after a long bus ride.

Chong Qing Restaurant (Map pp74-5; 727 Monivong Blvd; mains US$2-5) This restaurant is popular with Chinese residents in Phnom Penh – always a good sign – and specialises in Sichuan soup cooked at your table. For the uninitiated, the dining table has built-in pots shaped like Yin and Yang; one side is fiery chilli soup, the other a light broth, and ingredients can be dunked in either side.

THE AUTHOR'S CHOICE

Wah Kee Restaurant (Map pp78-9; 296 Monivong Blvd; mains US$1-5; 6pm-6am) If you get struck with the munchies after midnight, this all-night diner is the place to be. Cheap noodle dishes start at just US$1, sizzling spicy beef hot plates are delicious and there is plenty of fresh seafood waiting to be fished out of the tanks.

OVER THE BRIDGE

The reconstruction of the Chruoy Changvar (Japanese Friendship) Bridge spanning the Tonlé Sap river created a restaurant boom on the river's east bank. There are dozens of restaurants lining the highway – from the decidedly downmarket to the obviously over-the-top – but most are interesting places for a very Cambodian night out. These are restaurants frequented by well-to-do Khmers, and on the weekend are packed with literally thousands of people on a big night out. Most charge about US$2 to US$4 a dish (with around 300 dishes to choose from) and about US$2 for a big bottle of beer. Heading north, the restaurants start to appear about 1km from the bridge on the east bank. They range from small, family-run places to enormous fairy-light festooned complexes with fountains and neon signs. Many of the larger places include a resident band and the amps are often cranked up pretty high – remember to sit a fair distance from the stage.

Places come in and out of favour, but following are some of the most consistently popular. All are signposted from the main road. A *moto* should cost about US$1 each way from the city centre.

Heng Lay Restaurant (☎ 430888) One of the biggest places, it hosts leading comedians every night and is popular with Cambodians. It's very slapstick, but the food is well-regarded, if relatively expensive.

Hang Neak Restaurant (☎ 369878) Another huge place, this restaurant has a large wall mount of Angkor Wat, and is popular with Chinese gamblers who can't be bothered visiting the real thing. It has good food and enough seating to get away from the loud music.

Rum Chang Restaurant Still a hotspot for Khmer food, there is no band here and the location overlooking the Mekong is very pleasant.

Boeng Bopha Restaurant The food here is similar to elsewhere, but this is a popular place for a younger crowd out drinking.

Ta Oeu Restaurant This simple place is popular for its value-for-money food, which has a reputation as being authentic and tasty.

Hua Nam Restaurant (Map pp74–5; ☎ 364005; 753 Monivong Blvd; mains US$5 & up, up, up) This place is a heavyweight Chinese dining experience, including delicacies such as goose webs and abalone. But meals here are very expensive by local standards.

Thai

Chiang Mai Riverside (Map pp78–9; 227 Sisowath Quay; mains US$2–5) The name gives away the prime riverfront location of this popular Thai restaurant, which serves the true taste of Thailand. On offer are tasty fish cakes and a good range of curries.

Baan Thai (Map pp78–9; ☎ 362991; 2 Ph 306; mains US$3–5) The name, Thai House, might not rate as highly original, but the setting is, housed within a classic Khmer house. It offers a choice of traditional floor seating or tables and chairs, and there is a lunchtime canteen downstairs for those eating on the cheap.

Boat Noodle Restaurant (Map pp78–9; Ph 294; mains 2500–10,000r) Still the cheapest Thai restaurant in town, this place draws Cambodians and Thais in search of a memorable meal. Soups and noodles are a bargain, but nothing will break the bank.

EID Restaurant (Map pp78–9; Ph 310; mains US$1–3) Twice relocated in the last few years, who is to say it won't move again! This is a long-running Thai eatery with a good selection of US$1 specials for a quick snack.

Vietnamese

Pho Shop (Map pp78–9; Sihanouk Blvd; mains 3000r) For cheap and delicious *pho bo* (Vietnamese beef noodle soup), try this local restaurant on the corner of Sihanouk Blvd and Ph 21. It does genuine *pho* with all the accompaniments. A bowl costs just 3000r.

An Nam (Map pp78–9; ☎ 212460; 118 Samdech Sothearos Blvd; mains US$2–5) Currently the classiest Vietnamese restaurant in town, An Nam has a good range of dishes from central Vietnam and beyond. It looks more like a diner than a refined restaurant á la Ho Chi Minh City or Hanoi.

Indonesian

Bali Café (Map pp78–9; ☎ 982211; 379 Sisowath Quay; mains US$2–4) Bringing a bit of Bali to the riverfront of Phnom Penh, this huge upstairs restaurant has a serious selection of Indonesian food. All the favourites are found here from *nasi goreng* (fried rice) to *gado gado* (vegetable salad with peanut sauce), and there are some special set menus.

Indian & Nepalese

Chi Cha (Map pp78-9; ☎ 366065; 27 Ph 110; set menus US$2) Not Indian or Nepalese, but Bangladeshi, this curry house turns out the cheapest subcontinent selections in town, including bargain *thalis* (set meals).

Lumbini Restaurant (Map pp78-9; ☎ 212544; 51 Ph 214; mains US$5) This Nepalese-run restaurant offers a healthy range of Indian and Nepalese food, including delicious dhal and succulent chicken tikka.

Curry Pot (Map pp78-9; Ph 93; mains US$2-4) Slap, bang in the middle of backpackersville, this little curry house turns out some of the best curries in town, but service can be a little slow. Upstairs is a rooftop bar if you want a warm-up drink.

Shiva Shakti (Map pp78-9; 70 Sihanouk Blvd; mains US$5-10) For indulgent Indian cuisine, this richly decorated restaurant has a refined menu of subcontinental specialities. Expect to pay nearer to US$15 for a full spread.

Italian

Happy Herb's (Map pp78-9; ☎ 362349; 345 Sisowath Quay; mains from US$4) This is a Phnom Penh institution thanks to its special pizzas. Those wanting to pass some time in a daze can ask the waiter for a 'happy' pizza, while those wanting to lose some days might request 'very happy'. The non-marijuana pizzas are equally good and don't mess with the mind.

Nike's Pizza House (Map pp78-9; 160 Ph 63; mains from US$4) Definitely one of the better pizza houses in town, contrary to what you might think looking from the outside. There are nearly 50 variations to choose from and the menu includes pastas, side salads and gnocchi. Free delivery.

Ecstatic Pizza (Map pp74-5; ☎ 365089; 193 Norodom Blvd; mains US$3-5) Don't go getting the wrong idea just because of Happy Herb's! This is another place with a strong reputation for well-prepared pizza, located a fair way south of the Independence Monument.

Pop Café (Map pp78-9; 371 Sisowath Quay; US$2-6) Blink and you'll miss it, but this teeny tiny café offers authentic Italian cooking with the Mekong River as a backdrop. Soups, pastas and regional dishes make up the small menu.

Luna D'Autumno (Map pp78-9; ☎ 220895; 6C Ph 29; mains US$4-10) The capital's newest Italian eatery is housed in a beautiful building with a lush tropical garden. The outdoor kitchen fires up the most authentic pizzas in town and indoors is a sophisticated restaurant with a huge walk-in wine cellar. Already hugely popular in Hanoi, it looks set for success in Cambodia.

Japanese

As is the case almost everywhere, Japanese food in Phnom Penh is expensive.

Origami (Map pp78-9; 88 Samdech Sothearos Blvd; set menus US$6-15) The best-value Japanese restaurant in town, this little place is full of character thanks to the charismatic owner. Set menus include the cracking-value origami set (US$6), beautifully presented sushi, sashimi (US$15) and tempura sets, and there is a small Japanese-style *tatami* (woven matting) dining area.

Nagasaki (Map pp78-9; ☎ 218394; 39 Sihanouk Blvd; mains US$5-15) The ambience is authentic, the individual rooms are decorated with *tatami* for group dining. The food has a good reputation, but there's something galling about paying Tokyo prices for a meal in Phnom Penh.

French

Comme a la Maison (Map pp78-9; ☎ 360801; 13 Ph 57; mains US$3-8) Just like the name suggests, it's like eating at home, although you'd be lucky if you ate this well every night. Succulent steaks, healthy salads and plenty of provincial French dishes make this a worthwhile detour for those seeking the Gallic touch.

Le Deauville (Map pp78-9; ☎ 012 371227; Ph 94; mains US$4-8) The accent is predominantly French, with a menu of steaks and salads. Located on the northern side of Wat Phnom, it is often heaving with well-heeled expats.

Restaurant 102 (Map pp78-9; ☎ 990880; 1A Ph 102; mains US$6-20+) If Cambodia awarded Michelin stars, this place would be near the front of the queue thanks to indulgent flavours such as scallops flambéed in brandy and imported chateaubriand. Expect a Parisienne-sized bill though.

International

The number of international restaurants in Phnom Penh is multiplying by the year as

THE AUTHOR'S CHOICE

Boddhi Tree (Map pp74-5; 50 Ph 113; www.bod dhitree.com; mains US$1.50-4) Located opposite Tuol Sleng Museum; many a visitor to that harrowing place have ended up here seeking solace and silence to reflect. Set in a lush garden that is a world away from the former prison opposite, this is one place that is definitely worth a stop. Asian dishes, sandwiches, salads, tapas and desserts, all are freshly prepared, packed full of flavour and available here.

tourism really takes off and between them they offer a tantalising array of cuisines.

Foreign Correspondents' Club (FCC; Map pp78-9; ☎ 724014; 363 Sisowath Quay; mains US$5-10, set menus US$10) The F, as expats like to call it, is housed in a grand old colonial-era building. It has a popular restaurant and bar on the 3rd floor with impeccable views of the Tonlé Sap river to the east and the National Museum to the west. Dishes come from all corners of the globe and the daily set menus are a good option for the undecided. There are also a couple of rooms to stay (p92).

Sa Restaurant (☎ 012 556503; 1 Ph 184; mains US$4-12) Occupying the cutest little colonial-era building in town, this small restaurant has a rooftop terrace for cool breezes and a classic view of the Royal Palace. Dishes are predominantly French and include a good selection of imported cuts, as well as innovative entrées.

Heading north along the riverfront, the international restaurants here come thick and fast.

Riverside Bistro (Map pp78-9; ☎ 213898; 273 Sisowath Quay; mains US$3-7) Sitting on a strategic corner, this is another classic French villa from the colonial period, and the wicker chairs tend to hold customers longer than anticipated. The menu has an eclectic mix of healthy portions from around the world, particularly Central Europe. The Riverside is also a popular bar later in the night and there are two pool tables here.

La Croisette (Map pp78-9; ☎ 012 418178; 241 Sisowath Quay; mains US$3-7) A French-style bistro, La Croisette specialises in unique brochettes (kebabs), as well as a good selection of steaks and freshwater fish, all accompanied by well-dressed salads.

Mekong River Restaurant (Map pp78-9; ☎ 991150; cnr Ph 118 & Sisowath Quay; mains US$2-9) A relative newcomer on the riverfront, the US$6 three-course set menus are great value and include several Asian and international choices. There is also tapas for inveterate snackers.

Riverhouse Restaurant & Lounge (Map pp78-9; ☎ 212302; cnr Ph 110 & Sisowath Quay; mains US$5-15) This place is popular with overseas residents thanks to its sophisticated menu of French and Cambodian cuisine. It gets very busy at the weekend when diners come here to warm up for a night at the lounge upstairs (p101).

Lyon D'Or (Map pp78-9; ☎ 217710; 12 Ph 110; mains US$3-10; 😮) Right next door to the Riverhouse, this French-style bistro has a huge menu of European and Asian food, including sizeable steaks, as well as mountains of couscous for a taste of North Africa.

Tok Thom (Map pp78-9; 17 Ph 104; mains US$3-7; 🕙 Tue-Sun) The name means big table and this brings the Belgian concept of shared dining to Phnom Penh. Everyone sits along one table à la beer house and the menu includes some good snacks and lively seafood.

Topaz (Map pp78-9; ☎ 211054; 100 Samdech Sothearos Blvd; mains US$9) This upmarket restaurant is popular with businesspeople and diplomats. It has a sophisticated ambience, and while the food is certainly good, the European dishes are expensive in their context.

Tamarind Bar (Map pp78-9; ☎ 012 727197; 31 Ph 240; mains US$3-9) Set in a lovely old French-era building, this atmospheric restaurant has an inviting blend of North African, French and tapas on the menu. Downstairs is a richly decorated bar, while way up on the rooftop is a great open-air dining area for the dry season.

Tell Restaurant (Map pp78-9; ☎ 430650; 13 Ph 90; mains US$5-15) Although it may be surprising to find a Swiss-German restaurant lurking behind Hotel Le Royal, the surprises don't stop there. The portions are gargantuan and include a fine selection of steaks and fish, laced with pernod-tinted sauces. There are also several Asian selections and the owners have taken their time to translate the menu into Khmer, a rarity at international spots. Fondues and raclettes for those who want to indulge.

Del Gusto Café (Map pp74-5; ☎ 012 565501; 43 Ph 95; mains US$2-4) This is set in a lovingly restored colonial-era villa that's hidden away behind towering tropical plants. Recently opened by the Boddhi Tree (opposite) owner, the menu here is more Mediterranean, with breads and dips, set to a soundtrack of jazz and classical music.

Khmer Restaurant (Map pp78-9; ☎ 216336; 6 Ph 57; mains US$2-4) Yeah, yeah, you're thinking what's this doing under International. It may look like nothing from the outside, but on the inside lies one of the best Western menus in town, with great salads and sandwiches, pub-style grub and desserts like brownies and crumbles. It has long been popular with NGOs based in the area.

Nature & Sea (Map pp78-9; ☎ 012 662184; 78 Ph 51; mains US$2-4) Definitely a candidate for the city's smallest eatery, at night it spills out onto the street attracting a healthy crowd for the healthy food. Here you'll get great fruit shakes with fresh produce from Vietnam and Cambodia, as well as wholewheat savoury pancakes and delicious seafish.

Fast Food

All Asian food is fast, but here we are talking about the sort of places that do burgers, French fries and the sort. The good news is that at present none of the big fast-food chains grace Phnom Penh, just a few copycats including Lucky Burger (Map pp78–9), part of Lucky Supermarket (p100).

More popular than these copycats are the Khmer burger joints opening around town that pull in students between and after classes. There is a whole strip of them on Samdech Sothearos Blvd south of the Royal Palace, including Mondo Burger (Map pp78–9). Don't expect McDonalds, but at least the food has flavour.

California 2 Guesthouse (Map pp78-9; ☎ 982182; www.cafecaliforniaphnompenh.com; 317 Sisowath Quay; mains US$2-4) A popular stop for bikers, Cambodia's very own biker café even, this place has a small menu of burgers, steaks and Mexican favourites. Very, very cheap beer!

Mex (Map pp78-9; ☎ 360535; 116 Norodom Blvd; mains US$1.50-4) The restaurant has had a serious atmosphere by-pass in recent years, but the takeaway menu (free delivery) may be an option if you want to eat Mexican.

Cafés

Garden Center Café (Map pp78-9; ☎ 363002; 23 Ph 57; mains US$3-6) Excessively popular with expats for its massive breakfasts and homecooked

lunches and dinners, the portions here are huge, and most meals include a side salad. The menu includes a lot of Western food, superb Sunday roasts, a selection of Thai dishes and some great desserts.

Jars of Clay (Map pp74-5; ☎ 300281; 39 Ph 155; cakes US$1, mains US$2-3; ☺ Tue-Sat) If the rigours of Psar Tuol Tom Pong (p104) are too much or you've just got too much shopping to carry, this little café is a great escape. The homebaked cakes are tasty, plus there are light bites like Ploughman's lunches and filled potatoes. Drinks include a thirst-quenching apple and ginger crush.

Java Café (Map pp78-9; ☎ 987420; 56 Sihanouk Blvd; mains US$2-5) It is easy to while away time on the breezy balcony here thanks to a creative menu of salads and sandwiches, innovative and wholesome burgers and daily specials. Drinks are a speciality, including – surprise, surprise – coffee from several continents and great shakes.

The Shop (Map pp78-9; 39 Ph 40; mains US$2-5) Anyone who loves delis back home will enjoy a visit to this little eatery. There is a daily selection of sandwiches and salads, plus some superb pasties if you leave the space. Don't forget the lively shakes such as banana, date and molasses.

A recent phenomenon in Phnom Penh is the arrival of the bubble tea café. Bubble tea has taken off in a big way and is basically a milkshake with glutinous jellies floating in the bottom. It's slightly on the sweet side, but worth a try. These places are quite up-market and fill the niche that a wine bar might in the West. Two of the best are the **Chit Chat Café** (Map pp78-9; ☎ 221535; 146 Sihanouk Blvd; bubble tea 5000r) and the **Mondulkiri Café** (Map pp78-9; 84 Ph 63; bubble tea 5000r).

Backpacker Cafés

There are few backpacker cafés of the sort so popular in nearby Vietnam, unless you include the restaurants in the more popular guesthouses.

Mama's Restaurant (Map pp78-9; Ph 111; mains 2000-4000r) It may have moved up the road a block or so, but the food here remains one of the best deals in town, including a bit of Khmer, Thai, French and even African. A real bargain.

Red Corner (Map pp78-9; Ph 93; meals US$2-3) This popular restaurant-bar has a lively menu of subcontinental and Southeast Asian food, as well as large portions of Western food like chicken and steaks.

Lazy Gecko Café (Map pp78-9; 23 Ph 93, Boeng Kak; mains US$2-5) A popular escape from the guesthouse balconies on the nearby lake, this little place has popular BBQs, big Sunday roasts and the full monty of comfort food from home.

Bakeries

Kiwi Bakery (Map pp78-9; ☎ 215784; 83 Ph 63) For good value, fresh breads and cakes look no further than here. Established by a Khmer family returning home after years of running a bakery in New Zealand, it has everything from jam tarts and gingerbread men to cheesecakes and eclairs.

Among the aforementioned restaurants and cafés, the Shop (p99) has a great selection of breads and pastries, as does Comme a la Maison (p97).

Most of the city's finest hotels also operate bakery outlets with extravagant pastries, but prices are higher than elsewhere. Drop in after 6pm when they offer a 50% discount and gorge away. The larger supermarkets also stock their own range of breads and cakes, freshly baked on the premises.

Self-Catering

Self-catering is easy enough in Phnom Penh, but it often works out considerably more expensive than eating like the locals. The markets are well stocked with fruit and vegetables, fish and meat, all at reasonable prices if you are prepared to bargain a little. Local baguettes are widely available around town, and usually cost about 500r. For something to fill them, Phnom Penh's supermarkets are remarkably well stocked. Imported items aren't that expensive as taxes aren't always paid, so for just US$2 to US$4 there are treats such as German meats, French cheeses and American snacks.

Lucky Supermarket (Map pp78-9; 160 Sihanouk Blvd; ⏰ 7am-9pm) Affectionately known as the unlucky market by some, this is the biggest supermarket chain in town with a serious range of products and several branches, including one in the new Sorya Shopping Mall on Ph 63.

Pencil Supermarket (Map pp78-9; Ph 214; ⏰ 7am-9pm) This popular Thai-run place is perhaps the largest supermarket in town right now and is well stocked.

Bayon Market (Map pp78-9; 133 Monivong Blvd) It may be a smaller supermarket, but Bayon Market has the best range of products, including some nice surprises that don't turn up elsewhere in the city, such as McVities biscuits and Orangina.

Thai Huot Supermarket (Map pp78-9; 103 Monivong Blvd) This is the place for Francophones or French travellers who are missing home, as it stocks almost exclusively French products, including Bonne Maman jam and creamy chocolate.

Many petrol stations include shops with a good selection of imported products; most Starmart shops at Caltex petrol stations on major junctions in the city are now open 24 hours. La Boutique shops located at Total petrol stations are also worth keeping an eye out for.

DRINKING

Phnom Penh has some great bars and it's definitely worth at least one big night on the town when staying here. Many popular bars are clustered along the riverfront, but one or two of the best are tucked away in the back streets. Many of the wooden guesthouse platforms built over Boeng Kak double as great sunset bars with cheap drinks and offer much more atmosphere than other guesthouse bars around town. Most bars are open until around midnight.

Keep an eye out for happy hours around town as these include two-for-the-price-of-one offers and the like that can save quite a bit of cash. Standard drink prices are US$1 to US$2 for a can of beer and US$1 to US$3 for spirits.

Elephant Bar (Map pp78-9; Hotel Le Royal, cnr Monivong Blvd & Ph 92) This joint has one of the best-known happy hours in town, from 4pm to 8pm. Drinks are two-for-one, including cocktails like Singapore Slings.

Foreign Correspondents' Club (FCC; Map pp78-9; ☎ 724014; 363 Sisowath Quay; ⏰ breakfast-late) This is a popular stop for tourists and expats alike thanks to big views and bigger breezes. Both here and the FCC's restaurant (p98) have a touch of colonial about the ambience, but the drinks list is contemporary. Happy hour is from 5pm to 7pm.

There are plenty of other top spots on or around the riverfront.

Cambodia Club (Map pp78-9; 359 Sisowath Quay; ⏰ breakfast-late) With a prime location opposite

FCC, this bar was always destined for big things and has now expanded, giving it a huge section of riverfront balcony. Better still, a club has just opened as we speak, with some serious sounds in a seriously sound-proofed environment.

Riverhouse Restaurant & Lounge (Map pp78-9; ☎ 212302; cnr Ph 110 & Sisowath Quay; ☻ lunch-late) Located above its noted restaurant (p98), this lavishly decorated lounge bar is popular for early evening drinks overlooking the river and late night drinks and a dance on the weekend when they unleash the DJs.

Salt Lounge (Map pp78-9; ☎ 012 289905; 217 Ph 136) This is minimalist heaven – a trendy little cocktail bar all finished in whites and chromes. A new bar in town, it should do well, as the concept is original for Phnom Penh, plus it is the most gay-friendly bar in town today.

Pink Elephant (Map pp78-9; 343 Sisowath Quay) One of the original riverfront pubs, it draws a lively crowd thanks to good tunes, cheap beer, tasty bar meals and free pool. The only drawback are the hordes of 'soo-sine, Bangkok Poh, you wan buy flower, one doll-aah' kids passing by all night. Enter the spirit (or consume the spirit) and it's all good fun.

Cantina (Map pp78-9; 347 Sisowath Quay) Almost next door to the Pink Elephant, Cantina is another popular drinking spot. It has a deserved reputation for good Mexican food.

Ginger Monkey (Map pp78-9; 29 Ph 178) Set in the home of a master sculptor, this bar is covered in replica bas-reliefs and carvings from Angkor. Good location, lively crowd, pavement seating and a generous happy hour from 5pm to 9pm with two-for-one cocktails.

Other drinking holes are spread out across town, although Ph 51 is taking off as a lively strip; many of the smaller places here tend to be hostess bars and are not that couple-friendly.

Heart of Darkness (Map pp78-9; 26 Ph 51) Long the place to be in Phnom Penh come midnight, the Heart, as locals call it, is now more a nightclub than a bar. It's lost the dark, edgy feel it once had, but remains one of Southeast Asia's classic night spots. Quiet before 10pm, it heaves at the hinges come the witching hour. The music is great if you only go once, but the disco diet soon gets repetitive. It is very gay friendly, but large gangs of rich, young Khmers, children of the elite, aren't averse to picking fights with foreigners on a busy night. Back off or you'll meet the bodyguards. The Heart usually stays open until the last person leaves.

Walkabout (Map pp78-9; ☎ 211715; cnr Ph 51 & Ph 174; ☻ 24hr) A couple of blocks down from the Heart, this huge bar has a loyal crowd during the day and draws an army of working girls and dedicated drinkers by night. Check out Friday's 'Joker Draw' in which some lucky soul might walk away with thousands of dollars in cash. Now boasting two bars, this place never closes.

Elsewhere (Map pp78-9; 175 Ph 51; ☻ Thu-Tue) Much further south on Ph 51 and a world away from the madness around the Heart is the oasis that is Elsewhere. Set in a beautiful French colonial-era villa with lavish gardens, this is the perfect spot to while away a warm evening. Low tables, lower cushions and a free plunge pool make this a top spot for the late afternoon happy hour.

Rubies (Map pp78-9; cnr Ph 240 & Ph 19) Anyone on a quest for the grape rather than grain should drop in here. It is a small bar with a big personality, thanks to its wood-finished interior. The lengthy wine list includes the best selection of Australian exiles in town.

Café Sonteipheap (Map pp74-5; 234 Ph 63) This friendly bar-café is one of the most welcoming in Phnom Penh. Warm service, cool décor and a good soundtrack make it worth the journey south. Check out the Brit-style pub quiz every Monday or the regular comedy or cabaret nights. It may have relocated by the time you read this…

Teukei Bar (Map pp78-9; 23 Ph 111; ☻ Mon-Sat) Also known as Gecko Bar, this is a place to relax to ambient sounds and reggae cuts. The food here is also good, including fresh seafish and spicy *merguez* sausage. Potent rum punches are a speciality at US$1.50 and luckily the bar is just stumbling distance from several popular guesthouses.

Tom's Irish Pub (Map pp78-9; 170 Ph 63) One of Phnom Penh's original Irish bars, there isn't much that is Irish about it, but it remains a popular drinking hole with resident NGOs living in this part of town.

Sharky's (Map pp78-9; 126 Ph 130) Billing itself as a rock'n'roll music bar, Sharky's has plenty of pool tables and plenty more working girls, which attracts some and repels others. Whatever your cup of tea, the bar

FLOWER POWER

Anyone who spends a night or two on the town in Phnom Penh will soon be familiar with young girls and boys entering popular bars and restaurants to sell decorative flowers. The kids are incredibly sweet and most people succumb to their charms and buy a flower or two. All these late nights for young children might not be so bad if they were benefiting from their hard-earned cash, but usually they are not. Look down the road and there will be a *moto* (small motorcycle) driver with an ice bucket full of these flowers waiting to ferry the children to another popular spot. Yet again, the charms of children are exploited for the benefit of adults who should know better but are too poor to worry about it. By all means buy, but bear in mind the child may not reap the reward.

menu is one of the best in town. Shooters and test tubes are a speciality here.

Martini (Map pp74-5; 45 Ph 95) One of Phnom Penh's original dodgy nightspots, Martini has recently been forced to relocate not once, but twice due to annoying its neighbours with noise. The old recipe prevails with a beer garden showing movies and a dark dance space. Drinkers are often outnumbered by working girls and it can be intimidating for the uninitiated. This is one of the best-value places to get a late-night feed, as there is a food court in the beer garden.

Other good spots:

Gym Bar (Map pp78-9; 42 Ph 178) Phnom Penh's only real sports bar with giant screens and a big crowd for the big games in the world of rugby and football.

Howie's Bar (Map pp78-9; 30 Ph 51) Just a couple of doors down from the Heart, this small bar is popular with expats looking for a little bolthole when the Heart gets too packed.

Rising Sun (Map pp78-9; ☎ 986270; 20 Ph 178) A blend of English pub and backpacker café, this place has professional pub grub.

ENTERTAINMENT

For news on what's happening here while you are in town, check the back page of the Friday edition of the *Cambodia Daily,* or look at the latest issue of the *Phnom Penh Post* or the monthly *Bayon Pearnik.*

Nightclubs

There aren't many out and out nightclubs in Phnom Penh and the few there are tend to be playgrounds of the privileged, attracting children of the country's political elite who aren't the nicest people to hang out with. Among the many bars listed previously, the best dance spots are the Heart of Darkness (p101) on any night of the week, the Riverhouse Lounge (p101) on weekends and the newcomer Cambodia Club (p100).

Manhattan Club (Map pp74-5; ☎ 427402; Ph 84; admission free; ☽ until daylight) Manhattan is Cambodia's longest running full-on club with banging techno tunes, and is usually heaving most nights. Drinks are pretty pricey (US$5 a beer), so if you are feeling thirsty, pop across the road to the drink stalls where beer is available for just US$1 a can.

Cinemas

There has been a renaissance of the cinema scene in Phnom Penh, following an appeal for the reopening of certain historic cinemas by King Sihanouk in 2001. However, there are almost no English-language films on offer, just a steady diet of low-budget Khmer films about zombies, vampires and ghosts.

Movie Street (Map pp78-9; ☎ 012 913899; 116 Sihanouk Blvd; tickets US$10-12; ☽ 9am-1am) This video shop near the Independence Monument offers private rooms with large TVs for that personal cinema experience. It pretty much has all the latest titles from Hollywood, the UK and Europe.

French Cultural Centre (Map pp78-9; Ph 184) The cultural centre has frequent movie screenings in French during the week, usually kicking off at 6pm. Check at the centre, where a monthly programme is available.

Classical Dance & Arts

Check the latest information on performances at the **Chatomuk Theatre** (Map pp74-5; Sisowath Quay), just north of Hotel Cambodiana. Officially, it has been turned into a government conference centre, but it's occasionally the venue for displays of traditional dance, as is the Royal University of Fine Arts (p85) campus on Ph 70 in the north of the city.

Apsara Arts Association (☎ 990621; 71 Ph 598) Alternate performances of classical dance and folk dance (US$3) are held here every Saturday at 7pm. Visitors are also welcome from 7.30am to 10.30am and from 2pm to

5pm Monday to Saturday to watch the students in training (admission by donation).

Sovanna Phum Arts Association (Map pp74-5; ☎ 987564; 111 Ph 360) Impressive traditional shadow puppet performances are held here at 7.30pm on Friday nights. Tickets are usually US$5 depending on the story being told. On alternate Fridays there are classical dance performances costing US$5.

It is possible to watch students training at the Royal University of Fine Arts (p85). However, it is important to remember that this is a school of learning – noise and flash photography should be kept to a minimum.

Live Music

Live music is pretty limited in Phnom Penh compared with the bigger Asian capitals. Several of the larger hotels have lobby bands from the Philippines, including the Intercontinental Hotel (p93) and Hotel Cambodiana (p93), but it is often more muzac than music.

Memphis Pub (Map pp78-9; 3 Ph 118; ⏰ 5pm-1am) This place often looks closed due to the soundproof doors, but it is best live music venue in town right now. They have live rock'n'roll from Tuesday to Saturday nights, including a Wednesday jam session.

Riverside Bistro (p98) is another reliable venue for live music.

SHOPPING

There is some great shopping to be had in Phnom Penh, but don't forget to bargain in the markets or you'll have your 'head shaved', local-speak for being ripped off. Most markets are open from around 6.30am to 5.30pm. Some shops keep shorter hours by opening later.

Art & Antiques

There are plenty of shops selling locally produced paintings along Ph 178, opposite the National Museum. It used to be a pretty sorry selection of the amateurish

---

SHOPPING FOR A CAUSE

There are a host of tasteful shops selling handicrafts and textiles to raise money for projects to assist disadvantaged Cambodians. These are a good place to spend some dollars, as it helps to put a little bit back into the country.

NCDP Handicrafts (Map pp78-9; ☎ 213734; 3 Norodom Blvd) This shop was set up by the National Centre for Disabled Persons (NCDP). The collection has come along in leaps and bounds in the last couple of years and the shop stocks some exquisite silk scarves, throws, bags and cushions. Other items include *krama* (scarves), shirts, wallets and purses, notebooks and greeting cards.

Wat Than Handicrafts (Map pp74-5; ☎ 216321; Norodom Blvd) Located in the grounds of Wat Than, this handicrafts shop is along similar lines to NCDP, with an emphasis on products made from Khmer silk. Proceeds go to help land mine and polio victims.

Tabitha (Map pp74-5; Ph 51) This is another NGO that is really driving up the quality of silk design in Cambodia with a fantastic collection of bags, tableware, bedroom decorations and children's toys. Proceeds go towards rural community development, such as well drilling.

Colours of Cambodia (Map pp78-9; 373 Sisowath Quay) Tucked away underneath FCC, this is a popular gift shop helping disabled people in Cambodia. It specialises in silk products, but also offers wood carvings, T-shirts and jewellery.

Rajana Main store (Map pp74-5; 170 Ph 450); Market store (Map pp74-5; Psar Tuol Tom Pong) There are two convenient branches of Rajana, both aimed at promoting fair wages and training. They have a beautiful selection of cards, some quirky metalware products, quality jewellery, bamboo crafts and a range of condiments from Cambodia.

Nyemo (Map pp78-9; 33 Ph 310) Helping disadvantaged women return to work, Nyemo's focus is on quality silk. It has a convenient new outlet next door to Rajana in Psar Tuol Tom Pong.

Khemara Handicrafts (Map pp78-9; 18 Ph 302) Run by a local NGO and women's self-help groups, this place has a nice garden setting. Downstairs is a café, while the shop upstairs is a relaxing place for some hassle-free browsing through the silk collection and other handicrafts.

Villageworks (Map pp74-5; 118 Ph 113) Opposite Tuol Sleng Museum, this shop has the inevitable silk, as well as some delightful handmade cards and coconut shell utensils, although some might be a little taken aback by all the Christian religious carvings in a Buddhist country.

Angkor paintings seen all over the country, but now with a new generation of artists coming up, the selection is much better. It is necessary to bargain vigorously. There are also lots of reproduction cement busts of famous Angkorian sculptures available along this stretch, which would look great on the mantelpiece back home.

Reyum (Map pp78-9; ☎ 217149; www.reyum.org; 47 Ph 178) If you happen to be browsing Ph 178, drop in on Reyum, a nonprofit institute of arts and culture that hosts regular exhibitions on all aspects of Cambodia.

There are several boutiques and antique shops around the city, including some very expensive ones in the city's luxury hotels. When it comes to genuine antiques, **Hanuman Fine Arts Shop** (Map pp74-5; ☎ 211916; 13b Ph 334) has a large collection of classic Buddhas, old silverware and ancient textiles, while **Orient** (Map pp78-9; ☎ 215308; 245 Sisowath Quay) has a range of Asian furniture and pottery from China and the region beyond.

Markets
PSAR THMEI
ផ្សារថ្មី

The dark-yellow Art Deco **Psar Thmei** (New Market; Map pp78-9; north of Ph 63) is also referred to as the Central Market, a reference to its location and size. The central domed hall resembles a Babylonian ziggurat and some claim it ranks as one of the largest domes in the world. It has four wings filled with stalls selling gold and silver jewellery, antique coins, fake name-brand watches, clothing and other such items. For photographers, the fresh food section affords many opportunities. There are a host of good-value food stalls for a local lunch, located on the western side, which faces Monivong Blvd.

Psar Thmei is undoubtedly the best market for browsing. However, it is definitely not the best place to buy things at because it has a reputation among Cambodians for overcharging on everything.

PSAR TUOL TOM PONG
ផ្សារទួលទំពូង

More commonly referred to by foreigners as the Russian Market (it is where the Russians shopped during the 1980s) **Psar Tuol Tom Pong** (Map pp74-5; south of Mao Tse Toung Blvd)

is the best place in town for souvenir and clothes shopping. It has a large range of real and fake antiquities, including miniature Buddhas, wood carvings, betel-nut boxes, silk, silver jewellery, musical instruments and so on. Bargain hard as thousands of tourists pass through here each month.

This is also the market where all the Western clothing made in garment factories around Phnom Penh turns up. There is a good range of trousers, skirts, shirts, T-shirts, boxer shorts and shoes, all at just 10% of the price paid back home. Popular brands include Gap, Colombia, Calvin Klein, Quiksilver, Aigle and Next, but more are coming to Cambodia all the time.

Also available are inexpensive DVDs, CDs and computer programmes, as well as a host of other goodies. This is the one market all visitors should come to at least once during a trip to Phnom Penh.

PSAR O RUSSEI
ផ្សារអូរូស្សី

Not to be confused with Psar Tuol Tom Pong (left), **Psar O Russei** (Map pp78-9; Ph 182) sells luxury foodstuffs, costume jewellery, imported toiletries, secondhand clothes and everything else you can imagine from hundreds of stalls. The market is housed in a huge new building that looks like a shopping mall from the outside and is a real labyrinth of a place.

Also worth checking out:

Psar Olympic (Map pp74-5) Items for sale include bicycle parts, clothes, electronics and assorted edibles. This is quite a modern market set in a covered location.

Psar Chaa (Map pp78-9) This is a scruffy place that deals in household goods, clothes and jewellery. There are small restaurants, food vendors and jewellery stalls, as well as some good fresh-fruit stalls outside.

Silk

Apart from the legendary Psar Tuol Tom Pong (left), which is stocked to the ceiling with silk, there are several boutiques specialising in silk furnishings and clothing:

Ambre (Map pp78-9; ☎ 217935; 37 Ph 178) The stylish silk clothing here is popular with members of the extended royal family, and the French-Cambodian designer is rapidly gaining an international reputation.

Couleurs D'Asie (Map pp74-5; 19 Ph 360) Specialising in sumptuous home design, this is the place for hangings, bedspreads and throws.

Jasmine (Map pp78-9; 73 Ph 240) Elegant evening wear and sartorial silk creations are the recipe here, much of it for export to overseas partners.

Kambuja (Map pp78-9; 165 Ph 110) The newest fashion boutique in town, this blends the best of Cambodian materials together with innovative international designs.

GETTING THERE & AWAY

Air

For information on international and domestic air services to/from Phnom Penh, see p288.

Boat

There are numerous fast-boat companies that operate from the **tourist boat dock** (Map pp78-9; Sisowath Quay) at the eastern end of Ph 106. Boats go to Siem Reap (p113) up the Tonlé Sap river then Tonlé Sap lake, but there are no longer services up the Mekong from Phnom Penh. Boats up the Mekong to Kratie (p252) and Stung Treng (p256) now start in Kompong Cham (p248), which is easily accessible by road from Phnom Penh. For more details on boat services up the Mekong, see p254.

The fast boats to Siem Reap (US$18 to US$25, five to six hours) are losing customers fast now that the road is in such good condition. When it costs US$4 for an air-conditioned bus or US$20ish to be bundled on the roof of a boat, it is not hard to understand why. It is definitely better to save your boat experience for the Mekong or the Siem Reap–Battambang run if you have the choice.

Several companies have daily services departing at 7am and usually take it in turns to make the run. The first stretch of the journey along the river is scenic, but once the boat hits the lake, the fun is over as it is a vast inland sea with not a village in sight.

Express services to Siem Reap are overcrowded, and often appear to have little in the way of safety gear. Most tourists prefer to sit on the roof of the express boats, but don't forget a head covering and sunscreen as thick as paint. Less-nimble travellers or fair-skinned folk might prefer to be inside. Unfortunately, not everyone can sit inside, as companies sell twice as many tickets as there are seats! In the dry season, the boats are very small and dangerously overcrowded to the point that one or two have sunk.

For all the details on the international boat services connecting Phnom Penh with the Mekong Delta in Vietnam, see p292.

Bus

Bus services have improved dramatically with the advent of rebuilt roads in Cambodia, and most major towns are now accessible by air-conditioned bus from Phnom Penh.

Phnom Penh Public Transport (PPPT; Map pp78-9; ☎ 210359; Psar Thmei) is the longest running company and serves Battambang (14,000r, five hours), Kompong Cham (8000r, two hours), Kompong Chhnang (5500r, two hours), Kratie (18,000r, six hours), Neak Luong (5000r, two hours), Poipet (20,000r, eight hours), Siem Reap (14,000r, six hours), Sihanoukville (14,000r, four hours) and Takeo (5500r, two hours).

Mekong Express (Map pp78-9; ☎ 427518; 87 Sisowath Quay) operates more upmarket services to Battambang and Siem Reap complete with in-drive hostesses. Tickets cost US$6.

There are many other bus companies that charge about the same price and take the same amount of time. These include the following:

Capitol Transport (Map pp78-9; ☎ 217627; 14 Ph 182) Services to Battambang, Poipet, Siem Reap and Sihanoukville.

GST (Map pp78-9; ☎ 012 895550; Psar Thmei) Services to Battambang, Poipet, Siem Reap, Sihanoukville and Sisophon.

Hour Lean (Map pp74-5; ☎ 880761; Ph 230) Services to Battambang, Kampot, Kompong Cham, Kratie, Poipet, Siem Reap, Sihanoukville, Svay Rieng and Takeo.

Narin Transport (Map pp78-9; ☎ 991995; 50 Ph 125) Services to Siem Reap.

Neak Krohorm (Map pp78-9; ☎ 219496; 127 Ph 108) Services to Battambang, Poipet, Siem Reap and Sisophon.

Most of the Battambang-bound buses drop off and pick up in Pursat, and some Siem Reap buses do the same in Kompong Thom.

HO CHI MINH CITY

Several bus companies run bus services between Phnom Penh and Ho Chi Minh City in Vietnam. PPPT (above) runs the only daily direct bus service departing Phnom Penh at 6.30am. **PPPT services** (☎ 08-920 3624; 309 Pham Ngu Lao, Ho Chi Minh City) depart Ho Chi Minh City at 6am and cost US$9. Capitol Transport and Narin Transport have cheap services with a change of bus at the border for US$5 to US$6. For more details see p291.

Taxi, Pick-up & Minibus

Taxis, pick-ups and minibuses leave Phnom Penh for destinations all over the country, but are fast losing ground to cheaper and more comfortable buses as the road network improves. Vehicles for Svay Rieng and Vietnam leave from Chbah Ampeau taxi park (Map pp74–5) on the eastern side of Monivong Bridge in the south of town, while those for most other destinations leave from around Psar Thmei. Different vehicles run different routes depending on the quality of the road, but the fast share taxis are more popular than the bumpy pick-ups and overcrowded minibuses. The following prices are those quoted for the most commonly used vehicle on that particular route, but are indicative rather than definitive, as even Khmers have to bargain a bit.

Share taxis run to Sihanoukville (10,000r, 2½ hours), Kampot (10,000r, two hours), Kompong Thom (10,000r, 2½ hours), Siem Reap (20,000r, five hours), Battambang (20,000r, four hours), Pursat (15,000r, three hours), Kompong Cham (10,000r, two hours) and Kratie (25,000r, five hours).

It is also possible to hire share taxis by the day. Rates start at US$25 for around Phnom Penh and nearby destinations, and then go up according to distance and the language skills of the driver.

Pick-ups still take on some of the long-distance runs to places such as Mondulkiri (US$10, eight hours) and Stung Treng (US$10, 10 hours), for Ratanakiri or the Lao border.

Minibuses aren't much fun and are best avoided where there are larger air-con buses or faster share taxis available.

Train

Train travel may be pretty cheap, even with the foreigner price set at three times the Khmer price, but it is definitely not the most time-effective way to travel. Trains are extremely slow, travelling at about 20km/h. Yes, for a few minutes you can outrun the train! There is one train a day on both the line south to Sihanoukville and the line west to Battambang. If the trains leave Phnom Penh Monday, they return Tuesday and so on, so always check the latest schedule at the station a couple of days ahead.

Trains for Takeo (3400r, three hours, 75km), Kampot (7500r, six hours, 166km) and Sihanoukville (12,300r, 12 hours, 270km) leave at 6.20am every other day.

Trains to Battambang (12,400r, 14 to 16 hours, 274km) and Pursat (7500r, eight hours, 165km) also depart at 6.20am every other day.

Phnom Penh's train station (Map pp78–9) is located at the western end of Ph 106 and Ph 108, in a grand old colonial-era building that is a shambles inside. Even if you don't plan on taking the train, it is interesting to see the crazy kafuffle around departure time each day.

GETTING AROUND

Being such a small city, Phnom Penh is not too bad to get around, although traffic is getting worse by the year and traffic jams are common around rush hour in the morning and evening, particularly around Monivong and Norodom Blvds.

To/From the Airport

Phnom Penh International Airport is 7km west of central Phnom Penh, via Russian Blvd. Official taxis from the airport to the city centre cost US$7 and unofficial taxis are no longer allowed to wait at the terminal. Taxi drivers will take you to only one destination for this price, so make sure that they take you to where you want to go, not where they want you to go. Official *motos* into town have been fixed at US$2, but if you walk outside the airport you can pick up a regular *moto* for more like US$1. The journey usually takes about 30 minutes.

Heading to the airport from central Phnom Penh, a taxi should cost no more than US$5 and a *moto* between US$1 and US$1.50.

Bicycle

It is possible to hire bicycles at some of the guesthouses around town for about US$1 a day, but take a look at the chaotic traffic conditions before venturing forth. Once you get used to the anarchy, it can be a fun way to get around, if a little dusty.

Bus

Local buses don't exist in Phnom Penh. Most Cambodians use *motos* or *cyclos* (pedicabs) to get around the city. With the long, straight boulevards criss-crossing the city, it would be perfect for trams or trolley

---

WE'RE ON A ROAD TO NOWHERE

Taking a ride on a *moto* (small motorcycle with driver) or *cyclo* (pedicab) is not quite as easy as it looks. Drivers who loiter around guesthouses, hotels, restaurants and bars may speak streetwise English and know the city well, but elsewhere the knowledge and understanding required to get you to your destination dries up fast. Flag a *moto* or *cyclo* down on the street or grab one from outside the market, and you could end up pretty much anywhere in the city. You name your destination, and they nod confidently, eager for the extra money a foreigner may bring, but not having the first clue of where you want to go. They start driving or pedalling furiously down the road and await your instructions. You don't give them any instructions, as you think they know where they are going. Before you realise it, you are halfway to Thailand or Vietnam. The moral of the story is always carry a map of Phnom Penh and keep a close eye on the driver unless he speaks enough English to understand where the hell you want to go.

---

buses, but developments like this are some years away.

Car & Motorcycle

Car hire is available through travel agencies, guesthouses and hotels in Phnom Penh. Everything from cars (from US$20) to 4WDs (from US$50) are available for travelling around the city, but prices rise if you venture beyond.

There are numerous motorbike hire places around town. Bear in mind that motorbike theft is a problem in Phnom Penh, and if the bike gets stolen you will be liable. Ask for a lock and use it, plus keep the bike in guarded parking areas (300r) where possible, such as outside markets. The best places for motorbike hire are **Lucky! Lucky!** (Map pp78-9; ☎ 212788; 413 Monivong Blvd) and **New! New!** (Map pp78-9; 417 Monivong Blvd) right next door to each other on the main drag in town. A 100cc Honda costs US$3 to US$4 per day or US$20 per week and 250cc dirt bikes cost US$7 per day or US$40 a week. Lucky! Lucky! operates a second drop-in rental desk, **Lucky! Lucky! 2** (Ph 93), at Boeng Kak.

Cyclo

Cyclos (pedicabs) are still common on the streets of Phnom Penh, but have lost a lot of ground to the *moto*. Travelling by *cyclo* is a more relaxing way to see the sights in the centre of town, but they are just too slow for going from one end of the city to another. For a day of sightseeing, think around US$6 to US$8 depending on exactly where you go and how many hours of pedalling it includes. Late at night, *cyclos* would have to be considered a security hazard for all but the shortest of journeys, but most

drivers are asleep in their *cyclos* at this time anyway. Costs are generally similar to *moto* fares, although negotiate if picking one up at popular spots around town.

Moto

Motos are generally recognisable by the baseball caps favoured by the drivers. In areas frequented by foreigners, *moto* drivers generally speak English and sometimes a little French. Elsewhere around town it can be difficult to find anyone who understands where you want to go – see the boxed text above for ways to survive. Most short trips are about 1000r and more again at night, although if you want to get from one end of the city to the other, you have to pay more. Prices are rarely negotiated in advance when taking rides. However, those staying in a luxury hotel must negotiate before they hop on or they will find themselves well and truly ripped off. Likewise, night owls taking a *moto* home from popular drinking holes should consider negotiating to avoid an expensive surprise.

Many of the *moto* drivers who wait outside the popular guesthouses and hotels have good English and are able to act as guides for a daily rate of about US$6 to US$8 depending on the destinations.

Remorque-moto

Also commonly known as *tuk tuks*, these motorbike and carriages have hit Phnom Penh in the past few years and are here to stay. They come in every shape and size from China, India and Thailand, and there are home-grown ones from Siem Reap. Average fares are about double those of *motos*, but this increases if you pack on the passengers.

Taxi

Phnom Penh has no metered taxis of the sort found in Thailand or Vietnam. **Bailey's Taxis** (☎ 012 890000) and **Taxi Vantha** (☎ 012 855000) offer taxis 24 hours a day, but have a limited number of cars. They do the run from town to the airport for US$5 and charge about US$1 per kilometre elsewhere. Note the price for the journey from the airport to town is fixed at US$7.

Private taxis tend to wait outside popular nightspots, but it is important to agree on a price in advance.

AROUND PHNOM PENH

There are several attractions around Phnom Penh that make good day trips, although they are kind of low key when compared with what's on offer in other parts of the country. The Angkorian temple of Tonlé Bati and the hilltop pagoda of Phnom Chisor are best visited in one trip, and can be built into a journey south to either Takeo (p204) or Kampot (p195). Udong, once the capital of Cambodia, is also a potential day trip and can be combined with a visit to Kompong Chhnang (p209), known for being a 'genuine' Cambodian town.

There is a clean, comfortable and cheap bus network operated by the PPPT (p105) covering most of the following places. For experienced riders, motorcycles (p107) are another interesting way to visit these attractions, as there are plenty of small villages along the way. If time is more important than money, you can rent a taxi to whisk you around for between US$25 and US$35 a day, depending on the destination. Some of the more popular guesthouses offer inexpensive tours with or without a guide to most of the places covered here.

KIEN SVAY
កៀនស្វាយ

Kien Svay is a very popular picnic area on a small tributary of the Mekong. Hundreds of bamboo huts have been built over the water and Khmers love to come here and sit around gossiping and munching on the weekend.

Kien Svay is a peculiarly Cambodian institution, a mixture of the universal love of picnicking by the water and the unique Khmer fondness for lounging about on mats. It works like this: for 5000r an hour, picnickers rent an area on a raised open hut covered with reed mats. Be sure to agree on the price *before* you rent a space and note that it should only be about 2000r if you buy food (such as grilled chicken, river lobster, fried vegetables etc) from the family. The tiny boat trip to the huts should be included in the price.

All sorts of food is sold at Kien Svay, although it is necessary to bargain to ensure a fair price. Prices generally seem reasonable thanks to the massive competition – there are perhaps 50 or more sellers here. Popular dishes include grilled chicken and fish, river lobster and fresh fruit. The area is pretty deserted during the week, but this can make it a calmer time to picnic.

Getting There & Away

Kien Svay is a district in Kandal Province and the actual picnic spot is just before the small town of Koki, about 15km east of Phnom Penh. To get here from Phnom Penh, turn left off NH1, which links Phnom Penh with Ho Chi Minh City, through a wat-style gate at a point 15km east of the Monivong Bridge. You will know you are on the right track if you see plenty of beggars and hundreds of cars. Buses regularly depart for Kien Svay from Psar Thmei and cost just 1500r. The local way to get there would be to take a *remorque-moto* (trailer pulled by a motorcycle) from the Chbah Ampeau taxi park, just east of the Monivong Bridge. This would cost around 1000r, but the trip is very slow, if somewhat amusing. A round-trip *moto* should cost about US$4.

UDONG
ភ្នំឧត្ដុង្គ

Udong (the Victorious) served as the capital of Cambodia under several sovereigns between 1618 and 1866. A number of kings, including King Norodom, were crowned here. The main attractions these days are the two humps of Phnom Udong, which have several stupas on them. Both ends of the ridge have good views of the Cambodian countryside dotted with innumerable sugar palm trees. Udong is not a major attraction, but for those with the time it's worth seeing. It's generally very quiet, though picnickers tend to arrive from Phnom Penh on the weekends.

The smaller ridge has two structures – both heavily damaged – and several stupas on top. **Ta San Mosque** faces westward towards Mecca. Only the bullet- and shrapnel-pocked walls survived the years of Khmer Rouge rule, though there are plans to rebuild the entire structure. Across the plains to the south of the mosque you can see **Phnom Vihear Leu**, a small hill on which a *vihara* stands between two white poles. To the right of the *vihara* is a building used as a prison under Pol Pot's rule. To the left of the *vihara* and below it is a pagoda known as **Arey Ka Sap**.

The larger ridge, Phnom Preah Reach Throap (Hill of the Royal Fortune), is so named because a 16th-century Khmer king is said to have hidden the national treasury here during a war with the Thais. The most impressive structure on Phnom Preah Reach Throap is **Vihear Preah Ath Roes**. The *vihara* and the Buddha, dedicated in 1911 by King Sisowath, were blown up by the Khmer Rouge in 1977; only sections of the walls, the bases of eight enormous columns and the right arm and part of the right side of the Buddha remain.

About 120m northwest of Vihear Preah Ath Roes is a line of small *vihara*. The first is **Vihear Preah Ko**, a brick-roofed structure that contains a statue of Preah Ko, the sacred bull; the original statue was carried away by the Thais long ago. The second structure, which has a seated Buddha inside, is **Vihear Preah Keo**. The third is **Vihear Prak Neak**, its cracked walls topped with a thatched roof. Inside is a seated Buddha who is guarded by a *naga* (*prak neak* means 'protected by a *naga*').

At the northwestern extremity of the ridge stand three large stupas. The first is the cement **Chet Dey Mak Proum**, the final resting place of King Monivong (r 1927–41). Decorated with *garuda* (mythical half-man, half-bird creatures), floral designs and elephants, it has four faces on top. The middle stupa, **Tray Troeng**, is decorated with coloured tiles; it was built in 1891 by King Norodom to house the ashes of his father, King Ang Duong (r 1845–59). But some say King Ang Duong was buried next to

the Silver Pagoda in Phnom Penh. The third stupa, **Damrei Sam Poan**, was built by King Chey Chethar II (r 1618–26) for the ashes of his predecessor, King Soriyopor.

An east-facing staircase leads down the hillside from the stupa of King Monivong. Just north of its base is a **pavilion** decorated with graphic murals depicting Khmer Rouge atrocities.

At the base of the ridge, close to the path, is a **memorial** to the victims of Pol Pot that contains the bones of some of the people who were buried in approximately 100 mass graves, each containing about a dozen bodies. Instruments of torture were unearthed along with the bones when a number of the pits were disinterred in 1981 and 1982.

Eating

There are plenty of Cambodian snack stalls around the base of the hill, as well as some small restaurants back at the turn-off from NH5. For a good view of Phnom Udong, there are several restaurants opposite the Prek Kdam ferry about 9km back towards Phnom Penh. They are built on wooden platforms over the wet-season flood plains, but are only really convenient for those with their own transport.

Getting There & Away

Udong is 41km from the capital. To get here, head north out of Phnom Penh on NH5. Continue past the Prek Kdam ferry for 5km and turn left (south) at the signposted archway. Udong is 3.5km south of the turn-off; the access road goes through the village of Psar Dek Krom, and passes by a memorial to Pol Pot's victims and a structure known as the Blue Stupa, before arriving at a short staircase.

A cheap and convenient way to get to Udong is by air-con local bus (3000r, one hour) from Phnom Penh. Buses depart from near Psar Thmei and run regularly throughout the day. The bus drivers can drop you at the access road to Udong, from where you can arrange a *moto* to the base of the hill for less than US$1. Buses to/from Kompong Chhnang (p209) also stop here, so you can combine your visit to the temples with a visit to a Cambodian town that sees few tourists.

A taxi for the day trip from Phnom Penh will cost around US$25. *Moto* drivers also run people to Udong for about US$8 to US$10 for the day, but when compared with the bus this isn't the most pleasant way to go, as the road is pretty busy and very dusty.

TONLÉ BATI

ទន្លេបាទី

Tonlé Bati (admission incl a drink US$3) is the collective name for a pair of old Angkorian-era temples and a popular lakeside picnic area. Anyone who has already experienced the mighty temples of Angkor (p134) can probably survive without a visit, but if Angkor is yet to come, these attractive temples are worth a detour.

Sights
TA PROHM

តាព្រហ្ម

The laterite temple of Ta Prohm was built by King Jayavarman VII (r 1181–219) on the site of an ancient 6th-century Khmer shrine. Today the ruined temple is surrounded by colourful flowers and plants, affording some great photo opportunities.

The main sanctuary consists of five chambers, in each is a *linga* (phallic symbol) and all show signs of the destruction wrought by the Khmer Rouge.

Entering the sanctuary from the east gate, 15m ahead on the right is a bas-relief depicting a woman and a man who is bowing to another, larger woman. The smaller woman has just given birth and failed to show proper respect for the midwife (the larger woman). The new mother has been condemned to carry the afterbirth on her head in a box for the rest of her life. The husband is asking that his wife be forgiven.

Inside the north gate is a damaged statue of the Hindu god Preah Noreay. Women come here to pray for the birth of children.

YEAY PEAU

យាយពៅ

Yeay Peau temple, named after King Prohm's mother, is 150m north of Ta Prohm in the grounds of a modern pagoda. Legend has it that Peau gave birth to a son, Prohm. When Prohm discovered his father was King Preah Ket Mealea, he set off to live with the king.

After a few years, he returned to his mother but did not recognise her and, taken by her beauty, asked her to become his wife. He refused to believe Peau's protests that she was his mother.

Nearby is **Wat Tonlé Bati**, a modern cement structure heavily damaged by the Khmer Rouge. The only remnant of the pagoda's pre-1975 complement of statues is an 80cm-high metal Buddha's head.

LAKEFRONT

About 300m northwest of Ta Prohm, a long, narrow peninsula juts into Tonlé Bati. It used to be packed at weekends with vendors selling food, drink and fruit, but their high prices have led most Phnom Penh residents to give the place a miss or bring picnics. You are best to do likewise.

Getting There & Away

The access road heading to Ta Prohm is signposted on NH2 at a point 31km south of Phnom Penh. The temple is 2.5km from the highway.

Buses leave for Takeo at fairly regular intervals throughout the day and can drop passengers at the access road. The fare is 3000r. The first bus from Phnom Penh leaves at 7am and there are hourly services until 4pm. Buses returning from Takeo in the afternoon leave hourly from noon to 4pm and take about one hour to get to Tonlé Bati. If you are heading to the zoo at Phnom Tamao, these services also apply.

PHNOM TAMAO WILDLIFE SANCTUARY

ភ្នំតាម៉ៅ

Cambodia's foremost wildlife sanctuary, **Phnom Tamao** (admission US$2) is a home for animals confiscated from traffickers or saved from poachers traps. It occupies a vast site south of the capital and its animals are kept in varying conditions that are rapidly improving with help from international wildlife NGOs such as Wildaid. Spread out as it is, it feels like a zoo crossed with a safari park, and gradually some of this space is being used to provide a better habitat for the larger animals. The way things are moving, Phnom Tamao is set to become one of the region's best-run animal sanctuaries in coming years.

Popular enclosures include huge areas for the large tiger population and the beautiful sun bears, and there are elephants that sometimes take part in activities such as painting. There is also a walk-through area with macaques and deer and a huge menagerie, although the incredible birdlife sadly took a hammering during the 2004 bird flu outbreak .

If you don't like zoos you probably won't like this wildlife sanctuary, but remember that these animals have been rescued from traffickers and poachers and need a home. Visitors that come here will be doing their own small bit to help in the protection and survival of Cambodia's varied and wonderful wildlife.

Getting There & Away

Phnom Tamao is about 44km from Phnom Penh, down NH2. Take a left turn after the sign for the zoo (37km), and it is 6km further down a sandy track. On weekends, you can combine an air-con bus ride with a *remorque-moto*, but on weekdays it may be easier to rent a motorbike if you are used to riding. See opposite for details on bus times and prices.

PHNOM CHISOR
ភ្នំជីសូរ្យ

A temple from the Angkorian era, **Phnom Chisor** (admission US$3) is set upon a solitary hill in Takeo Province (p204). Try to get to Phnom Chisor early in the morning or late in the afternoon, as it is a very uncomfortable climb in the heat of the midday sun.

The main temple stands on the eastern side of the hilltop. Constructed of laterite and brick with carved lintels of sandstone, the complex is surrounded by the partially ruined walls of a 2.5m-wide gallery with windows.

Inscriptions found here date from the 11th century, when this site was known as Suryagiri. The wooden doors to the sanctuary in the centre of the complex, which open to the east, are decorated with carvings of figures standing on pigs. Inside the sanctuary are statues of Buddha.

On the plain to the east of Phnom Chisor are the sanctuaries of **Sen Thmol**, just below Phnom Chisor, and **Sen Ravang**, farther east, and the former sacred pond of **Tonlé Om**.

All three of these features form a straight line from Phnom Chisor in the direction of Angkor. During rituals held here 900 years ago, the king, his Brahmans and their entourage would climb a monumental 400 steps to Suryagiri from this direction.

There is a spectacular view of the temples and plains from the roofless gallery opposite the wooden doors to the central shrine. Near the main temple is a modern Buddhist *vihara* that is used by resident monks.

There are two paths up the 100m-high ridge, which takes about 15 minutes to climb. The northern path, which has a mild gradient, begins at a cement pavilion with windows shaped like the squared-off silhouette of a bell. The building is topped with a miniature replica of an Angkor-style tower. The steeper southern route, which begins 600m south of the northern path, consists of a long stairway. A good way to see the view in all directions is to go up the northern path and come down the southern stairway.

Getting There & Away

The eastward-bound access road to Phnom Chisor is signposted on the left about 52km south of central Phnom Penh and 27km north of Takeo town. It's about 5km from the highway to the base of the hill.

The cheapest way to get to Phnom Chisor is to take a Takeo bus from Phnom Penh and ask to be let off at the turnoff from NH2. This costs 4000r and from here you can take a *moto* to the bottom of the hill for less than US$1. See opposite for details on the bus schedule. Alternatively, you can charter a taxi for about US$30 to visit both Phnom Chisor and Tonlé Bati, or there is the option of hiring a motorcycle (p107) in Phnom Penh.

KIRIROM NATIONAL PARK
ឧទ្យានជាតិគីរីរម្យ

The hill station of Kirirom, set amid lush forest and pine groves, has been established as a national park. It is popular with Khmers at weekends as it is 675m above sea level with a climate notably cooler than Phnom Penh. There are several small **waterfalls** in the park, which are popular picnic spots for Khmers, and quite a lot of basic walking trails. For a more substantial walk, consider hooking up with a ranger (US$5 or so) for a two-hour hike up to **Phnom Dat Chivit** (End of the World Mountain) where an abrupt cliff-face offers an unbroken view of the **Chuor Phnom Damrei** (Elephant Mountains) and **Chuor Phnom Kravanh** (Cardamom Mountains) to the west. It is often possible to see wildlife on this trail, including black bears scavenging the pine trees for honey.

Kirirom is one of the few national parks to have a community tourism programme up and running. The **Mlup Baitong** (☎ 023-214409; mlup@online.com.kh) programme is based in nearby Chambok, where attractions include a 40m-high waterfall, traditional oxcart rides (Cambodia's original 4WDs) and nature walks. Proceeds from the educational walks are pumped back into the local community.

Sleeping

There are two options for staying at Kirirom and they are poles apart. The very basic **Kirirom Guesthouse** (r US$10) looks like it is on its last legs, but the rooms have clean sheets, a fan and attached bathroom if you get stuck here.

Kirirom Hillside Resort (www.kiriromresort.com; r US$40-55; ⬛) is located just beneath the entrance to the national park. This kitsch place is aimed at local and regional tourists wanting a taste of country life. The castle-like entrance and plastic dinosaurs put most Westerners off, but set in the spacious grounds are some Scandinavian-style bungalows in various shapes and sizes. Facilities include a swimming pool.

Getting There & Away

Kirirom National Park is 112km southwest of Phnom Penh, located about 25km to the west of NH4. Unless you have your own transport, it is not that easy to get there. One possibility is to catch a bus going to Sihanoukville and ask to be let off at Kirirom or Preah Suramarit Kossomak National Park (the full name in Khmer). However, you would still have to hire a *moto* to get around the park itself. The best way to visit is to hire a motorcycle (p107) in Phnom Penh or get a group together and charter a taxi for about US$50. Coming under your own steam, the turn-off for the park is about 85km from Phnom Penh, and is marked by a large sign on the right of the highway.

Siem Reap
សៀមរាប

SIEM REAP

Siem Reap (*see*-em ree-*ep*) is the gateway to Cambodia's spiritual and cultural heartbeat, the temples of Angkor. The town was a quiet, sleepy backwater until a few years ago, but it's quickly reinventing itself as a sophisticated centre for the new wave of visitors passing through each year. If Cambodia is hot right now, then Siem Reap is at boiling over, the one place everyone coming to Cambodia will hit during their visit.

Around the centre, it remains a charming town with rural qualities. Old French shop-houses, shady tree-lined boulevards and a gentle winding river are remnants of the past, while five-star hotels, air-con buses and international restaurants are pointers to the future. The gold rush of recent years continues unabated in Siem Reap: hotels and guesthouses going up every month, restaurants and bars every week. Tourism is the lifeblood of Siem Reap and without careful management it could become Siem Reapolinos, the not so Costa-del-Culture of Southeast Asia. However, there are promising signs that developers are learning from the mistakes that have blighted other regional hot spots, with restrictions on the height of hotels and bus sizes. Either way, Angkor is centre stage on the world travel map right now and there is no going back for its supply line, Siem Reap.

Siem Reap is just north of the western extent of Tonlé Sap lake. It's the perfect place to relax for several days and many visitors end up staying a week, thanks to a good range of facilities, friendly and fun-loving locals, and the world's most magnificent temples being slap-bang on the doorstep. Angkor is a place to be savoured, not rushed, and Siem Reap is the perfect place from which to plan your adventures.

HIGHLIGHTS

- See some of the world's rarest large water birds at the sanctuary of **Prek Toal** (p132)
- Float through the flooded forest of **Kompong Phhluk** (p133), an incredible village of bamboo skyscrapers
- See the forgotten temples of Angkor hiding in town behind the modern pagodas of **Wat Athvea** and **Wat Preah Inkosei** (p117).
- Discover the secrets of **Bar St** (p128), Siem Reap's quaffing capital where the action goes on all night
- Relax with a **massage** or **spa** (p119), the perfect medicine for weary bodies

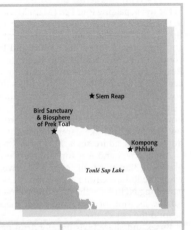

- TELEPHONE CODE: ☎ 063   - POPULATION: 750, 000   - AREA: 10,299 SQ KM

SIEM REAP

HISTORY

The name Siem Reap means 'Siamese Defeated', hardly the most tactful name for a major city near Thailand. Imagine Birmingham with the name 'Germany Defeated'? The empire of Angkor once included much of modern-day Thailand, but there's a touch of irony about the name, given that Thailand ultimately defeated Cambodia, and controlled Siem Reap and Angkor from 1794 to 1907.

Siem Reap was little more than a village when the first French explorers re-discovered Angkor in the 19th century. With the return of Angkor to Cambodian, or should that be French, control in 1907, Siem Reap began to grow, absorbing the first wave of tourists. The Grand Hotel d'Angkor opened its doors in 1929 and the temples of Angkor remained one of Asia's leading draws until the late-1960s, luring visitors like Charlie Chaplin and Jackie Kennedy. With the advent of war, Siem Reap entered a long slumber from which it only began to awake in the mid-1990s. It is now undoubtedly Cambodia's fastest growing town.

ORIENTATION

Siem Reap is still a small town at heart and easy enough to navigate in an hour or two. The centre is around Psar Chaa (Old Market), the administrative district along the western bank of the river, and accommodation is spread throughout town. National Hwy 6 (NH6) cuts across the northern part of the town, passing Psar Leu (Main Market) in the east of town, the Royal Residence and the Grand Hotel d'Angkor in the centre, and then heads out to the airport and beyond to the west. Stung Siem Reap (Siem Reap River) flows north–south through the centre of town, and has enough bridges that you won't have to worry too much about being on the wrong side. Like Phnom Penh, however, street numbering is haphazard to say the least, so take care when hunting down specific addresses.

Angkor Wat and Angkor Thom are only 6km and 8km north of town respectively, while the Roluos Group of temples is 13km east along NH6 – see the map on pp136–38 for the location of these and other places beyond the city centre.

Buses and share taxis usually drop passengers off at the taxi park about 2km east of the town centre, from where it is a short *moto* (small motorcycle with driver) ride to nearby guesthouses or hotels. Fast boats from Phnom Penh and Battambang arrive at Phnom Krom, about 11km south of town, and most places to stay include a free transfer by *moto* or minibus. Siem Reap airport is 7km west of town and there are plenty of taxis and *moto* available for transfers to the town centre. For more details, see p131.

INFORMATION

Pick up a copy of the *Siem Reap Angkor Visitors Guide*, which is packed with listings and comes out quarterly. Bear in mind that reviews are linked to advertisers.

Bookshops

Cheap books on Angkor and Cambodia are hawked by kids around the temples, and by amputees trying to make a clean start in Siem Reap. This can be a good way of assisting the disadvantaged during your visit.

Lazy Mango (Map pp116-17; ☎ 963875; Bar St) Siem Reap's largest secondhand bookstore with guides, novels and plenty on Cambodia.

Monument Books (Map pp116-17; ☎ 963647; Psar Chaa area) The latest branch of the Monument Books empire opened its doors when we were in town. There are also two branches at Siem Reap International Airport.

Emergency

Tourist police (Map pp136-38; ☎ 012 969991) There's an office at the main ticket checkpoint for the Angkor area. This is the place to come and complain if you are seriously mistreated while in Siem Reap, particularly if you fall victim to the 'scam bus' (p294) from Bangkok.

Internet Access

Internet shops have spread through town like wildfire and your nearest online fix will never be far away. Prices are US$1 per hour and most places also offer cheap Internet-based telephone calls. The greatest concentration is along Ph Sivatha and around the Psar Chaa area. Many guesthouses and hotels also offer affordable access.

Medical Services

Anyone who falls seriously ill or who has a major injury or bad accident in Siem Reap is best to seek treatment in Bangkok. It's best to avoid the provincial hospitals unless you want your condition to worsen.

Angkor Children's Hospital (Map pp116-17; ☎ 963409; ☽ 24hr) An international-standard paediatric hospital, the place to take your children if they fall sick.

Naga Medical Centre (Map pp136-38; ☎ 964500; NH6 west; ☽ 24hr) Arguably Siem Reap's best clinic for emergencies or consultation.

Money

For cash exchanges, markets are faster and less bureaucratic than the banks.

Cambodia Asia Bank (Map pp116-17; ☎ 964741; Ph Sivatha; ☽ 7.30am-9pm) Travellers cheques and credit-card cash advances at 2% commission, with long hours and an airport booth.

Cambodian Commercial Bank (CCB; Map pp116-17; ☎ 964392; 130 Ph Sivatha; ☽ 9am-4pm) Changes travellers cheques and offers cash advances at a 2% commission. Also has a useful booth at Psar Chaa.

Canadia Bank (Map pp116-17; ☎ 964808; Psar Chaa) Best all-rounder, with free cash advances on credit cards and the ability to change travellers cheques in most major currencies, at a 2% commission.

Mekong Bank (Map pp116-17; ☎ 964417; 43 Ph Sivatha) Arranges cash advances on credit cards for US$5 each and travellers cheques at the usual 2%. There's a handy after-hours booth that is open until 7pm.

Union Commercial Bank (Map pp116-17; ☎ 963534; Psar Chaa) Free credit-card cash advances here are a draw, plus it operates a popular branch at the main Angkor ticket checkpoint.

Post

The main post office is along the river, 500m south of the Grand Hotel d'Angkor. Services are getting more reliable these days, but it doesn't hurt to see your stamps franked; many people have reported mail going astray in the past. For urgent shipping requirements, there are several courier services in town:

DHL (Map pp116-17; ☎ 964949; Central Market)

EMS (Map pp116-17; ☎ 760000; Main Post Office)

TNT (Map pp116-17; ☎ 963758; Ta Prohm Hotel)

Telephone & Fax

Making international calls is straightforward. The cheapest way is to use the major Internet cafés, with calls starting at about US$0.25 per minute, but there can be a lot of echo and delay. The cheapest unblemished calls can be arranged through the many private booths advertising telephone services. There are a few public phone booths around town, including some around Psar Chaa. Phonecards are sold at shops and hotels. For domestic calls, it is cheaper to call from a private booth. Hotels impose hefty surcharges on calls, so check the rates before you dial.

If you need to send or receive faxes and are not based in a hotel that offers this service, try one of the many reasonably priced Internet cafés in the Psar Chaa area.

Tourist Information

The Tourism Office in Siem Reap is in a white building opposite the Grand Hotel d'Angkor. There's a sign saying 'Tourist Information', but this is a little optimistic unless you come as a paid-up client on one of its private tours. Khmer Angkor Tour Guides Association is also based here, and is a convenient place to arrange an official guide for Angkor – see p147 for more details. Guesthouses and hotels are often a more reliable source of information.

DANGERS & ANNOYANCES

There are a lot of commission scams in Siem Reap that involve certain guesthouses and small hotels paying *moto* and taxi drivers to deliver guests. This is hardly unique to Cambodia, but is worth knowing about in advance. Ways to avoid the scam include booking ahead via the Internet and arranging a pick-up, or sticking with a partner guesthouse if you are coming from Phnom Penh. Alternatively, just go with the flow and negotiate with the hotel or guesthouse on arrival.

For more on the commission scams facing those travelling to Siem Reap by land from Bangkok, see the boxed text on p294.

There are a lot of beggars around town and some visitors quickly develop beggar fatigue. However, try to remember that with no social security network and no government support, life is pretty tough for the poorest of the poor in Cambodia. There is no need to give to everybody, but there is also no need to treat them as if they don't exist. In the case of children, it is often better to offer food, as money usually ends up being passed on to someone else.

Out at the remote temple sites beyond Angkor, stick to clearly marked trails. There are still land mines at locations such as Phnom Kulen and Kbal Spean. For more information about Cambodia's land mines, see p274.

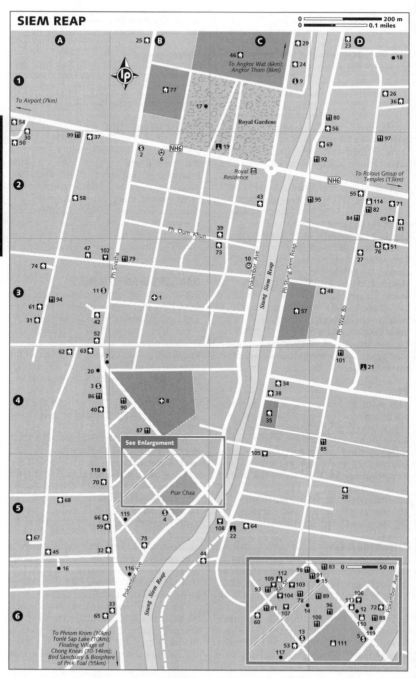

SIGHTS

Visitors come to Siem Reap to see Angkor. The sights in and around the town pale in comparison, but they are a potential diversion for those who find themselves templed out after a few days.

Wats

Modern temples around Siem Reap offer an interesting contrast to the ancient sandstone structures of Angkor. **Wat Bo** (Map pp116-17; 6am-6pm) is one of the town's oldest temples and has a collection of well-preserved wall paintings from the late-19th century depicting the *Reamker,* Cambodia's interpretation of the *Ramayana.* Another wat to consider is **Wat Preah Inkosei** (Map pp136-38; 6am-6pm), built on the site of an early Angkorian brick temple north of town, which still stands today in the compound.

Wat Athvea (Map pp136-38; 6am-6pm), south of the city centre, is an attractive pagoda on the site of an ancient temple . The old temple is still in very good condition and sees far fewer visitors than the main temples in the Angkor area, making it a peaceful spot in the late afternoon.

Wat Thmei (Map pp136-38; 6am-6pm), on the left fork of the road to Angkor Wat, has a small memorial stupa containing the skulls and bones of victims of the Khmer Rouge. It also has plenty of young monks wanting to practise their English.

Wat Dam Nak (Map pp116-17; 6am-6pm) was formerly a royal palace during the reign of King Sisowath, hence the name *dam nak* (palace). Today it is home to the Centre for Khmer Studies, an independent institution promoting a greater understanding of Khmer culture.

SIEM REAP

Artisans d'Angkor

Siem Reap is the epicentre of the drive to revitalise Cambodian traditional culture, which was dealt such a harsh blow by the Khmer Rouge and the years of instability that followed its rule.

Les Chantiers Écoles (Map pp116–17) is a school specialising in teaching wood- and stone-carving techniques to impoverished youngsters. The school has a beautiful shop on the premises, called **Artisans d'Angkor** (Map pp116–17; ☎ 380354; www.artisansdangkor.com), which sells everything from elegant stone and wood reproductions of Angkorian-era statues to household furniture. Tucked down a side road, the school can be quite hard to find, but it's now well signposted from Bakong Lodge (p122).

There is also a second shop opposite Angkor Wat and outlets at Phnom Penh and Siem Reap international airports. Profits from sales go back into funding the school and bringing more teenagers into the training programme.

Shadow Puppets

The creation of leather *sbei tuoi* (shadow puppets) is a traditional Khmer art form, and the figures make a memorable souvenir. Characters include gods and demons from the *Reamker*, as well as exquisite elephants with intricate armour. These are a very Cambodian keepsake. The House of Peace Association makes these puppets, and small puppets cost about US$10 while larger pieces can be as much as US$150. One workshop is located at Wat Preah Inkosei

(Map pp136–38) and a second (Map pp136–38) about 4km down NH6 on the way to the airport. La Noria Guesthouse (p128) hosts shadow puppet shows.

Miniature Replicas of Angkor's Temples

One of the more quirky places in town is the **garden** (Map pp116–17) of a local master sculptor, which houses miniature replicas of Angkor Wat, the Bayon and Banteay Srei. It is a bluffer's way to get that aerial shot of Angkor without chartering a helicopter, although the astute might question the presence of oversized insects in the shot. Entry costs US$1.

Les Chantiers Écoles Silk Farm

Les Chantiers Écoles (see Artisans d'Angkor, left) also maintains a silk farm about 16km west of Siem Reap, just off the road to Sisophon in the village of Puok. All stages of the production process can be seen here, from the cultivation of mulberry trees to the dyeing and weaving of silk. The work produced and sold here is some of the best in the country.

Tonlé Sap Exhibition

North of town, Krousar Thmey – a non-governmental organisation (NGO) supporting orphans – has an interesting **exhibition** (Map pp136–38; admission free) about the Tonlé Sap lake. The exhibition contains photos, models and fishing equipment from around the lake, as well as an informative video. After viewing the exhibition you can indulge in a massage (opposite).

WAR OF THE WAR MUSEUMS

Set up by local de-miner Aki Ra, the **Land Mine Museum** (Map pp136-38; donations accepted) is very popular with travellers for its informative displays on the curse of land mines in Cambodia. The museum includes extensive details about the types of mines used during the civil war in Cambodia. Back in 2000, critics claimed the museum was dangerous, as some live weapons were kept at the site. Local authorities persistently harassed Aki Ra, citing that his museum portrayed a negative image of the country, and he ended up behind bars on more than one occasion. The reasons later became clear: in 2001 the **War Museum** (Map pp136-38; admission US$3; ☺ 8am-5.30pm), run by a local military commander, opened near the airport. Clearly, Siem Reap wasn't big enough for two war museums and Aki Ra lost the civil war.

However, he has since bounced back and it is still possible to visit the Land Mine Museum: there is no charge so it is not operating as a museum. It can be found by following Stung Siem Reap about 1km north of Angkor Conservation. The new War Museum is heavily signposted on the road to the airport, and is overpriced for an uninspiring collection of old military equipment hauled out of former Khmer Rouge areas.

ACTIVITIES
Massage & Spa

Deserving of support is **Seeing Hands Massage 4** (Map pp116-17; ☎ 012 836487; massage per hr $4), training blind people in the art of massage. Located just off Ph Sivatha, some of the money raised assists blind people in Siem Reap Province. You may well need a massage if you have arrived by road from Poipet. **Krousar Thmey** (Map pp136-38; massage US$5) also has massage by the blind, at its interesting Tonlé Sap lake exhibition.

Foot massage is a big hit in Siem Reap – not surprising given all those steep stairways at the temples. If your feet are feeling frumpy, head to the strip running northwest of Psar Chaa where there are half a dozen or more places offering a massage for about US$5 an hour, including **Islands Traditional Khmer Massage** (Map pp116-17; ☎ 012 836487) and the brilliantly named Dr Feet.

Other more upmarket options:

Chai Massage (Map pp136-38; ☎ 380287; Vithei Charles de Gaulle; massage per hr US$20) Popular for authentic shiatsu (Japanese massage).

Frangipani (Map pp116-17; ☎ 012 982062) Located down a narrow alley between Psar Chaa and Bar St, this delightful little place offers massage and a whole range of spa treatments.

Many top-end hotels have in-house spas that are open to residents and nonresidents. Those with the best reputation include **Angkor Spa** (Map pp136–38) at Sofitel Royal Angkor (p124), **Sanctuary Spa** (Map pp116–17) at Shinta Mani (p124) and **Visaya Spa** (Map pp116–17) at FCC Angkor (p124).

Swimming

There are no public swimming pools in Siem Reap, but locals like to swim in the waters of the Western Baray (p169) at the weekend.

Many of the bigger hotels in Siem Reap have swimming pools and some allow access to the public. There are fairly small swimming pools at the **Angkoriana Hotel** (p124, US$6), and **Day Inn Angkor Resort** (p124, US$5). **Le Meridien Angkor** (p124) is good value at US$10. Best of all are the huge lagoon pools at the **Sofitel Royal Angkor Hotel** (p124, US$20), and the **Angkor Palace Spa Resort** (p125), which charges US$12 but includes a drink, and US$22 including lunch or dinner – this meal deal is good value.

FESTIVALS & EVENTS

Chaul Chnam (Khmer New Year) is in mid-April and throngs of Khmers flock to Angkor by bus, truck, car or bike. It's absolute madness at most temples, with a lot of water and talc being thrown about. Avoid it if you want a quiet, reflective Angkor experience.

Bon Om Tuk (Water Festival) is in late October or November. Boat races are held on Stung Siem Reap and hundreds of people flock to town to cheer on their team.

For more information on festivals and events celebrated in Cambodia, see p276.

SLEEPING

A vast number of family-run guesthouses charging US$3 to US$10 a room cater for budget travellers, while those looking for midrange accommodation can choose upmarket guesthouses from US$15, or small hotels, which start from US$20 per room. Those wanting air-con at a budget price may find better value at cheap hotels and upmarket guesthouses than in the budget guesthouses offering only a few air-con rooms.

There are plenty of midrange to top-end hotels around town and, as the construction boom continues unabated, these will soon be supplemented by further arrivals. In fact, it is no exaggeration to say that there are now as many places to stay in Siem Reap as there are temples at Angkor.

In the low season (April to September), it may be possible to negotiate discounts at many of these places. Top-end hotels usually publish high- and low-season rates.

Check out the website of **Siem Reap Angkor Hotel & Guesthouse Association** (www.angkorhotels .org) for a complete listing of guesthouses and hotels.

Budget

Touts for budget guesthouses wait at the taxi park, Phnom Krom docks (where the fast boat from Phnom Penh docks) and at the airport. Even if you have not yet decided where to stay in Siem Reap, do not be surprised to see a noticeboard displaying your name, as most guesthouses in Phnom Penh either have partners up here or sell your name on to another guesthouse! This system usually involves a free ride into town. There is no obligation to stay at their guesthouse if you don't like the look of the place, but the 'free lift' might suddenly cost US$1 or more.

SIEM REAP

Apart from the guesthouses listed here, there are heaps of other places around town with rooms ranging from US$3 and up. Many places offer small discounts for those planning longer stays.

PSAR CHAA AREA

Shadow of Angkor Guesthouse (Map pp116-17; ☎ 964774; r US$6-20; 🔀) Set in a breezy building dating from French colonial days, this is the only budget guesthouse with a central riverside location. The fan rooms are a smart, cheap way to share the dream, but the air-con rooms are larger and include a little more decorative flourish. Breakfast and snacks are served on the balcony.

Popular Guesthouse (Map pp116-17; ☎ 963578; chom@camnet.com.kh; r US$3-15; 🔀) As the name suggests, this place is popular with backpackers, thanks to a solid selection of rooms and a relaxed rooftop restaurant. Cheaper rooms are in the old wing and include bathrooms. The recently completed new wing is the place for those wanting extra touches like air-con, TV and hot water.

Bequest Angkor Hotel (Map pp116-17; ☎ 963317; r US$13; 🔀) Hotel standards at guesthouse prices is the good news for guests at this establishment. Bright rooms with TV, hot water, fridge and even telephone make for shiny, happy people.

Red Lodge (Map pp116-17; ☎ 012 707048; www.red lodgeangkor.com; r US$6-12; 🔀 💻) Hidden down the backstreets, but brazenly signposted from all over town, this guesthouse has a selection of fan and air-con rooms with bathroom, set in a modern villa. There's free breakfast, tea and coffee, and free bicycles make for a real deal. Its website is a good source of travel info.

PHLAUV SIVATHA AREA

Family Guesthouse (Map pp116-17; ☎ 760077; family gh@everyday.com.kh; r US$3-15; 🔀) Once all guesthouses in Siem Reap used to look like this, set in two-storey wooden houses with comfortingly creaky floors – a rare breed these days thanks to all the concrete construction. There are cheaper fan rooms in the old house, and air-con alternatives in the new wing. Family-run, obviously!

Naga Guesthouse (Map pp116-17; ☎ 963439; r US$2-4) One of the first guesthouses in town, all credit to this place for staying true to its roots and only offering basic fan rooms. It's

a big old wooden house, with high ceilings, and downstairs it has a pool table and small restaurant.

Mommy Guesthouse (Map pp116-17; ☎ 012 941755; r US$2-6) Another of the more traditional family-run guesthouses with a big heart, this friendly place has cheap rooms with fan and bathroom, although some air-con additions are planned. It's one of the few guesthouses to have a proper bar out front (one of the cheaper drinking holes in this part of town).

Smiley Guesthouse (Map pp116-17; ☎ 012 852955; r US$4-15; 🔀 💻) More a backpacker hotel than a guesthouse these days, it offers rooms in every shape and size from a single bed and a bathroom right through to satellite TV, hot water and a bathtub. It pays more attention to detail than some guesthouses and there's a popular restaurant serving Khmer and Western favourites.

Royal Hotel (Map pp116-17; ☎ 012 552491; r US$5-12; 🔀) This long-running hotel looks a little worn around the edges, but the rooms are good value for this very reason – US$7 brings hot water, US$10 air-con and US$12 a fridge.

Other possibilities here:

Long Live Angkor Guesthouse (Map pp116-17; ☎ 760286; r US$5-6) A clean place – rooms come with TV, and for hot water add US$1.

Orchidae Guesthouse (Map pp116-17; ☎ 012 849716; r US$2-10; 🔀) A lively little guesthouse just off the main drag, with a solid selection of rooms.

NH6 WEST AREA

Hello Guesthouse (Map pp116-17; ☎ 012 920556; r US$2-8; 🔀) The Siem Reap outpost of Okay Guesthouse (p90) in Phnom Penh, the rooms here are quite a bargain, with air-con options from US$7 and primitive fan rooms with share bathroom for US$2. There's a large restaurant with handy Khmer phrases pasted on the wall.

THE AUTHOR'S CHOICE

Jasmine Lodge (Map pp116-17; ☎ 760697; www.jasminelodge.com; r US$2-15; 🔀) A great little guesthouse that goes the extra mile to ensure guests are well looked after, this place has a range of clean fan rooms and some smarter air-con options. The rooftop restaurant has a free pool table.

Inside the grounds of the Royal Palace (p80), Phnom Penh

JULIET COOMBE

Cyclos (p107), Phnom Penh

JOHN BANAGAN

RICHARD I'ANSON

Stone relief carving at Wat Phnom (p83), Phnom Penh

BILL WASSMAN

Silver Pagoda (p80), Phnom Penh

Wat Ounalom (p84), Phnom Penh

TOM COCKREM

Food stalls at Psar Thmei (p104), Phnom Penh

RICHARD

Chenla Guesthouse (Map pp116-17; ☎ 963233; 012835488@mobitel.com.kh; r US$6-20; ❀) Another of the long-running guesthouses that has reinvested in its success and keeps on growing. Chenla is popular with Japanese travellers thanks to its range of rooms.

Earthwalkers (Map pp136-38; ☎ 012 967901; www .earthwalkers.no; dm US$4, s US$10-13, d US$12-15; ❀ 💻) Set up by a gang of young Norwegians who fell for Cambodia, this smart guesthouse has an international feel. Dorms are more expensive than many cheapies in town, but you may get a room to yourself and rates include breakfast. The rooms are meticulously clean and the downstairs bar is a great source of travel tips. Book online for a 10% discount.

And there's more…

Apsara Angkor Guesthouse (Map pp116-17; ☎ 012 779678; r US$2-20; ❀) An established pad that is often busy thanks to rooms at every rate.

Sidewalk Guesthouse (Map pp136-38; ☎ 012 893468; meanchanthon@bigpond.com.kh; r US$2-4) A small guesthouse on the airport road with little extras like free bicycle hire and bottomless tea and coffee.

EAST BANK OF THE RIVER

13th Villa (Map pp116-17; ☎ 012 756655; r US$3-12; ❀) In this case, the number 13 shouldn't prove unlucky for some. This is a modern guesthouse with large rooms – singles with shared bathroom are the cheapest, while US$7 brings the bonus of hot water for those who need a good scrub after a dusty day.

Two Dragons Guesthouse (Map pp116-17; ☎ 012 630297; r US$6-15; ❀) South of 13th Villa, in the midst of the guesthouse ghetto, is this new place with smart little rooms in a single-storey house. The owner runs one of the best Internet travel sites on Cambodia, so reliable travel info is guaranteed.

Samnark Preah Riem Guesthouse (Map pp116-17; ☎ 760378; preahriem@camnet.com.kh; r US$6-15; ❀) So the name is a bit of a mouthful, but it's worth trying to pronounce it, as the upstairs rooms here are very homely. Fan rooms finished in wood are US$8, while paying the top rate brings air-con and hot water.

Home Sweet Home Guesthouse (Map pp116-17; ☎ 963245; sweethome@camintel.com; r US$10-15; ❀) One of a family of spotless guesthouses, a family that includes the nearby European Guesthouse (Map pp116–17). The spacious rooms include all the trimmings and there are always spillover options, with three properties from which to choose.

Angkor Thom Hotel (Map pp116-17; ☎ 964862; r US$10-13; ❀) This hotel really stands out thanks to its slick rooms of two-star quality. Satellite TV, fridge and hot water are standard, and someone has thought about ambience – Angkor photos line the corridors.

And the budget beat goes on…

Green Town Guesthouse (Map pp116-17; ☎ 964974; r US$3-12; ❀) This sprawling guesthouse near the river offers no nonsense value for money, including real bargains in the old house.

Happy Guesthouse (Map pp116-17; ☎ 963815; r US$5-12; ❀) This friendly guesthouse has a lively garden café and a reasonable range of rooms.

Rosy Guesthouse (Map pp116-17; ☎ 965059; r US$7-15; ❀) Under new Western management; the rooms here are conscientiously cleaned and there is a bustling bar downstairs.

FURTHER AFIELD

Angkorian Lodge (Map pp136-38; ☎ 012 840033; r US$7-15; ❀) Located a few hundred metres north of Angkor Conservation on the opposite bank of the river. The bungalows here have a serene setting amid trees. The rooms are much the same as those of the competition, but the rate includes breakfast and it is definitely a peaceful option.

Garden Village (Map pp136-38; ☎ 012858647; garden village@asia.com; r US$2-12; ❀) Not far from town, but feeling a world away, this guesthouse is earning a popular following thanks to its reasonable rates and pretty garden restaurant.

7th Paradise Resort (☎ 012 996152; r US$5-10; ❀) Way, way out in the sticks, this miniresort needs a renewed injection of love and care, but where else can you find a swimming pool at these prices? It's about 10km out of town towards Thailand…not for night owls.

Midrange

There are some very good deals around, thanks to an explosion in Siem Reap's mid-range accommodation options. Most rates include a free arrival transfer from the airport or boat dock. Don't be afraid to venture 'further afield', as we call it, as some of the most memorable places are away from the centre.

PSAR CHAA AREA

Ivy Guesthouse (Map pp116-17; ☎ 012 800860; r US$15-25; ❀) The Ivy has gone upmarket with the move to its new location (just up the road from the old). Rooms are well equipped with TV and hot water, plus the decoration is a cut above average. It's still not far to the bar (p129).

Molly Malone's Guesthouse (Map pp116-17; ☎ 963533; r US$20-45; ☒) Siem Reap's first real Irish pub (p129) includes a small selection of guest rooms, creatively finished with four-poster beds. Almost every room has a different price depending on size and style, but the US$40 room with balcony offers a nice perspective on downtown Siem Reap.

Ta Prohm Hotel (Map pp116-17; ☎ 380117; tapro hm@camintel.com; s/d US$45/50; ☒) One of Siem Reap's original hotels. Rates here have been slashed in recent years, making it great value for such a central location. Offering three-star comfort, but limited style, the property overlooks Stung Siem Reap and is popular with tour groups.

PHLAUV SIVATHA AREA

Bakong Lodge (Map pp116-17; ☎ /fax 963419; www .bakong-guesthouse.com; 1 Ph Sivatha; s/d US$15/20; ☒) The prices have remained constant at this fine, family-run place, which was one of the first upmarket guesthouses to open its doors in Siem Reap. All rooms include the usual amenities and there is also a small lobby restaurant.

Red Piano (Map pp116-17; ☎ 963240; www.red piano cambodia.com; r US$18-30; ☒) Recently re-located down a quiet side road to a bright red modern villa, the rooms at this popular guesthouse retain their signature decoration with carved wooden beds and colourful wall hangings, plus standard comforts like TV and hot water. The Red Piano restaurant (p127) is nearby.

Golden Temple Villa (Map pp116-17; ☎ 012 943459; r US$8-30; ☒ ▣) Located down a small side street near Artisans d'Angkor, this slick guesthouse includes wood trim and some little touches like Angkor artwork on the walls. Rooms include the usual amenities and there is a lively bar downstairs.

Dead Fish Inn (Map pp116-17; ☎ 963060; www .deadfishtower.com; r US$5-25; ☒) Once visited, never forgotten thanks to a wicked sense of humour that sees all the rooms named after luxury hotel chains like Hilton and Sofitel. The rooms are quite individual, with raised platform beds and mini suites, but the cheaper ones are a little pokey.

Auberge Mont Royal (Map pp116-17; ☎ 964044; mont -royal@mobitel.com.kh; s/d standard US$25/30, deluxe

US$45/50; ☒) An attractive colonial-style villa, the Auberge is a little way off the main drag but offers sophisticated rooms with minibar and bathroom. There is a nice feel here, but don't forget to add 10% tax and US$2.50 for breakfast.

Green Garden Guesthouse (Map pp116-17; ☎ 963342; 012 890363@mobitel.com.kh; r US$15-25; ☒) This guesthouse has striven to improve its rooms in recent years and little extras include the smart use of silk on beds and curtains. There is, as you might guess, a lush garden outside.

There are plenty of other places on the popular Sivatha strip:

Funan Angkor Palace (Map pp116-17; ☎ 012 971676; 560 Ph Sivatha; US$10-18; ☒) This smart place has some huge US$18 deals that are worth a look.

Mandalay Inn (Map pp116-17; ☎ 963960; 148 Ph Sivatha; s/d/tr US$15/20/25; ☒) Burmese-run with big rooms hiding small touches like hairdryers.

Reaksmey Chanreas Hotel (Map pp116-17; ☎ 963557; 330 Ph Sivatha; r US$15-40; ☒) Recently renovated, and so good value at the lower end of things.

NH6 WEST AREA

Moon Inn (Map pp136-38; ☎ 760334; r US$15-30; ☒) Easy to miss if you don't look out for the signs on NH6, this big, new, family-run villa has attractive rooms. Walk to the top floor and you get a bargain for US$15, but all rooms include silk trim and are seriously spick-and-span. It's north of NH6 west.

Secret of the Elephants (Map pp136-38; ☎ 964328; info@angkor-travel.com; NH6 west; r incl breakfast US$30-40; ☒) Staying here is more about character than comfort, as the cheaper rooms only come with ceiling fan and there are no modern fangled gadgets like TV or fridge. Creative decoration may not be enough of an attraction for solo travellers, and it's better value for couples.

EAST BANK OF THE RIVER

Many of the hotels here are on or near the riverfront, a pleasant, shaded area of town.

La Noria Guesthouse (Map pp116-17; ☎ 964242; www.angkor-hotel-lanoria.com; s/d US$33/44; ☒ ▣ ▣) This delightful villa complex is set in a verdant garden with a new swimming pool. The small rooms are thoughtfully decorated and include their own veranda, but there's no TV or fridge. Prices include breakfast and tax. Sister hotel **Borann L'Auberge des Temples** (Map pp116-17; ☎ 964740;

borann@bigpond.com.kh; s/d US$33/44; 🅇 🖵 🅡) is almost identical.

Angkor Discover Inn (Map pp116-17; ☎ 762727; www.angkorinn.com; s/d/tw US$25/35/45; 🅇 🖵) A classy new addition to the hotel scene in this part of town, with a wood and laterite stone finish. The rooms have been decorated with care and attention. Singles and doubles are a touch on the small side, so opt for a twin.

Bopha Angkor Hotel (Map pp116-17; ☎ 964928; www.bopha-angkor.com; Ph Stung Siem Reap; r US$38-62; 🅇) Priding itself on five-star service at three-star prices, this hotel is better on the inside than the older exterior might suggest. All rooms are decorated with Khmer culture in mind and little extras include a turn-down service at night. The restaurant here enjoys an excellent reputation.

Big Lyna Villa (Map pp116-17; ☎ 964807; bec@camintel.com; r US$13-25; 🅇) Set in a traditional Khmer wooden house, the spacious rooms here offer some nice touches that use local handicrafts. Hot water kicks in if you shell out US$20 or more.

Koh Ker Hotel (Map pp116-17; ☎ /fax 963234; kohker@camintel.com; s/tw US$30/35; 🅇) The façade is business-like here, but the rooms are reasonable value given the smart facilities and decorative touches, including TV, minibar, safe and bathtub.

Other recommendations:

City River Hotel (☎ 763000; www.cityriverhotel.com; r US$35-50; 🅇) A smart new hotel, with tempting rates and a leading location overlooking the river.

Passaggio Hotel (☎ 760324; www.passaggio-hotel .com; r US$35-55; 🅇 🖵) This Swiss-managed hotel has two elegant suite rooms and smart standard rooms.

FURTHER AFIELD

Hanumanalaya (Map pp136-38; ☎ 760582; www.hanu manalaya.com; r US$35-65; 🅇 🖵) Billing itself as Angkor's boutique guesthouse, this traditional wooden home is lovingly decorated with Cambodian antiques and handicrafts. Rooms include all the nontraditional comforts like satellite TV and minibar and a choice of Asian or Western breakfast. In a new location, it is very close to Angkor Conservation and the river and guests are able to use the Sofitel Royal Angkor swimming pool for free.

La Villa Loti (Map pp136-38; ☎ 012 888403; www .lavillaloti.com; r US$35-50; 🅇) Also confusingly known as Coconut House, this charming

SIEM REAP

hotel is beautifully finished in local materials. Upstairs rooms generally have a better perspective than those downstairs, but it is worth paying extra for the large suites.

Pavillon Indochine (Map pp136-38; ☎ 012 849681; www.pavillon-indochine.com; r US$25-33, bungalows US$25; 🅇) The closest guesthouse to the temples of Angkor, this charming property has tasteful rooms with Chinese and Khmer furnishings and an attractive ambience. A bar and restaurant are attached.

Peace of Angkor Villa (Map pp136-38; ☎ 760475; www.peaceofangkor.com; r US$15-35; 🅇) Set in a spacious modern villa, this English-run place has neat rooms and plenty of photographs adorning the walls and corridors. The owners also operate an adventurous programme of tours.

Top End

Most of the hotels in this range levy an additional 10% government tax, and sometimes an extra 10% for service. Breakfast is included though, so there is no need to head off to the market for a baguette. Competition in this sector is starting to bring prices down, although booking through a travel agent can save considerable money on the walk-in rate and includes taxes. It is essential to book ahead at most of these places from November through to March.

Grand Hotel d'Angkor (Map pp116-17; ☎ 963888; www.raffles-grandhoteldangkor.com; s/d US$310/360; 🅇 🖵 🅡) For those with a sense of history, this hotel is hard to beat, welcoming guests like Charlie Chaplin and Jackie Kennedy since 1929. Owned by the Raffles group, it is one of the most luxurious in town and in these sorts of opulent surroundings you can imagine what it was like to be a tourist in colonial days. The rooms are packed with

---

THE AUTHOR'S CHOICE

La Résidence d'Angkor (Map pp116-17; ☎ 963390; www.pansea-angkor.com; Ph Stung Siem Reap; r US$280; 🅿 🖳 🖳) Home to perhaps the most charming rooms in town, this classic wooden resort-hotel is luxurious while modest throughout, including a minimalist reception and an inviting central swimming pool. The huge rooms are ergonomically designed and open plan, including the best baths in town – Jacuzzi-sized and finished in marble.

---

five-star features, including elegant beds and claw- and ball-feet bathtubs, but you sometimes get the feeling the place takes itself too seriously, and service can be a little austere.

Victoria Angkor Hotel (Map pp116-17; ☎ 760428; www.victoriahotels-asia.com; s/d US$285/320; 🅿 🖳 🖳) To the uninitiated, this striking hotel looks like a colonial relic from the same era as its grand neighbour, but it only opened its doors in 2003. The refined lobby gives way to one of the nicest swimming pools in Siem Reap, set in a courtyard garden with terrace bar. The rooms are smart and well-equipped, but the bathtubs are on the small side for bigger *barang* (foreigners).

Amansara (Map pp116-17; ☎ 760333; www.amanresorts.com; s/d US$700/775; 🅿 🖳 🖳) The Aman chain is associated with ultimate indulgence wherever its hotels may be and Siem Reap is no exception. Set in the old guest villa of former Prince Sihanouk, the suites here are some of the largest rooms in town and face on to a small swimming pool. The architecture is very 1960s, including a striking circular restaurant. Rates include meals and a tour of Angkor by *remorque-moto* (trailer pulled by a motorcycle). It's undoubtedly nice, although not as striking as the chain's Indonesian resorts like Amanjiwo and Amankila.

FCC Angkor (Map pp116-17; ☎ 760280; www.fcccambodia.com; Pokambor Ave; s/d US$140/160; 🅿 🖳 🖳) For the flavour of Amansara without the price tag, this new boutique hotel is fast earning a following in Siem Reap. Designed to sit side by side with its elegant restaurant (p128), the rooms are stylish and minimalist but very comfortable. There's high-speed Internet access in every room, plus a black-

tiled swimming pool and attached spa for winding down.

Day Inn Angkor Resort (Map pp116-17; ☎ 760500; www.dayinnangkor.com; Ph Oum Khun; s/d US$80/90; 🅿 🖳 🖳) A new resort nestled in the backstreets behind the post office. All the rooms here are set around a verdant garden courtyard with a generously sized swimming pool. It's functional four-star comfort with some flourish, and the discounts often available here make it enticingly good value.

Shinta Mani (Map pp116-17; ☎ 761998; www.sanctuaryresorts.com/shintamani; Ph Oum Khun; s/d US$144/160; 🅿 🖳 🖳) Established as a training institute to prepare for the opening of its Hotel de la Paix (opposite) resort on Ph Sivatha, this hotel's 18 rooms feature elegant bathrooms and sleigh beds as planned at the new venture. Don't be put off by the exterior (very two-star hotelish), as the interior and spa are well-conceived. The restaurant has a good name around town.

Sofitel Royal Angkor (Map pp136-38; ☎ 964600; www.sofitel.com; Vithei Charles de Gaulle; s/d US$280/320; 🅿 🖳 🖳) The first five-star resort hotel to open its doors in Siem Reap, the Sofitel brings a touch of the Thai islands on the road to Angkor. The rooms are à la Sofitel style worldwide, but memorable moments include a lush lagoon swimming pool with a swim-up bar and a luxury spa.

Le Meridien Angkor (Map pp136-38; ☎ 963900; www.lemeridien.com; s/d US$290/310; 🅿 🖳 🖳) The closest of the major hotel resorts to the temples of Angkor, with an exterior that looks like a Far East fortress. However, cross the threshold and it's an oasis of comfort inside. Rooms include split-level bathrooms opening to the bedrooms, and all the five-star features. The swimming pool complex is very Romanesque and fun for kids, plus there's an authentic Italian restaurant.

Angkor Century Hotel (Map pp116-17; ☎ 963777; www.angkorcentury.com; Ph Sivatha; s/d US$220/235; 🅿 🖳 🖳) The rooms at this four-star hotel are more about function than flair, in keeping with the businesslike exterior, but the lagoon swimming pool and courtyard garden are impressive. It boasts a walk-in humidor for serious cigar smokers.

Angkoriana Hotel (Map pp116-17; ☎ 760274; www.angkorianahotel.com; r US$65-90; 🅿 🖳 🖳) One of the cheaper top-end options, the Angkoriana has a lively location on the road to Angkor. The rooms are finished to a fairly typical three-star standard, but the swimming pool and bar area are designed to make you want to stick around.

Angkor Village (Map pp116–17; ☎ 965561; www .angkorvilla█.com; r US$96–159; ❄ ▢ ▨) Famous beyond the borders of Cambodia as a haven of peace and tranquillity. The wooden bungalow rooms here are set around a recessed restaurant and ornately sculpted water gardens. While the rooms are very comfortable, the rates reflect ambience rather than amenities. The new **Angkor Village Resort** (Map pp136–38; ☎ 963561; Ph Phum Traeng; ▨), out towards Angkor, is now welcoming guests and includes a pool that winds its lazy way through the grounds like a river and larger rooms with separate shower and toilet. Book ahead.

Angkor Palace Spa Resort (Map pp136–38; ☎ 760511; www.angkorpalaceresort.com; s/d US$125/ 145; ❄ ▢ ▨) Bringing the beauty of a Balinese resort to Siem Reap, this hotel occupies a vast corner of Siem Reap just off the road to the airport, covering twice the area of the Sofitel. The dramatic wooden lobby sets the tone for a stylish place that has one of the largest swimming pools in town. Rooms are also generous and include inviting open-plan bathrooms and classic beds. The rates are great value compared with some of the five-star competition.

La Maison d'Angkor (Map pp136–38; ☎ 965045; www .lamaisondangkor.com; NH6 west; r US$55–70; ❄ ▢ ▨) This attractive garden resort had just opened its doors when we were in town. The whitewashed bungalows are set around a seductive swimming pool and have inviting double beds but no twins as yet. Rooms include TV, fridge and a safe.

Damnak Angkor Village (Map pp136–38; ☎ 760032; www.damnakangkor.com; s/tw/tr US$90/100/115; ❄ ▢ ▨) A small resort with plenty of character, this place is tucked away down a side road on the way to the airport, north of NH6 west. There is an element of Angkor Village (above) here, with wood trim and tasteful furnishings all around.

Lotus Angkor Hotel (Map pp136–38; ☎ 965555; www .lotusangkor.com; r US$80–90; ❄ ▢ ▨) One of the newest hotels along the airport road. The rooms here are well furnished with wooden floors and smart bathrooms. It's popular with tour groups thanks to generous rates, and the swimming pool is a healthy size for exercise.

Other top-end hotels due to open soon include: the **Royal Angkor Resort** (Map pp136–38; NH6 west), constructed as a near copy of the venerable Hotel Le Royal in Phnom Penh; and **Hotel de la Paix** (Map pp116–17; www.sanctuaryresorts .com/delapaix; Ph Sivatha), part of the Sanctuary Resorts group.

EATING

The restaurant scene in Siem Reap has evolved at a dizzying pace and there is now something from every corner of the globe on dining tables around town, as well as the traditional taste of Cambodian cuisine. Many of the more established restaurants have been overrun by tour groups in recent years, making dining quite an impersonal experience, but the food remains good.

Some of the budget guesthouses have good menus offering a selection of local dishes and Western meals; while it's all too easy to get into the habit of ordering in-house, it hardly counts as the full Siem Reap experience.

Several of the midrange hotels and all the top-end places have restaurants, some of which warrant an individual listing in this section. When it comes to the luxury palaces and their gastronomic (by Cambodian standards astronomically priced) buffets, the Sofitel Royal Angkor still leads the pack, as you might expect from a French-run chain, but the Victoria Hotel also has a good reputation. For details on dinner and a performance of classical dance, as offered at several hotels and restaurants around town, see the Entertainment section (p129).

For more on the lunch options available in and around Angkor, see the boxed text on p144.

Khmer

Amok (Map pp116–17; ☎ 012 800309; The Alley; mains US$3–4) Named in honour of Cambodia's national dish, and across the alley from Khmer Kitchen Restaurant, Amok is a small, stylish restaurant with a big personality.

Arun Restaurant (Map pp116–17; ☎ 964227; mains US$2–3) Serving a popular selection of Khmer and Asian dishes, long-running Arun is one of the few local Khmer places not to have been inundated by tour groups. Fish with ginger is an old favourite here. Arun is north of NH6 east.

THE AUTHOR'S CHOICE

Khmer Kitchen Restaurant (Map pp116–17; ☎ 964154; The Alley; mains US$2–3) Tucked away down the up-and-coming alley situated between Bar St and Psar Chaa, this is a friendly little hole in the wall with a tasty range of Khmer and Thai dishes. Try the *mussaman* curries which are a hearty feed for US$2.50. Tables spill out into the street and recent customers include a certain Mick Jagger.

Bayon Restaurant (Map pp116–17; ☎ 012 855219; Ph Wat Bo; mains US$2–4) This huge restaurant caters primarily to tour groups, but has a deserved reputation for tasty and authentic dishes. Set around an inner courtyard, this place has slick service, as staff are used to dealing with dozens at a time.

Samapheap Restaurant (Map pp116–17; Ph Stung Siem Reap; mains US$2–5) A typical garden restaurant complete with twinkling fairy lights; the range of food here is some of the best in town. The seafood dishes with fresh green peppercorns are deservedly popular. Trouble is, all the tour companies know this. The trick is to come later when the groups have headed home, or to ask for a garden pavilion.

Banteay Srei Restaurant (Map pp136–38; NH6 west; mains US$2–4) This local place has a breezy garden to dine in and is more popular with Khmers than foreigners. Authentic Khmer cuisine also means plenty of *prahoc*, so watch out if fermented fish paste is not your thing!

Café Indochine (Map pp116–17; Ph Sivatha; mains US$4–7) Set in an elegant traditional villa on the main drag, this restaurant offers a blend of Asian and European flavours. The Khmer food is international more than authentic, but it's all about ambience here.

Madame Butterfly (Map pp136–38; ☎ 016 909607; NH6 west; mains US$4–8) Hidden away from the bustle of the airport road in an old wooden house hemmed in by vegetation, this Khmer restaurant has oodles of character. It offers a fusion of Asian cuisines in exotic surroundings. It's often busy with groups, but there are small tables on the veranda.

Viroth's Restaurant (Map pp116–17; ☎ 016 951800; Ph Wat Bo; mains US$3–6) Formerly occupying the Angkor Café, the owners have found strength in adversity and opened this charming garden restaurant in the east of town. Delicious Khmer food in a sophisticated setting suggests a bright future.

When it comes to cheaper Khmer eats, Psar Chaa has plenty of food stalls with signs and menus in English, and these are becoming increasingly lively, atmospheric places for a local meal at local-ish prices. Some dishes are on display, others are cooked to order, but nothing costs much more than US$1. There is another gaggle of inexpensive food stalls just north of the royal bridge on the east bank of the river, plus a long stretch of night stalls on Ph Sivatha, just north of the New Central Market. Alternatively, ask your driver for recommendations of the best stalls or holes in the walls, as these guys eat on the cheap every day.

Thai

Chivit Thai (Map pp116–17; ☎ 012 830761; 130 Ph Wat Bo; mains US$2–4) This is possibly the most atmospheric restaurant in town for Thai cuisine, as it is set in a green garden under traditional wooden pavilions. You can choose between floor dining or table dining and then spice up your life with some hot Thai favourites.

Sawasdee Restaurant (Map pp116–17; ☎ 012 983510; Ph Wat Bo; mains US$2–4) Sawasdee is a reliable stop for authentic Thai food, including tasty fish cakes and buzzing curries.

Krua Thai Restaurant (Map pp136–38; ☎ 963677; mains US$3–6) This new Thai restaurant is a little way out of town on an up-and-coming strip near Angkor Conservation. Choose between the wooden house and the flourishing garden for dining and don't forget the bargain breakfasts if you happen to be passing this way in the morning.

THE AUTHOR'S CHOICE

Dead Fish Tower (Map pp116–17; Ph Sivatha; mains US$2–4) Set in an incredible multilevel structure that looks like a cross between a barn and a big club, this is a fun place to get a flavoursome feed. Floor dining and tree-trunk tables are the go and the Thai teasers on the menu are extensive. They promise '…we don't serve dog, cat, rat or worm', so bad luck if you like any of those!

Vietnamese

Soup Dragon (Map pp116-17; ☎ 964933; Bar St; Vietnamese mains US$1-3, Western mains US$4-6) Hit the ground floor for classic Asian breakfasts like *pho* (Vietnamese rice-noodle soup) at 2500r, just the recipe for traipsing the temples. Upstairs is an upmarket restaurant with a huge menu of Asian and international dishes. The spicy fish in clay pot is divine and there's homemade ice cream to wrap things up. If you feel like a warm-up or a wind down, head for the rooftop bar (it donates 7% of its takings to Angkor Children's Hospital).

Japanese

Ginga (Map pp136-38; ☎ 963366; mains US$6-15) One of Phnom Penh's best known Japanese restaurants now has a branch in Siem Reap, opposite the stadium, that does steady business with tour groups from the homeland. A slice of Sapporo, but at a price.

Sanctuary 36.5°C (Map pp116-17; ☎ 964282; Psar Chaa; sets from US$5) A small Japanese restaurant opposite the old market. The bento boxes are good value for those in the market for sashimi or the like. It's more welcoming and less formal than upmarket Ginga.

Indian

Taj Mahal (Map pp116-17; ☎ 963353; Psar Chaa; mains US$2-5) This is one of the best Indian restaurants in town, with a serious subcontinental selection to satisfy seasoned curry lovers. The thalis (set meals) are good value for those who can't make up their mind.

Little India Restaurant (Map pp116-17; ☎ 012 652398; Psar Chaa; mains US$2-4) The oldest Indian in town – that's the restaurant, not the owner – the food here is consistently good, with its fair share of vegetarian options.

International

Red Piano (Map pp116-17; ☎ 963240; mains US$3-5) This popular Siem Reap institution, northwest of Psar Chaa, now has a commanding balcony overlooking downtown Siem Reap and plenty of space for diners to relax. The menu has a bit for everyone, with some Khmer dishes and a solid selection from beyond, plus it's a popular pub with its famous 'Tomb Raider' cocktail. The recently renovated Red Piano guesthouse (p122) is situated nearby down a quiet side street.

Balcony Café (Map pp116-17; mains US$1-6) Diagonally opposite the Red Piano restaurant

is another grand old building, housing the Balcony. The menu includes some power shakes and a small selection of Khmer dishes and Western snacks, but there's no alcohol served – that's almost commercial suicide in a town like this. Still, 20% of profits go to rural development, so forgive and forget.

Tell Restaurant (Map pp116-17; ☎ 63289; Ph Sivatha; mains US$1-6; ❄) One of the few air-con restaurants in town, something you may learn to appreciate if you are here in the hot season. The menu includes good-value Asian eats and some more-expensive Central European dishes. Big portions.

Kampuccino Pizza (Map pp116-17; ☎ 012 835762; mains US$2-6) This popular restaurant, northeast of Psar Chaa, has been around a while and it's expanded along the street thanks to an international menu with something from every corner of the globe. There's also good Khmer grub, like chicken with ginger.

Continental Café (Map pp116-17; ☎ 963723; mains US$3-6) Occupying a handsome building on the riverfront northeast of Psar Chaa, this restaurant-bar has an eclectic menu, including a selection from Cambodia, Thailand and Indonesia, as well as popular pizzas. A quiet retreat these days.

Le Gecko Mayonnaise (Map pp116-17; mains US$2-4) For those who like their crepes, this is the place to come, with a solid selection of savoury pancakes and sweet treats. Located north of Psar Chaa.

Ecstatic Pizza (Map pp116-17; ☎ 011 928531; mains US$3-6) For one of the better pizzas in town, head to this place near Psar Chaa, but remember, Ecstatic is more than a name – it's pizza à la ganja, which could put a grin as wide as the insane grin of the restaurant's logo on your face! Note, pizzas only include ganja if you ask for it!

TRAINING RESTAURANTS

There are several training schools in town striving to build the capacity of disadvantaged rural Cambodian teenagers by offering a ticket into the tourism industry. If you dine at these places, it gives the trainees a good opportunity to hone their skills with real customers.

Sala Bai (Map pp116-17; salabaiadmin@online.com.kh; set lunch Mon-Fri US$5) This school trains housekeepers, kitchen staff, receptionists and restaurant staff. It offers a small set menu daily and a few hotel rooms upstairs for those who want to give the project more support.

CVSG Training Restaurant (Map pp116-17; Ph Wat Bo; mains US$1-2) Run by the Japanese Cambodia Village Support Group (CVSG), children working here are orphans or have disabled parents. Profits go towards CVSG projects like drilling water wells. The set up is more basic than the others, but the food is authentic Khmer and very tasty.

École de Tourism Paul Dubrule (Map pp136-38; ☎ 963672; NH6 west; set lunch Tue-Fri US$6) Set in the refined surroundings of the Paul Dubrule Hotel and Tourism School, the set lunches here are excellent value, with three courses of international-standard cuisine. Paul Dubrule is one of the co-founders of the Accor hotel group, which includes the Sofitel, so the standards are very high!

Pissa Italiana (Map pp116-17; ☎ 012 440382; Bar St; pizzas US$3-7) This place was just opening when we were in town and promised to deliver authentic Italian, as the owner worked for the Sofitel Royal Angkor's pizza and pasta pub, Wayfarers.

FCC Angkor (Map pp116-17; ☎ 760280; mains US$4-10) Bringing the FCC touch to Siem Reap, this refined restaurant and bar is set in a beautiful building from the '60s, with the newly built hotel (p124) nearby. Diners are welcomed with a reflective pool and outdoor bar, while upstairs in the bar and restaurant proper the menu includes a serious range of Asian and international food. There's a daily set menu at US$10.

La Noria Guesthouse (Map pp116-17; ☎ 964242; mains US$3-6) The elevated, all-wood restaurant at this guesthouse (p122) offers a fine blend of Khmer and French cuisine, including delicious brochettes. The restaurant offers a shadow puppet show on Wednesday evenings and some of the $12 set-dinner fee is donated to a charity supporting local children.

Self-Catering

The markets are well stocked with fruit and fresh bread. For more-substantial treats like cheese and chocolate, try the local supermarkets. Eating in the market usually works out cheaper than self-catering, but some folks like to make up a picnic for longer days on the road.

Try these:

Angkor Market (Map pp116-17; Ph Sivatha) A new arrival in town, the market is under the same ownership as Bayon Market in Phnom Penh, so it has an excellent supply of international goodies.

Starmart (Map pp116-17; Caltex Starmart, NH6 west) Has a good selection of imports.

DRINKING

Siem Reap is really rockin' these days, a big change from just a few years ago when there were no real bars. One street now has so many drinking holes that it has earned the nickname Bar St and we are happy to go with that given the lack of street names in town! It is definitely worth hitting the bars at least once – each place has its own character, making it prime pub crawl territory.

Many of the bars here have happy hours, but so do some of the fancier hotels, which is a good way to sample the high life even if you are not staying at those places. Some of the best are the Elephant Bar (Map pp116–17) at Grand Hotel d'Angkor (p123), with happy hour from 4pm to 8pm when most drinks are two-for-one; L'Explorateur (Map pp116–17) at Victoria Angkor Hotel (p124), which kicks off late from 9pm to 11pm and is also two-for-one; and FCC Angkor (p124), with its Brunswick pro pool table, with happy hour from 5pm to 7pm.

Angkor What? (Map pp116-17; Bar St) One of the first, and still one of the most popular bars in town. This hole in the wall heaves from 9pm most nights and stays open until the last person leaves. Sorted sounds and a bulging bar keep the punters happy and a small slice of the profits supports the Angkor Children's Hospital, so drinking here helps someone's liver (if not your own).

Temple Bar (Map pp116–17; Bar St) Laterite stone and pediments give the exterior a temple feel, but the only worshipping going on here is 'all hail the ale'. Pavement tables, a generous happy hour from 4pm to 9pm with buy-two-get-one-free and some alternative rock have quickly earned it a loyal following.

Buddha Lounge (Map pp116–17; Bar St) Opposite the Temple and in a similar vein, the Buddha Lounge brings a touch of the Heart of Darkness to town, as the owner used to work in the famous Phnom Penh bar of that name (see p101). Spiritual décor and spirited drinks should bring success.

Linga Bar (Map pp116–17; The Alley) Siem Reap's first and currently only gay bar in town welcomes all-comers with a laid-back lounge look that wouldn't seem out of place in any major city. A cracking cocktail list, tapas tasters on the small menu and dance beats are helping to spread the word.

Molly Malone's (Map pp116–17; Bar St) This Irish pub brings a bit of the Emerald Isle to homesick Irish (and Brits and everyone else for whom Irish bars have become institutions!) in Siem Reap. Big bar menu, Guinness in cans and the word is that draught is soon on its way…

Ivy Bar (Map pp116–17; Psar Chaa) This well-known long-running English bar has recently relocated up the road, offering a spacious and sophisticated setting in which to take a drink at any time of day. The international bar menu is one of the best in town.

Laundry Bar (Map pp116–17; Psar Chaa) One of the few places to cut some dance moves in Siem Reap, Laundry is lavishly decorated and low lit, setting the scene for the late shift. It's busy at weekends or when they have guest DJs. This is definitely not a place to bring your dirty undies.

Abacus (Map pp116–17; near Ph Sivatha) Generating a buzz around town as the first complete dining, drinking and dancing establishment in town, this classy wooden villa is set in a spacious garden, giving it the feel of Balinese-style bar. A huge bar and lively owners keep customers on their toes.

Butterfly Garden Bar (Map pp116–17; admission US$1; ☺ 9am–5pm) The tropical garden here is home to hundreds of live butterflies flitting about under a huge net. It's a quiet spot in which to pass the time when it's hot, and the small menu includes drinks and international dishes.

Martini (Map pp116–17; Wat Dam Nak area) Nothing to do with its namesake in Phnom Penh (p102), this is probably the most popular Khmer nightclub in town, with a large beer garden and a dark, dark disco. Try some *rom vong*, the popular Cambodian dancing that involves everyone gliding around in circles and flapping their arms dementedly. We say everyone, but we mean foreigners – Khmers carry themselves with genuine grace.

ENTERTAINMENT

Several restaurants and hotels offer cultural performances during the evening, and for many visitors such shows offer the only opportunity to see Cambodian classical dance. While they may be tourist traps and nowhere near as sophisticated as a performance of the Royal Ballet in Phnom Penh, to the untrained eye it is nonetheless graceful and alluring. All prices include a buffet meal.

The most atmospheric show is at **Apsara Theatre** (Map pp116–17; admission US$22) at Angkor Village (p125), as the setting is a striking wooden pavilion finished in the style of a wat. Grand Hotel d'Angkor (p123) has an attractive performance house on the banks of Stung Siem Reap, opposite the hotel – admission is US$22.

Tonlé Sap Restaurant (Map pp116–17; ☎ 963388; NH6 west; show US$12; ☺ 7.30pm) offers a large, impersonal show that pulls in the big tour groups who chow down on Khmer and sukiyaki, as well as Malay, Japanese and European dishes.

There is also a weekly performance of shadow puppetry at La Noria Guesthouse (opposite).

Beatocello (Map pp136–38; www.beatocello.com), better known as Dr Beat Richner, performs original and Bach cello compositions on Saturday at 7.15pm at Jayavarman VII Children's Hospital . Entry is free, but donations are welcome as they will help the hospital in its mission to give free medical treatment to Siem Reap's children.

SHOPPING

Much of what is seen on sale in the markets of Siem Reap can also be purchased from children and vendors throughout the temple area. Some people get fed up with the endless sales pitches as they navigate the ancient wonders, while others enjoy the banter and a chance to interact with Cambodian people.

Whatever your view, it may be an idea to buy at least some items out at the temples, as many of the families there are descendants of the original inhabitants of Angkor and arguably have more right than anyone to make a living from these spectacular monuments.

It's often children out selling, and some visitors will argue that they should be at school instead. However, most do attend school at least half of the time, if their families can afford it.

Items touted at the temples include postcards, T-shirts, temple bas-relief rubbings, curious musical instruments, ornamental knives and crossbows – the latter may raise a few eyebrows with customs should you try to take one home! Bargain, but not too hard, and remember, you can't bargain at the fixed price shops in town.

When it comes to shopping in town, the Psar Chaa market (Map pp116–17) is well stocked with anything you may want to buy in Cambodia, and lots you don't. Silverware, silk, wood carvings, stone carvings, Buddhas, paintings, rubbings, notes and coins, T-shirts, table mats...the list goes on. There are bargains to be had if you haggle patiently and humorously. Do not buy old stone carvings that vendors claim are from Angkor. Whether or not they are real, buying these artefacts serves only to encourage their plunder and they will usually be confiscated by customs. Buy modern replicas and bury them in the garden for a few months – they will soon look the same.

Artisans d'Angkor (Map pp116-17; ☎ 380354; www.artisansdangkor.com) Sells high-quality souvenirs and its profits go to a cultural rehabilitation project. For more information see p118.

Made in Cambodia (Map pp116-17; opposite Psar Chaa) This is another shop with a higher purpose, specialising in quality silk products such as wallets, handbags, photo albums and the like. All profits are ploughed back into training and employment for members of Cambodia's disabled community.

Tabitha Cambodia (Map pp116-17; ☎ 760650; Ph Sivatha) Along similar lines to Made in Cambodia, with a beautiful range of silk scarves, cushion covers and throws to choose from. The proceeds go towards Tabitha projects like house building and well drilling.

Rajana (Map pp116-17; Bar St) Produces quirky wooden and metalware objects, silver jewellery and handmade cards, as well as selling

local condiments such as lemongrass, pepper and coffee. The organisation promotes fair trade and employment opportunities for Cambodians.

There are now lots of private handicraft, silk and souvenir shops in Siem Reap:

Senteurs d'Angkor (Map pp116-17; ☎ 964801) Opposite Psar Chaa; has an eclectic collection of silk, carvings, traditional beauty products and spices.

Tara & Kys Art Gallery (Map pp116-17; near Psar Chaa) Has some interesting artwork, postcards and T-shirts featuring that icon of Angkor, Jayavarman VII.

Quality photos can be printed cheaply in Siem Reap, and digital shots downloaded onto CD. The best of the photographic shops is **Siem Reap Thmei Photo** (Map pp116-17; Ph Wat Bo), a large Fuji lab.

GETTING THERE & AWAY
Air

There are direct international flights to Bangkok in Thailand; Vientiane, Luang Prabang and Pakse in Laos; Ho Chi Minh City (Saigon) and Hanoi in Vietnam; Kuala Lumpur in Malaysia; and Singapore. For more information on international flights to and from Siem Reap, see the Transport chapter (p288).

Domestic links are currently limited to Phnom Penh, which is served by Siem Reap Airways (US$65/105 one way/return), Royal Phnom Penh Airways (US$55/100) and President Airlines (US$65/95). Demand for the limited number of flights is high during peak season, so book as far in advance as possible.

Airline offices around town:

Bangkok Airways (Map pp136-38; ☎ 380191; NH6 west)
Lao Airlines (Map pp136-38; ☎ 963283; NH6 west)
Malaysia Airlines (☎ 964136; Siem Reap Airport)
President Airlines (Map pp136-38; ☎ 963887; NH6 west)
Siem Reap Airways (Map pp136-38; ☎ 380192; NH6 west)
Vietnam Airlines (Map pp136-38; ☎ 964488; NH6 west)

Boat

There are daily express boat services between Siem Reap with Phnom Penh (US$18 to US$25, five to six hours) and Battambang (US$15, three to eight hours depending on the season). The boat to Phnom Penh is a bit of a rip-off these days, given it is just as fast by road and about one-fifth the price. The Battambang trip is seriously scenic, but breakdowns are *very* common. See the

Phnom Penh (p105) and Battambang (p216) listings for more details.

Boats from Siem Reap leave from the Floating Village of Chong Kneas near Phnom Krom, 11km south of Siem Reap. The boats dock in different places at different times of the year; when the lake recedes in the dry season, both the port and floating village move with it. The worst time to arrive is May – the lake is extremely low at this time of year and exposes its clay base, which turns as slippery as ice once the rain starts.

Most of the guesthouses in town sell boat tickets. The boat companies tend to take it in turns to make the run between so don't be surprised if you end up on a different boat in each direction. Buying the ticket from your guesthouse usually includes a *moto* or minibus ride to the port. Otherwise, a *moto* out here costs about US$1. A taxi is more like US$5.

Bus, Car & Taxi

The road linking Siem Reap to Phnom Penh is now surfaced all the way, and aircon buses thunder up and down it daily. The road west to Sisophon, Thailand and Battambang is in a messy state in places and is served by some buses and plenty of share taxis.

There are several companies operating buses between Phnom Penh and Siem Reap and services depart between 6.30am and 12.30pm. The average cost of a ticket is US$4, depending on the company. Tickets can be bought at guesthouses or ticket booths in town. Leading companies include **Capitol Transport** (Map pp116-17; ☎ 963883), **GST** (Map pp116-17; ☎ 012 777442; Ph Sivatha), **Neak Krohorm** (Map pp116-17; ☎ 964924) located opposite Psar Chaa, and **Hour Lean** (Map pp116-17; ☎ 760103; Ph Sivatha), the latter offering the newest buses. **Mekong Express** (☎ 963662) offers a slightly more upmarket service with buses departing for Phnom Penh at 7.30am and 12.30pm. The services include an indrive hostess and a snack, and cost US$6. All buses now arrive and depart from the taxi park, about one kilometre east of Psar Leu on NH6 towards Phnom Penh.

Share taxis are a faster way to travel between Siem Reap and the capital. They can usually cover the distance in just four hours and charge about US$5 per person or US$35 for the whole car.

The 152km run to Thailand can take as little as three hours, but in the wet season you should double that and add some more on an off day. Buses through to Bangkok cost about US$10 to US$12 and can take from 10 to 14 hours. It is faster to go your own way. Share taxis run to Poipet (15,000r per seat, US$25 for the car, three to four hours) for those travelling independently, and to Sisophon (10,000r), for connections to Battambang. For more on the overland trip between Bangkok and Siem Reap, including the 'scam bus', see p293.

Share taxis and pick-ups depart from the taxi park about 2km out of town on NH6 towards Phnom Penh.

GETTING AROUND

For more on transport around Angkor, see p148. Following are insights on the most common forms of transport used for getting around Siem Reap.

To/From the Airport

Siem Reap International Airport is 7km from the town centre. Many of the hotels and guesthouses in Siem Reap have a free airport pick-up service if you have booked in advance. Official taxis are available outside the terminal for US$5. A trip to the city centre on the back of a *moto* will cost US$1.50.

Bicycle

Some of the guesthouses around town hire out bicycles, as do a few shops around Psar Chaa, usually for US$1 to US$2 a day.

Car & Motorcycle

Most hotels and guesthouses can organise car hire for the day, with a going rate of US$20 to US$25. Upmarket hotels may charge considerably more.

Foreigners are forbidden to rent motorcycles in and around Siem Reap. If you want to get around on your own motorcycle, you need to hire one in Phnom Penh and ride it to Siem Reap.

Moto

Moto are available at daily rates of US$6 to US$8. The average cost for a short trip within town is 1000r, more to places strung out along the roads to Angkor or the airport. It is not normally necessary to negotiate in advance, but it is wise at night or for those staying at luxury hotels.

Remorque-moto

These sweet little motorcycles with carriages are a nice way for couples to get about Siem Reap, although drivers like to inflate the prices. Try for US$1 on trips around town, although drivers may charge US$1.50 for a trip to the edges of town at night. Prices rise if you pile on in numbers!

AROUND SIEM REAP

BIRD SANCTUARY & BIOSPHERE OF PREK TOAL

ជំរកបក្សីព្រែកទាល

Prek Toal is one of three biospheres on Tonlé Sap lake, and the establishment of its bird sanctuary makes Prek Toal the most worthwhile and straightforward to visit. It is an ornithologist's fantasy, with a significant number of rare breeds gathered in one small area, including the huge lesser and greater adjutant storks, the milky stork and the spot-billed pelican.

Visitors during the dry season (December to May) will find the concentration of birds like something out of a Hitchcock film. As water starts to dry up elsewhere, the birds congregate here. Serious twitchers know that the best time to see birds is early morning or late afternoon and this means a very early start or an overnight at Prek Toal's environment office, where there are basic beds for US$7.

Getting to the sanctuary under your own steam requires you to take a 20-minute *moto* (US$1 or so) or taxi (US$5) ride to the floating village of Chong Kneas and then a boat to the environment office (around US$35 return, one hour each way). From here, a small boat (US$20 including a guide) will take you into the sanctuary, which is about one hour beyond.

Binoculars are available for those who don't carry their own, and sunscreen and head protection are essential, as it can get very hot in the dry season. For real enthusiasts, it may be best to head out of Siem Reap after lunch, to get to the sanctuary at around 4pm for an afternoon viewing. Stay overnight at the environment office,

and view the birds in the morning before returning to Siem Reap for lunch. The guides are equipped with booklets with the bird names in English, but they speak little English themselves.

One company in Siem Reap offers organised day-trip tours to help promote the benefits to the Cambodian people of responsible tourism, and financially contribute to the conservation of the area. **Osmose** (☎ 012 832812; osmose@bigpond.com.kh) runs day trips that cost US$60 per person with a minimum group of four. Tours offered by this nonprofit agency include transportation, entrance fees, guides, breakfast, lunch and water, making it a very reasonable deal.

There is another bird sanctuary, **Ang Trapeng Thmor Reserve**, just across the border in Banteay Meanchey Province in the Phnom Srok region, about 100km from Siem Reap. It's one of only two places in the world where it is possible to see the extremely rare sarus crane, as depicted on bas-reliefs at Bayon. These grey-feathered birds have immensely long legs and striking red heads. Take the road to Sisophon for about 72km before turning north. The reserve is based around a reservoir created by forced labour during the Khmer Rouge regime, and facilities are very basic.

FLOATING VILLAGE OF CHONG KNEAS

ភូមិបណ្ដែតចុងឃ្នាស

This famous floating village is now extremely popular with visitors wanting a break from the temples, and is an easy enough excursion for visitors wanting a break from the temples; it's simple to arrange yourself. Visitors arriving by fast boat get a preview, as the floating village is near Phnom Krom, where the boat docks. It is very scenic in the warm light of early morning or late afternoon and can be combined with a view of the sunset from the hilltop temple of Phnom Krom (see p171 for more details). The downside is that tour groups tend to take over, and boats end up chugging up and down the channels in convoy.

Visitors should also check out the **Gecko Environment Centre** (⊙ 8.30am-5.30pm), part of the floating village. It has displays on flora and fauna of the area, as well as information on communities living around the lake.

The village moves depending on the season and you will need to rent a boat to get around it properly. A local cooperative has fixed boat prices at US$10 per person to visit the floating village, a touch on the cheeky side for what is a short trip. If you are travelling by boat between Phnom Penh and Siem Reap you get to see it for free anyhow.

To get to the floating village from Siem Reap costs US$1 or so by *moto* each way (more if the driver waits), or US$5 by taxi. This trip takes 20 minutes.

FLOODED FOREST OF KOMPONG PHHLUK

កំពុងភ្លុក

More memorable than Chong Kneas, but also much harder to reach, is the flooded forest of Kompong Phhluk, alongside an other-worldly village built on stilts. The flooded forest is inundated every year when the lake rises to take the Mekong's overflow, and as the lake drops the petrified trees are revealed. Exploring this area by wooden dugout is very atmospheric. Further inland from the lake is the village of Kompong Phhluk itself, where most of the houses are built on stilts of about 6m or 7m high, looking like it has come straight out of a film set.

There are two ways to get to Kompong Phhluk. One is to come via the floating village of Chong Kneas, where a boat (one hour) can be arranged for about US$25, and the other is to come via the small town of Roluos by a combination of road (about US$5 by *moto*) and boat (US$5). All said the road/boat route will take about 1½ hours but it depends on the season, sometimes it's more by road, sometimes more by boat!

Temples of Angkor

Prepare for divine inspiration! The temples of Angkor, capital of Cambodia's ancient Khmer empire, are the perfect fusion of creative ambition and spiritual devotion. The Cambodian god-kings of old each strove to better their ancestors in size, scale and symmetry, culminating in the world's largest religious building – Angkor Wat, and one of the world's weirdest – the Bayon. The hundreds of temples surviving today are but the sacred skeleton of the vast political, religious and social centre of an empire that stretched from Burma to Vietnam, a city that, at its zenith, boasted a population of one million when London was a scrawny town of 50,000. The houses, public buildings and palaces were constructed of wood – now long decayed – because the right to dwell in structures of brick or stone was reserved for the gods.

'The temples of Angkor are the heart and soul of the Kingdom of Cambodia'

The temples of Angkor are the heart and soul of the Kingdom of Cambodia, a source of inspiration and national pride to all Khmers as they struggle to rebuild their lives after years of terror and trauma. Today, the temples are a point of pilgrimage for all Cambodians, and no traveller to the region will want to miss their extravagant beauty.

It is easy to spend as long as a week at Angkor, seeing the temples at a leisurely pace, returning to the principal attractions several times to see them at different times of day, and taking in newly emerging sites further afield. However, many travellers feel that four or five days is the ideal length of time to spend at Angkor. This is just about long enough to fit in all the highlights of the Angkor area, but even with only two days at your disposal you can pack in a lot (providing you make some early starts). One day at Angkor? Sacrilege! Don't even consider it.

HIGHLIGHTS

Must see temple of Angkor activities:

- Stare in awe at the mother of all temples, **Angkor Wat** (p150)
- Succumb to the enigmatic smiles of the 216 giant faces of the **Bayon** (p156), Angkor's strangest temple
- Experience nature running riot at the mysterious ruin of **Ta Prohm** (p162), the original *Tomb Raider* temple
- Marvel at the exquisite carvings adorning the tiny temple of **Banteay Srei** (p172), the finest seen at Angkor
- Venture into the jungles of Cambodia to discover the River of a Thousand Lingas at **Kbal Spean** (p174)

HISTORY
Early Years

The Angkorian period spans more than 600 years from AD 802 to 1432, during which the temples of Angkor were built and the Khmer empire consolidated its position as one of the great powers of Southeast Asia. This era encompasses periods of decline and revival, and wars with rival powers in Vietnam, Thailand and Myanmar. This brief history deals only with the periods that produced the temples we see at Angkor.

The Angkorian period began with the rule of Jayavarman II (r 802–50). He was the first to unify Cambodia's competing kingdoms before the birth of Angkor. His court was situated at Phnom Kulen (p175), 40km northeast of Angkor Wat, and later at Roluos (p170; known then as Hariharalaya), 13km east of Siem Reap.

TOP TEN KINGS OF ANGKOR

A mind-numbing array of kings ruled the Khmer empire from the 9th century to the 14th century. Many of the names are difficult to pronounce for foreigners but all include *varman*, which means 'armour' or 'protector'. Forget the small fish and focus on the big fish in our guide to the most powerful kings of Angkor, the dates they reigned and their most important achievements:

- **Jayavarman II** (802–50) Founder of the Khmer empire in 802

- **Indravarman I** (877–89) Builder of the first *baray* (reservoir), and of Preah Ko and Bakong

- **Yasovarman I** (889–910) Moved the capital to Angkor and built Lolei and Phnom Bakheng

- **Jayavarman IV** (928–42) Usurper king who moved the capital to Koh Ker

- **Rajendravarman II** (944–68) Builder of Eastern Mebon, Pre Rup and Phimeanakas

- **Jayavarman V** (968–1001) Saw construction of Ta Keo and Banteay Srei

- **Suryavarman I** (1002–49) Expanded the empire to perhaps its greatest extent

- **Udayadityavarman II** (1049–65) Builder of the pyramid Baphuon and the Western Mebon

- **Suryavarman II** (1112–52) Legendary builder of Angkor Wat and Beng Mealea

- **Jayavarman VII** (1181–219) The king of kings, building Angkor Thom, Preah Khan and Ta Prohm

---

Jayavarman II set a precedent that became a feature of the Angkorian period and accounts for the staggering architectural productivity of the Khmers at this time. He established himself as a 'god-king' *(devaraja)* whose all-reaching power embodied the godlike qualities of Shiva. Shiva's dwelling place is the mythical Mt Meru. Thus Jayavarman built a 'temple-mountain' at Phnom Kulen, symbolising the holy mountain at the centre of the universe.

Indravarman I (r 877–89) is believed to have been a usurper, and probably inherited the mantle of god-king through conquest. He built a 6.5 sq km *baray* (reservoir) at Roluos and established Preah Ko (p170). The *baray* was the first stage of an irrigation system that, eventually, was to extensively water the lands around Angkor. But it also had religious significance as, according to legend, Mt Meru is flanked by lakes. As is often the case, necessity and symbolism dovetail nicely. Indravarman's final work was Bakong (p170), a pyramidal representation of Mt Meru.

'Jayavarman established himself as a "god-king"'

For some reason, Indravarman I's son Yasovarman I (r 889–910) looked further afield to celebrate his divinity and glory in a temple-mountain of his own. After building Lolei (p171) on an artificial island in the *baray* established by his father, he began work on the Bakheng, siting it on the hill known today as Phnom Bakheng (p163), a favoured spot for viewing the sunset over Angkor Wat (p150). A raised highway was constructed to connect Phnom Bakheng with Roluos, 16km to the southeast, and a large *baray* was formed to the east of Phnom Bakheng – it is now known as the Eastern Baray (p168) and has entirely silted up. Yasovarman also established the temple-mountains of Phnom Krom (p171) and Phnom Bok (p172).

After the death of Yasovarman I, power briefly shifted from the Angkor region to Koh Ker (p233), around 80km to the northeast of Angkor, under another usurper – Jayavarman IV (r 928–42). In 944 power returned again to Angkor under the leadership of Rajendravarman II (r 944–68), who built the Eastern Mebon (p168) and Pre Rup (p169). The rule of his son Jayavarman V (r 968–1001) produced the temples Ta Keo (p165) and Banteay Srei (p172), the latter built by a Brahman rather than the king.

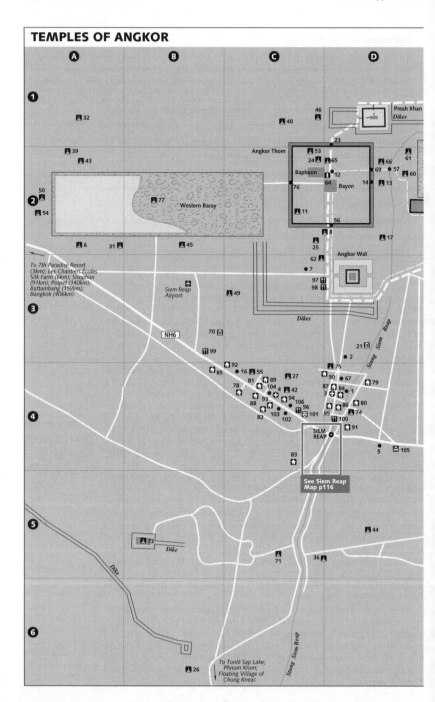

TEMPLES OF ANGKOR

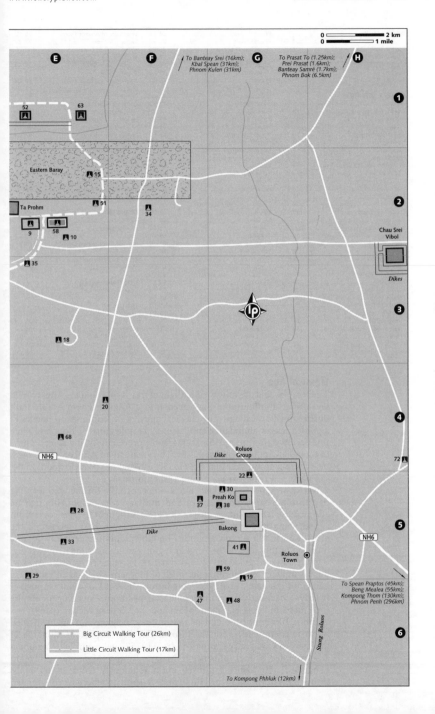

To Banteay Srei (16km);
Kbal Spean (31km);
Phnom Kulen (31km)

To Prasat To (1.25km);
Prei Prasat (1.6km);
Banteay Samré (1.7km);
Phnom Bok (6.5km)

0 — 2 km
0 — 1 mile

52

63

Eastern Baray

15

51

34

Ta Prohm

9

58

10

35

Chau Srei
Vibol

Dikes

18

20

68

NH6

Roluos
Group

Dike

22

72

30
Preah Ko

37

38

28

Bakong

33

Dike

41

Roluos
Town

NH6

29

59

19

To Spean Praptos (45km);
Beng Mealea (55km);
Kompong Thom (130km);
Phnom Penh (296km)

47

48

Stang Roluos

Big Circuit Walking Tour (26km)

Little Circuit Walking Tour (17km)

To Kompong Phhluk (12km)

Classical Age

The temples that are now the highlight of a visit to Angkor – Angkor Wat and those in and around the walled city of Angkor Thom – were built during the classical age. The classical appellation conjures up images of a golden age of abundance and leisurely temple construction, but while this period is marked by fits of remarkable productivity, it was also a time of turmoil, conquests and setbacks. The great city of Angkor Thom owes its existence to the fact that the old city of Angkor – which stood on the same site – was destroyed during a Cham invasion.

Suryavarman I (r 1002–49) was a usurper to the throne who won the day through strategic alliances and military conquests. Although he adopted the Hindu cult of the god-king, he is thought to have come from a Mahayana Buddhist background and may even have sponsored the growth of Buddhism in Cambodia. Buddhist sculpture certainly became more commonplace in the Angkor region during his time.

Little physical evidence of Suryavarman I's reign remains at Angkor, but his military exploits brought much of southern Thailand and southern Laos into the ambit of Angkorian control. His son Udayadityavarman II (r 1049–65) embarked on further military expeditions, extending the empire even more, building Baphuon (p159) and the Western Mebon (p169).

From 1066 until the end of the century, Angkor was again divided by various contenders for the throne. The first important monarch of this new era was Suryavarman II (r 1112–52), who unified Cambodia and extended Khmer influence to Malaya, Burma (Myanmar) and Siam (Thailand). He also set himself apart religiously from earlier kings through his devotion to the Hindu deity Vishnu, to whom he consecrated the largest and arguably most magnificent of all the Angkorian temples, Angkor Wat (p150).

The reign of Suryavarman II and the construction of Angkor Wat signifies one of the high-water marks of Khmer civilisation. However, there were signs that decline was waiting in the wings. It is thought that the hydraulic system of reservoirs and canals that supported the agriculture of Angkor had by this time been pushed beyond capacity, and was slowly starting to silt up due to overpopulation and deforestation. The construction of Angkor was a major strain on resources, and, on top of this, Suryavarman II led a disastrous campaign against the Dai Viet (Vietnamese) late in his reign.

In 1177 the Chams of southern Vietnam, then the Kingdom of Champa and long annexed by the Khmer empire, rose up and sacked Angkor. They burned the wooden city and plundered its wealth. Four years later Jayavarman VII (r 1181–219) struck back, emphatically driving the Chams out of Cambodia and reclaiming Angkor.

Jayavarman VII's reign has given scholars much to debate. It represents a radical departure from the reigns of his predecessors. For centuries the fount of royal divinity had reposed in the Hindu deity Shiva and, occasionally, Vishnu. Jayavarman VII, however, adopted Mahayana Buddhism and looked to Avalokiteshvara, the Buddha of Compassion, for patronage during his reign. In doing so he may well have been converting to a religion that already enjoyed wide popular support among his subjects. It may also be that the destruction of Angkor was such a blow to royal divinity that a new religious foundation was thought to be needed.

In his reign, Jayavarman VII embarked on a dizzying array of temple projects that centred on Baphuon, which was the site of the city destroyed by the Chams. Angkor Thom (p155), Jayavarman VII's new city, was surrounded by walls and a moat, which became another component of Angkor's complex irrigation system. The centrepiece of Angkor Thom was Bayon (p156), the temple-mountain studded with faces that, along with Angkor Wat, is the most famous of Angkor's temples. Other temples built during his reign include Ta Prohm (p162), Banteay Kdei (p165) and Preah Khan (p166). Further away, he rebuilt vast temple complexes such as Banteay Chhmar (p222) and Preah Khan (p231), making him by far the most prolific builder of Angkor's many kings.

'the construction of Angkor Wat signifies one of the high-water marks of Khmer civilisation'

He also embarked on a major public-works programme, building roads, schools and hospitals across the empire, drawing parallels with the might of the Roman empire. Remains of many of these roads and their magnificent bridges can still be seen across Cambodia today. Spean Praptos at Kompong Kdei, 60km southeast of Siem Reap on National Hwy 6 (NH6), is the most famous, but there are many more lost in the forest on the old Angkorian road from Beng Mealea to the great Preah Khan.

After the death of Jayavarman VII around 1219, the Khmer empire went into decline. The state religion reverted to Hinduism for a century or more and outbreaks of iconoclasm saw Buddhist sculpture adorning the Hindu temples vandalised or altered. The Thais sacked Angkor in 1351 and again with devastating efficiency in 1431. The Khmer court moved to Phnom Penh, only to return fleetingly to Angkor in the 16th century; in the meantime it was abandoned to pilgrims, holy men and the elements.

Angkor Rediscovered

The French 'discovery' of Angkor in the 1860s made an international splash and created a great deal of outside interest in Cambodia. But 'discovery', with all the romance it implied, was something of a misnomer.

When French explorer Henri Mouhot first stumbled across Angkor Wat it included a wealthy, working monastery with monks and slaves. Moreover, Portuguese travellers in the 16th century encountered Angkor, referring to it as the Walled City. A 17th-century Japanese pilgrim even drew a detailed plan of Angkor Wat, though he mistakenly recalled that he had seen it in India.

Still, it was the publication of *Voyage à Siam et dans le Cambodge* by Mouhot in 1868 that first brought Angkor to the public eye. Although the explorer himself made no such claims, by the 1870s he was being posthumously celebrated as the discoverer of the lost temple city of Cambodia. In fact, a French missionary known as Charles-Emile Bouillevaux had visited Angkor 10 years before Mouhot and had published his own account of his findings. It was roundly ignored. It was Mouhot's account, with its rich descriptions and tantalising pen-and-ink colour sketches of the temples, that turned the ruins into an international obsession.

From the time of Mouhot, Angkor became the target of financed French expeditions. A few individuals, such as John Thomson, a Scottish photographer who took the first photographs of the temples and was the first to posit the idea that the temples were symbolic representations of the mythical Mt Meru, managed to make their way to the region. For the most part, however, the temples were the preserve of French archaeological teams.

'the monuments of Angkor were left to the jungle for many centuries'

The first of these expeditions was led by Ernest Doudart de Lagrée, and its principal mission was to determine whether the Mekong River was navigable into China. Doudart de Lagrée died upstream in Yunnan, but not before taking his team on a detour to the temples of Angkor. The team assembled its findings at Angkor into *Voyage d'exploration en Indo-Chine*, which contained valuable archaeological detail.

Louis Delaporte, who had joined Doudart de Lagrée on the first mission, led the second expedition to Angkor. The aim was to produce plans of the monuments and return to France with examples of Angkorian art. Delaporte brought back some 70 pieces, and his sketches aroused the interest of some Parisian architects, who saw in the monuments of Angkor a bold clash of form and function. Architect Lucien Fournereau travelled to Angkor in 1887 and produced plans and meticulously executed cross-sections that were to stand as the best available until the 1960s.

In 1901, the **École Française d'Extrême-Orient** (EFEO; www.efeo.fr) began a long association with Angkor by funding an expedition to the Bayon. In 1907, Angkor, which had been under Thai control, was returned to Cambodia and the EFEO took responsibility for clearing and restoring the whole site. In the same year, the first tourists arrived in Angkor – an unprecedented 200 of them in three months. Angkor had been 'rescued' from the jungle and was assuming its place in the modern world.

ARCHAEOLOGY OF ANGKOR
Angkor Restored

With the exception of Angkor Wat, which was restored for use as a Buddhist shrine in the 16th century by the Khmer royalty, the monuments of Angkor were left to the jungle for many centuries. A large number of the monuments are made of sandstone, which tends to dissolve when in prolonged contact with dampness. Bat droppings took their toll, as did sporadic pilfering of sculptures and cut stones. In the case of some monuments, such as Ta Prohm, the jungle had stealthily waged an all-out invasion, and plant-life could only be removed at great risk to the structures it now supported in its web of roots.

TOP TEN BOOKS ON ANGKOR

Countless books on Angkor and the magical temples of Cambodia have been written over the years, but many of the older titles are either out of print or only available in French. More and more of these may be reissued in the coming years. However, in the meantime, plenty of new titles are in the pipeline, reflecting Angkor's rebirth as one of the world's cultural hotspots.

- *A Guide to the Angkor Monuments* (Maurice Glaize) – the definitive guide to Angkor, downloadable for free at www.theangkorguide.com

- *A Passage Through Angkor* (Mark Standen) – one of the best photographic records of the temples of Angkor

- *A Pilgrimage to Angkor* (Pierre Loti) – one of the most beautifully written books on Angkor, based on the author's 1910 journey

- *Angkor: an Introduction to the Temples* (Dawn Rooney) – probably the most popular contemporary guide available

- *Angkor Cities and Temples* (Claudes Jacques) – written by one of the foremost scholars on Angkor; a monumental work that has lovely photos

- *Angkor: Millennium of Glory* (various authors) – a fascinating introduction to the history, culture, sculpture and religion of the Angkor period

- *Angkor – Heart of an Asian Empire* (Bruno Dagens) – the story of the 'rediscovery' of Angkor, complete with lavish illustrations

- *Khmer Heritage in the Old Siamese Provinces of Cambodia* (Etienne Aymonier) – Aymonier journeyed through Cambodia in 1901 and visited many of the major temples

- *The Customs of Cambodia* (Chou Ta Kuan) – the account of a Chinese emissary who spent a year at Angkor in the late 13th century

- *Travels in Siam, Cambodia, Laos and Annam* (Henri Mouhot) – Mouhot was credited with 'rediscovering' Angkor, and this is his account of his adventures

---

Initial attempts to clear Angkor under the aegis of the EFEO were fraught with technical difficulties and theoretical disputes. On a technical front, the jungle tended to grow back as soon as it was cleared, and on a theoretical front, scholars debated the extent to which temples should be restored and whether later additions, such as Buddha images in Hindu temples, should be removed.

It was not until the late 1920s that a solution came along – anastylosis. This was the method the Dutch had used to restore Borobudur in Java. Put simply, it was a way of reconstructing monuments using the original materials and in keeping with the original form of the structure. New materials were permitted only where the originals could not be found, and were to be used discreetly. An example of this method can be seen on the right side of the causeway leading to the entrance of Angkor Wat – it is largely the result of French restoration work.

The first major restoration job was carried out on Banteay Srei in 1930. It was deemed such a success that many more extensive restoration projects were undertaken elsewhere around Angkor, culminating in the massive Angkor Wat restoration in the 1960s. Large cranes and earth-moving machines were brought in, and the operation was backed by a veritable army of surveying equipment.

The Khmer Rouge victory and Cambodia's subsequent slide into an intractable civil war resulted in far less damage to Angkor than many had assumed, as EFEO and Ministry of Culture teams had removed many of the statues from the temple sites for protection. Nevertheless, turmoil in

Cambodia resulted in a long interruption of restoration work, allowing the jungle to grow back and once again resume its assault on the monuments. The illegal trade of *objets d'art* on the world art market has also been a major threat to Angkor, although it is the more remote sites that have been targeted recently. Angkor has been under the jurisdiction of the UN Educational Scientific and Cultural Organisation (Unesco) since 1992 as a World Heritage site, and international and local efforts continue to preserve and reconstruct the monuments. In a sign of real progress, Angkor was removed from Unesco's endangered list in 2003.

However, many of Angkor's secrets remain to be discovered, as most of the work at the temples has concentrated on restoration efforts above the ground rather than archaeological surveys below. Underground is where the real story of Angkor and its people lies – the inscriptions on the temples give us only a partial picture of the gods to whom each structure was dedicated, and the kings who built them.

> 'The illegal trade of *objets d'art* on the world art market has also been a major threat to Angkor'

ARCHITECTURAL STYLES

From the time of the earliest Angkorian monuments at Roluos, Khmer architecture was continually evolving, often from the rule of one king to the next. Archaeologists therefore divide the monuments of Angkor into nine separate periods (see the boxed text, opposite), named after the foremost example of each period's architectural style.

To a certain extent, however, the evolution of Khmer architecture was the elaboration of a central theme: the idea of the temple-mountain, preferably set on a real mountain, but artificial if there weren't any mountains at hand. The earlier a temple was constructed the closer it adheres to this fundamental idea. Essentially, the mountain was represented by a blunt-topped tower mounted on a tiered base. At the summit was the central sanctuary, usually with an open door to the east, and three false doors at the remaining cardinal points of the compass.

By the time of the Bakheng period, this layout was being embellished. The summit of the central tower, for example, was crowned with five 'peaks', in a quincuncial arrangement – four cells at the points of the compass and one in the centre. Even Angkor Wat features this layout,

---

HIDDEN RICHES, POLITICAL HITCHES

Angkor Conservation is a Ministry of Culture compound on the banks of the Stung Siem Reap, about 400m east of the Sofitel Royal Angkor Hotel. It houses more than 5000 statues, *linga* (phallic symbols) and inscribed steles, stored here to protect them from the wanton looting that has blighted hundreds of sites around Angkor. The finest statuary is hidden away inside Angkor Conservation's warehouses, meticulously numbered and catalogued. Unfortunately, without the right contacts, getting a peek at the statues is a lost cause. Hopefully, some of the statuary will eventually go on public display in some sort of Angkor museum (to rival the National Museum in Phnom Penh).

Formerly housed in the Angkor Conservation compound, but now going it alone in offices spread throughout Siem Reap is Apsara Authority (Authority for the Protection and Management of Angkor and the region of Siem Reap). This organisation is responsible for the research, protection and conservation of cultural heritage around Angkor, as well as urban planning in Siem Reap and tourism development in the region. Quite a mandate, quite a challenge – especially now that the government is taking such a keen interest in its work. Angkor has become a money-spinner and the politicians in Phnom Penh want their share, with political appointees taking over from professionals in most departments. This may be good for personal enrichment but it doesn't bode well for the future of Angkor, where profits may well come before preservation.

ARCHITECTURAL STYLES AT ANGKOR	
Style	**Date**
Preah Ko	875–93
Bakheng	893–925
Koh Ker	921–45
Pre Rup	947–65
Banteay Srei	967–1000
Kleang	965–1010
Baphuon	1010–80
Angkor Wat	1100–75
Bayon	1177–230

though on a grand scale. Other features that came to be favoured included an entry tower and a causeway lined with *naga* (mythical serpent) balustrades or sculpture leading up to the temple.

As the temples grew in ambition, the central tower became a less-prominent feature, although it remained the focus of the temple. Courtyards enclosed by colonnaded galleries, with the galleries themselves richly decorated, came to surround the central tower. Smaller towers were placed on gates and on the corners of walls, their overall number generally having a religious or astrological significance.

These refinements and additions culminated in Angkor Wat, which effectively showcases the evolution of Angkorian architecture. The architecture of the Bayon period breaks with tradition to a certain extent in temples such as Ta Prohm and Preah Khan, in which the horizontal layout of galleries, corridors and courtyards seems to completely eclipse the central tower.

The curious narrowness of the corridors and doorways in these structures can be explained by the fact that Angkorian architects never mastered the flying buttress to build a full arch. They engineered arches by laying blocks on top of each other, until they met at a central point; known as false arches, they can support only very short spans.

'Angkor Wat effectively showcases the evolution of Angkorian architecture'

ORIENTATION

Angkor's monuments are spread throughout the forest. Heading north from Siem Reap, you first come to Angkor Wat, then the walled city of Angkor Thom. To the east and west of this city are two vast reservoirs, which helped to feed the Angkor Thom population. Further east are temples including Ta Prohm, Banteay Kdei and Pre Rup. North of Angkor Thom is Preah Kahn and way beyond in the northeast, Banteay Srei, Kbal Spean, Phnom Kulen and Beng Mealea. To the southeast of Siem Reap is the Roluos Group of early Angkorian temples.

Maps

There have been quite a number of detailed maps of the Angkor area published over the years, many of which appear in the books on Angkor recommended in the boxed text on p141. There are several free maps covering Angkor, including the *Siem Reap Angkor 3D Map*, which are available at certain hotels, guesthouses and restaurants in town. They offer no more detail than the maps in this book, but they are a handy pocket size. The May 1982 issue of *National Geographic* magazine (available in secondhand bookshops) included an excellent map that shows Angkor in its prime.

INFORMATION
Admission Fees

While the cost of entry to Angkor is relatively expensive by Cambodian standards, the fees represent excellent value. Visitors have a choice of a one-day pass (US$20), a three-day pass (US$40) or a one-week pass (US$60). Passes cannot be extended and days run consecutively, so plan your visit in advance. Purchase the entry pass from the large official entrance booth on the road to Angkor Wat. One passport-sized photo is required for multiday passes – there are instant cameras at the entrance booth, but bring your own photo if you don't want to queue. Visitors entering the monuments after 5pm get a free sunset, as the ticket starts from the following day. This fee includes access to all the monuments of Angkor in the Siem Reap area, but does not currently include the sacred mountain of Phnom Kulen (effectively run as a private enterprise by a local businessman) or the remote complexes of Beng Mealea and Koh Ker.

Entry tickets to the temples of Angkor are controlled by a local petroleum company called Sokimex, which in return for administrating the site takes 15% of the revenue. Just 10% goes to Apsara Authority (see the boxed text, p142), the body responsible for protecting and conserving the temples, and 75% goes to the Finance Ministry – it's anyone's guess what happens to it once it enters that black hole. Putting profit before preservation is, in our opinion, a scandal and the situation will hopefully change in the coming years. Ironically, the situation is better than it was a few years ago, when ticket scams were plentiful and almost nothing of the entry fee filtered through to the temples themselves.

Most of the major temples now have uniformed guards to check the tickets, which has reduced the opportunity for scams, although many

'Most of the major temples now have uniformed guards to check the tickets'

OUT TO LUNCH

Most of the tour groups buzzing around Angkor head back to Siem Reap for lunch. This is as good a reason as any to stick around the temples, taking advantage of the lack of crowds to explore some popular sites and enjoying a local lunch at one of the many stalls. Almost all of the major temples have some sort of nourishment available beyond the walls. Anyone travelling with a *moto* (small motorcycle with driver) or *remorque* (trailer pulled by a bicycle or motorcycle) should ask the driver for tips on cheap eats, as these guys eat around the temples every day. They know the best spots at which to eat, at the best price, and should be able to sort you out (assuming you are getting along well).

The most extensive selection of restaurants is lined up opposite the entrance to Angkor Wat, including several overpriced local restaurants with a range of Khmer food. There is also now a handy branch of Blue Pumpkin turning out sandwiches, salads and ice creams, as well as the usual divine fruit shakes, all to take away if required. **Chez Sophea** (☎ 012 858003) offers barbecued meats and fish, accompanied by a cracking homemade salad.

There are dozens of local noodle stalls just north of the Bayon, which are a good spot for a quick bite to eat. Other central temples with food available include Ta Prohm, Preah Khan and Ta Keo. Further afield, Banteay Srei has several small restaurants, complete with ornate wood furnishings freshly cut from Cambodia's forests. Further north at Kbal Spean, food stalls at the bottom of the hill can cook up fried rice or a noodle soup, plus there is the excellent Borey Sovann Restaurant, which is a great place to wind down before or after an ascent.

Water and soft drinks are available throughout the temple area, and many sellers lurk outside the temples, ready to pounce with offers of 'You wanna buy cold drink?' Sometimes they ask at just the right moment, on other occasions it is the 27th time in an hour that you've been approached and you are ready to scream. Try not to – you'll scare your fellow travellers and lose face with the locals.

WHEN NATURE CALLS

Angkor is now blessed with some of the finest public toilets in Asia. Designed in wooden chalets and complete with amenities like electronic flush, they wouldn't be out of place in a fancy hotel. The trouble is that the guardians often choose not to run the generators that power the toilets, meaning it is pretty dark inside the cubicles (but thankfully you can flush manually too!). Entrance is free if you show your Angkor pass, and they are found near most of the major temples.

Remember, in remote areas, don't stray off the path – being seen in a compromising position is infinitely better than stepping on a land mine.

---

would argue that the current arrangement with Sokimex is the biggest scam of all! Visitors found inside central temples without a ticket are fined US$30. Many of the smaller temples do not have uniformed guards checking passes. An Angkor pass is not required for excursions to villages around or beyond the Angkor area.

SUGGESTED ITINERARIES

The chief attractions of Angkor can be summed up as the mother of all temples, Angkor Wat; the vast walled city of Angkor Thom and the enigmatic faces of the Bayon; and iconic Ta Prohm, battling against the forces of nature. However, these are also the most popular attractions and can be very busy at certain times of the day. On a day trip to Angkor, it is best to concentrate on these three attractions – attempting too much is likely to reduce the whole experience to a dizzying stampede of sandstone. Other spectacular temples that should not be missed include Preah Khan, with its incredible cruciform corridors, and Banteay Srei, home to the most exquisite carving produced in the Angkorian period.

A curious lore of itineraries and times for visiting the monuments has developed at Angkor since tourism first began early in the 20th century. It is received wisdom that as Angkor Wat faces west, one should be there for the sunset, and in the case of the Bayon, which faces east, in the morning. Ta Prohm, most people seem to agree, can be visited in the middle of the day because of its umbrella of foliage. This is all well and good: Angkor Wat is indeed stunning at sunset and the Bayon is a good place to be come the morning. However, if you reverse the order, the temples will still look good – and you can avoid the crowds. For more on keeping away from the crowds, see the boxed text on p146.

'as Angkor Wat faces west, one should be there for the sunset'

Back in the early days of tourism, the problem of what to see and in what order came down to two basic temple itineraries: the Little (Petit) Circuit and the Big (Grand) Circuit. It's difficult to imagine that anyone follows these to the letter any more, but in their time they were an essential component of the Angkor experience and were often undertaken on the back of an elephant.

The circuits provide a useful guide on breaking a trip into bite-sized chunks. Angkor Wat, Ta Prohm and the principal monuments of Angkor Thom are impressive enough to warrant a morning or afternoon each, as are the remote sites of Kbal Spean and Beng Mealea, with Banteay Srei best combined with the latter in a long day trip. Banteay Srei can also be visited in a trip that includes Banteay Samré and a possible aside to the little-visited hilltop temple of Phnom Bok. Other temples that can be easily grouped together include Preah Khan, Preah Neak Pean, Ta Som, Eastern Mebon and Pre Rup; Chau Sey Tevoda, Thommanon, Ta Keo, Banteay Kdei and Sra Srang; and the Roluos Group to the east of Siem Reap.

Little Circuit

The 17km Little Circuit begins at Angkor Wat, and heads north to Phnom Bakheng, Baksei Chamkrong and Angkor Thom (including the city wall and gates, the Bayon, the Baphuon, the Royal Enclosure, Phimeanakas, Preah Palilay, Tep Pranam, the Preah Pithu Group, the Terrace of the Leper King, the Terrace of Elephants, the Central Sq, the North Kleang, the South Kleang and the 12 Towers of Prasat). It exits from Angkor Thom via Victory Gate (in the eastern wall), and continues to Chau Say Tevoda, Thommanon, Spean Thmor and Ta Keo. It then heads northeast of the road to Ta Nei, turns south to Ta Prohm, continues east to Banteay Kdei and Sra Srang, and finally returns to Angkor Wat via Prasat Kravan.

Big Circuit

The 26km Big Circuit is an extension of the Little Circuit: where the latter exits at the east gate of the walled city of Angkor Thom, the Big Circuit exits at the north gate and continues to Preah Khan and Preah Neak Pean, east to Ta Som then south via the Eastern Mebon to Pre Rup. From there it heads west and then southwest on its return to Angkor Wat.

AVOIDING THE HORDES

The days of serene and spiritual moments within the confines of empty temples are definitely over. Angkor is back on the tourist trail and is getting busier by the year. But it's not all bad news, as, with a little planning, it is still possible to escape from the hordes. However, one important thing to remember, particularly on the subject of sunrise and sunset, is that places are popular for a reason, and it is worth going with the flow at least once.

The most popular place for sunrise is Angkor Wat and particularly the area around the royal ponds. The Bayon is also popular, but sees far fewer visitors than Angkor Wat in the early hours. Sra Srang is usually pretty quiet, and a good sunrise here can be spectacular thanks to reflections in the extensive waters. Phnom Bakheng could be an attractive option, because the sun comes up behind Angkor Wat and you are far from the madding crowds who gather here at sunset. Phnom Krom is also impressive, but getting out here so early is a real pain.

The definitive sunset spot is the hilltop temple of Phnom Bakheng, but this has been getting well out of control lately, with as many as 1000 tourists clambering around the small structure. Better to check it out for sunrise or early morning and miss the crowds. Staying within the confines of Angkor Wat for sunset is a rewarding option, as it can be pretty peaceful when most tourists head off to Phnom Bakheng around 5pm or so. Angkor Wat's immense upper terraces also offer a good view across the forest canopy as the light shifts. Pre Rup is popular with some for an authentic rural sunset over the surrounding rice-fields, but this is starting to get busier (although nothing like the circus at Bakheng). Better is the hilltop temple of Phnom Krom, which offers commanding views across the Tonlé Sap lake, but involves a long drive back to town in the dark. The Western Baray takes the sunset in from the eastern end, across its vast waters, and is generally a quiet option.

When it comes to the most popular temples, the middle of the day is consistently the quietest time (the large groups head back to town for lunch), but it's also the hottest. This makes it tough going around relatively open temples such as Banteay Srei and the Bayon, but fine at well-covered temples such as Ta Prohm, Preah Khan and Beng Mealea, or even the bas-reliefs at Angkor Wat. The busiest times at Angkor Wat are from 6am to 7am and 3pm to 5pm, at the Bayon from 7.30am to 9.30am, and at Banteay Srei from mid-morning to mid-afternoon, while at other popular temples such as Ta Prohm and Preah Khan, it is hard to predict. At most other temples, it's just a case of pot luck. If you pull up outside and see a car park full of tour buses, you may want to move on to somewhere quieter. The wonderful thing about Angkor is that there is always another temple to see.

One Day

If you have only one day to visit Angkor, a good itinerary would be Angkor Wat for sunrise and then to stick around to explore the mighty temple while it is quieter. From there continue to the tree roots of Ta Prohm before breaking for lunch. In the afternoon, have a short look at the huge structure that is Preah Khan, before finishing the day at Angkor Thom and the beauty of the Bayon in the late afternoon light.

Two Days

A two-day itinerary might be very similar to the one above, but with more time to explore the temples. An important addition is petite Banteay Srei, with its fabulous carvings, and a surfaced road all the way out there. Finally, on the back circuit to Preah Khan it is worth visiting Preah Neak Pean and Ta Som – small temples with plenty of character – and taking in a sunset at Pre Rup.

Three to Five Days

If you have three to five days to explore Angkor, it is possible to see most of the important sites described in this chapter. One approach is to see as much as possible on the first day or two (as covered earlier) and then spend the final days combining visits to other sites such as Roluos and Banteay Samré, as well as revisiting the places you liked best from the first day. Some prefer a gradual build-up to the most spectacular monuments, progressing through more minor temples first. Another interesting option is a chronological approach, starting with the earliest Angkorian temples and working steadily forwards in time to Angkor Thom, taking stock of the evolution of Khmer architecture and artistry along the way.

It is also well worth making the trip to the River of a Thousand Lingas at Kbal Spean, offering the chance to stretch your legs amid natural and manmade splendour, or making a trip to the remote, vast and overgrown temple of Beng Mealea, both of which can be combined with Banteay Srei in one long day.

'Those with the time to spend a week at Angkor will be richly rewarded'

One Week

Those with the time to spend a week at Angkor will be richly rewarded. Not only is it possible to fit all the temples of the region into an itinerary, but it is also possible to take an odd day off for shopping or exploring around Siem Reap. Check out the aforementioned itineraries for some ideas on approach, but relax in the knowledge that you'll see it all. You may also want to throw in some of the more remote sites such as Koh Ker (p233), Prasat Preah Vihear (p235) or Banteay Chhmar (p222).

TOURS

Those on package tours or tailor-made trips will have their Angkor itinerary already organised, while most budget and midrange travellers prefer to take in the temples at their own pace. However, visitors with a flexible budget who have only a day or two at this incredible site may prefer something organised locally.

It is possible to link up with an official tour guide in Siem Reap. The **Khmer Angkor Tour Guides Association** (☎ 964347; khmerang@camintel.com; Tourism Office) represents all of Angkor's authorised guides. English- or French-speaking guides can be booked from US$20 a day; guides who speak other languages – such as Italian, German, Spanish, Japanese and Chinese – are available at a higher charge as there are fewer speakers.

For something just a little bit different, **Terre Cambodge** (☎ 964391; www
.terrecambodge.com) offers trips to a variety of remote sites around Angkor,
including boat trips on the Tonlé Sap lake aboard its wooden sampan.

GETTING THERE & AROUND

Visitors heading to the temples of Angkor – in other words pretty much
everybody coming to Cambodia – need to consider the most suitable way
to travel between the temples. Many of the best-known temples are no
more than a few kilometres from the walled city of Angkor Thom, which is
just 8km from Siem Reap, and can be visited using anything from a car or
motorcycle to a sturdy pair of walking boots. Tourists on organised trips
are likely to travel around the area by coach, minibus or car, but for the independent traveller there is a daunting range of alternatives to consider.

For the ultimate Angkor experience, try a pick and mix approach, with
a *moto* (small motorcycle with driver) one day to cover the more remote
sites, a bicycle for a couple of days to get around the central temples, and
an exploration on foot for a spot of peace and serenity.

All of these options could one day become irrelevant, as there have
been persistent and well-founded rumours of a Korean company winning
a contract to provide electric cars to get around the site. Disneyland
Cambodia? For now the outcry among local *moto* drivers and transport
companies has done enough to keep the company at bay and it is rumoured to be trying its luck at Koh Ker.

For the temples further away such as Banteay Srei or Beng Mealea,
prices are higher than those suggested here, due to extra fuel costs.

> 'A great
> way to get
> around the
> temples,
> bicycles are
> environ-
> mentally
> friendly'

Bicycle

A great way to get around the temples, bicycles are environmentally
friendly and are used by most locals living around the area. There are
few hills and the roads are in good condition, so there's no need for
much cycling experience. Moving about at a slower speed, you soon find
that you take in more than from out of a car window or on the back of
a speeding *moto*. Many guesthouses and hotels in town rent bikes for
around US$1 to US$2 per day.

Car

Cars are popular with some for getting about the temples. The obvious
advantage is protection from the elements, be it rain or the punishing
sun. Shared between several travellers, they can also be an economical
way to explore. The downside is that visitors are a little more isolated
from the sights, sounds and smells as they travel between temples. A car
for the day around the central temples is US$20 to US$25 and can be
arranged with hotels, guesthouses and agencies in town.

4WD

A 4WD isn't necessary for the vast majority of Angkor's temples. However, people planning adventures further afield to Preah Khan, Koh Ker
or other remote sites in Preah Vihear Province (p228) will need to arrange a 4WD if they don't want to be on a motorcycle for several long
days. Rates are higher the further you plan to go and the fancier the
vehicle. Think US$80 and up per day.

Cyclo

Some companies have introduced *cyclos* (pedicabs) for transporting tour
groups around the temples. This may be a good option for those who like

the idea of a bicycle – but who don't like the pedalling in the sun part. Rent a local *remorque-kang* (trailer pulled by a bicycle) for the day and the locals will sure get a surprise.

Elephant

Travelling by elephant was the traditional way to see the temples way back in the early days of tourism at Angkor, at the start of the 20th century. It is once again possible to take an elephant ride between the south gate of Angkor Thom and the Bayon (US$10) in the morning, or up to the summit of Phnom Bakheng for sunset (US$15). It is hardly reliving the days of the explorers, but some like to get that elephant-at-Angkor photo to show the folks back home. It can't be much fun for the elephants, hauling tourists up the steep path to Bakheng each day, but they are very well looked after.

Helicopter

For those with lots of holiday money, there are tourist flights around Angkor Wat (US$68) and the temples outside Angkor Thom (US$120) with **Helicopters Cambodia** (Map pp116-17; ☎ 012 814500, 016 839565; www.helicoptersnz.co.nz), which has an office near the Psar Chaa in Siem Reap. The company also offers charters to remote temples such as Prasat Preah Vihear and Preah Khan, with prices starting at US$1200 per hour plus 10% sales tax. Call your bank manager first.

Hot-Air Balloon

For a bird's eye view of Angkor Wat, try **Angkor Balloon** (☎ 012 844049). The balloon is on a fixed line and rises 200m above the landscape. It costs US$11 per person and carries up to 30 people.

Minibus

Minibuses are available from various travel agents around town. A 12-seat minibus costs from US$40 per day, while a 25- or 30-seat coaster bus is around US$80 per day.

Motorcycle

Many independent travellers end up visiting the temples by motorcycle. *Moto* drivers accost visitors from the moment they set foot in Siem Reap, but they often end up being knowledgeable and friendly, and good companions for a tour around the temples. They can drop you off and pick you up at allotted times and places and even tell you a bit of background about the temples as you zip around. Those on a really tight budget can just take individual *moto* rides from temple to temple and this may end up cheaper than the US$6 a day most drivers charge. Motorcycle rental in Siem Reap is currently prohibited, but some travellers bring a motorcycle from Phnom Penh. If you manage to get a bike up here, remember to observe the speed restrictions around Angkor, as this is a protected area. It is also important to leave the bike at a guarded parking area or with a stallholder outside each temple, otherwise it might well get stolen.

Remorque-moto

Siem Reap has a unique type of *remorque-moto* – a motorcycle with a twee little hooded carriage towed behind. These are becoming a very popular way to get around Angkor as fellow travellers can still talk to each other as they explore (unlike on the back of a *moto*). They also offer limited protection from the rain. As with *moto* drivers, some *remorque* drivers

'Travelling by elephant was the traditional way to see the temples way back in the early days of tourism at Angkor'

are very good companions for a tour of the temples. Prices start at about US$10 for the day, depending on the destination.

Walking

Why not forget all the fancy methods and simply explore on foot? There are obvious limitations to what can be seen on foot, as some temples are just too far from Siem Reap. However, it is easy enough to walk to Angkor Wat and the temples of Angkor Thom, and this is a great way to meet up with villagers in the area. Those who want to get away from the roads should try the peaceful walk along the walls of Angkor Thom. It is about 13km in total, and offers access to several small, remote temples and a lot of birdlife. Another rewarding walk is from Ta Nei to Ta Keo through the forest.

ANGKOR WAT

អង្គរវត្ត

Angkor Wat is simply unique, a stunning blend of spirituality and symmetry, an enduring example of man's devotion to his gods. Relish the very first approach, as that spine-tickling moment when you emerge on the inner causeway will rarely be felt again. It is the largest and undoubtedly the most breathtaking of the monuments at Angkor, and is widely believed to be the largest religious structure in the world. It is also the best-preserved temple at Angkor, as it was never abandoned to the elements, and repeat visits are rewarded with previously unnoticed details. It was probably built as a funerary temple for Suryavarman II (r 1112–52) to honour Vishnu, the Hindu deity with whom the king identified.

'Angkor Wat is famous for its beguiling *apsara* (heavenly nymphs)'

There is much about Angkor Wat that is unique among the temples of Angkor. The most significant point is that the temple is oriented towards the west. West is symbolically the direction of death, which once led a large number of scholars to conclude that Angkor Wat must have existed primarily as a tomb. This idea was supported by the fact that the magnificent bas-reliefs of the temple were designed to be viewed in an anticlockwise direction, a practice that has precedents in ancient Hindu funerary rites. Vishnu, however, is also frequently associated with the west, and it is now commonly accepted that Angkor Wat most likely served both as a temple and a mausoleum for Suryavarman II.

Angkor Wat is famous for its beguiling *apsara* (heavenly nymphs). There are more than 3000 carved into the walls of the temple, each of them unique, and there are more than 30 different hairstyles for budding stylists to check out. Many of these exquisite *apsara* were damaged during Indian efforts to clean the temples with chemicals during the 1980s, the ultimate bad acid trip, but they are now being restored by the teams of the **German Apsara Conservation Project** (GACP; www.gacp-angkor.de). The organisation operates a small information booth in the northwest corner of Angkor Wat, near the wat, where beautiful black-and-white postcards and images of Angkor are available.

SYMBOLISM

Visitors to Angkor Wat are struck by its imposing grandeur and, at close quarters, its fascinating decorative flourishes and extensive bas-reliefs; however, a scholar at the time of its construction would have revelled in its multilayered levels of meaning in much the same way as a contemporary literary scholar might delight in James Joyce's *Ulysses*.

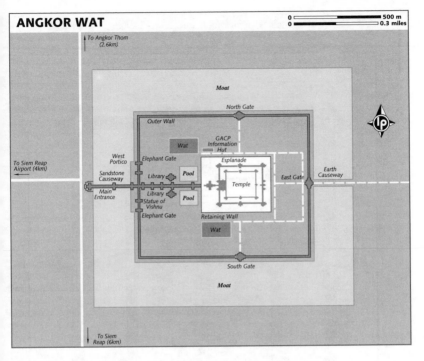

ANGKOR WAT

0 _____ 500 m
0 _____ 0.3 miles

To Angkor Thom
(2.6km)

Moat

North Gate

Outer Wall

GACP
Information
Hut

Wat

West
Portico

Esplanade

To Siem Reap
Airport (4km)

Elephant Gate

Sandstone
Causeway

Library

Pool

Temple

East Gate

Earth
Causeway

Main
Entrance

Library

Pool

Statue of
Vishnu

Elephant Gate

Retaining Wall

Wat

South Gate

Moat

To Siem
Reap (6km)

David Chandler, drawing on the research of Eleanor Moron, points
out in his book *History of Cambodia* that the spatial dimensions of
Angkor Wat parallel the lengths of the four ages (Yuga) of classical Hindu
thought. Thus the visitor to Angkor Wat who walks the causeway to the
main entrance and through the courtyards to the final main tower, which
once contained a statue of Vishnu, is metaphorically travelling back to
the first age of the creation of the universe.

Like the other temple-mountains of Angkor, Angkor Wat also repli-
cates the spatial universe in miniature. The central tower is Mt Meru, with
its surrounding smaller peaks, bounded in turn by continents (the lower
courtyards) and the oceans (the moat). The seven-headed *naga* becomes
a symbolic rainbow bridge for man to reach the abode of the gods.

ARCHITECTURAL LAYOUT

Angkor Wat is surrounded by a moat, 190m wide, which forms a giant
rectangle measuring 1.5km by 1.3km. It makes the moats around European castles look like kid's play. From the west, a sandstone causeway
crosses the moat; the holes in the paving stones held wooden pegs that
were used to lift and position the stones during construction. The pegs
were then sawn off and have since rotted away. The sandstone blocks
from which Angkor Wat was built were quarried more than 50km away
(from the district of Svay Leu at the eastern foot of Phnom Kulen) and
floated down the Stung Siem Reap (Siem Reap River) on rafts. The lo-
gistics of such an operation are mind-blowing, consuming the labour of
thousands – an unbelievable feat given the lack of cranes and trucks that
we take for granted in contemporary construction projects.

CENTRAL STRUCTURE OF ANGKOR WAT

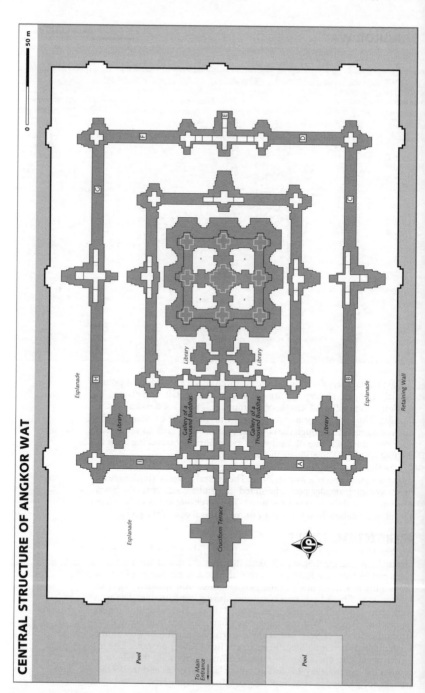

Bayon temple (p156), Angkor Thom

Entrance to the South Gate, Angkor Thom (p155)

Preah Ko temple (p170), Roluos Group

Elephants at the entrance to Angkor Thom (p155)

Ruins at Preah Khan temple (p166)

The jungle covered Ta Prohm temple (p162)

The rectangular outer wall, which measures 1025m by 800m, has a gate on each side, but the main entrance, a 235m-wide porch richly decorated with carvings and sculptures, is on the western side. In the gate tower to the right as you approach is a statue of Vishnu, 3.25m in height and hewn from a single block of sandstone. Vishnu's eight arms hold a mace, a spear, a disk, a conch and other items. You may even see locks of hair lying about. These are an offering by both young women and men preparing to get married or by people who seek to give thanks for their good fortune.

An avenue, 475m long and 9.5m wide and lined with *naga* balustrades, leads from the main entrance to the central temple, passing between two graceful libraries (the northern one still undergoing restoration by a Japanese team) and then two pools, the northern one a popular spot from which to watch sunrise.

The central temple complex consists of three storeys, each made of laterite, which enclose a square surrounded by intricately interlinked galleries. The Gallery of a Thousand Buddhas used to house hundreds of Buddha images before the war, but many of these were removed or stolen, leaving the broken remnants we see today.

The corners of the second and third storeys are marked by towers, each topped with pointed cupolas (domed structures). Rising 31m above the third level and 55m above the ground is the central tower, which gives the whole ensemble its sublime unity. At one time, the central sanctuary of Angkor Wat held a gold statue of Vishnu mounted on a *garuda* (a mythical half-man, half-bird creature) that represented the deified god-king Suryavarman II. The stairs to the upper level are immensely steep, because reaching the kingdom of the gods was no easy task; modern-day visitors should exercise due care and caution when clambering up or down, as the stairs have claimed victims before.

Once at the central tower, the pilgrimage is complete: soak up the breeze, take in the views and then find a quiet corner in which to contemplate the symmetry and symbolism of this Everest of temples.

> 'Soak up the breeze, take in the views and then find a quiet corner in which to contemplate the symmetry and symbolism of this Everest of temples'

BAS-RELIEFS

Stretching around the outside of the central temple complex is an 800m-long series of intricate and astonishing bas-reliefs. The carvings were once sheltered by the cloister's wooden roof, which long ago rotted away (except for one original beam in the western half of the north gallery; the other roofed sections are reconstructions). The following is a brief description of the epic events depicted on the panels in the gallery of bas-reliefs. They are described in the order in which you'll come to them if you begin on the western side and keep the bas-reliefs to your left. The majority of the bas-reliefs were completed in the 12th century, but in the 16th century several new reliefs were added to unfinished panels.

(A) Battle of Kurukshetra

The southern portion of the west gallery depicts a battle scene from the Hindu *Mahabharata* epic, in which the Kauravas (coming from the north) and the Pandavas (coming from the south) advance upon each other, meeting in furious battle. Infantry are shown on the lowest tier, with officers on elephant-back and chiefs on the second and third tiers. Some of the more interesting details (from left to right) include: a dead chief lying on a pile of arrows and surrounded by his grieving parents and troops; a warrior on an elephant who, by putting down his weapon, has accepted defeat; and a mortally wounded officer, falling from his carriage into the arms of his soldiers. Over the centuries, some sections have been polished (by the millions of hands that fall upon them) to look like black marble. The portico at the southwestern corner is decorated with sculptures representing subjects taken from the *Ramayana.*

(B) Army of Suryavarman II

The remarkable western section of the south gallery depicts a triumphal battle-march of Suryavarman II's army. In the southwestern corner about 2m from the floor is Suryavarman II on an elephant, wearing the royal tiara and armed with a battle-axe; he is shaded by 15 umbrellas and fanned by legions of servants. Further on is a procession of well-armed soldiers and officers on horseback; among them are bold and warlike chiefs on elephants. Just before the end of this panel is the rather disorderly Thai mercenary army, with their long headdresses and ragged marching, at that time allied with the Khmers in their conflict with the Chams. The Khmer troops have square breastplates and are armed with spears; the Thais wear skirts and carry tridents.

The rectangular holes seen in this stretch were created when, long ago, pieces of the scene – reputed to possess magical powers – were removed. Part of this panel was damaged by an artillery shell in 1971.

(C) Heaven & Hell

The eastern half of the south gallery, the ceiling of which was restored in the 1930s, depicts the punishments and rewards of the 37 heavens and 32 hells. On the left, the upper and middle tiers show fine gentlemen and ladies proceeding towards 18-armed Yama (the judge of the dead) seated on a bull; below him are his assistants, Dharma and Sitragupta. On the lower tier is the road to hell, along which the wicked are dragged by devils. To Yama's right, the tableau is divided into two parts by a horizontal line of *garuda* (half-man, half-bird creatures): above, the elect dwell in beautiful mansions, served by women, children and attendants; below, the condemned suffer horrible tortures.

'The eastern half of the south gallery depicts the punishments and rewards of the 37 heavens and 32 hells'

(D) Churning of the Ocean of Milk

The southern section of the east gallery is decorated by the most famous of the bas-relief scenes at Angkor Wat, the Churning of the Ocean of Milk. This brilliantly executed carving depicts 88 *asura* (devils; on the left), and 92 *deva* (gods) with crested helmets, churning up the sea to extract the elixir of immortality, which both sides covet. The demons hold the head of the serpent and the gods hold its tail. At the centre of the sea, the serpent is coiled around Mt Mandala, which in the tug of war between the demons and the gods turns and churns up the water. Vishnu, incarnated as a huge turtle, lends his shell to serve as the base and pivot of Mt Mandala. Brahma, Shiva, Hanuman (the monkey god) and Lakshmi (the goddess of beauty) all make appearances, while overhead a host of heavenly female spirits sing and dance in encouragement. Luckily for us the gods won through, as the *apsara* (heavenly nymphs) above were too much for the hot-blooded devils to take.

(E) Elephant Gate

This gate, which has no stairs leading to it, was used by the king and others for mounting and dismounting elephants directly from the gallery. North of the gate is a Khmer inscription recording the erection of a nearby stupa in the 18th century.

(F) Vishnu Conquers the Demons
The northern section of the east gallery shows a furious and desperate encounter between Vishnu, riding on a *garuda*, and innumerable *danava* (demons). Needless to say, he slays all comers. This gallery was only completed at a later date, most likely in the 16th century, and the carving is notably inferior to the original work from the 12th century.

(G) Krishna & the Demon King
The eastern section of the north gallery shows Vishnu incarnated as Krishna riding a *garuda*. He confronts a burning walled city, the residence of Bana, the demon king. The *garuda* puts out the fire and Bana is captured. In the final scene Krishna kneels before Shiva and asks that Bana's life be spared.

'In the final scene Krishna kneels before Shiva and asks that Bana's life be spared'

(H) Battle of the Gods & the Demons
The western section of the north gallery depicts the battle between the 21 gods of the Brahmanic pantheon with various demons. The gods are featured with their traditional attributes and mounts. Vishnu, for example, has four arms and is seated on a *garuda*, while Shiva rides a sacred goose.

(I) Battle of Lanka
The northern half of the west gallery shows scenes from the *Ramayana*. In the Battle of Lanka, Rama (on the shoulders of Hanuman), along with his army of monkeys, battles 10-headed Ravana, seducer of Rama's beautiful wife Sita. Ravana rides a chariot drawn by monsters and commands an army of giants.

ANGKOR THOM

អង្គរធំ

The fortified city of Angkor Thom (Great Angkor, or Great City), some 10 sq km in extent, was built by Angkor's greatest king, Jayavarman VII (r 1181–219), who came to power following the disastrous sacking of the previous Khmer capital by the Chams. At its height, it may have supported a population of one million people in the surrounding region. Centred on the Bayon, Angkor Thom is enclosed by a *jayagiri* (square wall) 8m high and 12km in length and encircled by a *jayasindhu* (moat) 100m wide, said to have been inhabited by fierce crocodiles. This is yet another monumental expression of Mt Meru surrounded by the oceans.

The city has five monumental gates, one each in the northern, western and southern walls and two in the eastern wall. The gates, which are 20m in height, are decorated with stone elephant trunks and crowned by four gargantuan faces of the Bodhisattva Avalokiteshvara facing the cardinal directions. In front of each gate stands giant statues of 54 gods (to the left of the causeway) and 54 demons (to the right of the causeway), a motif taken from the story of the Churning of the Ocean of Milk illustrated in the famous bas-relief at Angkor Wat. The south gate is most popular with visitors, as it has been fully restored and many of the heads (usually copies) remain in place. However, this gate is on the main road into Angkor Thom from Angkor Wat, and it gets very busy. More peaceful are the east and west gates, found at the end of uneven trails. The east gate was most recently used as a location on *Tomb Raider* where the bad guys broke into the 'tomb' by pulling down a giant (polystyrene!) *apsara*. The causeway at

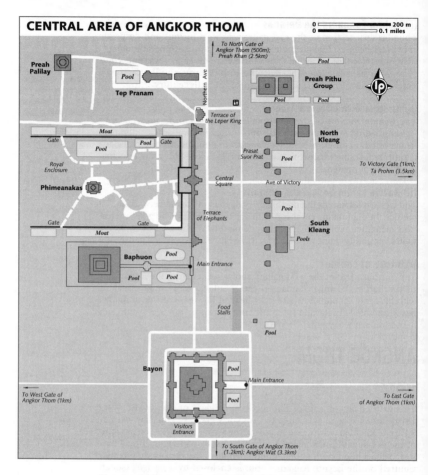

CENTRAL AREA OF ANGKOR THOM

the west gate has completely collapsed, leaving a jumble of ancient stones sticking out of the soil like victims of a terrible historical pile-up.

In the centre of the walled enclosure are the city's most important monuments, including the Bayon, the Baphuon, the Royal Enclosure, Phimeanakas and the Terrace of Elephants.

BAYON
បាយ័ន

Unique even among its cherished contemporaries, Bayon epitomises the creative genius and inflated ego of Cambodia's legendary king, Jayavarman VII. It's a place of stooped corridors, precipitous flights of stairs and, best of all, a collection of 54 gothic towers decorated with 216 coldly smiling, enormous faces of Avalokiteshvara that bear more than a passing resemblance to the great king himself. These huge heads glare down from every angle, exuding power and control with a hint of humanity – this was precisely the blend required to hold sway over such a vast empire, ensuring the disparate and far-flung population yielded to his magnanimous will. As you walk around, a dozen or more of the heads are visible at any one time – full-face or in profile, almost level with your eyes or staring down from on high.

Bayon is now known to have been built by Jayavarman VII, though for many years its origins were not known. Shrouded in dense jungle, it also took researchers some time to realise that it stands in the exact centre of the city of Angkor Thom. There is still much mystery associated with Bayon – such as its exact function and symbolism – and this seems only appropriate for a monument whose signature is an enigmatic smiling face.

A number of locals suggest that the Khmer empire was divided into 54 provinces at the time of Bayon's construction, hence the all-seeing eyes of Avalokiteshvara (or Jayavarman VII) were keeping watch on the kingdom's outlying subjects.

The eastward orientation of Bayon leads most people to visit it early in the morning, preferably just after sunrise, when the sun inches upwards, lighting face after face with warmth. Bayon, however, looks equally good in the late afternoon, and if you stay for the sunset you get the same effect as at sunrise, in reverse. A Japanese team is restoring several outer areas of the temple.

Architectural Layout

Unlike Angkor Wat, which looks impressive from all angles, the Bayon looks rather like a glorified pile of rubble from a distance. It's only when you enter the temple and make your way up to the third level that its magic becomes apparent.

The basic structure of the Bayon is a simple three levels, which correspond more or less to three distinct phases of building. This is because Jayavarman VII began construction of this temple at an advanced age, so was never confident it would be completed. Each time one phase was completed, he moved on to the next. The first two levels are square and adorned with bas-reliefs. They lead up to a third, circular level, where you will find the towers and their faces.

Bas-Reliefs

Bayon is decorated with a total of 1.2km of extraordinary bas-reliefs incorporating more than 11,000 figures. The famous carvings on the outer wall of the first level depict vivid scenes of everyday life in 12th-century Cambodia. The bas-reliefs on the second level do not have the epic proportions of those on the first level or the ones at Angkor, and tend to be fragmented. The reliefs described in this boxed text are those on the first level. The sequence assumes that you will enter the Bayon by the east gate and view the reliefs in a clockwise direction.

(A) THE CHAMS ON THE RUN

Just south of the east gate is a three-level panorama. On the first tier, Khmer soldiers march off to battle; check out the elephants and the ox carts, which are almost exactly like those used in Cambodia today. The second tier depicts the coffins being carried back from the battlefield. In the centre of the third tier, Jayavarman VII, shaded by parasols, is shown on horseback followed by legions of concubines (to the left).

(B) LINGA WORSHIP

The first panel north of the southeastern corner shows Hindus praying to a *linga* (phallic symbol). This image was probably originally a Buddha, later modified by a Hindu king.

'Unlike Angkor Wat, which looks impressive from all angles, the Bayon looks rather like a glorified pile of rubble from a distance'

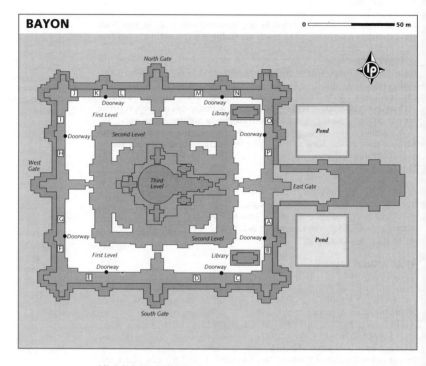

BAYON

0 ————— 50 m

North Gate

Doorway · Doorway

First Level · Library

Second Level · Doorway

Third Level

West Gate

East Gate

Second Level · Doorway

First Level · Library

Doorway · Doorway

South Gate

Pond

Pond

(C) A NAVAL BATTLE

The next panel has some of the best-carved reliefs. The scenes depict a naval battle between the Khmers and the Chams (the latter with head coverings) and everyday life by Tonlé Sap lake, where the battle was fought. Look for images of people picking lice from each other's hair, of hunters and, towards the western end of the panel, a woman giving birth.

(D) THE CHAMS VANQUISHED

In the next panel scenes from daily life continue and the battle shifts to the shore where the Chams are thrashed. Scenes include two people playing chess, a cockfight and women selling fish in the market. The scenes of meals being prepared and served are in celebration of the Khmer victory.

(E & F) A MILITARY PROCESSION

The last section of the south gallery, depicting a military procession, is unfinished, as is the panel showing elephants being led in from the mountains. Brahmans have been chased up two trees by tigers.

(G) CIVIL WAR?

This panel depicts scenes that some scholars maintain is a civil war. Groups of people, some armed, confront each other, and the violence escalates until elephants and warriors join the melee.

(H) THE ALL-SEEING KING

The fighting continues on a smaller scale in the next panel. An antelope is being swallowed by a gargantuan fish; among the smaller fish is a prawn, under which an inscription proclaims that the king will seek out those in hiding.

(I) VICTORY PARADE
This panel depicts a procession that includes the king (carrying a bow). Presumably it is a celebration of his victory.

(J) THE CIRCUS COMES TO TOWN
At the western corner of the northern wall is a Khmer circus. A strong man holds three dwarfs, and a man on his back is spinning a wheel with his feet; above is a group of tightrope walkers. To the right of the circus, the royal court watches from a terrace, below which is a procession of animals. Some of the reliefs in this section remain unfinished.

(K) A LAND OF PLENTY
The two rivers, one next to the doorpost and the other a few metres to the right, are teeming with fish.

(L, M & N) THE CHAMS RETREAT
On the lowest level of this unfinished three-tiered scene, the Cham armies are being defeated and expelled from the Khmer kingdom. The next panel depicts the Cham armies advancing, and the badly deteriorated panel shows the Chams (on the left) chasing the Khmers.

(O) THE CHAMS SACK ANGKOR
This panel shows the war of 1177, when the Khmers were defeated by the Chams, and Angkor was pillaged. The wounded Khmer king is being lowered from the back of an elephant and a wounded Khmer general is being carried on a hammock suspended from a pole. Directly above, despairing Khmers are getting drunk. The Chams (on the right) are in hot pursuit of their vanquished enemy.

(P) THE CHAMS ENTER ANGKOR
This panel depicts another meeting of the two armies. Notice the flag bearers among the Cham troops (on the right). The Chams were defeated in the war, which ended in 1181, as depicted on panel A.

BAPHUON
បាពួន

'Baphuon would have been one of the most spectacular of Angkor's temples in its heyday'

Baphuon would have been one of the most spectacular of Angkor's temples in its heyday. Located 200m northwest of Bayon, it's a pyramidal representation of mythical Mt Meru. Construction probably began under Suryavarman I and was later completed by Udayadityavarman II (r 1049–65). It marked the centre of the city that existed before the construction of Angkor Thom.

Baphuon was the centre of EFEO restoration efforts when the Cambodian civil war erupted and work paused for a quarter of a century. The temple was taken apart piece by piece, in keeping with the anastylosis method of renovation, but all the records were destroyed during the Khmer Rouge years, leaving experts with the world's largest jigsaw puzzle. The EFEO resumed a 10-year restoration programme in 1995, which should see the temple fully reopen to the public during 2005. Baphuon is approached by a 200m elevated walkway made of sandstone, and the central structure is 43m high.

On the western side of the temple, the retaining wall of the second level was fashioned – apparently in the 15th or 16th century – into a reclining Buddha 40m in length. The unfinished figure is difficult to make out, but the head is on the northern side of the wall and the gate is where the hips should be; to the left of the gate protrudes an arm. When it comes to the legs and feet – the latter are entirely gone – imagination must suffice. This huge project undertaken by the Buddhist faithful 500 years ago demonstrates that Angkor was never entirely abandoned.

ROYAL ENCLOSURE & PHIMEANAKAS
ភិមានអាកាស

'Phimeanakas means "Celestial Palace", and some scholars say that it was once topped by a golden spire'

Phimeanakas stands close to the centre of a walled area that once housed the royal palace, not that there's anything much left of the palace today except for two sandstone pools near the northern wall. Once the site of royal ablutions, these are now used as swimming holes by local children. It is fronted to the east by the Terrace of Elephants. Construction of the palace began under Rajendravarman II, although it was used by Jayavarman V and Udayadityavarman I. It was later added to and embellished by Jayavarman VII (who else?) and his successors.

Phimeanakas means 'Celestial Palace', and some scholars say that it was once topped by a golden spire. Today it only hints at its former splendour and looks a little worse for wear. The temple is another pyramidal representation of Mt Meru, with three levels. Most of the decorative features are broken or have disappeared. Still, it is worth trudging up to the second and third levels for good views of Baphuon.

PREAH PALILAY
ព្រះប៉ាលីឡៃ

Preah Palilay is one of the most atmospheric temples in Angkor Thom, located about 200m north of the Royal Enclosure's northern wall. It was erected during the rule of Jayavarman VII and originally housed a Buddha, which has long since vanished. There are several enormous trees looming large over the central sanctuary, which make for a fine photo.

TEP PRANAM
ទេព្យប្រណម្យ

Tep Pranam, an 82m by 34m cruciform Buddhist terrace 150m east of Preah Palilay, was once the base of a pagoda of lightweight construction. Nearby is a Buddha that's 4.5m high – it is a reconstruction of the original. A group of Buddhist nuns lives in a wooden structure close by.

PREAH PITHU GROUP
ព្រះពិធូ

Preah Pithu, which is across Northern Ave from Tep Pranam, is a group of 12th-century Hindu and Buddhist temples enclosed by a wall.

TERRACE OF THE LEPER KING
ទីលានព្រះគម្លង់

The Terrace of the Leper King, just north of the Terrace of Elephants, is a 7m-high platform. On top of the platform stands a nude, though sexless, statue. It is another of Angkor's mysteries. The original of the statue is in Phnom Penh's National Museum (p81), and various theories have been advanced to explain its meaning. Legend has it that at least two of the Angkor kings had leprosy, and the statue may represent one of them. A more likely explanation is that the statue is of Yama, the god of death, and that the Terrace of the Leper King housed the royal crematorium.

The front retaining walls of the terrace are decorated with at least five tiers of meticulously executed carvings of seated *apsara;* other figures include kings wearing pointed diadems, armed with short double-edged swords and accompanied by the court and princesses, the latter adorned with beautiful rows of pearls. The terrace, built in the late 12th century, between the construction of Angkor Wat and the Bayon, once supported a pavilion made of lightweight materials.

On the southern side of the Terrace of the Leper King (facing the Terrace of Elephants), there is access to the front wall of a hidden terrace that was covered up when the outer structure was built – a terrace within a terrace. The four tiers of *apsara* and other figures, including *naga,* look as fresh as if they had been carved yesterday, thanks to being covered up for centuries. Some of the figures carry fearsome expressions.

TERRACE OF ELEPHANTS
ទីលានជល់ដំរី

The 350m-long Terrace of Elephants was used as a giant viewing stand for public ceremonies and served as a base for the king's grand audience hall. As you stand here, try to imagine the pomp and grandeur of the Khmer empire at its height, with infantry, cavalry, horse-drawn chariots and elephants parading across the Central Sq in a colourful procession, pennants and standards aloft. Looking on is the god-king, crowned with a gold diadem, shaded by multitiered parasols and attended by mandarins and handmaidens bearing gold and silver utensils.

The Terrace of Elephants has five outworks extending towards the Central Sq – three in the centre and one at each end. The middle section of the retaining wall is decorated with life-size *garuda* and lions; towards either end are the two parts of the famous parade of elephants, complete with their Khmer mahouts.

'As you stand here, try to imagine the pomp and grandeur of the Khmer empire at its height'

KLEANGS & PRASAT SUOR PRAT
ឃ្លាំង/ប្រាសាទស្ងួព្រ័ត

Along the east side of Central Sq are two groups of buildings, the North Kleang and the South Kleang, that may at one time have been palaces. The North Kleang dates from the period of Jayavarman V (r 968–1001).

Along the Central Sq in front of the two Kleangs are 12 laterite towers – 10 in a row and two more at right angles facing the Ave of Victory – known as the Prasat Suor Prat or Temple of the Tightrope Dancers. Archaeologists believe the towers, which form an honour guard along Central Sq, were constructed by Jayavarman VII (r 1181–219). It is likely that each one originally contained either a *linga* or a statue. It is said artists performed for the king on tightropes or rope-bridges strung between these towers. It is also rumoured that they were used for public trials of sorts – during a dispute the two parties would be made to sit inside two towers, one party eventually succumbing to disease and hence proven guilty.

AROUND ANGKOR THOM

TA PROHM

តាព្រហ្ម

Ta Prohm is undoubtedly the most atmospheric ruin at Angkor and should be high on the hit list of every visitor. Its appeal lies in the fact that, unlike the other monuments of Angkor, it has been left to be swallowed by the jungle, and looks very much the way most of the monuments of Angkor appeared when European explorers first stumbled upon them. Well, that's the theory, but in fact the jungle is pegged back and only the largest trees are left in place, making it manicured rather than raw like Beng Mealea. Still, a visit to Ta Prohm is a unique, other-world experience. The temple is cloaked in dappled shadow, its crumbling towers and walls locked in the slow muscular embrace of vast root systems. If Angkor Wat, the Bayon and other temples are testimony to the genius of the ancient Khmers, Ta Prohm reminds us equally of the awesome fecundity and power of the jungle. There is a poetic cycle to this venerable ruin, with humans first conquering nature to rapidly create, and nature once again conquering humans to slowly destroy.

Built from 1186 and originally known as Rajavihara (Monastery of the King), Ta Prohm was a Buddhist temple dedicated to the mother of Jayavarman VII. It is one of the few temples in the Angkor region where an inscription provides information about the temple's dependents and inhabitants. The numbers quoted really are staggering, although possibly

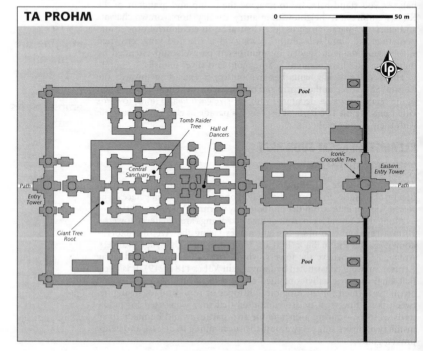

TA PROHM

0 ————————— 50 m

Pool

Tomb Raider Tree
Hall of Dancers

Iconic Crocodile Tree

Central Sanctuary

Eastern Entry Tower

Path
Entry Tower

Path

Giant Tree Root

Pool

include an element of exaggeration to glorify the king: close to 80,000 people were required to maintain or attend at the temple, among them more than 2700 officials and 615 dancers.

Ta Prohm is a temple of towers, close courtyards and narrow corridors. Many of the corridors are impassable, clogged with jumbled piles of delicately carved stone blocks dislodged by the roots of long-decayed trees. Bas-reliefs on bulging walls are carpeted by lichen, moss and creeping plants, and shrubs sprout from the roofs of monumental porches. Trees, hundreds of years old – some supported by flying buttresses – tower overhead, their leaves filtering the sunlight and casting a greenish pall over the whole scene. The most popular of the many strangulating root formations is that on the inside of the easternmost *gopura* (entrance pavilion) of the central enclosure. However, there are several other astounding growths including the famous *Tomb Raider* tree where Angelina Jolie picked a jasmine flower before falling through the earth into…Pinewood Studios. It used to be possible to climb onto the damaged galleries, but this is now prohibited to protect both the temple and visitor. Many of these precariously balanced stones weigh a tonne or more and would do some serious damage if they came down.

Because there's such a maze of rubble and vegetation, there are predictably some children who manage to duck the security and want to guide you through the temple. Some readers don't like this idea, some do. Either way, the fact of the matter is that these are mostly poor kids from poor families looking for the chance to make some money. It is easy to say that it is somehow wrong and that they should be at school or doing a traditional job, but most Westerners have never experienced poverty in a Cambodian sense, and the desperation it breeds. Some of the kids will certainly make more money than their parents ever did, struggling in the rice-fields under the shadow of land mines. If you don't want them to follow you around, politely tell them so, but try not to be rude or aggressive, as they are only young. If you want help to find some photo spots and the like, try and agree on a price (2000r or whatever) in advance. Throwing around dollar bills is not such a good idea, as it breeds expectancy and contempt.

For a culture clash of sorts, check out *Tomb Raider*, the action movie starring Angelina Jolie as Lara Croft. The temples of Angkor are culture personified; as for the movie…well, there's the clash.

BAKSEI CHAMKRONG
បក្សីចាំក្រុង

Located southwest of the south gate of Angkor Thom, Baksei Chamkrong is one of the few brick edifices in the immediate vicinity of Angkor. A well-proportioned though petite temple, it was once decorated with a covering of lime mortar. Like virtually all of the structures of Angkor, it opens to the east. In the early 10th century, Harshavarman I erected five statues in this temple: two of Shiva, one of Vishnu and two of Devi.

PHNOM BAKHENG
ភ្នំបាក់ខែង

Around 400m south of Angkor Thom, the main attraction of Phnom Bakheng is the sunset view of Angkor Wat. Unfortunately, and inevitably, the whole affair has turned into something of a circus, with crowds of tourists gasping up the steep slope of the hill and jockeying for space once on top. Coming down can be even worse as there is nothing at all in the way of lighting. Still, the sunset over the Tonlé Sap lake is very impressive from the hill. To get a decent picture of Angkor Wat in the

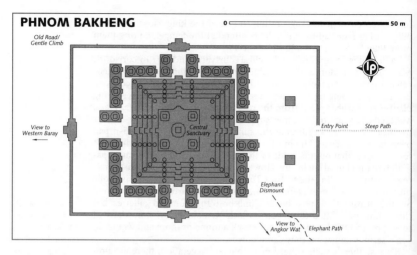

PHNOM BAKHENG

Old Road/Gentle Climb

View to Western Baray

Central Sanctuary

Entry Point   Steep Path

Elephant Dismount

View to Angkor Wat   Elephant Path

0 ▭▭▭ 50 m

warm glow of the late afternoon sun you will need at least a 300mm lens, as the temple is 1.3km away.

Phnom Bakheng is also home to the first of the temple-mountains built in the vicinity of Angkor. Yasovarman I (r 889–910) chose Phnom Bakheng over the Roluos area, where the earlier capital had been located.

The temple-mountain has five tiers, with seven levels (including the base and the summit). At the base are – or were – 44 towers. Each of the five tiers had 12 towers. The summit of the temple has four towers at the cardinal points of the compass as well as a central sanctuary. All of these numbers are of symbolic significance. The seven levels, for example, represent the seven Hindu heavens, while the total number of towers, excluding the Central Sanctuary, is 108, a particularly auspicious number and one that correlates to the lunar calendar.

It is now possible to arrange an elephant ride up the hill (US$15 one way), and the location certainly makes for a memorable journey, if you're OK the idea of elephants hauling themselves up the steep hill day after day. It is advisable to book in advance, as the rides are very popular with tour groups.

PRASAT KRAVAN
ប្រាសាទក្រវ៉ាន់

The five brick towers of Prasat Kravan, which are arranged in a north–south line and oriented to the east, were built for Hindu worship in 921. The structure is unusual in that it was not constructed by royalty; this accounts for its slightly remote location, away from the centre of the capital. Prasat Kravan is just south of the road between Angkor Wat and Banteay Kdei.

The Prasat Kravan Group was partially restored in 1968 and is particularly notable for the stunning brick carvings cut into the interior walls. The images of Vishnu in the largest central tower show the eight-armed deity on the back wall, taking the three gigantic steps with which he reclaimed the world on the left wall, and riding a *garuda* on the right wall. The northernmost tower displays bas-reliefs of Vishnu's consort, Lakshmi.

One of Vishnu's best-loved incarnations was when he appeared as the dwarf Vamana, and proceeded to reclaim the world from the evil demon-king Bali. The dwarf politely asked the demon-king for a comfortable patch of ground upon which to meditate, saying that the patch need only be big enough so that he could easily walk across it in three paces. The demon agreed, only to see the dwarf swell into a mighty giant who strode across the universe in three enormous steps. From this legend, Vishnu is sometimes known as the 'long strider'.

BANTEAY KDEI & SRA SRANG
ពន្លាយក/ស្រះស្រង់

Banteay Kdei, a massive Buddhist monastery from the latter part of the 12th century, is surrounded by four concentric walls. The outer wall measures 500m by 700m. Each of its four entrances is decorated with *garuda,* which hold aloft one of Jayavarman VII's favourite themes: the four faces of Avalokiteshvara. The inside of the central tower was never finished and much of the temple is in a ruinous state due to hasty construction. It is considerably less busy than nearby Ta Prohm and this alone can justify a visit.

Just east of Banteay Kdei is a basin of earlier construction, Sra Srang (Pool of Ablutions), measuring 800m by 400m. A tiny island in the middle once bore a wooden temple, of which only the stone base remains. This is a beautiful body of water from which to take in a quiet sunrise.

TA KEO
តាកែវ

Ta Keo is a stark, undecorated temple that undoubtedly would have been one of the finest of Angkor's structures, had it been finished. Built by Jayavarman V (r 968–1001), it was dedicated to Shiva and was the first Angkorian monument built entirely of sandstone. The summit of the central tower, which is surrounded by four lower towers, is almost 50m high. This quincuncial arrangement (with four towers at the corners of a square and a fifth tower in the centre) is typical of many Angkorian temple-mountains.

No-one is certain why work was never completed, but a likely cause may have been the death of Jayavarman V. However, some scholars have also attributed it to an inauspicious lightning strike during construction.

TA NEI
តានី

Ta Nei, 800m north of Ta Keo, was built by Jayavarman VII (r 1181–219). There is something of the spirit of Ta Prohm here, albeit on a lesser scale, with moss and tentacle-like roots covering many outer areas of this small temple. It now houses the Apsara Authority's training unit and can be accessed only by walking across the French-built dam. To get to the dam, take the long track on the left, just after Spean Thmor when coming from Siem Reap.

SPEAN THMOR
ស្ពានថ្ម

Spean Thmor (Stone Bridge), of which an arch and several piers remain, is 200m east of Thommanon. Jayavarman VII, the last great builder of Angkor, constructed many roads with these immense stone bridges spanning watercourses, but this is the only large bridge remaining in the immediate vicinity of Angkor. The bridge vividly highlights how the

'Ta Keo is a stark, undecorated temple that undoubtedly would have been one of the finest of Angkor's structures, had it been finished'

water level has dropped over the subsequent centuries and may offer another clue to the collapse of Angkor's extensive irrigation system. Just north of Spean Thmor is a large and surprisingly elegant water wheel.

There are more-spectacular examples elsewhere in Siem Reap Province, including Spean Praptos (19 arches) in Kompong Kdei on NH6 from Phnom Penh, and Spean Ta Ong, a 77m bridge complete with a beautiful *naga*, forgotten in the forest about 25km east of Beng Mealea.

CHAU SAY TEVODA
ចៅសាយទេវតា

Just east of Angkor Thom's east gate is Chau Say Tevoda. It was probably built during the second quarter of the 12th century and dedicated to Shiva and Vishnu. It has been under renovation by the Chinese for years to bring it up to the condition of its twin temple, Thommanon.

THOMMANON
ធម្មនុន

Thommanon is just north of Chau Say Tevoda. Although unique, the temple complements its neighbour, as it was built to a similar design around the same time. It was also dedicated to Shiva and Vishnu. Thommanon is in much better condition than the rather ruinous Chau Say Tevoda thanks to extensive work by the EFEO in the 1960s.

PREAH KHAN
ព្រះខ័ន

'The temple was dedicated to 515 divinities and during the course of a year 18 major festivals took place here'

The temple of Preah Khan (Sacred Sword) is one of the largest complexes at Angkor – a maze of vaulted corridors, fine carvings and lichen-clad stonework. It is a good counterpoint to Ta Prohm, although it generally gets fewer visitors. Preah Khan was built by Jayavarman VII (it probably served as his temporary residence while Angkor Thom was being built), and like Ta Prohm it is a place of towered enclosures and shoulder-hugging corridors. Unlike Ta Prohm, however, the temple of Preah Khan is in a reasonable state of preservation and ongoing restoration efforts by the **World Monuments Fund** (WMF; www.wmf.org) should ensure stabilisation.

The central sanctuary of the temple was dedicated in 1191 and a large stone stele, originally located within the first eastern enclosure, but now housed safely at Angkor Conservation, says much about Preah Khan's role as a centre for worship and learning. The temple was dedicated to 515 divinities and during the course of a year 18 major festivals took place here, requiring a team of thousands just to maintain the place.

Preah Khan covers a very large area, but the temple itself is within a rectangular enclosing wall of around 700m by 800m. Four processional walkways approach the gates of the temple, and these are bordered by another stunning depiction of the Churning of the Ocean of Milk, as in the approach to Angkor Thom, although most of the heads have disappeared. From the central sanctuary, four long, vaulted galleries extend in the cardinal directions. Many of the interior walls of Preah Khan were once coated with plaster that was held in place by holes in the stone. Today, many delicate carvings remain, including *essai* (wise men) and *apsara*.

The main entrance to Preah Khan is, as with most of the other Angkorian temples, in the east, but the standard practice is to enter at the west gate near the main road. You then walk the length of the temple to

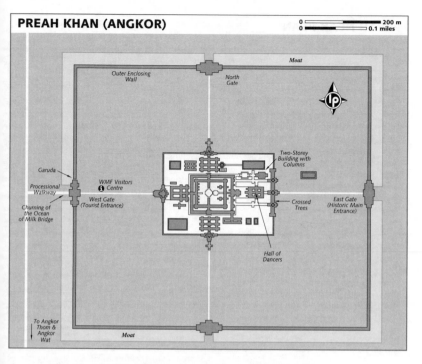

PREAH KHAN (ANGKOR)

the east gate before doubling back to the central sanctuary and making your way to the north gate (drivers usually offer to wait at the north gate). Approaching from the west, there is little clue to nature's genius, but on the outer retaining wall of the east gate, a pair of trees with monstrous roots embrace as they reach for the sky. There is also a curious Grecian-style two-storey structure inside the east gate, the purpose of which is unknown, but it looks like an exile from Athens.

PREAH NEAK PEAN

នាគព័ន្ធ

The late-12th-century Buddhist temple of Preah Neak Pean (Intertwined Naga; pronounced preah neak po-an) is a petite yet perfect temple constructed by...surely not him again...Jayavarman VII. It has a large square pool surrounded by four smaller square pools. In the centre of the central pool is a circular 'island' encircled by the two *naga* whose intertwined tails give the temple its name. Although it has been centuries since the small pools were last filled with water, it's a safe bet that when the Encore Angkor casino is eventually but inevitably developed in Las Vegas, Preah Neak Pean will provide the blueprint for the ultimate swimming complex.

In the pool around the central island there were once four statues, but only one remains, reconstructed from the debris by the French archaeologists who cleared the site. The curious figure has the body of a horse supported by a tangle of human legs. It relates to a legend that Avalokiteshvara once saved a group of shipwrecked followers from an island of ghouls by transforming himself into a flying horse.

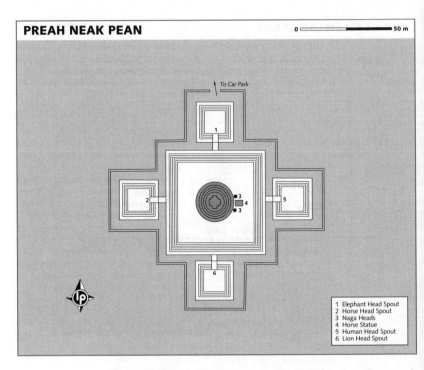

PREAH NEAK PEAN

0 ⊏⊐ 50 m

To Car Park

1 Elephant Head Spout
2 Horse Head Spout
3 Naga Heads
4 Horse Statue
5 Human Head Spout
6 Lion Head Spout

Water once flowed from the central pool into the four peripheral pools via ornamental spouts, which can still be seen in the pavilions at each axis of the pool. The spouts are in the form of an elephant's head, a horse's head, a lion's head and a human's head. The pool was used for ritual purification rites and the complex was once in the centre of a huge 3km-by-900m *baray* serving Preah Khan, now dried up and overgrown. It must have been truly spectacular to approach this island temple by boat.

TA SOM
តាសោម

Ta Som, which stands to the east of Preah Neak Pean, is yet another of the late-12th-century Buddhist temples of Jayavarman VII, the Donald Trump of ancient Cambodia. The central area of Ta Som is in a ruined state, but restoration by the World Monument Fund is getting closer to completion. The most impressive feature at Ta Som is the huge tree completely overwhelming the eastern *gopura*, providing one of the most popular photo opportunities in the Angkor area.

EASTERN BARAY & EASTERN MEBON
បារាយណ៍ខាងកើត/មេបុណ្យខាងកើត

The enormous one-time reservoir known as the Eastern Baray was excavated by Yasovarman I (r 889–910), who marked its four corners with steles. This basin, now entirely dried up, was the most important of the public works of Yasodharapura, Yasovarman I's capital, and is 7km by 1.8km. It was originally fed by Stung Siem Reap.

The Hindu temple known as the Eastern Mebon, erected by Rajendravarman II (r 944–68), would have been on an islet in the centre of the Eastern Baray, but is now very much on dry land. This temple is like a smaller version of Pre Rup, which was built 15 to 20 years later and lies to the south. The temple-mountain form is topped off by the now familiar quincuncial arrangement of towers. The elaborate brick shrines are dotted with neatly arranged holes, which attached the original plasterwork. The base of the temple is guarded at its corners by perfectly carved stone figures of harnessed elephants, many of which are still in a very good state of preservation.

PRE RUP
ប្រែរូប

Pre Rup, built by Rajendravarman II, is about 1.km south of the Eastern Mebon. Like its nearby predecessor, the temple consists of a pyramid-shaped temple-mountain with the uppermost of the three tiers carrying five square shrines arranged as a quincunx. The brick sanctuaries were also once decorated with a plaster coating, fragments of which still remain on the southwestern tower; there are some amazingly detailed lintel carvings here. Several of the outermost eastern towers are perilously close to collapse and are propped up by armies of wooden supports.

Pre Rup means 'Turning the Body' and refers to a traditional method of cremation in which a corpse's outline is traced in the cinders, first in one direction and then in the other; this suggests that the temple may have served as an early royal crematorium.

This is one of the most popular sunset spots around Angkor, as the view over the surrounding rice-fields of the Eastern Baray is beautiful.

> 'The base of the temple is guarded at its corners by perfectly carved stone figures of harnessed elephants'

BANTEAY SAMRÉ
បន្ទាយសំរែ

Banteay Samré dates from the same period as Angkor Wat and was built by Suryavarman II (r 1112–52). The temple is in a fairly healthy state of preservation due to some extensive renovation work, although its isolation has resulted in some looting during the past two decades. The area consists of a central temple with four wings, preceded by a hall and also accompanied by two libraries, the southern of which is remarkably well preserved. The whole ensemble is enclosed by two large concentric walls around what would have been the unique feature of an inner moat, sadly now dried up.

Banteay Samré is 400m east of the Eastern Baray, which in practical terms means following the road to Banteay Srei to the village of Pradak and continuing straight ahead rather than following the tarmac to the right. A visit here can be combined with a trip to Banteay Srei or Phnom Bok.

WESTERN BARAY
បារាយខាងលិច

The Western Baray, measuring an incredible 8km by 2.3km, was excavated by hand to provide water for the intensive cultivation of lands around Angkor. Just for the record, these enormous *baray* weren't dug out, but were huge dykes built up around the edges. In the centre of the basin is the ruin of the Western Mebon temple, where the giant bronze statue of Vishnu, now in the National Museum (p81) in Phnom Penh, was found. The Western

Mebon is accessible by boat from the dam on the southern shore. The *baray* is also the main local swimming pool around Siem Reap. There is a small beach of sorts at the western extreme (complete with picnic huts and inner tubes for rent), which attracts plenty of Khmers at weekends.

ROLUOS GROUP

រលួស

The monuments of Roluos, which served as Indravarman I's (r 877–89) capital, Hariharalaya, are among the earliest large, permanent temples built by the Khmers and mark the beginning of the age of Khmer classical art. Before the construction of Roluos, generally only lighter (and less-durable) construction materials such as brick were employed.

The temples can be found 13km east of Siem Reap along NH6 near the modern-day town of Roluos: Preah Ko is 600m south of NH6, while Bakong is 1.5km south of the highway. There are contemporary Buddhist monasteries at both Bakong and Lolei. For those who aren't travelling much beyond Siem Reap and Phnom Penh, it may be worth venturing into the genuine Cambodian town of Roluos for a refreshing drink.

'The towers of Preah Ko (Sacred Ox) feature three *nandi* (sacred oxen), all of whom look like they had a few steaks sliced off them down the years'

PREAH KO

ប្រះគោ

Preah Ko was erected by Indravarman I in the late 9th century, and was dedicated to Shiva. The six *prasat* (stone halls), aligned in two rows and decorated with carved sandstone and plaster reliefs, face east; the central tower of the front row is a great deal larger than the other towers. Preah Ko has some of the best surviving examples of plasterwork seen at Angkor and is currently under restoration by a German team. There are elaborate inscriptions in the ancient Hindu language of Sanskrit on the doorposts of each tower.

The towers of Preah Ko (Sacred Ox) feature three *nandi* (sacred oxen), all of whom look like a few steaks have been sliced off them over the years. Preah Ko was dedicated by Indravarman I to his deified ancestors in AD 880. The front towers relate to male ancestors or gods, the rear towers to female ancestors or goddesses. Lions guard the steps up to the temple.

BAKONG

បាគង

Bakong is the largest and most interesting of the Roluos Group temples, and has an active Buddhist monastery just to the north of the east entrance. It was built and dedicated to Shiva by Indravarman I. It's a representation of Mt Meru, and it served as the city's central temple. The east-facing complex consists of a five-tier central pyramid of sandstone, 60m square at the base, flanked by eight towers (or their remains) of brick and sandstone and by other minor sanctuaries. A number of the eight towers below the upper central tower are still partly covered by their original plasterwork.

The complex is enclosed by three concentric walls and a moat. There are well-preserved statues of stone elephants on each corner of the first three levels of the central temple. There are 12 stupas – four to a side – on the third tier. The sanctuary on the fifth level was a later addition during the reign of Suryavarman II, in the style of Angkor Wat's central tower.

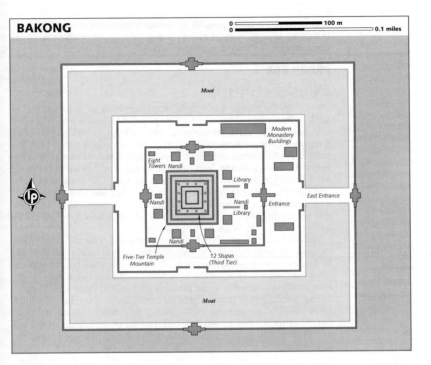

LOLEI
លលៃ

The four brick towers of Lolei, an almost exact replica of the towers of Preah Ko (although in much worse shape) were built on an islet in the centre of a large reservoir – now rice-fields – by Yasovarman I (r 889–910), the founder of the first city at Angkor. The sandstone carvings in the niches of the temples are worth a look and there are Sanskrit inscriptions on the doorposts. According to one of the inscriptions, the four towers were dedicated by Yasovarman I to his mother, his father and his maternal grandparents on 12 July 893.

AROUND ANGKOR

PHNOM KROM
ភ្នំក្រោម

The temple of Phnom Krom, 12km south of Siem Reap on a hill overlooking the Tonlé Sap lake, dates from the reign of Yasovarman I in the late 9th or early 10th century. The name means 'Lower Hill' and is a reference to its geographic location in relation to its sister temples of Phnom Bakheng and Phnom Bok. The three towers, dedicated (from north to south) to Vishnu, Shiva and Brahma, are in a ruined state, but this remains one of the more tranquil spots from which to view sunset, complete with an active wat. The fast boats from Phnom Penh dock

near here, but it is not possible to see the temple from beneath the hill.
If coming here by *moto* or car, try and get the driver to take you to the
summit, as it is a long, hot climb otherwise.

PHNOM BOK

ភ្នំបូក

Making up the triplicate of temple-mountains built by Yasovarman I in
the late 9th or early 10th century, this peaceful but remote location sees
few visitors. The small temple is in reasonable shape and includes two
frangipani trees growing out of a pair of ruinous towers – they look like
some sort of extravagant haircut when in full flower. However, it is the
views of Phnom Kulen to the north and the plains of Angkor to the south
from this 212m hill that make it worth the trip. The remains of a 5m
linga are also visible at the opposite end of the hill and it's believed there
were similar *linga* at Phnom Bakheng and Phnom Krom. Unfortunately,
it is not a sensible place for sunrise or sunset, as it would require a long
journey in the dark to get here or get back.

Phnom Bok is about 25km from Siem Reap and is clearly visible from
the road to Banteay Srei. It is accessible by continuing east on the road
to Banteay Samré for another 6km. It is possible to loop back to Siem
Reap via the temples of Roluos by heading south instead of west on the
return journey, offering some pleasant glimpses of rural life. There is
a long, winding trail (not suitable for bikes) snaking up the hill, which
takes about 20 minutes to climb, plus a new faster cement staircase,
but the latter is fairly exposed. Avoid the heat of the middle of the day
and carry plenty of water, which can be purchased near the base of the
mountain.

> 'The small
> temple in-
> cludes two
> frangipani
> trees grow-
> ing out of
> a pair of
> ruinous
> towers –
> they look
> like some
> sort of
> extravagant
> haircut
> when in full
> flower'

CHAU SREI VIBOL

ចៅស្រីវិបុល

This petite hilltop temple sees few visitors, as it is only easily accessible
by motorcycle. The central sanctuary is in a ruined state, but is nicely
complemented by the construction of a modern wat nearby. Surrounding
the base of the hill are laterite walls, each with a small entrance hall in
reasonable condition. To get here turn east off the reasonable dirt road
between Phnom Bok and Roluos at a point about 8km north of NH6,
or 5km south of Phnom Bok. From this point, the trail deteriorates and
crosses several small, rickety bridges, helping to explain why tour buses
don't make it here. The path also crosses a small Angkorian bridge, built
at the end of the 12th century, complete with *naga* balustrades. The
route is easy to lose, so keep asking locals for directions at junctions and
eventually you will find yourself in a monastic compound at the base of
the small hill.

BANTEAY SREI

បន្ទាយស្រី

Banteay Srei is considered by many to be the jewel in the crown of Angkorian art. A Hindu temple dedicated to Shiva, it is cut from stone of a
pinkish hue and includes some of the finest stone carving seen anywhere
on the planet. It is one of the smallest sites at Angkor, but what it lacks
in size it makes up for in stature. It is wonderfully well preserved and
many of its carvings are three-dimensional. Banteay Srei means 'Citadel

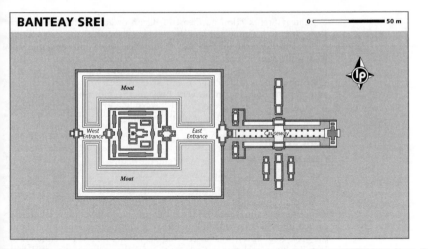

BANTEAY SREI

0 ▭▬ 50 m

Moat

West Entrance

East Entrance

Causeway

Moat

of the Women' and it is said that it must have been built by a woman, as the elaborate carvings are too fine for the hand of a man.

Construction on Banteay Srei began in 967 and it is one of the few temples around Angkor not to be commissioned by a king, but by a Brahman who may have been a tutor to Jayavarman V. The temple is square and has entrances at the east and west, the east approached by a causeway. Of interest are the lavishly decorated libraries and the three central towers, which are decorated with male and female divinities and beautiful filigree relief work.

Classic carvings at Banteay Srei include delicate women with lotus flowers in hand and traditional skirts clearly visible, as well as breathtaking re-creations of scenes from the epic *Ramayana* adorning the library pediments (carved inlays above a lintel). However, the sum of the parts is no greater than the whole – almost every inch of these interior buildings is covered in decoration. Standing watch over such perfect creations are the mythical guardians, all of which are copies of originals stored in the National Museum (p81).

Banteay Srei was the first major temple-restoration undertaken by the EFEO in 1930 using the anastylosis method. The project, as evidenced today, was a major success and soon led to other larger projects such as the restoration of Bayon. However, it was not the first time the temple had hit the headlines, because in 1923 Frenchman André Malraux was arrested in Phnom Penh for attempting to steal several of the site's major statues and pieces of sculpture. Ironically, Malraux was later appointed minister of culture under Charles de Gaulle.

When Banteay Srei was first rediscovered, it was assumed to be from the 13th or 14th centuries, as the refined carving must have come at the end of the Angkor period. It was later dated to 967, from inscriptions found at the site. However, some scholars are once again calling for a revision of this date, given that the style of this temple and its carvings are unlike anything else seen in the 10th century. New theories suggest that like the great cathedrals of Europe, some Angkorian temples may have been destroyed and then rebuilt, or altered beyond recognition, and that the inscription stele at Banteay Srei relates to an earlier structure on the site, not the delicate flower of a temple we see today.

Banteay Srei is 21km northeast of Bayon or about 32km from Siem Reap. It is well signposted and the road is surfaced all the way – a trip from Siem Reap should take just 45 minutes. *Moto* and *remorque* will want a bit of extra cash to come out here, so agree on a sum first. It is possible to combine a visit to Banteay Srei with a trip to the River of a Thousand Lingas at Kbal Spean and Beng Mealea, or to Banteay Samré and Phnom Bok. It can be very busy in the morning; lunchtime is quiet, but very hot; late afternoon is probably best, although not so late that the sun has dropped beneath the tree line.

KBAL SPEAN

ក្បាលស្ពាន

Kbal Spean is a spectacularly carved riverbed, set deep in the jungle to the northeast of Angkor. More commonly referred to in English as the 'River of a Thousand Lingas', the name actually means 'bridgehead', a reference to the natural rock bridge at the site. *Linga* have been elaborately carved into the riverbed, and images of Hindu deities are dotted about the area. Kbal Spean was 'discovered' in 1969, when EFEO ethnologist Jean Boulbet was shown the area by an *essai;* the area was soon off-limits due to the civil war, only becoming safe again in 1998.

'*Linga* have been elaborately carved into the riverbed, and images of Hindu deities are dotted about the area'

It is a 1.5km uphill walk to the carvings, along a pretty path that winds its way up into the jungle, passing by some interesting boulder formations along the way. Carry plenty of water up the hill, as there is none available beyond the parking area. The path eventually splits to the waterfall or the river carvings. It is best to start with the river carvings and work back down to the waterfall to cool off. There is an impressive carving of Vishnu on the upper section of the river, followed by a series of carvings at the bridgehead itself (including Shiva's mount, Nandi), many of which have been tragically hacked off in the past few years. This whole area is now roped off to protect the carvings from further damage.

Following the river down, there are several more impressive carvings of Vishnu, and Shiva with his consort Uma, and further downstream hundreds of *linga* appear on the riverbed. At the top of the waterfall, there are many animal images, including a cow and a frog, and a path winds around the boulders to a wooden staircase leading down to the base of the falls. Visitors between February and June will be disappointed to see very little water here. The best time to visit is between September and December.

Although Kbal Spean is of less spiritual significance to Khmers than Phnom Kulen, it is generally a more rewarding visit, as there is less litter and no whopping charge going to a private businessman. Admission to Kbal Spean is included in the general Angkor pass and the last entry to the site is at 3.30pm.

Kbal Spean is about 50km northeast of Siem Reap or about 18km beyond the temple of Banteay Srei. At the time of writing the road from Banteay Srei had generated into an impassable mess for most vehicles and only motorcycles could get through without taking a long diversion via Phnom Kulen. However, once the road is flattened again, it is an 18km drive from Banteay Srei. Lately it has been taking an hour or more. This road continues north to Anlong Veng (p226), formerly a stronghold of the Khmer Rouge.

Moto drivers will no doubt want a bit of extra money to take you here – a few extra dollars should do, or US$10 or so for the day, including a trip to Banteay Srei. Likewise, *remorque* drivers will probably up the price to about US$15. A surcharge is also charged to come out here by car.

LAND MINE ALERT!

At no point during a visit to Kbal Spean or Phnom Kulen should you leave well-trodden paths, as there are land mines in the area.

PHNOM KULEN
ភ្នំគូលែន

Phnom Kulen is considered by Khmers to be the most sacred mountain in Cambodia and is a popular place of pilgrimage during weekends and festivals. It played a significant role in the history of the Khmer empire, as it was from here in 802 that Jayavarman II proclaimed independence from Java, giving birth to modern-day Cambodia. There is a small wat at the summit of the mountain, which houses a large Buddha carved into the sandstone boulder upon which it is built. Nearby is a large waterfall and above it are smaller bathing areas and a number of carvings in the riverbed, including numerous *linga*. The bad news is that a private businessman bulldozed a road up here in 1999 and now charges a US$20 toll per foreign visitor, an outrageous fee compared with what you get for your money at Angkor. None of the toll goes towards preserving the site. You can buy a cheaper ticket for US$12 from the City Angkor Hotel in Siem Reap, surprise, surprise, owned by the same businessman!

The new road winds its way through some spectacular jungle scenery, emerging on the plateau after 20km ascent. The road eventually splits, the left fork leading to the picnic spot, waterfalls and ruins of a 9th-century temple, the right fork continuing over a bridge and some riverbed carvings to the reclining Buddha. This is the focal point of a pilgrimage here for Khmer people, so it is important to take off your shoes and any head covering before climbing the stairs to the sanctuary. The views from the 487m peak are tremendous, as you can see right across the forested plateau.

The waterfall is an attractive spot, but could be much more beautiful were it not for all the litter left here by families picnicking at the weekend. Near the top of the waterfall is a jungle-clad temple known as Prasat Krau Romeas, dating from the 9th century.

There are plenty of other Angkorian sites on Phnom Kulen, including as many as 20 minor temples around the plateau, the most important of which is Prasat Rong Chen, the first pyramid or temple-mountain to be constructed in the Angkor area. Most impressive of all are the giant stone animals or guardians of the mountain, known as Sra Damrei (Elephant Pond). These are very difficult to get to, with the route passing through mined sections of the mountain and the trail impossible in the wet season. The few people who make it, however, are rewarded with a life-size replica of a stone elephant – a full 4m long and 3m tall – and smaller statues of lions, a frog and a cow. These were constructed on the southern face of the mountain and from here there are spectacular views across the plains below. Getting here requires taking a *moto* from Wat Pre Ang Thom for about 12km on very rough trails through thick forest before arriving at a sheer rock face. From here it is a 1km walk to the animals through the forest. Don't try to find it on your own; expect to pay the *moto* driver about US$6 (with some hard negotiating) and carry plenty of water, as none is available.

Before the construction of the private road up Phnom Kulen, visitors had to scale the mountain and then walk across the top of the plateau to

'Phnom Kulen is considered by Khmers to be the most sacred mountain in Cambodia'

the reclining Buddha. This route takes more than two hours and is still an option. About 15km east of the new road up Kulen, the trail winds its way to a small pagoda called Wat Chou, set into the cliff face from which a *tuk chou* (spring) emerges. The water is considered holy and Khmers like to bottle it up to take home with them. This water source eventually flows into the Tonlé Sap lake and is thought to bless the waterways of Cambodia.

Phnom Kulen mountain is a huge plateau around 50km from Siem Reap and about 15km from Banteay Srei. To get here on the new toll road, take the well-signposted right fork just before Banteay Srei village and follow this, going straight ahead at the crossroads. Just before the road starts to climb the mountain, there is a barrier and it is here that the US$20 charge is levied.

To walk to the site, head east along the base of the mountain at the major crossroads. After about 15km, there is a wat-style gate on the left and a sandy trail. Follow this to a small community from where the climb begins. It is about a 2km climb, including a new staircase up the final cliffs, and then an hour or more in a westerly direction along the top of the plateau. This route of the pilgrims of old should cost nothing if you arrive after midday, although it takes considerably longer.

Moto drivers are likely to want about US$15 to bring you out here, and rented cars will hit passengers with a surcharge, more than double the going rate for Angkor; forget coming by *remorque* as the hill climb is just too tough.

BENG MEALEA

បឹងមាលា

'exploring this titanic of temples is Angkor's ultimate Indiana Jones experience'

Beng Mealea is a spectacular sight to behold. It's one of the most mysterious temples at Angkor, as nature has well and truly run riot here. Built to the same floorplan as Angkor Wat, exploring this titanic of temples is Angkor's ultimate Indiana Jones experience. Built in the 12th century under Suryavarman II (r 1112–52), Beng Mealea is enclosed by a massive moat measuring 1.2km by 900m, much of which has dried up today.

The temple has been utterly subsumed by jungle, and standing just a few metres away from the trees it is hard to tell what lies beneath. Entering from the south, visitors wend their way over piles of masonry, through long dark chambers and between hanging vines to arrive at the central tower, which has completely collapsed. Hidden away among the rubble and foliage are several impressive carvings, as well as a well-preserved library in the northeastern quadrant. The temple is a special place and it is worth taking the time to explore thoroughly. There is also now a large wooden walkway to the centre, constructed during the filming here of Jean-Jacques Annaud's *Two Brothers* (2004).

Beng Mealea is at the centre of an ancient Angkorian road connecting Angkor Thom and Preah Khan in Preah Vihear Province. A small Angkorian bridge just west of Chau Srei Vibol temple is the only remaining trace of the old Angkorian road between Beng Mealea and Angkor Thom; between Beng Mealea and Preah Khan there are at least 10 bridges abandoned in the forest. This is a way for extreme adventurers to get to Preah Khan temple (p231); however, don't undertake this journey lightly.

It now costs US$5 to visit Beng Mealea and there are additional small charges for cars and motorcycles – make sure you work out in advance who is paying this. It is best to undertake a long day trip combining Beng Mealea, Kbal Spean and Banteay Srei. At the very least include Banteay Srei, as you almost pass it along the way.

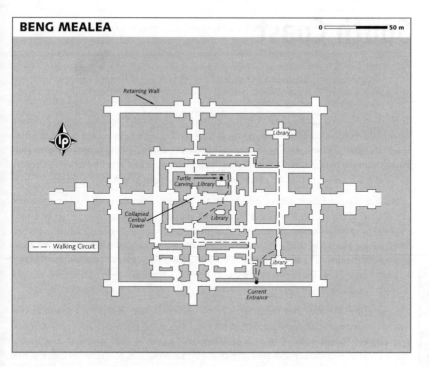

Beng Mealea is about 40km east of Bayon (as the crow flies) and 6.5km southeast of Phnom Kulen. By road it is about 80km from Siem Reap and is a two-hour trip.

There are two routes to Beng Mealea, but the shortest and fastest is currently via the small town of Dam Dek on NH6 towards Phnom Penh. Turn north immediately after the market and continue on this road for 25km. The main road bears left towards Phnom Kulen but don't take this road, go straight ahead instead. You will eventually come to a T-junction.

For the second, longer route, take the road towards Banteay Srei and follow the right fork to Phnom Kulen, continuing right at the major crossroads along the base of the holy mountain. Follow this route for about 35km until you leave Kulen behind and come to a T-junction.

This T-junction is where the two different routes meet. Veer left at this junction; it is another 10km or so northeast to the village of Beng Mealea and the temple is to the left at the main intersection in town. The final 10km or so used to be a mess of miserable sand and mud, but there is now even some tarmac – this is another of these private roads and partly privatised temples, where profit takes precedence over preservation. It usually costs US$2.50 for a car, US$1 for a motorbike, but that is each way, believe it or not!

REMOTE ANGKORIAN SITES

Information on the remote Angkorian sites of Banteay Chhmar (p222), Koh Ker (p233), Preah Khan (p231) and Prasat Preah Vihear (p235) is found in the Northwestern Cambodia chapter.

South Coast

The up-and-coming south coast is home to tropical white sand beaches, unspoilt desert islands, abandoned colonial-era resorts and several of Cambodia's nascent national parks. It also includes the birthplace of ancient Cambodian civilisation in the Angkor Borei region, dating from the 5th century. The area is beginning to take off and offers a cracking selection of diverse attractions that, with a little planning, can be seen in less than a week.

Much of the coastline is dotted with small fishing communities, living off the sea. The western portion of this region is wild and remote and includes the impenetrable jungle of Chuor Phnom Kravanh (Cardamom Mountains), while to the east is generally heavily settled, with the forest having yielded to farmland long ago. Tourism is proving itself the industry of the future, as many of the islands in this region are lined with perfect palm-fringed beaches and covered in a blanket of forest. They easily rival some of Thailand's finest, but even now there is not yet a beach bungalow in sight along the shimmering shores of Cambodia's forgotten islands.

Historically, the towns of Kampot and Kep were the most important centres in the region – Kampot as Cambodia's principal port and Kep as the leading beach town. Kampot was eclipsed following the founding of Sihanoukville port in 1959, and with the steady destruction of Kep during and after the civil war, Sihanoukville was soon to become the most popular beach town in Cambodia. Today, it remains the commercial and entertainment centre of the south coast. Krong Koh Kong is an up-and-coming commercial centre benefiting from its close proximity to Thailand and the construction of a new road, plugging it into the world from both the east and west.

SOUTH COAST

HIGHLIGHTS

- Soak up the sun in **Sihanoukville** (p184), home to blissful beaches, tropical islands, fresh seafood and a lively nightshift

- Journey up the jungle road to **Bokor hill station** (p199), with its eerie, abandoned buildings and breathtaking views over the coast of Cambodia

- Kick back in **Kampot** (p195), a pretty riverside town with some of Cambodia's best-preserved colonial architecture

- Explore abandoned villas and remote islands in the colonial-era beach resort of **Kep** (p201), a town that's slowly coming back to life

- Speed back in time on a fast boat along Angkorian canals to the ancient hill temple of **Phnom Da** (p206), set among lush paddy fields

Phnom Da

Bokor Hill Station

Sihanoukville

Kampot

Kep

| ▪ ELEVATION: 0–1800M | ▪ POPULATION: 2.6 MILLION | ▪ AREA: 27,817 SQ KM |

SOUTH COAST

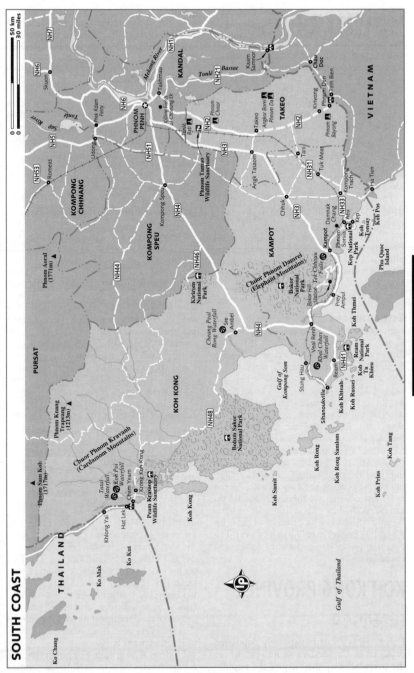

Getting There & Away

There is currently only one well-travelled international border crossing in the south coast region, linking Cambodia to Thailand via the checkpoint at Cham Yeam–Hat Lek connecting Koh Kong and Trat Provinces. There is a border crossing between Cambodia and Vietnam in Takeo Province, but this is definitely the least appealing crossing for the time being. There are rumours that the crossing between Kampot Province and Ha Tien will open sometime soon…keep your ear to the ground, as this will be a great way to connect Cambodia's south coast with the Mekong Delta and the island of Phu Quoc.

For those who aren't travelling overland from Thailand, Phnom Penh is the easiest gateway to the south coast. Highways connect the capital with Sihanoukville and Kampot and buses are cheap and frequent, plus there is the option of hire car or motorcycle. A train line also links these destinations but the speeds are more like those of a toy train set than of a real train.

Getting Around

For travellers arriving in Sihanoukville from Krong Koh Kong by boat, there is the option of continuing along the coast by road to Kampot. This sleepy riverside town makes a good base from which to explore Kep and beautiful Bokor National Park. From Kampot there is a direct road (National Highway 3; NH3) to Phnom Penh, or you can amble slowly via Takeo and the nearby ruined temples around Angkor Borei.

Visitors starting in Phnom Penh would be wiser to run the route in reverse, packing in all the sightseeing first before chillin' out on the beaches at Sihanoukville. All the hot spots covered on the south-coast loop can be reached by public transport or *moto* (small motorcycle with driver), but those on a healthier budget may like to rent a car. The circuit is pretty straightforward for experienced bikers.

KOH KONG PROVINCE

ខេត្តកោះកុង

Koh Kong is a vast but sparsely populated province in Cambodia's southwest, where the overwhelming majority of the population live along the coastline and where the mountains remain untamed. Not surprisingly, fishing is the main source of income for most residents. Tourism is tiny, as most people are simply passing through from Thailand to Sihanoukville, but there is definite potential for future growth thanks to the incredible beaches lining Botum Sakor National Park and nearby islands like Koh Kong (yes, confusingly enough, the province and island share the same name). Diving the relatively unexplored coastal waters and the concept of exploratory ecotourism in the upcountry jungle will eventually take off, but, for now, you are on your own.

Getting around the province is effectively limited to one road linking Krong Koh Kong to the rest of Cambodia, or a fast boat service to Sihanoukville. The Thai military bulldozed a road from the Thai border all the way through the jungle to join NH4 near Sre Ambel in 2002. This has put Krong Koh Kong just six hours from Phnom Penh and Sihanoukville in the dry season, revolutionising life for the residents of the town. Thailand is not well known for magnanimous gestures towards its smaller, 'inferior' neighbours, so it's possible that this road construction will carry a hidden cost, namely the destruction of much of Cambodia's pristine forest in this wilderness region. The price could end up being higher still for Cambodia, as the road cuts through Chuor Phnom Kravanh (Cardamom Mountains) – a unique ecosystem that provides a habitat for many endangered species.

KRONG KOH KONG

កោះកុង

☎ 035 / pop 29,500

It's not one of Cambodia's more exciting destinations, but Krong Koh Kong has seen an increasing numbers of travellers passing through when journeying between Cambodia and Thailand by land and sea. The Thai authorities funded a massive bridge, 1.9km in length, spanning Stung Koh Poi, which has improved traffic between the two countries. The new bridge, combined with the option of road transport out of town, means that travellers need not become stuck here, unless they want to be.

In time, Krong Koh Kong may become a base from which to explore Cambodia's nearby islands, but for now it remains primarily a transit stop. Those who hang around can head for a scruffy but quiet beach to the east of town, or two attractive waterfalls upstream.

It is a bit of a boom town for trade (both legal and illegal), attracting migrants from other parts of the country who are seeking opportunities in this fast-growing frontier area. The border area is popular with Thais, as casinos are a legal and thriving business in Cambodia, unlike in Thailand.

Orientation & Information

Krong Koh Kong is bordered to the west by Stung Koh Poi and the long bridge to Thailand. The town fans out from here to the east and the main road linking it the rest of Cambodia heads out to the northeast.

US dollars and Thai baht can both be used around town, but the baht is definitely king. Changing either currency into riel is easy at Psar Leu (Central Market) or at most guesthouses. The nearest banks that deal with travellers cheques and credit cards are in Sihanoukville or Thailand.

There is a **post office** (Ph 3) in town, but it is better to send mail from Thailand before crossing into Cambodia, or wait until Phnom Penh. There are plenty of private phone booths around town from where reasonably priced local calls can be made. Internet access is available at Asean Hotel (p182) and the Moto Bar (p183).

There is a tourist office on the waterfront about 1km south of the dock, but popular guesthouses like Cheap Charlie's (p182) and Otto's (p182) are more useful. Another good source of information is the unofficial website for Koh Kong (www.kohkong.com).

Sights & Activities
BEACHES

There are several beaches in the vicinity of Krong Koh Kong, including a beach (of sorts) a few kilometres south of town where the river estuary meets the sea. Locals like it and there are pedalos and jet skis for rent. If Cambodian drivers bring you out in a cold sweat, just imagine how scary it is seeing them handle a jet ski. Keep a safe distance away. This beach is also just downstream from town and there are no prizes for guessing where the town's effluent goes. Further afield are countless beaches that

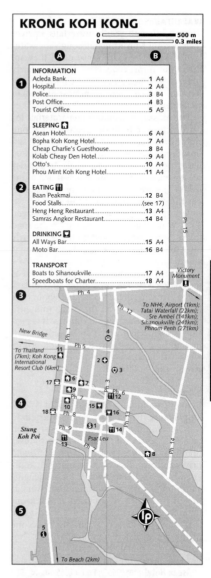

KRONG KOH KONG

0 ———— 500 m
0 ———— 0.3 miles

INFORMATION
Acleda Bank..............................1 A4
Hospital....................................2 A4
Police.......................................3 B4
Post Office...............................4 B3
Tourist Office...........................5 A5

SLEEPING
Asean Hotel.............................6 A4
Bopha Koh Kong Hotel..............7 A4
Cheap Charlie's Guesthouse......8 B4
Kolab Cheay Den Hotel.............9 A4
Otto's.....................................10 A4
Phou Mint Koh Kong Hotel.......11 A4

EATING
Baan Peakmai.........................12 B4
Food Stalls.........................(see 17)
Heng Heng Restaurant............13 A4
Samras Angkor Restaurant......14 B4

DRINKING
All Ways Bar...........................15 A4
Moto Bar................................16 B4

TRANSPORT
Boats to Sihanoukville.............17 A4
Speedboats for Charter...........18 A4

To NH4; Airport (1km);
Tatai Waterfall (22km);
Sre Ambel (141km);
Sihanoukville (241km);
Phnom Penh (271km)

New Bridge

To Thailand
(7km); Koh Kong
International
Resort Club (6km)

Stung
Koh Poi

Psar Leu

To Beach (2km)

SOUTH COAST

Victory
Monument

can be accessed by *moto* or boat. There are some impressive beaches on the western side of the island of Koh Kong, but these aren't so cheap to get to, particularly now that boat drivers have become accustomed to the idea of overcharging tourists. Try to pay no more than 800B to 1000B per boat for a round-trip charter.

WATERFALLS

There are some scenic waterfalls upriver from Krong Koh Kong, although the water level drops in the dry season and they are then less impressive. The water is fairly pure, as it comes down from Chuor Phnom Kravanh, where there are almost no human settlements.

The most spectacular is **Tatai Waterfall**, located nearly an hour upstream from Krong Koh Kong. Set in a lush jungle gorge, it is a thundering set of rapids in the wet season, plunging over a 4m rock shelf. In the dry season, visitors can walk across much of the ledge. The wet season is more spectacular, but the dry season is more fun, as it is possible to take a dip in the gentle-flowing river. Tatai Waterfall can be reached on the road to Sre Ambel, signposted on the left shortly after the first ferry crossing. The waterfall is about 1km from the main road.

There is a second set of rapids, known as the **Koh Poi Waterfall**, on a different tributary of the river. It's great to clamber about here in the dry season, as there are immense boulders to use as stepping stones. It is possible to visit this and the Tatai Waterfall in one boat trip from Krong Koh Kong. Negotiate hard with the driver and aim to pay around 800B to 1000B.

Sleeping

Being Cambodia's original 'Wild West', long before Pailin and Poipet started to muscle in on the gambling and prostitution business, several of the town's guesthouses double as brothels. Many places offer *moto* drivers a commission for bringing customers, which has led to a whole lot of shenanigans on the part of unscrupulous drivers. If they say somewhere is closed, check it out first, as it's more likely that the place is one that won't pay drivers a commission. None of the places listed here are brothels, but that doesn't mean that certain guests may not take prostitutes into them!

Asean Hotel (☎ 936667; Ph 1; r US$5-20; ❄ ▯) The town's newest hotel is a smart place in a smart location, overlooking the river and big enough to ensure everyone arriving by boat or road stands up and takes notice. It is nicely finished with a range of smart rooms from US$5 with fan, US$10 with air-con, US$15 with hot water and US$20 for a river view.

Phou Mint Koh Kong Hotel (☎ 936221; Ph 1; r US$5-15; ❄) Another of the newer hotels in town, this place occupies a prime position on the riverbank, midway between the boat dock and bridge. The rooms are spacious and clean, if a little plain. The cheapies include a fan, US$12 brings air-con and US$15 the added luxury of hot water.

Cheap Charlie's Guesthouse (☎ 016 853450; d with fan 50B) As cheap as it gets in this town. The rooms are basic with a capital B, but there is little room for complaint at this price. Small cells with shared bathroom are the order of the day, but the friendly family makes it feel like home. Cheap Charlie's is also a good source of traveller info and there is a lively little restaurant turning out a tasty mix of Asian and Western dishes.

Otto's (☎ 936163; Ph 7; r 80-120B) The closest of the budget options to the boat dock, this small wooden guesthouse has reliable rooms at a reasonable price, the more expensive ones including an attached bathroom. It's a good spot for travel information and there's a popular restaurant (opposite).

Kolab Cheay Den Hotel (☎ 936211; Ph 6; r 150-250B; ❄) In a quiet, backstreet location right near the boat dock, this clean, friendly minihotel offers a good deal with large, inexpensive rooms. Cheaper rooms include a fan and 250B adds air-con action.

Bopha Koh Kong Hotel (☎ 936073; s US$8, d US$13-25; ❄) This was top dog in town before the new riverfront hotels muscled in; the air-con singles here are a pretty good deal. The self-styled VIP rooms are big, but very important people won't be that impressed.

Koh Kong International Resort Club (☎ 66-39-588173; www.kohkonginter.com; r US$45-105) Cambodia's borders are now littered with casinos to help Thai gamblers part with their money (gambling is illegal in Thailand). This monster of a resort is one of the biggest, with rooms galore strung out along the Cambodian side of the border. Baht rates are usually about half the value of official US dollar prices. Think twice before splashing your cash on the undeniable comfort here, as the attached Koh Kong Safari World promotes orang-utan boxing. Sick stuff!

Eating

Dining options are pretty limited in Koh Kong, although Thai food is more common here than elsewhere in Cambodia. The best budget meals are the stalls in and around Psar Leu. There are also cheap stalls near the boat dock that turn out basic, cheap food.

Baan Peakmai (☎ 011 788771; Ph 6; mains 50-150B) A Thai-style garden restaurant that's the most alluring of the town's few eateries. The monster menu includes more than 30 vegetarian choices and a fair spread of seafood.

Samras Angkor Restaurant (Ph 9; mains 50-150B) Just come from Thailand and want to try something Khmer? This could be the place, a small local restaurant serving a good range of Cambodian cuisine. It comes complete with a karaoke backdrop, but it's easy enough to ignore if you are just here for the food.

Otto's (mains 60-200B) Set on the breezy veranda of the guesthouse (opposite), this Western-style restaurant makes a convenient stop for a quick breakfast before taking the boat to Sihanoukville. The dinner menu includes Thai food, several hearty vegetarian choices and a selection of central European dishes, including one of the best bratwurst you'll find in Cambodia.

Heng Heng Restaurant (Ph 2; mains 2000-6000r) This is a popular Khmer restaurant for tasty Chinese and Cambodian breakfasts of noodle soup and *bobor* (rice porridge), but it lacks the atmosphere to warrant a dinner stop here.

Entertainment

There are a couple of Western bars on the main drag in town – **Moto Bar** (☎ 936220; Ph 3) and All Ways Bar – but both seem more geared up to the Pattaya expat on a visa run than the average tourist passing through.

Getting There & Away

There were no flights between Phnom Penh and Krong Koh Kong at the time of writing.

The Thai-built road between Krong Koh Kong and Sre Ambel is a popular new route in and out of town. However, its condition, and therefore the amount of time it takes to get to Phnom Penh or Sihanoukville, varies dramatically with the season. Think six hours to both places in the dry season, and 10 hours or more in the wet. However, there are plans to seal this road during 2005 and then build bridges to span the four ferry crossings that currently slow things down, all of which will improve journey times dramatically. There are daily tourist buses to Phnom Penh or Sihanoukville, both departing around 9am and costing US$10. Share taxis are also available and charge about 40,000r a seat (space might be more accurate, as a whole seat is too much to hope for!).

There is also a very rough, remote route through the mountains of Koh Kong to Pailin or Battambang, passing through a wild and remote area formerly controlled by the Khmer Rouge. There is no such thing as regular public transport on this route; it should be attempted in the dry season only, by dirt bikers with oodles of off-road experience.

Otherwise, all transport goes by sea. Fast boats leave at 8am daily for Sihanoukville (600B, four hours). Boats leave Sihanoukville at noon.

For more details on travel between Thailand and Sihanoukville via the town of Krong Koh Kong, see p293.

Getting Around

Motos are the most popular form of transport around town and most short-hop fares cost 10B. Bicycles are another option and can be rented at Cheap Charlie's Guesthouse (opposite) for 50B per day.

With so much water around, boats are a crucial part of the transport network. Boats can also be chartered for trips to nearby islands, beaches and waterfalls. Negotiate hard to get a fair price. With the opening of the bridge, it is possible to take a *moto* (50B) or taxi (100B) the 7km to the border. There is a 10B toll for the bridge if you are travelling with your own wheels.

SRE AMBEL
ស្រែអំបិល

Located up a river estuary in southeastern Koh Kong Province, Sre Ambel is something of a smugglers' port. It used to offer an alternative way to get from Phnom Penh to Krong Koh Kong by boat, but this service has been suspended with the opening of the road. The road has certainly put Sre Ambel back on the map for commercial traffic, but it will take more than this to bring tourists here. The best hope is the **Chheang Peal Rong Waterfall**, about 10km north of Sre Ambel in the foothills of Chuor Phnom Kravanh. This is one of Cambodia's finest set of falls, with a series of five big drops ranging from about 15m to 30m. Each looks unique, giving the impression of five separate waterfalls, even though one follows on from the other. Some falls run over huge boulders, some over almost-sculpted cliff faces. Clambering around is tough, but it's worth it as there are some good swimming holes at the right time of year. Heed local advice about crocodiles, however, as this is the start of the wild, wild Cardamoms.

The easiest way to get here in the dry season is head out of Sre Ambel by road, cross the river at the first ferry crossing and then turn right. Follow this road up into the mountains until the massive waterfall appears on your left. However, with a lot of bridges down, the route can be tough to follow without a knowledgeable local, as it lies off the trail of an abandoned logging road. It is only possible to get here by boat during the wet season.

A minibus to Sre Ambel from Psar Dang Kor (Dang Kor Market) in Phnom Penh is 6000r; chartering a whole share taxi is US$15.

SIHANOUKVILLE
ក្រុងព្រះសីហនុ

☎ 034 / pop 155,000
Sihanoukville is the closest thing you get to the Costa del Cambodia, but fear not, development here is light years behind most Thai resorts, let alone Spain. The charmless town is fortunate enough to be hemmed in on all sides by palm-fringed, squeaky, white-sand beaches and undeveloped tropical islands. Visitor numbers have skyrocketed in the past few years and the coast here is set for a facelift, particularly if the much vaunted flights to Siem Reap actually take off.

Named in honour of the then-king, the town was hacked out of the jungle in the late 1950s to create the country's first and only deep-water port; the USA provided the money for NH4 linking Sihanoukville to Phnom Penh. During the 1960s, it experienced a mini tourism boom and some large hotels were constructed, but Kep remained the most popular beach resort. With the overthrow of Sihanouk in 1970, the town's name was changed to Kompong Som and didn't revert back to Sihanoukville until 1993. Cambodians refer to the town by both names –

royalists preferring to use Sihanoukville, and old-guard former communists choosing Kompong Som.

The big attractions around here are the four beaches ringing the headland. None of them qualify as the region's finest, but on weekdays it is still possible to have stretches of the beach to yourself. However, as traveller numbers increase, this seclusion is unlikely to last. Sihanoukville is extremely popular on weekends with well-to-do Khmers heading south from Phnom Penh. Beyond the immediate beaches surrounding the town are the virtually empty beaches of Ream National Park and Otres, and a dozen more islands that see less than 0.1% of the visitors received by their counterparts in Thailand.

The battle continues for the heart and soul of Sihanoukville. Some Cambodian businessmen and their associates from neighbouring countries want to turn the town into a concrete casino town of mega resorts, while some expats from nearby Pattaya want to turn it into a sort of sex, sea and sun go-go resort. On the other side, younger expats are hoping to make a new Ko Pha Ngan on Cambodia's southern coast with the birth of Serendipity Beach, while other investors rub their hands and hope for a Ko Samui gold rush and pleasant garden bungalows set among swaying palms. Whoever wins out in the end, it's certain that Sihanoukville is evolving fast. Like Siem Reap, this is another place in Cambodia that doesn't stay still.

ORIENTATION
The headland of Sihanoukville is spread over several kilometres. The slightly soulless centre of Sihanoukville is along the eastern end of Ph Ekareach, which doubles as the main drag linking the various beaches in town. Budget travellers have traditionally made for Weather Station Hill above the port, but this area is fast losing ground to the popular strip at the northern end of Occheuteal Beach, nicknamed Serendipity Beach, to the south of the city centre. West of town is tiny Koh Pos Beach and the larger Independence Beach, which is one of the quieter beaches during the week. Buses from Phnom Penh arrive in the centre of town, while boats from Krong Koh Kong arrive about 3km north of town.

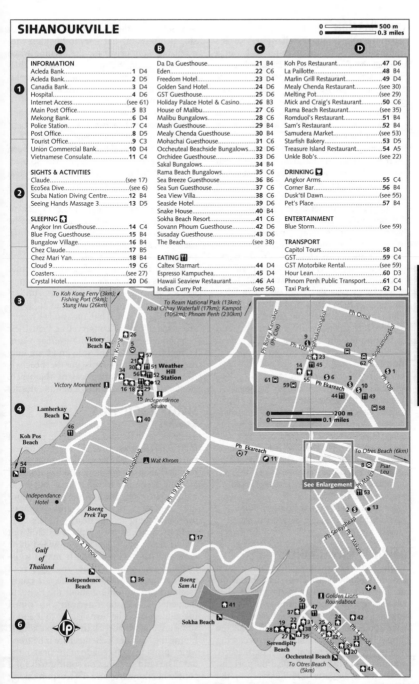

SIHANOUKVILLE

0 — 500 m
0 — 0.3 miles

A

INFORMATION
Acleda Bank...........................**1** D4
Acleda Bank...........................**2** D5
Canadia Bank.........................**3** D4
Hospital.................................**4** D6
Internet Access....................(see 61)
Main Post Office.....................**5** B3
Mekong Bank.........................**6** D4
Police Station.........................**7** C4
Post Office.............................**8** D5
Tourist Office.........................**9** C3
Union Commercial Bank..........**10** D4
Vietnamese Consulate............**11** C4

SIGHTS & ACTIVITIES
Claude................................(see 17)
EcoSea Dive.......................(see 6)
Scuba Nation Diving Centre....**12** B4
Seeing Hands Massage 3.........**13** D5

SLEEPING
Angkor Inn Guesthouse..........**14** C4
Blue Frog Guesthouse.............**15** B4
Bungalow Village...................**16** B4
Chez Claude..........................**17** B5
Chez Mari Yan.......................**18** B4
Cloud 9................................**19** C6
Coasters.............................(see 27)
Crystal Hotel.........................**20** D6

B

Da Da Guesthouse.................**21** B4
Eden....................................**22** C6
Freedom Hotel......................**23** B4
Golden Sand Hotel.................**24** D6
GST Guesthouse....................**25** D6
Holiday Palace Hotel & Casino...**26** B3
House of Malibu.....................**27** C6
Malibu Bungalows..................**28** C6
Mash Guesthouse...................**29** B4
Mealy Chenda Guesthouse......**30** B4
Mohachai Guesthouse.............**31** C6
Occheuteal Beachside Bungalows...**32** D6
Orchidee Guesthouse..............**33** D6
Sakal Bungalows....................**34** B4
Rama Beach Bungalows..........**35** C6
Sea Breeze Guesthouse...........**36** B6
Sea Sun Guesthouse...............**37** C6
Sea View Villa.......................**38** C6
Seaside Hotel........................**39** D6
Snake House..........................**40** B4
Sokha Beach Resort................**41** C6
Sovann Phoum Guesthouse......**42** D6
Susaday Guesthouse...............**43** D6
The Beach...........................(see 38)

EATING
Caltex Starmart......................**44** D4
Espresso Kampuchea...............**45** D4
Hawaii Seaview Restaurant......**46** A4
Indian Curry Pot..................(see 56)

C

Koh Pos Restaurant................**47** D6
La Paillotte...........................**48** B4
Marlin Grill Restaurant............**49** D4
Mealy Chenda Restaurant.....(see 30)
Melting Pot........................(see 29)
Mick and Craig's Restaurant....**50** C6
Rama Beach Restaurant.......(see 35)
Romduol's Restaurant.............**51** B4
Sam's Restaurant...................**52** B4
Samudera Market................(see 53)
Starfish Bakery......................**53** D5
Treasure Island Restaurant......**54** A5
Unkle Bob's.......................(see 22)

DRINKING
Angkor Arms.........................**55** C4
Corner Bar............................**56** B4
Dusk'til Dawn.....................(see 55)
Pet's Place............................**57** B4

ENTERTAINMENT
Blue Storm.........................(see 59)

TRANSPORT
Capitol Tours........................**58** D4
GST.....................................**59** C4
GST Motorbike Rental..........(see 59)
Hour Lean.............................**60** D3
Phnom Penh Public Transport...**61** C4
Taxi Park..............................**62** D4

SOUTH COAST

INFORMATION

Sihanoukville is always changing, so it's important to keep up to date. Seek out a copy of the *Sihanoukville Visitors Guide*, a pocket-sized directory that comes out twice a year and can be found at local hotels, guesthouses, restaurants and bars. There is a tourist office in the centre of town, but guesthouses and bars are generally a better source of information.

The main post office is near the port, and there is a small branch near Psar Leu, but reliability is not something for which either is known. Telephone calls can be made easily from small private booths around town.

Email and Internet access is available in Sihanoukville at about US$1 to US$1.50 per hour. There are several convenient places to get online around the bus stations in the centre of town, plus a few places in the backpacker quarter on Weather Station Hill.

There is a **Vietnamese consulate** (☎ 012 340495; Ph Ekareach; ✆ 8am-noon & 2-4pm Mon-Fri) in Sihanoukville, which offers probably the fastest Vietnamese visas available anywhere in the world. Staff can normally turn one around in 15 minutes, and they cost US$25.

Money

There are several banks in town.

Acleda Bank (☎ 320232; Ph Ekareach) The place for Western Union transfers for those needing cash in a hurry.

Canadia Bank (☎ 933490; Ph Ekareach) A useful option for people carrying non–US dollar travellers cheques, as it changes major currencies at a 2% commission. There are also free cash advances for MasterCard and Visa holders.

Mekong Bank (☎ 933867; Ph Ekareach) Offers cash advances on credit card for a minimum charge of US$5 per transaction, or 2% above US$250. It operates a Sunday service from 10am to 2.30pm.

Union Commercial Bank (☎ 933833; Ph Ekareach) An efficient place for credit-card cash advances, with no commission or charges.

DANGERS & ANNOYANCES

Theft and robbery is on the rise in and around Sihanoukville. There have been numerous incidences of theft on the beaches while people are out swimming. Don't take anything valuable to the beach, unless you have someone to keep an eye on it all the time. Night robberies have been occurring in Sihanoukville in recent years, particularly around the red-light district near the port and on the poorly lit parts of Ph Ekareach on the

way out to Weather Station Hill. It shouldn't stop people going out – try to hook up with a reliable *moto* driver for the evening when heading out on the town. Motorcycle theft is also a popular pastime in Sihanoukville. Anyone who rents a motorcycle should make sure it comes with a separate padlock.

Lone women should exercise caution when walking on the beaches after dark, particularly the section that connects Serendipity Beach to Occheuteal Beach, as there has been one high profile case of rape. Any solo females venturing further down Occheuteal to the bar shacks should definitely not walk alone.

Take care with the currents off Occheuteal during the wet season, as they can be deceptively strong. Several locals drown each year, although in general strong swimmers should have no problem.

It's not all one-way traffic when it comes to dangers and annoyances. One annoyance for locals in Sihanoukville is the underdressed foreigners wandering about town. Cambodia is not Thailand and Khmers are generally more conservative than their neighbours. Just look at the average Cambodian frolicking in the sea…most are fully dressed. Wearing bikinis on the beach is fine, but cover up when leaving the beach. Topless or nude bathing is a definite no-no.

SIGHTS & ACTIVITIES

Beaches

The beaches at Sihanoukville are in a state of flux, as developers move in to cash in on the tourism boom. The best all-rounder is **Occheuteal Beach**; the northern end has emerged as quite a popular traveller hang-out nicknamed **Serendipity Beach**, while further south it is popular with Khmers and midrange tourists staying in the nearby hotels. Serendipity Beach is a cool place to chill out with a drink, but it gets very crowded these days and has rocky waters. It may also be given a new name by the time you read this, because, as we write, there is a comical court case unfolding about the rights to the name. Chuck, the American who coined the name, claims he owns rights to it and is suing anyone who uses it in their marketing! Lining the back of Occheuteal are pine trees, which provide useful shade in the heat of the day. The sand stretches on southwards for a couple of kilometres and it's worth trekking

SOUTH COAST

down here if you want a bit of privacy. A new resort is slowly under construction in the central part of the beach.

Just around a small headland at the southern end of Occheuteal Beach is **Otres Beach**, a seemingly infinite strip of empty white sand. Government officials are eagerly dividing up land behind the beach, but for now there are still no bungalows and fewer visitors make it here than to other beaches around town. To get to Otres Beach, follow the road behind Occheuteal Beach before branching left then right around a small headland, or follow Ph Omoouy east out of town from Psar Leu for about 7km; both are rough tracks.

Sokha Beach is perhaps the prettiest and most popular beach at Sihanoukville, but it has been privatised with the opening of the huge Sokha Beach Resort (p190). Guests get to enjoy the privacy, but for everyone else, the small slither of beach at the eastern end isn't enough.

Victory Beach was the original backpacker beach and remains a favourite with budget travellers due to its proximity to Sihanoukville's most popular guesthouses. It's arguably the least appealing of all the beaches, as the port is located at its northern end – hardly making for the perfect tropical moment – and the beach itself is narrow and scruffy. South from here, around a small headland, is another small stretch of sand, usually also known as Victory Beach, but also signposted as **Lamherkay Beach**, after the old hotel near here.

Further south on the western tip of Sihanoukville's headland is tiny **Koh Pos Beach**, which has been taken over by Treasure Island Restaurant. This is a nice, shady beach, but with rough waters. Finally, there is **Independence Beach** running southeast from here – it's a good stretch of clean sand, but lacks shade and facilities. Above the northern end of the beach is the old **Independance Hotel** [sic], soon to reopen its doors as a four-star hotel after extensive renovations.

Diving

The marine life off the coast of Sihanoukville isn't as impressive as that of Thailand or Indonesia, thanks in part to dynamite fishing. However, further afield around the islands of **Koh Tang** and **Koh Prins** and nearby reefs, there are some interesting dive sites, although most remain relatively unexplored. Unfortunately,

this area can't be reached in a day using the slow fishing boats and so requires an overnight trip, which pushes up the costs.

There are currently three dive operators in Sihanoukville. In theory, they are open 9am to 12pm and 2pm to 5pm, but in practice hours are completely random.

Claude (☎ 012 824870; www.chezclaude.info; Chez Claude) Claude has been exploring the waters of Sihanoukville for more than a decade now, and specialises in longer trips to distant reefs.

EcoSea Dive (☎ 012 654104; www.ecosea.com; Ph Ekareach) One of the newer outfits offering Professional Association of Diving Instructors (PADI) courses, fun dives and snorkelling.

Scuba Nation Diving Center (☎ 012 604680; www .divecambodia.com; Weather Station Hill) The first Professional Association of Diving Instructors (PADI) centre to open in Cambodia. The multilingual instructors offer classes in English, Dutch, French and German.

Massage

There are lots of dodgy massage parlours in Sihanoukville, but for a legitimate venue, head to **Seeing Hands Massage 3** (☎ 012 794016; Ph Ekareach; per hr US$3. Massages are administered by trained blind masseurs. It raises money to assist Cambodia's visually impaired community.

Other Attractions

Kbal Chhay Waterfall is a popular excursion for Khmers visiting Sihanoukville, as it was used as a major location for the filming of the popular movie *Pos Keng Kong* (The Giant Snake; 2000), the most successful Cambodian-made film in the post–civil war era. The multiple falls are attractive, but not as spectacular or isolated as those near Krong Koh Kong. There is also a litter problem here that rather detracts from the natural beauty. Anyone who has seen or is planning to see the falls at Krong Koh Kong can probably give Kbal Chhay a miss. For anyone who has seen *Pos Keng Kong*, it's a must. The falls are located about 17km from the centre of Sihanoukville. The turn-off is signposted on the left from NH4, about 9km out of town. It costs around US$4 for a return trip by *moto*, but it's easy enough to navigate yourself on a rented motorcycle.

Just 2km north of the main port is a **fishing port**, which offers good photo opportunities at sunrise or sunset. Another 20km up the coast is the small fishing town of **Stung**

Hau, where the rusting remains of Cambodia's communist navy lie abandoned.

SLEEPING

For the budget traveller there's a wide range of inexpensive rooms in Sihanoukville, from US$3 with a bed and fan to US$10 with aircon, TV and hot-water bathroom. There is also a good selection for midrange visitors looking to spend between US$15 and US$30, as the arrival of some major casinos with cheap rooms has kept prices down. And the opening of Sokha Beach Resort brings some genuine international comfort to town. Most visitors want to stay as close to the beach as possible, because the beaches are the stars here. For those who are all beached out after Thailand, there is the town centre, but it is not the most charming place in Cambodia by any stretch of the imagination.

Budget

There are three main areas for budget accommodation here: the long-running area centred on Weather Station Hill above Victory Beach; the town centre; and the flavour of the moment, Serendipity Beach.

VICTORY BEACH

This was the original backpacker area and there are more than 20 guesthouses on the hill above the beach, many with barely a sign and offering just a few basic rooms.

Mealy Chenda Guesthouse (☎ 933472; dm US$2, r US$3-15; 🔀 🖳) Sihanoukville's original backpacker guesthouse is still going strong. Looking more like a hotel at first glance, it offers good-value rooms at budget prices. The cheapest rooms have a shared bathroom, those from US$5 and up include a TV, and the air-con rooms from US$12 have a balcony and sometimes a sea view. There's plenty of travel information available here, plus a good restaurant.

Da Da Guesthouse (☎ 012 879527; r US$2-8; 🔀) Another one of the longer-running places up on the hill. The friendly family offers a good selection of rooms from the very basic to slightly more sophisticated with TV and bathroom. Possibly the cheapest air-con in town.

Bungalow Village (☎ 933875; bungalows US$4-10) Occupying a strategic section of the hillside that's nearer the beach than most, the garden here gives this place charm. The

cheaper bungalows are smaller with local bathrooms, while the most expensive are bigger and include a balcony with a view.

Sakal Bungalows (☎ 012 806155; r US$3-8; 🔀) Right at the bottom of Weather Station Hill, just over the road from the beach, this sprawling setup has 28 rooms. Some are tepee-style bungalows, while others are located in the longhouse. All are clean, and the upper price brings air-con into the equation. Its restaurant and bar are pretty lively and worth a stop for nonguests on their way back from the beach.

Other spots:

Blue Frog Guesthouse (☎ 012 432799; r US$5-10; 🔀) This old wooden house has just been renovated and has a nice breezy veranda upstairs.

Mash Guesthouse (☎ 012 913714; r US$3-5; 🔀) A long-running place with a mix of rooms with some popular paint schemes.

SERENDIPITY BEACH

All of these places are built on land leased from the military police and may not be around permanently.

Eden (☎ 933585; r US$8-10) It doesn't get any more beachfront than at Eden, a smart wooden building with comfortable fan rooms. The location is great by day, but not quite so great by night, when the downstairs bar and next door Unkle Bob's both start pumping out tunes into the early hours.

Cloud 9 (☎ 012 479365; bungalow US$8-10) Not exactly Serendipity, but on the hillside over towards Sokha Beach, this attractive little resort has bungalows draped down the hillside to the sea. The bungalows are basic but comfortable and the location attracts a breeze. Includes a little bar near the water.

Mohachai Guesthouse (☎ 933586; r US$5-8) Located just a short stroll up the hill from the beach, there are now nearly 40 rooms here. Tiled floors and attached bathrooms are about as flash as it gets, and the staff is a good source of travel tips.

Sea Sun Guesthouse (☎ 012 357825; r US$3-10; 🔀) Midway between Golden Lions roundabout and Serendipity Beach, this place offers the best value for money in this part of town. Pokey bungalow rooms are just US$3, while bigger bungalows include TV and hot water and start at just US$5 with fan – quite a bargain. The big garden is a bit bare but promises room for expansion.

OCCHEUTEAL BEACH
This has traditionally been the turf of mid-range overseas tourists and Khmers, but budget places are making inroads.

Sovann Phoum Guesthouse (☎ 012 504537; Ph 1 Kanda; r US$5-10; ❄) Located a couple of blocks back from the thick of the action; the rooms here are clean, comfortable and a fair deal. All include TV and a bathroom, and a mini restaurant has just opened out the front.

GST Guesthouse (☎ 933816; r US$5-12; ❄) If the name sounds familiar, it's because there is a link with the bus company of the same name and that helps explain how the owners manage to fill their 44 rooms on a regular basis. The rooms, all single-storey bungalows, are in good shape and all rooms come with TV and attached bathroom.

Susaday Guesthouse (☎ 933907; susaday@camintel.com; Ph 14 Milthona; r US$10) It's hard to fault the location, right across from the beach, but the rooms themselves are quite basic and are twice the price of similar rooms found at other guesthouses.

TOWN CENTRE
There are dozens of places around the town centre, but given the attraction of the beach, it's not most people's first choice.

Angkor Inn Guesthouse (☎ 016 896204; Ph Sopheakmongkol; r US$4-5) Cheap and a little bit cheerful, this is a firmly established budget deal. Large TVs and small bathrooms are standard, plus there is the lure of great coffee across the road at Espresso Kampuchea.

Freedom Hotel (☎ 012 257953; Ph Sopheakmongkol; r US$5-20; ❄) The cheapest fan rooms are a little dark due to lack of windows, but the US$10 rooms are well kitted-out with TV, hot water and air-con. All room rates include a free beer at the bar downstairs!

Midrange

With the exception of weekends, when Khmers head down from Phnom Penh, there is generally a glut of midrange rooms available in Sihanoukville. This, coupled with some of the bigger hotels slashing their rates dramatically, means there are good deals to be had.

OCCHEUTEAL BEACH
This is the most popular part of town for bigger spenders, thanks to its location – a short stroll to the beach.

Occheuteal Beachside Bungalows (☎ 933895; r US$15; ❄) A new resort just a block back from the beach. The solid thatched bungalows here come complete with hot water, TV and a fridge. The staff is always on hand to help, plus there is a likeable little restaurant and bar.

Crystal Hotel (☎ 933880; crystal@camintel.com; Ph 14 Milthona; r US$20-30; ❄) OK, so the hotel looks a little strange from the outside, with all the reflective glass, but once inside the rooms are pretty smart and the building's design allows all a sea view (of sorts). Carpets, bathtubs and other little touches make it a touch smarter than some of the competition.

Seaside Hotel (☎ 933662; fax 933640; Ph 14 Milthona; r US$20-40; ❄) This is one of the town's most established hotels, and it looks like a junior version of the famous Hotel Cambodiana (p93) in Phnom Penh. It offers a variety of well-appointed rooms and is pretty popular with tour groups hitting the beach.

Orchidee Guesthouse (☎ 933639; www.orchidee-guesthouse.com; Ph 23 Tola; r US$10-25; ❄ 🖳 🖳) A short way from the beach, this place is popular with adventure tour groups – so it's often full. The rooms are more hotel than guesthouse and the new swimming pool is a welcome addition.

Golden Sand Hotel (☎ 933607; www.hotelgoldensand.com; r US$20-50; ❄ 🖳 🖳) This huge new hotel is currently the smartest place near Occheuteal. The rooms are so sparkling that you may need shades, but they're certainly comfortable. The swimming pool out front is popular, but in the public eye.

SERENDIPITY BEACH
House of Malibu (☎ 012 733334; r US$25-30; ❄) Running down to the sands of Serendipity Beach, Malibu offers the most charming accommodation in town for this kind of money. The rooms are all named after flowers and include hot showers, TV and a hearty breakfast in the elevated restaurant overlooking the sea. **Malibu Bungalows** (r US$25-30) is a newer operation on the hill between Sokha and Serendipity Beaches, offering attractive bungalows spilling down to the sea (although they don't include air-con and hot water). Over the road are more smart rooms like those at the original House of Malibu.

Rama Beach Bungalows (☎ 934088; r US$20-25; ❄) Occupying a prime slice of beachfront, this resort has smart but small bungalows with all the amenities. There really isn't a lot of room around the beds, so these may be better suited to solo travellers. The cheaper rooms are set further back, the pricier options in front.

Coasters (☎ 933776; coasters@camintel.com; r US$10-15) These solid bungalows are spread across the hillside above the beach, although the bar and restaurant run right to the water's edge. The bungalows have their own verandas for some quality contemplation, but are otherwise basic with fan and bathroom.

Sea View Villa (☎ 935555; r US$6-20; 🏠) The top-notch rooms here are huge, with open-plan bathrooms and enough space to play table tennis, making for a really good deal. There are also cheaper options available with fan, so there's something for everyone. It's just a few metres back from the beach.

The Beach (☎ 016 931970; r US$6-18; 🏠) Nestled between Sea View and Rama Beach, this little hideaway has some very stylish air-con rooms complete with TV, fridge and hot water. There is also a garden restaurant and bar for relaxing at night.

OTHER BEACHES

There are fewer options to be found on other beaches around town.

Snake House (☎ 012 673805; Lamherkay Beach; s/d US$15/20; 🏠) These stylish bungalows look something like Lombok's Sasak style colliding with Cambodia, but it works well. The large rooms are impressive value and include TV, fridge and smart bathrooms, as well as verandas for relaxing. The attached reptile house's restaurant (opposite) is far enough away that snake haters need not look under the bed each night.

Chez Mari Yan (☎ 933709; r US$5-20) Tucked away in a verdant garden that overlooks Victory Beach, this bungalow resort is more about rustic charm than straightforward comfort. The cheapest rooms are in a long-house, but it is worth investing more for a larger bungalow with a sea view. There's also a small restaurant and bar.

Holiday Palace Hotel & Casino (☎ 933808; fax 933809; Ph Krong; r US$15-45; 🏠 🖥) The first casino complex to set up shop in Sihanoukville does what all casino complexes do best – it slashes rates to draw in the punters. Looming large over Victory Beach, the US$15 rooms are of three-star standard, making them one of the best deals in Cambodia.

Chez Claude (☎ 012 824870; www.chezclaude.info; bungalows US$20-50; 🏠) For a commanding view over the town's beaches, it is hard to beat this hilltop resort above Sokha Beach. Rooms range from a traditional Cambodian house to an African *banda* (circular hut with thatch roof). All have atmosphere in abundance and hot water, but it is quite a hike to the beach.

Sea Breeze Guesthouse (☎ 320217; s/d/tr US$15/20/25; 🏠) A lonely looking place down on Independence Beach, this is a possible option for a bit of peace and quiet. Rooms come with all the touches like satellite TV and fridge, but it's a long, dark road to town for those who like to party at night.

Top End

Sokha Beach Resort (☎ 935999; www.sokhahotels .com; r US$130-250; 🏠 🖥 🖥) Cambodia's first five-star beach resort brings luxury to Sihanoukville. The rooms are elegantly designed with both bathtub and shower and include room safes and balconies, as well as all the other touches you expect at this end of the scale. The pool is resort sized, but better still is the private beach, long considered the best in town. Best news of all is that the rates have been aggressively discounted since it opened in 2004, so you may get a very good deal.

EATING

There's a healthy selection of restaurants and cafés in Sihanoukville. Most are open from about 7am for breakfast and close after dinner at around 9pm or 10pm. The backpacker area on Weather Station Hill claims a dozen or more restaurants, plus decent food at many of the guesthouses. The centre of gravity has definitely shifted to Serendipity Beach, which is also a good spot for beachside barbecues. However, other beaches around town have a couple of seafood restaurants, while the centre of town has a few places that can be useful for before or after a bus trip or during a night on the town. Most beaches attract vendors selling everything from pineapples and quail eggs to freshly grilled prawns and fish. You may find it all a bit of a hard sell if you are just trying to relax on the beach, but provided you bargain, this can be an inexpensive way to snack your way through the day.

Weather Station Hill

The original budget-dining centre of town. Places here offer a good range of tasty and inexpensive cuisines, served out of basic wooden shacks.

Mealy Chenda Restaurant (mains US$1-3) The rooftop restaurant at Mealy Chenda Guesthouse (p188) draws a mixed crowd at night, including local Khmers. The menu includes an evening seafood barbecue as well as backpacker breakfasts, but service can be slow if it's busy. A good spot for a sunset beer.

Romduol's Restaurant (mains 3000-5000r) The menu here is uncannily like that of Mealy Chenda, as it was set up by a former employee of the guesthouse. Located just across the road, dishes are competitively priced in riel rather than US dollars, and it fills up most nights.

Sam's Restaurant (mains US$1-3) One of the original guesthouses in town continues life as a small family-run restaurant. The menu strikes a nice balance between Khmer and Western food and it's a friendly place to hang out.

Melting Pot (☎ 012 913714; mains US$1-4) Merged with Mash Guesthouse (p188), this little eatery has a slightly more adventurous selection of Western food than its rivals, and offers popular Sunday lunches – good after a hard night on the town.

Indian Curry Pot (☎ 934040; dishes US$2-4) Recently relocated to the main strip on Weather Station Hill, this little hole in the wall offers some of the best curries in Sihanoukville. It's 100% halal, and has good-value buffets at the weekend.

La Paillotte (mains US$3-7) Bringing a touch of class to an otherwise budget backyard, this new restaurant is set under a giant thatched roof at the end of a winding path. The accent is predominantly French, with a good range of local seafood soaked in sauces. Out the front is a laid-back bar with a pool table.

Snake House (☎ 012 673805; mains US$2-5) 'Unique' is a used and abused term in tourism circles, but for once it is justified at this restaurant, near the guesthouse of the same name (opposite). The tables are set amid a flourishing reptile house with snakes from all over the world. The food, well, that's incidental when there's a python to your left, a cobra to your right and snakes right underneath your plate…yes, the glass-topped tables include snakes inside.

Serendipity & Occheuteal Beaches

A lot of visitors end up dining on Serendipity Beach, as the beachfront tables with candles are hard to beat for atmosphere. There is now a string of beach shacks turning out cheap food almost all the way to Occheuteal Beach with barbecued fish and seafood at reasonable prices at all of them.

Unkle Bob's (☎ 934072; mains US$1-4) One of the first places to open down here, Unkle Bob's has a prime location under the boughs of a creaking tree. This means shade by day and shadows by night. The menu is fairly standard, but includes a popular barbecue each night.

Rama Beach Restaurant (mains US$3-6) A cut above the competition, Rama Beach offers low-slung tables on the beach or upright dining under a pavilion. The menu mixes Asian favourites with tasty pastas, but it's all about the seafood here, including a good selection of shellfish.

Mick & Craig's Restaurant (☎ 012 727740; mains US$2-6) No prizes for guessing the names of the owners at this establishment, now relocated to the heart of the action near Serendipity. This outdoor restaurant is set under a thatched roof and has a good selection of breakfasts, including hearty vegetarian options, as well as a serious selection of good Western grub and popular specials. Food is served late (until around 11pm) and a small secondhand bookstore is attached.

Other Beaches

There are several seafood restaurants located on the beaches around Sihanoukville, including **Hawaii Seaview Restaurant** (Lamherkay Beach; mains US$2-6), but it is worth checking the price when you order, as much of the seafood is by the kilo and the bill can mount quickly.

Treasure Island Restaurant (☎ 012 755335; Koh Pos Beach; mains US$2-10) Occupying an isolated beach, this is a big seafood restaurant that's popular with Khmers and Asian tourists. Prices are generally reasonable, although shellfish goes by the kilo, so keep an eye on the weight. Most of it is fresh and housed in tanks – just point to what you want and the staff will fish it out. One litre bottles of Gordon's Gin are US$12 here, and Smirnoff Vodka is just US$8! Don't drive if you like your spirits!

Koh Pos Restaurant (Golden Lions roundabout; US$2-8) This restaurant's less than memorable location has done nothing to dent its popularity with Khmers. The wok-fried curried whole crab (about US$5 depending on the size of the crab) is a speciality.

Chez Claude (seafood mains US$5-8) Clinging to the top of Chez Claude's hilltop empire (p190), the predominantly seafood menu at this restaurant is one of the best in town. It includes claypot fish dishes with a French accent and local shellfish such as clams and scallops. The wine list is extensive, but you can just drop by for a sunset beer – the views are massive.

Town Centre

The town centre has more than its fair share of restaurants, but they can't deliver the sea view of the beachside places.

Starfish Bakery (☎ 012 952011; mains US$1-3; ⊗ breakfast & lunch) Tucked down a little side street off Ph 7 Makara, this garden café provides filling breakfasts and light lunches (such as salads and sandwiches), all in the name of a good cause. Like a grassroots nongovernmental organisation (NGO), the Starfish Project supports local disadvantaged Cambodians who have fallen upon hard times. The homemade cakes and a juice are a great way to break up the day.

Marlin Grill Restaurant (Ph Ekareach; mains US$2-5) Set underneath the Marlin Hotel, this bar-restaurant is popular with expats for its fast-food fixes such as burgers and steaks.

Self-caterers wanting to put together a picnic for a day out should head to **Samudera Market** (Ph 7 Makara), just by the turn-off to the Starfish Bakery. This has the best stock of international foods, including cheese, meats and chocolate. **Caltex Starmart** (Ph Ekareach) is another convenient option that stays open pretty late.

DRINKING

Nightlife in Sihanoukville continues to gather pace with more and more travellers crossing by land from Thailand. The late-opening spots are all in the centre of town or at Serendipity Beach, but there are a whole lot of beach shacks further south on Occheuteal that heave until the early hours. It is hard to recommend any by name, as they may not be around much longer, once the new resort opens in this part of town.

With the Angkor Brewery located on the outskirts of town, draught beer is very

cheap – it starts at US$0.50 at some of the budget restaurants on Weather Station Hill. Melting Pot (p191), Romduol's Restaurant (p191) and Mealy Chenda Restaurant (p191) all pull a drinking crowd into the evening, but for the real action it is better to hit a dedicated bar.

Pet's Place (☎ 012 472325; Weather Station Hill) A long-running bar that has moved all over town; it's come to rest here and is one of the most popular places in the old backpacker quarter. Cheap drinks and a pool table should keep it that way and there are rooms for rent (US$2 to US$5) for those that like the place so much they want to stay.

Corner Bar (Weather Station Hill) It does what the sign says and straddles the busiest corner in this part of town. A hot spot for catching English Premier League action, it stays open later than most on the hill.

Angkor Arms (www.angkorarms.com; Ph Ekareach) Probably the oldest bar in town, this place sells itself as a traditional British pub with darts and draught beer. There is air-con on the inside and a large outdoor area for those who want a drink au naturel. Happy hour is from 5pm to 7pm, and it's open late.

Dusk 'til Dawn (Ph Sopheakmongkol) Right next door to Angkor Arms, this place is located on the rooftop of a townhouse, up a rickety staircase. The name gives away its hardcore opening hours and it is usually the last place in town to close. Just mind the stairs on the way home!

Blue Storm (Ph Ekareach; entry free) The only real nightclub in town. It can be pretty quiet on weekdays, but it tends to be crammed at the weekends when young Khmers make for the beach. With DJs, VJs and slightly more-pricey drinks than elsewhere in town, don't come here expecting conversation.

Down on Serendipity Beach there are a couple of popular bars, including 24-hour Unkle Bob's (p191) that rocks on into the night. There's also the ever-popular Eden (p188), with an inviting bar to prop up and some horizontal deckchairs for taking things slowly.

GETTING THERE & AWAY
Air

Sihanoukville airport, 13km out of town near Ream, has been renovated, but there are currently no scheduled flights. There is much talk of local airlines offering flights to

Siem Reap for a temples-beach combo, but nothing has yet materialised.

Boat

There are daily boats departing Sihanoukville (500B, four hours) at noon for Krong Koh Kong. Most foreigners are charged US$15 or 600B. For more details on this boat service and crossing into Thailand, see p293.

Bus

NH4, the 230km road between Sihanoukville and Phnom Penh, is in excellent condition for its entire length. Phnom Penh Public Transport (PPPT), Hour Lean, GST and Capitol Tours operate large, comfortable, air-con buses between Sihanoukville and the capital (12,000r, four hours) Their ticket offices are located on Ph Ekareach in the centre of town. Most companies operate several services a day in both directions, starting around 7am and finishing about 1.30pm. All buses now arrive and depart from the taxi park, however, not the ticket offices.

Motorcycle

Some travellers with biking experience use motorcycles rented in Phnom Penh (p107) to get to Sihanoukville. However, while NH4 is an easy run, it's relatively dull by Cambodian standards, and quite dangerous due to the prevalence of high-speed overtaking on blind corners. A motorcycle is useful for exploring areas along the south coast and it is becoming increasingly popular to do a circuit that takes in Kampot, Kep and Bokor hill station. Note that foreigners are not permitted to hire motorcycles in Sihanoukville; if hired elsewhere they can be ridden here though (see right).

Share Taxi

Taxis between Phnom Penh and Sihanoukville leave from the southwest of the capital near Psar Dang Kor (Dang Kor Market) or Psar Thmei (New Market), and from Sihanoukville from the new taxi park. Taxis are worth considering only if you have somehow managed to miss the bus, or are in a real rush. Prices are negotiable, but you can expect to pay about US$20 a vehicle, 10,000r a head in cramped conditions or 15,000r each with just three in the back. Most drivers seem to think they're Michael Schumacher, so if you don't like blind over-

taking, you may want to sit in the back with some Valium.

The road is now surfaced all the way from Sihanoukville to Kampot (8000r, two hours, 105km). Taxis to Kampot also depart from the taxi park and it should be possible to charter a whole car for around US$15.

Train

The train service to Sihanoukville is extraordinarily slow when compared with the bus service. There is a daily cargo service willing to take foreign passengers, but anyone really wanting to try trains is better off travelling the shorter journey between Takeo and Kampot (p198).

GETTING AROUND
Bicycle

Cycling is a pleasant and environmentally friendly way to get around Sihanoukville. Some guesthouses around town offer rentals at around US$1 to US$2 for the day.

Moto

There are plenty of *motos* for hire in Sihanoukville, but it is a cut-throat business. Sihanoukville drivers are the most notorious in Cambodia for ripping off people, so it is necessary to haggle hard over the price of all journeys. From the guesthouse area to the market is about 2000r, to Sokha and Occheuteal Beaches around 3000r, plus a little extra at night. From the centre of town to any of the beaches should set you back about 2000r. From the backpacker area to the fast-boat dock, it is hard to get anything under US$1.

Motorcycle

At the time of going to press, authorities were no longer allowing foreigners to rent motorcycles in Sihanoukville. It remains to be seen if this ban will hold, so ask around for the latest at guesthouses, restaurants and bars.

Before the ban was put in place, the cheapest rentals in town were 100cc *motos* at US$3 per day (available through many guesthouses and restaurants). Slightly newer bikes cost US$4. If the ban is lifted, **GST** (☎ 933826; Ph Ekareach) in the town centre rents out bikes for US$4 per day, plus larger 250cc trail bikes for US$7 per day, just the thing for Bokor National Park.

SOUTH COAST

AROUND SIHANOUKVILLE

For the lowdown on what to see and do in Kirirom National Park, located midway between Sihanoukville and the capital, see p111.

ISLANDS

There are more than a dozen islands off the coast of Sihanoukville; all are extremely undeveloped by the standards of neighbouring Thailand. Only **Koh Russei** (Bamboo Island) has some basic bungalows. Many of the guesthouses, restaurants and bars around Sihanoukville arrange day trips to the most popular islands, including a spot of snorkelling and lunch.

Most of the islands nearer town are small, rocky and far from ideal for anything but limited snorkelling. Further afield are the large islands of **Koh Rong** and **Koh Rong Samlon**. Both are surrounded by blissfully empty, beautiful beaches and have freshwater sources, suggesting they will be a major focus for future development. Koh Rong Samlon includes a large heart-shaped bay with some shellfish cultivation, as well as some good beaches on its north coast. Koh Rong has a fantastic beach on the southwestern coast, stretching for 5km or more without a beach hut in sight. There are other good beaches around this huge island, and there's a bustling fishing community on the southeast with basic supplies available, plus fresh fish and crab. If one place is set to become the Ko Samui (Thailand) of Cambodia, this is it – don't worry though, it won't be for at least another five years!

Nearer the coast and to the south of Sihanoukville are several smaller islands that are an option if the open waters to Koh Rong are too choppy. **Koh Khteah** is the nearest, but very small, while **Koh Ta Khieu** has the better beaches, but is near Cambodia's navy headquarters.

REAM NATIONAL PARK
ឧទ្យានជាតិរាម

Also known as Preah Sihanouk National Park, Ream National Park was established in 1993 as a 210 sq km protected area and is home to many animal and bird species and an expanse of mangrove swamp and forests.

The park has boats that can transport visitors along the river to untouched beaches. Along the estuary you may see monkeys, eagles and even dolphins or porpoises, and from the empty sands on the coast it is possible to explore some nearby creeks that disappear into the forest.

Boat trips through the park are both adventurous and educational, providing you get an English-speaking ranger. The income generated should ensure that the rangers protect the park instead of selling its firewood or poaching its wildlife to make a living. Boats cost US$25 for up to four people and US$5 for every additional person, plus US$5 for the ranger. Sounds complicated? Guesthouses in Sihanoukville can make arrangements (including lunch).

Getting There & Away

Ream National Park is located about 13km east of the centre of Sihanoukville. To get to the park headquarters, take a *moto* from Sihanoukville for about US$2, or squeeze in a share taxi to Ream. The park's headquarters is a short distance down a turn-off from the *naga* (mythical serpent) statue in Ream. Look out for the Preah Sihanouk National Park sign carved in stone. The building (white with a green roof) is located right next to the little-used airport. Boats leave from a bridge about 5km further up NH4. Contact the rangers to organise a trip or try a guesthouse in town.

KAMPOT PROVINCE
ខេត្តកំពត

Kampot has emerged as one of the most popular provinces in Cambodia, thanks to an alluring combination of abandoned colonial towns, abundant natural attractions and easy access around the region.

Most of the attractions in Kampot can be absorbed in just a few days, including Bokor National Park and its abandoned hill station, the dilapidated but recovering seaside resort of Kep and the caves around Kompong Trach. However, the sleepy, atmospheric provincial capital of Kampot often holds people longer than expected.

It wasn't always this way. Kampot remained a dangerous province to visit until the mid-1990s due to the presence of Khmer Rouge units in the surrounding hills. A train travelling between Phnom Penh and Sihanoukville was ambushed in July 1994, and three foreigners and a large number of Khmers were kidnapped. As government forces closed in on Phnom Voal, where the prisoners were being held, the three Westerners were executed by the Khmer Rouge.

The province's economy never really recovered from the loss of its south-coast port status to Sihanoukville in 1959, and was in slow decline until the civil war. Agriculture gradually regained supremacy over trade in the province; a wide range of fruit and vegetables, herbs and spices are cultivated. Durian haters be warned: Kampot is Cambodia's main producer of this stinky fruit.

Road links between Kampot Province and Phnom Penh have come on in leaps and bounds in the past few years. NH3 to Phnom Penh is in pretty good condition for its whole length, while long-forgotten NH31 running down to Kep and Kompong Trach has been totally rebuilt. Heading west to Sihanoukville, there is more good news, with a widened road approaching motorway status by Cambodian standards. The Phnom Penh–Sihanoukville railway line runs right across the province, with the most scenic stretches found here. It is a long journey right through, but taking short sections – such as between Kampot and Takeo or Kampot and Veal Renh – is a nice way to get a taste of life on the rails without the hardships.

KAMPOT
កំពត

☎ 033 / pop 33,000

The sleepy riverside town of Kampot is slowly awakening. Visitors are discovering a charming place with a French architectural legacy and a relaxed atmosphere. Despite experiencing a commercial decline since the birth of Sihanoukville in 1959, Kampot is well known for producing some of the best pepper in the region. In the years before war took its toll, no self-respecting French restaurant worth its salt in Paris would be without Kampot pepper on the table. The town is the perfect base from which to explore the nearby crumbling beach resort of

Kep, the abandoned hill station of Bokor and the caves around Kompong Trach.

Orientation

Kampot is bordered to the west by the river, beyond which looms the massive shadow of Phnom Bokor. The centre of town is marked by a large roundabout. To the northwest is the market and to the north is the road to Phnom Penh. To the southeast is the road to Kep and Kompong Trach.

Information

The main post office is on the river to the south of the city centre, but it is safer to save any post for the capital. There are plenty of telephone booths around town that offer local and international calls.

INTERNET ACCESS

It is easy enough to get online in Kampot, with a string of Internet places along Ph 7 Makara; the going rate is currently 6000r an hour. Santepheap Internet is reliable.

MONEY

Acleda Bank (☎ 932880) Western Union representative for anyone in need of a quick money transfer.
Canadia Bank (☎ 932392) Cash and travellers cheques, plus credit-card cash advances with no fee; this is the best all-rounder in town.

TOURIST INFORMATION

There is a tourist office in town, but the staff has nothing in the way of hand-outs. Guesthouses and hotels are a far better source of information for the time being.

Sights & Activities

Most of the interesting activities are found beyond Kampot in Bokor, Kep or the Emmenthal-like countryside that is littered with caves.

KAMPOT TRADITIONAL MUSIC SCHOOL

Established to train orphaned and disabled children in the arts of traditional music and dance, the delicate sounds of **Kampot Traditional Music School** (◷ 7-11am & 2-5pm) can be heard beyond the compound. Visitors are more than welcome to come to see the students training, and it's open most evenings (from 6.30pm to 9pm) when students are training for folk dances and music. There is no charge but donations are welcome.

SOUTH COAST

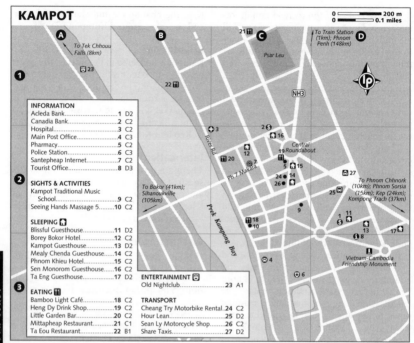

KAMPOT

MASSAGE

The latest outpost of the excellent Seeing Hands empire is **Seeing Hands Massage 5** (☎ 012 503012; per hr US$3; ⏰ 8am-6pm). Blind masseurs are trained in shiatsu massage and all profits go towards assisting blind people in Cambodia. The right medicine after the bumpy road to Bokor...

BOAT TRIPS

Kampot's riverside location makes it a good place to organise a short boat trip upstream. Ask around among local boat owners and you should be able to arrange something for about US$5 an hour. Several of the guesthouses and hotels around town can arrange something a little more organised – try the Mealy Chenda Guesthouse (right).

Sleeping

There is now some real competition in Kampot and there are a lot of good deals to be had. One thing worth bearing in mind is that after a wet or cloudy day trip up to Bokor hill station, a hot shower might well be in order.

Blissful Guesthouse (☎ 012 513024; dm/s/d US$2.50/3/4) Surrounded by a lush garden, this old wooden house is home to the most atmospheric guesthouse in Kampot. The rooms are basic, with a shared bathroom at the bottom end, but with a few thoughtful extra decorative touches. There is a great chill-out area for guests upstairs and a very popular bar-restaurant, open to all-comers, downstairs.

Mealy Chenda Guesthouse (☎ 932559; dm/s US$2/3, d US$4-6) With a new location closer to the action, this guesthouse is run by the same family as Mealy Chenda in Sihanoukville (p188). It's a vast building, and the rooms are equally cavernous. Plans include a rooftop restaurant and bar. It's a good place for travel information and transport services.

Borey Bokor Hotel (☎ 012 820826; s/d US$10/15, VIP r US$25; ❄) The top hotel in town. The rooms here are smart and include TV, fridge, hot water and air-con, all in spotless surroundings. VIP rooms are a little larger and include a bathtub, but they are not exactly fit for a king.

Sen Monorom Guesthouse (☎ 012 650330; r US$5-15; 🖭) No, we are not in Mondulkiri! This new guesthouse is an enticing deal for budget travellers wanting that extra dose of comfort. All rooms are the same – large and clean with big windows and satellite TV. Handing over US$5 spins the fan; make it US$15 and the air-con kicks in.

Ta Eng Guesthouse (☎ 012 330058; r US$2-5) This is the longest-running basic backpacker place in town. It has steadily expanded from a family homestay into a popular guesthouse with extra amenities like attached bathrooms. The friendly owner speaks French and English and looks after his guests.

Kampot Guesthouse (☎ 016 885255; r US$4-13; 🖭) One of the more upmarket guesthouses in town. Large budget rooms are a good deal at US$4, while the more expensive air-con rooms come with fancier furnishings and a bigger bathroom.

Phnom Khieu Hotel (☎ 012 820923; r US$5-12; 🖭) This ex-government hotel, located at the central roundabout, has good-value fan rooms with bathroom and TV, but there is an air of neglect hanging over the place. Time for a facelift!

Eating

There's a good range of international menus to complement the excellent local cuisine.

Several guesthouses and hotels have popular restaurants, including Mealy Chenda Guesthouse (opposite), which has a wide range of Khmer food and international treats from US$0.50 to US$2.50. Full breakfasts at US$2 are a steal here. Blissful Guesthouse (opposite) has a fine selection of food from US$1 to US$4, including some Mexican dishes and plenty of sandwiches and salads.

Ta Eou Restaurant (☎ 932422; River Rd; mains 4000-8000r) Location, location, location…this place has it, built on stilts over the river, and is a top place for a sunset meal with views across to Bokor. The English-language menu is extensive and includes fresh seafood dishes. Crab with fresh green peppercorns (around US$4, depending on the size of the crab) is tasty, as are the local broths.

Bamboo Light Café (☎ 012 602661; River Rd; curries US$2-4) Kampot's first Sri Lankan restaurant brings the spices of the subcontinent to town. Local expats rave about the fine flavours and the setting is slap-bang in the middle of the action on the riverfront.

Little Garden Bar (☎ 012 256901; www.littlegarden bar.com; River Rd; mains US$1-3) The first bar to come to Kampot a few years ago, this tranquil little haven now has a small menu of Khmer and international dishes. Set in the garden of an old French-period property, the cocktail list is impressive for this neck of the woods and wine is available by the glass. The owners have recently opened a new guesthouse next door with six swish rooms at US$10 a pop. Enquire at the restaurant for more details.

Mittapheap Restaurant (mains 4000-8000r) Opposite the market, this place has long been a favourite with officials from the French embassy – and who is to question the French when it comes to food? Great soups and Khmer staples, all at fair prices.

Heng Dy Drink Shop (☎ 932925) The spot for self-caterers planning to explore Bokor, this place at the central roundabout has a healthy selection of imported goods, including cheese, pâté and chocolate.

Drinking

Kampot may not be kicking just yet, but there is a lot more nightlife than there used to be. Diners at Little Garden Bar (above) and Mealy Chenda Guesthouse (opposite) often find themselves lingering for a drink. However, come the later hours, there is only one place to be in Kampot and that is Blissful Guesthouse (opposite), with its happening little bar downstairs. Cheap beer and plenty of spirits guarantee a good time.

For something completely different, the old nightclub in town, just across the river from the real action, has reopened as a sort of karaoke bar. It's mostly about drunk Khmer males making moves on local ladies of the night, but the outside terrace is quite a relaxing place to have a cheap bottle of Angkor (US$1.50).

Getting There & Away

Travellers with riding experience can get to Kampot on 250cc motorcycles from the capital; see p107 for rental details. It is also a good trip from Sihanoukville to Kampot by motorcycle. However, note that at the moment it is not possible to rent motorcycles in Sihanoukville; see p193. It is possible to rent motorcycles in Kampot; see p198.

For details on getting to Bokor National Park, Kep and Kompong Trach, see p200, p202 and p203 respectively.

SOUTH COAST

TAXI, PICK-UP & MINIBUS

Kampot is 148km from Phnom Penh and the condition of NH3 varies depending on how long it's been between repairs. At the time of writing, it is in sharp shape and the trip takes about two hours. Share taxis (10,000r) leave Kampot from a stand near the Total petrol station, just southeast of the roundabout; minibuses leave from the same place and cost 6000r. More comfortable is the new bus service to the capital operated by **Hour Lean** (☎ 012 939917), costing 10,000r.

There is also the same selection of vehicles making the 105km journey to Sihanoukville, a road which has been completely rebuilt in recent years. For more details, see p193.

From Kampot to Takeo is not so straightforward, as there are rarely any direct services. Jump in a vehicle going to Phnom Penh and ask to get off at Angk Tasaom, the turn-off for Takeo – the trip to this point should cost about 5000r by share taxi, less in a minibus. From here, take a *moto* (US$1) or a cheaper *remorque-moto* (trailer pulled by a motorcycle) for the 13km trip to Takeo.

TRAIN

In terms of time, taking the train is the least sensible option, but time is something many travellers have to spare. It takes about six hours to Phnom Penh (7500r) or Sihanoukville (4800r) and even with foreigner prices is still pretty cheap. Coming from Phnom Penh, the section between Takeo and Kampot is the most scenic, as the route passes near some interesting karst formations. Continuing on to Sihanoukville, it follows the base of Phnom Bokor (1080m) before looping around a quiet, unexplored region of Cambodia's coast.

The train runs between Phnom Penh and Sihanoukville on alternate days. The schedule is random, but if it leaves Phnom Penh on Monday, it will leave Sihanoukville on Tuesday. Check at the train station a couple of days before travelling.

Getting Around

The average fare for a *moto* ride around town is 1000r. Expect to pay a little extra at night. Kampot has many *remorque-kang* (trailers pulled by bicycles) and the average fare is similar to that of *motos*.

There are two excellent motorcycle rental shops in Kampot. **Sean Ly Motorcycle Shop**

(☎ 012 944687) rents out small bikes for US$3 a day and trail bikes for US$4 to US$5. It can also arrange cars/minibuses/pick-ups for US$20/25/30 per day for small groups who want to do a bit of exploring.

Cheang Try Motorbike Rental (☎ 012 974698) is located on the same strip as Sean Ly and small bikes are hired out for US$2 to US$3, trail bikes for US$4. Owner Cheang Try speaks good English and often guides tourists himself.

AROUND KAMPOT
Tek Chhouu Falls

ទឹកឈូវ

This pleasant bathing spot is a major hit with locals. Waterfall enthusiasts should prepare themselves for a disappointment, however, as these falls, 8km northwest of town, are really just a series of small rapids that don't even move all that rapidly in the dry season. A *moto* to Tek Chhouu should cost about US$1 each way.

There is a proper waterfall 18km further up a dirt track from Tek Chhouu, but access is not straightforward, as the trail is pretty bad. Ask about trail conditions before heading up there, and take a guide. A *moto* should cost about US$5 return.

Caves Around Kampot

There are more holes than a Swiss cheese in the limestone landscape around Kampot and a lot of the bigger caves can be explored with the help of local kids and a reliable torch (flashlight).

Phnom Chhnork is the most impressive because there's a 7th-century brick temple located inside the main chamber. The protection of the cave means the brickwork is in remarkable condition, giving the impression of a kitsch temple replica built more recently. Phnom Chhnork is about 10km from Kampot. Take the road to Kep and veer left after the short one-way section. Follow this road until the tourism signpost and park up in the local temple. Local kids can help guide you from here, for a small tip.

Phnom Sorsia is another cave complex on the way towards Kep. It is considered a holy place and there is a small wat at the bottom of the hill. Concrete steps wind their way past altars and statues on a circuit that takes you to several major caves.

The biggest cave is called **Rung Damrey Saa** (White Elephant Cave) because of a stalactite formation thought to resemble a white-elephant head. Further on the right is a sign pointing to **100 Rice Fields Cave**. By following a precarious path to a small hole in the cave wall, you are rewarded with a peep show of terraced paddy fields. The final cave is home to many bats that you can hear squeaking before you descend. The circuit ends near a small **stupa** from where there are impressive views. Coming from Kep or Kompong Trach, turn right 2.5km after the statue of the white horse. To get here from Kampot, turn left off the main road after 13.5km.

BOKOR NATIONAL PARK
ឧទ្យានជាតិបូកគោ

Officially known as Preah Monivong National Park but more commonly referred to as Bokor, **Bokor National Park** (admission per person US$5) is one of the country's largest protected areas. It has been open to visitors for several years, having long been kept off the map due to Khmer Rouge activity and more recently because of illegal loggers. A decade ago, there was talk of making this vast tropical forest a World Heritage site, but sadly, extensive illegal logging put an end to this initiative.

Within the park boundaries are the nascent tourist attractions of an abandoned French hill station and the Popokvil Falls, a two-tiered waterfall where you can swim

in the wet season. The park is home to significant numbers of birds and mammals, including elephants and tigers. However, most of the animals are nocturnal and inhabit the more remote areas of the park, so don't expect to see much wildlife. The park has a ranger post at the bottom of Phnom Bokor and a ranger station with accommodation at the old hill station. The entry fee will hopefully provide the rangers with much needed revenue to combat illegal logging.

Both the national park and the hill station are believed to be free of land mines, but, as always in Cambodia, do the sensible thing and stick to well-worn paths.

It is easiest to visit the park as a day trip from Kampot, but should you want to visit from Sihanoukville, it is best to overnight at Bokor or in Kampot, as it is a lot of ground to cover in one day.

Sights & Activities
BOKOR HILL STATION
ស្ថានីយដ្ឋានភ្នំបូកគោ

The old French hill station of Bokor (1080m) is known for its cool climate, secluded waterfalls and jungle vistas. The French authorities decided to construct a road to Bokor in 1917; the project took several years to complete and many Cambodian indentured labourers perished in the process. With the completion of the road, a small community was established that included a grand colonial hotel – the Bokor Palace – inaugurated in 1925.

The hill station was twice abandoned: first when Vietnamese and Khmer Issarak (Free Khmer) forces overran it in the late 1940s while fighting for independence against the French, and then in the early 1970s when the Lon Nol regime left it to Khmer Rouge forces that were steadily taking over the country-side. It has since remained uninhabited, save for the presence of either Vietnamese troops or Khmer Rouge guerrillas during much of the '80s and '90s. Its altitude and commanding views made it a spot of strategic importance to all sides during the long years of conflict in Cambodia, and it was one location the Vietnamese really had to fight for during their invasion in 1979. The Khmer Rouge held out for several months; one unit was ironically holed up in the Catholic church while the Vietnamese shot at them from the Bokor Palace only 500m away.

SOUTH COAST

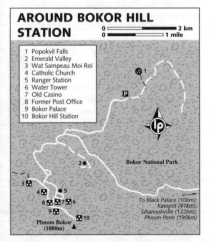

AROUND BOKOR HILL STATION

0 —————— 2 km
0 —————— 1 mile

1 Popokvil Falls
2 Emerald Valley
3 Wat Sampeau Moi Roi
4 Catholic Church
5 Ranger Station
6 Water Tower
7 Old Casino
8 Former Post Office
9 Bokor Palace
10 Bokor Hill Station

Bokor National Park

To Black Palace (10km);
Kampot (41km);
Sihanoukville (132km);
Phnom Penh (190km)

Phnom Bokor
(1080m)

The place has a genuine ghost-town feel, and the old **Catholic church** looks like it was locked up only yesterday. Inside, the altar remains intact and drawings of what appear to be Khmer Rouge fighters adorn the wall.

The old hotel, **Bokor Palace**, is straight out of the film *The Shining*. From what was once an outdoor terrace, there is a magnificent view over dense jungle stretching almost to the sea. It is possible to wander from the kitchens, up and down the corridors and through the ballroom to the suites above, imagining what the hotel was like in its heyday. On cold, foggy days it can get pretty creepy up there, as visibility drops to nothing and the wind howls through the building.

The ruin of **Wat Sampeau Moi Roi** is known locally as Five Boats Wat due to its five large rocks, which some say resemble boats (although what they were smoking at the time is up for debate). It was built in 1924 and, like Bokor Palace, affords tremendous views over the jungle to the coastline below. Other buildings dotted around include an old **casino** just opposite the ranger station, an abandoned **post office**, which looks like it has taken a mortar at some stage in its history, and an old **water tower** that looks like something out of *Close Encounters of the Third Kind*.

Debate rages over whether to redevelop the town. Environmentalists say it should be left untouched, while entrepreneurs eye its tried and tested potential. It would be sensible to create a compromise that allows a limited redevelopment of the old town area, thus generating much-needed funds to help protect the actual national park, much of which remains remote and defenceless. After all, it has come back from the dead once before, why not third time lucky?

POPOKVIL FALLS

ពពកវិល

This two-tiered waterfall is a fine place to bathe on a sunny day. The upper falls are 14m high and are the best place to swim. The lower falls are 18m high and can be reached by a path and wooden stairway that is signposted from the upper falls. The name translates as 'Swirling Clouds' and for much of the time there do indeed appear to be swirling clouds just above the falls. From the hill station, the falls are located about 15 minutes by road.

The road to the falls is 37km from Kampot. The road forks – left goes to the hill station, right to the falls. Follow the right road for about 3km before parking and walking just 100m to the top of the falls.

TREKKING

Trekking has a lot of potential at Bokor, although there is little in the way of organised trekking. There is a shady trail from Wat Sampeau Moi Roi to Popokvil Falls, which covers 11km and takes about three hours. This should not be undertaken alone, as there is always the possibility of an unexpected encounter with a three-legged tiger nicknamed Tripod who has been known to roam the ridge along here. Unfortunately, the park charges an absurdly high price for the services of a ranger (US$20), given the fact that none of them speak any English.

Sleeping

It is possible to stay up at Bokor hill station in the **ranger station** (dm per person US$5, r US$20) There are three dormitories with six bunks in each, and one room with a double and single bed. Bathroom facilities are shared and there is a basic communal kitchen for use by guests and rangers. There is now a limited menu on offer of the noodle or rice variety, but some visitors like to bring some food from Kampot. Running water and electricity continue until about 9pm, sometimes longer if there is a full house. It can get very cold at night so take some extra layers. If the ranger station is full, as sometimes happens at the weekend, rangers offer camp beds and a blanket for US$2.

Getting There & Away

Bokor National Park is 41km from Kampot, 132km from Sihanoukville and 190km from Phnom Penh. The access road is 7km west of Kampot, marked by an elaborate interchange system that must have seen its fair share of Peugeots and Citroëns in the resort's heyday. There is a ranger post and a ticket booth 1km beyond this interchange.

The road up to Bokor is one of Cambodia's most stunning, but it's in terrible condition along its length and is best covered on a motorcycle or in a sturdy 4WD. Cars and minibuses can also make it, but it's a rough ride. The road winds its way up through thick jungle and in places the

Koh Tonsay (p203), near Kampot

Fishing fleet, Kampot (p195)

NICK RAY

ANDREW BURKE

Abandoned colonial villa, Kep (p201)

NICK RAY

Riding the bamboo train (p217)

ANDREW BURKE

NICK RAY

Statue, Battambang Province (p212)

Pilgrims on their way to Prasat Preah Vihear (p235)

JOHN

foliage is trying to reclaim the road. Trees do get blown across the road from time to time. The road eventually emerges on top of the plateau, where the buildings appear and you catch the first glimpse of the wonderful view over the coast.

These first buildings made up Sihanouk's villa complex at Bokor, known as the Black Palace. From here the final 10km of road to the hill station is in marginally better shape, and the scenery is decidedly different. Check out the lush Emerald Valley, visible to the left of the main road just before you reach the hill station.

One of the most popular ways to visit Bokor is with a tour, organised through one of the guesthouses in town. Most of them run pick-ups daily up the mountain and charge from US$6 to US$8 per person, including a picnic lunch. The park entrance fee of US$5 is not included.

Moto drivers in Kampot take visitors up to Bokor for about US$10. It is possible to find English-speaking drivers with a little local knowledge hanging out at the guesthouses around town. However, be aware that it is punishing ride for the passenger, with so many potholes along the way.

Many experienced riders like to hire a motorcycle and take on the road themselves. The word 'experienced' should be stressed, as the road is not for beginners. Anyone riding the hill on the weekend should be very careful on the many hairpin bends, as there is a hell of a lot of traffic going up and down. Motorcycles can be hired in Kampot (p198).

Small groups of visitors will find it cheaper to rent a car or pick-up to get up here. See p198 for rentals, which are a bargain given the mess of a road that awaits.

Mountain biking is a final hardcore option. There are no decent bikes to rent as yet, but they may come. If the hill appears too ugly, it is possible to put the bike in the back of a pick-up, cut out the hard part and enjoy an adrenaline-fuelled descent, taking serious care on the corners.

KEP
កែប

☎ 036 / pop 4000

Kep is a permanent and poignant reminder of the devastation and destruction wrought on Cambodia during the long years of civil

war. The seaside resort of Kep-sur-Mer was founded as a colonial retreat for the French elite in 1908. Cambodian high rollers continued the tradition, flocking here to enjoy gambling and water sports, and during the 1960s it was home to Cambodia's leading zoo. The war was not kind to Kep and little remains except skeletons of buildings. What wasn't dismantled by the Khmer Rouge was looted by the Vietnamese 'liberators', or by locals selling materials to the Vietnamese in order to survive the 1979–80 famine.

Kep is on a small headland and has a 6km palm-fringed road extending along the coastline. On top of the hill near the beach is one of King Sihanouk's many palaces, constructed in the early 1990s. Before his overthrow in 1970, Kep was one of Sihanouk's favourite spots in Cambodia; he used to entertain visiting foreign dignitaries on an outlying island nicknamed Île des Ambassadeurs. He perhaps harboured thoughts of retirement here, but his poor health and Cambodia's political instability has meant that he's never actually stayed at the palace, which remains unfurnished.

After several false starts, Kep finally seems to be rising from the ashes, with several upmarket hotels open or under construction and plenty of budget bungalows popping up on the hillside above the former town. The beach itself is rather scruffy, but it never was a natural sandy bay – before the war, white sand was shipped in from Sihanoukville to keep up appearances. Thirty years on, it is crying out for a clean. Kep may be little more than a shadow of its former self, but there is a certain atmosphere that draws Cambodians back again and again.

Sleeping

There has been something of a building boom on the Kep accommodation scene. Many of the popular cheaper places are located on a verdant hill above the coast, while some of the more expensive places are located by the sea. Several upscale resorts were under construction at the time of writing which should bring a new level of sophistication to Kep.

Veranda Guesthouse (☎ 012 888619; veranda resort@mobitel.com.kh; bungalows US$4-15) Spread across the hill above town, this verdant resort is a great place to relax. The bungalows come in several shapes and sizes, starting

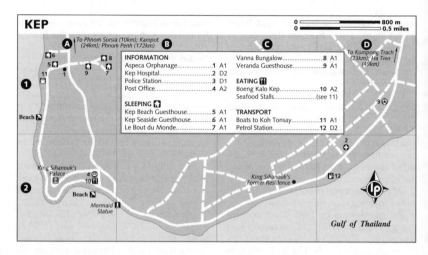

KEP

To Phnom Sorsia (10km); Kampot (24km); Phnom Penh (172km)

To Kompong Trach (23km); Ha Tien (49km)

Beach

King Sihanouk's Palace

King Sihanouk's Former Residence

Beach

Mermaid Statue

Gulf of Thailand

with small, basic ones for US$4 and rising up to US$10 to US$15 for large individual pads with striking bathrooms. Everything is elevated at Veranda, and the bungalows are connected to the central bar and restaurant by wooden walkways. A memorable spot.

Le Bout du Monde (☎ 012 955670; r 30,000-40,000r) The first to set up shop here on the hill, this French-run guesthouse is quite basic but atmospheric. Rooms include a bathroom and creative décor, but it is showing signs of age.

Vanna Bungalow (☎ 012 755038; r US$5-7) Perched across the track from the other two bungalow operations, this place has solid, comfortable bungalows at sensible prices. Set in pleasant gardens, there is also a basic restaurant here.

Kep Seaside Guesthouse (☎ 012 684241; s US$4, d US$5-7) The best of the budget beachside accommodation, this big guesthouse has large, breezy rooms right on the water's edge (however, there isn't exactly a sandy beach here). Room 10 is worth the US$7, as it's the only one with a full-frontal sea view.

Kep Beach Guesthouse (☎ 012 820831; r US$4-5) Basically basic, the cheapest rooms here are pretty small, but the US$5 rooms in the main house are better value. The friendly family speaks some English and French.

Eating

Lunch in Kep is all about fresh seafood and the crabs rule in this town. There are numerous bamboo shacks along the waterfront and

at about 5000r a kilo, it is one of the cheapest places in the country to indulge in fresh crab. Locals point out that some scales have been tweaked to register 1kg for every 600g. Definitely agree on a price in advance and make sure the seafood is fresh and freshly cooked.

Several of the aforementioned sleeping options also boast great little restaurants that are open to nonresidents. Veranda Guesthouse (p201) has a small restaurant with a big menu (mains US$2 to US$5), including more Italian dishes than you might expect in this corner of Cambodia. From its hilltop restaurant above town, Le Bout du Monde (left) was the first to offer seafood (mains US$2 to US$5) with a view.

Boeng Kalo Kep (☎ 012 680816; mains US$1.50-4) Down near the beach is this great little alternative to the picnic stalls that Cambodians so love – it's an open-fronted restaurant with some seriously tasty seafood. Try the generous portion of shrimp with black pepper or the excellent sweet-and-sour fish.

Getting There & Away

Kep is 24km from Kampot, 172km from Phnom Penh and 49km from the Vietnamese town of Ha Tien.

From Kampot it is possible to arrange a *moto* from US$6 per day, or rent a motorcycle – see p198 for details. Another option is to charter a share taxi from the centre of Kampot, but drivers are likely to charge US$20 for the day (because they could be making money on longer runs). Some of the more popular guesthouses also arrange cars or minibuses if there is enough demand.

Hour Lean operates two direct buses a day in either direction between Phnom Penh and Kep (10,000r, five hours), but it's a slow service.

Travellers wanting to continue to Kompong Trach from Kep can continue along the beach road out of town, before turning right at the main junction in Damnak Chang Aeu, home to Kep's train station.

Speaking of railways, it is possible – if daft – to get to Kep by train. Coming from Kampot is pretty insane, as the 24km journey is slow and there is only one train every two days. However, coming from Phnom Penh, it is quite possible to get off the train at Damnak Chang Aeu, and then take a *moto* into Kep.

AROUND KEP
Koh Tonsay
កោះទន្សាយ

Koh Tonsay (Rabbit Island) is a short boat ride off the coast of Kep and is so named because locals say it resembles a rabbit – an example of what too much local brew can do to your imagination. It has several beaches – all considerably nicer than those at Kep – and it is possible to stay with local families, as long as you can agree on a price for food and lodging (most families can arrange a seafood spread with a little notice). There are now a couple of basic guesthouses here that have proper beds and mosquito nets. Malaria is prevalent on most islands of Cambodia's coast, so come prepared with a bucketful of repellent (and see p310 for details on how to minimise risk of contraction).

Boats from Kep can be arranged at the first cluster of food stalls on the coast road. Expect to pay about US$20 a day for the boat, or about US$10 one way, although the price may depend on numbers. Most of the guesthouses in Kep can arrange boats, starting from about US$10 for one to three people and rising to US$20 for as many as eight people.

There are several other small islands beyond Koh Tonsay, including **Koh Pos** (Snake Island), but locals won't take foreigners much beyond here, as it's very close to the sea border with Vietnam. As this border is still a contentious issue between the two countries, don't expect a friendly welcome should you stray into Vietnamese waters; locals say machine-gun fire is more likely.

KOMPONG TRACH
កំពង់ត្រាច

Kompong Trach practically vanished from the map of Cambodia during the early 1990s, as Khmer Rouge forces were in control of the hills that surround the town. The end of the civil war brought it back to life and it is now drawing a small number of visitors to its caves and wats. The town itself has little to attract the visitor, but may grow in stature if and when the border with Vietnam at Ha Tien opens to overland traffic.

The main reason to come to Kompong Trach is to visit **Wat Kirisan**, a modern temple built at the foot of Phnom Sor (White Mountain), a karst formation riddled with numerous caves and passages. From the wat there is an underground passage to the centre of the karst formation, where there is another shrine. From here, other caves lead through the hill. It is easy to explore the basic passages unaided, provided you carry a torch, but anyone planning on delving deeper into the network of caves should find a local guide. To get to Wat Kirisan from Kompong Trach, take the dirt road opposite Acleda Bank for 2km to the foot of the karst formation. Follow the road to the right and the wat is a few hundred metres ahead on the left. Continue on this road a little further and there is another large cave located halfway up the hillside – the cave features an old iron ladder descending into the darkness. This is hard to find without local help, but once inside it leads to the **Cave of a Thousand Rice Fields**, so named because the limestone formations resemble the tiered paddy fields of Bali and the Philippines. A *moto* out here, plus the driver's assistance in exploring the caves, should cost about US$3 from Kompong Trach.

Getting There & Away
Kompong Trach is 37km east of Kampot along a decent road. Leaving Kampot, after 16km there is a fork in the road at the statue of a white horse, the left fork goes to Kompong Trach and the right to Kep. Most visitors make their way here from Kampot on rented motorcycles. NH31 connects Kompong Trach with Tani, and NH3 for travellers heading straight back to Phnom Penh.

SOUTH COAST

Another interesting option for motorcyclists is to take the excellent 32km laterite road that runs north to Chhuk, passing through some beautiful countryside.

It is also possible to get here by train, as the Phnom Penh–Kampot–Sihanoukville line passes through town.

TAKEO PROVINCE

ខេត្តតាកែវ

Often referred to as 'the cradle of Cambodian civilisation', Takeo Province includes several important pre-Angkorian sites built between the 5th and 8th centuries. This whole area was part of what Chinese annals called 'water Chenla', no doubt a reference to the extensive annual floods that still blanket much of the province. It would have been an important kingdom among several smaller states that existed at that time; its principal centre was at Angkor Borei, with other smaller religious centres at both Phnom Chisor and Phnom Bayong. Places such as Phnom Chisor continued to exact a strong pull on the kings of Angkor and many came to pay tribute to their ancestors in elaborate ceremonies.

Today, Takeo is primarily a province of farming and fishing that sees a healthy number of tourists visiting the temples of Tonlé Bati and Phnom Chisor near Phnom Penh. However, few visitors stay overnight in the provincial capital of Takeo. The town is not all that spectacular, but it's the closest provincial town to the capital, and it's easy to score a slice of real Cambodian life here.

NH2 runs south through the province and is in fairly good condition, as is recently reconstructed NH31 connecting Takeo and Kampot provinces. Elsewhere, roads are poor due to the damaging effects of heavy flooding in the wet season, and boats are almost as popular a form of transport as cars.

TAKEO

តាកែវ

☎ 032 / pop 39,000

Takeo, the provincial capital, is best used as a base from which to visit the old temples in the Angkor Borei area. However, as the temples can be seen in a day trip from Phnom Penh, there is no compelling reason to stay in Takeo. It lacks the architectural charm of some of the other provincial capitals, as it has less French legacy than elsewhere around the country. However, it is a convenient stop when travelling between Phnom Penh and Kampot. During the wet season, it becomes a pleasant lakeside town, with much of the surrounding countryside yielding to water.

Orientation & Information

Takeo is a small town hemmed in by a large lake to the north and a huge flood zone to the east. Come with cash, as there is nowhere to change travellers cheques in Takeo. For quick money transfers, **Acleda Bank** (☎ 932880; Ph 10) represents Western Union.

Telephone calls can be made from booths throughout town. Internet access is available in a small shop in front of the Mittapheap Hotel, charging 500r a minute.

The **tourist office** (☎ 931323) has helpful staff and is located opposite Psar Nat (Meeting Market), although the office lacks any information to take away.

Sights
TA MOK'S HOUSE
ផ្ទះតាម៉ុក

Commander of the Southwestern Zone during Khmer Rouge rule and, until his capture in 1999, military supremo of the ragged guerrilla movement, Ta Mok was born in Takeo Province. He built a large and elaborate house on an island in the lake north of town. He was extremely paranoid about security and was said to have had architects and builders executed upon completion of each floor, which included hidden rooms and escape passages. It was used as a government hotel during the 1980s, but is occupied by local police today. It is possible to look at the exterior, but not possible to go inside. Ta Mok is currently being held in T-3 prison in Phnom Penh, awaiting trial for crimes against humanity. He is likely to be one of the first in the dock if and when the long overdue Khmer Rouge trial moves forward.

Sleeping

There are some reasonable options to get your head down in Takeo, although the proximity of Phnom Penh means few foreigners actually spend the night here.

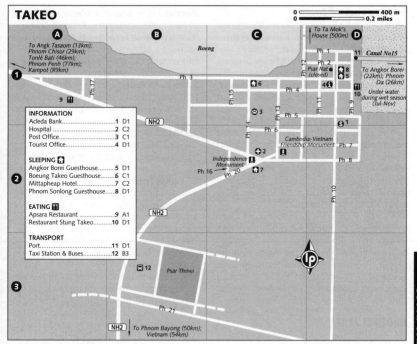

TAKEO

INFORMATION
Acleda Bank.................................**1** D1
Hospital **2** C2
Post Office...................................**3** C1
Tourist Office...............................**4** D1

SLEEPING
Angkor Borei Guesthouse..........**5** D1
Boeung Takeo Guesthouse.........**6** C1
Mittapheap Hotel.......................**7** C2
Phnom Sonlong Guesthouse......**8** D1

EATING
Apsara Restaurant **9** A1
Restaurant Stung Takeo..........**10** D1

TRANSPORT
Port..**11** D1
Taxi Station & Buses................**12** B3

SOUTH COAST

Boeung Takeo Guesthouse (☎ 931306; cnr Ph 3 & 14; r US$5-10; ⊠) Boasting the best location in town, overlooking the lake. All rooms here are essentially the same, but for US$10 you get a dose of air-con. Ask for a room with a view, as it is no more expensive. TV – yes, hot water – no.

Mittapheap Hotel (☎ 931205; Ph 20; r US$5-10; ⊠) This place may be an option for those who have a particular attraction to Cambodian Independence Monuments, as it overlooks Takeo's. Don't be put off by the old house at the front, as the owners have added a new wing in a leafy garden at the back, with the smartest air-con rooms in town.

There are a couple of cheaper options overlooking the empty Psar Nat.

Angkor Borei Guesthouse (☎ 931340; Ph 10; r US$4) This friendly little family-run place has a bewildering array of rooms available, all at the same price. Some are bigger, some are smaller, some have TV, some don't, but in the interests of equality everyone pays the same. Ask to have a look first!

Phnom Sonlong Guesthouse (☎ 931404; Ph 10; r US$3-4) Right next door to the Angkor Borei,

this guesthouse offers the same setup, only it charges a little less for rooms with just one bed. There also rooms with two beds. Some of the staff here speak English.

Eating

There are plenty of food stalls in the area around the Independence Monument. By night, this is also the place to snack on Cambodian desserts or enjoy a *tukalok* (fruit shake).

Restaurant Stung Takeo (☎ 016 957897; Ph 9; mains 3000-6000r) This place is built on stilts, as the whole area becomes a giant lake during the wet season. The restaurant overlooks the canal to Angkor Borei, and it's one of the most popular lunch stops in town. It's a good place to tuck into some Khmer food before making a trip to Angkor Borei and Phnom Da.

Apsara Restaurant (☎ 931329; NH2; mains 4000-8000r) This is an alternative spot for a good Cambodian meal during the dry season, when this part of town is less stinky than the area near the water. It has an English-language menu and some tasty local soups.

Getting There & Away

NH2, which links Phnom Penh with Takeo (77km), is in reasonable condition with just a few potholes to slow things down. PPPT and Hour Lean both run air-con buses between Phnom Penh and Takeo (5500r, two hours). They leave from Psar Thmei (New Market) in Phnom Penh and from Takeo they depart from in front of Psar Leu. These buses also go past Tonlé Bati and Phnom Chisor.

The price from Phnom Penh by share taxi is 6000r, by minibus 3000r. Travellers continuing by road to Kampot should take a *remorque-moto* (1000r) or *moto* (5000r) for the 13km journey to Angk Tasaom and then arrange a seat in a minibus or share taxi (5000r) on to Kampot.

There are also train services linking Takeo to Phnom Penh, Kampot and Sihanoukville. Trains from Phnom Penh pass through Takeo at around 9am on the way to Kampot (4100r, three hours, 89km). Coming from Kampot, they depart for Takeo at around 2pm every second day, depending on what time the train arrives from Sihanoukville.

AROUND TAKEO

For information on the temples around Phnom Chisor and Tonlé Bati, both in Takeo Province, see p111 and p110 respectively.

Angkor Borei & Phnom Da
អង្គរបុរី/ភ្នំដា

Angkor Borei was known as Vyadhapura when it served as the capital of 'water Chenla' in the 8th century, one of several competing kingdoms in the pre-Angkorian era. It is one of the earliest pre-Angkorian sites in Cambodia, dating back to the 5th century. Angkor Borei is actually a small modern town, but in this instance it is used to refer to the remains of an ancient walled city in the vicinity. The town has a small **museum** (admission US$1; ⏰ 8.30am-noon & 2-4.30pm), set up with assistance from the European Union (EU) in 1997. The museum houses a half-decent collection of Funan- and Chenla-era artefacts, although most pieces are copies of originals housed in the National Museum (p81) in Phnom Penh.

A few kilometres south of Angkor Borei is the hill of Phnom Da. Four artificial caves, built as shrines, are carved into the northeastern wall of the hill. On top of

Phnom Da is a square **laterite temple** open to the north, dating from the 8th century. The temple is forgettable compared with its bigger cousins around Angkor, but it's more about the journey to get here. Nearby is the smaller sandstone sanctuary of **Wat Asram Moha Russei**, a strange little structure that looks like it has been over-restored. In the wet season, it is only possible to reach Phnom Da by water, as the hill becomes an island spectacularly isolated by annual floods. The boats speed along ancient canals through a sea of green rice-fields.

GETTING THERE & AWAY

Angkor Borei and Phnom Da are about 20km east of Takeo town along Canal No 15, which is visible in the dry season and flooded the rest of the year. Most visitors charter an outboard from Takeo, which costs US$15 or US$18 depending on the engine size, taking around 35 minutes to Angkor Borei and another 15 minutes to Phnom Da. Alternatively, wait around the dock until locals gather to travel, and take a berth for 10,000r. There are also slower, larger boats to Angkor Borei that leave at 9am and 1pm and cost 1500r, taking almost two hours.

In the dry season it is also possible to visit by road, taking a route that passes south of Phnom Chisor. Expect to pay about 4000r in a share taxi or about US$5 for a round trip by *moto*. By boat is definitely the better option, as it is much more atmospheric.

Phnom Bayong
ភ្នំបាយ៉ង

Phnom Bayong is home to a small Chenla temple, built on the summit of a sizable hill in Kirivong district near the Vietnamese border. The temple itself doesn't justify a visit, but the views across Vietnam's pancake-flat Mekong Delta just might. NH2, which runs from Takeo to the border, is slowly being upgraded and the 50km journey from Takeo takes about 1½ hours. The turn-off in Kirivong is marked by a painted sign showing a temple – the temple is just a few kilometres from the main road. The walk to the summit takes about two hours; carry lots of water. A *moto* from Takeo will probably cost about US$8. Taking a share taxi towards Vietnam and arranging a local *moto* to the summit of the hill is a cheaper option (US$1).

Northwestern Cambodia

The northwest offers a blend of accessibility and adventure, with the timeless towns a gateway to the little-explored Cambodia beyond. Northwestern Cambodia covers a broad swath of the country running right around the Tonlé Sap, extending west and north right up to the border with Thailand. It includes some of Cambodia's most fertile land ('the rice bowl') as well as some of the country's most inhospitable mountain ranges – Chuor Phnom Kravanh (Cardamom Mountains) and Chuor Phnom Dangkrek (Dangkrek Mountains).

Of the region's atmospheric towns, Battambang attracts the most visitors. This is thanks to an alluring blend of classic colonial architecture and a host of sights beyond the town. Other rewarding towns include Kompong Thom, nestled on the banks of the Stung Sen and a base for the temples of Sambor Prei Kuk, and Pailin, a former Khmer Rouge stronghold.

Beyond the towns, the remote jungle conceals some of Cambodia's most inspiring temples, forgotten to all but the intrepid for more than three decades. Preah Khan and Prasat Preah Vihear are sublime spots, but are only for those with a serious thirst for adventure. This region also hosts some amazing natural wilderness, including the brooding Cardamom Mountains, home to rare wildlife, and the dry forests of northern Cambodia, home to rare birdlife.

Much of this region was plagued by war for considerably longer than other parts of the country; the northwest is a long way from Vietnam and very remote in places – both of these factors suited the Khmer Rouge. On a sobering note, this means there are many land mines in remote areas, so *do not stray from the path*.

HIGHLIGHTS

- Soak up some colonial-era charm in the riverside town of **Battambang** (p213), surrounded by teasing temples and rural scenes

- Explore Southeast Asia's first temple city, the impressive pre-Angkorian ruins of **Sambor Prei Kuk** (p240), near Kompong Thom

- Journey to the 10th-century capital of **Koh Ker** (p233), its many massive temples forgotten in the forests for more than a thousand years

- Live the ultimate adventure in an overland pilgrimage to the majestic mountaintop temple of **Prasat Preah Vihear** (p237)

- Discover the country's dark past with a dig around **Anlong Veng** (p226), the former Khmer Rouge stronghold where Pol Pot met his end

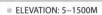 ELEVATION: 5–1500M |  POPULATION: 3.5 MILLION | AREA: 71,157 SQ KM

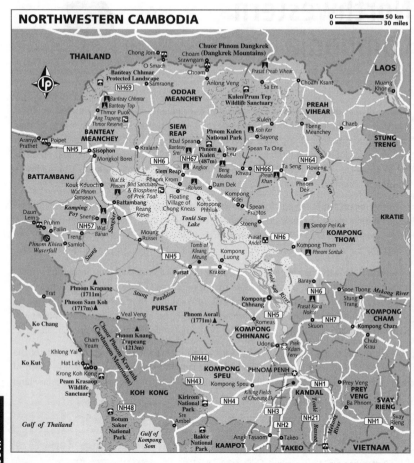

NORTHWESTERN CAMBODIA

Getting There & Away

Northwestern Cambodia has heaps of international border crossings to Thailand, giving more choice to overland travellers in the region. As well as the original border crossing at Poipet–Aranya Prathet (p293), 150km west of Siem Reap, there are three newer land crossings: the Pruhm–Daun Lem crossing (p295) is near Pailin, 100km southwest of Battambang; the O Smach–Chong Jom border (p294) is near Samraong, about 150km northwest of Siem Reap; and the Choam–Choam Srawngam crossing (p295) is near Anlong Veng, about 150km north of Siem Reap.

Travelling within Cambodia, the obvious gateways to the region are Siem Reap (p113) and Phnom Penh (p70), both with good road connections throughout the northwest. Phnom Penh is also connected to Battambang by railway and Siem Reap to Battambang by a memorable boat service.

Getting Around

Beyond National Hwy 5 (NH5) and NH6, much of this area remains extremely remote, and getting about can be tough. NH5 connects Phnom Penh, Kompong Chhnang, Pursat, Battambang and Sisophon to the south and west of the Tonlé Sap lake, while NH6 connects Siem Reap, Kompong Thom and Phnom Penh. Transport between the main towns is straightforward, but anywhere else requires a little more patience.

All areas of Cambodia are considered secure these days, but it pays to travel with company in remote areas, just to be safe. It never hurts to check on the latest security conditions before heading down a little-travelled road, particularly in the wilds of Preah Vihear Province

KOMPONG CHHNANG PROVINCE

ខេត្តកំពង់ឆ្នាំង

Kompong Chhnang is a relatively wealthy province thanks to its close proximity to the capital and to its extensive fishing and agricultural industries, which are supported by abundant water resources. There aren't a whole lot of places to visit, which has kept visitors to a minimum, although many pass through on their way to Battambang by road or Siem Reap by boat.

KOMPONG CHHNANG

កំពង់ឆ្នាំង

☎ 026 / pop 42,000

Kompong Chhnang is a tale of two cities: the bustling dockside viewed by those travelling to Siem Reap by fast boat, and the old French quarter with its pleasant parks and handsome buildings on the road from Phnom Penh. Connecting these very different parts is a long road lined with stilt houses and a maze of narrow walkways. The name Kompong Chhnang is from the local *chhnang* (claypots) made in villages around the town and sold throughout Cambodia, and from *kompong* (port), thanks to its location on the Tonlé Sap river. The town has nothing beyond atmosphere to offer the casual visitor, but for those with limited time who want a feel of provincial Cambodia, it is a straightforward stop between Phnom Penh and Battambang. It also makes for an easy day trip from the capital, stopping at the old royal capital of Udong (p108) along the way.

Information

Acleda Bank (☎ 988748; NH5) is the only bank in town. It represents Western Union for cash transfers, but can't change travellers cheques.

HONG KONG, DUBAI…KOMPONG CHHNANG?!

During much of the 1990s, plans were afoot to redevelop Kompong Chhnang's old Chinese-built runway, constructed during the Khmer Rouge regime to fly in supplies from China for their 'self-sufficient' paradise. The massive runway was never fully operational, but may well have been planned with an attack on Vietnam in mind, as the complex seems too sophisticated for cargo alone. Thousands are believed to have died during construction, as it was rumoured that the ultra-paranoid Khmer Rouge leadership had all workers on the project executed to keep its existence a secret. An investment consortium planned to turn this area into a free-trade zone and had hoped it would eventually rival Hong Kong and Dubai – a project that has never materialised.

Telephone and fax services are available at Kompong Chhnang's post office located in the old French quarter, but it's more straightforward to arrange phone calls from the private telephone booths dotted around town. **ODEC Internet** (☎ 988802; NH5; per min 400r) is located on the road towards Phnom Penh.

Sights & Activities

The riverfront area of Kompong Chhnang is interesting to explore. The town is surrounded by water for much of the year and there are a lot of floating communities and fisherfolk living on the river. Arranging some sort of **boat trip**, by negotiating directly with boat owners, may be a nice way to take it all in.

Across the river are several **old temples** dating from the Chenla period, including **Prasat Srei**, but these are only worth considering as the focus of a rural adventure, as they are very dilapidated. You can arrange a *moto* (small motorcycle with driver) driver in town for the day.

With Kompong Chhnang's claypot connection, it is hardly surprising that the town is well known for its undecorated but elegant **pottery**. There are several stalls selling pots, vases and more on the road to Phnom Penh.

NORTHWESTERN CAMBODIA

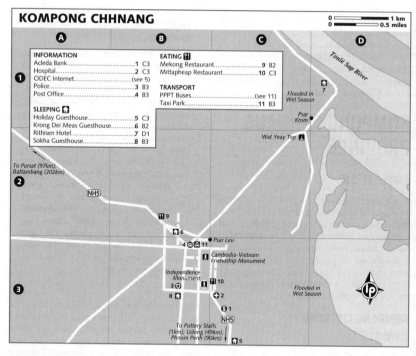

KOMPONG CHHNANG

| | | 0 — 1 km |
| | | 0 — 0.5 miles |

INFORMATION
Acleda Bank...............................**1** C3
Hospital.....................................**2** C3
ODEC Internet.........................(see 5)
Police.......................................**3** B3
Post Office...............................**4** B3

SLEEPING
Holiday Guesthouse..................**5** C3
Krong Dei Meas Guesthouse.....**6** B2
Rithisen Hotel...........................**7** D1
Sokha Guesthouse.....................**8** B3

EATING
Mekong Restaurant...................**9** B2
Mittapheap Restaurant.............**10** C3

TRANSPORT
PPPT Buses.............................(see 11)
Taxi Park.................................**11** B3

Tonlé Sap River

Flooded in Wet Season

Psar Krom

Wat Yeay Tep

To Pursat (97km); Battambang (202km)

NH5

9

6

Psar Leu

4 11

Cambodia-Vietnam Friendship Monument

Independence Monument

3

10

Flooded in Wet Season

8

2

1

NH5

To Pottery Stalls (1km); Udong (49km); Phnom Penh (90km)

5

Sleeping

Sokha Guesthouse (☎ 988622; r US$5-15; ☒) Popular with visiting nongovernmental organisation (NGO) workers, this is the most comfortable accommodation in town. It occupies several buildings in a sprawling, scenic garden in the south of town. The largest air-con rooms with TV, fridge and hot water can also be rented with fan only for US$8.

Holiday Guesthouse (☎ 988802; NH5; r US$2.50-10; ☒ ▢) Run by an extremely helpful Khmer teacher who used to work with the UN, this guesthouse has rooms with shared bathroom, but also has smarter fan and air-con rooms with bathroom for a tad more privacy. There's free use of computers (but there's a charge for Internet) for guests, and casual Khmer classes.

Rithisen Hotel (☎ 988632; r US$5-10; ☒) There is an inexplicably forlorn feel to this place, the only lodging in town that overlooks the Tonlé Sap river. Air-con runs from 6pm to 6am, so don't panic if it's not working during the day. There are some nice verandas for watching river life go by, but in the

dry season the aromas can get pretty strong when the river is low.

Krong Dei Meas Guesthouse (☎ 092 918800; s/d US$3/5) This is the cheapest deal in town, but it's a crashpad without much class. If you're a solo traveller it's worth considering, but couples will find better-value doubles at the other guesthouses and hotels.

Eating

There are plenty of food stalls at the markets in town – Psar Krom (Lower Market) is on the riverfront, while Psar Leu (Central Market) is in the town centre.

Mittapheap Restaurant (☎ 012 949297; NH5; mains 3000-6000r) This central restaurant has carved itself a niche serving Khmers travelling between Phnom Penh and Battambang, and that's always a sign of good-value, quality food. Mainly Khmer dishes, a sprinkling of Chinese and an English-language menu.

Mekong Restaurant (☎ 988882; NH5; mains 3000-8000r) Located on the road to Battambang, this restaurant has a small menu, including a good interpretation of a French beefsteak and all the Cambodian greatest hits.

Getting There & Away

Kompong Chhnang is 91km northwest of Phnom Penh on the smooth NH5. Phnom Penh Public Transport (PPPT) runs 11 bus services in either direction between Kompong Chhnang and Phnom Penh (5500r, two hours), generally departing on or close to the hour from 6.15am onwards. Minibuses cost just 3000r, but are more cramped.

Heading northwest toward Pursat (97km) and Battambang (202km), the road is in fantastic shape and air-con buses ply the route. Bus companies running between Phnom Penh and Battambang or Poipet drop off and pick up in Kompong Chhnang and other stops along the way. See p105 for details on bus companies.

Technically, Kompong Chhnang is on the railway, but the station is at Romeas, about 20km southwest of town. This can be a good place to kiss the slowest train in Asia goodbye when coming from Battambang. Staying on the train means a 10pm arrival in Phnom Penh, but getting off here offers the chance to get to the capital earlier or to stay the night in Kompong Chhnang and explore another provincial town.

PURSAT PROVINCE

ខេត្តពោធិ៍សាត់

Pursat is Cambodia's fourth-largest province, stretching from the Thai border eastwards to the Tonlé Sap lake. It encompasses part of Chuor Phnom Kravanh (Cardamom Mountains), one of the most remote areas of the country. Livelihoods in Pursat include fishing and farming in the north of the province and the harvesting of sandalwood oil, which fetches huge prices in Asia, but sandalwood trees are disappearing fast in Cambodia. Illegal logging and poaching remain serious problems in remote areas. Few travellers ever see much more than the provincial capital, but getting around the province is much easier with the new-look NH5.

PURSAT

ពោធិ៍សាត់

☎ 052 / pop 57,000

There's not a whole lot to do in Pursat, so most tourists here are those stopping for lunch on the road between Phnom Penh and Battambang. From the main road, it looks like a tedious town, but if you dig a little deeper you'll find it improves along the banks of the river towards the older part of town. Pursat is the best base for those wanting to explore the floating town of Kompong Luong on the Tonlé Sap lake, or the lush forests in nearby Chuor Phnom Kravanh.

Information

Make sure you carry cash, as there is nowhere to change travellers cheques here. **Acleda Bank** (☎ 951434; NH5), just west of the river, is a small bank representing Western Union for easy money transfers.

There are several phone and fax outlets near Psar Leu, and a post office on the riverbank. Expensive Internet access and cheap Internet telephone calls are available at **Tien Chanhong Internet** (Ph 1; per min 500r), just north of the market.

There is a tourist office behind all the government buildings on the river's west bank. The director is a helpful chap who knows the province well – because Khmers love to picnic, he has even written his own guidebook (in Khmer) called *Pursat and Picnics*.

Sleeping & Eating

Phnom Pich Hotel (☎ 951515; Ph 1; r US$5-15; ❄) A smart, modern hotel with fan-cooled rooms at the cheap end and fully equipped air-con rooms from US$10. Rooms are spacious and clean and the hotel's attached restaurant is one of the most popular restaurants in town.

New Tounsour Hotel (☎ 951506; Ph 2; r S$5-10; ❄) This friendly, long-running hotel offers a similar deal to the Phnom Pich Hotel – toss a coin (if you can find one in this coinless country) to choose between them. The décor is very plush, as several of the rooms have been upgraded in recent years.

Sopheak Mongkol Guesthouse (NH5 east; r US$3-5) It's currently the cheapest place in town, but the rooms are a bit basic compared with what's available for a couple of bucks more at other hotels.

Vimean Sourkea Hotel (☎ 951466; Ph 1; r with fan/air-con US$4/8; ❄) From the outside, this hotel looks as though it has seen better days, but once inside it improves – the air-con rooms with hot water provide the cheapest cool air in town.

There are plenty of cheap roadside diners on NH5, offering tasty, quick meals for as little as 2000r.

Magic Fish Restaurant (Ph 1; mains 3000-6000r) Located in the far north of town, this place turns out pretty good food in a riverside setting. Look for the modern yellow building on the right as you drive north from town, as there is no sign in English.

Getting There & Away

The road between Phnom Penh and Battambang is in super shape and this has put Pursat back on the map. Bus companies running between Phnom Penh (US$2, three hours, 188km) and Battambang (US$1.50, 1½ hours, 105km) or Poipet (244km) drop off and pick up in Pursat and other stops along the way. See p105 for details of bus companies.

One train per day comes through Pursat, heading to Phnom Penh or Battambang on alternate days. It is really only worth considering from Battambang (4900r for foreigners, five hours) just for the experience…the train takes longer to cover the 105km than buses take to run all the way to Phnom Penh. It is a bad idea to head by train to Battambang, as it doesn't arrive until around 10pm. The train to Battambang comes through Pursat any time after about 12.30pm (usually later!), while the train from Battambang leaves at 6am, usually arriving at Pursat around 11am, but never earlier.

AROUND PURSAT
Kompong Luong
កំពង់ល្វង

pop 10,000

The floating town of Kompong Luong on the Tonlé Sap lake is one of the most interesting places to visit in Pursat Province. It's a town whose population lives permanently on the lake, spread across hundreds of boats. The town moves with the lake's water level, as recognised by a faded signpost on NH5 to Krakor, which states that the distance to Kompong Luong is maximum 7km, minimum 2km. Not much fun for the postman!

Kompong Luong boasts pretty much all the facilities found in other Cambodian towns except the ubiquitous cars and motorcycles, which comes as something of a relief. That said, it isn't exactly Venice! There

are floating restaurants, schools, medical clinics and karaoke bars but, unlike Venice, the residents here don't have to worry about sinking, as everything has a boat as its base. There are plenty of places to stop for an iced coffee or a beer and just soak up the atmosphere of life on the water. There is not anywhere to stay, although if you want to get some photographs early in the morning you may be able to cut a deal to stay with one of the villagers (offer about 10,000r for a bed).

The population of Kompong Luong is predominantly Vietnamese, so you may find the welcome slightly more subdued than in most rural Cambodian towns. This isn't so much a reflection of hostility on the part of the Vietnamese; it's a reflection of their ambiguous status in Cambodian society, which has taught them to be wary of outsiders. Khmer Rouge massacres of Vietnamese villagers living around the Tonlé Sap lake were commonplace during the first half of the 1990s, and even as late as 1998 more than 20 Vietnamese were killed in a village near Kompong Chhnang.

Expect to pay about US$5 to charter a motorboat around Kompong Luong for an hour (significantly less for a paddle-powered boat).

GETTING THERE & AWAY

Kompong Luong is between 39km and 44km east of Pursat depending on the time of year. Hook up with a *moto* driver in Pursat for about US$6 to US$8 for the day – the trip takes about 45 minutes each way by road.

From April to June, when the Tonlé Sap lake is very low, the small fast boats ferrying tourists between Phnom Penh and Siem Reap occasionally stop at Kompong Luong for refuelling…at the floating petrol station, of course!

BATTAMBANG PROVINCE
ខេត្តបាត់ដំបង

This province has changed hands between Thailand and Cambodia on several occasions in the past few centuries. Cambodian control returned in 1907 but as recently as WWII the Thais cut a deal with the Japanese to take control again for several years. Before Cambodia's civil war, Battambang was the largest and richest province in Cambodia, but ceded a large chunk of its territory to Banteay Meanchey for the creation of the new province. It shares a long border with Thailand, a short border with the Tonlé Sap lake and is the fifth-largest province in the country.

Battambang was untouched for much of the early 1970s, as fighting raged elsewhere around the country. For this reason the whole area was viewed with much suspicion by Khmer Rouge leaders and was the victim of successive purges carried out by Pol Pot loyalists. Life was little better after the war, as the ongoing guerrilla war and the proliferation of thousands of land mines devastated the agricultural industry that had built the province's economy. However, it is slowly recovering as demining groups free up land for agriculture and the many refugees who returned here during the 1990s are permanently settled. Tourism has a lot of potential, as not only is the provincial capital a popular stop, but there are extensive examples of Angkorian heritage in the surrounding countryside.

Travel around the province has traditionally been slow due to poor roads. NH5, passing through the heart of the province, is in top condition, but NH57 to Pailin is a real disaster.

BATTAMBANG
 បាត់ដំបង

☎ 053 / pop 140,000

Cambodia's second-largest city is an elegant riverside town, home to some of the best-preserved French period architecture in the country and to warm and friendly inhabitants. Battambang is now back on the overland travel map and it makes a great base from which to explore nearby temples and scenic villages. There is a very popular boat service connecting Battambang and Siem Reap, probably the most scenic river trip in the country.

Orientation

Although it is a major city, Battambang is fairly compact and easily negotiable on foot. The centre of town is Psar Nat (Meeting Market) and all commercial activity and most of the city's hotels are located within a few blocks of here. This central area is bordered to the west by the railway line and to the east by Stung Sangker. Across the river are several large properties serving as administrative centres for the large numbers of NGOs represented in the province.

Information

The main post office faces the riverfront – you can make international telephone calls here but it is much cheaper to use an Internet telephone service.

INTERNET ACCESS

Straightforward Internet access is available at riverfront places for US$1 an hour.

Anana Computer (Ph 1) Charges just 2000r between noon and 2pm and 3000r at other times.

KCT Internet Café (per hr 6000r) Offers the fastest connection in town. There are two branches in town, one on the riverfront and one on the leading dining strip.

MONEY

There are several banks in town, offering a healthy range of services.

Acleda Bank (☎ 370122) Located on the east bank of Stung Sangker, this bank is good for quick money through Western Union.

Cambodian Commercial Bank (☎ 952266) Close to the train station, this bank offers credit-card cash advances for US$5, and changes travellers cheques at 2%.

Canadia Bank (☎ 952267) North of Psar Nat, this bank can change travellers cheques in most major currencies for 2% commission, and offers free credit-card cash advances.

Union Commercial Bank (☎ 952552; Ph 1) A few doors down from Canadia, occupying the riverfront corner, this bank offers free credit-card cash advances.

TOURIST INFORMATION

There is a small provincial tourist office near the Governor's Residence – it has little to offer in the way of handouts, but staff can tell you quite a lot about places of interest near Battambang.

Many of the *moto* drivers who hang out at popular hotels like Chhaya and Royal speak excellent English and have a good knowledge of the province. They can take you beyond the tourist sites to experience a slice of local life in the farming communities around the town.

Veteran Cambodia adventurer Ray Zepp has written a guidebook to the Battambang region called *Around Battambang* (US$5), available at selected hotels and restaurants in town. His latest publication has a lot of detail

BATTAMBANG

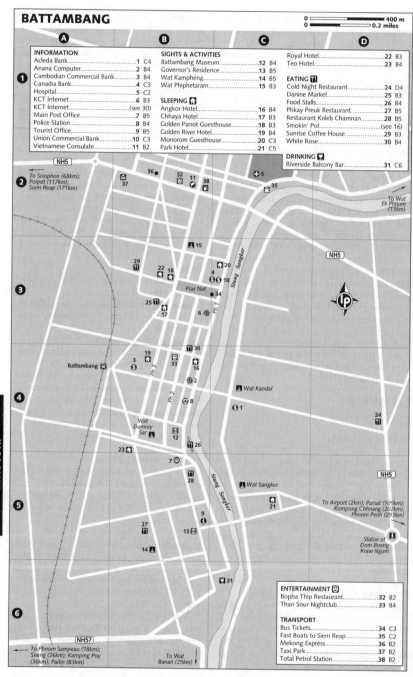

INFORMATION	
Acleda Bank	1 C4
Anana Computer	2 B4
Cambodian Commercial Bank	3 B4
Canadia Bank	4 C3
Hospital	5 C2
KCT Internet	6 B3
KCT Internet	(see 30)
Main Post Office	7 B5
Police Station	8 B4
Tourist Office	9 B5
Union Commercial Bank	10 C3
Vietnamese Consulate	11 B2

SIGHTS & ACTIVITIES	
Battambang Museum	12 B4
Governor's Residence	13 B5
Wat Kampheng	14 B5
Wat Phiphetaram	15 B3

SLEEPING	
Angkor Hotel	16 B4
Chhaya Hotel	17 B3
Golden Parrot Guesthouse	18 B3
Golden River Hotel	19 B4
Monorom Guesthouse	20 C3
Park Hotel	21 C5

Royal Hotel	22 B3
Teo Hotel	23 B4

EATING	
Cold Night Restaurant	24 D4
Danine Market	25 B3
Food Stalls	26 B4
Phkay Preuk Restaurant	27 B5
Restaurant Koleb Chamnan	28 B5
Smokin' Pot	(see 16)
Sunrise Coffee House	29 B3
White Rose	30 B4

DRINKING	
Riverside Balcony Bar	31 C6

ENTERTAINMENT	
Bopha Thip Restaurant	32 B2
Than Sour Nightclub	33 B4

TRANSPORT	
Bus Tickets	34 C3
Fast Boats to Siem Reap	35 C2
Mekong Express	36 B2
Taxi Park	37 B2
Total Petrol Station	38 B2

NORTHWESTERN CAMBODIA

To Sisophon (68km); Poipet (117km); Siem Reap (171km)

To Wat Ek Phnom (13km)

NH5

Stung Sangker

Psar Nat

Battambang

Wat Kandal

Wat Damrey Sar

Wat Sangker

To Airport (2km); Pursat (105km); Kompong Chhnang (202km); Phnom Penh (293km)

Statue of Dom Boeng Kraw Ngum

NH5

NH57

To Phnom Sampeau (18km); Sneng (26km); Kamping Poy (36km); Pailin (83km)

To Wat Banan (25km)

0   400 m
0   0.2 miles

on local wats, as well as the important Angkorian temples in Battambang. It's a useful companion for a longer stay in the area. The cause is very worthwhile as all proceeds go to the Monks HIV project, which trains monks to spread the message of compassion towards HIV/AIDS sufferers and promotes education and awareness about prevention.

Sights & Activities

It languished behind closed doors for many years due to a lack of visitors, but the **Battambang Museum** (admission US$1; ⌚ 8-11am & 2-5pm Mon-Fri) is once again open for business. It houses an attractive but limited collection of fine-carved lintels and statuary from all over Battambang Province, including pieces from Wat Banan and Sneng.

Much of Battambang's charm lies in the network of old **French shop houses** nestled along much of the riverbank. The **Governor's Residence** is also a handsome legacy of the French presence in Cambodia, although the huge new laterite gateway has obscured the view. The residence isn't this open to the public, but you can stroll the grounds or take a photo from the outside.

There are a huge number of wats around town, including **Wat Phiphetaram** (north of the market) and **Wat Kampheng** (south of the Teo Hotel), where a number of the monks speak English and are glad for the chance to practise conversation. Beyond the town are a number of attractions including hilltop temples, Angkorian-era wats and a large lake.

Smokin' Pot (☎ 012 821400) offers morning cooking classes (held at the restaurant – see p216) for those wanting to learn how to prepare Khmer and Thai dishes. Courses run from 9.30am to 12.30pm, involve a trip to the local market for the ingredients and include three dishes. A fun morning out and lunch is just US$7, including a small souvenir recipe book.

Sleeping

Prices at Battambang's hotels are fairly uniform so expect to pay US$5 for a spacious double with bathroom, TV and fridge, and US$10 for the added luxuries of air-con and hot water.

Chhaya Hotel (☎ 952170; 118 Ph 3; r US$4-10; ✷) Now one of the largest hotels in town, Chhaya has emerged as the leading backpacker choice in the city centre. All rooms

include TV and bathroom, but the more expensive options have hot water and air-con. This is also a reliable place to link up with English-speaking *moto* drivers to explore the province and to arrange onward transport.

Royal Hotel (☎ 016 912034; r US$4-20; ✷) Popular with independent travellers and small tour groups, the Royal has the widest range of rooms in town. Fans and bathrooms are standard at the budget end, while the most expensive rooms are more like suites. There's also a popular rooftop restaurant here, with good views over Battambang.

Angkor Hotel (☎ 952310; Ph 1; r US$11-13; ✷) It boasts a great location on the riverfront, but the building is a modern blight incongruously clinging to the end of some fine old buildings. All rooms are essentially the same, with TV and fridge, the price difference based on hot or cold water. Ask for one of the five rooms with a river view.

Monorom Guesthouse (☎ 012 878389; Ph 1; s/d/tr US$4/5/7) The rooms at this big, riverfront guesthouse are a touch on the musty side, but the price is right for such a popular location. Rooms include TV and a bathroom, but no hot water.

Teo Hotel (☎ 952288; Ph 3; s/d US$11/13) The largest hotel in town, this place is often crawling with government delegations and NGOs. Rooms include all the necessities for a comfy night's sleep and there is a restaurant downstairs for convenience.

Golden Parrot Guesthouse (☎ 016 961103; Ph 3; r US$3-5) Also once known as the Chantrea Hotel; the cheapest rooms here are up several flights of stairs. Rooms on the lower floors include a TV and all rooms at Chantrea provide good value for money.

Golden River Hotel (☎ 730165; 234 Ph 3; r US$5-10; ✷) Looks can be deceiving here, as a small entrance gives way to a big place with 38 rooms. It's a friendly hotel with good-value air-con singles for just US$8.

Park Hotel (☎ 953773; NH5; r US$5-11) The rooms at this brand new hotel are in very good shape. The only drawback is the location, on the less-popular east bank of the river.

Eating

White Rose (Ph 2; mains 2000-6000r) For a mammoth menu of inexpensive food and fine *tukalok* (fruit shakes), try this place, known as Colap So in Khmer. The menu includes tasty Khmer dishes and Vietnamese favourites, plus the Cambodian sandwiches sold throughout the day make a useful picnic for trips around the province.

Smokin' Pot (☎ 012 821400; mains 3000-6000r) Battambang's first, and one of Cambodia's only, cooking schools doubles as a good restaurant turning out Khmer and Thai food. It's a popular stop for an evening beer, and if you like the food, you can come back the following day to learn the secrets (see p215).

Phkay Preuk Restaurant (☎ 952870; Ph 3; mains US$1.50-3) The family that owns this sprawling Thai-style garden restaurant now has branches in Siem Reap, Sisophon and Poipet. The Thai and Cambodian food is well prepared and the dessert menu includes ice-cream sundaes (made with Walls ice cream, for homesick Brits!).

Sunrise Coffee House (☎ 953426; mains US$1-3; ☾ closed Sun) This little café is an unexpected surprise in Battambang, with a tantalising range of breakfasts and lunches, including pancakes, sandwiches and salads. The menu has plenty of creative coffee kicks and the tastiest homemade cakes this side of Siem Reap, making it a good stop for preparing a picnic.

Restaurant Koleb Chamnan (Ph 1; mains US$1-3) If you want to eat near the river, this restaurant has a beer garden with a live band most nights and is popular with locals after dark. Nearby are a host of food stalls that set up for business in the late afternoon and make a good place to watch life go by.

Cold Night Restaurant (☎ 012 994746; mains US$2-4) Anyone who is willing to venture a bit further afield (east of Wat Kandal) will find this restaurant has a massive menu of about 300 dishes. There is a wide selection of Asian food and a surprising amount of Western food, including burgers and pastas, plus a local version of pizzas.

Cheaper dining is available in and around Psar Nat, where all the Cambodian market stall favourites are available for about 2000r or so. Be aware that some places seem to specialise in what can only be described as 'unusable bits' soup.

Danine Market (☎ 952331; 116 Ph 117) Self-caterers can also hit this market, which is the best stocked in town.

Drinking & Entertainment

For such a large city, Battambang's nightlife is thin on the ground, especially compared with Phnom Penh and Siem Reap. Khmer nightclubs are an endangered species in Cambodia, but somehow struggle on in Battambang.

Riverside Balcony Bar (Ph 1; drinks US$0.75-2.50) Set in a gorgeous old wooden house high above the southern section of the riverfront, this is by far the best bar in town. It has a wonderful atmosphere by night and serves basic Western food, as well as inexpensive drinks. Famous customers have included Angelina Jolie, so you never know who you might run into here. Closed Monday and Tuesday.

Than Sour Nightclub (Ph 2) Somewhat optimistically meaning 'Paradise', Than Sour has been forced to brighten its lights so that nothing dodgy goes on in the dark. Be prepared to come under attack by the many 'beer girls' using their charms to encourage you to drink their particular brand.

Bopha Thip Restaurant (drinks US$1-3) This place is even bigger than Than Sour and usually has a live band to get the punters grooving – to *rom vong* (Cambodian circle dancing).

Getting There & Away
AIR

With the reconstruction of the road to Phnom Penh, there are no longer any scheduled services to Battambang.

BOAT

There is a fast-boat service between Battambang and Siem Reap along the Stung Sangker, which is a scenically stunning way to avoid the bumpy roads, but can take forever. This journey is arguably the most spectacular in Cambodia, as the boat passes through protected wetlands and narrow waterways.

Express boats make the run when the water is high enough between the months of August and January (US$15, three to eight hours!). However, if a smaller boat is available, opt for that, as the big boats are extremely unpopular with local communities along the river. Drivers snag fishing nets, send large waves over small boats and, in the worst case, have been know to cause deaths by capsizing small craft. From February to June, when the water level is too low for bigger boats, six-person speedboats travel this route for the same price, but navigating the shallow waters can take several hours longer, making for an all-day trip. Even these boats can disrupt local fishermen, so try to convey that the need for speed is less pressing than the need not to upset the locals.

BUS & TAXI

The 293km road to Phnom Penh is now the Cambodian equivalent of a motorway and journey times have dropped dramatically to just four to five hours. **GST** (☎ 012 414441), **Hour Lean** (☎ 012 307252) and **Neak Krohorm** (☎ 012 627299) have buses departing from 6.30am, costing US$3. GST has the most options, including a lunchtime service. For something more comfortable, consider **Mekong Express** (☎ 012 702330), costing US$4.50. All buses have air-con, run at fixed times with a fixed price and guarantee a seat. Tickets for all bus companies are available from ticket booths at the eastern end of Psar Nat near the river.

For the shorter stretch (1½ hours) to Sisophon (68km) to connect with Poipet (117km) or Siem Reap, there are plenty of share taxis running this route. Aim to pay 6000r for a seat – better still, buy two for US$3 and some extra comfort.

For details on the insanely bad road to Pailin, see p220.

TRAIN

It is a harsh 274km journey to Phnom Penh of at least 14 hours, assuming the train encounters no problems on the way. The train leaves at 6am, running up one day and down the next day, and the foreigner price is 12,400r. Check the schedule a day or two in advance. Taking the train is really masochistic given the journey time by road of four to five hours; save the train experience for the shorter south-coast stretch from Takeo to Kampot (p198) instead. There is also a train from Battambang to Sisophon (4000r, four hours), which departs at 7am, but it's about four times slower than by taxi.

Getting Around

MOTO

Battambang is compact enough to explore on foot. That said, *moto* are cheap and plentiful. Short rides are 1000r but it costs a little more at night. Taking a driver for the day starts at US$6 and up, depending on the distance travelled.

MOTORCYCLE

There are no official rental shops, but guesthouses can often set up visitors with a bike

for US$5 to US$7. Hotels can also set up guests with taxi rentals for the day – handy during the wet season when a motorcycle is too exposed to the elements.

NORRY

These are a sort of local train built from wood and powered by an electric motor. They can be used for short hops up and down the lines between Battambang and Pursat or Sisophon, and are a fun experience providing you don't run into a train! Foreigners usually call them bamboo trains and *moto* drivers include a quick ride in rural runs beyond town. Sadly, rumour has it that they will soon be banned from the line.

REMORQUE-KANG

Instead of *cyclos* (pedicabs), Battambang has *remorque-kang* (trailers pulled by bicycles). Aim to pay about the same as for *motos*.

AROUND BATTAMBANG

Before setting out on trips around Battambang, try to link up with an English-speaking *moto* driver, as it really adds to the experience. The following prices are indicative only, as settling on a price is all about the specific itinerary and your negotiating skills. *Moto* excursions that include jaunts through the countryside will cost a little more than prices quoted here. Several places can be combined in a day trip, such as Wat Phnom Sampeau, Kamping Poy and Sneng, or Wat Phnom Sampeau and Wat Banan.

NH57 (the road from Battambang to Pailin along which many of the attractions are located) was once called NH10 – despite its recent renumbering, many locals still refer to it as NH10. If you are heading to Pailin in a group of two or more, it could work out to be reasonable value to charter a taxi there for around US$30, and include Wat Phnom Sampeau and Sneng along the way.

Wat Ek Phnom
វត្ដឯកភ្នំ

Wat Ek Phnom is an atmospheric but dilapidated 11th-century temple dating from the reign of Suryavarman I. It is something of a disappointment after Angkor, but the attractive ride out here on a winding road following the banks of Stung Sangker makes the trip worth the time, especially towards sunset.

It is a very popular picnic and pilgrimage spot for Khmers during festival times. Take a *moto* (US$3) for the 25km round trip.

Wat Phnom Sampeau

ភ្នំសំពៅ

Wat Phnom Sampeau, a hilltop temple on top of a striking limestone outcrop, is 18km southwest of Battambang. It was formerly the front line in the government's defence of Battambang.

There is a long, hot climb to reach the summit, which is topped by both a small wat and a stupa. Nearby are a couple of large field guns, a hangover from the long civil war. Unless you are on a fitness drive, it may be better to take the winding road up the left side of the mountain and come down the main stairs. The gentler, winding road comes out at a grisly killing field located in a couple of caves. A small staircase leads down to a platform covered in the skulls and bones of victims. Look up to the right and there is a skylight hole where victims were bludgeoned before being thrown into the cave beneath.

There is another mountain nearby, called Crocodile Mountain, which was often occupied by the Khmer Rouge during the civil war. From here they would lob shells at government troops guarding Wat Phnom Sampeau.

A return *moto* to Wat Phnom Sampeau costs about US$4, including wait time.

Wat Banan

វត្តបាណន់

Wat Banan has five towers pointing skyward and is like a smaller version of the rather more illustrious Angkor Wat (p150). Locals claim it was, in fact, the inspiration for Angkor Wat, but this is a tad optimistic as there are considerable differences in size and scale.

Built in the 11th century by Udayadit-yavarman II, son of Suryavarman I, it is in a considerably better state of repair than Wat Ek Phnom, and its hillside location offers incredible views across the surrounding countryside. There are several impressive carved lintels above the doorways to each tower, although most are now housed in Battambang Museum (p215). There is also a large field gun, dating back to the bad old days when the government had to defend this hill from the Khmer Rouge.

Wat Banan is 25km south of Battambang and the round trip out here costs US$4. A visit to Wat Banan can be combined in a loop (US$6 to US$10) with Wat Phnom Sampeau, as there is a pleasant country road a few kilometres north of Wat Banan that leads west across to NH57.

Kamping Poy

កំពីងពួយ

Kamping Poy is the site of both a recreational lake and one of the Khmer Rouge's grander schemes – a massive hand-built dam stretching for about 8km between two hillsides. Some locals claim the dam was intended as a sort of final solution for enemies of the revolution, who were to be invited to witness its inauguration but would instead be drowned following the detonation of dynamite charges. It was more likely another step on the road to re-creating the complex irrigation network that Cambodia enjoyed under the kings of Angkor. Whatever the truth, as many as 10,000 Cambodians are thought to have perished during its construction, worked to death under the shadow of executions, malnutrition and disease. Today the lake is a popular swimming spot for locals at the weekend. It is possible to rent a local boat for a short trip around the lake. Try to negotiate a price of something like 4000r per hour.

Kamping Poy is 36km southwest of Battambang down a rough road that starts on the right just beyond Wat Phnom Sampeau. It is best combined with a visit to Wat Banan. A *moto* for a full day here should be about US$7 or US$8.

Sneng

ស្ងឹង

This is a small, nondescript town on NH57 to Pailin, but it's home to two small yet interesting temples. **Prasat Yeay Ten** dates from the end of the 10th century and, although little more than a pile of blocks, has three elaborately carved lintels above the doorways that have somehow survived the ravages of time and war. The temple clings to the left-hand side of the highway, so close to the road that it could pass as an Angkorian-era tollbooth!

Behind Prasat Yeay Ten is a contemporary wat, and tucked away at the back of this compound are three **brick sanctuaries** with some beautifully preserved carving adorning the entrances. The sanctuaries look like pre-Angkorian Chenla temples, but given the limited Chenla presence in western Cambodia, it is possible they date from the same period as Prasat Kravan (p164) at Angkor, around the early part of the 10th century.

Sneng is about 26km southwest of Battambang. By *moto* it can be combined with Wat Phnom Sampeau and Kamping Poy in a long and bumpy day trip (US$8 to US$10) or it makes a convenient stop for those chartering a taxi to Pailin.

PAILIN
ប៉ៃលិន

☎ 053 / pop 22,000

Pailin has an attractive location amid the foothills of Chuor Phnom Kravanh, but the town itself lacks major attractions unless you know a bit about gemstones or like hanging out with geriatrics responsible for mass murder. It may start to see more traffic now that the nearby border crossing at Pruhm–Daun Lem is open to international traffic.

This small town near the Thai border has bountiful gem and timber resources, long the economic crutch that kept the Khmer Rouge hobbling along. It was used as a base from which to launch regular dry-season offensives against government positions in and around the province of Battambang. Government forces managed to take Pailin in the summer of 1994, but the Khmer Rouge massed for a counter attack and chased the army all the way up to Wat Phnom Sampeau. However, in August 1996, Ieng Sary, former brother No 3 during the Khmer Rouge regime and Khmer Rouge supremo in these parts, defected to the government side, bringing with him up to 3000 fighters and their dependants. This was critical in bringing about the eventual demise of the Khmer Rouge, as it cut off much-needed sources of revenue for fighters in the north and allowed the army to concentrate its resources on one front.

Pailin's fortunes rose dramatically in the late 1990s as gem dealers flocked into town and casinos opened to milk cash from Thai gamblers. However, much of this freewheelin' activity has moved back to the border area where large casinos are more convenient for Thais. Today, Pailin is a

---

> **DON'T STRAY FROM THE PATH**
>
> The area around Pailin and Samlot is one of the most heavily mined in Cambodia. Much of the region between Pailin and Battambang was the frontline in the government's war on the Khmer Rouge, and districts such as Treng and Ratanak Mondul were mined year after year. Similarly, the border with Thailand is riddled with mines. The upshot of this is that you should stick to roads and paths where others have travelled and do not stray from them for any reason. Ignoring this rule could cost you a leg or your life in this part of the country.

---

subdued Wild West town in which former leaders of the Khmer Rouge seek haven, avoiding the long arm of international law.

Information

There is a branch of **Canadia Bank** (NH57) for cash transactions, but it does not change travellers cheques.

There are several telephone kiosks around Psar Pailin.

Sights & Activities

The hillock of **Phnom Yat** marks the gateway to town, and atop the summit is the eponymous **Wat Phnom Yat**. The wat is nothing to write home about, but there is an attractive old stupa here dating back to the early part of the 20th century. There are clear views across Pailin from here and it's a top spot for sunrise or sunset. At the base of the hill is **Wat Khaong Kang**, an important centre for Buddhist teaching before the war. It has since reopened for business.

The **Phnom Khieu Waterfall** is in the lower reaches of Chuor Phnom Kravanh on Phnom Khieu (Blue Mountain), and draws Khmers at holiday time. It is about 20km southwest of town and requires the service of a *moto* driver, as the road disappears into a path up into the forest. Getting here involves a round-trip hike of about 6km, taking five or six hours. There are other **swimming holes** around the Pailin area that make for worthwhile excursions during a longer visit to this region.

Down on the Thai border are a couple of major casinos – the **Caesar International Resort** and the **Pailin Casino** – where well-to-do Pailin

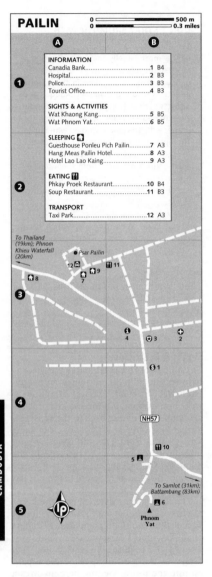

PAILIN

INFORMATION	
Canadia Bank	1 B4
Hospital	2 B3
Police	3 B3
Tourist Office	4 B3

SIGHTS & ACTIVITIES	
Wat Khaong Kang	5 B5
Wat Phnom Yat	6 B5

SLEEPING	
Guesthouse Ponleu Pich Pailin	7 A3
Hang Meas Pailin Hotel	8 A3
Hotel Lao Lao Kaing	9 A3

EATING	
Phkay Proek Restaurant	10 B4
Soup Restaurant	11 B3

TRANSPORT	
Taxi Park	12 A3

To Thailand (19km); Phnom Khieu Waterfall (20km)

Psar Pailin

NH57

To Samlot (31km); Battambang (83km)

Phnom Yat

residents like to be seen at night. They are only really worth considering if you're spending more than a couple of nights in town.

Sleeping & Eating

Hang Meas Pailin Hotel (☎ 012 936746; s/d US$11/13; ☒) This is the fanciest place in town, offering smart rooms with comforts like TV,

fridge and hot water. There is a restaurant with tasty food where live bands and comedians perform regularly. There's also karaoke, making it a veritable entertainment mecca in this part of the world.

Guesthouse Ponleu Pich Pailin (r 100B) The rooms here are clean and bright, and it's the best of the cheap deals in town. It may not seem spectacular, but when you've seen some of the other cells around town...

Hotel Lao Lao Kaing (r 100B) A reasonable alternative, although the hotel part of the name is a touch ambitious. Squat bathrooms and a fan smack of guesthouse.

Dining options are pretty limited in Pailin. Apart from the fancy surrounds of the Hang Meas Pailin Hotel and the rather less-fancy local market, there are only a smattering of restaurants in town.

Phkay Proek Restaurant (mains 40-100B) The Khmer and Thai food served here is reliably tasty. The restaurant is part of an extended family of restaurants that have taken the northwest by storm, with branches in Battambang, Sisophon and Poipet.

The no-name soup restaurant east of the market is a popular spot for breakfast and serves the full range of Khmer and Chinese soups. Later in the day it offers *soup chhnang dei* (cook-your-own soup) for US$4.

Getting There & Away

Pailin lies 83km southwest of Battambang, just 19km from the border with Thailand.

The road between Pailin and Battambang has gone to pieces (again), making it a hard ride. Share taxis (150B, four hours) and pick-ups (120/80B inside/on the back, four hours) make the journey between Battambang and Pailin. These prices are a little higher than elsewhere in Cambodia – given the distance – but until recently, Cambodian cabbies considered the trip to Pailin as the equivalent of driving to Hades itself!

For hardcore motorcyclists with plenty of off-road experience, there is also a new logging road running from the Pailin area south to Krong Koh Kong. It starts in the Treng district, about 25km east of Pailin, and runs through former Khmer Rouge strongholds such as Samlot and Veal Veng. It's a dawn-to-dusk ride in the dry season and shouldn't be attempted in the wet season. Veal Veng (about 275km) is the place to refuel. There is not yet any public transport on this run.

NORTHWESTERN CAMBODIA

AROUND PAILIN
Samlot
សំឡូត

Famous for a 1967 peasant rebellion that marked the first major skirmish of the long civil war, Samlot was also one of the last areas to succumb to government control in this part of Cambodia. The Sangkum government did not take kindly to such a wanton act of disobedience and local authorities massacred hundreds of peasants in reprisal. To be fair to King Sihanouk, it was likely a local army initiative, but it did much to dent his image in these parts and helped to ensure peasant support for the Khmer Rouge here for three decades. It also kick-started a purge of leftist teachers, pushing remaining urban leftists in Phnom Penh – such as Khieu Samphan, Hou Youn and Hu Nim – into the jungle.

Today, Samlot is little more than a small village with a small set of rapids, creatively billed as a **waterfall**, which locals head to for picnics. It's a scenic spot, but hardly in the A-list of worldwide waterfalls – you'll find it a couple of kilometres from town off the road back to Treng and NH57.

Life is improving, however, as actor Angelina Jolie has decided to pretty much sponsor the village in its fight for recovery, building a school and health clinic, among other initiatives.

The best way to get to Samlot is by *moto* from Pailin (US$5 return).

BANTEAY MEANCHEY PROVINCE
ខេត្តបន្ទាយមានជ័យ

This is one of Cambodia's newest provinces, created in the 1980s from the northern chunk of Battambang. The name Banteay Meanchey means 'Fortress of Victory' – this may refer to the fact that it was one area of Battambang Province that the government was able to control during the long civil war, as there are few mountains in the province. Traditionally, rice and staple fruit and vegetables have been grown in Banteay Meanchey. However, thanks to a shared border with Thailand, new opportunities are emerging for trade, and

several locals-only borders are fast developing as centres of commerce. Poipet has found the best niche of all as the gambling centre of Cambodia and there are now half a dozen or more major casinos.

Travel in the province is improving fast. The nightmare road from Poipet through Sisophon to Siem Reap is in an averagely bad state, improving in some sections, deteriorating in others, while NH5 south to Battambang is in wholesome shape all the way.

SISOPHON
ស៊ីសុផុន

☎ 054 / pop 98,000

Sisophon, often called Svay by locals, is not one of Cambodia's more inspiring towns; few visitors linger longer than for lunch on the journey between Thailand and the temples of Angkor. However, a number of travellers do find themselves having to spend the night here, particularly in the wet season when the roads can be unholy. Sisophon also provides a useful base for visits to the Angkorian temples of Banteay Chhmar and Banteay Top, about 50km north of town. Thai baht is the currency of choice here, but, as in the rest of Cambodia, US dollars are never scorned.

Information
There is nowhere to change travellers cheques in Sisophon, so come armed with cash. There is a branch of **Acleda Bank** (☎ 958821) if a Western Union money transfer is required. Telephone services can be arranged at kiosks throughout town. There is a tourist office in town; however, it never seems to be open and is cunningly designed with the entrance at the rear so that nobody notices.

Sleeping & Eating
Phnom Svay Hotel (☎ 012 656565; NH5 west; r US$6-10; 🛌) Marking the start of the road to Poipet, this well-tended hotel offers the best value in town. Affectionately known as 'The Birthday Cake' thanks to its extravagant exterior, it is popular with aid workers and small tour groups. All rooms include TV and hot water.

Roeung Rong Hotel (☎ 958823; NH5 west; s US$6-9, d US$7-10; 🛌) Just down the road from Phnom Svay is this small family-run hotel, sounding worryingly like the 'wrong room' hotel. Don't worry, for many they prove to

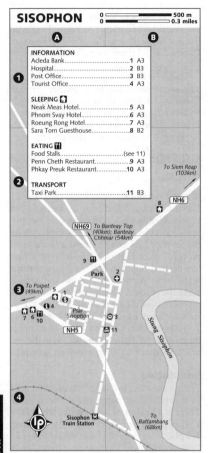

SISOPHON

INFORMATION	
Acleda Bank.....................................1	A3
Hospital..2	B3
Post Office......................................3	B3
Tourist Office..................................4	A3

SLEEPING	
Neak Meas Hotel...........................5	A3
Phnom Svay Hotel.........................6	A3
Roeung Rong Hotel.......................7	A3
Sara Torn Guesthouse..................8	B2

EATING	
Food Stalls................................(see 11)	
Penn Cheth Restaurant.................9	A3
Phkay Preuk Restaurant...............10	A3

TRANSPORT	
Taxi Park......................................11	B3

have the right rooms, with satellite TV and bathrooms…cold water only, though.

Neak Meas Hotel (☎ 012 937215; s/d US$12/15; 🔁) This hotel has the biggest and just about the best rooms in town, including carpets! The bad news for light sleepers is that it also has a karaoke bar and disco attached in the vast compound. There's no hot water in the showers, either.

There are several cheap but not-that-cheerful guesthouses on the road towards Siem Reap. Pick of the pack is the **Sara Torn Guesthouse** (NH6 east; s/d 100/150B) with spacious fan-cooled rooms and a pleasant veranda area to while away an evening.

The choice of restaurants in Sisophon is pretty limited. Those on a tight budget

can chow down at inexpensive food stalls found all over town, particularly in the area around the taxi park.

Phkay Preuk Restaurant (mains 60-100B) Phkay Preuk is a veritable northwestern empire, with branches in Siem Reap, Battambang and Poipet. Almost next door to the Phnom Svay Hotel, this reliable restaurant offers a range of Thai dishes, as well as familiar Khmer favourites. It may look closed from the front, but the dining goes on out back.

Penn Cheth Restaurant (NH69; mains 3000-6000r) This huge diner on the road to Banteay Chhmar used to do a roaring trade with soldiers stationed here, but it's as quiet as the rest of Sisophon these days.

Entertainment

Peace has not been so kind to the night scene in Sisophon, and without the soldiers to fill them most of the nightclubs have closed down. However, the Neak Meas Hotel (left) offers karaoke rooms for those who dare, as well as a small beer garden (of sorts). There is also a raging disco at the hotel, but this doesn't seem to attract the punters like the karaoke.

Getting There & Away

The roads to Siem Reap and Poipet bounce back and forth from good to bad every year. Share taxis travel from Sisophon to Poipet (5000r, one hour), to Siem Reap (10,000r, two hours) and to Battambang (6000r, 1½ hours).

There are also local trains to Battambang (4000r, four hours) leaving some time after 1pm each day. There aren't any trains to Poipet, as the Khmer Rouge ripped up the tracks long ago.

BANTEAY CHHMAR
បន្ទាយឆ្មារ

Vast and remote, Banteay Chhmar (Narrow Fortress) has been repeatedly looted over the years and many of its treasures carted off to private collections around the world. The massive temple complex is yet another that was constructed by Cambodia's most prolific builder, Jayavarman VII (r 1181–219), on the site of an earlier 9th-century temple. Built at the height of the Khmer empire's indulgence, this area would have been one of the most important in Cambodia after

Angkor Thom and Preah Khan. There is some debate over its origins, with some scholars suggesting it was built in tribute to Jayavarman VII's son Indravarman and the leading Cambodian generals responsible for the defeat of the Chams. Other sources suggest it may have been built as a funerary temple for the grandmother of the king.

Originally enclosed by a 9km-long wall, it housed one of the largest and most impressive Buddhist monasteries of the Angkorian period. This is one of the few temples in Cambodia to feature the faces of Avalok-iteshvara, as seen at Bayon (p156) in Angkor Thom. However, many of the towers have collapsed over the centuries and it is now only possible to make out a few towers with their mysterious expressions.

The temple was deservedly renowned for its intricate carvings, including scenes of daily life in the Angkorian period similar to those at Bayon. Unique to Banteay Chhmar was a sequence of eight multi-armed Avalok-iteshvaras adorning an outer gallery, but six of these were hacked up and trucked into Thailand in a brazen act of looting in 1998. The two that remain are spectacular and offer a glimpse of how this temple must have looked before it was pillaged.

Fortunately, Cambodian and Thai authorities have begun to clamp down on the illicit trade in Cambodian antiquities and many of the items plundered in 1998 were intercepted on the road to Bangkok and have since been returned to Cambodia. Unfortunately, it's too little, too late for Banteay Chhmar.

This temple was pretty much off limits during the civil war, until 1999. Like Beng Mealea (p176), to the east of Angkor, the romantic image of the all-powerful jungle slowly consuming the ancient buildings pointed to massive potential for visitors. However, the authorities decided to clear away the jungle encroaching on the stonework, and while this has undoubtedly made exploring the temple a safer experience, it has taken away some of the magic. Tourists with a genuine interest in Cambodia's temples will enjoy a visit here, as will travellers who want to see more of rural Cambodia than Siem Reap has to offer. However, don't expect anything quite as spectacular as the principal temples at Angkor.

There are as many as a dozen smaller temples in the vicinity of Banteay Chhmar,

all in a ruinous state. These include Prasat Mebon, Prasat Ta Prohm, Prasat Prom Muk Buon, Prasat Yeay Choun, Prasat Pranang Ta Sok and Prasat Chiem Trey.

BANTEAY TOP
បន្ទាយទ័ព

Banteay Top (Fortress of the Army) may only be a small temple, but there is something special about the atmosphere here. The temple was constructed around the time of Banteay Chhmar, quite possibly as a tribute to the army of Jayavarman VII. They had reaffirmed Cambodian dominance over the region in a comprehensive defeat of the Chams.

Set among the rice paddies, one of the damaged towers almost appears to have been partially rebuilt and looks decidedly precarious, like a bony finger pointing skyward. This temple is about 14km southeast of Banteay Chhmar on a poor dirt road. The turn-off from NH69 is marked by a stone plinth with gold inscription, about 9km south of Banteay Chhmar.

Sleeping & Eating
The small number of visitors coming to Banteay Chhmar usually stay in Sisophon or Siem Reap. The nearest accommodation to Banteay Chhmar is found in Thmor Puok, about 15km south of the temple. **Ly Hour Guesthouse** (tw 180B) offers basic rooms with fans. This small town has power from 6pm to 11pm only and there is no generator, so it can get sticky at night.

There are a few food stalls clustered around the bedraggled market in the village of Banteay Chhmar, just beyond the temple's moat. Those who are squeamish about food hygiene should consider a picnic.

Getting There & Away
NH69 from Sisophon to Banteay Chhmar is sometimes good, sometimes bad, depending on how recently it has been flattened. The 39km section from Sisophon to Thmor Puok sees frequent traffic, but it thins out on the last 15km to Banteay Chhmar. All said, it takes about an hour on a trail bike and about two hours by *moto* or car. Arranging a *moto* to come here for the day is around US$10. Try the hotels in Sisophon (p221) if you want to rent a motorcycle. It is also possible to get to Banteay Chhmar by

taking a pick-up from Sisophon to Thmor Puok (5000/3000r inside/on the back) and arranging a *moto* for the round trip from there (US$5). Some pick-ups may even carry on to Samraong, passing through Banteay Chhmar village, but this is rare.

It is also possible to get here in a long day trip from Siem Reap by car (about US$70). It's too far to be sensible by *moto*. It takes around five hours or so to get to Banteay Chhmar, so leave Siem Reap very early.

POIPET
ប៉ោយប៉ែត

☎ 054 / pop 45,000

Viva Poipet! Long the armpit of Cambodia, famous for nothing but mud and mess, Poipet is reinventing itself as the Las Vegas of Cambodia, home to more than half a dozen major casino resorts. With gambling illegal in Thailand, Poipet has emerged as the most popular border destination for neighbourly flutters, eclipsing Krong Koh Kong and Pailin. Names such as Star Vegas and Tropicana don't make it quite as sophisticated as the US desert metropolis just yet, but it is growing fast.

As recently as 1996, the town was under intermittent mortar fire from the Khmer Rouge and so was always a transient place with a transient look. Town roadworks aren't proceeding as fast as resort building, so during the wet season the roads become rivers of mud and detritus. There is no reason to spend any time here unless you have the urge to part with large amounts of money.

Poipet is also emerging as scam central and many tourists are being ripped off on overland travel to Siem Reap and Battambang. For more on this, see the boxed text on p294. Don't judge Cambodia on your first experiences in Poipet, because the rest of the country does not carry on like this. In time, let's hope the good folk of Poipet realise that the bad folk are doing their community and reputation no favours through such behaviour – they may then put their house in order.

Orientation & Information
Poipet is little more than one straight road, stretching for a few kilometres along NH5 in the direction of Sisophon and Siem Reap. The Thai immigration office lies on the west bank of the O Chrou stream, with the Cambodian immigration office on the east. The border area is dotted with huge casino resorts and once inside Cambodia, taxis and transport to Siem Reap wait beyond the new central roundabout. Strung out along this road are guesthouses, hotels, banks and shops, but nothing that is likely to tempt you to stick around.

For changing travellers cheques, there's a handy branch of **Canadia Bank** (☎ 967107; NH5) not far from the border post. Changing cash is faster at shops or restaurants. For those who really want to send their Cambodian postcards before they leave Cambodia, there is a small post office looking on to the central roundabout.

Sleeping & Eating
Many of the cheaper hotels in Poipet have been hijacked by the casinos to house their large staff, so the places covered here are those where rooms are actually available to visitors. When the big casinos first opened their doors, they preferred not to rent out rooms to non-gamblers, and advertised minimum stakes of 50,000B (more than US$1000), which was a touch expensive for a sorry town like this. However, since Thai Prime Minister Thaksin Shinawatra said he would sack any government employees caught on security cameras setting a bad example by crossing the border to gamble, numbers have dropped slightly and the big resorts all advertise rooms from about 750B to 2000B – good value, given the facilities. For the record, the casinos include Tropicana, Poipet Resort, Holiday Palace, Golden Crown and Star Vegas.

Should you, for some masochistic reason, feel inclined to stay in Poipet, note that room rates rise at weekends, when Thai gamblers flood the town.

Ngy Heng Hotel (☎ 967101; NH5; r with fan/air-con 200/400B; ❄) One of the few cheaper places that hasn't been co-opted by the casinos. The rooms here offer clean comfort at a good rate; air-con rooms include hot showers and all rooms have a TV.

Orkiday Angkor Hotel (☎ 967502; oa_tour@online .com.kh; r US$10-20; ❄) You can't miss this big new hotel, looking over Poipet's only roundabout. The rooms are brand-spanking new and include all the amenities – it's a good option if you are unlucky enough to get caught in town for the night.

There are a couple of hole-in-the-wall restaurants near the border area and plenty of street stalls here. It is also the last place to find cheap treats and drinks from Thailand for the journey further into Cambodia, as east of here the price goes up and the selection goes down.

Getting There & Away

Poipet is connected by road to Thailand to the west and Sisophon to the east. For more details of travelling between Thailand and Cambodia via Poipet, see p293. With some dedicated negotiating, a seat in a share taxi to Sisophon should be 50B. Taxis also run direct to Siem Reap (150B per seat, 1000B for the taxi, three to four hours) or direct to Battambang (100B, 2½ hours). These times are all for the dry season – it can take much, much longer in the wet season.

ODDAR MEANCHEY PROVINCE

ខេត្តឧត្តរមានជ័យ

This is the newest of Cambodia's provinces, carved out of the sections of Siem Reap Province that the government did not control for much of the 1980s and 1990s. The name means 'Victory Province', a little idealistic for much of that period, but suitable enough by 1999. This is a dirt-poor province thanks to the sorrow of war, and produces very little apart from opportunities for aid organisations. Sharing a lengthy border with Thailand could eventually prove a road to riches for some local entrepreneurs. Illegal logging was rampant for a few years but seems to have stopped for now. There are few attractions for tourists in this province, although some visitors are drawn to the former Khmer Rouge town of Anlong Veng, with its many associations with Pol Pot and other leading figures from the movement.

Getting around the province is tough during the wet season, as there are no sealed roads. The road from Siem Reap to Anlong Veng is due to be rebuilt with Thai assistance, but remains a mess for now. The Cambodian military have built a good border road linking Anlong Veng to Prasat Preah

> **LAND MINE ALERT!**
>
> Oddar Meanchey is one of the most heavily mined provinces in Cambodia and most of the mines were laid in the past decade. Do not, under any circumstances, stray from previously trodden paths. Those with their own transport should travel only on roads or trails regularly used by locals.

Vihear and Samraong and there are two international border crossings open near Anlong Veng – Choam–Choam Srawngam and O Smach–Chong Jom – all of this could help put this province on the tourist map, at least for passing through, and that's better than nothing.

SAMRAONG

សំរោង

There are towns called Samraong throughout Cambodia, as the name means 'Dense Jungle' (sadly, a rarity in this area today). This Samraong is the provincial capital of Oddar Meanchey Province and it's slowly emerging after decades of isolation – resulting from its frontline position in the long civil war. There is nothing for foreigners to see or do up here, unless they happen to be in development work – something much in demand around here. This could change with the advent of the new international border crossing 20km north of town in O Smach.

Sleeping & Eating

There are only slim pickings on the accommodation front. You'll find a few guesthouses clustered near the scruffy little market, which is conveniently located right next to the taxi park. **Meanchey Guesthouse** (r US$2.50-6) is the best of the bunch, popular with visiting NGOs and offering cheap rooms with share bathroom and bigger rooms with private bathroom.

There are several food stalls around the market offering saucepans of pre-cooked food for about 2000r a serve. Poke your head in and see what takes your fancy. For something more sophisticated, try the **Santepheap Restaurant** (mains 3000-6000r), arguably the best restaurant in town (although the competition is thin on the ground).

Getting There & Away

Most visitors make it to Samraong from Kralanh, a small town on NH6 midway between Siem Reap and Sisophon. Getting to Kralanh from either Siem Reap or Sisophon is about 6000r by share taxi (one hour in the dry season). From Kralanh it is another 65km north to Samraong (8000r, two to three hours) on a boneshaking road that is gradually improving. It is possible to find through-taxis from Siem Reap (15,000r) if you leave early enough. It is sometimes possible to travel between Banteay Chhmar and Samraong (two hours), but few trucks go this way. There are also roads linking Samraong to Anlong Veng (15,000r, two hours), or to Thailand via the border crossing at O Smach (10,000r, one hour).

O SMACH
អូរស្មាច់

O Smach shot to fame in July 1997, as Funcinpec forces regrouped here after the coup. Perched on the mountain, soldiers under the command of General Neak Bun Chhay were able to hold out against the superior forces of the Cambodian People's Party (CPP) until a peace agreement was brokered that allowed the 1998 elections to go ahead.

With the advent of peace, the military moved in and cleared locals off safe land to sell it to a casino developer. Each year, the casino attracts thousands of Thais. Meanwhile, the locals who were evicted were forced to relocate to mined land that the military claimed to have cleared. All too often in Cambodia the strong exploit the weak, but this episode was particularly heartless and brought to international attention the issue of military land grabs in 'peacetime' Cambodia.

Some foreign visitors are starting to use the new international border crossing here, but it remains a trickle rather than a torrent. For more details on the O Smach–Chong Jom border crossing, see p294.

ANLONG VENG
អន្លង់វែង

For almost a decade, this was the ultimate of Khmer Rouge strongholds – home to Pol Pot, Nuon Chea, Khieu Samphan and Ta Mok, the most notorious leaders of Democratic Kampuchea. Anlong Veng fell to government forces in April 1998, at the same time that Pol Pot mysteriously died near the Thai border. Soon after, Prime Minister Hun Sen ordered that a major road be bulldozed through the jungle to ensure the population didn't have second thoughts about ending the war.

Today Anlong Veng is expanding fast, shedding its image as a dusty, poor town to attract migrants from other parts of the kingdom. It has also begun to attract some visitors thanks to the macabre lure of all things associated with the Khmer Rouge. The average visitor will find little of interest here compared with what's on offer around Angkor, but for those with a keen interest in contemporary Cambodian history it is an important part of the picture. And now that there's an international border crossing just 10km north at Choam–Choam Srawngam, more foreigners may begin to pass through town. The Thai side of the border is pretty isolated compared with other crossings in the northwest though. North of town along the ridge of Chuor Phnom Dangkrek are the houses of several former leaders of the Khmer Rouge, as well as some dense jungle and compelling views.

Information

There are no banks in Anlong Veng, so come with cash (US dollars or riel). International telephone calls are possible, but there is no Internet access yet.

Sights & Activities

The one-legged military chief of the Khmer Rouge, Ta Mok, ruled the movement in its final years, and his **residence** (admission of US$1 sometimes requested) is open to visitors. He doesn't need the home just now, as he is a guest of the Cambodian government in T-3, a Phnom Penh prison, awaiting trial for genocide. His residence is a large pad, but little remains of the original furnishings, as it was badly looted by government soldiers. There are several evocative Angkorian paintings adorning the upper walls, and downstairs is a large garage, which used to house his luxury 4WD.

Some of the guards around the house are former Khmer Rouge soldiers and have an alternative story to tell about Ta Mok. To them, he was harsh but fair, a builder of

CAMBODIA'S UNDERGROUND WAR

Cambodia is a country scarred by years of conflict and some of the deepest scars lie just inches beneath the surface. The legacy of land mines in Cambodia is one of the worst anywhere in the world, with an estimated four to six million dotted about the countryside. These insidious inventions are not just weapons of war, but weapons against peace, as they recognise no ceasefire.

As many as 40,000 Cambodians have lost limbs due to mines. Cambodia has one of the world's highest number of amputees per capita – about one in 275 people. After snake bites, malaria, tuberculosis, diarrhoea, HIV/Aids and traffic accidents, mines are one of Cambodia's top killers. Land mines litter the country, buried in rice-fields and on roadsides and, even after extensive mine awareness campaigns, they still claim 25 to 35 victims a month. This is a vast improvement on a decade ago, when the figure was more like 300, but still entirely unacceptable for a country officially at peace. To make matters more complicated, areas that appear safe in the dry season become unsafe in the wet season as the earth softens. It is not uncommon for Cambodian farmers to settle on land during the dry season, only to have their dreams of a new life shattered in the wet season when a family member has a leg blown off by a land mine.

The cost to an extensively mined country is enormous. In a developing country like Cambodia, the UN estimates that the lifetime rehabilitation of a land mine victim costs US$3000. With 40,000 victims, the cost is around US$120 million. Then there are indirect costs, such as those resulting from the deaths of grazing livestock. Mines hamper rural development too. Much of Cambodia's agricultural land is mined, making it impossible to farm and sometimes causing food shortages.

There are a number of groups working in Cambodia to alleviate the problem of mines. The Cambodian Mine Action Centre (CMAC) is an all-Cambodian government agency operating with technical support from overseas governments. Hazardous Areas Life (Support) Organisation (HALO Trust) was one of the pioneers of mine clearing in Cambodia, and now has many teams working in provinces such as Pursat, Banteay Meanchey and Siem Reap. The Mines Advisory Group (MAG) is a British outfit that trains Cambodians in mine clearance. It has launched programmes to train mine victims and all-women teams in mine clearance. It has also pioneered mine awareness programmes throughout the country involving puppet shows for children and posters in rural communes.

Most sensible travellers will not be wandering around mined areas while they are in Cambodia. Nevertheless, there are some points worth bearing in mind while you are in the country:

▪ Always check with locals that paths are not mined.

▪ Never leave a well-trodden path in remote areas.

▪ Never touch anything that looks remotely like a mine.

▪ If you find yourself accidentally in a mined area, retrace your steps only if you can clearly see your footprints; if not, you should stay where you are and call for help – as advisory groups put it, `better to spend a day standing in a minefield than a lifetime as an amputee'.

▪ If someone is injured in a minefield, even if they are crying out for help, do not rush in; find someone who knows how to safely enter a mined area.

▪ Do not leave the roadside in remote areas, even for the call of nature, your limbs are more important than your modesty.

There have been some breakthroughs in the campaign to ban land mines in recent years. In 1997 more than 100 countries signed a treaty banning the production, stockpiling, sale and use of land mines. Some important international players in land mine production signed the treaty, including Italy, France and the UK. However, the world's major producers, including China, Russia and the USA, refused to sign, so even as you read this, land mines continue to be produced.

Cambodia was a signatory to the treaty and while it is commendable that it has signed, the treaty does little to alleviate the everyday nightmare of life in heavily mined rural provinces. Mine clearance in Cambodia is, tragically, too often a step-by-step process. For the majority of Cambodians, the underground war goes on. You can learn more about landmines from the Nobel Peace Prize–winner **International Campaign to Ban Landmines** (ICBL; www.icbl.org).

orphanages and schools, and a leader who kept order, in stark contrast to the anarchic atmosphere that prevailed once the government took over. However, there may be a hefty bias among his former followers, as to most Cambodians Ta Mok is known as 'The Butcher'. He is and was widely known to have been Pol Pot's military enforcer, responsible for thousands of deaths in successive purges during the terrible years of Democratic Kampuchea.

Across the swamp that's in front of the house is a small island with the remains of a toilet outhouse. This is all that remains of **Pol Pot's residence** in Anlong Veng.

There used to be a dilapidated **Angkorian temple** behind Anlong Veng's high school, but this was destroyed by Ta Mok and his army in their search for ancient statues to sell to the Thais. Sadly, this is not an isolated case and many a small temple that survived the centuries has succumbed to modern greed in the past couple of decades.

Otherwise, the 'attractions' of Anlong Veng are all found in the north of town along the Thai border. The road north begins to climb the escarpment about 8km out of town. Look out for the intricate **carvings of Khmer Rouge soldiers** cut from a huge boulder in the middle of the trail. The images have been decapitated by government forces, but remain striking for their detail and the fact that they have been hewn entirely from the surrounding rock. It is ironic to see that those responsible for such destruction were capable of such creativity, with the right motivation.

Once at the top of the plateau, it is possible to visit the **cremation site of Pol Pot**. He was hastily burned on a pile of old tyres and rubbish, satisfyingly apt given the suffering he inflicted on millions of Cambodians. But, unfortunately, an autopsy was never carried out, fuelling rumours about his manner of demise that persist today.

Strung out along the border itself are the **safehouses** of Pol Pot, Khieu Samphan and Son Sen, located close enough to Thailand that they could flee if the government attacked. As always, the Khmer Rouge was often its own worst enemy, and in 1997 Pol Pot ordered former defence minister Son Sen and all of his family be murdered and their bodies run over by trucks. This incident led to Pol Pot's overthrow by Ta Mok,

and his Khmer Rouge show trial. All the remaining houses are shells, as everything of value was long ago looted by soldiers.

Anyone interested in visiting these bizarre sites should link up with a *moto* driver, as much of the border area is heavily mined.

Sleeping & Eating

Because of the deteriorating road and the resulting extended journey times, quite a few visitors find themselves overnighting in town. There isn't an overwhelming choice of guesthouses from which to choose, but the **Reaksmey Angkor Guesthouse** (r 15,000-25,000r) stands out as the pick of the pack. Rooms are clean, have mosquito nets and include a bathroom.

The restaurant scene is similarly limited. There are several local joints around the central roundabout that can cook up local dishes at low prices – these are popular with pick-up and taxi drivers passing through town.

Getting There & Away

Anlong Veng lies about 142km north of Siem Reap on NH67, a miserable dirt road awaiting a facelift. Journey times vary from four to six hours depending on the season. Share taxis take on the torment for about 15,000r per seat. Approaching by motorcycle, follow the surfaced road from Siem Reap to Banteay Srei temple before continuing north past Kbal Spean. Much of the scenery is monotonous dry forest, but midway through the journey is a verdant section of jungle to divert the mind.

Anlong Veng is also connected by reasonable roads to Samraong (15,000r) in the west and Prasat Preah Vihear to the east. Transport is irregular to the latter, but there are always a couple of pick-ups leaving early that can drop you at Sa Em (about 15,000r), the turn-off to the temple.

PREAH VIHEAR PROVINCE

ខេត្តព្រះវិហារ

Vast Preah Vihear Province shares borders with Thailand and Laos to the north, as well as Siem Reap, Oddar Meanchey, Stung Treng and Kompong Thom within Cambo-

dia. Much of the province is extremely remote and heavily forested. However, large
logging companies are doing their best to
change this, carving huge tracts of pristine
tropical hardwoods out of the landscape.
The province remains desperately poor,
thanks in part to a disastrous infrastructure where there are no major roads in existence. The 'road' linking the provincial
capital, Tbeng Meanchey, to Choam Ksant
in the north is only passable for half the
year, and that's stretching the definition
of passable.

However, Preah Vihear's future may be
brighter, as within the province's lengthy
boundaries are found three of the most
impressive legacies from the Angkorian
era: the mountain temple of Prasat Preah
Vihear, the 10th-century capital of Koh Ker
and the mighty Preah Khan. Koh Ker is
now easily accessible from Siem Reap via
Beng Mealea, but the other two remain
difficult to visit, requiring long and tough
overland journeys and the distinct possibility of a night in the forest. In the wet
season, they are simply unreachable. However, there are plans to upgrade roads leading to each of these incredible locations,
which, in time, could ensure the temples
of Preah Vihear Province become one of
the most important stops on a visit to
Cambodia.

Hidden Cambodia (www.hiddencambodia.com) operates dirt bike tours to these temples during the dry season or for something more
upmarket, try the temple safari offered by
Hanuman Tourism (www.hanumantourism.com).

For now, travel around the province is
only for the most resilient of souls. With
the exception of the new tollroad to Koh
Ker from Siem Reap and the new border
road that links Anlong Veng with Choam
Ksant, the rest of the province has no roads,
just a miserable collection of sandy trails
impersonating roads.

TBENG MEANCHEY
ត្បូងឃ្មុំមានជ័យ

☎ 064 / pop 22,000

Tbeng Meanchey is one of the more out-
of-the-way provincial capitals in Cambodia
and this has kept visitors to a minimum.
Locals refer to the town as Preah Vihear,
a fact that has confused many a foreigner

> **LAND MINE ALERT!**
>
> Preah Vihear Province is one of the most
> heavily mined provinces in Cambodia and
> most of the mines were laid in the past dec-
> ade. Do not, under any circumstances, stray
> from previously trodden paths. Those with
> their own transport should travel only on
> roads or trails regularly used by locals.

attempting the arduous overland journey
to Prasat Preah Vihear, the famous temple
115km further north. Foreigners often refer
to the town as TBY.

Tbeng Meanchey is sprawling and dusty
and consists of little more than two major
dirt roads running north to south. There
is not much to draw the visitor to the town
itself, but it has come to prominence as
the eastern gateway to Koh Ker or Preah
Khan and as a staging post on the long
haul to the mountaintop temple of Prasat
Preah Vihear. This new-found importance
may not last long as new roads are completed linking Siem Reap direct to these
remote temples – TBY could become For-
gottensville once more! The big news for
locals in Tbeng Meanchey, and a bonus
for foreign visitors, is that the town now
has 24-hour electricity to keep those fans
a-spinning.

Information
Bring US dollars as there is nothing in the
way of financial institutions in this town.
There is mobile phone coverage even this
far north and calls can be arranged from
booths near the market.

Sights
The silk-weaving centre **Joom Noon Silk Project**
(www.joomnoon.com) was established by Vietnam
Veterans of America Foundation (VVAF) as
a training school for amputees or impoverished Cambodians. Supplying an artificial
limb is step one in the rehabilitation process, and step two is offering these individuals the chance to make a living. The centre
produces fine hand-woven silk scarves and
sarongs for export to Australia, Japan and the
USA. It is possible to visit the silk-weaving
centre, located about 600m east of the *naga*
(mythical serpent) fountain in the south
of town.

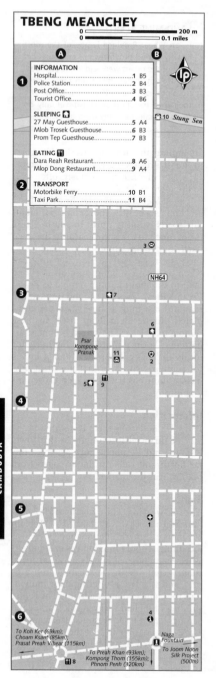

TBENG MEANCHEY

INFORMATION
Hospital	1 B5
Police Station	2 B4
Post Office	3 B3
Tourist Office	4 B6

SLEEPING
27 May Guesthouse	5 A4
Mlob Trosek Guesthouse	6 B3
Prom Tep Guesthouse	7 B3

EATING
Dara Reah Restaurant	8 A6
Mlop Dong Restaurant	9 A4

TRANSPORT
Motorbike Ferry	10 B1
Taxi Park	11 B4

Sleeping & Eating

Prom Tep Guesthouse (☎ 012 964645; r US$5-10; ❄)
The closest thing to a hotel in this part of
Preah Vihear. The rooms here are spacious
and comfortable – satellite TV comes as
standard, the bathrooms include Western-
style toilets and it's the only place in town
with air-con (if it's working).

Mlob Trosek Guesthouse (☎ 012 952035; r 15,000r)
Another TBY favourite, with a large, green
garden, clean enough rooms with bathroom
and plenty of secure parking. The newer
rooms at the rear are lighter and brighter
than those near the front and also have
genuine lino floors, the sort of thing you
look out for in these parts…if you want to
practice your breakdance moves.

27 May Guesthouse (r 5000-15,000r) The chea-
pies with share bathroom are little more
than cells, but rooms don't come cheaper
than US$1.25. The 15,000r rooms are bigger
and have a bathroom inside. It can get noisy
here, being near the market and taxi park.

With the exception of the run-down
market and a couple of street stalls, there
are only a couple of eateries in town.

Mlop Dong Restaurant (mains 3000-6000r) Has
inexpensive food, and the range of dishes is
heartening for this part of the world. It is a
popular stop for expats living in TBY, and
after dinner this is about the closest thing
to a pub this town boasts.

Dara Reah Restaurant (mains 3000-8000r) This
is a larger garden restaurant that's popular
with well-to-do locals. It has good grub (for
this part of the world) and some nice pavilions for small groups.

Getting There & Away

Tbeng Meanchey is 155km north of Kompong Thom on NH64. Pick-ups (15,000/
7000r inside/on the back, four to five hours)
run the route daily, but share taxis (20,000r)
are faster and more comfortable. The road
is in horrendous condition as the logging
freeze means no-one has done any maintenance for a few years. The final 30km
stretch to Tbeng Meanchey climbs over a
series of hills, which can get very nasty in
the wet season with minor rivers to ford.

For all the details on heading north to
Prasat Preah Vihear or west to the temples of
Koh Ker, see p237 and p234 respectively.

For details on the remote trail east to
Stung Treng via Chaeb, see p258.

PREAH KHAN
ប្រះខ័ន

The vast laterite and sandstone temple of Preah Khan is the largest temple enclosure ever constructed during the Angkorian period. Originally dedicated to Hindu deities, it was reconsecrated to Mahayana Buddhist worship during a monumental reconstruction undertaken by Jayavarman VII in the late 12th and early 13th centuries.

Its history is shrouded in mystery, but it was long an important religious site and some of the structures here date back to the 9th century. Both Suryavarman II, builder of Angkor Wat, and Jayavarman VII lived here at times during their lives. This suggests Preah Khan was something of a second city in the Angkorian empire, supporting a large rural population as well as the royal court's urban elite. Jayavarman VII was likely to have been based here during the disastrous occupation of Angkor by the Chams from 1177 and may have already commanded significant regional support among the population in this area,

helping him to later consolidate control of Angkor.

Preah Khan was connected to the temples of Angkor by a 120km laterite highway, complete with ornate *naga* bridges, many examples of which remain today, forgotten in the forests of northwestern Cambodia. Some scholars suggest it was also linked by an ancient road to the pre-Angkorian centre of Sambor Prei Kuk, which continued as a centre of learning throughout the Angkorian era. This indicates Preah Khan was of significant importance throughout the period of the Khmer empire.

The complex covers a total area of almost 5 sq km, and includes a massive *baray* (reservoir), which is 3km long. There is currently no entry charge, but this may change when new roads are built. At the eastern end of the *baray* is a small pyramid temple called **Prasat Damrei** (Elephant Temple). Much of the outer structure is no longer standing, but there are several impressive carvings of *devedas* (goddesses) on the remaining entrance wall. At the summit of the hill were a number of exquisitely carved

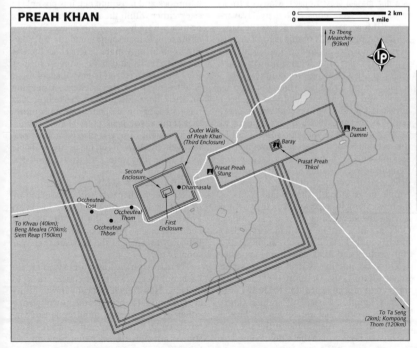

PREAH KHAN

0   2 km
0   1 mile

To Tbeng Meanchey (93km)

Outer Walls of Preah Khan (Third Enclosure)

Prasat Damrei

Baray

Second Enclosure

Prasat Preah Stung

Prasat Preah Thkol

Dharmasala

Occheuteal Tooi

Occheuteal Thom

First Enclosure

To Khvau (40km); Beng Mealea (70km); Siem Reap (150km)

Occheuteal Thbon

To Ta Seng (2km); Kompong Thom (120km)

elephants guarding the shrine, but only two remain today, one partially buried in the mud, the other adorned with local offerings. Two others can be seen on display in the National Museum (p81) in Phnom Penh and the Musée Guimet in Paris.

In the centre of the *baray* is an island temple called **Prasat Preah Thkol** (known by locals as Mebon), which is similar in style to the Western Mebon (p169) at Angkor. At the western end of the *baray* is **Prasat Preah Stung** (known by locals as Prasat Muk Buon – Temple of the Four Faces), perhaps the most memorable temple at Preah Khan. Prasat Preah Stung has all the hallmarks of Jayavarman VII, with the enigmatic faces seen at the Bayon (p156) carved into its central tower. The temple is fairly overgrown, but it is possible to clamber around and explore.

It is a further 400m southwest to the walls of Preah Khan itself, which are surrounded by a moat similar to that around the walled city of Angkor Thom. Much of the moat has vanished under weed and the bridges here no longer have *naga*. Entering through the eastern *gopura* (entrance pavilion) there is a **dharmasala** (rest house). Many of these rest houses were constructed by Jayavarman VII for weary pilgrims across the Angkorian empire. Much of this central area is overgrown by forest, giving it an authentic, abandoned feel, but local authorities are undertaking a clearing programme.

The central structure, which included libraries and a pond for ablutions, has been devastated by looting in recent years. As recently as the mid-1990s, it was thought to be in reasonable shape, but some time in the second half of the decade, thieves arrived seeking buried statues under each *prang* (temple tower). Assaulted with pneumatic drills and mechanical diggers, the ancient temple never stood a chance and many of the towers simply collapsed in on themselves, leaving the depressing mess we see today. Once again, a temple that had survived so much couldn't stand the onslaught of the 20th century and its all-consuming appetite.

This was not the first looting to strike Preah Khan. Louis Delaporte, in charge of the second official expedition to study Cambodia's temples, carted off tonnes (literally!) of carvings that are now in the Musée Guimet in Paris. Also found at the site was the bust of Jayavarman that's now housed in Phnom Penh's National Museum and widely copied as a souvenir for tourists. The body of the statue was discovered a few years ago by locals who realised the strangely shaped stone must have significance and alerted authorities. The head and body were finally rejoined in 1999.

Most locals refer to this temple as Prasat Bakan; scholars officially refer to is as Bakan Svay Rolay, combining the local name for the temple and the district name. Khmers in Siem Reap often refer to it as Preah Khan, Kompong Svay.

Locals say there are no land mines in the vicinity of Preah Khan, but stick to marked paths just to be on the safe side.

Sleeping & Eating

To get the most out of a visit to Preah Khan really requires an overnight stay at the nearby village of Ta Seng. Making a day trip from Kompong Thom, Tbeng Meanchey or Siem Reap requires at least 10 hours on the road, usually more, and that doesn't leave a whole lot of time for exploring. There is no guesthouse in Ta Seng as yet, but with a hammock and mosquito net, it is possible to sleep either within the Preah Khan complex or in a private house in the village. Sleeping at the temple may sound romantic, but staying in Ta Seng is more practical, as there is some electricity and basic supplies such as food and water. Expect to pay villagers about 5000r a night for the privilege of sleeping on their floor. Sleeping at the temple also means taking on the kamikaze mosquitoes that come at you from every angle throughout the night. There is always at least one that gets through! Basic meals are available in Ta Seng, plus water, soft drinks and beer.

Getting There & Away

Unless you particularly enjoy travelling by ox cart, it is extremely difficult to get to Preah Khan between the months of May and November. The best time to visit is from February to April, as the trails are then reasonably dry.

There is no public transport to Preah Khan itself, but there are very infrequent trucks to Ta Seng. However, realistically most visitors are going to get here under their own steam – either by *moto*, rented motorcycle or chartered 4WD. Only *very* experienced bikers should attempt this on rental motorcycles,

Food seller on the Phnom Penh to Battambang railway line (p217)

ANDREW BURKE

JULIET COOMBE

Drinks vendor near Angkor Wat (p150)

Monks receiving alms, Phnom Penh (p70)

COREY WISE

An elephant and its handler in a Pnong village, Mondulkiri Province (p264)

Passengers on the roof of the fast boat from Phnom Penh to Siem Reap (p105)

A farmer and his ox, Kompong Cham (p248)

as conditions are extremely tough from every side. The ox-cart trails snake their way through remote forest in areas that are still mined. It may be sensible to take a local *moto* driver to lead the way, even if you have your own bike; this should cost about US$10 per day plus petrol. Take a wrong turn in this neck of the woods and you'll end up in the middle of nowhere. Do not attempt to visit in the wet season, as the whole area is prone to serious flooding and there are several rivers to cross.

By road, getting to Preah Khan is quickest on motorcycle from Kompong Thom, although most *moto* drivers aren't familiar with the route. Take NH6 towards Siem Reap out of Kompong Thom for 5km and then follow NH64 (the right fork that goes to Tbeng Meanchey). After about 80km a small track leads west from the village of Phnom Dek through the forest to Ta Seng and Preah Khan. The trail starts from pretty much opposite the right fork to Rovieng district. Rumour has it that this road will be upgraded during 2005. The total distance is about 120km from Kompong Thom and the journey should take about four to five hours in the dry season.

Coming from Tbeng Meanchey, head south on NH64 for 37km before turning right at the 'Preah Khan 56km' sign. This is an unpleasant 56km for motorcycles, as it is deep sand for much of the way, but it's the easiest way for 4WDs in the dry season. This route takes four to five hours and leads to Ta Seng via Prasat Damrei.

Coming from Siem Reap there are several choices. By car requires a long journey down NH6 to Stoeng, before heading north on a bad dirt road to Ta Seng and Preah Khan. This could be the approach of choice for now, as the government is rebuilding the road here (before the 2003 election, they promised this in return for votes).

By motorcycle there are two ways from Siem Reap. Easiest is to follow NH6 southeast to Kompong Kdei before heading north on a good dirt road to the village of Khvau. From Khvau, it is 40km east to Preah Khan on a miserable ox-cart track. This can just about be done in a 'dawn-till-dusk' day trip from Siem Reap in the dry season. Don't bank on it, though.

Or get your kicks on Route 66 (NH66). More adventurous and romantic is to follow the old Angkor road from Beng Mealea (p176) east to Preah Khan, which includes about 10 Angkorian bridges dating from the 12th and 13th centuries. From Beng Mealea, the road vanishes into a rough ox-cart track to nowhere, but some huge bridges in the middle of this empty forest make the gain worth the pain. **Spean Ta Ong**, a magical place, is 77m long with about 15 arches, and is 7km west of the village of Khvau. There are well-founded rumours that this old Angkorian road will be the next to be 'privatised' like the road to Koh Ker, whereby a well-connected businessman rebuilds the road and then charges visitors to use it. Nice idea, only there is no tender process and the businessmen always seem to be prominent allies of the ruling CPP.

If hitting the road seems like just too much effort, head for the skies – charter a chopper from Siem Reap for the ultimate view. See p149 for details.

KOH KER

កោះកេរ្ដិ៍

Abandoned to the forests of the north, **Koh Ker** (admission using the toll road US$10, approaching from the west free), a former 10th-century capital of the Angkorian empire, was long one of the most remote and inaccessible temple sites in Cambodia. However, this has all changed with the opening of a new tollroad from Beng Mealea that puts Koh Ker only three to four hours from Siem Reap (day-trip distance). To really appreciate the temples of Koh Ker, it is necessary to spend the night, as a day trip leaves little time to explore. There are some very strange development plans afoot that may see visitors driven around the complex in electric cars from Korea, the same ones that were planned for Angkor before sanity prevailed. Watch this space and ask around in Siem Reap.

Also known as Chok Gargyar, Koh Ker was the capital during the reign of Jayavarman IV (r 928–42), who, having seized the throne from a rival, left Angkor and moved his capital here, where it remained throughout his reign. His son and successor Harshavarman I moved the capital back to Angkor in 944.

There are a remarkable number of religious buildings in the Koh Ker region, considering the short space of time that it was the capital of the empire. There are more than 30 major

---

LAND MINE ALERT!

There were countless land mines in the area around Koh Ker, but most have now been cleared. However, err on the side of caution and do not, under any circumstances, stray from previously trodden paths during a visit to this temple.

---

structures and experts believe there may have been as many as 100 minor sacred buildings in the region. It was also a prolific period for gigantic sculpture and several of the most impressive pieces in the National Museum (p81) in Phnom Penh come from Koh Ker, including a huge *garuda* (mythical half-man, half-bird creature) greeting visitors in the entrance hall, and a unique carving depicting a pair of wrestling monkey-kings.

The principal monument at Koh Ker is **Prasat Thom**, sometimes called Prasat Kompeng, a 40m-high sandstone-faced pyramid of seven levels. This striking structure offers some spectacular views across the forest from its summit. Look out for a giant *garuda* under the collapsed chamber up here. Some 40 inscriptions, dating from 932 to 1010, have been found at Prasat Thom, offering an insight into Cambodian history at this time. Heading northeast, the compound includes the obligatory libraries, as well as a host of smaller brick sanctuaries. Beyond the inner wall and across a *naga*-flanked causeway lies **Prasat Krahom** (Red Temple), the second-largest structure at Koh Ker. Named after the red bricks from which it is constructed, Prasat Krahom is famous for its carved lions (sadly, none of which remain today), similar to those found at Prasat Tao (p240) in the Sambor Prei Kuk Group near Kompong Thom. Prasat Krahom has a wonderful atmosphere when approached from Siem Reap, looking like it is totally lost in the jungle.

South of this central group is a large *baray* known as the **Rahal**, fed by Stung Sen, which would have supplied water to irrigate the land in this arid area. There are many other temples in the area, and most are now safe and accessible thanks to mine clearing in the area. However, no visitor will fail to notice the Danger Mines! signs just beyond each temple. Don't wander off into the forest!

Some of the more interesting temples include: **Prasat Bram**, the first you come to on the

road from Siem Reap, named in honour of its five towers, two of which are smothered by strangler figs; **Prasat Neang Khmau**, with some fine lintels decorating its otherwise bland exterior; **Prasat Chen**, where the statue of the wrestling monkeys was discovered; and **Prasat Leung**, which contains one of the largest and best-preserved Shiva *linga* (phallic symbol) seen anywhere in Cambodia.

Koh Ker is one of the least-studied temple areas from the Angkorian period. Louis Delaporte visited in 1880 during his extensive investigations into Angkorian temples. It was surveyed in 1921 by the great Henri Parmentier for an article in the *Bulletin de l'École D'Extreme Orient,* but no restoration work was ever undertaken here. Archaeological surveys were carried out by Cambodian teams in the 1950s and 1960s, but all records vanished during the destruction of the 1970s, helping to preserve this complex as something of an enigma.

Sleeping & Eating

Nowhere and nothing (to get straight to the point). Bring a hammock and mosquito net, as conditions are very basic, whether you choose to stay around the temples or in the tiny village of Koh Ker. Locals can prepare some very basic food such as rice and noodles, but carry enough food and water to be self-sufficient in case you get lost on the way. There are more supplies and a better chance of something resembling a bed in Sayong, about 9km southeast. With the completion of the new tollroad, it is likely that some new guesthouses and hotels will open during the lifetime of this book.

Getting There & Away

Mean roads long kept Koh Ker off the travel map, but the new private toll road from Beng Mealea (61km) puts the temple complex just two hours from Siem Reap by car. The road from Beng Mealea follows the route of an ancient Angkorian highway that runs through Svay Leu district and on to Koh Ker. Koh Ker is now easy day-trip distance from Siem Reap (146km) and visitor numbers look set to soar. Arrange transport in Siem Reap (p131), but expect high prices due to the distances involved, perhaps US$20 for a *moto* or US$60 and up for a car.

There are two more routes to Koh Ker – one from Siem Reap and the more popular one from Tbeng Meanchey – both passing through the strategic village of Sayong. They are worth knowing about as you are not required to pay the US$10 temple fee. From Sayong to Koh Ker, a *moto* should cost around US$8 to US$10 for the day. For now, these alternative routes are only possible in the dry season.

The route from Siem Reap is to head 60km southeast on NH6 to Kompong Kdei where there is a beautiful Angkorian-era bridge, Spean Praptos. From here there is a good dirt road north to the village of Khvau (40km) and then a mire of a road north to Koh Ker (55km). There is regular public transport to Khvau, with a change in Kompong Kdei. From Khvau it can get a little tricky, but in the dry season there are some tractor-trucks known locally as *coyonnes* that head to Sayong.

The most popular route has been to approach Koh Ker from the east, starting in the provincial capital of Tbeng Meanchey (69km). The trail goes west via the small town of Kulen and road conditions are now much improved from the hell of old. The best news about this route is that it can be partly covered by public transport. There are pick-ups to Kulen (8000/4000r inside/on the back), from where pick-ups or Russian 4WDs continue to Sayong (8000r), gateway to Koh Ker. Serious bikers can take on this route, although it helps to take a local *moto* driver as a guide. The services of a *moto* the whole way, whether guide or driver, are about US$10 per day plus petrol. This is money well earned on these roads.

CHOAM KSANT
ជាំក្សាន្ត

Choam Ksant, a major trade hub for northern Preah Vihear Province, is little more than a large village that has recently fallen off the overland trail to Prasat Preah Vihear because the new road diverts past it. Much of the town engages in petty trade with Thailand, as there is a local border market at Anh Seh, 20km north of town in the Chuor Phnom Dangkrek. The Cambodians transport pigs into Thailand, while the Thais shift a whole host of consumer goods into Cambodia. The border is closed to foreigners and there is nothing of interest to see up there, except some big views. The town is quite affluent with wide, neat streets, and in the remote forests nearby lie the remains of several temples, including the historically important **Prasat Neak Buos**. However, explore with care, as there are lots of mines in the area.

Choam Ksant has a few basic guesthouses for those hardy enough to make it here, offering electricity for only a few hours in the evening. **Heng Heng Guesthouse** (r 8000-10,000r) is the smartest option, located opposite the new market. It has a couple of rooms with bathroom, including a toilet raised like a throne. There are a few basic food stalls around the old and new markets, as well as more street stalls around the village.

Road connections are good towards Prasat Preah Vihear and Anlong Veng, but miserable south to Tbeng Meanchey. There really isn't much need for travellers to come here anymore now that there is a more direct route from Tbeng Meanchey to Prasat Preah Vihear.

PRASAT PREAH VIHEAR
ប្រាសាទព្រះវិហារ

The imposing temple-mountain of Prasat Preah Vihear has the most dramatic location of all of the Angkorian monuments, perched atop a cliff face of Chuor Phnom Dangkrek, towering 550m above the plains below. The views from this most mountainous of temple-mountains are breathtaking: lowland Cambodia stretching as far as the eye can see, and the holy mountain of Phnom Kulen (p175) looming in the distance.

Prasat Preah Vihear was built by a succession of seven Khmer monarchs, beginning with Yasovarman I (r 889–910) and ending with Suryavarman II (r 1112–52), builder of Angkor Wat. This progressive construction is easily appreciated once at the temple itself, as there is a series of sanctuaries rising to the summit of the cliff. Some scholars have contended that the site may have been founded earlier still, as evidenced by inscriptions linking it to the son of Jayavarman II, the first of Angkor's *devaraja* (god-kings). He transported holy stone here from the ancient Cambodian temple of Wat Phu Champasak in Laos.

Known as Khao Phra Wiharn by Thais, translating as 'Sacred Monastery', Prasat

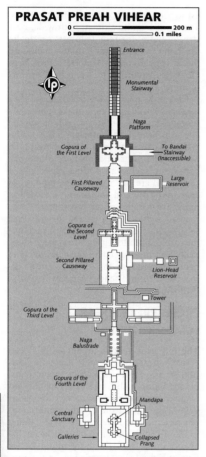

PRASAT PREAH VIHEAR

0 — 200 m
0 — 0.1 miles

Entrance

Monumental Stairway

Naga Platform

Gopura of the First Level

To Bandai Stairway (Inaccessible)

First Pillared Causeway

Large Reservoir

Gopura of the Second Level

Second Pillared Causeway

Lion-Head Reservoir

Tower

Gopura of the Third Level

Naga Balustrade

Gopura of the Fourth Level

Mandapa

Central Sanctuary

Galleries

Collapsed Prang

NORTHWESTERN CAMBODIA

Preah Vihear was an important place of pilgrimage during the Angkorian period. It was constructed, like other principal temple-mountains from this period, to represent Mt Meru and was dedicated to the Hindu deity Shiva. The complex includes five principal *gopura,* the best preserved of which are the those at a higher level. The central sanctuary is constructed right on the edge of the mountain and in places the foundation stones of the temple are just a few centimetres from the cliff face, further proof of the architectural genius of the ancient Khmers. The site is in reasonable condition and includes many exquisitely carved lintels, particularly around the third, and largest, *gopura.* Look out

for an early rendition of the Churning of the Ocean of Milk, as later perfected at Angkor Wat, on the southern doorway. However, it is the location that really draws the visitors.

For generations, Prasat Preah Vihear has been the subject of tensions between Cambodia and Thailand, which periodically boil over. Much of this area was occupied by Thailand for several centuries, but was returned to Cambodian sovereignty during the French protectorate under the treaty of 1907. In 1959, the Thai military seized the temple from Cambodia and then–Prime Minister Sihanouk took the dispute to the International Court, gaining worldwide recognition for Cambodian sovereignty in a 1962 ruling.

That was that, at least for a few decades, and the only time that Prasat Preah Vihear made international news was in 1979 when the Thai military pushed more than 40,000 starving, diseased Cambodian refugees across the border in what was then the worst case of forced repatriation in UN history. The whole area was mined and the refugees stumbled right back into the middle of Armageddon. Many people died from horrific injuries, starvation and disease before the occupying Vietnamese army could cut a safe passage through to the survivors and escort them on the long walk south to Kompong Thom. No doubt many then ended up imprisoned in Phnom Penh, for a time, for having fled the country in the first place.

Prasat Preah Vihear hit the headlines again in May 1998, because the Khmer Rouge regrouped there after the fall of Anlong Veng and staged a last stand, a stand that turned to surrender.

With peace came an agreement between the Cambodians and Thais to open the temple to tourism. The Thais built a huge road up the mountain and began to appropriate Cambodian territory along the ill-defined border. Today, there is a large visitors centre and car park built on what was – not so long ago – Cambodian land. The Thais now want their territory to extend right up to the temple steps; they also want to close the small Cambodian market that has grown up at the base of the temple. The stand-off resulted in the temple being closed to visitors from the Thai side in December 2001 – it only reopened to visitors in 2003.

Currently, it is open to visitors from both sides of the border. It costs US$10 to visit from the Thai side – US$5 to the Thais for visiting the 'national park' and US$5 to the Khmers as the temple fee. From the Cambodian side, only the temple fee is levied, but they often forget to charge at all, so surprised are they to see foreigners arriving from this side.

For more on the carvings of Prasat Preah Vihear and the temple's history, look out for vendors selling *Preah Vihear* by Vittorio Roveda, a readable souvenir book accompanied by some attractive photographs.

Getting There & Away

The easy way to get to Prasat Preah Vihear is from Thailand, as there are paved roads right up to the back door. Anyone coming from Thailand will no doubt be armed with a copy of Lonely Planet *Thailand,* which contains all the details for this route via the town of Kantharalak. However, getting here from the Cambodia side is a unique and challenging experience, an adventure that will make an explorer of any of us. The struggle outlined here may soon become unnecessary, as the Cambodian government is in the process of rebuilding roads here from Anlong Veng and Tbeng Meanchey. This could put Prasat Preah Vihear within four hours of Siem Reap on a good road, although it is not going to happen overnight.

Getting to Prasat Preah Vihear via the village of Sa Em is seriously difficult and shouldn't be attempted by anyone who isn't willing to put up with misery along the way. It can only be done between December and May, because in the wet season roads are impassable in this part of the country. The Sa Em trip can be done as an overnight trip from Siem Reap or Tbeng Meanchey or as part of a three-day trip between Siem Reap and Phnom Penh. Bear in mind that if you are travelling by public transport, you will need to take a *moto* for the short leg from Sa Em to the base of the mountain (US$1 to US$2).

Getting to Sa Em and Prasat Preah Vihear from Tbeng Meanchey is no picnic. A new road was completed in 2003, linking the two, but it has since degenerated into a mess of mythical proportions under the

---

LAND MINE ALERT!

Prasat Preah Vihear was the scene of heavy fighting as recently as 1998 and numerous land mines were used by the Khmer Rouge to defend this strategic location against government forces. As long as clearance continues, do not stray from marked paths during a visit to this temple, as several locals have been killed or maimed in recent years.

---

weight of fuel-smuggling trucks from the Thai border. Plan on about five hours to reach Prasat Preah Vihear (115km). This road is often completely impassable in the wet season, when vehicles end up having to go via Siem Reap instead. Some pickups take on this route and it costs around 20,000r for a seat.

From Siem Reap, it is first necessary to get to Anlong Veng (see p228 for details of this trip). From Anlong Veng (103km), there are pick-ups running the decent road towards Sa Em (10,000r, two hours).

Either way, once you get to the base of the mountain, the approach is the same. From the checkpoint below, there is a rollercoaster of a road up the mountain that is only suitable for highly experienced drivers or bikers, as there are gradients of 35% and loose stones everywhere – an unforgiving combination. Anyone coming without their own wheels has a few options: take a two-hour walk up the same road carrying plenty of water; arrange a *moto* for about US$5, or charter the police 4WD to give you a lift. The latter is usually US$25, but if the police are going up anyway, they may sell you a seat for US$5.

Once at the summit of the mountain, you have the satisfaction of knowing that you have undertaken a modern-day pilgrimage that is almost the equal of any undertaken at the height of the Angkorian empire. On the downside, you also have the deeply disheartening sight of hundreds of tourists who have steamed up to the temple in air-conditioned coaches along a sealed superhighway in Thailand – they will never know what you have been through.

To really get a bird's-eye view of the temple – and arrive in style – take a helicopter from Siem Reap. For more, see p149.

NORTHWESTERN CAMBODIA

KOMPONG THOM PROVINCE

ខេត្តកំពង់ធំ

Kompong Thom is Cambodia's second-largest province and is starting to draw more visitors thanks to the temples of Sambor Prei Kuk and other lesser-known Angkorian sites. During French rule, it was home to a large minority group called the Stieng, but they have long been assimilated into Khmer society. Farming and fishing are the mainstay of the population, and Stung Sen winds its way through the province and into the Tonlé Sap river in the west.

The province was hard hit by the long civil war. It came under particularly fierce US bombardment in the early 1970s, in an effort to reopen the severed road between Phnom Penh and Siem Reap.

There are only two roads that visitors tend to use in Kompong Thom Province: smooth and sexy NH6, which links Phnom Penh and Siem Reap, and rough and ready NH64 north to Tbeng Meanchey and Preah Vihear Province.

KOMPONG THOM

កំពង់ធំ

☎ 062 / pop 66,000

Kompong Thom is a bustling commercial centre on the banks of Stung Sen that is strategically located on NH6 midway between Phnom Penh and Siem Reap. It is another one of those towns in which overland travellers stop for a bite to eat, but rarely hang around long enough to get a feel for the place. Despite the improved road between the capital and the temples of Angkor, Kompong Thom remains the ideal base from which to explore the pre-Angkorian Chenla capital of Sambor Prei Kuk and a gateway to the incredible remote temples of Preah Khan, Koh Ker and Prasat Preah Vihear.

Information

There is nowhere to change travellers cheques or obtain cash advances in Kompong Thom, so bring plenty of cash. **Acleda Bank** (☎ 961243; NH6 east) can arrange Western Union money transfers.

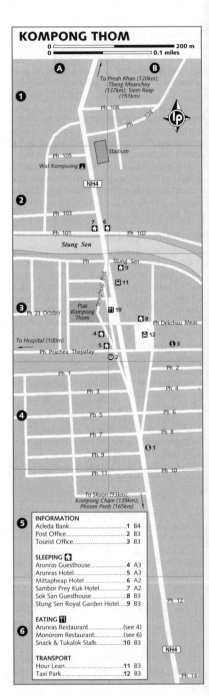

KOMPONG THOM

0 ——————— 200 m
0 ——————— 0.1 miles

To Preah Khan (120km);
Tbeng Meanchey
(137km); Siem Reap
(151km)

Ph 106
Ph 104

Ph 105   Stadium
Wat Kompuong

NH4

Ph 103
7 6
Ph 101   Ph 102
Stung Sen

Ph   Stung Sen
11

Psar
Ph 23 October   Kompong   10
Thom   8 Ph Dekchau Meas
4   12
To Hospital (100m)   5   3
Ph Prachea Thepatay   2

Ph 1   Ph 2
Ph 3   Ph 4
Ph 5   Ph 6
Ph 7   Ph 8
1
Ph 9
Ph 11   Ph 10

To Skuon (93km);
Kompong Cham (139km);
Phnom Penh (165km)

INFORMATION	
Acleda Bank	1 B4
Post Office	2 B3
Tourist Office	3 B3

SLEEPING	
Arunras Guesthouse	4 A3
Arunras Hotel	5 A3
Mittapheap Hotel	6 A2
Sambor Prey Kuk Hotel	7 A2
Sok San Guesthouse	8 B3
Stung Sen Royal Garden Hotel	9 B3

EATING	
Arunras Restaurant	(see 4)
Monorom Restaurant	(see 6)
Snack & Tukalok Stalls	10 B3

TRANSPORT	
Hour Lean	11 B3
Taxi Park	12 B3

Ph 12

NH4

Ph 14

NORTHWESTERN CAMBODIA

There are telephone kiosks all around the market, offering national and international calls. There is also a **post office** (Ph Prachea Thepatay) opposite the Arunras Hotel.

There is a tourist office on Ph Prachea Thepatay; it's upstairs in an old wooden building and the staff here speak a little English and better French.

Sleeping

Due to Kompong Thom's central location on NH6, there's a wide range of accommodation available in to suit every budget.

Arunras Hotel (☎ 961294; Ph Prachea Thepatay; r US$6-12; 🗷) Formerly the Neak Meas Hotel, it has been given a total overhaul and is now the first and only hotel in Kompong Thom with a lift (elevator). It may not sound like much, but this is big news in a small town. The rooms are very smart, including a master panel by the bed, satellite TV, fridge and hot water. Definitely the best deal in town.

Arunras Guesthouse (☎ 961238; 46 Sereipheap Blvd; s/tw with fan 12,000/17,000r, tw with air-con US$8; 🗷) Probably the most popular place in town for budget travellers. The rooms include TV and bathroom, making for a good deal. However, when it comes to air-con, smarter rooms are available at the town's hotels.

Mittapheap Hotel (☎ 961213; NH6 north; r US$5-10; 🗷) Part of the Mittapheap empire, which includes sister hotels in Kompong Cham and Kratie, this smart little hotel has comfortable rooms at the right price.

Stung Sen Royal Garden Hotel (☎ 961228; Ph Stung Sen; r US$15-25; 🗷) The name conjures up a pretty plush pad and it is a comfortable hotel (for the provinces). Rooms come fully furnished and the gargantuan suites are a good investment for an extra five bucks. It is popular with package groups passing through town on a trip to Sambor Prei Kuk.

Sambor Prey Kuk Hotel (☎ 961359; NH6 north; s US$3-8, d US$5-10; 🗷) It may not be in the same league as the newer hotels in town, but this place is worth consideration by solo travellers – the singles are exceedingly good value.

There are bargain basement guesthouses on Ph Dekchau Meas running east from the market, but some make more money as brothels and are right opposite the taxi park for early morning horn action. Best of the lot is **Sok San Guesthouse** (8 Ph Dekchau Meas; r 6000-10,000r). Don't be put off by the old cow-shed rooms near the entrance, as there is a newer block at the back with tidy enough rooms with bathroom that offer very good value for money. Don't even think about staying in the cow shed just to save 4000r!

Eating

There aren't a whole lot of restaurants in town, but there are plenty of snack stalls and *tukalok* sellers in front of the market and these are the cheapest places at which to pick up light bites.

Arunras Restaurant (46 Sereipheap Blvd; mains 3000-6000r) Located beneath Arunras Guesthouse, this is the most popular restaurant in town, turning out cheap and tasty food for itinerant travellers. The large menu includes the full range of Cambodian cuisine, plus a few dishes of Chinese and Western influence for good measure. Try the deep-fried fresh honeycomb if it's in season.

Monorom Restaurant (☎ 961213; NH6 north; mains 3000-8000r) Next door to Mittapheap Hotel, this local restaurant is a top spot for breakfast and is popular with locals throughout the day.

Entertainment

Kompong Thom is not the nightlife capital of Cambodia, but the Arunras Hotel (left) does have a live band in its restaurant most nights. The music is mainly Khmer, but the band throws in the odd English or French track. It is a good place to practise your Khmer dance moves without being seen by too many fellow foreigners!

Getting There & Away

Strategically situated on NH6, Kompong Thom is 165km north of Phnom Penh and 150km southeast of Siem Reap. After a rebuild that was long overdue, this road is now in good shape. Bus companies running between Phnom Penh and Siem Reap often drop off and pick up passengers when passing through. Share taxis are faster and cost 10,000r to Phnom Penh (2½ hours), and about US$3 to Siem Reap.

Heading north to Tbeng Meanchey, often referred to as Preah Vihear by locals, pickups (15,000/7000r inside/on the back, four to five hours) are the most common form of transport, but share taxis also do occasional runs (20,000r). For more on the unholy road conditions see p230.

NORTHWESTERN CAMBODIA

AROUND KOMPONG THOM
Sambor Prei Kuk
សំបូរព្រៃគុក

Sambor Prei Kuk is the most impressive group of pre-Angkorian monuments in Cambodia. There are more than 100 small temples scattered through the forest, and they are some of the oldest structures in the country. Originally called Isanapura, Sambor Prei Kuk was the capital of Chenla during the reign of the early-7th-century King Isanavarman, and continued to be an important learning centre during the Angkorian era.

The central complex of temples consists of four groups of edifices, most of which are made of brick, and whose design prefigures a number of later developments in Khmer art. Years of monsoon rains have not been kind to the delicate brick carvings on the exterior, but it is somehow more reassuring to know they have been assailed by the elements rather than by the malice of man (as seen at later, looted Angkorian sites).

The principle group, known as **Prasat Sambor** and visible from the road, is dedicated to

Gambhireshvara, one of Shiva's many incarnations. The other groups are all dedicated to Shiva himself. Several of Prasat Sambor's towers retain carvings in a reasonable condition and there is a series of large *yoni* (female fertility symbols) around the central tower that appear to date from a later period, demonstrating the continuity between pre-Angkorian and Angkorian culture.

Prasat Tao, boasting the largest of the Sambor Prei Kuk structures, means 'Lion Temple' and there are two excellent examples of Chenla carving in the form of two large and elaborately coiffured lions.

The last major group is **Prasat Yeay Peau**. This is arguably the most atmospheric complex, as it feels more lost in the forest than the others. The eastern gateway stands precariously under the weight of a massive tree, its ancient bricks interwoven with the tree's probing and extensive roots.

In the future, generations of Cambodian brochure writers will no doubt attempt to draw comparison with Bagan in Myanmar (Burma), but this is an optimistic description, to say the least. However, there is a

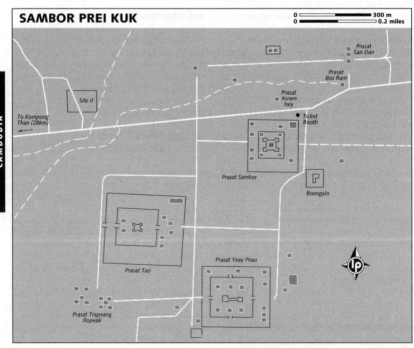

SAMBOR PREI KUK

0 ————— 300 m
0 ————— 0.2 miles

Prasat San Dan

Prasat Bos Ram

Prasat Asram Isey

Site II

To Kompong Than (28km)

Ticket Booth

Prasat Sambor

Boengalo

Prasat Tao

Prasat Yeay Peau

Prasat Trapeang Ropeak

serene and soothing atmosphere about the place.

Sambor Prei Kuk is best visited on the way to Siem Reap as it offers a chronological insight into the development of temple architecture in Cambodia. Coming from Siem Reap, you might have seen enough temples to last a lifetime, but Sambor Prei Kuk is sufficiently different from Angkor to warrant a visit for those interested in Cambodia's rich architectural legacy.

At the time of writing, there is no entrance charge, but visitor details are taken down in a small notebook and a 'donation' requested. It is surely only a matter of time before an official charge is introduced.

GETTING THERE & AWAY

The road that links Sambor Prei Kuk to NH64 is one of the best dirt roads in the country…sadly, the same cannot be said for NH64 itself. To get here from Kompong Thom, follow NH6 north in the direction of Siem Reap for 5km before continuing straight on NH64 towards Tbeng Meanchey. The road to Sambor Prei Kuk starts on the right after a further 11km and is marked by an elaborate laterite sign. The next 14km are bliss.

Visitors without transport can arrange a *moto* out here; the round trip should cost about US$6, or US$8 for the whole day. It takes about one hour to get here by car, and slightly less by motorcycle.

Prasat Andet
ប្រាសាទអណ្ដែត

Dating from the same period as Sambor Prei Kuk (7th century), this small, ruinous brick temple is set amid the grounds of a modern wat. Prasat Andet would have been the focal point of an important commercial centre trading on the Tonlé Sap, and some researchers believe it continued to play such a role during the time of Angkor. Today, very little remains and it is only worth the visit for dedicated temple-trackers with time on their hands. It is 29km west of Kompong Thom, and about 2km south of NH6.

Phnom Sontuk
ភ្នំសន្ទុក

Phnom Sontuk is the most important holy mountain in this region and the hillside is decorated with Buddha images and a series of pagodas. It is an attractive location, set high above the surrounding countryside, but this means there are a lot of stairs to climb – 980, in fact. The stairs wind their way up through a forest and emerge at a colourful **pagoda** that has many small shrines (quite unlike other shrines around Cambodia). There are a number of interesting sandstone boulders balanced around the wat, into which have been carved images of Buddha. Just beneath the southern summit of the mountain are several large **reclining Buddhas** – some modern incarnations cast in cement, others carved into the mountain itself centuries ago. There is an active wat on the mountain and the local monks are always interested in receiving foreign tourists. For travellers spending the night in Kompong Thom, Phnom Sontuk could be a good place from which to catch a magnificent sunset, but this means coming down the mountain in the dark.

GETTING THERE & AWAY

Phnom Sontuk is 20km from Kompong Thom. Follow NH6 for 18km in the direction of Phnom Penh and turn left down a sandy trail leading to the mountain. Those coming from Phnom Penh in their own transport should try to fit it in on the way to Kompong Thom so that there is no need for backtracking. A round trip by *moto* costs around US$4, depending on wait time. Those with trail bikes and a healthy dose of experience can ride up the hill by following the trail to the left of the stairs and veering right when the trail goes up what looks like a rocky dried-out stream-bed.

Prasat Kuha Nokor
ប្រាសាទគុហានគរ

This 11th-century temple constructed during the reign of Suryavarman I is in extremely good condition thanks to a lengthy renovation before the civil war. It is set in the grounds of a modern wat and is an easy enough stop for those with their own transport, although a headache for those travelling by bus or share taxi. From Phnom Penh, the journey will take about two hours, and from Kompong Thom about an hour. The temple is signposted from NH6, about 22km north of Skuon, and is 2km from the main road. From NH6, you can get a *moto* to the temple.

Eastern Cambodia

Eastern Cambodia is a vast area stretching from the Lao border in the north, down the long frontier of Vietnam to the east. It is a region of stark contrasts: the hilly, forested northeast looming large over the flat agricultural plains that characterise the rest of the country further to the south. The Mekong River and its tributaries pass through the densely populated agricultural lowlands, which often flood. For much of the eastern region the massive Mekong and its tributaries form the main transport routes and provide a livelihood for many people.

If a wildlife encounter fires your imagination, then it's to the northeast you must come. The provinces of Mondulkiri and Ratanakiri, best visited from November to March, are home to some of Cambodia's most beautiful landscapes, as well as tigers, leopards and elephants. Kouprey, an extremely rare wild ox and the country's national symbol, used to inhabit the region, but is sadly thought to be extinct. In the Mekong River live dwindling numbers of freshwater Irrawaddy dolphins which can be viewed year-round near Kratie.

It is also possible to live the wild life in the northeast of Cambodia, as the area is home to many ethnic minority groups known as Khmer Leu (Upper Khmer) or *chunchiet* (ethnic minorities). With different dialects, different lifestyles and different looks, these people are a world away from their lowland Khmer neighbours. Trekking, biking and kayaking are all activities beginning to take off in this remote corner of Cambodia. On the down side, illegal logging is also a major problem in the provinces of the northeast, and has replaced rubber as the major industry in the region.

HIGHLIGHTS

- Sneak a peek at the rare freshwater Irrawaddy dolphins in the **Mekong River** (p254) near Kratie

- Discover another world amid the rolling hills of **Mondulkiri** (p264), home to many of Cambodia's ethnic minorities

- Take the plunge into the crystal-clear waters of **Boeng Yeak Lom** (p261), the best swimming pool in the country, surrounded by lush forest

- Trek through the jungle on an **elephant** (p259) near Ban Lung in Ratanakiri Province, still the traditional form of transport for the hill tribes

- Take a **boat trip** (p250) on the scenic stretch of the Mekong between Kompong Cham and Stung Treng, a scenic stretch of river with countless islands and villages

| ■ ELEVATION: 5 – 1500M | ■ POPULATION: 5.4 MILLION | ■ AREA: 68,472 SQ KM |

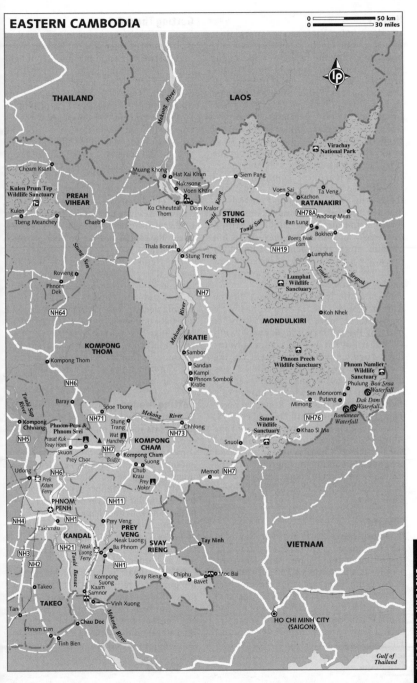

EASTERN CAMBODIA

0 _____ 50 km
0 _____ 30 miles

THAILAND

LAOS

Choam Ksant

Kulen Prum Tep
Wildlife Sanctuary

PREAH
VIHEAR

Kulen

Tbeng Meanchey

Chaeb

Muang Khong

Hat Xai Khun

Nakasong

Voen Kham

Ko Chheuteal
Thom

Dom Kralor

Siem Pang

Voen Sai

Virachay
National Park

Ta Veng

Kachon

RATANAKIRI

NH78A

Andong Meas

STUNG
TRENG

Thala Boravit

Stung Treng

Tonle San

Ban Lung

Boeng Yeak
Lom

Bokheo

NH19

Lumphat

Steung Sen

Rovieng

Phnom
Dek

NH64

NH7

Lumphat
Wildlife
Sanctuary

Koh Nhek

MONDULKIRI

KOMPONG
THOM

KRATIE

Mekong River

Sambor

Kompong Thom

NH6

Sandan

Kampi

Phnom Sombok

Kratie

Phnom Prech
Wildlife Sanctuary

Phnom Namlier
Wildlife
Sanctuary

Baray

Spoe Tbong

Mekong River

Phnom Pros &
Phnom Srei

Stung
Trang

Chhlong

Sen Monorom

Phulung

Putang

Mimong

Bou Sraa
Waterfall

Dak Dam
Waterfall

Kompong
Chhnang

NH71

Wat
Hanchey

Prasat Kuk-
Yeay Hom

NH7

NH5

Skuon

Prey Chor

Bridge

KOMPONG
CHAM

NH73

Kompong Cham

Suong

Snuol
Wildlife
Sanctuary

NH76

Khao Si Ma

Snuol

Romanear
Waterfall

Udong

NH6

Prek
Kdam
Ferry

Chub
Krau

Prey
Nokor

Memot

NH7

PHNOM
PENH

NH11

NH4

Takhmau

Prey Veng

KANDAL

NH21

Neak
Luong
Ferry

Neak Luong

Ba Phnom

PREY
VENG

SVAY
RIENG

Tay Ninh

VIETNAM

NH3

NH2

Kompong
Suong

Kaam
Samnor

Svay Rieng

Chiphu

Bavet

Moc Bai

TAKEO

Takeo

Tani

Vinh Xuong

Phnam Den

Chau Doc

Tinh Bien

HO CHI MINH CITY
(SAIGON)

Gulf of
Thailand

EASTERN CAMBODIA

History

In the 1960s Vietnamese communist forces sought sanctuary in eastern Cambodia to escape the fire power and might of the American army, and much of the area wa's heavily under the influence of the Vietnamese. Prince Sihanouk became increasingly anti-American as the 1960s progressed, and cut a deal to tacitly supply the Vietnamese communists with weapons from the Chinese, via the port of Sihanoukville. By the end of the decade, as the USA began its bombing raids and incursions, the Vietnamese communists had moved deep into the country. Following the overthrow of Sihanouk, Lon Nol demanded that all Vietnamese communist forces withdraw from Cambodia within one week, an ultimatum they could not possibly meet, and open war erupted. In just a few months, much of eastern Cambodia fell to the Vietnamese communists and their Khmer Rouge allies.

During the much of the rule of the Khmer Rouge, the eastern zones were known to be more moderate than other parts of the country and it wasn't until 1977 that Pol Pot and the central government tried to impose their will on the east. Militarily, eastern Cambodia was independent and strong, and the centre's crackdown provoked what amounted to a civil war between Khmer Rouge factions. This tussle lingered until December 1978, when the Vietnamese invasion forced the Khmer Rouge leadership to flee to the Thai border. The east became one of the safest areas of the country during much of the 1980s, as the Khmer Rouge kept well away from areas that were close to the Vietnamese border.

Climate

It is business as usual in the lowlands of eastern Cambodia, with a climate similar to that of the capital, Phnom Penh. However, venture to the northeast and it is another story, as the higher elevations mean lower temperatures. It doesn't ever really get that cool during the day, but you might find yourself chilling out at night if you don't pack a warm top in the winter months. The wet season in the northeastern areas tend to be wetter than that of lowland Cambodia.

Getting There & Away

Eastern Cambodia is home to several of the important international border crossings between Cambodia and its neighbours. The Mekong River border at Dom Kralor–Voen Kham shared with Laos to the north is an ever more popular route for adventurous travellers. East of Phnom Penh are two border crossings with Vietnam, the old favourite Bavet–Moc Bai crossing on the road to Ho Chi Minh City, and the Mekong River crossing at Kaam Samnor–Vinh Xuong. See p292 for more on border crossings.

For those already in Cambodia, Phnom Penh is the usual gateway to the region, with a host of newly renovated roads fanning out to the major cities, plus regular flights between the capital and the popular province of Ratanakiri.

As overland travel takes off in Cambodia, it is possible to reach many of the more remote provinces by a combination of boat and road travel. A round trip from Phnom Penh to Ratanakiri by land can take less than one week (if you set a fast pace). Mondulkiri is more straightforward and, with good connections, a round trip can be done in four days. But be aware that you can sometimes end up stranded in the wet season.

Getting Around

Eastern Cambodia is one of the more remote parts of the country and conditions vary widely between wet and dry seasons. Getting around the lowlands is easy enough, as many of the roads have been upgraded and buses, minibuses and taxis ply the routes. National Highway (NH) 1 to Vietnam has been comprehensively overhauled and is in fine shape all the way to the Vietnamese border. NH7 has been rebuilt as far as Kratie, but further north work is still in progress towards Stung Treng and the Lao border.

The northeast is a different matter, as the punishing rains of the wet season leave many of the roads in a sorry state. A good road can turn bad in a matter of months and journey times become hit and miss. Boat travel on the Mekong River remains a savvy option during the wet season, while in the dry season, taxis, jeeps and pick-ups do the trick.

EASTERN CAMBODIA

SVAY RIENG PROVINCE

ខេត្តស្វាយរៀង

This small province occupies a jut of land sticking into Vietnam, an area known as the parrot's beak. During the Vietnam War, American forces were convinced that this was where the Vietnamese communists' version of the Pentagon was situated. While there were undoubtedly a lot of Vietnamese communists hiding in Cambodia during much of the war, there was no such thing as a Pentagon. In 1969 the Americans began unauthorised bombing in this area and in 1970 joined forces with South Vietnamese forces for a ground assault.

Svay Rieng is considered one of Cambodia's poorest provinces because of the poor quality of its land. Most of the population eke out a subsistence living based on farming and fishing. There is really nothing to attract visitors here, which is why 99.9% zoom through on NH1, which passes right through the heart of the province to Vietnam.

SVAY RIENG

ស្វាយរៀង

☎ 044 / pop 21,000

Svay Rieng is a blink-and-you'll-miss-it provincial capital that many travellers whistle past when making the journey between Phnom Penh and Ho Chi Minh City. It is much like Cambodia's other sleepy towns, but if you feel the urge to recharge the batteries between the nightlife capitals of Phnom Penh and Saigon, this is the most convenient place to do it. There is quite literally nothing to do here. Winding its way through town is Tonlé Wayko, a tributary of the Mekong.

Information

This is a town where cash is king, so come with US dollars or riel. **Acleda Bank** (☎ 945545), a few blocks west of the Independence Monument, is the place to organise Western Union money transfers.

Sleeping

The choice is hardly overwhelming in this part of Cambodia. At the budget end, there are several guesthouses clustered around a junction in the centre of town, just a few hundred metres west of the Independence Monument. There are two fully fledged hotels in town that offer air-con, satellite TV and bathroom, both overlooking the Independence Monument.

Vimean Monorom Hotel (☎ 945817; NH1; r US$5-10; ☒) This place has a dash of the Soviet about its exterior, but the rooms are large, comfortable and good value. Cheaper rooms come with a fan; double your money for some air-con action.

Tonlay Waikor Hotel (☎ 945718; NH1; r US$10; ☒) This huge hotel, ever proud of its carpets, used to charge more than the competition. Prices are now enticing and you're sure to feel secure here, as it's owned by the National Police Chief.

Samaki Guesthouse (☎ 011 888412; Ph 113; r with/without bathroom US$4/3) Best of a mediocre group of guesthouses; the owners are friendly and helpful here. Cheaper rooms involve running the gauntlet with a share bathroom.

Santepheap Guesthouse (☎ 011 682760; Ph 113; r with/without bathroom US$5/4) The next best guesthouse, but the extra bucks might be well spent upgrading to one of the hotels.

Eating

Boeng Meas Restaurant (NH1; mains US$1; ☒ 6.30am-9.30pm) Built on stilts near the riverside, this little wooden restaurant is considered by many Khmers to be the best in town. All the Khmer favourites are helpfully listed on the English menu and service is swift.

Thun Thean Reksmey Restaurant (Ph 113; mains 3000-6000r; ☒ 6.30am-9.30pm) Long a favourite spot with nongovernmental organisation (NGO) workers in town, this family run restaurant has tasty food and a welcoming atmosphere.

There are cheap food stalls around Psar Svay Rieng (Svay Rieng Market) for those wanting a faster feed, as well as some snack stalls alongside the river at night.

Entertainment

Dream on! There used to be a couple of Khmer nightclubs in the big hotels, but these have succumbed to the power of karaoke. Some of the riverfront stalls sell beers and could be the place for a quiet drink.

Getting There & Away

Share taxis for Svay Rieng leave from Phnom Penh's Chbah Ampeau taxi park in the southeast of the city. The cost is about 8000r per person. Hour Lean (p105) operate buses direct from Phnom Penh to Svay Rieng (8000r, three hours, one departure a day).

Travelling to Svay Rieng from the Bavet border crossing with Vietnam may be more difficult because taxi drivers prefer the more lucrative option of taking foreigners all the way to Phnom Penh. Stuff yourself into a taxi with other travellers and ask to be dropped off at Svay Rieng (US$1 to US$2). Taxis usually drop people off near Psar Svay Rieng.

PREY VENG PROVINCE

ខេត្តព្រៃវែង

Prey Veng is a small but heavily populated agricultural region nestled on the east bank of the Mekong. Rubber played a large part in Prey Veng's prewar economy, but most of the plantations are no longer commercially viable. There is little of significance to be seen in the province today, but it may have played a significant role in Cambodian history, as one of the earliest pre-Angkorian kingdoms was located in the area around Ba Phnom. It is a province that has experienced few visitors; the provincial capital is a sleepy place on NH11, recently rebuilt as a road link between NH1 and NH7.

PREY VENG

ព្រៃវែង

☎ 043 / pop 55,000

Few travellers make it to Prey Veng, a sleepy backwater on NH11 between Neak Luong and Kompong Cham. Not a lot happens here and most of the population is tucked up in bed by 9pm. Those who want to escape their fellow tourists may enjoy a visit to Prey Veng, as it offers an alternative route between Phnom Penh and Kompong Cham.

There are a few decaying colonial structures around town, attesting to a once-important centre. During most of the year a vast lake marks the western edge of town, but from March to August this evaporates and the local farmers cultivate rice.

Information

Come with riel or US dollars as other currencies are not so popular around here.

Acleda Bank (☎ 944555) represents Western Union for those needing quick transfers.

Sights

In short, not a lot. There is a small **museum** in the middle of town, but it's locked up for most of the year. Don't be put off, however, as it is so small that you can see everything it has to offer by peering through the window.

Sleeping

The cheaper rooms in Prey Veng have fans, while those with higher prices have air-con.

Angkor Thom Hotel (☎ 012 953165; r US$5-10; ❄) Setting a new standard for Prey Veng, this smart little hotel has 27 spotless rooms to choose from, all with bathroom.

Chan Kiry Guesthouse (☎ 011 746014; r US$5-10; ❄) Occupying a breezy location on a promontory that juts out into the lake during the wet season, this guesthouse could do with a facelift to bring the rooms up to the standard of the setting. Satellite TV and a bathroom are standard.

Mittapheap Hotel (☎ 012 997757; r US$4-10; ❄) Sitting on the central crossroads in town, this popular little place is the old timer among Prey Veng's hotels. The rooms are clean and, like the competition, good value for money.

Rong Damrey Hotel (☎ 011 761052; r US$5-10; ❄) Tucked away in the northeastern corner of town behind the local stadium (looks more like a field mind you), this is a clean, comfortable establishment. Work was underway on a new wing when we swung by, so it could once again be the smartest in town by the time you read this.

Apart from the food stalls around Psar Prey Veng (Prey Veng Market) and a couple of basic holes-in-the-wall, there is only one real restaurant in town.

Eating

Mittapheap Restaurant (☎ 011 939213; mains 3000-4000r) Owned by the same family as the nearby Mittapheap Hotel (above), this restaurant has an effusive manager who ensures lightning quick service. It is a friendly, fun place with inexpensive Khmer, Chinese and Vietnamese food.

Getting There & Away

Prey Veng is 90km east of Phnom Penh and 78km south of Kompong Cham, but that used to feel like a world away thanks to the miserable condition of NH11. However, this road was comprehensively overhauled in 2003 and is now as good as any road in the country. Minibuses (6000r) depart when full and share taxis (8000r) link Phnom Penh (two hours) with Prey Veng, but this will get much faster once the huge bridge at Neak Luong is completed in 2007 to 2008. Prey Veng and Kompong Cham are connected by minibuses (4000r) and share taxis (6000r), taking about 1½ hours.

The smart new road is a mixed blessing for motorbikers: it is a lot faster to get here, but a whole lot less interesting than the rollercoaster road of old.

NEAK LUONG
អ្នកលឿង

☎ 043 / pop 22,000

Neak Luong is the point at which travellers speeding between Phnom Penh and the Vietnamese border have to slow to a stop to cross the mighty Mekong River. The car ferry chugs back and forth giving kids ample time to try to sell you strange-looking insects and other unidentifiable food on sticks. Coming from Vietnam, it is an overwhelming welcome to Cambodia. The first bridge to span the Mekong's girth in Cambodia is in Kompong Cham. Construction on a second here at Neak Luong is getting underway and it should open sometime in 2007 or 2008.

Neak Luong rates a mention as one of the locations depicted in *The Killing Fields* (1984). In August 1973, American B-52s mistakenly razed it to the ground in an attempt to halt a Khmer Rouge advance on Phnom Penh. The intensive bombardment killed 137 civilians and wounded 268. The US government tried to cover it up by keeping the media out, but Sydney Schanberg, played by Sam Waterstone in the film, managed to travel to the city by river and publicise the true scale of the tragedy. The US ambassador offered compensation of US$100 per family and the navigator of the B-52 was fined US$700, which pretty much summed up the American attitude to the price of Cambodian lives in this most miserable of sideshows.

The most straightforward way to get here is to take an air-con bus (4500r, hourly) from Psar Thmei in Phnom Penh and pay the foot passenger toll (100r) to cross the Mekong on the ferry. From Neak Luong, it is possible to continue east to Svay Rieng (64km), north to Prey Veng (30km) or south to the Kaam Samnor border, gateway to Vietnam and the Mekong Delta – for more on the route between Phnom Penh and Chau Doc, see p295.

BA PHNOM
បាភ្នំ

Ba Phnom is one of the earliest religious and cultural sites in the Kingdom of Cambodia, dating back to the 5th century and the time of the mysterious Funan. Some scholars consider it a birthplace of the Cambodian nation, in the same way that Phnom Kulen is revered as the first capital of Angkor. It remained an important place of pilgrimage for kings of the subsequent empires of Chenla and Angkor and continued to be a place of spiritual significance into the 19th century, but its past conceals a darker side. According to French records, human sacrifices were carried out here and were only finally stamped out in 1872.

Today there is little left to see considering the site's extensive history. At the eastern extremity of the small group of hills lie the kitsch ruins of an 11th-century temple known as **Preah Vihear Chann**. The temple was evidently destroyed by the ravages of time, but has been rebuilt by the local monastery using a few original blocks and a whole lot of cement, all set under a corrugated roof.

There is a modern **wat** at the base of the hill and a series of concrete steps lead up the slope to some small **pagodas** on the summit. It is only really worth the detour for those who have a keen interest in early Cambodian history; for the casual visitor there is unfortunately little to see.

Getting There & Away

To get to Ba Phnom from Phnom Penh, head east on NH1 and turn north at Kompong Suong, just over 9km east of Neak Luong. Follow this dirt road for 3km before turning right and bearing east along the base of the hill. After another 7km, turn left under a wat-style arch and head to the bottom of the hill. Those without wheels can engage the services of a *moto* (small motorcycle with driver) in Neak Luong for about US$4 round trip.

EASTERN CAMBODIA

KOMPONG CHAM PROVINCE

ខេត្តកំពង់ចាម

The most heavily populated province in Cambodia, Kompong Cham has also supplied a steady stream of Cambodia's current political heavyweights including Prime Minister Hun Sen and Senate Head Chea Sim. Most Kompong Cham residents enjoy quieter lives, living off the land or fishing along the Mekong River. Rubber was the major prewar industry and there are huge plantations stretching eastwards from the Mekong. Some of these are being redeveloped for industrial use and there are even encouraging signs of young saplings being planted around Memot. Some of Cambodia's finest silk is also produced in this province and most of the country's *krama* (scarves) originate here.

Kompong Cham Province draws a fair number of visitors thanks to its role as a gateway to the northeast. Attractions include several pre-Angkorian and Angkorian temples, as well as some pleasant riverbank rides for cyclists or motorbikers. Getting about has became a lot easier thanks to the excellent condition of NH7 all the way to Kratie. Beyond the main roads, travel is not too bad, as the large population has helped to prioritise tertiary road improvements.

KOMPONG CHAM

កំពង់ចាម

☎ 042 / pop 46,000

Long considered Cambodia's third city after Phnom Penh and Battambang, lately Kompong Cham has been somewhat left in the dust by the fast-growing tourist towns of Siem Reap and Sihanoukville. More a quiet town than a bustling city, it is a peaceful provincial capital spread along the banks of the Mekong River. It was an important trading post during the French period, the legacy evident as you wander through the streets of bruised yet beautiful buildings. Kompong Cham remains an important travel hub for road and river, and acts as a gateway to eastern and northeastern Cambodia. This role has been enhanced in recent

years with the opening of the first bridge to span the Mekong's width in Cambodia, dramatically cutting journey times to popular destinations like Kratie and Mondulkiri.

Orientation

Kompong Cham may be one of Cambodia's larger cities, but that doesn't make it very big. Navigating on foot is straightforward. Arriving from Phnom Penh, all roads east end up at the Mekong River, near many of the guesthouses and hotels. The market is a few blocks west of the river.

Information

Mr Vannat is an experienced local guide, and if you sip an evening drink overlooking the Mekong, he'll likely find you before long. He speaks English and French.

ABC Computer (☎ 941477; 11 Ph Ang Duong; per hr US$1) Internet access.

Acleda Bank (☎ 941703; 31 Ph Khemarak Phomin) The local representative for Western Union if you need cash fast.

Canadia Bank (☎ 941361; Preah Monivong Blvd) Can handle cash and travellers cheques in various currencies, Visa and MasterCard cash advances and Moneygram transfers.

Sights

WAT NOKOR

វត្តនគរ

Just outside town is an 11th-century Mahayana Buddhist shrine of sandstone and laterite, which today houses an active Theravada wat. It is a kitsch kind of place, a temple within a temple, and many of the older building's archways have been incorporated into the new building as shrines for worship. On weekdays, there are only a few monks in the complex and it is peaceful to wander among the many alcoves and their hidden shrines. There is also a large reclining Buddha.

To get here, head out of town on the road to Phnom Penh, and take the left fork at the large roundabout about 1km from town. The temple is at the end of this dirt road.

KOH PAEN

កោះប៉ែន

Koh Paen is a rural island in the Mekong River, connected to the southern reaches of Kompong Cham town by an elaborate bamboo bridge in the dry season or a local ferry in the wet season. The bamboo bridge

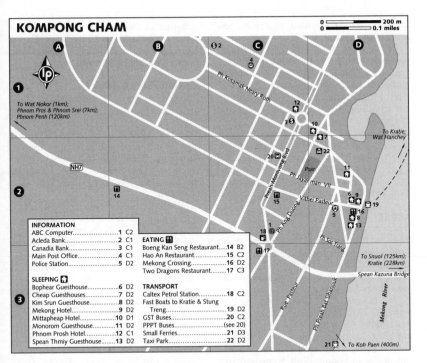

KOMPONG CHAM

0 ————— 200 m
0 ————— 0.1 miles

To Wat Nokor (1km);
Phnom Pros & Phnom Srei (7km);
Phnom Penh (120km)

NH7

To Kratie;
Wat Hanchey

Psar

To Snuol (125km);
Kratie (228km)

Spean Kazuna Bridge

Rue Pasteur

Mekong River

21 ⬋ To Koh Paen (400km)

INFORMATION	
ABC Computer.....................1	C2
Acleda Bank.........................2	C1
Canadia Bank.......................3	C1
Main Post Office...................4	C1
Police Station.......................5	D2

SLEEPING 🏠	
Bophear Guesthouse............6	D2
Cheap Guesthouses..............7	D2
Kim Srun Guesthouse...........8	D2
Mekong Hotel......................9	D2
Mittapheap Hotel...............10	D1
Monorom Guesthouse.........11	D2
Phnom Prosh Hotel.............12	C1
Spean Thmiy Guesthouse....13	D2

EATING 🍴	
Boeng Kan Seng Restaurant....14	B2
Hao An Restaurant...............15	C2
Mekong Crossing.................16	D2
Two Dragons Restaurant......17	C3

TRANSPORT	
Caltex Petrol Station...............18	C2
Fast Boats to Kratie & Stung	
Treng..................................19	D2
GST Buses...........................20	C2
PPPT Buses...................(see 20)	
Small Ferries.......................21	D3
Taxi Park.............................22	D2

is an attraction in itself, totally built by
hand each year and looking like it is made
of matchsticks from afar. There are plenty
of local wats on the island and locals make
a living fishing, as well as growing tobacco
and sesame. During the dry season, several
sandbars, the closest thing to a beach in this
part of Cambodia, appear around the island.
The best way to get about the island is by
bicycle, which is possible to arrange through
some of the budget guesthouses in town.

Sleeping

Many visitors prefer to stay on the riverfront,
with a view over the Mekong. There are several guesthouses and a hotel here – the only
drawback is the noise of the boat horns at an
ungodly hour of the morning.

Mekong Hotel (☎ 941536; Ph Preah Bat Sihanouk;
r US$5-10; ❄) Still the best all-rounder in
town, this vast hotel has a great riverfront
location. All rooms have satellite TV, and
10 bucks earns a date with air-con and hot
water, but remember to ask for a Mekong
view. The corridors are so large, they are
begging for an ultimate Frisbee session.

Spean Thmiy Guesthouse (95 Ph Preah Bat Sihanouk; s/tw US$4/5) This place has a bird's-eye
view of the mighty Mekong bridge, hardly a
surprise given the hotel's name means 'New
Bridge'. US$4 with a bathroom is a fair deal
and there is a nice outdoor veranda.

Kim Srun Guesthouse (☎ 941507; 81 Ph Preah Bat
Sihanouk; s/d US$3/5) Double up here, as the sin-
gles are rather too cell-like for comfort. Run
by a friendly family, this is one of the more
homely places to stay in town.

Bophea Guesthouse (☎ 012 796803; Vithei Pasteur;
r US$2-3) A long-running budget option just
one block up from the river; the rooms are a
real bargain here. The cheaper rates miss out
on a bathroom, so it is worth being liberal
with that extra dollar for the big rooms with a
bathroom. There are also bicycles for rent.

Mittapheap Hotel (☎ 941565; fax 941536; 18 Ph Kosamak Neary Roth; r US$5-10; ❄) Has the same own-
ers as the Mekong Hotel. The neat rooms
here are a good deal, arguably the smartest in
town, and include TV and hot water.

Monorom Guesthouse (☎ 941441; s US$4-8, d
US$5-10; ❄) The old house at the front might
look like it is on its last legs, but don't be

EASTERN CAMBODIA

put off as the guesthouse is in a clean, new wing at the back.

Phnom Prosh Hotel (☎ 941444; Ph Kosamak Neary Roth; r US$5-10; 🅿) Famously owned by a nephew of Samdech Hun Sen, Cambodia's prime minister – that should mean security isn't a problem here! The rooms have all the trimmings like satellite TV, fridge and hot water.

One street off the market has a whole row of cheap guesthouses advertising rooms for 5000r, although most 'guests' seem to pay by the hour, so it could get noisy. Rooms are cells, but if money's too tight to mention, consider taking one for a night.

Eating

There are several good restaurants in town and a lot of cheaper hole-in-the-wall places dotted around the market. There are a host of stop-and-dip food stalls in the market and a number of *tukalok* (fruit shake) stalls near the police station.

The advent of the bridge over the Mekong in 2002 brought a whole bunch of restaurants on stilts on the other side of the river. Many are mini versions of those huge restaurants across the Chrouy Changvar Bridge in Phnom Penh. Some have live bands, others go for karaoke and all have a good range of Khmer favourites.

Hao An Restaurant (☎ 941234; Preah Monivong Blvd; mains 4000-10,000r) A glitzy looking establishment by Kompong Cham standards, this place has pretty reasonable prices. The service is slick and there is always a regiment of 'beer girls' to ensure you don't go thirsty.

Two Dragons Restaurant (Ph Ang Duong; mains 4000-8000r) Smaller and more simple, but with equally good food, this family-run restaurant is a popular stop for Khmer staples.

Boeng Kan Seng Restaurant (NH7; mains 4000-10,000r) This place has an enticing location near a small lake on the outskirts of town. Highlights on the eclectic menu include tasty shrimps in batter with sweet chilli sauce.

Mekong Crossing (☎ 012 427432; 12 Vithei Pasteur; mains US$2-4) This little restaurant-pub is in spitting distance of the Mekong River and has a good mix of Khmer curries and Western favourites like burgers and sandwiches. This is the closest thing to a bar in town by night.

Earlier in the evening, locals and expats gather on the waterfront outside the Mekong Hotel, where a number of stalls sell cheap drinks and cold beers in the evening.

Getting There & Away

Kompong Cham is 120km northeast of the capital and the road is in good shape for the length of the journey. Phnom Penh Public Transport (PPPT; p105) and GST (p105) offer hourly air-con bus services between Kompong Cham and the capital (7000r, two hours). Overcrowded minibuses also do the run (5000r) as do superfast share taxis (10,000r).

NH7 to Kratie has been completely rebuilt in the past few years. PPPT has bus services from Phnom Penh to Suong, Memot and Kratie that pick up punters in Kompong Cham if space allows. The bus to Kratie (15,000r, three hours) passes through at 10.30am.

Boat services have taken a real hammering with the advent of new roads in this region. There are no longer any boats to Phnom Penh and now only one boat a day to Kratie (US$7, three hours) at 7.30am. Between July and January, this boat continues up to Stung Treng (US$15, seven hours).

There are still some slow cargo boats plying the waters north and south of Kompong Cham. They are extremely slow, but pretty cheap and a good way to get some reading done if you sling a hammock on the upper deck. Ask about departures at the boat dock in front of the Mekong Hotel as there are no real schedules.

Getting Around

Most *moto* journeys around town are only 1000r, and a little more at night. Bicycles or motorcycles may be arranged through negotiations with staff at your guesthouse or hotel.

AROUND KOMPONG CHAM
Phnom Pros & Phnom Srei
ភ្នំប្រុសភ្នំស្រី

Phnom Pros and Phnom Srei translate as 'Man Hill' and 'Woman Hill' respectively. Local legend has it that two teams, one of men and the other of women, toiled by night to be the first to construct a stupa on

---

THE EIGHT-LEGGED FOOD ROUTINE

Locals in the small Cambodian town of Skuon (otherwise known affectionately as Spiderville) eat eight-legged furry friends for breakfast, lunch and dinner. Most tourists travelling between Siem Reap and Phnom Penh pass through Skuon without ever realising they have been there. This is hardly surprising, as it has nothing much to attract visitors, but it is the centre of one of Cambodia's more exotic culinary delights – the deep-fried spider.

Pick-up trucks usually pause in Spiderville, so take a careful look at the eight-legged goodies the food sellers are offering. The creatures, decidedly dead, are piled high on platters, but don't get too cocky: there are usually live samples lurking nearby.

The spiders are hunted in holes in the hills to the north of Skuon and are quite an interesting dining experience. They are best treated like a crab and eaten by cracking the body open and pulling the legs off one by one, bringing the juiciest flesh out with them – a cathartic experience indeed for arachnophobes. They taste a bit like…mmm chicken. Alternatively, for a memorable photo, just bite the thing in half and hope for the best. Watch out for the abdomen, which seems to be filled with some pretty nasty-tasting brown sludge, which could be anything from eggs to excrement.

No-one seems to know exactly how this micro-industry developed around Skuon, although some have suggested that the population may have developed a taste for these creatures during the years of Khmer Rouge rule, when food was in short supply.

---

the summit of their hill by daybreak. The women built a big fire, which the men took to be the rising sun and gave up work. The women, having won, no longer had to ask for the man's hand in marriage, which had previously been the tradition.

Phnom Srei has good views of the countryside during the wet season. Phnom Pros is an interesting place for a cold drink, as a band of inquisitive monkeys populate the trees. The hills are about 7km out of town on the road to Phnom Penh and can be reached by *moto* for about US$3 (round trip) depending on wait time.

Wat Hanchey
វត្តហាន់ជ័យ

Wat Hanchey is a hilltop pagoda that was an important centre of worship during the Chenla period, and today offers some of the best Mekong views in Cambodia. As well as a large, contemporary wat, there is a brick sanctuary dating from the 8th century and the foundations of several others. During the time of the Chenla empire, this may have been an important transit stop on journeys between the ancient cities of Thala Boravit (near Stung Treng to the north) and Angkor Borei (near Takeo to the south), and Sambor Prei Kuk (near Kompong Thom to the west) and Banteay Prei Nokor (near Memot to the east).

The simplest way to get to Wat Hanchey is to charter an outboard from outside the Mekong Hotel (p249) in Kompong Cham. Boats with a 15HP engine cost around 40,000r, while faster boats with a 40HP engine are 50,000r. Solo travellers who want to save money can jump on the fast boat to Kratie at 7.30am and ask to be let off here (5000r, 30 minutes). After sniffing around for a while, walk south to the village and find a minibus or pick-up truck heading back to Kompong Cham.

Local expats like to cycle up here in the dry season through the pretty riverbank villages. If you can get your hands on a decent bicycle, this might be a good way to pass a day.

Rubber Plantations
ចំការកៅស៊ូ

Kompong Cham was the heartland of the Cambodian rubber industry and rubber plantations still stretch across the province. Many of these are no longer commercially tapped, but are tapped by locals for a variety of uses. However, some of the largest plantations remain active and can be visited by interested groups, usually French tourists on a tour of their colonial past. The most commonly visited is **Chup Rubber Plantation**, a large plantation in Tbong Khmom district, about 15km east of Kompong Cham.

Prasat Kuk Yeay Hom
ប្រាសាទកុកយាយហម

This is a ruined Angkorian structure languishing in the rice paddies of Kompong Cham, forgotten by all but the most slavish of temple devotees. Locals suggest it was damaged during the US bombing campaign of the early 1970s. Not exactly a regional highlight, it is about 7km from Prey Chor between Skuon and Kompong Cham. Local *moto* drivers can guide visitors after they abandon the bus in Prey Chor.

MEMOT
មេមត់

☎ 042 / pop 35,000

Pronounced more like may-*moot*, this is a surprisingly large town set amid the rubber plantations of eastern Kompong Cham Province. Very few visitors stop here as there is little of interest unless you happen to work for Michelin, but plenty pass through on the way to Mondulkiri or Kratie.

There is one small attraction in town for those with a keen interest in prehistory, namely the **Memot Centre of Archaeology** (NH7; admission free; ✆ 8–11am & 2–5pm). It houses a small exhibition on Iron Age circular earthwork villages, many of which have been discovered in the Memot region. It's only really for the initiated, but breaks the long overland journey east if you have your own transport. The gate may look closed, but the guardians can usually let you in.

There is no real need to stay here with the new, improved road connections, but those that get stuck should hit the **Reaksmey Angkor Chum Guesthouse** (☎ 012 317272; NH7; r US$4–10; 🌂), a smart new place with cheap, clean fan rooms with TV, optional air-con and a central location.

There are several hole-in-the-wall diners for passing traffic, but the most popular is the **Soy Try Restaurant** (☎ 012 708095; mains 3000–6000r), with an inexpensive range of Khmer standards.

Buses connect Memot with Kompong Cham (5000r, 1½ hours, several a day), but faster and more frequent are share taxis (7000r). Heading on to Snuol, where you can connect to Mondulkiri, a share taxi should cost about 6000r.

KRATIE PROVINCE
ខេត្តក្រចេះ

Kratie is a heavily forested province spanning the Mekong River, whose banks are home to most of the province's population. Beyond the river it's a remote and wild area that has seen few outsiders. Most visitors are here to view the rare freshwater dolphins found 15km north of the provincial capital, and for good reason, as other attractions are thin on the ground. However, the town of Kratie is a charming little place and makes a good base to check out the surrounding countryside.

This was one of the first areas to fall to Khmer Rouge control in the civil war, although for several years it was in fact the Vietnamese communists who were running the show. The port of Chhlong in southwest Kratie somehow held out against the communists until 1975, probably a useful way for the Khmer Rouge to acquire arms from corrupt government forces. It was also one of the first provincial capitals to fall to the liberating Vietnamese forces in the overthrow of the Khmer Rouge on 30 December 1978.

In the past, getting about was easier by boat than by road, as most roads in the province were pretty horrible. However, Kratie is now connected to Kompong Cham by two good roads: reconstructed NH7 which winds through Snuol before boomeranging back towards Phnom Penh, and the pretty road south to Chhlong and the district of Suong. The long haul north to Stung Treng has long been a truly nasty piece of work, but is earmarked for upgrade by the Chinese sometime during the lifetime of this book.

KRATIE
ក្រចេះ

☎ 072 / pop 79,000

Kratie is the best place in the country to see the rare Irrawaddy dolphins, which live in the Mekong River in ever-diminishing numbers – for that reason alone it is well worth a stop when travelling by land between Phnom Penh and Ratanakiri or the Lao border. A compact but populous riverside town, Kratie (pronounced kra-*cheh*) is well preserved as it was spared the war-time bombing that destroyed so many other provincial centres. It was one of the first towns to be 'liberated' by the Khmer Rouge (actually it was the North Vietnamese, but the Khmer Rouge later took the credit) in the summer of 1970. There are some dramatic sunsets over the Mekong and some very old Khmer houses on the northern reaches of Rue Preah Sihanouk.

Information

Telephone services are available at kiosks around the market, but there is no Internet access as yet. There is a tourist office by the river in the south of town. In theory it is open 8am to 11.30am and 2pm to 5pm, but don't count on it!

For general information on getting around the province, the Star Guesthouse (below) is hard to beat. For a humorous look at Kratie up close and personal, pick up a copy of *Plumbing the Depths of Kratie – A Wet Season Guide* by Zenia Davies for US$1.

Acleda Bank (☎ 971707) can change cash, but that's it for now.

Sleeping

The cheapest places to stay in Kratie are the guesthouses along Rue Preah Sihanouk near the market.

Santepheap Hotel (☎ 971537; Ph Preah Sumarit; r US$5-15; ❄) Arguably the best all-rounder in town, this large hotel has cheaper fan-cooled rooms at the back and swankier air-con rooms in the main building with the added extra of hot water. All rooms include satellite TV, but those at the back might be more prone to the gentle wail of karaoke below.

Star Guesthouse (☎ 971663; Ph Preah Sihanouk; r US$2-5) The best of the budget deals in town, this friendly guesthouse has a good selection of rooms at low, low prices. The young staff speak excellent English and the small **restaurant** (mains US$1-2) here turns out tasty and inexpensive food. The cheapest rooms involve a bathroom for the masses, but the biggest US$5 room has commanding views of the market. Reliable travel information is available here.

You Hong Guesthouse (☎ 012 957003; 91 Ph 8; r US$2-5) One of the newer kids on the block, this guesthouse offers great value for money. The rooms are basic but very clean, and downstairs is a small **restaurant** (mains US$1-2) with plenty of travel information plastered to the walls.

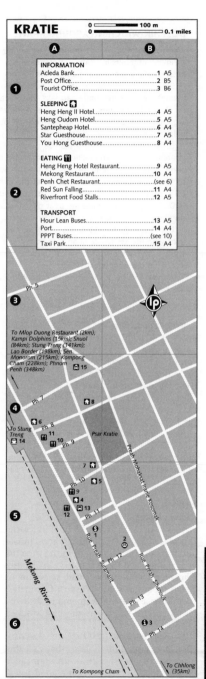

KRATIE

0 — 100 m
0 — 0.1 miles

INFORMATION
Acleda Bank...1 A5
Post Office...2 B5
Tourist Office.......................................3 B6

SLEEPING 🏠
Heng Heng II Hotel...............................4 A5
Heng Oudom Hotel...............................5 A5
Santepheap Hotel................................6 A4
Star Guesthouse...................................7 A5
You Hong Guesthouse..........................8 A4

EATING 🍴
Heng Heng Hotel Restaurant.................9 A5
Mekong Restaurant.............................10 A4
Penh Chet Restaurant.......................(see 6)
Red Sun Falling.................................11 A4
Riverfront Food Stalls.........................12 A5

TRANSPORT
Hour Lean Buses................................13 A5
Port...14 A4
PPPT Buses....................................(see 10)
Taxi Park..15 A4

To Mlop Duong Restaurant (2km); Kampi Dolphins (15km); Snuol (84km); Stung Treng (141km); Lao Border (198km); Sen Monorom (215km); Kompong Cham (228km); Phnom Penh (348km)

To Stung Treng

Psar Kratie

Mekong River

To Kompong Cham

To Chhlong (35km)

DOLPHIN-WATCHING AROUND KRATIE

The freshwater Irrawaddy dolphin *(trey pisaut)* is an endangered species throughout Asia, with shrinking numbers inhabiting stretches of the Mekong in Cambodia and Laos and others found in isolated pockets in Bangladesh and Myanmar.

Before the civil war, locals say, Cambodia was home to as many as 1000 dolphins and their habitat included the Tonlé Sap lake. However, during the Pol Pot regime, many were hunted for their oils and their numbers have plummeted. Dynamite fishing, whereby lazy locals chuck a grenade in the river because they can't be bothered to wait around for a catch, hasn't exactly helped the dolphins' plight either.

Locals and experts alike believe there may be as many as 75 Irrawaddy dolphins left on stretches of the Mekong River north of Kratie. It is possible to see them at a place called Kampi, about 15km north of Kratie, on the road to Stung Treng. There are local motorboats available to shuttle visitors out to the middle of the river to view the dolphins at close quarters. It costs US$3 per person, fixed price, under the supervision of the Mekong Dolphin Conservation Project (MDCP). Try to encourage the boat driver to use the engine as little as possible once near the dolphins, as the noise is sure to disturb them.

Locals say the best time of year to see the dolphins is at the height of the dry season; however, with the assistance of an able boat driver, it is just as easy to spot a few in the wet season. There is no particular time of day that's best suited to spotting, although early morning and late afternoon draw the most visitors.

A *moto* for the 30km round trip should be around US$4 depending on how long the driver has to wait.

Heng Oudom Hotel (☎ 971629; Ph 10; s US$3-4, d US$5-10; ❄) This new pad has some very good deals for those travelling solo, as all rooms are essentially the same but the price depends of how many of the amenities you sign up for, like TV and air-con. Clean and smart, the rooms may be a step up from the guesthouses, but the atmosphere is a definite step down.

Heng Heng II Hotel (☎ 971405; Ph Preah Sumarit; r US$5-10; ❄) This hotel started life as a guesthouse, but its new wing delivers some of the smartest rooms in town. Each is spacious and includes TV and hot water.

Eating

Red Sun Falling (Ph Preah Sumarit; mains US$1-3) A welcome sight on arrival by boat in Kratie, this place has fine furnishings, good music and a small bookshop, setting the tone for a relaxing place to sit and take in Kratie. The menu includes a small selection of Asian food and some Western favourites, including excellent homemade brownies. By night, the bar is the best stocked in town.

Mekong Restaurant (☎ 971438; Ph 9; dishes 4000-8000r) A reliable little hole in the wall, this place has an English menu with a fair range of local food, as well as some good inter-pretations of *barang* (foreigner) favourites such as French fries.

Mlop Duong Restaurant (NH7; mains US$1-3) If you have bolted down from the Lao border, this garden restaurant may be your first chance for a Khmer-style night out, complete with a local live band. The drawback is that service can be slow to the point of indifferent with about an hour passing between each dish – perhaps they thought we were French?

Cheap dining can be had on the riverfront during the evening when food stalls set up shop overlooking the Mekong, and this area doubles up as a super spot for a sunset drink. By day, the market has the usual range of cheap food stalls hawking Cambodian, Chinese and Vietnamese dishes for next to nothing.

Several of the hotels have good restaurants attached; try the Heng Heng II Hotel or the Santepheap Hotel, home to the **Penh Chet Restaurant** (☎ 971537; Ph Preah Sumarit; mains US$1-3).

Getting There & Away

NH7 puts Kratie 348km northeast of Phnom Penh and 141km south of Stung Treng. The road south to Phnom Penh is now surfaced all the way, cutting journey times dramatically. **PPPT** (☎ 012 523400) and **Hour Lean** (☎ 012 535387) each run one bus a day to the capital at 7.30am (18,000r, six hours). More frequent and faster are the share taxis that cost about 15,000r per place to Kompong Cham and 25,000r to Phnom Penh. Some taxis take NH7 all the way for speed, others take the dirt road south through Chhlong to Suong district to save money on petrol. Both take about the same time and that means just four or so hours to the capital.

For motorbikers, there is a more scenic dry-season route that follows the Mekong River. Take the river road north out of Kompong Cham as far as Stung Trang district (no, not Stung Treng – that's way north of Kratie) and cross the Mekong on a small ferry before continuing up the east bank of the Mekong through Chhlong to Kratie. This is a very beautiful route through small rural villages and takes from four to six hours on a trail bike, depending on conditions and experience.

For the lowdown on getting from Kratie to Mondulkiri Province, check out p266.

For full and unpleasant details of the road north to Stung Treng and for details of boats running between Kratie and Stung Treng, see p257.

Fast boats used to be the most popular way to get to Kratie, but in a sign of the times they no longer run to Phnom Penh – although it is possible to take one as far as Kompong Cham (US$7, three hours). One boat departs early at 7am and during the wet season a second departs at lunchtime having done the run down from Stung Treng.

Getting Around
A *moto* ride around Kratie town is the usual 1000r or so depending how far into the suburbs you venture. Most of the guesthouses and hotels can arrange motorbikes (with driver US$6 to US$10, without driver US$5) and should also be able to set visitors up with a bicycle.

AROUND KRATIE
Phnom Sombok
ភ្នំសំបុក

Phnom Sombok is a small hill with an active wat, located on the road from Kratie to Kampi. The hill offers the best views across

the Mekong on this stretch of the river and a visit here can easily be combined with a trip to see the dolphins for an extra buck or so.

Sambor
សំប័រ

Sambor was the site of a thriving pre-Angkorian city during the time of Sambor Prei Kuk and the Chenla empire. Not a stone remains in the modern town of Sambor, which is locally famous for the largest **wat** in Cambodia, complete with 108 columns. Constructed on the site of a 19th-century wooden temple, the new one is something of a minor place of pilgrimage for residents of Kratie Province. To get to Sambor, follow the Stung Treng road north to Sandan, before veering left along a reasonable 10km stretch of road – it's about 35km in total.

SNUOL
ស្នួល

☎ 072 / pop 19,000
This was a sorry little town before the coming of the road. It still feels a little like it has fallen off the map, but the new road provides a quick way out. A lot of folk end up having at least one meal here, as it is common to have to change vehicles when journeying between Mondulkiri Province and towns on the Mekong.

Mittapheap Guesthouse (NH7; r 10,000r), just south of the market, has simple rooms, but think of it as a last resort as the partitions don't even reach to the ceiling.

Muoy Heang Restaurant (NH7; mains 2000-5000r) is a filthy hole in the wall, but turns out tasty food, something in short supply in this little town. It also has a basic bathroom out the back.

Snuol is approximately 125km southwest of Mondulkiri Province and 135km east of Kompong Cham. It is only about 15km north of the Vietnamese border, but this crossing is not open to foreigners. Pick-ups to Sen Monorom (inside/on the back 20,000/15,000r, four hours) aren't all that regular and are easier to find in the early part of the morning. Taxis connect Snuol with Kompong Cham (10,000r, 1½ hours) and Kratie (5000r, one hour).

STUNG TRENG PROVINCE

ខេត្តស្ទឹងត្រែង

This remote province is emerging as a major commercial crossroads for trade between Cambodia, Laos, Thailand and Vietnam. It is a forgotten place, but once the roads south are finished, it will once again be properly plugged into the rest of the country. Much of Stung Treng's traffic travels by water, as several major rivers traverse the province, including Tonlé Kong, Tonlé San, Tonlé Srepok and, of course, the Mekong. However, the roads are improving and NH19 east to Ratanakiri is scheduled for an upgrade.

Visitor attractions are extremely limited for now, but as tourism takes off elsewhere in Cambodia, it is possible that boat trips up the Mekong's tributaries, to places like Siem Pang, will be a different way to see some remote areas. The population of Stung Treng includes several minority groups and the western chunk of massive Virachay National Park, accessible from Siem Pang – two factors that suggest there is some tourism potential as the province's infrastructure develops. Part of its problem is being sandwiched between Ratanakiri, one of Cambodia's most interesting provinces, and southern Laos, an area rich in attractions – why hang around Stung Treng? Right now, anywhere outside the provincial capital is pretty much the end of the earth.

STUNG TRENG

ស្ទឹងត្រែង

☎ 074 / pop 24,500

Stung Treng has experienced a surge in visitor numbers with the opening of the Cambodian–Lao border just 50km north of town, and while there aren't a whole lot of reasons to stick around, it makes a sensible overnight stop on the overland route to Ratanakiri. It is a bustling little trading town located on the banks of Tonlé San, which flows into the mighty Mekong on the western outskirts of the city limits. Some locals call Tonlé San Tonlé Kong or Tonlé Sekong as these two rivers merge 10km east of town. Chinese contractors are currently

constructing a bridge across this river, which will form a key link in the new road between Kratie and the Lao border.

Information

Familiar story: there are no banks in Stung Treng, but US dollars are happily accepted everywhere. It might also be the last chance to get rid of any excess Lao kip. For telephone services, try the mobile phone kiosks sprinkled around the market. Internet access has come to Stung Treng and there are several shops advertising access around the market. However, it is slow for the money at US$4 per hour.

There is no longer any need to arrange any paperwork to exit Cambodia into Laos. Anyone who tries to tell you otherwise is fishing for money.

The **tourist office** (☎ 973967) is found in the government compound located in the south of town. It is a mini city of portacabins and in and among it all is Mom Rotha, the provincial director of tourism, who speaks some English.

Sights

THALA BORAVIT
ថ្លាបូរវិត

Thala Boravit was an important Chenla-period trading town on the river route connecting the ancient city of Champasak and the holy site of Wat Phu with the southern reaches of the Chenla empire, including the ancient cities of Sambor Prei Kuk (Isanapura) and Angkor Borei. For all its past glories, there is very little to see today. It is hardly worth the effort for the casual visitor, but temple fiends may feel the urge to tick it off. Thala Boravit is on the west bank of the Mekong River and irregular boats cross from Stung Treng throughout the day. It should be easy enough to wait for locals to fill up the regular boats (1000r), rather than charter an outboard (US$5 or so). It is from here that the jungle road to Kompong Thom or Tbeng Meanchey starts via the village of Chaeb. See p258 for more details.

Sleeping

The cheap guesthouses are not all that inspiring, so it's worth the extra couple of dollars to go for a hotel.

Sok Sambath Hotel (☎ 973790; r US$6-15; ⚡) The smartest pad in town, this hotel offers well-tended rooms with TV and creature comforts like hot water for those who are prepared to spend the extra dollars. The fan rooms are essentially the same and good value at US$7 for two.

Riverside Restaurant & Guesthouse (☎ 012 439454; r US$3) Many travellers make this their first stop in town, thanks to the lively little **restaurant** (mains US$1-3) downstairs, the rooftop bar upstairs and the cheap rooms. All rooms are US$3 here, regardless of how many squeeze in, and include a basic bathroom. The menu downstairs includes some Khmer food, a bit of Chinese and a few international dishes. The staff here are a good source of travel information on Laos, Ratanakiri and Kratie.

Sekong Hotel (☎ 973762; r US$3-15; ⚡) This rambling ex-government hotel has a dizzying selection of rooms. Cheapest are the big, basic rooms in a block at the rear, but for just US$3 or US$4 there is little room to complain. Spend another dollar and you get a TV, US$7 brings hot water and US$15 air-con. The more expensive rooms are uninspiring compared with the Sok Sambath Hotel.

Mohasal Hotel (☎ 973999; r US$5-10; ⚡) Tucked away in the deep south of town, this quiet place has cavernous air-con rooms with bathroom that could be worth considering if you want to get away from it all. They come complete with ornately carved wooden beds.

Eating

New World Restaurant (☎ 011 908584; US$1-2) One block west of the market, this new restaurant offers a mix of Asian flavours from Cambodia, Thailand and China, plus a fair selection of beers with which to wash down the meal.

Mekong Blue (☎ 973977; www.mekongblue.com; US$1-2) Mekong Blue was originally established as a silk weaving centre in Stung Treng and is famous throughout Cambodia for its high-quality designs. A new gallery was opening just after our visit and promises to include a relaxing café for light meals and sumptuous décor. It is halfway between town and the airport.

Cheap food stalls can be found on the riverfront and around the market. When it comes to real restaurants, there are only limited options.

Getting There & Away

Flights to Stung Treng were no longer operating at time of writing.

NH7 south to Kratie (141km) is a nasty piece of work for much of its length, passing through some very remote country. It is reasonable within Stung Treng Province (30km), but thereafter degenerates into a hellish mix of broken bitumen, small rocks and sandy gullies. The Chinese government has agreed to repair this road and work should be ongoing through to 2007, but for now it is a last reminder of how bad all of Cambodia's roads used to be. Share taxis make the run daily to Kratie (30,000r, five hours). Until the road is repaired, take the boat instead.

For details on the journey south of Kratie by either road or boat, see the Getting There & Away sections under Kratie (p254) and Kompong Cham (p250).

For the scoop on the sometimes good, often bad road between Stung Treng and Ban Lung in Ratanakiri, see p261.

Fast boats run daily between Kratie and Stung Treng from July through to December (25,000r, three hours), leaving Stung Treng at 7.30am and Kratie around 11.30am.

During the rest of the year, small long-tail rocket boats (US$15 per person, three hours) make the trip, as the river becomes perilous with rocks and sandbars appearing everywhere. Do not be talked into taking one of these boats in the afternoon, as they have no lights and travelling at high speeds on the Mekong in the dark is dicing with death. Several locals die on this stretch each year and several tourists have lost everything when the boats have collided with objects of immovable force.

For the inside story on the border crossing with Laos, see p292.

There is also a trail that leads across northern Cambodia from Stung Treng to either Tbeng Meanchey or Kompong Thom. It is unwise for the average traveller to take this route, but for adventure addicts who don't mind a very long and bumpy bike ride it is an option. First, cross the Mekong to Thala Boravit from where a jungle trail leads west to the large village of Chaeb. If trail conditions are bad you may need to overnight in Chaeb in the wat or with some locals. From Chaeb, there is an old logging road west that joins with the main road from Kompong Thom to Tbeng Meanchey. A *moto* to or from Tbeng Meanchey should cost about US$20, as the drivers need to cover the cost of their return. Only highly experienced bikers should undertake this route on their own machine and will need to be ready to spend a night in the jungle if things go wrong. This route should not be attempted in the wet season.

RATANAKIRI PROVINCE

ខេត្តរតនគីរី

Ethnic minorities, elephants, waterfalls and jungle combine to make this one of the most popular provinces in the northeast of Cambodia. Many of the inhabitants come from minority groups known as Khmer Leu (Upper Khmer), including Kreung, Tompoun and Jarai. These tribes each have their own distinct language and customs, although today they dress as most other poor Cambodians and lack the colourful clothing seen in Thailand and Vietnam. This could be a blessing in disguise, as it may spare the tourist onslaught seen in northern Thailand. There is also a large Lao population throughout the province and multiple languages will be heard in villages such as Voen Sai.

The province played its part in Cambodia's contemporary tragedy, serving as a base for the Khmer Rouge leadership during much of the 1960s. Pol Pot and Ieng Sary fled here in 1963 and established headquarters in Ta Veng in the north of the province.

Gem mining and tourism form the lifeblood of the province. There is good quality zircon mined in several parts of the province and the prices are low compared to the west (Ratanakiri actually translates as 'hill of the precious stones'). However, in the long run, tourism is the future thanks to the abundant natural attractions the province has been blessed with. Boeng Yeak Lom, a volcanic lake, is outstanding, but in time the massive Virachay National Park may prove popular too.

Roads in Ratanakiri are not as impressive as the sights – dry season means chewing on dust, wet season means sloshing about in mud; take your pick. Boats are a popular means of transport for scenic trips, but the province is too isolated to make river travel into Stung Treng a realistic option.

BAN LUNG

បានលុង

☎ 075 / pop 17,000

Ban Lung is the dusty provincial capital of Ratanakiri Province and the most popular base from which to explore the natural attractions of the area. The town was originally known as Labansiek before the war, but the district name of Ban Lung has gradually slipped into use among locals. The town itself is not exactly inspiring, but with attractions such as Boeng Yeak Lom just a short distance away, no-one is complaining. Many of the minorities from the surrounding villages come to Ban Lung to buy and sell at the market, making it one of the more lively commercial centres in the provinces.

Information

There are no banks in Ban Lung, but you can change US dollars into riel at jewellers' shops in the market. Some of the hotels in town can also change travellers cheques, although at a hefty commission.

There is a post office on the road to Bokheo that offers international phone services, but the mobile-phone kiosks around the market area are cheaper. Internet access is available in town; currently rates are high, speed low. Ratanak Hotel (p260) is the cheapest at US$4 an hour.

There is a small provincial tourist office in the centre of town, but visitors will find their guesthouse or hotel to be of more use in the quest for knowledge. Check out www.yaklom.com for more on what to do in Ratanakiri.

Activities

There are no real sights in town, but plenty beyond. For details on lakes, waterfalls and gem mines beyond Ban Lung, see p261.

ELEPHANT RIDES

Most guesthouses and hotels can arrange short elephant rides from nearby villages to local waterfalls. One of the most popular rides is from the village of Kateung to the spectacular waterfall of Ka Tieng. The ride takes about one hour, passing through beautiful rubber plantations, and the elephant crosses the river above the waterfall, making for a top photo opportunity. The usual charge is US$10 per person per hour. For longer elephant rides, Mondulkiri Province (p265) remains the more popular option.

TREKKING

Trekking has really started to take off around Ratanakiri, but it is important to make clear arrangements with your guide to ensure you get what is expected out of

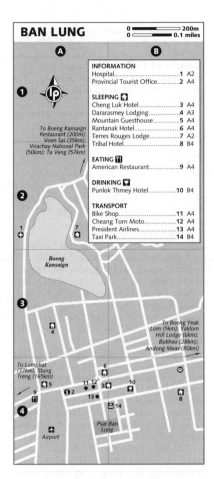

a trip. There are lots of popular routes that take in minority villages and scenic spots around the province, including Kreung villages near the road to Ta Veng, and Jarai villages up in Andong Meas district.

Many visitors opt for a trek into Virachay National Park, but be aware that most of these treks barely scrape the park itself, and spend much of the time in the park buffer zone. There are plans to develop bigger treks into the park, but it will take time to establish facilities along the way, as it is one of the most wild and remote areas in Cambodia. The cost of a trek depends on the route, but figure on US$15 to US$25 a day for a good guide and more on top for transport, food and lodging along the way. Budget travellers really need to link up with a group to make it affordable. The best places to arrange trekking are the Ratanak Hotel (below) for budget travellers, and Terres Rouges (below) and Yaklom Hill Lodge (below) for those with a little more money to play with.

For details on the excellent community trek around Boeng Yeak Lom, Ratanakiri's spectacular crater lake, see opposite.

Sleeping

Ratanakiri is now firmly established on the overland map of Cambodia and the choice of guesthouses and hotels is growing by the year. All places offer free pick-up from the airport.

Ratanak Hotel (☎ 974033; r US$5-10; 🍴 🖥) Currently the most popular place in town for budget travellers, this hotel is under the energetic eye of Mr Leng, who keeps things running smoothly. The rooms are large and include TV and hot water at the higher end, attracting some small tour groups from Europe. Renovations are underway to ensure it keeps up with the new hotels in town. The downstairs **restaurant** (mains US$1-3) turns out some of the best food in town, including the signature *phnom pleung* (hill of fire), a beef and vegetable DIY tabletop barbecue.

Terres Rouges Lodge (☎ 974051; terouges@camintel.com; r US$30-45) Imperiously set in the former governor's residence, this lavish wooden house remains the pacesetter for style and charm in the wilds of the northeast. Rooms are tastefully finished with touch of Khmer and Chinese flourish and include hot showers, although not air-con. Set amid a flourishing garden is the **restaurant** (mains US$2-5) which offers a solid menu of Asian and European favourites.

Yaklom Hill Lodge (☎ 012 644240; www.yaklom.com; r incl breakfast US$10-22; 🍴) Billing itself as Ratanakiri's ecolodge, this place offers a completely different experience from the places in town. Set amid lush gardens about 6km east of town, all the rooms here are in wooden bungalows with ethnic minority handicrafts for decoration. There is no electricity during the day, but at night the fan and lights are working. There is an atmospheric **restaurant** (mains US$2-4) serving Thai and Khmer food.

Cheng Luk Hotel (☎ 974121; r US$5-10; 🍴) Right across the road from the Ratanak, this relative newcomer has bright and clean rooms with hot-water showers, making for a smart stay. Facilities include satellite TV, but there is no restaurant here.

Tribal Hotel (☎ 974074; tribalhotel@camintel.com; r US$3-15; 🍴) Undoubtedly the biggest hotel in town. There is a healthy selection of rooms catering to all budgets. The main house is the place to go for comfort seekers, with hot water on tap, plus satellite TV and a fridge. These rooms tend to be popular with visiting NGOs. Budget rooms are set in smaller blocks dotted around the huge garden and include singles with bathroom for US$3 and doubles for US$5. The garden includes a big **restaurant** (mains US$1-3) with a good selection of Khmer and Asian cuisine.

Dararasmey Lodging (☎ 012 456820; r US$5-10; 🍴) The building may look a bit cotton candy from the outside, but as one of the new pads in town, there is some quality comfort on the inside. All rooms are well furnished and include satellite TV, but it is a little out the way compared with the hotels on the main drag.

Mountain Guesthouse (☎ 974047; s/d US$3/4) Set in a wooden house near the airport, this place has been around an eternity and is currently under new management. The rooms are a bit on the basic side, with only shared bathroom available, but they are some of the cheapest in town.

Eating

Beyond the hotels, dining options are somewhat limited. The cheapest food in town is found in and around Psar Ban Lung (Ban Lung Market) and this is also the area to find *tukalok* (fruit shakes) and desserts by night.

American Restaurant (mains US$1-2) During the UN time in Cambodia, this was the only place to eat in town and is still going strong. Various foreign visitors have contributed to the menu, which includes some very local interpretations of hamburgers and a selection of Khmer dishes. Steer clear of the lobster thermidor this far from the coast. Lunch specials are popular with NGOs from the area, including a local soup and main dish.

Boeng Kansaign Restaurant (mains US$1-2) For location it is hard to beat this restaurant on the shores of the lake. Khmer and Chinese dishes make up the menu and the breeze across the water is blissful on a hot day.

EASTERN CAMBODIA

Entertainment

Yes, it exists! Ratanak Hotel (opposite) has opened a bar opposite the main hotel, and Mr Leng has an impressive collection of tunes donated by customers over the years. Beers and some spirits are available.

Punlok Thmey Hotel (☎ 974110; beers from US$1) Where Khmer men head for a nightcap. It is a beer garden, karaoke parlour and part-time brothel and tends to stay open until about 1am.

Getting There & Away

President Airlines (☎ 974059) flies to Ban Lung from Phnom Penh (one way/return US$60/110) several times a week, but last-minute cancellations are common, so be prepared for a long road journey if you have a fixed schedule.

The road between Ban Lung and Stung Treng is in miserable shape again at the time of writing but it is scheduled for a complete rebuild during the lifetime of this book. Share taxi (30,000r, 4½ hours) is the way to go as pick-ups (inside/on the back 25,000/15,000r, seven hours) are much slower. Wet-season journey times are considerably longer. One way or the other, it is now possible to make the overland journey to or from Phnom Penh in just two days. For those in a hurry, there are now direct taxis running between Ban Lung and Kratie (50,000r, nine to 11 hours), although this is punishment in the extreme until the roads are finished.

There is no real road linking Ratanakiri to Mondulkiri, contrary to what older maps may show. There is a road as far as Lumphat, but after crossing Tonlé Srepok by ferry, it descends into a series of sandy ox-cart tracks until Koh Nhek in northern Mondulkiri Province. A trickle of hardcore bikers have been using this route over the past few years, but it really isn't for the average traveller – only attempt it if you have years of biking experience or are an extremely hardy soul with an iron backside.

Realistically, it is a two-day journey between Ban Lung and Sen Monorom, with an overnight stay in Koh Nhek. The Cambodian military are currently rebuilding the road from Sen Monorom to Koh Nhek, which should make the journey possible in one day. It is almost impossible in the wet season and pretty tough in the dry, but has improved with the return of settlers from refugee areas. Anyone seriously considering this option should link up with a local who knows the route, as there are lots of opportunities to get lost. Cross at the truck ferry a few kilometres upstream from Lumphat and stick to the trail that's been used the most. A range of motorbike spares, copious amounts of water, old US 1:50,000 military maps of the area and a compass should make for a smoother journey.

Getting Around

Motorbikes, jeeps and pick-ups are available for hire from most guesthouses in town. Korean motorbikes from Ratanak Hotel (opposite) are just US$5 a day and newer Suzukis are US$7. Ratanak Hotel also offers a 4WD pick-up for just US$30 a day with driver, which is a good deal for small groups. Other guesthouses and hotels offer comparable prices. Terres Rouges Lodge (opposite) offers old Sanyang motorbikes for US$7 a day, or US$12 with driver, and jeeps for US$50.

Cheang Torn Moto (☎ 012 960533) has some 250cc dirt bikes available for US$10 per day. Local guides with motorbikes offer their services around the province and rates range from US$8 to US$15 depending on their experience, level of English and where you want to go.

There are also pick-ups and jeeps available for charter at the taxi park. Figure on a price of US$30 to US$50 depending on how far you want to go and how far you are willing to negotiate.

For something cheaper and more environmentally friendly, consider a bicycle (US$1 per day), available from some hotels and the bike shop on the main drag.

AROUND BAN LUNG

Try to link up with a responsible local guide when exploring Ratanakiri, as the minority people around the province are sensitive to outsiders just stomping in and out of their villages. Contact **Yeak Laom Community Based Ecotourism** (☎ 012 981226; yeak_laom@camintel.com) for a knowledgeable indigenous guide.

Boeng Yeak Lom
ប៊ឹងយក្សឡោម

The protected area of **Yeak Lom** (admission US$1) includes an intriguing circular crater-lake, believed to have been formed 700,000 years ago, situated amid pristine jungle. Some people swear it must have been formed by a meteor strike as the circle is so perfect. The indigenous minority people in the area have long considered Yeak Lom a sacred place and their legends talk of mysterious creatures that inhabit the waters of the lake. It is one of the most peaceful, beautiful locations Cambodia has to offer and the water is extremely clear with visibility of up to 5m. It is a great place to take a dip early in the morning or late in the afternoon. There is a small **visitors centre** (admission free) nearby that has information on ethnic minorities in the province, local handicrafts for sale and suggested walks around the lake. The area is administered by the local Tompuon minority and proceeds from the entry fee go towards improving life in the nearby villages.

Community walks offer an insight into the life of the Tompuon people, including their relationship with the land; contact Yeak Laom Community Based Ecotourism to arrange a walk with an English-speaking indigenous guide (US$3 to US$7 per person depending on numbers). Profits are ploughed back into the community.

Boeng Yeak Lom is 5km east of Ban Lung. Turn right off the road to Bokheo at the statue of the minority family. *Motos* are available for around US$2 return, but expect to pay more if the driver has to wait around. It takes almost an hour to get here on foot from Ban Lung.

Waterfalls

There are numerous waterfalls in the province, but many are difficult to reach in the wet season and lacking much water in the dry season. The three most commonly visited are **Chaa Ong** (admission 2000r), **Ka Tieng** (admission free) and **Kinchaan** (admission 2000r), and these are now signposted from the main road towards Stung Treng, about 5km west of town. The most spectacular of the three is Chaa Ong, as it is set in a jungle gorge and you can clamber behind the waterfall or venture underneath for a power shower. Ka Tieng is the most fun, as it drops over a rock shelf allowing you to clamber all the way behind. There are some vines on the far side that are strong enough to swing on for some Tarzan action.

Tuk Chrouu Bram-pul (Sean Lae Waterfall; admission 2000r) is a popular waterfall with seven gentle

tiers, located about 35km southeast of Ban Lung, but the trail to get here is tough at any time and pretty much impossible in the wet season. A visit here can be combined with a visit to the current hot spot for **gem mining** in Chum Rum Bei. This involves a walk of several kilometres through the forest, as motorbikes cannot make it. Take a local guide for this combination trip, but check in Ban Lung that the mines are still active.

Voen Sai

វើនសៃ

pop 3000

Located on the banks of Tonlé San, Voen Sai is a pleasant little community of Chinese, Lao and Kreung villagers. Originally, the town was located on the north bank of the river and known as Virachay, but these days the main settlement is on the south bank. The north side of the river is the most interesting, with an **old Chinese settlement** that dates back more than 100 years and several **Lao and chunchiet villages** nearby. It is possible to cross the river for 500r on a small ferry and walk west for a couple of kilometres, passing through a Chinese village, a Lao community and a small *chunchiet* area, before emerging on a wealthy Chinese village complete with large wooden houses and inhabitants who still speak Chinese. Check out how clean it is compared to the surrounding villages.

Voen Sai is also home to Virachay National Park headquarters, although there is very little information available and it is easier to organise a trek into the park out of Ban Lung.

Voen Sai is about 35km northwest of Ban Lung on an average-to-poor road. There is an old Soviet bonerattler (2000r, two to three hours) that leaves about 7am from Psar Ban Lung, returning some time around midday. It is easy enough to get here under your own steam on a motorbike.

Chunchiet Cemeteries

កន្លែងបញ្ចុះសពពួកជនជាតិ

There are many *chunchiet* cemeteries scattered throughout the forests of Ratanakiri. **Kachon** is a one-hour boat ride east of Voen Sai and has an impressive **Tompuon cemetery** (admission US$1) in the forest beyond the village. Family groups are buried side by side in the forest and there are effigies of the deceased. When a lengthy period of mourning is complete, villagers hold a big celebration and add two carved wooden likenesses of elephant tusks to the structures. Some of these tombs date back many years and have been abandoned to the jungle. Newer tombs of wealthy individuals have been cast in concrete and show some modern influences like shades and mobile phones. Sadly, some unscrupulous art collectors and amateur anthropologists from Europe have reportedly been buying up the old effigies from poor villagers, something tantamount to cultural rape. Remember that this is a sacred site for local Tompuon people – touch nothing and act respectfully.

Expect to pay around US$10 to US$15 for the boat trip from the Voen Sai riverbank to Kachon, including a jaunt to the Chinese and Lao villages opposite Voen Sai. To get to the cemetery, walk through the health centre located at the riverbank and turn right. The cemetery is just a couple of hundred metres from the village. It is also possible to get to Kachon by road – head south out of Voen Sai and turn left at the first major junction.

Ta Veng
តាវែង

Ta Veng is an insignificant village on the southern bank of Tonlé San, but acts as an alternative gateway to Virachay National Park. It was in the Ta Veng district that Pol Pot, Ieng Sary and other leaders of the Khmer Rouge established their guerrilla base in the 1960s. Locals say nothing remains of the remote base today, although in a dismal sign of decline, they point out that Ta Veng had electricity before the war.

Ta Veng is about 57km north of Ban Lung on a rollercoaster road through the mountains that affords some of the province's finest views. There are some very steep climbs in sections and for this reason it wouldn't be much fun in the rain. No scheduled pick-ups run up here so it is necessary to come by motorbike or charter a vehicle. The road passes through several **minority villages**, where it is possible to break the journey.

It is possible to arrange small boats in Ta Veng for gentle river jaunts; try US$5 in the local area or US$30 for the three-hour trip to Voen Sai.

Andong Meas
អណ្ដូងមាស

pop 1500

Andong Meas district is growing in popularity thanks to a combination of minority villages, **Jarai cemeteries** and a short river trip. There is a pleasant trail from Andong Meas to a Jarai cemetery on the banks of the Tonlé San. From here it is possible to return to Andong Meas by river for about US$10 for the whole boat. Andong Meas lies about 80km northeast of Ban Lung on a reasonable road taking two hours. Transport prices are slightly higher to here due to the distance involved.

Virachay National Park
ឧទ្យានជាតិវិរៈជ័យ

Virachay National Park is the largest protected area in Cambodia, stretching east to Vietnam, north to Laos and west to Stung Treng Province. The park has never been fully explored and is likely home to a number of larger mammals, including elephants, leopards and tigers. Optimists speculate that there may even be isolated rhinoceroses or kouprey (wild oxen), but this is unlikely. Rangers also claim there are **waterfalls**, some as high as 100m, but these are many days' hike from the park boundary. See p259 for more details on arranging a trek into the park.

A new ecotourism programme is currently under development at the park, focusing on small-scale culture, nature and adventure trekking. The programme aims to involve and benefit local communities. Trips currently being planned combine jungle trekking with overnight camping, river journeys and village-based accommodation. One part of the project includes a small visitor and information centre at the **Virachay National Park Headquarters** (☎ 974176; www.bpamp.org.kh) in Ban Lung, located at the Department of Environment. Visitors can book park excursions here, pay the necessary fees and receive the latest information. All visitors who wish to enter the park will be required to have an entry permit and to be accompanied by a park ranger guide and community guide.

The park is actually more accessible from the Stung Treng side, although it's all relative really. Siem Pang acts as the western gateway to the park and it is easier to spot wildlife in this section. Siem Pang is accessible by motorbike in the dry season, about a three-hour ride from Voen Sai. It is also connected to Stung Treng by longtail rocket boat (30,000r), but have a look at how rocky the Tonlé Kong is before you sign up.

Lumphat
 លុមផាត់

pop 2000

The former provincial capital of Lumphat is something of a ghost town these days thanks to sustained US bombing raids in the early 1970s. This is also the last gasp of civilisation, if it can even be called that, for hardcore bikers heading south on the tough trails to Mondulkiri Province.

To get here from Ban Lung, take the road to Stung Treng for about 15km before heading south. The 35km journey takes around an hour and pick-ups do a few runs from Ban Lung for 5000r.

MONDULKIRI PROVINCE
ខេត្តមណ្ឌលគីរី

Mondulkiri means 'Meeting of the Hills', a suitable name for such a hilly province. Nestled against Cambodia's eastern border, Mondulkiri really is another Cambodia, with scenery and a climate quite unlike anywhere else in the country. In the dry season it is a little like Wales with sunshine; in the wet season, like Tasmania with dreadful roads. There are endless grassy hills with the occasional clump of pines huddled together against the winds. At an average elevation of 800m, it can get quite chilly at night, so carry something warm.

Mondulkiri is the most sparsely populated province in the country, with just two people per sq km. Almost half of the 35,000 inhabitants come from the Pnong minority group, with other minorities making up much of the rest of the population. The lack of people adds to something of a wild-east atmosphere and there are certainly a lot of wild animals, including tigers, elephants, bears and leopards, in the more remote parts of the province.

There has recently been an influx of refugees returning from the Thai border area, which has pushed the province forward a little. Rice farming is picking up, but hunting remains the profession of choice for many minorities. Roads are bad throughout the province, but several have been earmarked for improvement, which could help speed up travel. The road from Phnom Penh is now in pretty good shape most of the way, bringing journey times down to seven hours, and this is driving an influx of domestic tourists each weekend.

SEN MONOROM
សែនមនោរម្យ

☎ 073 / **pop 7000**

Sen Monorom, the provincial capital of Mondulkiri, is a charming little community set amid rolling hills. The centre of town, a village really, has two lakes, leading some dreamers to call it 'The Switzerland of Cambodia'. The area around Sen Monorom has plenty of minority villages and picturesque waterfalls, making it a pleasant place to pass a few nights. Many of the Pnong people from nearby villages come into Sen Monorom to trade, and the distinctive baskets they carry on their backs makes them easy to distinguish from the immigrant Khmers. High winds billow throughout the year and it can get pretty fresh at night, so bring some warm clothing.

The big news is that tarmac has finally come to town and several roads were being surfaced at the time of writing. It might have been a good idea to tarmac the runway first?

Information

Bring a suitable amount of cash as this is no place for travellers cheques or plastic. Prices are slightly higher than in other parts of the country, as everything has to be shipped in from Phnom Penh or Vietnam.

There are plenty of mobile phones in Sen Monorom these days and calls are easy to make. There is currently no Internet access in Mondulkiri.

There is a small tourist office in town and staff speak good English and French. They can arrange elephant treks and overnight stays in minority villages, as can the leading guesthouses in town.

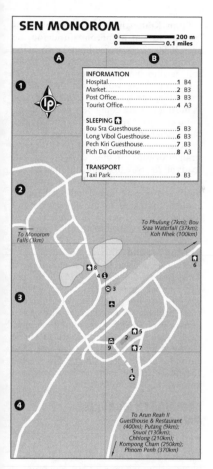

SEN MONOROM

0   200 m
0   0.1 miles

INFORMATION
Hospital...................................1 B4
Market....................................2 B3
Post Office..............................3 B3
Tourist Office..........................4 A3

SLEEPING
Bou Sra Guesthouse..................5 B3
Long Vibol Guesthouse.............6 B3
Pech Kiri Guesthouse................7 B3
Pich Da Guesthouse..................8 A3

TRANSPORT
Taxi Park................................9 B3

To Phulung (7km); Bou Sraa Waterfall (37km); Koh Nhek (100km)

To Monorom Falls (3km)

To Arun Reah II Guesthouse & Restaurant (400m); Putang (9km); Snuol (130km); Chhlong (210km); Kompong Cham (250km); Phnom Penh (370km)

Another man who knows the province very well is Long Vibol, an all-round Mr Fix-it who works for the Red Cross, runs a guesthouse, is a dentist and wedding photographer and, of more relevance perhaps, an English-speaking tour guide.

Activities

ELEPHANT TREKS

The villages of Phulung, 7km northeast of Sen Monorom, and Putang, 9km southwest of town, are the most popular places to arrange an elephant trek. Most of the guesthouses around town, as well as the tourist office, can arrange day treks for around US$25 to US$30, including lunch and transport to and from the village. It can get pretty uncomfortable up on top of an elephant after a couple of hours, so carry a pillow to ease the strain.

It is also possible to negotiate a longer trek with an overnight stay in a Pnong village. Long Vibol organises overnight elephant treks with a night camping in the forest, costing US$60 per person. Pech Kiri Guesthouse (below) offers an elephant trek to Kbal Preah Waterfall, including overnight on wooden platforms, which costs US$80 per person.

Sleeping & Eating

Sen Monorom has electricity from around 6pm to 10pm only, so a torch is useful for late-night ablutions, although some places run a generator through the night. Hot water is more important in this part of the country, as the temperature can drop dramatically at night. Places without hot-water showers can usually provide flasks of boiling water for bathing. There is no need for air-con in this neck of the woods.

Pech Kiri Guesthouse (☎ 012 932102; r US$3-10) The original and, for a long time, the only guesthouse in town is still doing well under the lively direction of Madame Deu. Cheap rooms with shared bathroom are in the main house, the older bungalows with bathroom are a very good deal at US$5, and the newest bungalows (costing US$10) are big and spacious. There is a nice garden here, but unfortunately the car park is now the biggest part of the complex. The **restaurant** (mains US$1-3) here has good Khmer food and does a tasty version of guacamole using local avocadoes.

Long Vibol Guesthouse (☎ 012 944647; s/d/tw US$5/10/15) Vibol has long been the most knowledgeable guide on the Mondulkiri tourist scene, and his guesthouse just keeps on growing. Rooms are spaciously spread across the blossoming garden and the large twin rooms have hot-water showers. Needless to say, this place is a great source of information on exploring Mondulkiri and a good place to arrange trekking. Its **restaurant** (mains US$1-3) is one of the most popular in town, and attracts well-to-do Khmers as well as foreigners.

Arun Reah II Guesthouse & Restaurant (☎ 012 856667; r US$5-10) The first place everyone sees when approaching town, this bungalow village boasts some fine views across the hills of Mondulkiri. The bungalows are seriously

EASTERN CAMBODIA

sweet and very good value, including bathroom, TV, free water and a torch. Hot-water rooms cost US$8 and the US$10 rooms are cavernous. There is a big **restaurant** (mains US$1-3) out front that can be a little quiet, but beer is always available.

Pich Da Guesthouse (☎ 012 484727; r US$5-7) One of the new breed of guesthouses that have sprung up to cater for Khmers; rooms are spread over two floors in a large concrete house. They are clean enough, include a bathroom and a restaurant is underway in the garden.

Bou Sra Guesthouse (☎ 012 527144; r US$5-10) Sitting in the centre of town near the market, this new guesthouse has big double rooms with tasteful bamboo furnishings, plus the bonus of cotton sheets rather than the shiny sheets often seen in this corner of Cambodia.

Getting There & Away

The airstrip at Sen Monorom has been closed since 2000 and local officials don't expect it to be reopened in the near future. For now, visitors who want to get to this unique region have to come overland, and this has been pretty straightforward since the completion of the new jungle highway by the Cambodian military in 2002.

There are two ways to get to Mondulkiri, both of which include the same section of old logging road from Snuol to Sen Monorom, and a third, harsh trail north to Ratanakiri – see p261 for more details on this hardcore route. The stretch from Snuol to Sen Monorom passes through some wild jungle after Khao Si Ma district and is one of the most dramatic and beautiful roads in Cambodia.

There is usually at least one pick-up a day heading from Phnom Penh to Sen Monorom (inside/on the back US$10/5, eight hours) in the dry season, leaving from Psar Thmei soon after 6am, but it's best to head to the market the day before you want to travel and arrange a seat with a driver, as places are limited.

Coming from Kompong Cham, there are few direct pick-ups to Sen Monorom, so it is usually necessary to first go to Snuol (10,000r by taxi, 1½ hours). From Snuol, there are pick-ups to Sen Monorom (inside/on the back 20,000/15,000r, three hours). Starting early from Kompong Cham, it should be easy enough to cover this in a day.

From Kratie there are direct pick-ups heading to Sen Monorom (inside/on the back 30,000/20,000r, five hours) early in the morning. Anyone leaving later will probably need to change vehicles in Snuol.

Getting from Mondulkiri Province to any of these destinations is generally easier, as most locals are going beyond Snuol and so no change is required, plus guesthouses can arrange for the pick-ups to pick up!

Experienced bikers will find it a pretty straightforward run these days, on surfaced roads all the way to Snuol and then decent enough dirt roads through to Sen Monorom. If it doesn't sound half challenging enough compared to the old days, don't worry: once you get to Mondulkiri there are still plenty of bad roads to be found.

Getting Around

The cheapest place to rent a motorbike is Arun Reah II Guesthouse (p265; US$5 per day). Other guesthouses charge US$10, but this may drop. There are no 250cc dirt bikes available for rent here, so hire one in Phnom Penh (p106) if you want more muscle. Russian jeeps and pick-up trucks can be chartered for the day. It costs about US$40 around Sen Monorom in the dry season, around US$60 or more to Bou Sraa, and more again in the wet season.

AROUND SEN MONOROM
Monorom Falls
ទឹកជ្រោះមនោរម្យ

This small waterfall is the closest thing to a public swimming pool for Sen Monorom. It has an attractive location in the forest, about 3km northwest of town. *Motos* can take people out here for about US$3 for the round trip. If walking, head straight on beyond Sihanouk's abandoned villa and when the trail eventually forks, take the left-hand side.

Bou Sraa Waterfall
ទឹកជ្រោះប៊ូស្រា

This double-drop waterfall is one of the largest in Cambodia and famous throughout the country. It is an unforgiving 37km journey east of Sen Monorom, but the reward is worth the effort. The upper tier of Bou Sraa drops some 10m and the lower tier drops 25m. To get to the bottom of the upper falls, take a left turn just before the river that feeds the falls. To get to the bottom of the lower falls, cross the river and take a left further down the track; it takes about 20 minutes to get down. A little way on is the Pnong village of Pichinda where there is a tiny **guesthouse** (r 10,000r) and **restaurant** (mains US$1-2). There are also some food and drink supplies available in the village.

GETTING THERE & AWAY

The road from Bou Sraa to Sen Monorom has long been appalling. It is one of the worst stretches of road in the country – and there's a lot of competition. There are two large rivers to cross, three if you include the one at the top of the falls, and several deep gullies. Most vehicles take more than two hours to complete the journey. All this was supposed to be a thing of the past, as the road is persistently rumoured to be getting an upgrade – believe it when you see it!

To get here, hire a *moto* driver for the day or charter a Russian jeep in a group. Coming alone by motorcycle is tough and should only be undertaken by highly experienced riders. Be especially careful if crossing the river above the Bou Sraa Falls, as the riverbed is as slippery as ice. Going over the top of the falls, motorbike and all, is not good for your health. See 'The Motorcycle Diaries' in *Lonely Planet Unpacked* for more on how this nearly happened to this author in 1999.

Other Waterfalls

Other popular waterfalls in Mondulkiri include **Romanear Waterfall**, 18km southeast of Sen Monorom, and **Dak Dam Waterfall**, 25km east of Sen Monorom. Both are very difficult to find without assistance, so it's best to take a *moto* driver or local guide. Romanear is a low, wide waterfall with some convenient swimming holes. There is also a second Romanear Waterfall, known rather originally as **Romanear II**, which is near the main road between Sen Monorom and Snuol. Dak Dam is similar to the Monorom Falls, albeit with a greater volume of water. The waterfall is

several kilometres beyond the Pnong village of Dak Dam and locals are able to lead the way if you can make yourself understood.

MIMONG
ម៊ីម៉ុង

Welcome to the wild east, where the gold rush lives on! Mimong district is famous for its **gold mines** and this has drawn speculators from as far away as Vietnam and China on the trail of wealth. The population of this overgrown village may actually be equal to that of Sen Monorom. Miners descend into the pits on ancient mine carts that are connected to dodgy-looking winches, sometimes going to a depth of 100m or more. It's not for the faint-hearted and several miners die in accidents each year.

The main problem is getting here, as the road is so bad that it takes about four hours to cover the 40km from Sen Monorom. The road improves slightly on the other side of Mimong and it is possible to carry on to link up with NH7 to Kratie to the west taking another four hours. There is also a major set of falls in the Mimong area called **Tan Lung Waterfall**, but this is also a nightmare to reach.

KOH NHEK
កោះញែក

pop 6000

This is the final frontier as far as Mondulkiri goes, a remote village in the far north of the province, but a strategic place on the difficult overland route between Sen Monorom and Ratanakiri. There is a big house in town with a friendly owner who accepts foreigners for 10,000r and can prepare some basic food. Ask for '*dam svay*' or 'mango tree' and most villagers can point the way. There are also basic supplies in the village, including beer – well-earned once you get here.

The Cambodian military are currently rebuilding the road to Koh Nhek which should improve journey times. It usually takes seven or more hours from Sen Monorom and another four or so hours on to Ban Lung.

DIRECTORY

Directory

CONTENTS

ACCOMMODATION

The accommodation situation in Cambodia has improved immensely during the past decade and everything is available from the classic budget crashpad to the plush palace. Most hotels in Cambodia quote in US dollars, but some smaller places in the provinces quote in riel. We quote prices based on the currency quoted to us at the time of research. In Phnom Penh, Siem Reap and Sihanoukville there are options to suit all wallets. Elsewhere around Cambodia, the choice is limited to budget and midrange options, but these places provide great value for money.

PRACTICALITIES

■ The usual voltage is 220V, 50 cycles, but power surges and power cuts are common, particularly in the provinces. Electrical sockets are usually two-prong, flat or round pin.

■ Most guesthouses and hotels have cheap laundry services, but check they have a dryer if the weather is bad. There are laundry shops in every town.

■ The *Cambodia Daily* is a popular English-language newspaper, while the *Phnom Penh Post* offers in-depth analysis every two weeks. Readable magazines include the humorous *Bayon Pearnik* and the travel magazine the *Cambodia Scene*.

■ BBC World Service broadcasts on 100.00FM. Cambodian radio and TV stations are mainly government-controlled and specialise in karaoke videos and soap operas. TV5 broadcasts in French.

■ Phone numbers in this chapter and the Transport chapter (p288) include local area codes.

■ Cambodians use the metric system for everything except precious metals and gems where they prefer the Chinese system.

In this guide, budget accommodation refers to guesthouses where the majority of rooms are within the US$2 to US$10 range, midrange generally runs from US$10 up to US$50 and top end is considered US$50 and up, up, up.

Budget guesthouses used to be restricted to Phnom Penh, Siem Reap and Sihanoukville, but as tourism takes off in the provinces, there are also options in most other provincial capitals such as Kampot, Kratie and Stung Treng. Costs hover around US$2 to US$5 for a bed. In many rural parts of Cambodia, the standard rate for the cheapest hotels is US$5, usually with bathroom and satellite TV. There may be a few places starting at 10,000r that make more by the hour as brothels than they do by the night – don't count on much sleep!

In Phnom Penh, Siem Reap and Sihanoukville, which see a steady flow of tourist traffic, hotels improve significantly once you start spending more than US$10 a night. For US$15 or less it is usually possible to find an air-con room with satellite TV and attached bathroom. If you spend between US$20 and US$50 it is possible to arrange something very comfortable with the possible lure of a swimming pool. Most smaller provincial cities also offer air-conditioned comfort in the US$10 to US$15 range.

Top-end accommodation is available only in Phnom Penh, Siem Reap, Sihanoukville and the border casinos along the Thai frontier (p219). There are now a host of international-standard hotels in Siem Reap, several in Phnom Penh and one in Sihanoukville, some operated by familiar international brands such as Le Meridien, Raffles and Sofitel. Most quote hefty walk-in rates and whack 10% taxes and 10% service on as well. Book through a travel agent for a lower rate including taxes and service.

Some guesthouses in Cambodia do not have hot water, but most places have at least a few more expensive rooms where it is available. Smaller places in remote areas may have bathrooms where a large jar or cement trough is filled with water for bathing purposes – don't climb into it, just sluice the water with the plastic scoop or metal bowl. However, most guesthouses have cold showers these days.

While many of the swish new hotels have lifts, older hotels often don't and the cheapest rooms are at the end of several flights of stairs. It's a win-win-win situation: cheaper rooms, a bit of exercise and better views!

There is often confusion over the terms 'singles', 'doubles', 'double occupancy' and 'twins', so let's try and make sense of it here. A single contains one bed, even if two people sleep in it. If there are two beds in the room, that is a twin, even if only one person occupies it. If two people stay in the same room, that is double occupancy. In some hotels 'doubles' means twin beds, while in others it means double occupancy.

ACTIVITIES

Tourism in Cambodia is catching up fast, but there are still fewer activities on offer than elsewhere in the region. Phnom Penh is an exception – the large population of foreigners has led to a boom in leisure activities, such as go-carting, jet-skiing, tenpin bowling and a variety of conventional sports like swimming and tennis. See p85 for details.

Bird-Watching

Bird-watching is set to be a big draw for Cambodia, as it is home to some of the region's rarest large water birds including adjutants, storks and pelicans. For more on the birds of Cambodia see p55, and for the lowdown on bird sanctuaries see p132.

Boat Trips

With so much water around the country, it is hardly surprising that boat trips are popular with tourists. Some of these are functional yet fun, such as travelling up the Tonlé Sap river to Siem Reap (p130), or up the Mekong River to Kratie (p254). But others are the traditional tourist trips, such as those available in Phnom Penh (p85), Siem Reap (p130) and Sihanoukville (p193).

Cycling

With a reputation for some of the worst roads in Asia, it is hardly surprising that cycling hasn't been a huge hit here so far. However, those who do cycle will experience an adrenaline-packed adventure and get much closer to the local people. Some of the main roads are getting busier and others remain dusty, but there are some great routes for those willing to put in the effort. The south coast of Cambodia remains a rewarding region for cyclists, while the northeast holds future promise for serious mountain bikers. The most popular place for cycling is around the majestic temples of Angkor where the roads are paved and the forest thick. Bikes are available for hire in most towns in Cambodia for US$1 a day, but serious tourers need to bring their own machine.

For some inspired insights into surviving the crazy world that is cycling through Cambodia, visit **Biking Southeast Asia with Mr Pumpy** (www.mrpumpy.net).

Dirt Biking

For experienced riders, Cambodia is one of the most rewarding off-road biking destinations in the world. The roads are generally considered some of the worst in Asia – read that as the best in Asia for die-hard biking enthusiasts. There are incredible rides all over the country, particularly the north and northeast, but it is best to stay away from the main highways as traffic and dust make it a choking experience. For more on dirt biking, see p291, or for something more organised, have a look at **Hidden Cambodia** (www.hiddencambodia.com).

Diving & Snorkelling
Snorkelling and diving are available off the coast of Sihanoukville. The jury is still out about the quality of the dive sites, but while it may not be as spectacular as Thailand or Indonesia, there is still plenty in the deep blue yonder. It is best to venture further afield to dive sites such as Koh Tang (p187) and Koh Prins (p187), staying overnight on a boat. There are many unexplored areas off the coast between Koh Kong and Sihanoukville that could one day put Cambodia on the dive map of Asia.

Golf
Cambodia is definitely not the golfing capital of Asia with just two full courses (p86). However, as one of the more obscure golfing destinations, it might earn brownie points during a schmoozing tournament back home. Both courses are near Phnom Penh, but plans are afoot to develop a golf course near Siem Reap in the near future.

Trekking & Walking
Trekking is not the first thing you associate with Cambodia due to the presence of land mines, but there are several relatively safe areas of the country, including the nascent national parks. The northeastern provinces of Ratanakiri (p258) and Mondulkiri (p264) were never mined and with their wild, natural scenery, abundant waterfalls and ethnic minority populations, they are emerging as the country's leading trekking destinations. Always take a guide, however, as there are some unexploded bombs in these areas from the American bombing campaign of the early 1970s. Elephant treks are also possible in these northeastern provinces.

Cambodia is steadily establishing a network of national parks with visitor facilities, and Bokor National Park (p199), Kirirom National Park (p111) and Ream National Park (p194) all promise trekking potential.

Finally, Angkor is emerging as a good place for gentle walks between the temples; this is one way to experience peace and solitude as visitor numbers skyrocket.

BUSINESS HOURS
Most Cambodians get up very early and it is not unusual to see people out and about exercising at 5.30am if you are heading home – ahem, sorry, getting up – at that time. Government offices, which are open from Monday to Saturday, theoretically begin the working day at 7.30am, break for a siesta from 11.30am to 2pm, and end the day at 5pm. However, it is a safe bet that few people will be around early in the morning or after 4pm, as their real income is earned elsewhere.

Banking hours vary slightly according to the bank, but most banks keep core hours of 8.30am to 3.30pm Monday to Friday, plus Saturday morning. Tourist attractions such as museums are normally open seven days a week and these days staff have had their arms twisted to stay open through lunch.

Local restaurants are generally open from about 6.30am until 9pm and international restaurants until a little later. Many bars are open all day, but some open only for the night shift, especially if they don't serve food.

Local markets operate seven days a week and usually open and close with the sun, running from 6.30am to 5.30pm. Markets shut up shop for a few days during the major holidays of Chaul Chnam (Khmer New Year), P'chum Ben (Festival of the Dead) and Chinese New Year. Shops tend to open from about 7am until 7pm, sometimes later.

CHILDREN
Children can live it up in Cambodia as they are always the centre of attention and almost everybody wants to play with them. For the full picture on surviving and thriving on the road with kids, check out Lonely Planet's *Travel with Children* by Cathy Lanigan, for a rundown on health precautions for kids and advice on travel during pregnancy.

Practicalities
When it comes to feeding and caring for babies, pretty much everything you'll need is available in Phnom Penh and Siem Reap,

but supplies dry up quickly elsewhere. Cot beds are available in international standard midrange and top-end hotels, but not elsewhere. There are no safety seats in rented cars or taxis, but some restaurants can supply a high chair when it comes to eating.

Breastfeeding in public is very common in Cambodia, so there is no need to worry about crossing a cultural boundary. But there are few facilities for changing babies other than the usual bathrooms, so pack a baby bag everywhere you go. For kiddies too young to handle chopsticks, most restaurants also have cutlery.

The main worry throughout Cambodia is keeping an eye on what strange things infants are putting in their mouths. Their natural curiosity can be a lot more costly in a country where dysentery, typhoid and hepatitis are commonplace. Keeping their hydration levels up and insisting they use sunscreen, despite their protests, is also important.

Phnom Penh, Siem Reap and other urban areas of Cambodia are pretty straightforward these days, although be very aware of the chaotic traffic conditions in the capital – better to restrict your child's movements than have them wander into danger. Rural Cambodia is not a good travel destination for children as there are many land mines littering the countryside. No matter how many warnings a child is given, can you be certain they won't stray from the path?

Sights & Activities
There is plenty to keep kids happy in Phnom Penh, Siem Reap and Sihanoukville, but in the smaller provincial towns the boredom factor might creep in. Phnom Penh has a good selection of swimming pools (p87) and even a couple of go-kart tracks (p86). Boat trips on the river should be a hit, but best of all is the Phnom Tamao Wildlife Sanctuary (p110), about 45km south of the city, with tigers, sun bears and elephants.

At Angkor (p134) the temples may be too much for younger children, but will be appreciated by inquisitive older children. Younger ones might prefer crumbling ruins like Ta Prohm (p162) or Beng Mealea (p176) to the more museum-like renovated temples. *Remorque-motos* (motorbikes with a cute little hooded trailer hitched to the back) are a fun way for families to get around the Angkor area (p149).

The national parks don't have enough visible wildlife to deliver, but some have impressive waterfalls, including Kirirom National Park (p111) and Bokor National Park (p199). Another area for attractive waterfalls is the northeast and the provinces of Mondulkiri (p264) and Ratanakiri (p258), where kids can also ride elephants.

Cambodia has a long coastline and Sihanoukville (p184) is the number one beach spot. There are plenty of local children hanging out on the beach, many of them trying to make a living and this can be an interesting bonding experience for kids. But pay close to attention to any playtime in the sea, as there are some deceptively strong currents in the wet season.

CLIMATE CHARTS
Life in Cambodia is fairly steamy in the lowlands, with a classic tropical climate. It gets a little cooler up in the hills of the northeast, but even there it rarely gets cold.

Average daily temperatures range from the high 20s in the 'cool' season of December and January, to the high 30s and beyond in the hot season months of April and May. The rain kicks in around June and falls thick and fast throughout August and September, bringing the landscape back to life ready for a new harvest.

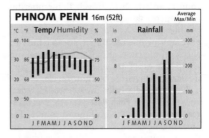

COURSES
Cooking
For the full story on cooking courses see p66.

Language
The only language courses available in Cambodia at present are in Khmer and are aimed at expat residents of Phnom Penh rather than travellers. If you are going to be based in Phnom Penh for some time, however, it would be well worth learning

basic Khmer. Ring the **Cambodia Development Research Institute** (☎ 023-368053; 56 Ph 315) for information about classes or try the Institute of Foreign Languages at the **Royal University of Phnom Penh** (Map pp74-5; ☎ 012 866826; Russian Blvd). Also check out the notice board at the Foreign Correspondents' Club (FCC; p98), where one-hour lessons are often advertised by private tutors.

CUSTOMS

If Cambodia has customs allowances, it is close-lipped about them. A 'reasonable amount' of duty-free items are allowed into the country. Travellers arriving by air might bear in mind that alcohol and cigarettes are on sale at prices well below duty-free prices on the streets of Phnom Penh – a branded box of 200 cigarettes costs just US$8! International spirits start as low as US$7 a litre!

Like any other country, Cambodia does not allow travellers to import weapons, explosives or narcotics – some would say there are enough in the country already. It is illegal to take ancient stone sculptures from the Angkor period out of the country.

DANGERS & ANNOYANCES

As memories of war grow ever more distant, Cambodia has become a much safer country in which to travel. Remembering the golden rule – stick to marked paths in remote areas – you'd be very unlucky to have any problems. But it doesn't hurt to check on the latest situation before making a trip few other travellers undertake, particularly if travelling by motorcycle.

The **Cambodia Daily** (www.cambodiadaily.com) and the **Phnom Penh Post** (www.phnompenhpost .com) newspapers are both good sources for breaking news on Cambodia – check out their websites before you hit the road.

Begging

Begging is common throughout Cambodia, although much more evident in Phnom Penh and Siem Reap than elsewhere. There are many reasons for begging in a society as poor as Cambodia, some more visually evident than others, such as amputees who may have lost their legs in frontline battles during the civil war. It is entirely up to individual visitors whether to give or not, and to decide how much to offer, but remember

---

> ### TRAVEL ADVISORY WEBSITES
>
> Travel advisories on government-run websites update nationals on the latest security situation in any given country, including Cambodia. They are useful to check out for dangerous countries or dangerous times, but they tend to be pretty conservative, stressing dangers where they don't always exist…otherwise known as covering your back or 'I told you so'. Cynics might argue travel advisories should come with a government warning themselves, saying 'take this with a pinch of salt'.
>
> **Australia** (www.dfat.gov.au/travel)
> **Canada** (www.voyage.gc.ca/dest/index.asp)
> **Germany** (www.auswaertiges-amt.de/www/de /laenderinfos/reise_warnung_html)
> **Japan** (www.mofa.go.jp/anzen/)
> **Netherlands** (www.minbuza.nl/default.asp?CMS _ITEM=MBZ458731)
> **New Zealand** (www.mft.govt.nz/travel/)
> **UK** (www.fco.gov.uk/travel)
> **USA** (www.travel.state.gov)

---

that it is common practice for Buddhists to give to those more needy than themselves.

Big brown eyes, runny noses and grubby hands…the sight of children begging is familiar throughout the developing world, and Cambodia is no exception. There are many child beggars around Phnom Penh and the temples of Angkor, and with their angelic faces it is often difficult to resist giving them some money. However, things to think about include: giving to child beggars may create a cycle of dependency that can continue into adulthood; the children may not benefit directly from the money, as they are often made to beg by a begging 'pimp' or their family; and some child beggars, particularly around central Phnom Penh, may use the money to buy glue to feed their sniffing habit. One way to help these impoverished children is to buy them some food or drink, or give them some of your time and attention – it is amazing how quickly they will forget about begging once they are being taught something simple like a whistle, a trick or a game.

The most common beggars around the country are land mine victims. Many of these victims sustained these injuries fighting, while others have had their legs blown off while working or playing innocently in the fields. You may tire of their attention after a few days in Cambodia, but try to remember that in a country with no social security network, begging is often all they can do to survive.

When giving to beggars, try to offer smaller denominations to avoid making foreigners more of a target than they already are.

Checkpoints

During the long years of civil war there were checkpoints on roads throughout the country. These were supposed to enhance security on provincial roads, but in reality they worsened the situation as the soldiers stationed at checkpoints learned to extort money from every vehicle passing through. However, the situation has improved vastly in recent years and none of the commonly travelled routes have checkpoints. Where there are checkpoints on major roads, spot checks may be carried out to make sure drivers have paid their road tax or are not carrying illegal guns.

If you are travelling in a taxi or pick-up truck in remote areas of Cambodia and come across a checkpoint, the driver should take care of the payment. If you are on a motorbike, you are unlikely to be stopped. However, should you ever find money being demanded of you, try to negotiate the sum to an acceptable level. Do not under any circumstances attempt to take photos of the individuals concerned as things could turn nasty.

Scams

There are fewer scams in Cambodia than neighbouring countries, but now that tourism is really taking off this might change. Most current scams are fairly harmless, involving a bit of commission here and there for taxi or *moto* drivers, particularly in Siem Reap. More annoying are the 'cheap' buses from Bangkok to Siem Reap, deservedly nicknamed the 'The Scam Bus' for crossing the wrong borders, driving slowly and selling passengers to guesthouses (p294).

There have been one or two reports of police set-ups in Phnom Penh, involving planted drugs. This seems to be very rare, but if you fall victim to the ploy, it will require patience and persistence to sort out, inevitably involving embassies and the like.

It may be best to pay them off before more police get involved at the local station, as the price will only rise when there are more people to pay off.

Cambodia is renowned for its precious stones, particularly the rubies and sapphires that are mined around the Pailin area in western Cambodia. However, there are lots of chemically treated copies around, as much of the high quality stuff is snapped up by international buyers. The long and the short of it is: don't buy unless you really know your stones.

Security

Cambodia is a pretty safe country to travel these days. Remembering the golden rule – *stick to marked paths in remote areas* – it is now possible to travel throughout Cambodia with no more difficulty than in neighbouring Thailand or Vietnam. Politically, Cambodia has proven an unpredictable country and this makes it hard to guarantee safety of travel at any given time. Suffice to say that you are no longer a target just because you are a tourist.

For many years the security situation was the Achilles heel of Cambodia's tourism industry. Certainly, during Cambodia's civil war, personal security was an issue of greater concern than in neighbouring countries. For most of the 1990s the Khmer Rouge had a policy of targeting Western tourists. A number were killed, and this naturally scared visitors away, while those that came found their movements restricted. The coup of July 1997 and the series of riots and extra-judicial killings that followed the elections of July 1998 further sullied Cambodia's international reputation. This culture of violence persists, but politicians are at last learning that it's not internationally popular.

Cambodia is something of a lawless society in which arms are often preferred to eloquence when settling a dispute. This 'wild east' atmosphere rarely affects tourists, but it is worth knowing about as you can expect to hear gunshots from time to time (usually someone firing into the air when drunk). Phnom Penh (p77) is arguably one of the more dangerous places in Cambodia since peace has come to the provinces; it is here that the most guns are concentrated and the most robberies take place. This is closely followed by Sihanoukville (p186), which has sadly developed a reputation for robbery and sneak theft. Elsewhere in the provinces you would be very unlucky to have any incident befall you, as the vast majority of Khmers are immensely hospitable, honest and helpful. More importantly, perhaps, the majority of Khmers are experiencing peace for the first time in more than 30 years and don't want anything to disturb it.

Trying to pinpoint any lingering areas of concern around the country is always difficult as circumstances change quickly. Pailin and large parts of Oddar Meanchey and Preah Vihear Provinces were Khmer Rouge controlled until just a few years ago, but are now considered safe. However, if and when a trial for surviving Khmer Rouge leaders moves forward, it may be a different story – just because the former rebels now wear Britney Spears T-shirts instead of Mao caps, doesn't mean they have forgotten the fight.

Should anyone be unlucky enough to be robbed, it is important to note that the Cambodian police are the best that money can buy. Any help, such as a police report, is going to cost you. The going rate depends on the size of the claim, but US$20 is a common charge.

Snakes

Visitors to Ta Prohm at Angkor and other overgrown archaeological sites should beware of snakes, including the small but deadly light-green Haluman snake, which often emerges after rainstorms to hunt for insects. They are very well camouflaged so keep your eyes peeled. For details of what to do in case of snake bite, see p313.

Theft & Street Crime

Given the number of guns in Cambodia, there is less armed theft than one might expect. Still, hold-ups and motorcycle theft are a potential danger in Phnom Penh (p77) and Sihanoukville (p186). There is no need to be paranoid, just cautious. Walking or riding alone late at night is not ideal, certainly not in rural areas.

Pickpocketing and theft by stealth is more a problem in Vietnam than in Cambodia, but it pays to be careful. The current hotspots are crowded pick-up trucks on popular tourist routes such as Siem Reap to Poipet or Phnom Penh, and the markets of Phnom Penh. Don't make it any easier for thieves by putting your passport and wads of cash in your back pocket. As a precaution, keep a 'secret' stash of cash separate from the bulk of your funds.

Traffic Accidents

Traffic conditions in Cambodia are chaotic, although no worse than in many other underdeveloped countries. If you are riding a bike in Phnom Penh you should stay very alert and take nothing for granted. Traffic moves in all directions on both sides of the road, so don't be surprised to see vehicles bearing down on you. The horn is used to alert other drivers of a vehicle's presence – get out of the way if you hear a car or truck behind you.

None of the *moto* drivers in Cambodia use or provide safety helmets. Fortunately most of them drive at sensible speeds. If you encounter a reckless driver, ask them to slow down or pay them and find another *moto*.

Having a major traffic accident in Phnom Penh would be bad enough, but if you have one in rural Cambodia, you are in big trouble. Somehow you will have to get back to Phnom Penh for medical treatment.

The basic rule is to drive carefully – there have already been too many shattered dreams (Honda Dreams?) in Cambodia, and there's no need to add to them. See p291 for safety tips.

Undetonated Mines, Mortars & Bombs

Never touch any rockets, artillery shells, mortars, mines, bombs or other war material you may come across. A favourite tactic of the Khmer Rouge was to lay mines along roads and in rice-fields in an effort to maim and kill civilians, thus – so the twisted logic concludes – furthering the rebel cause by demoralising the government. The only concrete results of this policy are the many limbless people you see all over Cambodia.

The most heavily mined part of the country is the Battambang and Pailin area, but mines are a problem all over Cambodia. In short: *do not stray from well-marked paths under any circumstances.* If you are planning any walks, even in safer areas such as the remote northeast, it is imperative you take a guide as there may be unexploded ordnance (UXO) from the American bombing campaign of the early 1970s.

Violence

Violence against foreigners is extremely rare and is not something you should waste much time worrying about, but it pays to take care in crowded bars or nightclubs in Phnom Penh (p77). If you get into a stand-off with rich young Khmers in a bar or club, swallow your pride and back down. Still think you can 'ave em'? Many carry guns, enough said.

DISABLED TRAVELLERS

Broken pavements (sidewalks), potholed roads and stairs as steep as ladders at Angkor ensure that for most people with mobility impairments, Cambodia is not going to be an easy country to travel. Few buildings in Cambodia have been designed with the disabled in mind, although new projects, such as the international airports at Phnom Penh and Siem Reap, and top-end hotels, include ramps for wheelchair access. Transport in the provinces is usually very overcrowded, but taxi hire from point to point is an affordable option.

On the positive side, the Cambodian people are usually very helpful towards all foreigners, and local labour is cheap if you need someone to accompany you at all times. Most guesthouses and small hotels have ground-floor rooms that are reasonably easy to access.

The biggest headache is also the main attraction – the temples of Angkor. Causeways are uneven, obstacles common and staircases daunting, even for able-bodied people. It is likely to be some years before things improve, although some ramping was introduced at Angkor Wat and Bayon for the visit of King Sihanouk and the then–Chinese Premier Jiang Zemin in 2000.

Wheelchair travellers will need to undertake a lot of research before visiting Cambodia. There is now a growing network of information sources that can put you in touch with others who have wheeled through Cambodia before. Try contacting the following:

Mobility International USA (☎ 54-1343 1284; www
.miusa.org)
Royal Association for Disability and Rehabilitation (Radar; ☎ 020-7250 3222; www.radar.org.uk)
Society for Accessible Travel & Hospitality (SATH; ☎ 212-447 7284; www.sath.org)

The website for **Lonely Planet** (www.lonelyplanet
.com) has a Thorn Tree section, which is also a good place to seek the advice of other travellers.

DISCOUNT CARDS

Senior travellers and students are not eligible for discounts in Cambodia – all foreigners who are rich enough to make it to Cambodia are rich enough to pay as far as Cambodians are concerned.

EMBASSIES & CONSULATES
Cambodian Embassies & Consulates

Cambodian diplomatic representation abroad is still thin on the ground, though the situation is gradually improving. However, as visas are available on arrival at airports and the borders with Thailand and Vietnam, most visitors don't need to visit a Cambodian embassy in advance.

When crossing overland from Laos to Cambodia, it is essential to arrange a Cambodian visa in Vientiane or Bangkok, as visas are not currently available at this border.

Cambodian diplomatic missions abroad include the following:
Australia (☎ 02-6273 1259; 5 Canterbury Cres, Deakin, ACT 2600)
China (☎ 010-6532 1889; 9 Dongzhimenwai Dajie, Beijing 100600)
France (☎ 01-45 03 47 20; 4 Rue Adolphe Yvon, 75116 Paris)
Germany (☎ 30-48 63 79 01; Benjamin-Vogelsdorf Str 2, 13187 Berlin)
Hong Kong (☎ 2546 0718; Unit 616, 6th fl, 3 Salisbury Rd, Tsim Sha Tsui, Kowloon)
India (☎ 011-649 5091; N-14 Panscheel Park, New Delhi 110017)
Indonesia (☎ 021-919 2895; 4th fl, Panin Bank Plaza, Jalan 52 Palmerah Utara, Jakarta 11480)
Japan (☎ 03-5412 8521; 8-6-9 Akasaka, Minato-ku, Tokyo 1070052)
Laos (☎ 21-314952; Tha Deau, Bon That Khao, Vientiane)
Malaysia (☎ 02-818 9918; 83/JKR 2809 Lingkungan, U Thant, 55000, Kuala Lumpur)
Singapore (☎ 299 3028; 152 Beach Rd, Gateway East, 189721, Singapore)
Thailand (☎ 02-254 6630; 185 Rajadamri Rd, Bangkok 10330)
USA (☎ 202-726 7742; 4500 16th St, NW, Washington DC 20011)
Vietnam Hanoi (☎ 04-825 3788; 71 Tran Hung Dao St); Ho Chi Minh City (☎ 08-829 2751; 41 Phung Khac Khoan St)

DIRECTORY

Embassies & Consulates in Cambodia

Quite a few countries have embassies in Phnom Penh, though some travellers will find that their nearest embassy is in Bangkok. It's important to realise what your country's embassy can and can't do to help you if you get into trouble. Generally speaking, it won't be much help if the trouble you're in is remotely your own fault. Remember that you are bound by the laws of the country you are in. Your embassy won't be sympathetic if you end up in jail after committing a crime, even if such actions are legal in your own country.

In genuine emergencies you might get some assistance, but only if other channels have been exhausted. If you have all your money and documents stolen, it might assist with getting a new passport, but a loan for onward travel is out of the question.

Those intending to visit Laos should note that Lao visas are available in Phnom Penh for US$30 and take two working days. For Vietnam, one-month, single-entry visas cost US$35 and take just one day, faster still at the Vietnamese consulate in Sihanoukville.

Embassies in Phnom Penh:

Australia (Map pp78-9; ☎ 023-213470; 11 Ph 254)
Canada (Map pp78-9; ☎ 023-213470; 11 Ph 254)
China (Map pp74-5; ☎ 023-720920; 256 Mao Tse Toung Blvd)
France (Map pp74-5; ☎ 023-430020; 1 Monivong Blvd)
Germany (Map pp78-9; ☎ 023-216193; 76-78 Ph 214)
India (Map pp74-5; ☎ 023-210912; 777 Monivong Blvd)
Indonesia (Map pp78-9; ☎ 023-216148; 90 Norodom Blvd)
Japan (Map pp74-5; ☎ 023-217161; 194 Norodom Blvd)
Laos (Map pp74-5; ☎ 023-982632; 15-17 Mao Tse Toung Blvd)
Malaysia (Map pp78-9; ☎ 023-216176; 161 Ph 51)
Myanmar (Map pp74-5; ☎ 023-213664; 181 Norodom Blvd)
Philippines (Map pp78-9; ☎ 023-215145; 33 Ph 294)
Thailand (Map pp74-5; ☎ 023-363869; 196 Norodom Blvd)
UK (Map pp74-5; ☎ 023-427124; 27-29 Ph 75)
USA (Map pp78-9; ☎ 023-216436; 27 Ph 240) A new embassy is scheduled to open near Wat Phnom in 2006.
Vietnam Phnom Penh (Map pp74-5; ☎ 023-362531; fax 362314; 436 Monivong Blvd); Sihanoukville (Map p185; ☎ 012-340495; Ph Ekareach)

FESTIVALS & EVENTS

The festivals of Cambodia take place according to the lunar calendar so the dates vary from year to year. Check against any Cambodian calendar for the dates.

> **FESTIVAL WARNING**
>
> In the run-up to major festivals such as P'chum Ben or Chaul Chnam, there is a palpable increase in the number of robberies, particularly in Phnom Penh (p77). Cambodians need money to buy gifts for relatives or pay off debts, and for some individuals theft is the quick way to get this money. Be more vigilant at night at these times and don't take valuables out with you unnecessarily.

Special prayers are held at Khmer pagodas when the moon is full or just the thinnest sliver, marking Buddhist Day.

Chaul Chnam Chen The Chinese inhabitants of Cambodia celebrate their New Year somewhere between late January and mid-February – for the Vietnamese, this is Tet. As many of Phnom Penh's businesses are run by Chinese, commerce grinds to a halt around this time, and there are dragon dances all over town.

Chaul Chnam Held in mid-April, this is a three-day celebration of Khmer New Year, Christmas, New Year and birthdays all rolled into one. Cambodians make offerings at wats, clean out their homes and exchange gifts. It is a lively time to visit the country as, like the Thais, Khmers go wild with water and talcum powder, leaving a lot of bemused tourists looking like plaster-cast figures. It is not the best time of year to visit the temples of Angkor as half the population turns up, leaving you no peace to explore and reflect.

Chat Preah Nengkal Held in early May, this is the Royal Ploughing ceremony, a ritual agricultural festival led by the royal family. It takes place in front of the National Museum (p81), near the Royal Palace in Phnom Penh, and the royal oxen are said to have a nose for whether it will be a good harvest or a bad one.

Visakha Puja Celebrated collectively as Buddha's birth, enlightenment and *parinibbana* (passing away); activities are centred on wats. The festival falls on the eighth day of the fourth moon (around May or June) and is best observed at Angkor Wat, where you can see candlelit processions of monks.

P'chum Ben This festival falls between mid-September and early October and is a kind of All Souls' Day, when respects are paid to the dead through offerings made at wats. This includes paper money, as well as food and drink, all passed through the medium of the monks.

Bon Om Tuk Held in early November, this celebrates the epic victory of Jayavarman VII over the Chams who occupied Angkor in 1177. It also marks the natural phenomenon of the reversal of the current of the Tonlé Sap river (with the onset of the dry season, water backed up on the Tonlé Sap lake begins to empty into the Mekong). This is one of the most important festivals in the Khmer calendar and a wonderful, if hectic, time to be in Phnom Penh or Siem Reap, as boat races are held on the Tonlé Sap and Siem Reap rivers.

FOOD

Cambodian cuisine may be less well known than that of its popular neighbours Thailand and Vietnam, but it is no less tasty. See p61 for the full story on Cambodian cuisine.

GAY & LESBIAN TRAVELLERS

While Cambodian culture is tolerant of homosexuality, the gay and lesbian scene here is certainly nothing like that in Thailand. The former King Norodom Sihanouk was a keen supporter of equal rights for same-sex partners and this seems to have encouraged a more open attitude among younger Cambodians. Both Phnom Penh and Siem Reap have a few gay-friendly bars, but it is a low-key scene compared with other parts of Asia.

With the vast number of same-sex travel partners – gay or otherwise – checking into hotels across Cambodia, there is little consideration over how travelling foreigners are related. However, it is prudent not to flaunt your sexuality. As with heterosexual couples, passionate public displays of affection are considered a basic no-no.

Utopia (www.utopia-asia.com) features gay travel information and contacts, including detailed sections on the legality of homosexuality in Cambodia and some local gay terminology.

HOLIDAYS
Public Holidays

During public holidays and festivals, banks, ministries and embassies close down, so plan ahead if visiting Cambodia during these times. Cambodians also roll over holidays if they fall on a weekend and take a day or two extra during major festivals (see opposite). Add this to the fact that they take a holiday for international days here and there and it soon becomes apparent that Cambodia has more public holidays than any other nation on earth!

International New Year's Day 1 January
Victory Over the Genocide 7 January
International Women's Day 8 March
International Workers' Day 1 May
International Children's Day 1 May
Constitution Day 24 September
Paris Peace Accords 23 October
King's Birthday 30 October to 1 November
Independence Day 9 November
International Human Rights Day 10 December

INSURANCE

A travel insurance policy that covers theft, property loss and medical expenses is more essential for Cambodia than for most other parts of Southeast Asia. Theft is less of a problem in Cambodia than some might imagine, but in the event of serious medical problems or an accident, it may be necessary to be airlifted to Bangkok, an expense that stretches beyond the average traveller's budget.

There are a wide variety of travel insurance policies available, and it's wise to check with a reliable travel agent as to which is most suitable for Cambodia. The policies handled by **STA Travel** (www.statravel.com) are usually good value.

When buying your travel insurance *always* check the small print:

- Some policies specifically exclude 'dangerous activities' such as scuba diving and riding a motorcycle. If you are going to be riding a motorbike in Cambodia, check that you will be covered.
- Check whether the medical coverage is on a pay first, claim later basis; if this is the case, keep all documents relating to any medical treatment.
- In the case of Cambodia, it is essential to check that medical coverage includes the cost of emergency evacuation.

INSURANCE ALERT!

Do not visit Cambodia without medical insurance. Hospitals are extremely basic in the provinces and even in Phnom Penh the facilities are generally not up to the standards you may be accustomed to. Anyone who has a serious injury or illness while in Cambodia may require emergency evacuation to Bangkok. With an insurance policy costing no more than the equivalent of a bottle of beer a day, this evacuation is free. Without an insurance policy, it will cost between US$10,000 and US$20,000 – somewhat more than the average traveller's budget. Don't gamble with your health in Cambodia or you may end up another statistic!

INTERNET ACCESS

Internet access is available in most towns throughout the country. In Phnom Penh prices just keep dropping, thankfully, and now average US$0.50 to US$1 per hour. Siem Reap is a little more expensive at US$1 to US$1.50 per hour, while in other provinces it can range from US$2 an hour to as much as US$5 an hour, thanks to expensive domestic phone calls.

If you're travelling with a laptop computer, be aware that your modem may not work once you leave your home country. The safest option is to buy a reputable 'global' modem before you leave home, or buy a local PC-card modem if you're spending an extended time in Cambodia. For more information on travelling with a portable computer, see www.teleadapt.com.

Remember that Cambodia's power supply voltage will vary from that at home, risking damage to your equipment. The best investment is a universal AC adapter, which will enable you to plug it in anywhere without frying the innards.

Visitors carrying a portable computer who are looking for a direct connection to a server have several choices. The easiest way is to pick up one of the prepaid Internet cards offered by Online or Everyday, available from shops and some restaurants. They come in a range of values from US$10 to US$50 and can be purchased from shops, hotels and petrol stations. Those who like contracts and paperwork can try **Online** (Map pp78-9; ☎ 023-430000; 15 Norodom Blvd), **Camintel** (Map pp74-5; ☎ 023-986789; 1 Sisowath Quay) or **Telesurf** (Map pp78-9; ☎ 012 800800; 33 Sihanouk Blvd), all in Phnom Penh. Prices are high by international standards and if you are using a mobile phone from remote areas, the connection is poor.

THE ABUSE OF INNOCENCE

The sexual abuse of children by foreign paedophiles is a serious problem in Cambodia. Moral grounds alone should be enough to deter foreigners from seeking under-age sexual partners in Cambodia, but unfortunately basic morality appears to be absent in some individuals. Paedophiles are treated as criminals in Cambodia and several have served or are serving jail sentences as a result. There is no such thing as isolation units for sex offenders in Cambodia. Countries such as Australia, France, Germany, the UK and the USA have also introduced much-needed legislation that sees nationals prosecuted in their home country for having under-age sex abroad.

This abuse of a child's innocence is disgusting and is, slowly but surely, being combated, although in a country as poor as Cambodia, money can tempt people into selling babies for adoption and children for sex. The trafficking of innocent children has many shapes and forms, and the sex trade is just the thin end of the wedge. Poor parents have been known to rent their children out as beggars, labourers or sellers; many child prostitutes in Cambodia are Vietnamese and have been sold into the business by family back in Vietnam. Once in the trade, it is difficult to escape a life of violence and abuse. Gang rapes and beatings are common experiences for many adult prostitutes, and for a child to be subject to this animalistic behaviour is horrific. Drugs are also being used to keep children dependent on their pimps, with bosses giving out *yama* (a dirty meta-amphetamine) or heroin to dull their senses. All in all, it is the sickest of many sick trades and needs to be stopped immediately.

Visitors can do their bit to fight this menace by keeping an eye out for any suspicious behaviour on the part of foreigners. Don't ignore it – try and pass on any relevant information such as the name and nationality of the individual to the embassy concerned. There is also a **Cambodian hotline** (☎ 023-720555) and a confidential **nongovernmental-organisation (NGO) hotline** (☎ 012 888840) for those with information on sexual abuse or the exploitation of children. **End Child Prostitution and Trafficking** (Ecpat; www.ecpat .org) is a global network aimed at stopping child prostitution, child pornography and the trafficking of children for sexual purposes, and has affiliates in most Western countries.

LEGAL MATTERS

Marijuana is not legal in Cambodia and police are beginning to take a harder line on it, although usually for their own benefit rather than a desire to uphold the law. There have been several busts (and a few set-ups too) of foreigner-owned bars and restaurants where ganja was smoked – the days of free bowls in guesthouses are now in the past. Marijuana is traditionally used in some Khmer food, so it will continue to be around for a long time, but if you are a smoker, be discreet. It's probably only a matter of time before the Cambodian police turn the regular busting of foreigners into a lucrative sideline.

This advice applies equally to other narcotic substances, which are also illegal. And think twice about visiting an opium parlour with an unfamiliar *moto* driver as it may end with you getting robbed after passing out.

MAPS

The best all-rounder for Cambodia is the Gecko *Cambodia Road Map*. At 1:750,000 scale as it has lots of detail and accurate place names. Other popular foldout maps include Nelles *Cambodia, Laos and Vietnam Map* at 1:1,500,000, although the detail is limited, and the Periplus *Cambodia Travel Map* at 1:1,000,000, with city maps of Phnom Penh and Siem Reap.

There are lots of free maps, subsidised by advertising, that are available in Phnom Penh and Siem Reap at leading hotels, guesthouses, restaurants and bars.

For serious map buffs or cartographers, Psar Thmei (New Market) in Phnom Penh is well stocked with Vietnamese and Khmer-produced maps of towns and provinces, as well as US military maps from the 1970s at a scale of 1:50,000. Roads have generally deteriorated rather than improved since the civil war, so much of the information remains accurate more than three decades on.

MONEY

Cambodia's currency is the riel, abbreviated in this guide by a lower-case 'r' written after the sum. Cambodia's second currency (some would say its first) is the US dollar, which is accepted everywhere and by everyone, though change may arrive in riel. Dollar bills with a small tear are unlikely to be accepted by Cambodians, so it's worth scrutinising the

---

YABA DABA DO? YABA DABA DON'T!

Watch out for *yaba*, the 'crazy' drug from Thailand, known rather ominously in Cambodia as *yama* (the Hindu god of death). Known as ice or crystal meth back home, it's not just any old diet pill from the pharmacist, but homemade meta-amphetamines produced in labs in Cambodia and the region beyond. The pills are often laced with toxic substances, such as mercury, lithium or whatever else the maker can find. *Yama* is a dirty drug and more addictive than users would like to admit, provoking powerful hallucinations, sleep deprivation and psychosis. Steer clear of the stuff unless you plan on an indefinite extension to your trip.

Also be very careful about buying 'cocaine'. One look at the map and the distance between Colombia and Cambodia should be enough to make you dubious, but it's much worse than that. Most of what is sold as coke, particularly in Phnom Penh, is actually pure heroin and far stronger than any smack found on the streets back home. Bang this up your hooter and you are in serious trouble – several backpackers die each year in the lakeside guesthouse ghetto of Boeng Kak in Phnom Penh.

---

change you are given to make sure you don't have bad bills. In the west of the country, the Thai baht (B) is also commonplace. If three currencies seems a little excessive, perhaps it's because the Cambodians are making up for lost time: during the Pol Pot era, the country had *no* currency. The Khmer Rouge abolished money and blew up the National Bank building in Phnom Penh.

The sinking fortunes of the riel meant that, until recently, it was hardly worth the paper it was printed on. The government has responded by creating new higher-value denominations, although notes of 20,000r and higher are still a fairly rare sight. The riel comes in notes of the following denominations: 50r, 100r, 200r, 500r, 1000r, 2000r, 5000r, 10,000r, 20,000r, 50,000r and 100,000r.

Throughout this book, prices are in the currency quoted to the average punter. This is usually US dollars or riel, but in the west it is often baht. While this may seem inconsistent, this is the way it's done in Cambodia and the sooner you get used to thinking comparatively in riel, dollars or baht, the easier your travels will be.

For a sprinkling of exchange rates at the time of going to print, see the Quick Reference section in the inside front cover of this book.

ATMs

Hard as it may be to believe, there are still no credit card–compatible ATMs in Cambodia. There are well-founded rumours of ANZ bank entering the market soon and blitzing the country with ATMs, which should make life easier for locals and foreign visitors alike…unless they dispense in riels!

Black Market

The black market no longer exists in Cambodia when it comes to changing money. Exchange rates on the street are the same as those offered by the banks, you just miss out on the queues and paperwork.

Cash

The US dollar remains king in Cambodia. Armed with enough cash, you won't need to visit a bank at all because it is possible to change small amounts of dollars for riel at hotels, restaurants and markets. Hardened travellers argue that your trip ends up being slightly more expensive if you rely on US dollars rather than riel, but in reality there's very little in it. However, it never hurts to support the local currency against the greenback. It is always handy to have about US$10 worth of riel kicking around, as it is good for *motos* (small motorcycles with drivers) and markets. Pay for something cheap in US dollars and the change comes in riel; gradually enough riel will accumulate in your wallet to pay for small items anyway. In remote areas of the north and northeast, locals often prefer riel.

The only other currency that can be useful is Thai baht (in the west of the country). Prices in towns such as Krong Koh Kong, Poipet and Sisophon are often quoted in baht, and even in Battambang it is as common as the dollar.

There are no banks at any of the land border crossings into Cambodia, meaning credit cards and travellers cheques are effectively useless on arrival. In the interests of making life as simple as possible, organise a supply of US dollars before arriving in Cambodia. Cash in other major currencies can be changed at banks or markets in Phnom Penh or Siem Reap. However, most banks tend to offer a miserable rate for any non-dollar transaction so it can be better to use moneychangers, which are found in and around every major market. Even at markets, the rate for other currencies is relatively poor compared with the US dollar.

The Foreign Trade Bank (p76) can arrange transfers and has partner banks in the USA, Europe, Asia and Australia, with relevant addresses and account details helpfully listed on a free handout, available at all branches. Western Union and Moneygram are both now represented in Cambodia for fast, if more expensive, money transfers. Western Union is represented by Acleda Bank and Cambodia Asia Bank, and Moneygram is represented by Canadia Bank.

Credit Cards

Top-end hotels, airline offices and upmarket boutiques and restaurants generally accept most major credit cards (Visa, MasterCard, JCB), but they usually pass the charges straight on to the customer, meaning an extra 3%.

Cash advances on credit cards are available in Phnom Penh, Siem Reap, Sihanoukville, Kampot, Battambang and Kompong Cham. Canadia Bank and Union Commercial Bank offer free cash advances, but most other banks advertise a minimum charge of US$5. Acleda Bank claims to be upgrading its services from 2005 to include cash advances, and it operates the most extensive network of branches in the country.

Several travel agents and hotels in Phnom Penh and Siem Reap arrange cash advances for about 5% commission; this can be particularly useful if you get caught short at the weekend.

Tipping

Tipping is not traditionally expected here, but in a country as poor as Cambodia, tips can go a long way. Salaries remain extremely low and service is often superb thanks to a Khmer commitment to hospitality. Hence a tip of just US$1 might be half a day's wages for some. Many of the upmarket hotels levy a 10% service charge, but this doesn't always make it to the staff. If you stay a couple of nights in the same hotel, try to remember to tip the staff that clean your room. Consider tipping drivers and guides, as the time they spend on the road means time away from home and family.

It is considered proper to make a small donation at the end of a visit to a wat, especially if a monk has shown you around; most wats have contribution boxes for this purpose.

Travellers Cheques

Travellers cheques can be changed at only a limited number of banks in Phnom Penh, Siem Reap, Sihanoukville, Battambang and Kompong Cham. If you are travelling up-country, you should change enough money before you go. It is best to have cheques in US dollars, though it is also possible to change most major currencies at branches of Canadia Bank. Generally, you will pay about 2% commission to change travellers cheques. Acleda Bank claims it will be able to change travellers cheques by the time of publication and it operates the most extensive network of branches in the country.

PHOTOGRAPHY & VIDEO
Airport Security

The X-ray machines at Phnom Penh and Siem Reap airports are film-safe. If you are carrying 1000 ASA or higher film, you should store it separately and ask to have it inspected by hand.

Film & Equipment

Print film and processing is pretty cheap in Cambodia. A roll of Kodak or Fuji film (36 exposures) costs just US$2 for ASA 100 or US$3 for ASA 400. Printing is also cheap with most laboratories charging about US$4 for a roll. The Fuji labs are generally the best quality, but the Konica ones are sometimes a little cheaper.

Slide film is also available at competitive prices in Phnom Penh. It costs US$5 for a roll of Kodak Elite or Fuji Sensia, and US$6 for Fuji's Velvia or Provia range. Purchase as much as you need in Phnom Penh, as it is pretty hard to come by elsewhere in the country. Do not have slide film processed in Cambodia unless it is really urgent. Many shops claim to be able to process slide film,

but you'll more than likely end up with black and white X-ray–style shots.

Most processing shops in Phnom Penh and Siem Reap can also now burn digital images onto CD to free up space on your memory card, as well as print top quality photos straight from your camera or CD. Cheap memory cards are available all over the place.

General camera supplies can be purchased in Phnom Penh. Camera batteries are easy to replace, providing you don't require anything too obscure; don't forget to carry spares if you are heading off the trail. There is a great range of new cameras in the capital at bargain prices, as most come in tax and duty free, including all the leading brands.

Camera film is available all over the city – just pick your brand and there will be a shop within a few hundred metres. The best place for developing photos from film or from digital is **City Colour Photo** (Map pp78-9; 123 Monivong Blvd), which also stocks cheap cameras and memory sticks.

If you carry a video camera, make sure you have the necessary charger, plugs and transformer for Cambodia. Take care with some of the electrical wiring in guesthouses around the country, as it can be pretty amateurish. In Phnom Penh and Siem Reap, it is possible to obtain video tapes for most formats, but elsewhere around the country you are unlikely to find much of use. It is often worth buying a few tapes duty-free before you start your trip.

Photographing People

The usual rules apply: be polite about photographing and video taping people; don't push cameras into their faces; and have some respect for monks and people at prayer. It shouldn't be necessary to say this, but unfortunately there are a lot of amateur photographers out there who think that they're on assignment for *National Geographic*. In general, the Khmers are remarkably courteous people and if you ask nicely, they'll agree to have their photograph taken. The same goes for video taping – ask permission first, although in rural areas you will often find children desperate to get in front of the lens and astonished at seeing themselves played back on a LCD screen. It is the closest most of them will get to being on TV.

DIRECTORY

Restrictions

Although the Cambodian armed forces don't seem too concerned about foreigners photographing bridges and so on (most of these were built by foreigners using foreign aid anyway), it would still be sensible to exercise some restraint. Charging up to an armed convoy and snapping away might result in unpleasant consequences.

Technical Tips

The best light conditions in Cambodia begin around 20 minutes after sunrise and last for just one to two hours, roughly corresponding to 6am to 8am. The same applies for the late afternoon light, which begins to assume a radiant warm quality around an hour before sunset. From 10am to around 4pm you can expect the light to be harsh and bleaching – there's not much you can do with it unless you have a polariser. Bear in mind that you have much more leeway with exposures in print film than you do in slide film. Snaps taken in poor light conditions often turn out OK in the printing process; with slides you either get it right or you don't. For endless tips on better travel photography, pick up a copy of Lonely Planet's *Travel Photography*.

POST

Post is now routed by air through Bangkok and other regional centres, which makes Cambodian post faster now than it used to be when parcels went via Moscow. But Cambodia is by no means a more reliable, place from which to send mail and parcels.

The postal service is very hit and miss from Cambodia; send anything valuable by courier or from another country. Make sure postcards and letters are franked before they vanish from your sight.

Postal rates are listed in post offices in the major towns and cities. Postcards cost 1500r to 2100r to send internationally. Letters and parcels sent farther afield than Asia can take up to two or three weeks to reach their destination. Use a courier to speed things up: **DHL** (Map pp74-5; ☎ 023-427726; www.dhl.com; 28 Monivong Blvd), **FedEx** (Map pp74-5; ☎ 023-216712; www.fedex.com; 701D Monivong Blvd), **TNT** (Map pp78-9; ☎ 023-211880; www.tnt.com; 151 Ph 154) and **UPS** (Map pp78-9; ☎ 023-427511; www.ups.com; 27 Ph 134). All have offices in Phnom Penh and some have branch offices in Siem Reap

(p115). A slightly cheaper courier option is **EMS** (Map pp78-9; ☎ 023-723511; Main Post Office, Ph 13), with offices at every major post office in the country.

Phnom Penh's main post office (p77) has a poste restante box at the far-left end of the post counter. Basically anybody can pick up your mail, so it's not a good idea to have anything valuable sent there. It costs 100r per item received. Long-term travellers are better off getting their stuff sent to Bangkok.

SHOPPING

There is some excellent shopping to be had in Cambodia, particularly in Phnom Penh (p103) and Siem Reap (p129). As well as the inevitable range of souvenirs, there are many high-quality handicrafts made to support disadvantaged groups in Cambodia.

Antiques

Cambodia has a reasonable range of antiques, although a lot disappeared or was destroyed during the war years. Popular items include textiles, silver, swords, coins, ceramics and furniture, but when buying antiques be very careful of fakes – they are extremely common in this part of the world. If the prices seem too good to be true, then they usually are and you'll end up with a well-aged, modern copy. This is particularly the case with 'old' bronzes from 'the time of Angkor' and a lot of 'ancient' Chinese pieces. It is important to remember that ancient sandstone carvings from the Angkorian or pre-Angkorian periods cannot legally be taken out of the country.

For those coming to settle in Cambodia for any length of time, there are some very nice pieces of antique furniture available in markets and shops in Phnom Penh (p103), with Chinese, French and Khmer influences all evident.

Bargaining

It is important to haggle over purchases made in local markets in Phnom Penh (p104) and Siem Reap (p129), otherwise the stallholder may 'shave your head', the local vernacular for 'rip you off'. Bargaining is the rule in markets, when arranging share taxis and pick-ups and in cheaper guesthouses. The Khmers are not ruthless hagglers, so care should be taken to not come on too strong. A persuasive smile and a little friendly quibbling is usually enough to get a good price. Try to remember that the aim is not to get the lowest possible price, but a price that is acceptable to both you and the seller. Remember back home, we pay astronomical sums for items, especially clothes, that have been made in poorer countries for next to nothing, and we don't even get the chance to bargain for them, just the opportunity to contribute to a corporate director's retirement fund. At least there is room for discussion in Cambodia, so try not to abuse the situation. And remember, in many cases a few hundred riel is more important to a Cambodian with a family to support than to a traveller on an extended vacation. After all, no-one bargains over a beer in a busy backpacker bar, so why bargain so hard over a cheap bottle of water?

Artwork

The choice of art was, until recently, limited to the poor-quality Angkor paintings seen throughout the country. However, the selection is improving in Phnom Penh and Siem Reap. Psar Chaa (p130) in Siem Reap and the art shops on Ph 178 in Phnom Penh (p103) are good hunting grounds, and there are a number of upmarket galleries in hotels in the capital.

Clothing

Many international brands are made in factories around Phnom Penh, including Colombia, Gap, Levis and Quiksilver; there is a lot of leakage, with items turning up in Psar Tuol Tom Pong (p104) in Phnom Penh at very reasonable prices.

Sculpture

The beauty and intricacy of Cambodian sculpture is evident for all to see around the temples of Angkor (p134) and in the National Museum (p81) in Phnom Penh. There are many skilled stone carvers within Cambodia today, and replica sculpture is widely available in Phnom Penh and Siem Reap. Popular items include busts of Jayavarman VII and statues of Hindu deities such as Shiva, Vishnu and Harihara. Do not attempt to buy ancient stone sculpture in Cambodia: looting is a huge problem in remote parts of the country and it would be grossly irresponsible for any visitor to add to the problem.

Silk & Textiles

Cambodia is world renowned for its exquisite silk, much of which is still traditionally hand-woven and dyed using natural colours from plants and minerals. The best silk comes from Kompong Cham and Takeo Provinces, but not all the silk sold in Cambodia originates here (some is imported from China and Vietnam). Concerted efforts are underway to reintroduce mulberry trees and locally cultivated silk across the country. There are silk farms in Siem Reap and some of the other provincial centres renowned for silk. Some of the best places to buy silk include Artisans d'Angkor (p118) in Siem Reap, which also operates branches at the international airports, at recommended shops in Phnom Penh and Siem Reap that support disabled and impoverished Cambodians, and at Psar Tuol Tom Pong (p104) in Phnom Penh. In the provinces, there are several high quality silk operations, including Mekong Blue (p257) in Stung Treng and Joom Noon (p229) in Tbeng Meanchey.

Silver

Cambodian silver is valued overseas for the detail of hand-carving on most of the pieces. However, not all silver has that much silver content, so it is important to be careful what you buy. Cambodian silver ranges from copies with no silver, to 50% silver alloy, right up to pure silver. Reputable establishments will often tell you the purity of their silver, but market sellers might try to pull a fast one. The easiest way for novices to determine the quality is to feel the weight. Pure silver should be heavier than alloys or plate.

Woodcarving

Woodcarving is a rich tradition in Cambodia and there are many wooden items that make nice decorative pieces. Reproduction Buddhas are very popular with visitors and there is no restriction on taking Buddha images out of the country. There are also wooden copies available of most of the principal Angkorian sculptures, as well as finely carved animals. Weaving wheels are quite popular and are often elaborately decorated, making nice wall mounts. Betel nut boxes are plentiful, as are jewellery boxes inlaid with mother of pearl, lacquer or metalwork.

TELEPHONE & FAX

Cambodia's land-line system was totally devastated by the long civil war, leaving the country with a poor communications infrastructure. The advent of mobile phones has allowed Cambodia to catch up with its regional neighbours by jumping headlong into the technology revolution. Mobile phones are everywhere in Cambodia, but landline access in major towns is also improving, connecting more of the country to the outside world than ever before.

Domestic Calls

Local calls are usually pretty cheap, even from hotel rooms. Calling from province to province is considerably more expensive by fixed lines. The easiest way to call in most urban areas is to head to one of the many small private booths on the kerbside, usually plastered with numbers like 012 and 016 and prices like 300r. Operators have a selection of mobile phones and leased lines to ensure that any domestic number you want to call is cheap. Local phone calls can also be made on the MPTC and Camintel public payphones, which are sometimes still seen in places like Phnom Penh, Siem Reap,

Sihanoukville and Kompong Cham. It can sometimes be difficult to get through to numbers outside Phnom Penh, and there is no directory inquiries service. Some hotels have telephone directories for the capital if you need to track down a number. Try to find a copy of the **Yellow Pages** (www.yellow pages.com.kh) which has a pretty comprehensive coverage of businesses, services and government offices.

Fax

Sending faxes is getting cheaper as telephone charges drop. The cheapest fax services are those via the Internet; these can be arranged at Internet cafés for around US$1 to US$2 a page. Some of the more popular midrange hotels have reliable business centres, but be aware that Cambodia's top-end hotels have expensive business centres where sending a fax will cost three times the price charged elsewhere.

International Calls

There is now a whole lot more choice when it comes to calling overseas than in the bad old days of all calls going via Moscow. There are several telephone cards available for cardphones, several prepaid calling cards for use from any telephone, private booths run from mobile phones and the growing world of Internet phone calls. Calling from hotels attracts a surcharge and the more expensive the hotel, the heftier the hit. As a general rule, whichever way you choose to ring, it is a little cheaper to make a call at weekends.

The cheapest way to call internationally is via Internet phone. Most of the shops and cafés around the country providing Internet services also offer Internet calls. Calls usually cost between 200r and 2000r per minute, depending on the destination. Calling the USA and Europe is generally the cheapest, but there is a hefty surcharge for connecting to mobile numbers. While the price is undoubtedly right, the major drawback is that there is often a significant delay on the phone, making for a conversation of many 'hellos?' and 'pardons?'

It is straightforward to place an international call from Ministry of Post & Telecommunications (MPTC) or Camintel phone booths. Purchase a phonecard, which in larger cities can be bought at hotels, restaurants, post offices and many

DOMESTIC TELEPHONE AREA CODES	
Banteay Meanchey Province	☎ 054
Battambang Province	☎ 053
Kampot Province	☎ 033
Kandal Province	☎ 024
Kep Province	☎ 036
Koh Kong Province	☎ 035
Kompong Cham Province	☎ 042
Kompong Chhnang Province	☎ 026
Kompong Speu Province	☎ 025
Kompong Thom Province	☎ 062
Kratie Province	☎ 072
Mondulkiri Province	☎ 073
Oddar Meanchey Province	☎ 065
Phnom Penh	☎ 023
Preah Vihear Province	☎ 064
Prey Veng Province	☎ 043
Pursat Province	☎ 052
Ratanakiri Province	☎ 075
Siem Reap Province	☎ 063
Sihanoukville Province	☎ 034
Stung Treng Province	☎ 074
Svay Rieng Province	☎ 044
Takeo Province	☎ 032

shops. Phonecards come in denominations of US$5 to US$50.

Before inserting the card into a public phone, always check that there is a readout on the liquid crystal display (LCD) unit. If there isn't, it probably means the phone is broken or there is a power cut – inserting the card at these times can wipe the value off the card.

If dialling from a mobile or using card-phones, instead of using the original international access code of ☎ 001, try ☎ 007, which works out cheaper. The name is not Bond, but Tele2, a private operator that has recently set up shop in Cambodia.

Making calls from Battambang and the west of Cambodia is cheaper and the lines are clearer than in other parts of the country, as the lines are plugged into the Thailand network. Calls to Thailand are only 10B a minute and calls to the rest of the world work out at about US$2 a minute or less.

Mobile Phones

Telephone numbers starting with ☎ 011, 012 or 016 are mobile phone numbers. If you are travelling with a mobile phone on international roaming, just select a network upon arrival, dial away and await a hefty phone bill once you return home. Note: Cambodian roaming charges are extraordinarily high.

Those who are planning on spending longer in Cambodia will want to hook up with a local network. Those with their own phone need only purchase a SIM card for one of the local service providers, but if you are travelling with a locked phone linked to your network back home, then you can't switch SIM cards. However, mobile phones are very cheap in Cambodia and second-hand ones are widely available. Most of the local companies offer fixed-contract deals with monthly bills, or pay-as-you-go cards for those who want flexibility. All offer regular promotions, so it is worth shopping around. Local companies based in Phnom Penh include the following:

Camshin (Map pp74–5; ☎ 023-367801; www.camshin .com; 66 Mao Tse Toung Blvd)

Mobitel (Map pp78–9; ☎ 012 800800; www.mobitel .com.kh; 33 Sihanouk Blvd)

Samart (Map pp78–9; ☎ 016 810001; www.hellogsm .com.kh; 58 Norodom Blvd)

TIME

Cambodia, like Laos, Vietnam and Thailand, is seven hours ahead of Greenwich Mean Time or Universal Time Coordinated (GMT/UTC). When it is midday in Cambodia it is 10pm the previous evening in San Francisco, 1am in New York, 5am in London, 6am in Paris and 3pm in Sydney.

TOILETS

Although the occasional squat toilet turns up here and there, particularly in the most budget of budget guesthouses, in general, Cambodian toilets are of the sit-down variety. If you end up in the sticks, you will find that hygiene conditions deteriorate somewhat, but rural Cambodian bathrooms are often in a better state than those in rural China or India.

The issue of toilets and what to do with used toilet paper is a cause for concern. Generally, if there's a wastepaper basket next to the toilet, that is where the toilet paper goes, as many sewage systems cannot handle toilet paper. Toilet paper is seldom provided in the toilets at bus and train stations or in other public buildings, so keep a stash with you at all times.

Public toilets are rare, the only ones in the country being along Phnom Penh's riverfront and some beautiful wooden structures dotted about the temples of Angkor. The charge is usually 500r for a public toilet, although they are free at Angkor. Most local restaurants have some sort of toilet; pay 500r if you are not eating or drinking anything.

Should you find nature calling in rural areas, don't let modesty drive you into the bushes: *there may be land mines not far from the road or track*. Stay on the roadside and do the deed, or grin and bear it until the next town.

TOURIST INFORMATION

Cambodia has only a handful of tourist offices, and those encountered by the independent traveller in Phnom Penh and Siem Reap are generally unhelpful unless you look like you're going to spend money. However, in the provinces it is a different story, as the staff are often shocked and excited to see visitors. They may have to drag the director out of a nearby karaoke bar, even at 10am, but once it is made clear that you are a genuine tourist, they will usually

DIRECTORY

tell you everything there is to know about places of interest. More and more towns are ambitiously opening tourist offices, but they generally have little in the way of brochures or handouts. You'll find some tourist offices listed in the relevant destination sections in this book, but lower your expectations compared with regional powerhouses like Malaysia and Singapore. Generally guesthouses and free local magazines are much more useful than tourist offices.

Cambodia has no official tourist offices abroad and it is unlikely that Cambodian embassies will be of much assistance in planning a trip, besides issuing a visa.

VISAS

Most nationalities receive a one-month visa on arrival at Phnom Penh and Siem Reap international airports. The cost is US$20 for a tourist visa and US$25 for a business visa. One passport photo is required and you'll be 'fined' US$1 to 100B if you don't have one. Those seeking work in Cambodia should opt for the business visa as, officially, it is easily extended for long periods and, unofficially, can be extended indefinitely, including multiple entries and exits. A tourist visa can be extended only once and only for one month, and does not allow for re-entry.

Visas are now available at most of the land borders. Entering from Thailand, visas are available on arrival at the land crossings at Anlong Veng, Krong Koh Kong, O Smach, Pailin and Poipet. Travellers planning a day trip to Prasat Preah Vihear from Thailand do not require visas, but may be asked to leave their passport on the Thai side of the border to ensure they don't continue on into Cambodia. Travellers are sometimes overcharged when crossing at land borders with Thailand, as immigration officials demand payment in baht and round up the figure considerably. Arranging a visa in advance in Bangkok avoids this potential problem.

Travellers arriving overland from Vietnam can get a visa on arrival at the popular Bavet and Kaam Samnor crossings on NH1 and the Mekong River respectively. However, if crossing by the obscure border at Phnom Den, arrange a visa in advance in Hanoi or Ho Chi Minh City.

The land border with Laos is now an established crossing, but it is still necessary to arrange a Cambodian visa in advance. This can be done in Bangkok or Vientiane.

Overstaying your visa currently costs a whopping US$5 a day.

Visa Extensions

Visa extensions are issued by a new immigration office located directly across the road from Phnom Penh International Airport (p106). Tourist visas can be extended only once for one month, whereas business visas can be extended indefinitely, as long as you come with a bulging wallet. You can probably even arrange citizenship if you bring enough greenbacks.

There are two ways of getting an extension – one official and one unofficial – and unsurprisingly the time and money involved differ greatly. Officially, a one-month extension costs US$30, three months US$60, six months US$100, and one year US$150; using the official route your passport will be held for 25 days and there will be more paperwork than a communist bureaucrat could dream up. This is fine for expatriates with an employer to make the arrangements, but those on their own really need to go unofficial. They don't call it corruption in Cambodia but 'under the table', and you can have your passport back the next day for inflated prices of US$39 for one month, US$69 for three months, US$145 for six months and US$275 for one year. Once you are one of the 'unofficials', it is pretty straightforward to extend the visa ad infinitum. Recommended travel agencies and some motorbike rental shops in Phnom Penh can help with arrangements, sometimes at a discounted price.

One passport photograph is required for visa extensions and there is a US$1 charge for the application form.

WOMEN TRAVELLERS

Women will generally find Cambodia a hassle-free place to travel, although some of the guys in the guesthouse industry will try their luck from time to time. Foreign women are unlikely to be targeted by local men, but at the same time it pays to be careful. As is the case anywhere in the world, walking or riding a bike alone late at night is risky, and if you're planning a trip off the beaten trail it would be best to find a travel companion.

Despite the prevalence of sex workers and women's employment as 'beer girls', dancing companions and the like, foreign women will probably find Khmer men to be courteous and polite. It's best to keep things this way by being restrained in your dress; flaunting a pierced belly button is likely to get the blood racing among Khmer males. Khmer women dress fairly conservatively, and it's best to follow suit, particularly when visiting wats. In general, long-sleeved shirts and long trousers or skirts are preferred. It is also worth having trousers for heading out at night on *motos*, as short skirts aren't too practical.

Tampons and sanitary napkins are widely available in the major cities and provincial capitals, but if you are heading into very remote areas for a few days, it is worth having your own supply.

WORK

Jobs are available throughout Cambodia, but apart from English teaching or helping out in guesthouses, bars or restaurants, most are for professionals and arranged in advance. There is a lot of teaching work available for English-language speakers, although the salary is directly linked to experience. Anyone with an English-language teaching certificate can earn considerably more than those with no qualifications.

For information about work opportunities with NGOs call into the CCC (right), which has a notice board for positions vacant and may also be able to give advice on where to look. If you are thinking of applying for work with NGOs, you should bring copies of your education certificates and work references. However, most of the jobs available are likely to be on a voluntary basis, as most recruiting for specialised positions is done in home countries or through international organisations.

Other places to look for work include the classifieds sections of the *Phnom Penh Post* and the *Cambodia Daily*, and on the notice board at the FCC (p98) in Phnom Penh.

Do not expect to make a lot of money working in Cambodia, but if you want to learn more about the country and help the locals improve their standard of living, it can be a very worthwhile experience.

Volunteering

There are fewer opportunities for volunteering than one might imagine in a country as impoverished as Cambodia. This is partly due to the sheer number of professional development workers based here, and development is a pretty lucrative industry these days.

Cambodia hosts a huge number of NGOs, some of whom do require volunteers from time to time. The best way to find out who exactly is represented in the country is to drop in on the **Cooperation Committee for Cambodia** (CCC; Map pp78-9; ☎ 023-214152; 35 Ph 178) in Phnom Penh. This organisation has a handy list of all NGOs, both Cambodian and international, and is extremely helpful.

One organisation that does encourage volunteers is the **Starfish Project** (www.starfishcambodia.org) based at the Starfish Bakery (p192) in Sihanoukville. Other places that can readily benefit from volunteers are the orphanages in Phnom Penh, Siem Reap and other towns in Cambodia, as some of these are in a very rundown condition. Even just stopping by can brighten up the children's day.

The other avenue is professional volunteering through an organisation back home that offers one- or two-year placements in Cambodia. One of the largest is **Voluntary Service Overseas** (VSO; www.vso.org.uk) in the UK, but other countries have their own organisations, including **Australian Volunteers International** (AVI; www.australianvolunteers.com) and **Volunteer Service Abroad** (VSA; www.vsa.org.nz). The UN also operates its own volunteer programme; details are available at www.unv.org. Other general volunteer sites with links all over the place include www.worldvolunteerweb.com and www.volunteerabroad.com.

Transport

CONTENTS

GETTING THERE & AWAY

ENTERING THE COUNTRY

Cambodia has two international gateways for arrival by air, Phnom Penh and Siem Reap, and a healthy selection of land borders with neighbouring Thailand, Vietnam and Laos. Formalities at Cambodia's international airports are traditionally smoother than at land borders, as the volume of traffic is greater. Crossing at land borders is relatively easy, but immigration officers may try and wangle some extra cash, either for your visa or via some other scam. Stand your ground. Anyone without a photo for their visa form will be charged about US$1 at the airport, and as much as 100B at land borders with Thailand.

Arrival by air is popular for those on a short holiday in Cambodia, as travelling overland to or from Cambodia puts a significant dent in your time in the country. Travellers on longer trips usually enter and exit by land, as road and river transport is very cheap in Cambodia.

Passport

Not only is a passport essential but you also need to make sure that it's valid for at least

THINGS CHANGE!

The information in this chapter is particularly vulnerable to change: prices for international travel are volatile, routes are introduced and cancelled, schedules change, special deals come and go, and rules and visa requirements are amended. You should check directly with your airline or a travel agent to make sure you understand how a fare (and ticket you may buy) works, and be aware of the security requirements for international travel.

The upshot of this is that you should get opinions, quotes and advice from as many airlines and travel agents as possible before you spend your hard-earned cash. The details given in this chapter should be regarded as pointers and are not a substitute for your own careful and up-to-date research.

six months beyond the *end* of your trip – Cambodian immigration will not issue a visa if you have less than six months' validity left on your passport.

It's also important to make sure that there is plenty of space left in your passport. Do not set off on a six-month trek across Asia with only two blank pages left – a Cambodian visa alone takes up one page. It is sometimes possible to have extra pages added to your passport, but most people will be required to get a new passport. This is possible for most foreign nationals in Cambodia, but it can be time consuming and costly, as many embassies process new passports in Bangkok.

Losing a passport is not the end of the world, but it is a serious inconvenience. To expedite the issuing of a new passport, keep a copy of your passport details somewhere separate from your passport.

For the story on visas, see p286.

AIR
Airports & Airlines
Phnom Penh International Airport (PNH; ☎ 023-890520; www.cambodia-airports.com/phnompenh/en) is the gateway to the Cambodian capital,

while **Siem Reap International Airport** (REP; ☎ 063-380283; www.cambodia-airports.com/siemreap /en) serves visitors to the temples of Angkor. Cambodia has an open-skies policy, which means any airline can fly into and out of the country. This fact is encouraging more and more airlines to offer flights to Siem Reap.

Flights to Cambodia are quite limited, pricey for the short distances involved and most link with neighbouring capitals. Bangkok has the most flights to Cambodia, and it is usually possible to get on a flight with any of the airlines at short notice, although flying Bangkok Airways to Siem Reap can get very busy from November to March. If you are heading to Cambodia for a short holiday and want a minimum of fuss, Thai Airways offers the easiest connections from major cities in Europe, the USA and Australia. Singapore Airlines' regional wing, Silk Air, is another good option, with at least one flight a day connecting Cambodia to Singapore. Other regional centres with flights to Cambodia are Ho Chi Minh City (Saigon), Vientiane, Kuala Lumpur, Hong Kong, Guangzhou and Shanghai.

Airlines in Cambodia tend to open up and close down regularly. This means that those who have the choice should enter the country on an international carrier such as Bangkok Airways, Silk Air, Thai Airways or Vietnam Airlines rather than a local carrier.

AIRLINES FLYING TO/FROM CAMBODIA

Air France (Map pp78-9; ☎ 219220; www.airfrance .com; Hong Kong Center, Samdech Sothearos Blvd, Phnom Penh) Airline code AF, hub city Paris.

Bangkok Airways (Map pp78-9; ☎ 023-426624; www .bangkokair.com; 61 Ph 214, Phnom Penh) Airline code PG, hub city Bangkok.

China Southern Airlines (Map pp74-5; ☎ 023-430877; www.cs-air.com; Phnom Penh Hotel, 53 Monivong Blvd, Phnom Penh) Airline code CZ, hub city Guangzhou.

Dragonair (Map pp74-5; ☎ 023-424300; www.dragon air.com; A4 Regency Sq, Intercontinental Hotel, cnr Mao Tse Toung & Monireth Blvds, Phnom Penh) Airline code KA, hub city Hong Kong.

First Cambodia Airlines (Map pp78-9; ☎ 023-221666; 107 Norodom Blvd, Phnom Penh) Airline code F6, hub city Phnom Penh.

Lao Airlines (Map pp78-9; ☎ 023-216563; www .laoairlines.com; 58 Sihanouk Blvd, Phnom Penh) Airline code QV, hub city Vientiane.

Malaysia Airlines (Map pp78-9; ☎ 023-426688; www .malaysiaairlines.com; Diamond Hotel, 172 Monivong Blvd, Phnom Penh) Airline code MY, hub city Kuala Lumpur.

President Airlines (Map pp74-5; ☎ 023-993088; A14 Regency Sq, Intercontinental Hotel, cnr Mao Tse Toung & Monireth Blvds, Phnom Penh) Airline code TO, hub city Phnom Penh. Represents EVA Air in Cambodia.

Royal Phnom Penh Airways (Map pp78-9; ☎ 023-990564; 209 Ph 19, Phnom Penh) Airline code RL, hub city Phnom Penh.

Shanghai Airlines (Map pp78-9; ☎ 023-723999; www .shanghai-air.com; 19 Ph 106, Phnom Penh) Airline code FM, hub city Shanghai.

Siem Reap Airways (Map pp78-9; ☎ 023-723963; 61 Ph 214, Phnom Penh) Airline code FT, hub city Phnom Penh.

Silk Air (Map pp74-5; ☎ 023-426807; www.silkair.com; Himawari, 313 Sisowath Quay, Phnom Penh) Airline code MI, hub city Singapore.

Thai Airways (Map pp74-5; ☎ 023-890292; www .thaiair.com; A15 Regency Sq, Intercontinental Hotel, cnr Mao Tse Toung & Monireth Blvds, Phnom Penh) Airline code TG, hub city Bangkok.

Vietnam Airlines (Map pp78-9; ☎ 023-363396; www .vietnamairlines.com; 41 Ph 214, Phnom Penh) Airline code VN, hub cities Hanoi and Ho Chi Minh City.

Tickets

When buying airline tickets, it is always worth shopping around. Buying direct from the airline is usually more expensive, unless the airline has a special promotion. As a rule, it is better to book as early as possible, as prices only get higher as the seats fill up.

The time of year you travel has a major impact on flight prices. If you are starting out from Europe, North America or Australia, figure on prices rising dramatically over Christmas and between July and August, and dropping significantly during lax periods of business like February, June and October.

Thailand is the most convenient gateway to Cambodia when travelling from outside the region. In Bangkok, the Banglamphu area, especially Khao San Rd, is a good place to buy tickets to Cambodia. Those who are travelling into Cambodia by air through Vietnam can easily pick up tickets in Ho Chi Minh City.

When buying tickets in Cambodia, the biggest agents are in Phnom Penh (p77), although many now operate branch offices in Siem Reap. Agents can normally save you a few dollars on the airline price, much more for long-haul flights or business class seats.

TRANSPORT

TRANSPORT

INTERNATIONAL DEPARTURE TAX

There is a departure tax of US$25, payable by cash or credit card, on all international flights out of Phnom Penh International Airport and Siem Reap International Airport.

Asia

All travellers heading to Cambodia by air will have to either pass through or fly from one of the regional air centres. Bangkok is the most likely option, but Ho Chi Minh City, Hanoi, Kuala Lumpur, Singapore and Hong Kong are also popular.

CHINA

China Southern Airlines has flights between Phnom Penh and Guangzhou in southern China (US$260/370 one way/return). Shanghai Airlines has flights connecting Phnom Penh with Shanghai (US$300/395 one way/return). Both airlines offer onward connections throughout China.

HONG KONG

Dragonair and First Cambodia Airlines connect Hong Kong and Phnom Penh (US$240/450 one way/return), and Dragonair has good onward connections to mainland China.

LAOS

Lao Airlines (US$150/250 one way/return) and Vietnam Airlines (US$155/310 one way/return) connect Phnom Penh and Vientiane, with an onward service to Hanoi. Lao Airlines also offers flights from Phnom Penh (US$78/149 one way/return) and Siem Reap (US$68/130 one way/return) to Pakse in southern Laos, sometimes continuing to Vientiane. Siem Reap Airways now offers several flights a week between Luang Prabang and Siem Reap.

MALAYSIA

Malaysia Airlines and First Cambodia Airlines fly between Kuala Lumpur and Phnom Penh (US$205/330 one way/return). Malaysia Airlines also offers services to Siem Reap from Kuala Lumpur.

SINGAPORE

Silk Air connects Singapore with Phnom Penh and Siem Reap (US$260/420 one way/return). First Cambodia Airlines also serves the Singapore to Phnom Penh route.

TAIWAN

EVA Air (www.evaair.com) has flights between Phnom Penh and Taipei (US$232/390 one way/return).

THAILAND

Flights between Phnom Penh and Bangkok (US$120 to US$35 one way, US$170 to US$240 return) operate daily with Thai Airways, Bangkok Airways and President Airlines.

Bangkok Airways also offers daily flights between Siem Reap and Bangkok (US$140/280 one way/return), from Siem Reap to Phuket (US$205/410 one way/return) and from Siem Reap to Ko Samui (US$230/460 one way/return), via Bangkok.

VIETNAM

Vietnam Airlines does the short hop between Ho Chi Minh City and Phnom Penh (US$75/130 one way/return) and also offers flights from the Cambodian capital to Hanoi (US$185/360 one way/return) via Ho Chi Minh City or Vientiane (in Laos).

Vietnam Airlines also offers daily flights between Siem Reap and both Hanoi and Ho Chi Minh City.

Australia

Fares between Australia and Asia are relatively expensive considering the distances involved. All flights between Australia and Cambodia involve stopovers in Bangkok, Kuala Lumpur or Singapore. Vietnam Airlines sometimes offers cut-price deals via Ho Chi Minh City.

There are usually peak and off-peak rates for flights from Australia to Southeast Asia. The peak season is December to January. Flights are often heavily booked at this time, as well as more expensive.

Good places to pick up tickets in Australia include the following:

Flight Centre (☎ 133 133; www.flightcentre.com.au)
STA Travel (☎ 1300 733 035; www.statravel.com.au)

Canada

Discount tickets from Canada tend to cost about 10% more than those sold in the USA. From the Canada's western side, the best deals are available via Hong Kong or

Bangkok. From the eastern side, it may be cheaper to go through London. For the lowdown on cheap fares, contact **Travel Cuts** (☎ 800-667-2887; www.travelcuts.com).

Continental Europe
Although London is the discount travel capital of Europe, major airlines and big travel agents usually have offers from all the major cities on the continent.

Recommended agents include:

Airfair (☎ 020 620 5121; www.airfair.nl) Operating from the Netherlands.

Barcelo Viajes (☎ 902 116 226; www.barceloviajes.com) Operates within Spain.

CTS Viaggi (☎ 06 462 0431; www.cts.it) This is an Italian outfit.

Just Travel (☎ 089 747 3330; www.justtravel.de) Says it is 'your English-language travel agent in Germany'.

Nouvelles Frontières (☎ 0825 000 747; www.nouvelles -frontieres.fr) This agency operates from France.

OTU Voyages (www.otu.fr) This French agency specialises in student and youth travellers.

STA Travel (☎ 01805 456 422; www.statravel.com) STA has branches in cities throughout Europe.

Voyageurs du Monde (☎ 01 40 15 11 15; www.vdm .com) Another French outfit.

New Zealand
The best way to get from New Zealand to Cambodia is to use one of the leading Asian carriers like Malaysia Airlines, Singapore Airlines or Thai Airways. Good agencies to start shopping around for tickets:

Flight Centre (☎ 0800 243 544; www.flightcentre.co.nz)

STA Travel (☎ 0508 782 872; www.statravel.co.nz)

UK & Ireland
Discount air travel is big business in London and there are some great fares to Asia, although the prices through to Cambodia are nowhere near as cheap as are those to Bangkok or Hong Kong. Many of the cheapest fares from London to Bangkok are with carriers from the Middle East, with long stopovers en route. Eva Air often has the cheapest direct flights to Bangkok, although look out for low season specials right through to Cambodia, particularly with Singapore Airlines and their regional wing, Silk Air.

There are oodles of agencies in the UK.

Flightbookers (☎ 0870 010 7000; www.ebookers.com)

North-South Travel (☎ 0124 560 8291; www.north southtravel.co.uk) North-South Travel donates part of its profit to projects in the developing world.

STA Travel (☎ 0870 160 0599; www.statravel.co.uk)

Trailfinders (☎ 0845 058 5858; www.trailfinders.co.uk)

Travel Bag (☎ 0870 890 1456; www.travelbag.co.uk)

USA
Discount travel agents in the USA are known as consolidators, although you won't see a sign on the door saying 'Consolidator'. San Francisco is the ticket-consolidator capital of America, although some good deals can be found in Los Angeles, New York and other big cities. Hong Kong is a handy gateway for those coming from the west coast, although many of the cheaper flights end up passing through Bangkok. Singapore Airlines and Thai Airways both now offer non-stop services to New York. Otherwise you can go via the west coast or via Europe.

Useful online options in the USA include the following:

American Express Travel (www.itn.net)

CheapTickets (www.cheaptickets.com)

Lowest Fare (www.lowestfare.com)

STA Travel (www.sta.com)

Travelocity (www.travelocity.com)

LAND
For years overland travellers were restricted to entering or exiting Cambodia at the Bavet–Moc Bai border crossing with Vietnam. However, several new land crossings between Cambodia and its neighbours have opened. There are now land crossings with Laos, Thailand and Vietnam.

Bus
It is possible to use buses to cross into Cambodia from Thailand or Vietnam. The most popular way to/from Vietnam is a cheap tourist shuttle via Bavet on the Cambodian side and Moc Bai in Vietnam. From Thailand, many travellers take the nightmare 'scam bus' (p294) from Bangkok to Siem Reap via the Poipet–Aranya Prathet border crossing.

Car & Motorcycle
Car drivers and motorcycle riders will need registration papers, insurance documents and an International Driving Licence to bring vehicles into Cambodia. It is complicated to bring in a car, but relatively straightforward to bring in a motorcycle, as long as you have a *carnet de passage* (vehicle passport). This acts as a temporary import-duty waiver and should save a lot of hassles when dealing

with Cambodian customs. Increasing numbers of international bikers are crossing into Cambodia, while most of the foreign cars that tend to make it are Thai-registered.

River

There is a river border crossing between Cambodia and Vietnam on the banks of the Mekong. There are regular passenger boats plying the route between Phnom Penh and Chau Doc in Vietnam, via the Kaam Samnor–Vinh Xuong border crossing. There is also a luxury fast boat service operated by **Victoria Hotels** (www.victoriahotels-asia.com), and two river boats running all the way to the temples of Angkor in Cambodia, operated by **Pandaw Cruises** (www.pandaw.com). Both services use the Kaam Samnor–Vinh Xuong border crossing.

Border Crossings

Cambodia shares one border crossing with Laos, five crossings with Thailand and three with Vietnam. Visas are now available at all the land crossings with Thailand and two of those with Vietnam, but not at the land crossing with Laos.

There are very few money-changing facilities at any of these crossings, so be sure to have some small-denomination US dollars handy. The black market is also an option for local currencies – Vietnamese dong, Lao kip and Thai baht. Remember that black marketeers have a well-deserved reputation for short-changing and outright theft.

Cambodian immigration officers at the land border crossings have a bad reputation for petty extortion. Travellers are occasionally asked for an 'immigration fee' of some kind, particularly when entering or exiting via the Lao border. Other scams include overcharging for the visa in Thai baht (anywhere between 1000B and 13,000B) and forcing tourists to change US dollars into riel at a poor rate. Hold your breath, stand your ground, don't start a fight and remember that not all Cambodians are as mercenary as the men in blue.

Senior government officials in Phnom Penh are trying to crackdown on overcharging for visas and general petty extortion at the borders as it gives Cambodia a bad image. In order to help bring an end to this, we suggest you ask for the name of any official demanding extra money at the

---

BORDER CROSSINGS

Laos
- Dom Kralor–Voen Kham

Thailand
- Cham Yeam–Hat Lek
- Choam–Choam Srawngam
- O Smach–Chong Jom
- Poipet–Aranya Prathet
- Pruhm–Daun Lem

Vietnam
- Bavet–Moc Bai
- Kaam Samnor–Vinh Xuong
- Phnom Den–Tinh Bien

---

border and mention you will pass it on to the ministers of Interior and Tourism.

LAOS

Cambodia and Laos share a remote frontier that includes some of the wildest areas of both countries. There is only one border crossing open to foreigners and given the remoteness of the region, it is unlikely any more will open in the near future.

Dom Kralor–Voen Kham

The border between Cambodia and Laos officially opened to foreigners in 2000 and hours are 7am to 5pm daily. It is rapidly growing in popularity as an adventurous and cheap way to combine travel to northeastern Cambodia and southern Laos. On the Cambodian side of the border, there are confusingly two possible places to cross the border: one on the river (Koh Chheuteal Thom) and one on the old road from Stung Treng (Dom Kralor). Currently most travellers cross at Koh Chheuteal Thom, but with a new road under construction, that will soon change to Dom Kralor.

To enter Cambodia using this route, it is necessary to arrange a Cambodian visa in Bangkok or Vientiane. Likewise, those exiting Cambodia for Laos should arrange a Lao visa in advance in Phnom Penh. Both sides of the border seem to charge an overtime fee for those crossing at lunch time or after dark, although the exact sum (usually US$1 to US$2) depends on gentle but persuasive bargaining.

To leave Cambodia, you will need to get to the remote town of Stung Treng (p256). From Stung Treng there are regular boats heading north up the Mekong to the border. Longtail rocket boats (US$30 for the boat, US$5 per person, one hour) can be chartered at any hour and take up to six people.

Cambodian immigration is on the west bank of the Mekong and Lao immigration is on the east bank. Once in Voen Kham in Laos, there are outboards running up to the island of Don Khone (US$5, 20 minutes), although they drop you on the wrong side of the island, as they can't traverse the falls.

Those heading further north can take a motorcycle taxi to Nakasong for about US$4 or US$5 where it is possible to arrange a boat to Don Det or Don Khone, or arrange a *jamboh* (three-wheeled motorcycle taxi) on to Hat Xai Khun for the boat across to Don Khong.

Coming to Cambodia from Laos, the options outlined above can be run in reverse. The cheapest way is to take one of the dirt cheap boat trips advertised on Don Khone and Don Khong, costing just US$2, which includes the waterfalls and dolphin viewing. Once you get back to Voen Kham from viewing the dolphins, jump ship and arrange a longtail rocket boat south to Stung Treng. There are always plenty of Cambodian outboards hanging around the dock at Voen Kham, but they seem to have fixed the price at US$10 per person, double what it costs to travel in the other direction. Roll on the new road to Stung Treng, which will mean cheap buses instead.

THAILAND
Cambodia and Thailand share a lengthy border and there are now five legal international border crossings, and many more options for locals. Land borders with Thailand are open from 7am to 8pm daily. Visas are available at all crossings for US$20 or 1000B – it doesn't take a rocket scientist to work out that for as long as the Thai baht stays below an exchange rate of 50B to US$1, dollars is the way to go. For the latest sagas on land crossings between Thailand and Cambodia, visit www.talesofasia.com.

Poipet–Aranya Prathet
The original land border crossing between Cambodia and Thailand has earned itself a bad reputation in recent years, with scams galore to help tourists part with their money. The 'scam bus' (p294) promoted on Khao San Rd in Bangkok is now legendary throughout Asia, but many travellers still succumb to the charms of cheap tickets.

There are two slow trains a day from Hualamphong train station in Bangkok to the Thai border town of Aranya Prathet (48B, six hours); take the 5.50am service unless you want to spend the night in a border town. There are also regular bus services from Bangkok's Mo Chit northern terminal to Aranya Prathet (180/140B 1st/2nd class, four to five hours). From Aranya Prathet, take a *tuk-tuk* (motorised three-wheeled pedicab) for the final six kilometres to the border for about 50B. Do not enlist the services of any touts when crossing the border and once in Poipet on the Cambodian side, arrange a seat in a share taxi to Siem Reap (three to five hours) for about 150B or the whole taxi for 1000B. Alternatively, just go as far as Sisophon by taxi (50B per seat, 400B for the whole taxi) and from there negotiate your onward travel to Siem Reap, Battambang or Banteay Chhmar. The road to Siem Reap still hasn't been overhauled and gets very, very ugly during the wet season. It is rumoured that an unnamed airline is paying an unstated commission to an unnamed political party to leave this road until last for an upgrade – well why else hasn't it been overhauled? It should be the number one priority for trade and tourism.

Leaving Cambodia, it is easy enough to get to Poipet from Siem Reap (p131), Battambang (p217) or even Phnom Penh (p105). By land there is no departure tax to leave Cambodia. From Poipet, take a *tuk-tuk* to Aranya Prathet, from where there are regular buses to Bangkok between 4am and 10pm.

Cham Yeam–Hat Lek
The Cham Yeam–Hat Lek border crossing between Cambodia's Krong Koh Kong and Trat in Thailand is popular with tourists and there tend to be fewer scams along the way.

Coming from Bangkok, take a bus to Trat (189B, five to six hours) from the city's Eastern bus station. Buses depart regularly

---

THE SCAM BUS

Poipet is a Wild West kind of place and has attracted a lot of unsavoury characters clinging to the coat-tails of the economic boom. Unfortunately, many of these are involved in the travel business and carry on like some sort of mafia, giving Cambodia a bad name. Welcome to the scam bus, notorious throughout Asia for ripping off foreigners. Anyone staying in Khao San Rd in Bangkok will soon notice the cheap tickets to Siem Reap and the temples of Angkor on offer. Prices start from around 100B, but as locals can't travel this route for less than 250B, the alarm bells should start to ring. Once travellers get to the border, someone will 'help' arrange the visas and pretend the visa fee is now 1300B rather than US$20. That's 400B down and counting...

Once inside Cambodia, a new game begins, drive as slowly as possible to Siem Reap. The road from Poipet to Siem Reap is good enough to cover in about three to four hours in the dry season, but somehow the bus driver will make sure you get there after dark arriving at a back-street guesthouse of their choice. Any attempt to leave this guesthouse will lead to a major confrontation with the guesthouse owners, as they have already agreed to a commission with the transport company and it's non-refundable. So the cheap bus ends up costing you time and money, deservedly earning its name the scam bus. Lately, it has got even worse, with Thai and Cambodian companies colluding to take travellers through the Pruhm–Daun Lem border crossing (opposite) near Pailin, a massive diversion on miserable roads. Coming this way ensures that you arrive in Siem Reap in the middle of the night, in no mood to go looking for another guesthouse.

Travelling independently is the way to go, using public buses on the Thai side and share taxis on the Cambodian side. Sure it will cost more, but this way you keep your options open. Remember the phrase 'too good to be true'? That's the scam bus through and through.

---

from 6am until 11.30pm. The 11.30pm bus arrives in Trat early enough to get to Krong Koh Kong in time to catch the 8am fast boat to Sihanoukville. Another convenient option for travellers staying in the Khao San Rd area is to take one of the minibuses bound for Koh Chang, getting off at Trat.

From Trat, take a minibus straight to the Thai border at Hat Lek for 100B. The border opens at 7am so it is possible to stay the night in Trat and, with an early enough start, still make the boat to Sihanoukville. Alternatively, cross later in the day and stay the night in Krong Koh Kong and see the waterfalls (p182) north of there. Once in Cambodia you can take a *moto* (motorcycle with driver; 50B) or taxi (100B) to Krong Koh Kong over the bridge.

Fast boats from Krong Koh Kong to Siha-noukville (600B for tourists, four hours) leave at 8am and depart Sihanoukville at 12pm when heading in the other direction. A word of warning: the sea can be dangerously rough at times and these boats were designed for river travel, not sailing the open seas! From Sihanoukville (p193) there are cheap air-con buses to Phnom Penh (p105).

It is also possible to travel by road on from Krong Koh Kong to Phnom Penh or Sihanoukville. There is a scheduled minibus service costing 500B that claims to leave at 9am every day, but for more flexibility negotiate with a share taxi. It should cost about US$10 or 400B for a seat to either destination, but it is probably worth buying two seats for comfort. The road is still not surfaced and can get pretty messy in the wet season.

Leaving Cambodia, there is no real reason to stay in Krong Koh Kong. Jump off the boat in Krong Koh Kong and take either a taxi or *moto* across the bridge to the border. Once in Thailand you can take a minibus to Trat from where there are regular buses to Bangkok. Alternatively, stay the night in Trat and then head to Ko Chang or the surrounding islands the following day.

Other Crossings

Three other more out of the way crossings are open for international traffic. The **0 Smach–Chong Jom** crossing connects Cambodia's Oddar Meanchey Province and Thailand's Surin Province with Siem Reap. There are five buses per day from Surin to Chong Jom (30B, two hours). Once on the Cambodian side, it is possible to arrange a taxi on to Siem Reap (US$30, five to seven hours).

Alternatively, head to Samraong (US$5, 30 minutes) and arrange local transport from there on to Siem Reap (p113) or Anlong Veng (p226).

The new crossing north of Anlong Veng, **Choam–Choam Srawngam** puts you into a pretty remote part of Thailand and hence transport connections are, for once, harder on the Thai side. Pick-up trucks (3000/2000r inside/on the back) leave Anlong Veng early, heading to the Cambodian border town of Choam at around 6am. Once on the Thai side, there are supposedly several onward buses a day, but they are quite spaced out. Coming in the other direction from Thailand, the closest major town is Si Saket, from where there are several buses a day to the border.

The border near Pailin in western Cambodia is open for business as well. Some foreigners are unexpectedly crossing the border at **Pruhm–Daun Lem**, courtesy of the 'scam bus' (opposite). To travel this way independently, take a bus from Bangkok to Chantaburi (148B, four hours) and then a minibus from there to Daun Lem (100B, 1½ hours). Cross the Cambodian border into Pruhm and then arrange a share taxi into Pailin (200B for the whole car, 50B per person). From Pailin it is possible to get to Battambang (200B, four hours) by share taxi on a real joke of a road. Run this route in reverse to exit Cambodia; prices should be the same with a bit of bargaining here and there.

There is also a border at **Prasat Preah Vihear** (p235), the stunning Cambodian temple perched atop the Phnom Dangkrek mountain range. This is currently just a day crossing for tourists wanting to visit the temple from the Thai side, the only straightforward way to get there for now.

VIETNAM

Cambodia and Vietnam share a long frontier with plenty of border crossings for locals. Foreigners are currently permitted to cross at only three points, but the Cambodian border at Ha Tien near the south coast is apparently scheduled to open during the lifetime of this book. Cambodian visas are available at the Bavet–Moc Bai and Kaam Samnor–Vinh Xuong border crossings, but not at the Phnom Den–Tinh Bien border. Vietnamese visas should be arranged in advance, as they are not available on arrival. Luckily, Cambodia is the cheapest place in the world to pick up Vietnamese visas! It is no longer necessary to stipulate your exact point of entry and exit on the Vietnam visa, or the exact date of arrival, making for the sort of carefree travel overlanders prefer.

Bavet–Moc Bai

The original land crossing between Vietnam and Cambodia has seen steady traffic for more than a decade. The trip by bus between Phnom Penh and Ho Chi Minh City takes between five and six hours, usually involving a change of bus at the border.

Most travellers use the minibus services run by Capitol Guesthouse (p90) or Narin Guesthouse (p90) in Phnom Penh, costing just US$6 all the way to Ho Chi Minh City with a change of buses at the border. In Vietnam, transport can be arranged through backpacker travel agencies such as Sinh Café and Kim Café. Phnom Penh Public Transport (PPPT) offer a daily through-bus (p105), departing Phnom Penh at 6.30am and Ho Chi Minh City at 6am, costing US$9.

For the independently minded, local buses on the Vietnamese side head to Tay Ninh from Ho Chi Minh City (3000d); ask to be let off at the turn-off for Moc Bai. *Moto* drivers can take you the rest of the way to the border for about US$1. On the Cambodian side you can take a share taxi from Bavet as far as Neak Luong (US$2), cross the Mekong by ferry (100r for foot passengers) and take an air-con bus to Phnom Penh (4000r).

Kaam Samnor–Vinh Xuong

Cambodia and Vietnam opened their border on the Mekong in 2000 and it is now very popular with independent travellers. It is a far more interesting trip than taking the road, as it involves a fast boat on the Mekong in Cambodia and travel along some very picturesque areas of the Mekong Delta in Vietnam. Coming from Ho Chi Minh City, it is possible to book a cheap Mekong Delta tour through to Chau Doc and then make your own way from there.

Adventurous travellers like to plot their own course. Leaving Cambodia, take a bus from Psar Thmei in Phnom Penh to Neak

TRANSPORT

Luong (4500r, regular departures, 1½ hours) then jump off the bus on the west bank of the Mekong (don't take the ferry across the river!) and ask around for outboards to Kaam Samnor (one hour). They depart from a small pier about 300m south of the ferry. It costs US$15 to charter the whole boat, but those with a little time on their hands can wait until it fills with locals and pay 10,000r (US$2.50) for a place. The border posts at Kaam Samnor are some way apart so hire a *moto* (US$1) to carry you from building to building to deal with the lengthy bureaucracy. There are separate offices for immigration and customs on both sides of the border, so it can end up taking as much as an hour to navigate. Luggage has to be x-rayed on the Vietnamese side of the border! Once officially in Vietnam at the village of Vinh Xuong, take a *xe om (moto)* to Chau Doc (US$4, one hour). From Chau Doc, there are frequent buses to Cantho and Ho Chi Minh City, as well as more-expensive boat services. Those entering Cambodia via Vinh Xuong can just run the aforementioned route in reverse.

There are two boat companies offering direct services between Phnom Penh and Chau Doc. The more upmarket **Blue Cruiser** (☎ 016 824343; 93 Sisowath Quay; US$35) departs Chau Doc at 8.30am and Phnom Penh at 1.30pm. **Hang Chau** (☎ 012 883542; US$15) pulls out from Chau Doc at 9am and departs Phnom Penh's tourist boat dock at 2pm. Both take three hours or so. **Victoria Hotels** (www.victoriahotels-asia.com; US$65) also has a boat making several runs a week between Phnom Penh and its luxury Victoria Chau Doc Hotel.

Lastly there are two companies offering luxury cruises between Ho Chi Minh City and Siem Reap via the Kaam Samnor–Vinh Xuong border crossing. International player **Pandaw Cruises** (www.pandaw.com) is an expensive option favoured by high-end tour companies. Cambodian company **Toum Teav Cruises** (www.cf-mekong.com) is smaller and is well regarded for its personal service and excellent food.

Phnom Den–Tinh Bien

This border crossing sees little traffic for now, as anyone in Chau Doc in Vietnam tends to use the Kaam Samnor–Vinh Xuong crossing direct to Phnom Penh. It's pretty remote and the roads are in bad shape so give it a miss for now. It lies about 60km southeast of Takeo town in Cambodia, along bumpy NH2.

TOURS

In the early days of tourism in Cambodia, organised tours were a near necessity. The situation has changed dramatically and it is now much easier to organise your own trip. Budget and midrange travellers in particular can go it alone, as arrangements are cheap and easy on the ground. If you are on a tight schedule, it can pay to book a domestic flight in advance if planning to link the temples of Angkor and Siem Reap with Cambodia's capital Phnom Penh. Once at Angkor, guides and all forms of transport under the sun are plentiful.

Shop around before booking a tour, as there is lots of competition and some companies, such as those listed here, offer more interesting itineraries than others.

Australia

Adventure World (☎ 02-8913 0755; www.adventure world.com.au) Offers adventure tours of Cambodia, as well as neighbouring Vietnam and Laos.

Intrepid Travel (☎ 1300 360 667; www.intrepidtravel .com.au) Small group tours for all budgets with an environmental, social and cultural edge.

Peregrine (☎ 02-9290 2770; www.peregrine.net.au) Small group and private tours supporting responsible tourism.

France

Compagnie des Indes & Orients (☎ 01-5363-3340; www.compagniesdumonde.com) Offers organised tours covering more of Cambodia than most.

Intermedes (☎ 01-4561-9090; www.intermedes.com) Offers specialised private tours.

La Route des Indes (☎ 01-4260-6090; www.laroutedes indes.com) High-end tours with an academic edge.

UK

Audley Travel (☎ 1604-234855; www.audleytravel.com) Specialises in tailor-made tours to all corners of Cambodia.

Exodus (☎ 020-8675-5550; www.exodus.co.uk) One of the UK's biggest adventure travel companies.

Explore (☎ 01252-760100; www.exploreworldwide.com) Small-group adventure travel company.

Mekong Travel (☎ 01494-674456; www.mekong-travel .com) Specialising in Southeast Asian travel; also offers eco-tours.

Symbiosis (☎ 020-7924 5906; www.symbiosis-travel .com) Small group and private tours in Asia, including diving and cycling trips.

Wild Frontiers (☎ 020-7376 3968; www.wildfrontiers
.co.uk) Adventure travel company specialising in small-
group and private tours.

USA
Asia Transpacific Journeys (☎ 800-642 2742; www
.asiatranspacific.com) Specialises in group and private tours
in Asia and the Pacific.
Distant Horizons (☎ 800 333 1240; www.distant
-horizons.com) Educational tours for discerning travellers.
Geographic Expeditions (☎ 800-777 8183; www
.geoex.com) Small-group adventure travel company.

GETTING AROUND

AIR
Airlines in Cambodia
Domestic flights offer a quick way to travel
around the country. The problem is that
the airlines themselves seem to come and
go pretty quickly. There are currently three
domestic airlines operating in Cambodia.
Siem Reap Airways (p289) serves the Phnom
Penh to Siem Reap route with modern ATRs
from France; **President Airlines** (p289) flies from
Phnom Penh to Siem Reap and Ratanakiri
Province, sometimes with a Boeing 737 to
the former, always with an old Antonov to
the latter; and **Royal Phnom Penh Airways** (p289)
operates flights between Phnom Penh and
Siem Reap and the capital and Ratanakiri
Province, but with a fleet of older Chinese
planes.

There are up to six flights a day between
Phnom Penh and Siem Reap and it is usu-
ally possible to get on a flight at short notice.
However, tickets for Siem Reap Airways
(US$65/105 one way/return) book out fast
in peak season, as fewer agents will book
with President Airlines (US$60/95) and
Royal Phnom Penh Airways (US$55/100).
President Airlines also flies to Ratanakiri
Province (US$65/105); however, during
peak season, demand for flights often ex-
ceeds supply.

There used to be regular services to Battambang, Koh Kong, Mondulkiri and Stung
Treng, but no airline was serving these routes
at the time of writing.

The baggage allowance for domestic
flights is only 10kg for each passenger,
but unless you are way over the limit it
is unlikely you will have to pay for excess
baggage.

DOMESTIC DEPARTURE TAX

The airport tax for domestic flights is US$6
from Phnom Penh and Siem Reap airports,
and just US$4 from regional airports.

Helicopter
Helicopters Cambodia (p149) is based in Siem
Reap and has a reliable chopper available
for rent. It mostly operates scenic flights
around Angkor, but can be chartered for
any journey.

BICYCLE
Cambodia is a great country for adventurous cyclists to explore. Needless to say, a
mountain bike is obligatory. Basic cycling
safety equipment and authentic spare parts
are also in short supply, so bring all this
from home. A bell is essential – the louder
the better. Many roads remain in bad condition, but there is usually a flat trail along
the side. Travelling at such a gentle speed
allows for much more interaction with the
locals. Although bicycles are common in
Cambodian villages, cycling tourists are still
very much a novelty and will be wildly welcomed in most small villages. In many parts
of the country there are new dirt tracks
being laid down for motorcycles and bicycles, and these are a wonderful way to travel
into remote parts of Cambodia.

Much of Cambodia is pancake flat or
only moderately hilly. Safety, however, is
a considerable concern on the newer surfaced roads, as local traffic travels at high
speed. Bicycles can be transported around
the country in the back of pick-ups or on
the roof of minibuses.

Cycling around Angkor (p148) is an awesome experience as it really helps to get a
measure of the size and scale of the temple
complex. Mountain biking is likely to take
off in Mondulkiri and Ratanakiri Provinces
over the coming years, as there are some
great trails off the beaten track. Guesthouses and hotels throughout Cambodia
rent out bicycles for US$1 to US$2 per day
and a repair stall is never far away.

For the full story on cycle touring in Cambodia, see Lonely Planet's *Cycling Vietnam,
Laos & Cambodia*, which has the lowdown
on planning a major ride. It outlines 14
days' worth of rides in Cambodia, including

TRANSPORT

TRANSPORT

a five-day ride from Phnom Penh to Ho Chi Minh City in Vietnam, travelling via Kompong Cham (p248) and Prey Veng (p246).

BOAT

Cambodia's 1900km of navigable waterways are a key element in the country's transportation system, particularly given the state of many roads and the railways. North of Phnom Penh, the Mekong is easily navigable as far north as Kratie (p252), and from July to January even large boats can make it as far as Stung Treng (p256). There are fast boat services between Siem Reap and Battambang (p213), and the Tonlé Sap lake is also navigable year-round, although only by smaller boats between March and July.

Traditionally the most popular boat services with foreigners were those that run between Phnom Penh and Siem Reap (p113). The express services do the trip in as little as five hours but the boats between Phnom Penh and Siem Reap are horrendously overcrowded and foreigners are charged almost twice the price of Khmers for the 'privilege' of sitting on the roof. It is not the most interesting boat journey in Cambodia, as the Tonlé Sap lake is like a vast sea, offering little scenery. It's much smarter to take a bus (p131) on the new road instead.

The boat services up the Mekong from the capital (p105) and the small boat between Siem Reap and Battambang (p216) are more rewarding, as the river scenery is truly memorable. Furthermore, should a breakdown occur, as will happen from time to time, it is easier to disembark from a river than from the middle of a lake. Whichever fast boat journey takes your fancy, you may well end up on the roof so remember to use sun block and wear a head covering.

There are now longtail rocket boats operating on northern stretches of the Mekong between Kratie (p254) and the Lao border. These are superfast, but are super dangerous if overcrowded or travelling after dark. Only use them for short journeys such as the Lao border to Stung Treng (p257) and never risk departing late if it means travelling at night.

Many travellers use the fast boat between Sihanoukville and Krong Koh Kong (p294) to travel between Thailand and Cambodia.

BUS

The range of road transport is extensive in Cambodia. On sealed roads, large air-conditioned buses are the best choice. Elsewhere in the country, a pick-up truck, share taxi or minibus is the way to go.

Bus services have come on in leaps and bounds in the last few years and the situation is getting even better as more roads are upgraded. The services used most regularly by foreigners are those from Phnom Penh to Siem Reap, Battambang, Sihanoukville and Kompong Cham, and the tourist buses from Siem Reap to Poipet.

There is a clean and comfortable bus service to towns and villages in the vicinity of Phnom Penh, such as Udong and Phnom Chisor. Operated by the Phnom Penh Public Transport (PPPT; p105), these services are very cheap and English-speaking staff can direct you onto the right bus.

Minibuses serve most provincial routes, but are not widely used by Western visitors. They are very cheap, but often uncomfortably overcrowded and driven by maniacs, like the meanest of *matatus* (minibus taxis) in East Africa. Only really consider them if there is no alternative.

CAR & MOTORCYCLE

Car and motorcycle rental are comparatively cheap in Cambodia and many visitors rent a car or motorcycle for greater flexibility to visit out-of-the-way places and to stop when and where they choose. Almost all car rental in Cambodia includes a driver, which is good news given the abysmal state of many roads and the prominence of the psychopathic driver gene among many Cambodian road users.

Driving Licence

A standard driving licence is not much use in Cambodia. In theory, to drive a car you need an International Driving Licence, usually issued through your automobile association back home. It is very unlikely that a driving licence will be of any use to most travellers to Cambodia, save for those coming to work with one of the many foreign organisations in Cambodia.

When it comes to renting motorcycles, it's a case of no licence required. If you can drive the bike out of the shop, you can drive it anywhere, or so the logic goes.

HIGHWAYS FROM HELL?

Cambodia has long been home to the most miserable road system in Asia, with many of the country's so-called national highways (NH) in a horrendous state of disrepair. Many would argue that Cambodia is up there among the contenders for worst roads in the world, along with the DR Congo and Mozambique. Many of the roads around the country have not been maintained since the 1960s, and in some places the damage from war, weather, and wear and tear has been hideous. However, all this has started to change with the huge rebuilding programme nearing completion on Cambodia's highways, including NH1, NH2, NH3, NH5, NH6 and NH7, a miracle funded by international aid.

While this makes travelling on the main roads much easier, beyond these highways, driving through Cambodia remains something like a steeplechase: some fast bits, some bumpy bits, and many vehicles failing before the finish line.

Black-cab drivers in London pride themselves on knowing every street in the city; indeed, the only way they get the job is to pass a tough test called 'the knowledge'. But that's nothing compared to the average Cambodian cabbie, who has to know every pothole in the road just to keep his vehicle alive. Experienced drivers can shave an hour or two off longer journeys, while an amateur can break an axle just a few kilometres down the road. Unfortunately, there is no real trick to telling who can drive and who can't before you start the journey. However, the choice of vehicle helps and for the most part you'll find you are best off in a pumped-up share taxi with super shocks than in a pick-up truck or minibus – with the suspension jacked up, these Toyota Camrys just fly over the holes!

While bouncing and bumping their way around Cambodia, many a traveller has engaged in debate as to which is the worst of the many diabolical roads in the country. A Lonely Planet poll has come up with yet another 'top five' now our old favourites are all being repaired – Cambodia's highways from hell:

■ **Kratie to Stung Treng** This is the last section of major highway still under reconstruction, lots of broken rocks and deep sand. It's 141km of pain and anguish.

■ **Sen Monorom to Ban Lung** Yes, it looks mighty tempting to link Mondulkiri Province and Ratanakiri Province by land, but the trails here eat *motos* for breakfast and it's easy to get lost.

■ **Pailin to Koh Kong** An old logging road cuts through the heart of the Chuor Phnom Kravanh (Cardamom Mountains), but the emphasis is on 'old'. With no maintenance, this is truly the badlands, where the law of the jungle rules.

■ **Tbeng Meanchey to Preah Vihear** Not so long ago a new road, it has been comprehensively trashed by fuel smuggling trucks. Survive that stretch and the Chuor Phnom Dangkrek (Dangkrek Mountains) await with 35% gradients!

■ **Tbeng Meanchey to Preah Khan** More sand than the Sahara, at least that's how it feels after 56km of struggling to keep the vehicle straight. Another one to be studiously avoided.

The good news is that there are already some impressive highways in the country, including NH4 to Sihanoukville and the rebuilt roads to Battambang and Siem Reap. The bad news, if you wanted more, is that in the wet season it gets a lot, lot worse, particularly in the remote provinces. Try travelling from Stung Treng cross-country to Tbeng Meanchey in September and you may, in time, come to appreciate Cambodia's other roads.

Fuel & Spare Parts

Fuel is relatively expensive in Cambodia, at around 3000r (US$0.75) a litre. Fuel is readily available throughout the country, but prices rise in rural areas. Even the most isolated communities usually have some-one selling petrol out of Fanta or Johnnie Walker bottles. Some sellers mix this fuel with kerosene to make a quick profit – use it sparingly, in emergencies only.

When it comes to spare parts, Cambodia is flooded with Japanese motorcycles, so it

ROAD DISTANCES (KM)

	Ban Lung	Battambang	Kampot	Kompong Cham	Kompong Chhnang	Kompong Thom	Kratie	Phnom Penh	Poipet	Prey Veng	Pursat	Sen Monorom	Siem Reap	Sihanoukville	Sisophon	Stung Treng	Svay Rieng	Takeo	Tbeng Meanchey
Ban Lung	---																		
Battambang	928	---																	
Kampot	783	441	---																
Kompong Cham	515	413	263	---															
Kompong Chhnang	726	202	239	211	---														
Kompong Thom	654	322	313	139	256	---													
Kratie	287	641	496	228	439	367	---												
Phnom Penh	635	293	148	120	91	165	348	---											
Poipet	957	117	558	442	319	303	670	410	---										
Prey Veng	580	384	239	78	182	217	293	90	520	---									
Pursat	823	105	336	308	97	353	536	188	222	279	---								
Sen Monorom	155	663	518	250	461	389	215	370	692	315	558	---							
Siem Reap	805	171	464	290	373	151	664	317	152	407	276	540	---						
Sihanoukville	865	523	105	350	321	395	578	230	640	321	418	600	546	---					
Sisophon	908	68	509	393	270	254	621	361	49	471	173	643	103	591	---				
Stung Treng	165	782	637	369	580	508	141	489	811	434	677	356	659	719	762	---			
Svay Rieng	675	418	273	173	216	290	388	125	535	95	313	410	441	355	486	529	---		
Takeo	710	368	85	195	166	240	423	75	485	166	263	445	391	190	436	564	200	---	
Tbeng Meanchey	791	459	450	276	393	137	504	302	440	354	490	526	288	532	391	645	467	377	---

is easy to get parts for Hondas, Yamahas or Suzukis, but finding a part for a Harley or a Ducati is another matter. The same goes for cars – spares for Japanese cars are easy to come by, but if you are driving something obscure, bring substantial spares.

Hire

CAR

Car hire is generally only available with a driver and is only really useful for sightseeing around Phnom Penh and Angkor. Some tourists with a healthy budget also arrange cars or 4WDs with drivers for touring the provinces. Hiring a car with a driver is about US$20 for a day in and around Cambodia's towns. Heading into the provinces it rises to US$40 or more, depending on the destination, and for those staying overnight, the driver will also need looking after. Hiring 4WDs will cost around US$50 to US$100 a day, depending on the model and the distance travelled. Driving yourself is just about possible but also inadvisable due to chaotic road conditions, personal liability in the case of an accident and higher charges.

MOTORCYCLE

Motorcycles are available for rent in Phnom Penh, Kampot and most popular tourist destinations. In Siem Reap, motorcycle rental is currently illegal, so anyone planning any rides around Siem Reap needs to arrange a bike in Phnom Penh (p107). At the time of writing, authorities were also no longer allowing foreigners to rent bikes, but it remains to see if this ban holds. In other provincial towns, it is usually possible to rent a small motorcycle after a bit of negotiation. Costs are US$3 per day for a 100cc motorcycle and US$7 for a 250cc dirt bike in Phnom Penh and Sihanoukville. This rises to US$5 to US$10 in most other provincial centres.

Drive with due care and attention, as medical facilities are less than adequate in Cambodia and traffic is erratic, particularly in Phnom Penh, where anarchy would be too constructive a word to describe how people drive. If you have never ridden a motorcycle before, the capital is not the best place to start, but once out of the city it does get easier. If you're jumping in at the deep end, make sure you are under the supervision of someone who knows how to ride.

The advantage of motorcycle travel is that it allows for complete freedom of movement and you can stop in small villages that Westerners rarely visit. It is possible to take motorcycles upcountry for tours, but only experienced off-road bikers should take to these roads with a dirt bike. Even riders with more experience should take care if intending to ride into remote regions – roads in Cambodia are not the same as roads at home! Anyone planning a longer ride should try out the bike around Phnom Penh for a day or so to make sure it is in good health.

For those with experience, Cambodia has some of the best roads in the world for dirt biking, particularly in the provinces of Preah Vihear (p228), Mondulkiri (p264) and Ratanakiri (p258). For those who don't want to ride that far, the road up to Bokor hill station (p199) near Kampot is very exhilarating.

Hidden Cambodia (www.hiddencambodia.com) is a Siem Reap-based company specialising in motorcycle trips throughout Cambodia. It operates an annual dry-season programme that includes the remote temples of northern Cambodia and beyond.

Dancing Roads (www.dancingroads.com) is a similar outfit based in Phnom Penh, offering tours around the capital and gentle tours further afield to the south coast.

Insurance

If you are travelling in a tourist vehicle with a driver, then it is usually insured. When it comes to motorcycles, many rental bikes are not insured and you will have to sign a contract agreeing to a valuation for the bike if it is stolen. Make sure you have a strong lock and always leave it in guarded parking where available.

Do not even consider renting a motorcycle if you are daft enough to be travelling in Cambodia without insurance. The cost of treating serious injuries is bankrupting for budget travellers.

Road Conditions & Hazards

Whether travelling or living in Cambodia, it is easy to lull yourself into a false sense of security and assume that down every rural road is yet another friendly village.

However, even with the demise of the Khmer Rouge, odd incidents of banditry and robbery occur in rural areas. When travelling in your own vehicle, and particularly by motorcycle in rural areas, make certain you check the latest security information in communities along the way. Many Cambodians do not travel beyond the village or town limits at night for fear of robbery, and it would be advisable to follow suit. The risks may be low for a foreigner on a bike, but there is no sense in courting potential danger.

Expatriates working in Phnom Penh may end up driving a 4WD or car, but will certainly need to drive with more care than at home. In Phnom Penh traffic is a law unto itself and in the provinces roads can resemble roller coasters. Residents and tourists with their own wheels should not attempt inter-provincial travel at night. Be particularly careful about children on the road – you'll find kids hanging out in the middle of a major highway. Livestock on the road are also a menace; hit a cow on a motorcycle and you'll both be shepherd's pie.

Other general security suggestions for those travelling by motorcycle:

- Try to get hold of a helmet for long journeys or high-speed riding.
- Carry a basic repair kit, including some tyre levers, a puncture repair kit and a pump.
- Always carry a rope for towing on longer journeys in case you break down.
- In remote areas always carry several litres of water, as you never know when you will run out.
- Travel in small groups, not alone.
- When in a group, stay close together in case of any incident or accident.
- Don't be a cheapskate with petrol – running out of fuel in a rural area could jeopardise your health, especially if water runs out too.
- Do not smoke marijuana or drink alcohol and drive, as it impairs your skills.
- Keep your eyes firmly fixed on the road; Cambodian potholes eat people for fun.

Road Rules

If there are road rules in Cambodia it is doubtful that anyone is following them. Size matters and the biggest vehicle wins by default. The best advice if you drive a car or ride a motorcycle in Cambodia is to take nothing for granted and assume that your fellow motorists are visually challenged psychopaths. Seriously though, in Cambodia traffic drives on the right. There are few traffic lights at junctions in Phnom Penh, so most traffic turns left into the oncoming traffic, edging along the left-hand side of the road until a gap becomes apparent. For the uninitiated it looks like a disaster waiting to happen, but Cambodians are quite used to the system. Foreigners should stop at crossings and develop a habit of constant vigilance.

Phnom Penh is the one place where, amid all the chaos, traffic police take issue with Westerners breaking even the most trivial road rules (p77). Make sure you don't turn left at a 'no left turn' sign or travel with your headlights on during the day (although strangely, it doesn't seem to be illegal for Cambodians to travel without headlights at night).

HITCHING

Hitching is never entirely safe in any country, and we don't recommend it. Travellers who decide to hitch should understand that they are taking a small but potentially serious risk. People who do choose to hitch will be safer if they travel in pairs and let someone know where they are planning to go. Hitching with truck drivers is a possibility, but it is very uncomfortable and should be considered extremely unsafe for lone women. Expect to pay for the ride.

LOCAL TRANSPORT

Bus

There are no local bus networks in Cambodia, even in the capital Phnom Penh.

Cyclo

As in Vietnam and Laos, the *samlor* or *cyclo* (pedicab) is a cheap way to get around urban areas. In Phnom Penh *cyclo* drivers can either be flagged down on main roads or found loitering around markets and major hotels. It is necessary to bargain the fare if taking a *cyclo* from outside an expensive hotel or popular restaurant or bar. Fares range from 1000r to US$1 (about 4000r). There are few *cyclos* in the provinces and in Phnom Penh the *cyclo* is fast losing ground to the *moto*.

WARNING

Moto drivers and *cyclo* riders with little or no English may not understand where you want them to go even though they nod vigorously. This is a particular headache in a big city like Phnom Penh – see the boxed text, p107.

Lorry

No, not a big truck, but the Cambodian name for a local train made from wood and powered by a motorcycle, quite literally the motorcycle's rear wheel touching the track and propelling it along. In the Battambang area, they are known as a norry or bamboo train to tourists and they are powered by an electric motor. Great fun until you meet another train coming the other way – aaaaargh!

Moto

Motos, also known as *motodops,* are small motorcycle taxis and their drivers almost universally wear a baseball cap. They are a quick way of making short hops around towns and cities. Prices range from 1000r to US$1 or more, depending on the distance and the town; expect to pay more at night. *Moto* drivers assume you know the cost of a trip and prices are rarely agreed before starting. However, if it's late at night or if you're staying at a fancy hotel, it may be worth negotiating the fare to avoid a protracted argument at the journey's end.

Outboards

Outboards (pronounced out-boor) are the equivalent of Venice's *vaporetto,* a sort of local river bus or taxi. Found all over the country, they are small fibreglass boats with 15hp and 40hp engines, and can carry up to six people for local or longer trips. They

---

THE MOTO BURN

Be careful not to put your leg near the exhaust pipe of a *moto* after long journeys; many travellers have received nasty burns, which can take a long time to heal in the sticky weather and often require antibiotics.

rarely run to schedules, but locals wait patiently for them to fill up. Those with time on their hands can join the wait, those in a hurry can charter the whole boat and take off. A new variation are the longtail rocket boats imported from Thailand that connect small towns on the upper stretches of the Mekong. Rocket is the definitive word and their safety is questionable.

Remorque-kang

The *remorque-kang* is a trailer pulled by a bicycle, effectively a kind of *cyclo* with the passenger travelling behind. The coming of the *moto* has led to a dwindling in numbers, but they are still widely seen in Battambang (p213), Kampot (p195) and Kratie (p252). Fares are about the same as *moto* rides.

Remorque-moto

The *remorque-moto* is a large trailer hitched to a motorcycle and pretty much operates as a low-tech local bus with oh-so-natural air-conditioning. They are used throughout rural Cambodia to transport people and goods, and are often seen on the edge of towns ready to ferry farmers back to the countryside. *Remorque-motos* offer a cheap way to sightsee in some of the provinces, as long as you can make the driver understand where you want to get off. Fares are very cheap, at around 100r per kilometre.

Siem Reap has its very own tourist version of the *remorque-moto*, with a cute little canopied trailer hitched to the back for two people in comfort or as many as you can pile on at night. These make a great way to get to the temples, as you get the breeze of the bike but some protection from the elements. Phnom Penh also now has its share of *remorque-motos*, more commonly known as *tuk-tuks* in the capital. These come in every shape and size from several different countries in the region.

Rotei Ses

Rotei means 'cart' or 'carriage' and *ses* is 'horse', but the term is used for any cart pulled by an animal. Cambodia's original 4WD, ox carts are a common form of transport in remote parts of the country, as they are the only things that can get through thick mud in the height of the wet season. They are usually pulled by water buffalo or cows. Horse-and-carts are commonly seen

in rural Cambodia, although very few tourists like the idea of being pulled along by one of these pitiful horses.

Taxi

Taxi hire is getting easier in Cambodia, but there are still next to no metered taxis. There are many private operators working throughout Cambodia. Guesthouses, hotels and travel agents can arrange them for sightseeing in and around towns. Even in Phnom Penh, however, it can be almost impossible to find a taxi for short hops unless you've booked a car in advance or are leaving popular nightspots late at night.

PICK-UP, SHARE TAXI & JEEP

These days the pick-up and jeep are losing ground to the pumped up Toyota Camrys that have their suspension jacked up like monster trucks. When using pick-up trucks or share taxis, it is an advantage to travel in numbers, as you can buy spare seats to make the journey more comfortable. Double the price for the front seat and quadruple it for the back seats. It is important to remember that there aren't necessarily fixed prices on every route, so you have to negotiate and prices do fluctuate with the price of petrol – after all, the cost of petrol has doubled in the last few years!

Pick-ups and share taxis take on the bad roads that buses would breakdown on and some of the busier roads that buses serve. Share taxis are widely available for hire and for major destinations they can be hired individually or you can pay for a seat and wait for other passengers to turn up. Guesthouses are also very helpful when it comes to arranging share taxis, at a price of course.

When it comes to pick-ups, passengers can sit in the cab or, if money is short and comfort an alien concept, out on the back; trucks depart when seriously full. Passengers sitting out back should carry a scarf to protect from the dust and sunscreen to protect against the sun. In the wet season a raincoat is as good as compulsory. Arranging pick-ups directly is less expensive than getting a guesthouse to organise it, but involves considerable aggravation. Haggle patiently to ensure a fair price.

In the remote northeast of the country, where the roads are so bad they actually

TRANSPORT

look sculpted, sturdy Russian jeeps and high-clearance pick-ups are the transport of choice. These seem to keep moving in even the most nightmarish conditions.

In very remote areas, particularly in the wet season, when the roads are even more abysmal than usual, huge six-wheel-drive Russian military trucks serve as periodic transport. These are known as *lan damrei* (elephant trucks).

TRAIN

Cambodia's rail system is, like the road network, one of the most notorious in Asia. It is fun to try out the trains, but only for shorter sections of the network; the best sections being between Kampot and Sihanoukville (p198) or Pursat and Battambang (p212). Trains travel at an average speed of 20km/h and mechanical problems can mean making unscheduled overnight stops. Bridges are not always maintained and the ride is often as bumpy as on some of the roads as the tracks are so warped. That said, the locals who use the trains regularly are particularly welcoming to foreigners who choose to travel this way.

The rail network consists of about 645km of single-track metre-gauge lines. The 382km

northwestern line, built before WWII, links Phnom Penh with Pursat (165km), Battambang (274km) and Sisophon (302km). The last stretch to Poipet was pulled up by the Khmer Rouge in the 1970s. The 263km southwestern line, which was completed in 1969, connects Phnom Penh with Takeo (75km), Kampot (166km) and the port of Sihanoukville (228km).

The civil war during much of the 1980s and 1990s led to some unique developments in the Cambodian rail system. Each train was equipped with a tin-roofed, armoured carriage sporting a huge machine gun and numerous gun ports in its sides. In addition, the first two flat-bed carriages of the train operated as mine sweepers. Travel on the first carriage was free and on the second carriage half-price and, despite the risks, these options were extremely popular with the locals. Gladly for the Cambodian people, these precautions are no longer necessary.

Costs

For Khmers train travel costs about 15r a kilometre (less than half a US cent), and although it still works out to be ludicrously cheap, foreigner prices are now levied at three times the Khmer price, without three times the level of service.

Health Dr Trish Batchelor

CONTENTS

Your health is more at risk in Cambodia than most other parts of Southeast Asia, due to poor sanitation and a lack of effective medical treatment facilities. Once you venture into rural areas you should consider yourself very much on your own, as even where pharmacies and hospitals are available you may have trouble making yourself understood.

If you feel particularly unwell, try to see a doctor rather than visit a hospital; hospitals are pretty primitive and diagnosis can be hit and miss. If you fall seriously ill in Cambodia you should return to Phnom Penh, as it is the only place in the country with decent emergency treatment. Pharmacies in the larger towns are remarkably well stocked and you don't need a prescription to get your hands on anything from antibiotics to antimalarials. Prices are very reasonable, but do check the expiry date, as some medicine may have been on the shelves for a long time.

Don't let this make you paranoid. Travel health depends on your level of predeparture preparation, your daily health care while travelling and how you handle any medical problem that may develop. While the potential dangers can seem quite frightening, in reality few travellers experience anything more than upset stomachs.

BEFORE YOU GO

INSURANCE

Make sure that you have adequate health insurance. See p277 for details.

RECOMMENDED VACCINATIONS

Plan ahead for getting your vaccinations (see the boxed text, p306): some of them require more than one injection over a period of time, while others should not be given together. Note that some vaccinations should not be given during pregnancy or to people with allergies – discuss these issues with your doctor.

It is recommended that you seek medical advice at least six weeks before travel. Be aware that there is often a greater risk of disease among children and during pregnancy.

Record all vaccinations on an International Certificate of Vaccination, available from your doctor or government health department. It is a good idea to carry this proof of your vaccinations when travelling in Cambodia.

FURTHER READING

If you are planning on travelling in remote areas for a long period of time, you may consider taking a more detailed health guide, such as Lonely Planet's *Healthy Travel: Asia & India,* which is a handy pocket-sized guide that's packed with useful information including pre-trip planning, emergency first aid, immunisation and disease information, and what to do if you get sick on the road. *Where There Is No Doctor,* by David Werner, is a very detailed guide intended for those going to work in an underdeveloped country.

Lonely Planet's *Travel with Children,* by Cathy Lanigan, includes advice on travel health for younger children.

OTHER PREPARATIONS

Make sure you're healthy before you start travelling. If you're going on a long trip, make a visit to a dentist before you depart. If you wear glasses, take a spare pair and your prescription.

REQUIRED & RECOMMENDED VACCINATIONS

Vaccinations you may want to consider for a trip to Cambodia are listed here, but it is imperative that you discuss your needs with your doctor. For more details about the diseases themselves, see the individual entries later in this section.

- **Diphtheria & Tetanus** Vaccinations for these two diseases are usually combined. After an initial course of three injections (usually given in childhood), boosters are necessary every 10 years.

- **Hepatitis A** This vaccine provides long-term immunity after an initial injection and a booster at six to 12 months. Alternatively, an injection of gamma globulin can provide short-term protection against hepatitis A – two to six months, depending on the dose. It is reasonably effective and, unlike the vaccine, is protective immediately, but because it is a blood product, there are current concerns about its long-term safety. The hepatitis A vaccine is also available in a combined form with the hepatitis B vaccine – three injections over a six-month period are required.

- **Hepatitis B** Travellers who should consider vaccination against hepatitis B include those on a long trip, as well as those visiting countries where there are high levels of hepatitis B infection (such as Cambodia), where blood transfusions may not be adequately screened or where sexual contact or needle sharing is a possibility. Vaccination involves three injections, with a booster at 12 months. More-rapid courses are available if necessary.

- **Japanese B Encephalitis** Consider vaccination against this disease if spending a month or longer in Cambodia, when making repeated trips or if visiting during an epidemic. It involves three injections over 30 days.

- **Polio** Everyone should keep up-to-date with this vaccination, normally given in childhood. A booster every 10 years maintains immunity.

- **Rabies** Vaccination should be considered by those spending a month or longer in Cambodia, especially if they are cycling, handling animals, caving or travelling to remote areas. It's also recommended for children, as they may not report a bite. Vaccination involves having three injections over 21 to 28 days. Vaccinated people who are bitten or scratched by an animal will require two booster injections of vaccine; those not vaccinated require more.

- **Tuberculosis** The risk of travellers contracting TB is usually very low, unless you will be living with, or closely associated with, local people. Vaccination against TB (BCG) is recommended for children and young adults who will be living in high-risk areas, including Cambodia, for three months or more.

- **Typhoid** Vaccination against typhoid may be required if you are travelling for more than a couple of weeks in Cambodia.

- **Yellow Fever** A yellow fever vaccine is now the only vaccine that is a legal requirement for entry into Cambodia when coming from an infected area. This refers to a direct flight from an infected area, but there are no direct flights from Africa or South America, the most likely places of infection.

If you require a particular medication, ensure that you take an adequate supply, as it may not be available locally. Take part of the packaging that shows the generic name rather than the brand, which will make getting replacements easier. To avoid any problems, it's a good idea to have a legible prescription or letter from your doctor to show that you legally use the medication.

Medical Kit Check List

Following is a list of items you should consider including in your medical kit – consult your pharmacist for brands available in your country.

- aspirin or paracetamol (acetaminophen in the USA) – for pain or fever
- antihistamine – for allergies, eg hay fever; to ease the itch from insect bites or stings; and to prevent motion sickness

- cold and flu tablets, throat lozenges and nasal decongestant
- multivitamins – consider for long trips, when dietary vitamin intake may be inadequate
- antibiotics – consider including these if you're travelling well off the beaten track; see your doctor before you go, as they must be prescribed, and carry the prescription with you
- loperamide or diphenoxylate, which are 'blockers' for diarrhoea
- prochlorperazine or metaclopramide – for nausea and vomiting
- rehydration mixture – to prevent dehydration, which may occur, for example, during bouts of diarrhoea; particularly important when travelling with children
- insect repellent, sunscreen, lip balm and eye drops
- calamine lotion, sting relief spray or aloe vera – to ease irritation from sunburn and insect bites or stings
- antifungal cream or powder – for fungal skin infections and thrush
- antiseptic (such as povidone-iodine) for cuts and grazes
- bandages, Band-Aids (plasters) and other wound dressings
- water purification tablets or iodine
- scissors, tweezers and a thermometer – note that mercury thermometers are prohibited by airlines
- sterile kit (sealed medical kit containing syringes and needles) – highly recommended, as Cambodia has medical hygiene problems

IN TRANSIT

DEEP VEIN THROMBOSIS (DVT)

Deep vein thrombosis (DVT) occurs when blood clots form in the legs during plane flights, chiefly because of prolonged immobility. The longer the flight, the greater the risk. Though most blood clots are reabsorbed uneventfully, some may break off and travel through the blood vessels to the lungs, where they may cause life-threatening complications.

The chief symptom of DVT is swelling or pain of the foot, ankle, or calf, usually on just one side. When a blood clot travels to the lungs, it may cause chest pain and difficulty in breathing. Travellers with any of these symptoms should immediately seek medical attention.

To prevent the development of DVT on long flights you should walk about the cabin, perform isometric compressions of the leg muscles (ie contract the leg muscles while sitting), drink plenty of fluids, and avoid alcohol and tobacco.

JET LAG & MOTION SICKNESS

Jet lag is experienced when a person travels by air across more than three time zones (each time zone usually represents a one-hour time difference). It occurs because many of the functions of the human body (such as temperature, pulse rate and emptying of the bladder and bowels) are regulated by internal 24-hour cycles. When we travel long distances rapidly, our bodies take time to adjust to the 'new time' of our destination, and we may experience fatigue, disorientation, insomnia, anxiety, impaired concentration and loss of appetite. These effects will usually be gone within three days of arrival, but to minimise the impact of jet lag:

- Rest for a couple of days prior to date of departure.
- Try to select flight schedules that minimise sleep deprivation; arriving late in the day means you can go to sleep soon after you arrive. For very long flights, try to organise a stopover.
- Avoid excessive eating (which bloats the stomach) and alcohol intake (which causes dehydration) during the flight. Instead, drink plenty of noncarbonated, nonalcoholic drinks such as fruit juice or water.
- Avoid smoking during the journey.
- Make yourself comfortable by wearing loose-fitting clothes and perhaps bringing an eye mask and earplugs to help you sleep.
- On the flight, try to sleep at the appropriate time for the time zone you are travelling to.

Eating lightly before and during a trip will reduce the chances of motion sickness. If you are prone to motion sickness, try to find a place that minimises movement – near the wing on aircraft, close to midships on boats, near the centre on buses. Fresh air usually helps; reading and cigarette smoke

HEALTH

don't. Commercial motion-sickness preparations, which can cause drowsiness, have to be taken before the trip commences. Ginger (available in capsule form) and peppermint (including mint-flavoured sweets) are natural preventatives of motion sickness.

IN CAMBODIA

AVAILABILITY & COST OF HEALTH CARE

Self-diagnosis and treatment of health problems can be risky, so you should always seek professional medical help. Although we do give drug dosages in this section, they are for emergency use only. Correct diagnosis is vital.

An embassy, consulate or five-star hotel can usually recommend a local doctor or clinic. Antibiotics should ideally be administered only under medical supervision. Take only the recommended dose at the prescribed intervals and use the whole course, even if the illness seems to be cured earlier. Stop immediately if there are any serious reactions and don't use the antibiotic at all if you are unsure that you have the correct one. Some people are allergic to commonly prescribed antibiotics such as penicillin or sulpha drugs; carry this information (eg on a bracelet) when travelling.

The best clinics and hospitals in Cambodia are found in Phnom Penh (p76) and Siem Reap (p114). A consultation usually costs in the region of US$20 plus medi-

---

EVERYDAY HEALTH

Normal body temperature is up to 37°C (98.6°F); more than 2°C (4°F) higher indicates a high fever. The normal adult pulse rate is 60 to 100 beats per minute (children 80 to 100, babies 100 to 140). As a general rule, the pulse increases about 20 beats per minute for each 1°C (2°F) rise in fever.

Respiration (breathing) rate is also an indicator of illness. Count the number of breaths per minute: between 12 and 20 is normal for adults and older children (up to 30 for younger children, 40 for babies). People with a high fever or serious respiratory illness breathe more quickly than normal. More than 40 shallow breaths a minute may indicate pneumonia.

---

cine. Elsewhere, facilities are more basic, although a private clinic is usually preferable to a government hospital. Where possible, return to Phnom Penh or Siem Reap and get a professional opinion there, or for serious injuries or illnesses, seek treatment in Bangkok.

INFECTIOUS DISEASES
Dengue

This viral disease is transmitted by mosquitoes and occurs mainly in tropical and subtropical areas of the world. Generally, there is only a small risk to travellers, except during epidemics, which are usually seasonal (during and just after the wet season). With unstable weather patterns thought to be responsible for large outbreaks of dengue fever in Southeast Asia, travellers to Cambodia may be especially at risk of infection.

Unlike the malaria mosquito, the *Aedes aegypti* mosquito, which transmits the dengue virus, is most active during the day and is found mainly in urban areas.

Signs and symptoms of dengue fever include a sudden onset of high fever, headache, joint and muscle pains (hence its old name, 'breakbone fever') and nausea and vomiting. A rash of small red spots appears three to four days after the onset of fever. Dengue is commonly mistaken for other infectious diseases, including influenza.

You should seek medical attention if you think you may be infected. A blood test can diagnose infection, but there is no specific treatment for the disease. Aspirin should be avoided, as it increases the risk of haemorrhaging, but plenty of rest is advised. Recovery may be prolonged, with tiredness lasting for several weeks. Severe complications are rare in travellers but include dengue haemorrhagic fever (DHF), which can be fatal without prompt medical treatment. DHF is thought to be a result of secondary infection due to a different strain (there are four major strains) and usually affects residents of the country rather than travellers.

There is no vaccine against dengue fever. The best prevention is to avoid mosquito bites at all times – see Malaria, p310, for more details.

Fungal Infections

Fungal infections occur more commonly in hot weather and are usually on the scalp, between the toes (athlete's foot) or fingers, in the groin and on the body (ringworm). You get ringworm (which is a fungal infection, not a worm) from infected animals or other people. Moisture encourages these infections.

To prevent fungal infections wear loose, comfortable clothes, avoid artificial fibres, wash frequently and dry yourself carefully. If you do get an infection, wash the infected area at least daily with a disinfectant or medicated soap and water, and rinse and dry well. Apply an antifungal cream or powder like tolnaftate (Tinaderm). Try to expose the infected area to air or sunlight as much as possible. Wash all towels and underwear in hot water, change them often and let them dry in the sun.

Hepatitis

Hepatitis is a general term for inflammation of the liver. It is a common disease worldwide. There are several different viruses that cause hepatitis, and they differ in the way that they are transmitted. The symptoms are similar in all forms of the illness, and include fever, chills, headache, fatigue, feelings of weakness and aches and pains, followed by loss of appetite, nausea, vomiting, abdominal pain, dark urine, light-coloured faeces, jaundiced (yellow) skin and yellowing of the whites of the eyes. People who have had hepatitis should avoid alcohol for some time after the illness, as the liver needs time to recover.

Hepatitis A is transmitted by ingesting contaminated food or water. You should seek medical advice, but there is not much you can do apart from resting, drinking lots of fluids, eating lightly and avoiding fatty foods. Hepatitis E is transmitted in the same way as hepatitis A; it can be particularly serious in pregnant women.

There are almost 300 million chronic carriers of hepatitis B in the world. It is spread through contact with infected blood, blood products or body fluids; for example, through sexual contact, unsterilised needles and blood transfusions, or contact with blood via small breaks in the skin. Other risk situations include shaving, tattooing or body piercing with contaminated equipment. The symptoms of hepatitis B may be more severe than type A and the disease can lead to long-term problems such as chronic liver damage, liver cancer or a long-term carrier state. Hepatitis C and D are spread in the same way as hepatitis B and can also lead to long-term complications.

There are vaccines against hepatitis A and B, but there are currently no vaccines against the other types of hepatitis. Following the basic rules about food and water (hepatitis A and E) and avoiding risk situations (hepatitis B, C and D) are important preventative measures.

HIV/AIDS

Infection with the human immunodeficiency virus (HIV) may lead to acquired immune deficiency syndrome (AIDS), which is a fatal disease. Any exposure to blood, blood products or body fluids may put the individual at risk.

The disease is often transmitted through sexual contact or dirty needles, so vaccinations, acupuncture, tattooing and body piercing can be potentially as dangerous as intravenous drug use. HIV/AIDS can also be spread through infected-blood transfusions; although the blood centre in Phnom Penh does screen blood used for transfusions, it is unlikely to be done in many of the provinces.

If you do need an injection, ask to see the syringe unwrapped in front of you, or take a needle and syringe pack with you. Fear of HIV infection should never preclude any treatment for serious medical conditions.

According to WHO figures, Cambodian rates of infection are highest among sex workers. The group's HIV prevalence increased from 10% in 1992 to over 40% in 1996. Another group with a high prevalence rate is the military.

Intestinal Worms

These parasites are most common in rural, tropical Cambodia. The various worms have different ways of infecting people. Some may be ingested in food such as undercooked meat (eg tapeworms) and some enter through your skin (eg hookworms). Infestations may not show up for some time, and although they are generally not serious, if left untreated they may cause severe health problems later. Consider having a stool test when you return home to check for worms and for your doctor to determine the appropriate treatment.

HEALTH

Japanese B Encephalitis

This viral infection of the brain is transmitted by mosquitoes. Most cases occur in locals living in rural areas, as the virus exists in pigs and wading birds. Symptoms include fever, headache and alteration in consciousness. Hospitalisation is needed for correct diagnosis and treatment. There is a high mortality rate among those who have symptoms; of those who survive many are intellectually disabled.

Malaria

This serious and potentially fatal disease is spread by mosquitoes. If you are travelling in endemic areas it is extremely important to avoid mosquito bites and to take tablets to prevent the disease developing if you become infected. There is no malaria in Phnom Penh, Siem Reap and most other major urban areas in Cambodia, so visitors on short trips to the most popular places do not need to take medication. Malaria self-test kits are widely available in Cambodia, but are not that reliable.

Symptoms of malaria include fever, chills and sweating, headache, aching joints, diarrhoea and stomach pains, usually preceded by a vague feeling of ill health. Seek medical help immediately if malaria is suspected, as, without treatment, the disease can rapidly become more serious or even fatal.

If medical care is not available, malaria tablets can be used for treatment. You need to use a different malaria tablet to the one you were taking when you contracted the disease, as obviously the first type didn't work. If travelling widely in rural areas of Cambodia, it is worth visiting a pharmacy to purchase a treatment dose – this will save you from complications in the event of an emergency. Antimalarials are available cheaply throughout Cambodia, although buy them from a clinic to be sure they are not fakes.

Travellers are advised to prevent mosquito bites at all times. The main messages:

- Wear light-coloured clothing.
- Wear long trousers and long-sleeved shirts.
- Use mosquito repellents containing the compound DEET on exposed areas (prolonged overuse of DEET may be harmful, especially to children, but its use is considered preferable to being bitten by disease-transmitting mosquitoes).
- Avoid perfumes or aftershave.
- Use a mosquito net impregnated with mosquito repellent (permethrin) – it may be worth taking your own.
- Impregnate clothes with permethrin to effectively deter mosquitoes and other insects.

MALARIA MEDICATION

Antimalarial drugs do not prevent you from being infected but they kill the malaria parasites during their developmental stage, significantly reducing the risk of becoming very ill or dying. Expert advice on medication should be sought, as there are many factors to consider, including the area to be visited, the risk of exposure to malaria-carrying mosquitoes, the side effects of medication, your medical history and whether you are a child or an adult and whether you're pregnant. Travellers heading to isolated areas in Cambodia should carry a treatment dose of medication for use if symptoms occur. A new drug called Malarine, supplied and subsidised by the European Union (EU) and WHO, is available in pharmacies throughout Cambodia for just 7900r, and is undoubtedly the most effective malaria killer available in Cambodia today. See a doctor for advice about the dosage appropriate for you.

Schistosomiasis

Also known as bilharzia, this disease is transmitted by minute worms. They infect certain varieties of freshwater snails found in rivers, streams, lakes and, in particular, dams. The worms multiply and are eventually discharged into the water.

The worm enters through the skin and attaches itself to the intestines or bladder. The first symptom may be feeling generally unwell, or a tingling and sometimes a light rash around the area where the worm entered. Weeks later a high fever may develop. Once the disease is established, abdominal pain and blood in the urine are other signs. The infection often causes no symptoms until the disease is well established (several months to years after exposure), when damage to internal organs is irreversible.

The main method of preventing the disease is avoiding swimming or bathing in fresh water where bilharzia is present. Even deep water can be infected. If you do get wet, dry off quickly and dry your clothes as well.

A blood test is the most reliable way to diagnose the disease, but the test will not show positive until a number of weeks after exposure.

Sexually Transmitted Infections (STIs)

Gonorrhoea, herpes and syphilis are among these infections. Sores, blisters or a rash around the genitals and discharges or pain when urinating are common symptoms. With some STIs, such as wart virus or chlamydia, symptoms may be less marked or not observed at all, especially in women. Syphilis symptoms eventually disappear completely, but the disease continues and can cause severe problems in later years. While abstinence from sexual contact is the only 100% effective prevention, using condoms is also effective. Reliable condoms are widely available throughout urban areas of Cambodia. Different STIs each require specific antibiotics. The treatment of gonorrhoea and syphilis is with antibiotics. There is no cure for herpes or AIDS (see p309).

Typhoid

Typhoid fever is a dangerous gut infection caused by contaminated water and food. Medical help must be sought.

In its initial stages sufferers may feel they have a bad cold or flu on the way, as early symptoms are a headache, body aches and a fever that rises a little each day until it is around 40°C (104°F) or higher. The victim's pulse is often slow relative to the degree of fever present – unlike a normal fever where the pulse increases. There may also be vomiting, abdominal pain, diarrhoea or constipation.

In the second week the high fever and slow pulse continue, and a few pink spots may appear on the body; trembling, delirium, weakness, weight loss and dehydration may occur. Complications such as pneumonia, perforated bowel or meningitis may also present themselves.

TRAVELLER'S DIARRHOEA

Simple things like a change of water, food or climate can all cause a mild bout of diarrhoea, but a few rushed toilet trips with no other symptoms are not indicative of a major problem. Almost everyone gets a mild bout of the runs on a longer visit to Cambodia.

Dehydration is the main danger with diarrhoea, particularly in children or the elderly as dehydration can occur quite quickly. Under all circumstances *fluid replacement* (at least equal to the volume being lost) is the most important thing to remember. Weak black tea with a little sugar, soda water, or soft drinks allowed to go flat and diluted 50% with clean water are all good. You need to drink at least the same volume of fluid that you are losing in bowel movements and vomiting. Urine is the best guide to the adequacy of replacement – if you have small amounts of concentrated urine, you need to drink more. Keep drinking small amounts often. Stick to a bland diet as you recover.

With severe diarrhoea, a rehydrating solution is preferable to replace lost minerals and salts. Commercially available oral rehydration salts are very useful; add them to boiled or bottled water. In an emergency you can make up a solution of six teaspoons of sugar and a half-teaspoon of salt to a litre of boiled or bottled water.

Gut-paralysing drugs such as Lomotil or Imodium can be used to bring relief from the symptoms of diarrhoea, although they do not actually cure the problem. Only use these drugs if you do not have access to toilets, eg if you *must* travel. For children under 12 years the use of Lomotil and Imodium is not recommended. Do not use these drugs if the person has a high fever or is severely dehydrated.

In certain situations antibiotics may be required: diarrhoea with blood or mucus (dysentery), any diarrhoea with fever, profuse watery diarrhoea, persistent diarrhoea not improving after 48 hours and severe diarrhoea. These suggest a more serious cause of diarrhoea, and gut-paralysing drugs should be avoided.

In these situations, a stool test may be necessary to diagnose what bug is causing your diarrhoea, so you should seek medical help urgently. Where this is not possible the recommended drugs for bacterial diarrhoea – the most likely cause of severe diarrhoea in travellers – are norfloxacin (400mg twice daily for three days), or ciprofloxacin (500mg twice daily for five days). These are not recommended for children or pregnant women. The drug of choice for

HEALTH

children would be co-trimoxazole (Bactrim, Septrin or Resprim) with dosage dependent on weight. A five-day course is given. Ampicillin or amoxycillin may be given in pregnancy, but medical care is necessary.

Amoebic Dysentery & Giardiasis

Two other causes of persistent diarrhoea in travellers are amoebic dysentery and giardiasis.

Amoebic dysentery, caused by the protozoan *Entamoeba histolytica*, is characterised by a gradual onset of low-grade diarrhoea, often with blood and mucus. Cramping abdominal pain and vomiting are less likely than in other types of diarrhoea, and fever may not be present. Amoebic dysentery will persist until treated and can recur and cause other health problems.

Giardiasis is caused by a common parasite, *Giardia lamblia*. Symptoms include stomach cramps, nausea, a bloated stomach, watery, foul-smelling diarrhoea and frequent gas. Giardiasis can appear several weeks after you have been exposed to the parasite. The symptoms may disappear for a few days and then return; this can go on for several weeks.

You should seek medical advice if you think you have giardiasis or amoebic dysentery, but where this is not possible, tinidazole (Fasigyn) or metronidazole (Flagyl) are the recommended drugs to take, although the side effects of Flagyl are severe. Treatment is a 2g single dose of Fasigyn or 250mg of Flagyl three times daily for five to 10 days.

ENVIRONMENTAL HAZARDS
Food

There is an old adage that says 'If you can cook it, boil it or peel it you can eat it…otherwise forget it'. Vegetables and fruit should be washed with purified water or peeled where possible. Beware of ice cream that is sold in the street or anywhere it might have been melted and refrozen; if there's any doubt (eg a power cut in the last day or two), steer well clear. Shellfish such as mussels, oysters and clams should be avoided, as should undercooked meat, particularly in the form of mince. Steaming does not make shellfish safe for eating.

If a place looks clean and well run and the vendor also looks clean and healthy,

---

A BANANA A DAY…

If your diet is poor or limited in variety, if you're travelling hard and fast and therefore missing meals or if you simply lose your appetite, you can soon start to lose weight and place your health at risk.

Make sure your diet is well balanced. Cooked eggs, tofu, beans, lentils and nuts are all safe ways to get protein. Fruit you can peel (bananas, oranges or mandarins, for example) is usually safe and a good source of vitamins. Melons can harbour bacteria in their flesh and are best avoided. Try to eat plenty of grains (including rice) and bread. Remember that although food is generally safer if it is well cooked, overcooked food loses much of its nutritional value. If your diet isn't well balanced or if your food intake is insufficient, it's a good idea to take vitamin and iron pills.

In hot climates make sure you drink enough – don't rely on feeling thirsty to indicate when you should drink. Not needing to urinate or voiding small amounts of very dark yellow urine is a danger sign. Always carry a water bottle with you on long trips. See below for information on heat exhaustion.

---

then the food is probably safe. In general, places that are packed with travellers or locals will be fine, while empty restaurants might be empty for a reason. The food in busy restaurants is cooked and eaten quite quickly with little standing around and is probably not reheated.

Heat Exhaustion

Dehydration and salt deficiency can cause heat exhaustion. Take time to acclimatise to high temperatures, drink sufficient liquids and do not do anything too physically demanding.

Salt deficiency is characterised by fatigue, lethargy, headaches, giddiness and muscle cramps; salt tablets may help, but adding extra salt to your food is better.

Anhidrotic heat exhaustion is a rare form of heat exhaustion that is caused by an inability to sweat. It tends to affect people who have been in a hot climate for some time, rather than newcomers. It can progress to heatstroke. Treatment involves removal to a cooler climate or immediate cold showers and wet sheets.

Heatstroke

This serious, occasionally fatal condition can occur if the body's heat-regulating mechanism breaks down, causing the body temperature to rise to dangerous levels. Long, continuous periods of exposure to high temperatures and insufficient fluids can leave you vulnerable to heatstroke.

The symptoms are feeling unwell, not sweating very much (or at all) and a high body temperature (39°C to 41°C, or 102°F to 106°F). Where sweating has ceased, the skin becomes flushed and red. Severe, throbbing headaches and lack of coordination will also occur, and the sufferer may be confused or aggressive. Eventually the victim will become delirious or convulse. Hospitalisation is essential, but in the interim get victims out of the sun, remove their clothing, cover them with a wet sheet or towel and then fan continually. Give fluids if they are conscious.

Insect Bites & Stings

Bedbugs live in various places, but particularly in dirty mattresses and bedding, evidenced by spots of blood on bedclothes or on the wall. Bedbugs leave itchy bites in neat rows. Calamine lotion or Stingose spray may help.

All lice cause itching and discomfort. They make themselves at home in your hair (head lice), your clothing (body lice) or in your pubic hair (crabs). You catch lice through direct contact with infected people or by sharing combs, clothing and the like. Powder or shampoo treatment will kill the lice, and infected clothing should be washed in very hot, soapy water and left to dry in the sun.

Bee and wasp stings are usually painful rather than dangerous. However, in people who are allergic to them, severe breathing difficulties may occur and urgent medical care is then required. Calamine lotion or Stingose spray will relieve itching, and ice packs will reduce the pain and swelling.

Avoid contact with jellyfish, which have stinging tentacles – seek local advice on the safest swimming waters. Dousing in vinegar will deactivate any stingers that have not 'fired'. Calamine lotion, antihistamines and analgesics may reduce the reaction and relieve the pain.

Leeches may be present in damp rainforest conditions; they attach themselves to your skin to suck your blood. Trekkers often get them on their legs or in their boots. Salt or a lighted cigarette end will make them fall off. Do not pull them off, as the bite is then more likely to become infected. Clean and apply pressure if the point of attachment is bleeding. An insect repellent may keep them away, and walkers in leech-infested areas should consider having their boots and trousers impregnated with benzyl benzoate and dibutylphthalate (available from pharmacies in Cambodia).

You should always check all over your body if you have been walking through a potentially tick-infested area, as ticks can cause skin infections and other more serious diseases. If a tick is found attached, press down around the tick's head with tweezers, grab the head and gently pull upwards. Try to avoid pulling the rear of the body as this may squeeze the tick's gut contents through the attached mouth parts into the skin, increasing the risk of infection and disease. Smearing chemicals on the tick will not make it let go and this is not recommended.

To minimise your chances of being bitten by a snake, always wear boots, socks and long trousers when walking through undergrowth where snakes may be present. Don't put your hands into holes and crevices, and be careful if collecting firewood.

Snake bites do not cause instantaneous death and antivenins are usually available. Immediately wrap the bitten limb tightly, as you would for a sprained ankle, and then attach a splint to immobilise it. Keep the victim still and seek medical help, if possible with the dead snake for identification. However, do not attempt to catch the snake

---

NOT A GOOD PLACE FOR CONTACTS

People wearing contact lenses should be aware that Cambodia is an extremely dusty country and this can cause much irritation when travelling. It is generally bearable in cars, but when travelling by motorcycle or pick-up, it is most definitely not. Pack a pair of glasses.

if there is any possibility of being bitten. Tourniquets and sucking out the poison are now comprehensively discredited.

Prickly Heat

Prickly heat is an itchy rash caused by excessive perspiration trapped under the skin. It usually strikes people who have just arrived in a hot climate. Keeping cool, bathing often, drying the skin and using a mild talcum or prickly heat powder, or resorting to the use of air-conditioning, may help.

Sunburn

You can get sunburnt surprisingly quickly, even through cloud. Use a sunscreen, a hat, and a barrier cream for your nose and lips. Calamine lotion or Stingose are good for mild sunburn. Protect your eyes with good-quality sunglasses.

Water

The number one rule is *be careful of the water and ice,* even though both are almost always factory-produced, a legacy of the French. If you don't know for certain that the water is safe, assume the worst. Reputable brands of bottled water or soft drinks are generally fine, but you can't safely drink tap water. Only use water from containers with a serrated seal. Take care with fruit juice, particularly if water may have been added. Milk should be treated with suspicion, as it is often unpasteurised, though boiled milk is fine if it is kept hygienically. Tea and coffee should be OK, since the water should have been boiled.

The simplest way of purifying water is to boil it thoroughly. Vigorous boiling should be satisfactory; however, at high altitude water boils at a lower temperature, so germs are less likely to be killed. Make sure you boil it for longer in these environments.

Consider purchasing a water filter for a long trip. There are two main kinds of filter. Total filters take out all parasites, bacteria and viruses and make water safe to drink. They are often expensive, but they can be more cost effective than buying bottled water. Simple filters (which can even be a nylon mesh bag) take out dirt and larger foreign bodies from the water so that chemical solutions work much more effectively; if water is dirty, chemical solutions may not

work at all. It's very important when buying a filter to read the specifications, so that you know exactly what it removes from the water and what it doesn't. Simple filtering will not remove all dangerous organisms, so if you cannot boil this water it should be treated chemically. Chlorine tablets (Puritabs, Steritabs or other brands) will kill many pathogens, but not some parasites like giardia and amoebic cysts. Iodine is more effective in purifying water and is available in tablet form (such as Potable Aqua). Follow the directions carefully and remember that too much iodine can be harmful.

WOMEN'S HEALTH
Gynaecological Problems

Antibiotic use, synthetic underwear, sweating and contraceptive pills can lead to fungal vaginal infections, especially when travelling in hot climates. Thrush (yeast infection or vaginal candidiasis) is characterised by a rash, itching and discharge. Nystatin, miconazole or clotrimazole pessaries or vaginal cream are the usual treatment. Maintaining good personal hygiene and wearing loose-fitting clothes and cotton underwear may help prevent these infections.

STIs are a major cause of vaginal problems. Symptoms include a smelly discharge, painful intercourse and sometimes a burning sensation when urinating. Medical attention should be sought and male sexual partners must also be treated. For more details see p311. Besides abstinence, the best thing is to practise safe sex using condoms.

Pregnancy

Most miscarriages occur during the first three months of pregnancy. Miscarriage is common and can occasionally lead to severe bleeding. The last three months should also be spent within reasonable distance of good medical care. A baby born as early as 24 weeks stands a chance of survival, but only in a good modern hospital. Pregnant women should avoid all unnecessary medication, although vaccinations and malarial prophylactics should still be taken where needed. Additional care should be taken to prevent illness and particular attention should be paid to diet and nutrition. Alcohol and nicotine, for example, should be avoided.

Language

CONTENTS

The Khmer or Cambodian language is spoken by approximately nine million people in Cambodia, and is understood by many in bordering countries. Written Khmer is based on the ancient Brahmi script of southern India. Arguably one of the oldest languages in Southeast Asia, Khmer inscriptions have been dated back to the 7th century AD. Although separate and distinct from its Thai, Lao and Burmese neighbours, Khmer shares with them the common roots of Sanskrit and Pali – a heritage of centuries of linguistic and cultural interaction and of their shared faith in Theravada Buddhism. More recently, many French words have entered the Khmer language during the colonial period, especially medical and technical terms.

Unlike the languages of neighbouring countries, Khmer is non tonal, meaning that there are no special intonations within words that alter their meaning. This may be a relief for travellers in the region who have been frustrated in their attempts at tonal languages such as Thai, Vietnamese and Lao. However, the lack of tones is easily offset by the complexity of the Khmer pronunciation. There are 33 consonants, often paired in seemingly bizarre combinations, and some 24 vowels and diphthongs. Further complicating the language is the haphazard transliteration system left over from the days of French rule, which does not reflect accurate pronunciation of Khmer words by English speakers.

On the positive side, Khmer grammar is very simple. There are no verb conjugations or gender inflections, no endings for single or plural, masculine or feminine. Adding a few words changes sentence tense to past, present or future.

A bit of Khmer will go a long way – no matter how rough it is. The Khmers sincerely appreciate any effort to learn their language and are very supportive of visitors who give it even a halfhearted try. You'll find that as your skill and vocabulary increase, so does your social standing: people go out of their way to compliment you, moto fares and prices at markets drop, and you may even win a few friends.

Though English is fast becoming Cambodia's second language, the Khmer still cling to the Francophone pronunciation of the Roman alphabet and most foreign words. This is helpful to remember when spelling Western words and names aloud; thus 'ay-bee-cee' becomes 'ah-bey-sey' and so on. French speakers will definitely have an advantage when addressing the older generation, as most educated Khmers studied French at some point during their schooling. Many household items retain their French names as well, especially those which were introduced to Cambodia by the French, such as *robinet* (tap, faucet) and *ampoule* (light bulb).

Recommend reading for those interested in further study of spoken and written Khmer are *Cambodian System of Writing and Beginning Reader*, *Modern Spoken Cambodian* and any other books by Frank Huffman.

Dialects

Although the Khmer language as spoken in Phnom Penh is generally intelligible to Khmers nationwide, there are several distinct dialects in other areas of the country. Most notably, the Khmers of Takeo Province tend to modify or slur hard consonant/vowel combinations, especially those that contain 'r'; thus *bram* (five) becomes *pe-am*, *sraa* (alcohol) becomes *se-aa*, and *baraang*

(French/foreigner) becomes *be-ang*. In Siem Reap, sharp-eared travellers will notice a very Lao-sounding lilt to the local speech. Here, certain vowels are modified, such as *poan* (thousand), which becomes *peuan*, and *kh'sia* (pipe), which becomes *kh'seua*.

TRANSLITERATION

The transliteration system used in this chapter has been designed for basic communication rather than linguistic perfection. Several Khmer vowels, however, have no English equivalent, thus they can only be approximated by English spellings. Other words are written to convey the way they are pronounced and not necessarily according to the actual vowels used in the words. (Khmer place names in this book written in the Roman alphabet will follow their common or standard spellings.)

PRONUNCIATION

The pronunciation guide below covers the trickier parts of the transliteration system used in this chapter. It uses the Roman alphabet to give the closest equivalent to the sounds of the Khmer language. The best way to improve your pronunciation is to listen carefully to native speakers.

Vowels

Vowels and diphthongs with an **h** at the end should be pronounced hard and aspirated (with a puff of air).

aa	as the 'a' in 'father'
i	as in 'kit'
uh	as the 'u' in 'but'
ii	as the 'ee' in 'feet'
ei	a combination of **uh** and **ii** above, ie 'uh-ii'
eu	similar to the 'eu' in French *peuple*; try saying 'oo' while keeping the lips spread flat rather than rounded
euh	as **eu** above; pronounced short and hard
oh	as the 'o' in 'hose'; pronounced short and hard
ow	as in 'glow'
u	as the 'u' in 'flute'; pronounced short and hard
uu	as the 'oo' in 'zoo'
ua	as the 'ou' in 'tour'
uah	as **ua** above; pronounced short and hard

aa-œ	a tricky one that has no English equivalent; like a combination of **aa** and **œ**. When placed in between consonants it's often pronounced like 'ao'.
œ	as 'er' in 'her', but more open
eua	combination of **eu** and **a**
ia	as 'ee-ya'; like the 'ee' in 'beer' without the 'r'
e	as in 'they'
ai	as in 'aisle'
ae	as the 'a' in 'cat'
ay	as **ai** above, but slightly more nasal
ey	as in 'prey'
ao	as the 'ow' in 'cow'
av	no English equivalent; sounds like a very nasal **ao**. The final 'v' is not pronounced.
euv	no English equivalent; sounds like a very nasal **eu**. The final 'v' is not pronounced.
ohm	as the 'ome' in 'home'
am	as the 'um' in 'glum'
oam	a combination of 'o' and 'am'
a, ah	shorter and harder than **aa** above
eah	combination of 'e' and 'ah'; pronounced short and hard
ih	as the 'ee' in 'teeth'; pronounced short and hard
eh	as the 'a' in 'date'; pronounced short and hard
awh	as the 'aw' in 'jaw'; pronounced short and hard
oah	a combination of 'o' and 'ah'; pronounced short and hard
aw	as the 'aw' in 'jaw'

Consonants

Khmer uses some consonant combinations that may sound rather bizarre to Western ears and be equally difficult for Western tongues, eg 'j-r' in *j'rook* (pig), or 'ch-ng' in *ch'ngain* (delicious). For ease of pronunciation, in this guide these types of consonants are separated with an apostrophe.

k	as the 'g' in 'go'
kh	as the 'k' in 'kind'
ng	as the 'ng' in 'sing'; a difficult sound for Westerners to emulate. Practise by repeating 'singing-nging-nging-nging' until you can say 'nging' clearly.
j	as in 'jump'
ch	as in 'cheese'

ny	as in the final syllable of 'onion', ie 'nyun'
t	a hard, unaspirated 't' sound with no direct equivalent in English. Similar to the 't' in 'stand'.
th	as the 't' in 'two', never as the 'th' in 'thanks'
p	a hard, unaspirated 'p' sound, as the final 'p' in 'puppy'
ph	as the 'p' in 'pond', never as the 'ph' in 'phone'
r	as in 'rum', but hard and rolling, with the tongue flapping against the palate. In rapid conversation it is often omitted entirely.
w	as in 'would'. Contrary to the common transliteration system, there is no equivalent to the English 'v' sound in Khmer.

ACCOMMODATION

Where is a (cheap) hotel?
sahnthaakia/ohtail (thaok) neuv ai naa?
សណ្ឋាគារ/អូតែល(ថោក)នៅឯណា?

I've already found a hotel.
kh'nyohm mian ohtail hao-y
ខ្ញុំមានអូតែលហើយ

I'm staying at ...
kh'nyohm snahk neuv ...
ខ្ញុំស្នាក់នៅ ...

Could you write down the address, please?
sohm sawse aasayathaan ao-y kh'nyohm
សូមសរសេរអាស័យដ្ឋានឲ្យខ្ញុំ

I'd like a room ... *kh'nyohm sohm bantohp ...* ខ្ញុំសុំបន្ទប់ ...
  for one person
  samruhp muy niak សំរាប់មួយនាក់
  for two people
  samruhp pii niak សំរាប់ពីរនាក់
  with a bathroom
  dail mian bantohp tuhk ដែលមានបន្ទប់ទឹក
  with a fan
  dail mian dawnghahl ដែលមានកង្ហារ
  with a window
  dail mian bawng-uit ដែលមានបង្អួច

I'm going to stay for ...
kh'nyohm nuhng snahk tii nih ...
ខ្ញុំនឹងស្នាក់ទីនេះ ...
  one day
  muy th'ngay មួយថ្ងៃ
  one week
  muy aatuht មួយអាទិត្យ

Do you have a room?
niak mian bantohp tohmne te?
អ្នកមានបន្ទប់ទំនេរទេ?

How much is it per day?
damlay muy th'ngay pohnmaan?
តំលៃមួយថ្ងៃប៉ុន្មាន?

Does the price include breakfast?
damlay bantohp khuht teang m'hohp pel pruhk reu?
តំលៃបន្ទប់គិតទាំងម្ហូបពេលព្រឹកឬ?

Can I see the room?
kh'nyohm aa-it mœl bantohp baan te?
ខ្ញុំអាចមើលបន្ទប់បានទេ?

I don't like this room.
kh'nyohm muhn johl juht bantohp nih te
ខ្ញុំមិនចូលចិត្តបន្ទប់នេះទេ

Do you have a better room?
niak mian bantohp l'aw jiang nih te?
អ្នកមានបន្ទប់ល្អជាងនេះទេ?

I'll take this room.
kh'nyohm yohk bantohp nih
ខ្ញុំយកបន្ទប់នេះ

Can I leave my things here until ...?
kh'nyohm aa-it ph'nyaa-œ tohk eiwuhn r'bawh kh'nyohm neuv tii nih dawl ... baan te?
ខ្ញុំអាចផ្ញើរវៀរបស់ខ្ញុំនៅទីនេះដល់ ... បានទេ?
  this afternoon
  l'ngiak nih ល្ងាចនេះ
  this evening
  yohp nih យប់នេះ

CONVERSATION & ESSENTIALS
Forms of Address

The Khmer language reflects the social standing of the speaker and subject through various personal pronouns and 'politeness words'. These range from the simple *baat* for men and *jaa* for women, placed at the end of a sentence, meaning 'yes' or 'I agree', to the very formal and archaic *Reachasahp* or 'Royal language', a separate vocabulary reserved for addressing the King and very high officials. Many of the pronouns are determined on the basis of the subject's age and sex in relation to the speaker. Foreigners are not expected to know all of these forms. The easiest and most general personal pronoun is *niak* (you), which may be used in most situations, with either sex. Men of your age or older may be called *lowk* (Mister). Women of your age or older can be called *bawng srei* (older sister) or for more formal situations, *lowk srei* (Madam). *Bawng* is a good informal, neutral pronoun for men or women who are (or appear to be) older than you. For third person, male or female, singular or plural, the respectful form is *koat* and the common form is *ke*.

Hello.
  johm riab sua/sua s'dei ជំរាបសួរ/សួស្ដី
Goodbye.
  lia suhn hao-y លាសិនហើយ
See you later.
  juab kh'nia th'ngay krao-y ជួបគ្នាថ្ងៃក្រោយ
Yes.
  baat បាទ
  (used by men)
  jaa ចាស
  (used by women)
No.
  te ទេ
Please.
  sohm សូម
Thank you.
  aw kohn អរគុណ
You're welcome.
  awt ei te/sohm anjœ-in អត់អីទេ/សូមអញ្ជើញ
Excuse me/I'm sorry.
  sohm toh សុំទោស
Pardon? (What did you say?)
  niak niyey thaa mait? អ្នកនិយាយថាម៉េច?
Hi. How are you?
  niak sohk sabaay te? អ្នកសុខសប្បាយទេ?
I'm fine.
  kh'nyohm sohk sabaay ខ្ញុំសុខសប្បាយ
Where are you going?
  niak teuv naa? អ្នកទៅណា?

(NB This is a very common question used when meeting people, even strangers; an exact answer is not necessary.)

What's your name?
  niak ch'muah ei? អ្នកឈ្មោះអី?
My name is ...
  kh'nyohm ch'muah ... ខ្ញុំឈ្មោះ ...
Where are you from?
  niak mao pii prateh naa? អ្នកមកពីប្រទេសណា?
I'm from ...
  kh'nyohm mao pii ... ខ្ញុំមកពី ...
I'm staying at ...
  kh'nyohm snhak neuv ... ខ្ញុំស្នាក់នៅ ...
May I take your photo?
  kh'nyohm aa-it thawt ruup niak baan te? ខ្ញុំអាចថតរូបអ្នកបានទេ?

DIRECTIONS
How can I get to ...?
  phleuv naa teuv ..? ផ្លូវណាទៅ ...?
Is it far?
  wia neuv ch'ngaay te? វានៅឆ្ងាយទេ?
Is it near?
  wia neuv juht te? វានៅជិតទេ?
Is it near here?
  wia neuv juht nih te? វានៅជិតនេះទេ?
Go straight ahead.
  teuv trawng ទៅត្រង់
Turn left.
  bawt ch'weng បត់ឆ្វេង
Turn right.
  bawt s'dam បត់ស្ដាំ
at the corner
  neuv kait j'rohng នៅកាច់ជ្រុង
in front of
  neuv khaang mohk នៅខាងមុខ
next to
  neuv joab នៅជាប់
behind
  neuv khaang krao-y នៅខាងក្រោយ
opposite
  neuv tohl mohk នៅទល់មុខ

north
  khaang jœng ខាងជើង
south
  khaang d'bowng ខាងត្បូង
east
  khaang kaot ខាងកើត
west
  khaang leit ខាងលិច

HEALTH
Where is a ...
  ... neuv ai naa? ... នៅឯណា?
  dentist
  paet th'mein ពេទ្យធ្មេញ
  doctor
  kruu paet គ្រូពេទ្យ
  hospital
  mohntrii paet មន្ទីរពេទ្យ
  pharmacy
  kuhnlaing luak th'nam/ កន្លែងលក់ថ្នាំ/
  ohsawt s'thaan ឱសថស្ថាន

I'm ill.
  kh'nyohm cheu ខ្ញុំឈឺ
My ... hurts.
  ... r'bawh kh'nyohm cheu ... របស់ខ្ញុំឈឺ
I feel nauseous.
  kh'nyohm jawng k'uat ខ្ញុំចង់ក្អួត

EMERGENCIES

Help!
juay kh'nyohm phawng! ជួយខ្ញុំផង!

It's an emergency!
nih jia reuang bawntoan! នេះជារឿងបន្ទាន់!

Call a doctor!
juay hav kruu paet mao! ជួយហៅគ្រូពេទ្យមក!

Call the police!
juay hav polih mao! ជួយហៅប៉ូលិសមក!

Could you help me please?
niak aa-it juay kh'nyohm អ្នកអាចជួយខ្ញុំបានទេ?
baan te?

Could I please use the telephone?
kh'nyohm braa-œ ខ្ញុំប្រើទូរស័ព្ទបានទេ?
turasahp baan te?

I've been robbed.
kh'nyohm treuv jao plawn ខ្ញុំត្រូវចោរប្លន់.

Stop!
chohp! ឈប់!

Watch out!
prawyaht! ប្រយ័ត្ន!

Where are the toilets?
bawngkohn neuv ai naa? បង្គន់នៅឯណា?

I wish to contact my embassy/consulate.
kh'nyohm jawng hav s'thaantuut/kohngsuhl r'bawh
prawteh kh'nyohm
ខ្ញុំចង់ហៅស្ថានទូត/កុងស៊ុលរបស់ប្រទេសខ្ញុំ

I feel weak.
kh'nyohm awh kamlahng ខ្ញុំអស់កំលាំង

I keep vomiting.
kh'nyohm k'uat j'raa-œn ខ្ញុំក្អួតច្រើន

I feel dizzy.
kh'nyohm wuhl mohk ខ្ញុំវិលមុខ

I'm allergic to ...
kh'nyohm muhn treuv thiat ...
ខ្ញុំមិនត្រូវជាតុ ...

  penicillin
  penicillin បេនីស៊ីលីន
  antibiotics
  awntiibiowtik អង់ទីប៊ីយោទិក

I need medicine for ...
kh'nyohm treuv kaa th'nam samruhp ...
ខ្ញុំត្រូវការថ្នាំសំរាប់ ...

  diarrhoea
  rowk joh riak រោគចុះរាក
  dysentery
  rowk mual រោគមូល
  fever
  krohn/k'dav kh'luan គ្រុន/ក្ដៅខ្លួន

  pain
  cheu ឈឺ

antiseptic
  th'nam samlahp me rowk ថ្នាំសំលាប់មេរោគ

aspirin
  parasetamol ប៉ារ៉ាសេតាម៉ុល

codeine
  codiin ខូឌីន

condoms
  sraom ahnaamai ស្រោមអនាម័យ

medicine
  th'nam ថ្នាំ

mosquito repellent
  th'nam kaa pia ថ្នាំការពារមូស
  muh

quinine
  kiiniin គីនីន

razor blade
  kambuht kao pohk moat កាំបិតកោរពុកមាត់

sanitary napkins
  samlei ahnaamai សំឡើអនាម័យ

shampoo
  sabuu kawk sawk សាប៊ូកក់សក់

shaving cream
  kraim samruhp kao pohk ក្រែមសំរាប់កោរពុកមាត់
  moat

sunblock cream
  kraim kaa pia pohnleu ក្រែមការពារពន្លឺថ្ងៃ
  th'ngay

toilet paper
  krawdah ahnaamai ក្រដាស់អនាម័យ

LANGUAGE DIFFICULTIES

Does any one here speak English?
tii nih mian niak jeh phiasaa awngle te?
ទីនេះមានអ្នកចេះភាសាអង់គ្លេសទេ?

Do you understand?
niak yuhl te/niak s'dap baan te?
អ្នកយល់ទេ/អ្នកស្ដាប់បានទេ?

I understand.
kh'nyohm yuhl/kh'nyohm s'dap baan
ខ្ញុំយល់ /ខ្ញុំស្ដាប់បាន

I don't understand.
kh'nyohm muhn yuhl te/kh'nyohm s'dap muhn baan te
ខ្ញុំមិនយល់ទេ/ខ្ញុំស្ដាប់មិនបានទេ

What does this mean?
nih mian nuh-y thaa mait?
នេះមានន័យថាម៉េច?

What is this called?
nih ke hav thaa mait?
នេះគេហៅថាម៉េច?

Please speak slowly.
sohm niyay yeut yeut
សូមនិយាយយឺតៗ

Please write that word down for me.
sohm sawse piak nu ao-y kh'nyohm
សូមសរសេរពាក្យនោះឱ្យខ្ញុំ

Please translate for me.
sohm bawk brai ao-y kh'nyohm
សូមបកប្រែឱ្យខ្ញុំ

NUMBERS & AMOUNTS

Khmers count in increments of five. Thus, after reaching the number five *(bram)*, the cycle begins again with the addition of one, ie 'five-one' *(bram muy)*, 'five-two' *(bram pii)* and so on to 10, which begins a new cycle. This system is a bit awkward at first (for example, 18, which has three parts: 10, five and three) but with practice it can be mastered.

You may be confused by a colloquial form of counting that reverses the word order for numbers between 10 and 20 and separates the two words with *duhn: pii duhn dawp* for 12, *bei duhn dawp* for 13, *bram buan duhn dawp* for 19 and so on. This form is often used in markets, so listen keenly.

1	*muy*	មួយ
2	*pii*	ពីរ
3	*bei*	បី
4	*buan*	បួន
5	*bram*	ប្រាំ
6	*bram muy*	ប្រាំមួយ
7	*bram pii/puhl*	ប្រាំពីរ
8	*bram bei*	ប្រាំបី
9	*bram buan*	ប្រាំបួន
10	*dawp*	ដប់
11	*dawp muy*	ដប់មួយ
12	*dawp pii*	ដប់ពីរ
16	*dawp bram muy*	ដប់ប្រាំមួយ
20	*m'phei*	ម្ភៃ
21	*m'phei muy*	ម្ភៃមួយ
30	*saamsuhp*	សាមសិប
40	*saisuhp*	សែសិប
100	*muy roy*	មួយរយ
1000	*muy poan*	មួយពាន់
1,000,000	*muy lian*	មួយលាន

1st	*tii muy*	ទីមួយ
2nd	*tii pii*	ទីពីរ
3rd	*tii bei*	ទីបី
4th	*tii buan*	ទីបួន
10th	*tii dawp*	ទីដប់

SHOPPING & SERVICES

Where is a/the ...

... neuv ai naa?		... នៅឯណា?
bank		
th'niakia		ធនាគារ
cinema		
rowng kohn		រោងកុន
consulate		
kohng sul		កុងស៊ុល
embassy		
s'thaantuut		ស្ថានទូត
hospital		
mohntii paet		មន្ទីរពេទ្យ
market		
p'saa		ផ្សារ
museum		
saramohntii		សារមន្ទី
park		
suan		សួន
police station		
poh polih/		ប៉ុស្តិ៍ប៉ូលីស/
s'thaanii nohkohbaal		ស្ថានីយនគរបាល
post office		
praisuhnii		ប្រៃសណីយ
public telephone		
turasahp saathiaranah		ទូរស័ព្ទសាធារណៈ
public toilet		
bawngkohn saathiaranah		បង្គន់សាធារណៈ
temple		
wawt		វត្ត

How far is the ...?
... ch'ngaay pohnmaan? ... ឆ្ងាយប៉ុន្មាន?
I want to see the ...
kh'nyohm jawng teuv mœl ... ខ្ញុំចង់ទៅមើល ...
I'm looking for the ...
kh'nyohm rohk ... ខ្ញុំរក ...
How much is it?
nih th'lay pohnmaan? នេះថ្លៃប៉ុន្មាន?
That's too much.
th'lay pek ថ្លៃពេក
I'll give you ...
kh'nyohm ao-y ... ខ្ញុំឱ្យ ...
No more than ...
muhn lœh pii ... មិនលើសពី ...
What's your best price?
niak dait pohnmaan? អ្នកដាច់ប៉ុន្មាន?

What time does it open?
wia baok maong pohnmaan?
វាបើកម៉ោងប៉ុន្មាន?
What time does it close?
wia buht maong pohnmaan?
វាបិតម៉ោងប៉ុន្មាន?
I want to change US dollars.
kh'nyohm jawng dow dolaa amerik
ខ្ញុំចង់ដូរដុល្លាអាមេរិក
What is the exchange rate for US dollars?
muy dolaa dow baan pohnmaan?
មួយដុល្លាដូរបានប៉ុន្មាន?

TIME & DAYS

What time is it?
eileuv nih maong pohnmaan?
ឥឡូវនេះម៉ោងប៉ុន្មាន?

in the morning	*pel pruhk*	ពេលព្រឹក
in the afternoon	*pel r'sial*	ពេលរសៀល
in the evening	*pel l'ngiat*	ពេលល្ងាច
at night	*pel yohp*	ពេលយប់
today	*th'ngay nih*	ថ្ងៃនេះ
tomorrow	*th'ngay s'aik*	ថ្ងៃស្អែក
yesterday	*m'suhl mein*	ម្សិលមិញ

Monday	*th'ngay jahn*	ថ្ងៃចន្ទ
Tuesday	*th'ngay ahngkia*	ថ្ងៃអង្គារ
Wednesday	*th'ngay poht*	ថ្ងៃពុធ
Thursday	*th'ngay prohoah*	ថ្ងៃព្រហស្បតិ៍
Friday	*th'ngay sohk*	ថ្ងៃសុក្រ
Saturday	*th'ngay sav*	ថ្ងៃសៅរ៍
Sunday	*th'ngay aatuht*	ថ្ងៃអាទិត្យ

TRANSPORT

Where is the ...?

	... neuv ai naa?	... នៅឯណា?
airport	*wial yohn hawh*	វាលយន្តហោះ
bus station	*kuhnlaing laan ch'nual*	កន្លែងឡានឈ្នួល
bus stop	*jamnawt laan ch'nual*	ចំណតឡានឈ្នួល
train station	*s'thaanii roht plœng*	ស្ថានីយរថភ្លើង

What time does the ... leave?

	... jein maong pohnmaan?	... ចេញម៉ោងប៉ុន្មាន?
bus	*laan ch'nual*	ឡានឈ្នួល
train	*roht plœng*	រថភ្លើង
plane	*yohn hawh/k'pal hawh*	យន្តហោះ/កប៉ាល់ហោះ

What time does the last bus leave?
laan ch'nual johng krao-y jein teuv maong pohnmaan?
ឡានឈ្នួល ចុងក្រោយចេញទៅម៉ោងប៉ុន្មាន?
I want to get off (here)!
kh'nyohm jawng joh (tii nih)!
ខ្ញុំចង់ចុះ (ទីនេះ)!
How much is it to ...?
teuv ... th'lay pohnmaan?
ទៅ ... ថ្លៃប៉ុន្មាន?
Please take me to ...
sohm juun kh' nyohm teuv ...
សូមជូនខ្ញុំទៅ ...
this address
aadreh/aasayathaan nih
អាសយដ្ឋាននេះ
Here is fine, thank you.
chohp neuv tii nih kaw baan
ឈប់នៅទីនេះក៏បាន

Glossary

apsara – heavenly nymph or angelic dancer, often represented in Khmer sculpture
Asean – Association of Southeast Asian Nations
Avalokiteshvara – the Buddha of Compassion and the inspiration for Jayavarman VII's Angkor Thom

barang – foreigner
baray – reservoir
boeng – lake

CCB – Cambodian Commercial Bank
CCC – Cooperation Committee for Cambodia
CFF – Cambodian Freedom Fighters
chunchiet – ethnic minorities
CPP – Cambodian People's Party
cyclo – pedicab; bicycle rickshaw

devaraja – cult of the god-king, established by Jayavarman II, in which the monarch has universal power
devedas – goddesses

EFEO – École Française d'Extrême Orient
essai – wise man or traditional medicine man

Funcinpec – National United Front for an Independent, Neutral, Peaceful and Cooperative Cambodia

garuda – mythical half-man, half-bird creature
gopura – entrance pavilion in traditional Hindu architecture

Hinayana – literally, 'Small Vehicle'; a school of Buddhism also known as *Theravada*
Hun Sen – Cambodia's prime minister (1998 to present)

Jayavarman II – the king (r 802–50) who established the cult of the god-king, kicking off a period of amazing architectural productivity that resulted in the extraordinary temples of Angkor
Jayavarman VII – the king (r 1181–201) who drove the Chams out of Cambodia before embarking on an ambitious construction programme, of which the walled city of Angkor Thom was part

Kampuchea – the name Cambodians use for their country; to non-Khmers, it is associated with the bloody rule of the Khmer Rouge, which insisted that the outside world adopt the name Democratic Kampuchea from 1975 to 1979

Khmer – a person of Cambodian descent; the language of Cambodia
Khmer Krom – ethnic Khmers living in Vietnam
Khmer Loeu – Upper Khmer or ethnic minorities in northeastern Cambodia
Khmer Rouge – a revolutionary organisation that seized power in 1975 and implemented a brutal social restructuring, resulting in the suffering and death of millions of Cambodians in the following four years
kouprey – extremely rare wild ox of Southeast Asia
krama – scarf

linga – phallic symbols

Mahayana – literally, 'Great Vehicle'; a school of Buddhism (also known as the Northern School) that built upon and extended the early Buddhist teachings; see also *Theravada*
moto – small motorcycle with driver; a common form of transport in Cambodia
Mt Meru – the mythical dwelling of the Hindu god Shiva
MPTC – Cambodian Ministry of Post and Telecommunications

naga – mythical serpent, often multiheaded; a symbol used extensively in Angkorian architecture
nandi – sacred ox
NCDP – National Centre for Disabled Persons
NGO – nongovernmental organisation
NH – national highway
Norodom Ranariddh, Prince – son of King Sihanouk and leader of *Funcinpec*
Norodom Sihanouk, King – king of Cambodia, film director and constant presence in Cambodian politics

Pali – ancient Indian language that, along with Sanskrit, is the root of modern *Khmer*
Party of Democratic Kampuchea – the political party of the *Khmer Rouge*
phlauv – street; abbreviated to Ph
phnom – mountain
Pol Pot – the former leader of the Khmer Rouge who is roundly blamed for the suffering and deaths of millions of Cambodians; also known as Saloth Sar
prang – temple tower
prasat – stone or brick hall with religious or royal significance
preah – sacred
psar – market

RAC – Royal Air Cambodge
Ramayana – an epic Sanskrit poem composed around 300 BC featuring the mythical Ramachandra, the incarnation of the god Vishnu
RCAF – Royal Cambodian Armed Forces
remorque-kang – trailer pulled by a bicycle
remorque-moto – trailer pulled by a motorcycle
rom vong – Cambodian circle dancing

Sangkum Reastr Niyum – People's Socialist Community; a national movement, led by King Sihanouk, that ruled the country during the 1950s and 1960s
Sanskrit – ancient Hindu language that, along with Pali, is the root of modern Khmer language
SNC – Supreme National Council
stung – river
Suryavarman II – the king (r 1112–52) responsible for building Angkor Wat and for expanding and unifying the Khmer empire

Theravada – a school of Buddhism (also known as the Southern School or Hinayana) found in Myanmar (Burma), Thailand, Laos and Cambodia; this school confined itself to the early Buddhist teachings; see also *Mahayana*
tonlé – large river

UNDP – UN Development Programme
Unesco – UN Educational Scientific and Cultural Organization
UNHCR – UN High Commissioner for Refugees
Untac – UN Transitional Authority in Cambodia

vihara – temple sanctuary

WHO – World Health Organization

Year Zero – 1975; the year the Khmer Rouge seized power
yoni – female fertility symbol

Behind the Scenes

THIS BOOK

Nick Ray wrote this 5th edition of *Cambodia*, and also authored the previous two editions. Dr Trish Batchelor provided text for the Health chapter.

THANKS from the Author

As always, a huge and heartfelt thanks to the people of Cambodia, whose warmth and humour, stoicism and spirit make it a happy yet humbling place to be. Biggest thanks are reserved for my wonderful wife Kulikar Sotho, as without her support and encouragement, this work would not be possible. And to our young son Julian for brightening our lives immeasurably. I look forward to introducing him to more of the country as he gets older.

A big, fat thanks to my Mum and Dad for all their support and their many visits out here, including for the wedding. And many thanks to all the others who made it over for the Cambodian leg of the wedding, including the three musketeers aka best men, Chris Johnson, Andrew Dear and Andrew Burke; Valerie and John Belcher; Sue Evans; Andrew Johnson and Jane Coyle; Elliot Jacobs and Lara Fisher; Janina Mundy; Chris and George Dear; Linda and Steve Prince; Gren and Elaine Kershaw; Alison and Andrew Scarth; Sue, Dick and James Gillian; Rose Rabone; Anthony Dupont; Simon Sweet and all the 'local' guests. And thank you to my Cambodian family for welcoming me so warmly, including Ma Sotho and Milean.

Thanks to fellow travellers and residents in Cambodia who have joined me on many trips including John McGeoghan, Philippe Janowski and Chris Gow. Thanks to the many Cambodians who have helped me with information or company, including Vannak, Bunthon, Rith and Tra.

Finally, thanks to the Lonely Planet team who have worked on this edition. The author may be the public face, but a huge amount of work behind the scenes goes into making this a better book and I thank you for your help.

CREDITS

Commissioning Editor: Kalya Ryan
Coordinating Editor: Carly Hall
Coordinating Cartographer: Natasha Velleley
Coordinating Layout Designer: Yvonne Bischofberger
Managing Cartographer: Mark Griffiths
Assisting Editors: Joanne Newell, Brooke Lyons, Kyla Gillzan, Kate Evans, Holly Alexander and Helen Christinis
Assisting Cartographers: Sarah Sloane, Corey Hutchinson, Emma McNicol and Helen Rowley
Assisting Layout Designers: Jacqueline McLeod, Michael Ruff and Katherine Marsh
Cover Designer: Kristin Guthrie
Colour Designer: Jim Hsu
Project Manager: Rachel Imeson
Language Content Coordinator: Quentin Frayne

Thanks to Jason Roberts for his Khmer expertise, Vivek Wagle for the blurb and Meg Worby for helping with the manuscript assessment. And a pat on the back for Kerryn Burgess, Melanie Dankel, Rebecca Lalor and Mark Germanchis.

THE LONELY PLANET STORY

The story begins with a classic travel adventure: Tony and Maureen Wheeler's 1972 journey across Europe and Asia to Australia. There was no useful information about the overland trail then, so Tony and Maureen published the first Lonely Planet guidebook to meet a growing need.

From a kitchen table, Lonely Planet has grown to become the largest independent travel publisher in the world, with offices in Melbourne (Australia), Oakland (USA) and London (UK). Today Lonely Planet guidebooks cover the globe. There is an ever-growing list of books and information in a variety of media. Some things haven't changed. The main aim is still to make it possible for adventurous travellers to get out there – to explore and better understand the world.

At Lonely Planet we believe travellers can make a positive contribution to the countries they visit – if they respect their host communities and spend their money wisely. Every year 5% of company profit is donated to charities around the world.

THANKS from Lonely Planet

Many thanks to the following travellers who used the last edition and wrote to us with helpful hints, useful advice and interesting anecdotes.

A Gep Aadriaanse, Helen Abbott, Charlotta & Robert Acevski, Weng Adam, Blair Adams, Johan Adams, Rudi Adriaenssen, Michel Albregts, Leon Alexanian, Ron Allen, Miguel Almirall, Lene Cecilie Andersen, Simon Anderson, Stuart Anderson, Jorgen Andersson, Martin Angiset, Mike Anthony, Jacob Antonsen, Tony Armstrong, Jennifer Arnett, Warren Askew, Christine Atteneder, Cathy Austin-Crowe **B** Chris Bain, Julie Baker, Leon Baker, Mirte Bakker, Shirley Ballinger, Stephen Balut, Ted Bancroft, Carina Bang, Cristiano Barberis, Rebecca Barnes, David Barrett, Don Barrett, Maarten Bax, Christopher Beaton, Michael Bechtel, Samuel Bechtold, Daniel Beck, Judith Becker, Stefan & Tanya Becker, Inger-Anne Becker Wold, Andrew & Cath Beech, Peter Beirinckx, Tom Bell, Will Bell, Fred Bemak, Maria & Tony Benfield, Dave Bennett, Nicola Bennett, Christian Berberski, Megan Berkle, Anna & Ian Betts, Sharmila Beverwijk, Nilema Bhakta-Jones, Maryline Billieux, Rolf Birrenbach, Liz & Mike Bissett, David Bitkower, Paul Blakemore, Robert Blaker, Robert G Bloemers, Andreas Blom, Paul Blom, Knut Bodeewes, Traci R Bogan, Michael Boller, Lilia Bonacorsi, Stephane Bone, Liz Bonham, Deborah Booth, Luis Borgeaud, Felicia Borsari, Eef Bos, Maria Botelho, Sophie Bottomley, Sophal Bou, Julian D Bound, Claire Bowen, Viv Bowra, Andy Boyd, Audrey & Roy Bradford, Derek Branum, Helen Bray, David Breun, George Brooke, Jennifer Broom, Cecile Brouwer, Alden Brown, Greg Brown, Stuart Brown, Dave Browne, Jayne Browning, Uri Brownshtien, Erik Brunekreef, Mary Bryant, Andrew Bunbury, Naomi Burgoyne, David Burns, Marco Buschman, Alett Bush, Scott Byrnes **C** Martin Caminada, Didier Carpentier, Susie Carr, Claire Carroll, Chris Carter, Felicity Carus, Matt Casey, Heino Caspelherr, David Caukill, Esteban Cavalli, C M J Chamuleau, Elisa Charra, Alex Charter, Dominique Chasseriaud, Erika Cherry, Lucy Chesser, Cameron Cheung, Aster Chin, Jan Christensen, Bryan Christner, Uwe Christner, Ream Chuon, Joe Cirvello, Vanessa Clark, Dean Clarke, Veronica Conley, Kay Cook, Robert Cook, Trevor Cook, Suzie Corser, Jane Costello, Margiotta Cristian, Peter & Ursula Crossley, Rey Cruz, Gabor Csonka, Carole Cusack, Chris Custer **D** Michael Dagoe, Clive Dale, Ricardo Dalmas, Jane Dancey, Stephane Dartoux, Mireille Dauphiñais, Dwayne Davidson, Amanda Davies, John Davies, Stuart Davis, Amber Dawson, Mark Dawson, James Dayson, Eddy de Bie, Sjors de Groot, Chris de Havilland, Nicole de Jong, Jan de Jongh, Derek de Souza, Barry de Vent, Steve Deadman, Truus Delissen-van Haeften, Luca Demichelis, Chamae Deosil, Jessica Derynck, Joost R Dessaur, Marty Deveney, Helen Dias, Trisha Dick, Lydia Dixon, Caroline Doggart, Carsten Dohrmann, Ineke Dohrmann, Keith Dokho, Chris Donawa, Lucy Donn, Rosemary Dooley, Sebastian Down, Anne Doyle, John Doyle, Jenny Drezin, Marcel Driessen, Aoife Duggan, Barney Duly, Stuart Duncan, Vivienne Duncan, Russell Dunne, Jo Duthie, Karen Dwyer **E** Maxine Easey, Larry Eav, Christian Ebner, Yael Edrey, Roland Ehrat, Nilgun Ekener, David Eklof, Joanne Elmer, Idoia Elortegui, Dee Eltaief, Karen Emmerson, Mirjam Enderle, Stephan Engelkamp, Paul Engels, Matt & Eileen Erskine, Erik Eskin, Jon Essex, Hannah Evans, James Evans, Lucy Evans **F** Charles Failmezger, Erin Farnbach, D'Arcy Faulkner, Ingeborg Trones Faye, David Fearn, Izhar Fed, Magdalena & Krysztof Fedorowicz, Adrian Felton, Claudio Ferraroni, Kate Fewins, Jason Field, Saskia Fijma, Michael Filippov, Alessandro Fiorio, Sophy Fisher, Karen Flam, Petra Fleck, Desirée Fleer, Jim Fletcher, Stan Fletcher, Lawrence Edwin Fogelberg, Suzie Fong, Sylvain Foret, Kathy Fossati, Jenny Fox, Siobhan Fox, Mathilde Frahm, Andre Franken, Gerdy Frantzke, Nicole Freeman, Andrew & Stefanie Freeston, Mark French, Daniel Friberg, Frank Froboese, Alexandra Fuchs, Marianne & Fabio Fukushima, Maya Fukutani, Richard Fulchiron **G** Susanne Galla, Randy Gallimore, Ruth Gamston, Luis Ivan Garcia, Deborah Gardiner, Jonathan Garrett, Dana Garrison, Georgia Garvey, Nick Gay, Michael Geisthor, Lia Genovese, Jennifer Gerrity, Daniel Gerster, Joris Geurts, Stephanie Gibbons, Bob & Eunice Goetz, Florian Gomm, Tastil Gonzalez, Chris Grabe, David Granger, Stephane Grant, K Grat, Charlotte Green, Gerald Gregory, William Griffin, Shaun Griffiths, Victoria Griffiths, Jos Groffils, Vicky Grossmith, Eric Grouse, Haydn Gunningham **H** Robert Hall, Garryck Hampton, Dave Hancock, Scott Hancock, Paul Hannon, Julian Hansen, Rasmus Juel Hansen, David Harries, Peter Harrin, Chris & Anne Harris, Brenda Hart, John Hart, Shereen Harvey, Elizabeth Haselgrove, Wendlandt Hasselle, Julie Hatfield, Helen Hatzimaggo, Christian Hautmann, Chris Hawke, Madeleine Healy, Linda Heaphy, Kerstin & Stefan Heine, Paul Heinrich, Horst-Dieter Heitmann, Sissel Elisabet Helminsen, Susan Henderson, Aly Hendriks, Helena Henkin, Anita Herzig, Caroline and Ric Hettinga, Nicola Hill, Michiel Hillenius, Bonnie Hittmann, John Hlashwe, Craig Hodges, Michael Hohn, Matthew Holt, Julian Hopkins, Anne Horsley, Jane Hough, Leon Houppermans, Edward Housley, Jill Ho-You, Tan Li Huang, Anneke Hudig, Anneke & Floor Oskam Hudig, Gordon Hudson, Thomas Hudson, Tom Hudson, Michael Huelsmann, Debbie Hughes, Carolyn & Jarrod Hunt-Wackett **I** Blanche Iberg **J** Bastiaan Jaarsma, Gary Jackson, Steve Jackson, Tobias Jackson, Danny Jacqmot, Jenny Jagsander, Jasmine Jasavala, Neil Jenkinson, Michael Jennings, Christian Jentz, K K Jhunjhunwala, Soames Job, Dennis Berthou Johansen, Carolyn Jones, Dax Jones, Paul W Jones, Tess Jongepier **K** Merike Kalm, Paul Kane, Sophie Kavoukis, David Kerkhoff, Gil Kezwer, Carlo Kielstra, Rebecca Kinakin, Rune Kirkeby, Danne Kjellin, Willem Klaassen, A L Koetsier, Karina Kohnert, Amy Kohrman, Minna & Tomi Kommeri, Ilkka Koskinen, Frank Koughan, Marieke Krijnen, Lars Kroon, Marianne Kruyskamp, Joe Kuhn, Diaz Kun, Irit Kurer **L** Dominic Lackschewitz, K K Lahiri, Blake LaMar, John Laney, Nina Laney, Margareta Langbacka Walker, Elliot Lange, Lynda Laros, Doretta Lau, Henriette Lavaulx-Vrecourt, Scott Lawrance, Shane Lawson, Vicky Leah, Sigal Lederman, Heidi Lee, Jim Lee, Stephan Lee, Gerard Leenen, Michael Lees, Francois Legendre, Neil Leighton, Ang Chew Leng, Jesse Lenna, Miki Lentin, Andra Leo, Sabrina Leombruni, Mikelson Leong, Craig Leversha, Mark Levitin, Brian & Lorna Lewis, Nicholas Liang, Matthew Lightfoot, Peter Lilley, Henry Lim, Carrie Lindsay, Julia Lippold, Kay Littlehales, Neil & Kim Locker, Christine Loft, Susan Lomow, Alexander Lorenz, Joanne Louis, Gary Lowe, Ron & Elaine Lowe, Katherine Lu, Darren Ludgate, Traci Lund-Pederson, Robert Lyall **M** Ian Macandrew, Richard Mace, Sue MacMaster, Amandeep Singh Madra, John

Maes, Feysal Maghoo, Liz Mair, Cedric Maizieres, Margarita Malkina, Richard Mallett, Patrick Manion, Elena Maringelli, Tanja Märkle, Sonalle Maroo, Tim Marshall, Claire Martin, Holtz Martin, Silke & Raynald Martin, Nick Mason, Kristina L Mayer, Corina Mayhew, Erin McAuley, Annie McCann, Shane McCarthy, John McCormack, Ian Mcdivett, Paula McDonald, Nathan McEwan, Ciaran McGarrigle, Stephen Mcguckin, Sarah & Sean McHugh, Clair Betty McKenzie, Soren McKenzie, Catherine McKinlay, Doug McLaggan, John Mcleod, Terry McNally, Shane McNamara, Margaret Mcphate, Tora Mehlsen, Susanne Meier, Marieke Meijer, Stefan Meivers, Sascha & Nicole Mendgen, Marek Mengel, Gerard Menkhorst, Pamela Mercier, Gorsky Mikael, Paul Miller, Neal Mitcheison, Melanie Mitchell, Philip Mitchell, Barbara Moccetti, Dennis Mogerman, Janice & Jock Moilliet, Marie-Loe Molenaar, Hans Mommer, Michael Montague, Monica Montebelli, Tink Moonen-de Graaff Stoffers, Celeste Moore, Patti Moore, Kathy Morefield, David Morgan, Jane Morgan, Steffi Morgner, Nick Morley, Scott Morrison, Peter Morrissey, Julia Morton, Moira Mount, Olrik R Muehlbach, Sebastian Mulder, Sonja Munnix, Michelle Murray, Phil & Rhonda Murray, June & Harry Myers **N** Dan Nadel, Connie Nanasy, Dale Ne, Torquil Neilson, Steven Neuse, Ilya & Tessa Neutjens-Van Iersel, Eileen Ni Mhaonaigh, Martin Nigg, Philippa Nigg, Daniel Nilsson, Gerben Nissink, Gerlinde Nooteboom, Marcus Norman, Rachel Nunn **O** Robert Oakes, Patricia Oey, Richard Oldham, Anne O'Leary, Dax Oliver, Deanne O'Nyons, Greig Oppenheimer, Dougald O'Reilly, Noey O'Rielly, Ingvild & Jan Helge Ostensen, Luciënne Oud **P** Marc Paelinck, Alex Paglinawan, Kiran Parghi, Nicholas Park, Nick Park, Tae Sung Park, Lesley & Ron Parker, Pauline Patton, Michelle Pauling, Bryan Pearson, Jill Peary, David Peck, Renate Pelzl, Jose Carlos Pereira, Maraya Perinat, Fredrik Persson, Thekla Pesta, Hugh Peterkin, Franko Petri, Truls Erik Pettersen, Ng Keng Phoy, Belinda Pike, Sara Pines, Maria Eugenia Beirer Pirez, Elius Play, Thomas Polfeldt, Doreen Pon, Lisa Kim Poole, Eva Poon, Adrian Portal, Chris Power, Megha Prem, Janet Preston, Andrew Primrose, Mark Princi, Onno & Esther Prins, Amparo Prior, Ben Prozesky, Karen Pszonka, Catherine Purvis, Bernard Puttaert **Q** Bernard Quin, Jason Quinlan, Dan Quinton **R** John Rajeski, Neil Ramsey, Dustin Reason, Carole Reay, Neil Reddy, Dietrich Rehnert, Leighton Reid, Jean-Luc Renevot, Simon Richards, Emma Richardson, Bjorn Richter, Katja Rieger, Klaus Riepl, Matthew A Rifkin, Liz Rinker, James Roberts, G.J. Robertson, Martin Robinson, Gabriel Rodriguez, Jodie Rogers, Jesper Rogner, Na'ama Ronen, Heikki Ronka, Karin Rosander, Barrett Ross, David Rostron, Jasper Rothuizen, Elizabeth Rowin, Daniel Rozas, Caroline Rubeli, Joan Rubin, Shimon Rumelt, Rob Russell, Denise Ruygrok, Roger Ryan, Andrea Ryder **S** Jill Saccardo, Christopher Sacken, Nurit Sadan, Hella Sæter, Rachel Salt, Darren Salter, Ben Sand, Suzanne & Faruque Sarkar, Rosie Scallon, Alison Schafer, Tobias Scheschkowski, Thomas Schillemans, Regula Schmidhauser,

Patrice Schneider, Frank P Schneidewind, Bec Schopen, Dan Sebastian, Wolfgang Seel, Hannes Seibold, Malcolm Sell, Alon Seren, Andy Sexton, Gavin Sexton, Iain Shaw, Nigel & Vera Shaw, Walter Shaw, Ally Shedden, Alan Sheridan, Liz Shield, Andrea, Bob & Ellen Shimwell, Peter Shinglewood, J H Shone, Andy Siegman, Pierre Simard, Brad Simmons, David Simpson, Reto Sinniger, Lem Skidmore, Silvij Skok, Jeroen Slikker, Andrew Sloan, Tobias Slordahl, Herbert Smit, Charles O Smith, Diana Smith, Sophie Smith, Espen Smith-Petersen, Robbert Kiem Hwat So, Maxine Soames, Aity Soekidjo, Steve Solomon, Marvin Sommer, Soren Ulrik Sonder, Lorenzo Sonelli, Pierre Soum, Mathijs Spoor, Flora Sproule, Robert JH Stagg, Mark Stainforth, John Statham, Lynn Stephenson, Tara Stern, Liad Stockfish, Eduard Stomp, Lili Strachan, Rob Street, Tom Stuart, Marie Stumpf, Fiona Sullivan, Heather Sweeney **T** Paul Tait, Katia Taller, Muei Hoon Tan, Anna Tapp, Tilo Tappesser, Florenc Tavard, Liz Taylor, Susie Taylor, Genevieve Tearle, Marie Teo, Kris Terauds, Maria Terenzio, Jasper Termeer, Tom Ternes, Cor W. Teunissen, Samir Thapa, Sookie Tharm, James Thompson, James R. Thompson, Kate Thompson, Les Thompson, Kirsten Thomson, May Soo Thoo, Rob Thorner, Ben Tibbalds, Thurain Tin, Evelyn To, Paul Tourigny, Meryan Tozer, Colin Trestrail, Ben Tsen, Alexia & Paul Turner, Larry Twohig, Andy Tybell, Rachel Tyler **U** Christian Ulrich, Elle Umbers, Kimleng Un, Michele Usuelli **V** Lauro Valera, Lore van Dale, Kim van den Berg, Pieternelle van den Lerkhove, Daniel van der Sleet, Michiel van der Want, Keith van Eaton, Marc van Echelpoel, Natalie van Eckendonk, Teun van Metelen, R F van Ombergen, Wouter van Zandwijk, Eric Vanbiervliet, Al & Trudy Veenstra, Bart Verbanck, Eleni Vlahakis, Ursula Voelpel, Sabrina Vogt, Barli (Christoph) von Toggenburg, Vincent Vu **W** Francesca Wade, Bert Wagendorp, Ian Wainwright, Lorna Wakefield, Vivien Margaret Walden, Bernadette Walker, C Walker, Chris Walker, Clive Walker, Peggy Walker, Richard C. Walker, Charmian Walker-Smith, Katherine Wang, Désiree Warning, Glenn Waters, Giles & Sophie Watkins, Brian Weber, David Week, Andrew Weir, Jane Welsh, Pauline Wennett, Sarah Wentworth, Arlo Werkhoven, Rachel & Andy Westnidge, Perry Whalley, Matthew Wheeler, Alex White, Caroline White, Nina White, Pam White, Melanie Wielens, Joni Wierer, Charmaine S. Williams, Sherron Williams, John Wilson, Kathryn Wilson, Fred & Jane Wolfe, Clayton Wood, Clayton Wood, Stephen Woods, Mark Woollam, Eoin Wrenn, Karolin Wreschniok **Y** Mike Yeomans, Daniel Young, Biao Yu **Z** Peter Zeidelhack, Gabriella Zipper, Sonja Zivkovic

ACKNOWLEDGMENTS

Many thanks to the following for the use of their content:
Globe on back cover © Mountain High Maps 1993 Digital Wisdom, Inc.

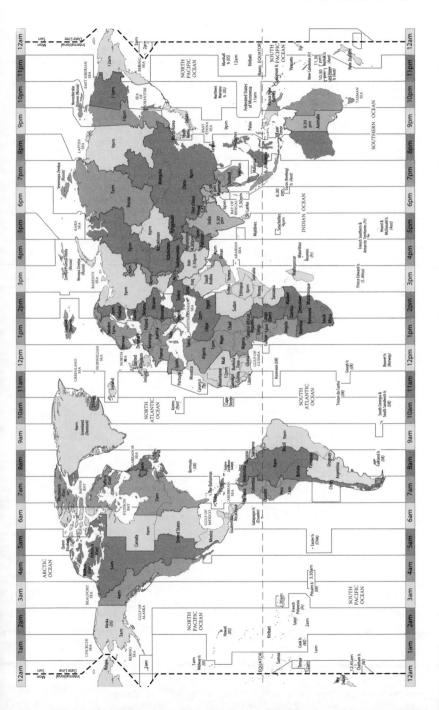

330

Index

INDEX

INDEX

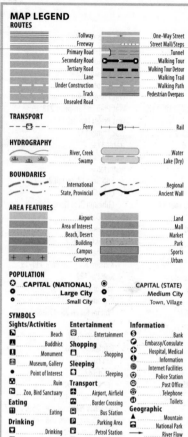

MAP LEGEND

ROUTES

........................Tollway
........................Freeway
........................Primary Road
........................Secondary Road
........................Tertiary Road
........................Lane
........................Under Construction
........................Track
........................Unsealed Road

........................One-Way Street
........................Street Mall/Steps
........................Tunnel
........................Walking Tour
........................Walking Tour Detour
........................Walking Trail
........................Walking Path
........................Pedestrian Overpass

TRANSPORT

........................Ferry
........................Rail

HYDROGRAPHY

........................River, Creek
........................Swamp
........................Water
........................Lake (Dry)

BOUNDARIES

........................International
........................State, Provincial
........................Regional
........................Ancient Wall

AREA FEATURES

........................Airport
........................Area of Interest
........................Beach, Desert
........................Building
........................Campus
........................Cemetery
........................Land
........................Mall
........................Market
........................Park
........................Sports
........................Urban

POPULATION

◎ **CAPITAL (NATIONAL)**
● **Large City**
● Small City

◉ CAPITAL (STATE)
● Medium City
○ Town, Village

SYMBOLS

Sights/Activities
🏖 ....Beach
🛕 ....Buddhist
🏛 ....Monument
🏛 ....Museum, Gallery
● ....Point of Interest
🏰 ....Ruin
🐦 ....Zoo, Bird Sanctuary

Eating
🍴 ....Eating

Drinking
☕ ....Drinking
☕ ....Café

Entertainment
🎭 ....Entertainment

Shopping
🛍 ....Shopping

Sleeping
🛏 ....Sleeping

Transport
✈ ....Airport, Airfield
🚏 ....Border Crossing
🚌 ....Bus Station
🅿 ....Parking Area
⛽ ....Petrol Station
🚕 ....Taxi Rank

Information
💲 ....Bank
📧 ....Embassy/Consulate
➕ ....Hospital, Medical
ⓘ ....Information
@ ....Internet Facilities
🚓 ....Police Station
✉ ....Post Office
☎ ....Telephone
🚻 ....Toilets

Geographic
▲ ....Mountain
🏕 ....National Park
→ ....River Flow
🌀 ....Waterfall

LONELY PLANET OFFICES

Australia

Head Office
Locked Bag 1, Footscray, Victoria 3011
☎ 03 8379 8000, fax 03 8379 8111
talk2us@lonelyplanet.com.au

USA

150 Linden St, Oakland, CA 94607
☎ 510 893 8555, toll free 800 275 8555
fax 510 893 8572, info@lonelyplanet.com

UK

72-82 Rosebery Ave,
Clerkenwell, London EC1R 4RW
☎ 020 7841 9000, fax 020 7841 9001
go@lonelyplanet.co.uk

Published by Lonely Planet Publications Pty Ltd
ABN 36 005 607 983

FLATHEAD VALLEY COMMUNITY COLLEGE LIBRARY